A HISTORY OF
CHRISTIAN DOCTRINE

A HISTORY OF CHRISTIAN DOCTRINE

In Succession to the Earlier Work of
G. P. FISHER
Published in the
International Theological Library Series

Edited by
HUBERT CUNLIFFE-JONES

Assisted by
BENJAMIN DREWERY

FORTRESS PRESS   PHILADELPHIA

First Fortress Press Edition 1980
Second Printing 1981

Library of Congress Cataloging in Publication Data

Main entry under title:

A History of Christian doctrine.

Bibliography: p.
Includes indexes.
1. Theology, Doctrinal—History—Addresses,
essays, lectures. I. Cunliffe-Jones, Hubert.
II. Drewery, Benjamin. III. Fisher, George Park,
1827–1909. History of Christian doctrine.
BT21.2.H57 1980   230'.09   79–21689
ISBN 0-8006-0626-4

Preface

This history has been unconscionably long in the making. Commissioned in the sixties, it was initially planned in 1968, and the editor hoped to receive the scripts from his contributors by December 1970.

The only contributor who actually achieved this was the late Dom David Knowles, to whom tribute must be paid. He was, of course, a very distinguished medieval historian, and I was by no means sure of winning his consent; but in his retirement, as he had never written on the history of doctrine, he welcomed the opportunity of focussing the results of his long experience on this aspect of medieval history.

With regard to the other contributors, the editor had a lot to learn about unexpected commitments which hindered the fulfilment of promises, the incidence of illness, and the varied attitudes of contributors to the completion of material. In the event, one major contributor was obliged to withdraw almost completely, and I am deeply grateful to those who accepted assignments to take over smaller parts of the whole section.

To those who have had to wait for the publication of their work because the manuscript was still incomplete, I present my apologies. Two contributors in particular, who sent in their material without undue delay, Professor Lampe and Dr. Ware, and who have taken the opportunity to revise their material before publication, have in this way rendered the book a further service.

The editor has not sought to restrict the variety of points of view from which the history is presented, because history is a normative study, not (except in detail) an exact one, and it demands continual reassessment. But in the result, what the contributors have presented should prove, for the most part, to be an acceptable general introduction to the period concerned and sometimes even a pioneering work in uncharted fields. But the final contributor, covering the centuries in which the need for reassessment is clearly greatest, has offered instead a presentation which is indeed acute, stimulating, and the product of very great learning, but which because it is not likely to win universal assent will need, for the purpose of a general introduction, to be supplemented from other sources. The questions however which he raises, and the authors to which he particularly calls attention, certainly need to be taken into account in any satisfactory understanding of Christian doctrine in the last three centuries.

The whole enterprise owes an immense debt to my colleague in the department of Ecclesiastical History, the Rev. Benjamin Drewery. When I retired from the Chair of Theology in the University of Manchester in July 1973, there seemed a real possibility that the whole enterprise, with all the precious freight then on board, might well founder. But he came to its aid. In addition to what he has written on Luther, and on the Council of Trent, he has brought to the work not only an intense interest in the history of Christian doctrine and a concern that this book should be finished, but an editorial experience and skill that has been invaluable. It has been a happy experience for me to have as collaborator in the working out of the final stages of the book, a colleague with whom I had such a common mind, and who was so energetic in his labours. In addition, he brought to its assistance the willing and interested technical help of the secretary of the Ecclesiastical History department, Miss Gillian Shepherd, to whom we give our warmest thanks. To the secretary of the department of Theology, Mrs. Dorothy Johnson, who saw me through the earlier stages of the enterprise, I am also deeply indebted.

My overriding indebtedness is to the publishers, T. and T. Clark Ltd., first for their initial commissioning of the work, then for their patience and understanding during the long delays in the fulfilment of that commission, even though they knew from the start that the completion of the work would present them with an immensely difficult publishing responsibility.

H. Cunliffe-Jones.

Table of Contents

Table of Contents

List of Contributors

The Rev. Professor Hubert Cunliffe-Jones, B.Litt., M.A.(Theol.), D.D.
Emeritus Professor of Theology, University of Manchester.

The Rev. Professor Geoffrey William Hugo Lampe, M.C., D.D., F.B.A.
Regius Professor of Divinity, University of Cambridge.

The very Rev. Archimandrite Kallistos Ware, M.A., D.Phil.
Spalding Lecturer in Eastern Orthodox Studies, University of Oxford.

The late Dom David Knowles, Litt.D., F.B.A.
formerly Emeritus Regius Professor of Modern History, University of
Cambridge.

The Rev. Professor Ernest Gordon Rupp, M.A., D.D., F.B.A.
Emeritus Dixie Professor of Ecclesiastical History, University of
Cambridge.

The Rev. Benjamin Drewery, M.A.
Bishop Fraser Senior Lecturer in Ecclesiastical History, University of
Manchester.

The Rev. Basil Hall, M.A., Ph.D., D.D., F.R.Hist.S., F.S.A.
Dean of St. John's College, Cambridge.

The Rev. Thomas Henry Louis Parker, M.A., D.D.
Reader in Theology, University of Durham.

The Rev. Professor Hugh Frederic Woodhouse, M.A., D.D.
Archbishop King's Professor of Divinity, University of Dublin.

The Rev. Robert Buick Knox, M.A., B.D., Ph.D.
Nivison Professor of Church History, Westminster College, Cambridge.

The Rev. John Henry Somerset Kent, M.A., Ph.D.
Professor of Theology, University of Bristol.

Bibliographical Note

G. P. Fisher set an excellent precedent for historians of Christian doctrine in giving no bibliography in his *History of Christian Doctrine*. But reviewers, teachers, students, may expect one.

Bibliographies are important but they are not stable and easily go out of date. All bibliographies are constantly being reassessed. In our studying everyone requires a listening ear and a perceptive eye to become aware of new work of real quality. Yet older books, even if they may go out of fashion for a time, often need to be rediscovered.

There are some references to books here and there in the text. But for the student who is beginning we would recommend the bibliographies in F. L. Cross and E. A. Livingstone: *The Oxford Dictionary of the Christian Church* 2nd Edition O.U.P. 1974 (or alternatively Douglas, J. D. (ed.): *The New International Dictionary of the Christian Church* Paternoster (1974)).

Students should search the catalogue under the name of the person that specifically interests them in the library of any educational or public institution handy to them that takes theological studies seriously.

Acknowledgements

The Editor expresses his thanks to T. and T. Clark Ltd. for entrusting him with the responsibility of preparing this volume and the encouragement which T. G. Clark Esq., T. G. Ramsay Clark Esq., and Dr. Geoffrey F. Green have given to him.

The Editors and Publishers express their gratitude to the following Publishers for permission to use copyright material:

The Clarendon Press, Oxford; R. F. Evans: *Pelagius – Inquiries and Reappraisals*; A. and C. Black Ltd.; Faber and Faber Ltd.; The Faith Press Ltd.; Basil Blackwell; James Clarke and Co. Ltd.; S.P.C.K.; Cambridge University Press.

The Rev. B. Drewery wishes to express his thanks to the Rev. Dr. W. Peter Stephens, of Wesley College, Bristol, for the loan of an (unpublished) paper on Luther's doctrine of the Two Kingdoms.

He also wishes to acknowledge above all the unwearying kindness of his tutor, colleague and friend, the Rev. Professor E. Gordon Rupp, without whose oral and published guidance and instructions he could not have written one word.

The Editors are deeply indebted to Professor C. N. L. Brooke, Dixie Professor of Ecclesiastical History at Cambridge, who has revised the proofs of the late Dom David Knowles' contribution.

Introduction

H. Cunliffe-Jones

The first edition of G. P. Fisher's *History of Christian Doctrine* was published in 1896. After more than seventy years, it is high time that a new treatment of the history, with consideration of nearly a hundred additional years of theological reflection, should be undertaken. But Fisher's *History* has held its place, and deservedly held its place, right up to the present, as the best one-volume *History of Christian Doctrine* available for the student.

1. TRIBUTE TO G. P. FISHER

It is fitting that the new edition should begin by paying a tribute to Fisher, whose work even if it needs now to be superseded deserves the highest respect.

George Park Fisher was born on August 10th, 1827, and died on December 20th, 1909. He was a Congregational Minister and historian and was the son of Lewis Whiting and Nancy Fisher, and a grandson of Lewis and Luther Fisher, whose descent is traced to the family of Samuel Fisher, the noted Quaker apologist and martyr, contemporary and friend of George Fox. He was born in Wrentham, Massachusetts, where he attended the State schools until he graduated from Brown University in 1847. Then he studied at Yale Divinity School where Nathaniel W. Taylor was his teacher of Systematic Theology. He went for a time to Auburn Theological Seminary, but he completed his three years' theological course in 1851 at Andover, Massachusetts, where Professor Edward A. Park was the leading influence. He had the best training that the leaders of 'New England Theology' could offer. It was unusual, then, for theological students to do graduate study abroad, but Fisher spent the years 1852 to 1854 in Germany, where he became acquainted with the theological authorities of the time and received thorough training in the methods of historical research.

On his return in 1854 he was called to the Livingstone Professorship of Divinity in Yale College. In 1861 he resigned the Pastorate of the College Church to accept a Professorship of Ecclesiastical History in the Divinity School where he taught continuously till 1901. His books reflect his interest both in general history, *Outlines of Universal History* 1885, *The Colonial Era* 1892; in church history, notably his *History of the Christian Church* 1887; and in the history of Christian theology, particularly the *History of Christian Doctrine* 1896.

A contemporary, Frederick Lynch, called attention both to the comprehensiveness and accuracy of Fisher's written works, and the characteristic that made them unexciting as books to be read through. 'His knowledge was beyond belief. There seemed to be nothing he did not know. Probably no student in the many years Professor Fisher taught at Yale ever asked him a question he could not answer. His histories, "The History of the Christian Church", "The History of Christian Doctrine", and "The History of the Reformation", partake of this defect as well as of this excellence – they are so packed with fact that the flow of style is impeded and the imagination does not find scope for free play.'

On the other hand it is quite clear that he came to life outside his writing. Professor Williston Walker paid tribute to him: 'Professor Fisher was a prince of teachers in the classroom. He could illuminate a past age by vivid characterization, or portray the traits of a leader in the Church with graphic and penetrating discrimination. His contact with students was always stimulating. His wit was keen and searching, but not unkindly. His judgment was sane, careful and impartial. He was also a man who rejoiced in the society of his friends, and who in turn won admiration and affection in a remarkable degree. Possessed of an almost marvellous memory, a story-teller of exceptional ability, keen, vivacious, and witty intercourse with him had not only unusual stimulus but a rare charm. He was a delightful companion. His acquaintance on both sides of the Atlantic was such as few scholars possess and his friends loved him no less than they honoured him and delighted to be with him.'

In short, G. P. Fisher was an outstanding scholar and teacher of his own time, whose knowledge went wide and deep, and whose presentation of it was factual, concise and clear. His comprehensiveness can be exaggerated. For example, a reader will look in vain in Fisher's own *History of Christian Doctrine* for anything on Lutheranism after 1580. But this only shows that he had to draw the line somewhere. All in all, he deserves to be honoured, when the time has at long last come to survey the ground afresh to serve the need of a radically changed and changing situation.

2. THIS VOLUME FOLLOWS THE BROAD LINES OF FISHER'S OWN WORK

(a) Apart from the fact that he does not bring the Church into his starting-point, where Fisher started we can start too. 'Christianity,' wrote Fisher, 'is the Revelation of God through Jesus Christ whereby reconciliation and a new spiritual life in fellowship with himself are brought to mankind . . . herein Christianity is differentiated from systems of Philosophy . . . Christianity is composed of teachings which are to be proclaimed, and which call for a clear and connected interpretation . . . The History of Christian Doctrine is the record of the series of attempts made in successive periods to embody the contents of the Gospel in clear and self-consistent propositions.'

The modification of this starting-point which is necessary, is to add the awareness of the corporate life of the Church to Fisher's individualism. Fisher's individualism is in some ways curious because during the nineteenth century the sense of the importance of the Church and of a true Doctrine of the Church was steadily growing, and Fisher must have known this by the time he wrote. But it did not influence his treatment. Still the agreement in starting-point is quite real.

(b) Fisher discussed the question whether the History of Christian Doctrine should have a wider or a more restricted scope. He does this in terms of the question whether it should cover the history of dogma or whether it should more broadly consider the history of Christian theology in general. 'It may be the aim simply to exhibit the history of dogmas; that is, of the definitions of doctrine which have been arrived at either in the Church at large, or in leading branches of it – definitions which, when once reached, were held to be authoritative. A dogma is a distinct conception and perspicuous statement of the doctrine professed by the body, or by a considerable body, of Christian people.'

When Fisher wrote, the distinctive exposition of the history of dogma by Adolf von Harnack was widely influential; but he turned away from it as in principle narrowing. He preferred the alternative. 'It may undertake to trace the history of theology, not only so far as theological inquiry and discussion have issued in articles of faith, but likewise so far as movements of religious thought are of signal interest, and are often not unlikely to influence sooner or later the moulding of the Christian creed. The present volume will include a survey, as full as is practicable within the space at command, of the course of modern theology down to the present day.'

Here the present edition follows, out of conviction, Fisher's own line. The history of dogma has its own value, and it is still being freshly expounded. But it is only part of a wider concern, and excludes some of the most important questions that need to be considered in the history of Christian theology.

(c) Fisher discusses the practice of dividing Doctrinal History into two parts, the General and Special History of Doctrine, and of completing the account of each period under both aspects before advancing to the next. 'Under the General History there is presented a sketch of the characteristics of the period with a notice of the principal themes of discussion and of the principal writers to whom we are to resort for materials. The General History is an outline map of the period to be traversed. Under the Special History the matter is collected under the *loci* or rubrics of the theological system.' He himself had used this method in his lectures, but in preparing the volume for publication he abandoned it for a straight General History. The truth is that General and Special History of Doctrine represent different possible methods of studying the History of Christian Theology.

(i) The method of General History enables the continuity and sequence of the historical process to be brought out.

(ii) The method of Special History enables the different themes of the Christian creed to be traced in their historical development.

(iii) A variant of the method of Special History is to write it in terms of the biographies of the great figures, focussing the total thinking of great theologians in one chapter disentangled both from the movement of General History, and from the topical approach which inevitably separates the different aspects.

All these matters in the hands of skilled practitioners are valuable. In this volume we follow Fisher in seeking to trace the General History of Christian Theology.

(d) One of the valuable features in Fisher's own Introduction was a brief survey of the history of the History of Christian Theology. This is a matter urgently needing further research so that we can trace the sequence of those who have pioneered in the study of the History of Christian Theology. Here we need a new lead. We need someone to survey and tell us the methodology that is appropriate to the study of the History of Christian theology in a new ecumenical atmosphere in which there is a new awareness of the vast extent of the subject, and of the very varied nature of the theological and ecclesiastical traditions. Here we can note a few of the outstanding landmarks:

(i) The Centuriators of Magdeburg. This was a history of the first thirteen centuries of the Church produced by Lutheran theologians at Magdeburg under the guidance of Matthew Flacius (1520–1575). He was a 'genuine' Lutheran, and published between 1559 and 1574 in thirteen folio volumes – one for each century – the *Historia Ecclesiae Christi*. It was inaccurate and it took liberties with the texts of original documents. Its attitude was that of a rigid Lutheran doctrinal position, and it was consciously and powerfully anti-Roman in its treatment of the evidence. But it was a landmark in the history of Christian theology because of the breadth of conception it showed of what history and the history of Christian theology involved. It is important in spite of its limitation as giving some vision of the scope of the history of Christian theology.

(ii) Fisher calls attention to John Forbes of Corse who wrote the *Institutiones Historicae Theologicae* (Amsterdam 1645). The purpose of this was to demonstrate how the reformed Church agreed in its doctrine with the doctrine of the Patristic Church.

John Forbes' work has been criticized because it did not open the door to a critical history. But it was important as acknowledging an appeal to Patristic theology as a legitimate test of Christian truth. The combination of Reformation convictions and Patristic testimony make the reading of it a stimulating experience.

(iii) Dionysius Petavius (1583–1652) whose main work was the *De Theologicis Dogmatibus* (Volume I to III 1644, Volume IV 1650). Petavius was an outstanding dogmatic theologian, one of the most brilliant and learned of his age. He was strictly an orthodox Catholic in outlook, but he was one of the first (a) to accept the idea of development in theology and (b) to concede that much patristic teaching was imperfect when it was judged by later standards of developed theology.

(iv) For the eighteenth century Johann Salomo Semler (1725–1791) may stand as a representative historian of Doctrine. He goes to the other extreme from the Catholic vision of the stability of dogma by perceiving in history only a moving, steadily changing element; the essence of dogma is only restless change. History for him is governed by the arbitrary powers of subjectivity. At the same time his work represents the first critical examination of primitive Christianity and the development of dogma. It is based on the assumption that Christianity can be regarded only as a historical phenomenon to be studied historically and without dogmatic presuppositions, and that its historical manifestation must be analysed in the context of its historical milieu: that milieu is Jewish, and everything 'Christian' can be traced to it. Semler's criticism is negative; but negative criticism is a necessary first stage in the movement toward a truly objective and positive mode of historical consideration.

(v) Gotthold Ephraim Lessing (1729–1781), whose influence in the subsequent period has been so great, took the opposite line. He raised in a new radical way searching questions about the uncertainty of historical knowledge. He insisted that 'the accidental truths of history can never become a proof of necessary truths of revelation'. His thought was not particularly original, but he formulated it in a striking and unforgettable way. He bequeathed to the nineteenth century the idea of progressive revelation and to the twentieth century the unsolved problem of uniting history and revelation.

(vi) The great teacher of History of Doctrine in the nineteenth century was Ferdinand Christian Baur (1792–1860). Baur's discussion of the methods appropriate to the study of the History of Christian theology is to be found primarily in *Die Epochen der kirchlichen Geschichtsschreibung*, which serves as an introduction to Baur's five-volumed Church History. This work comprises an extensive analysis of various types and periods of Church historiography and concludes with a section in which Baur presents his own principles as well as his theology of the Church. A similar and extensive introduction is provided in the first volume of *Vorlesungen über die christliche Dogmengeschichte*, where Baur considers the position of history of dogma in the theological disciplines, the object, methods, and periods of dogma, the relation of the history of dogma to the history of philosophy, and the history of the study of the history of dogma – its origin and development into a science. Baur regards the historical part as an intrinsically important independent reality in shaping the historical present.

Both faith and historical knowledge are involved in the work of the historian of doctrine. On the one hand historical critical theology is dependent on authentic subjective faith, for it is only through the freedom thus achieved that the historical theologian is able to transpose himself critically into the objectivity of the historical data. On the other hand faith is dependent on, or must be instructed by, historical knowledge, since the content of faith is mediated historically and knowable through critical history, and since authentic faith requires the continual prodding and testing of historical criticism, for its certainty is of a different order from the empirical certainties of this world.

Whether Baur came to the point of claiming that faith is not only subjective but actually penetrates to a transcendent reality not apart from but within the objectivity of the historical process is not clear. His uncertainty at this point is in one way to his credit, as many of his contemporaries foreclosed the issue in the direction of denying the Transcendent. But he has bequeathed his uncertainty to the twentieth century, and we have not solved the problem in any satisfactory intellectual manner.

(vii) It is not proposed to develop further in this introduction even this minute sketch of the history of the History of Christian Theology that is a clear and urgent desideration. There are many aspects of the late nineteenth-century history of Christian theology which need investigation – e.g. the tendentious Lutheran histories of Albrecht Ritschl (1822–1889); and among

British thinkers: the treatment of development by Andrew Martin Fairbairn (1838–1912) in Division I – 'The law of development in Theology and the Church' – of his study of *The Place of Christ in Modern Theology*; or the immanentist perspective of Alexander V. G. Allen: *The continuity of Christian Thought: A Study of Modern Theology in the light of its history* (1884). A rude shock was given to all such perspectives by the publication of the first volume of Karl Barth's *Church Dogmatics* in 1932 with its incisive division of historical Christian thinking into three groups: Roman Catholic theology, Reformation theology, and Neo-Protestant theology. Since then the pendulum has moved back to various new considerations of natural theology; also the growing ecumenical movement, and the decline of religious allegiance in the older established centres of Christian dominance, have produced many different changes of perspective.

Two things may be said:

i. the history of the History of Christian Theology needs to be written from some kind of stable perspective, even if that stability is only of a temporary kind. How can it be written from an objective standpoint if the perspective in which we live is constantly changing?

ii. the writing of such a perspective would be more convincingly undertaken if the question of the legitimacy of the appeal to the Transcendent from within an historical perspective had been settled.

Nevertheless, we must continue to hope that someone, thoroughly equipped, will undertake the work.

3. BUT THIS VOLUME IS DIFFERENT IN A NUMBER OF WAYS FROM FISHER'S OWN WORK

(a) It aims to point out the main aspects of the history without being comprehensive in detail.

There are disadvantages in Fisher's very comprehensiveness. His accuracy, and the fact that everything was to be found in it, was so useful that students preparing for examinations deemed it unnecessary to proceed to the texts on which the History was based. This is not a good way of studying the History of Christian theology, even if G. P. Fisher's own work is a first-rate example of the type of text-book that enabled it to be followed. All general histories should be studied with reference to the primary texts.

This volume will presuppose that the student will not be content with it but will turn to the texts to make his own judgment as to whether the History is rightly done or not. For the comprehensiveness in detail that the student does in fact often need, he is advised to turn to other sources, e.g. to the *Oxford Dictionary of the Christian Church* edited by F. L. Cross, of which the second edition was published in 1974.

(b) It is written from a series of points of view which seek to do justice to all standpoints of Christian tradition. One of the reasons why this new edition of Fisher is a composite production is that it is not possible now to call on any one scholar to prepare the History of Christian Doctrine because the different aspects of the History are now too specialized. Fisher presented the History of Christian Doctrine from a single point of view. There are advantages in a multiple approach.

History of Christian theology as a University discipline must cover the whole spectrum of Christian theology impartially: Greek Orthodox, Roman Catholic, Anglican, Classical Protestant, Decentralized Protestant and Radical Protestant. There is no one perspective from which the History of Christian theology must be seen. The attainment of a reasonable perspective which may be accepted by all qualified students of the subject is a matter not of one point of view but of continuing dialogue between representatives of different theological and ecclesiastical traditions. It is not a question of anyone suppressing his own convictions or his own perspective. These must be expressed. But so far as anyone can, he must approach the material in its own right and see that his own predilections do not distort the material. In any case he must offer his contribution to the History of Doctrine as a contribution to be set in the context of treatments from other points of view.

From the point of view of students the advantage of a multiple approach is that they can no longer acquiesce in the supposition that history is just a series of facts universally accepted. History is rather essentially fact plus interpretation, and where interpretations differ widely there may well be different opinions about what the facts actually are. If the reader of this history finds the approaches of the contributors contrasting, or finds himself at variance with the approach of any one, that should be a spur to clarify his own understanding of what the right interpretation is, and how it illuminates the facts.

(c) It takes account of much research and interpretation that has been done since Fisher's time, and points to new research that is still needed.

In the first place, it reflects the current awareness of the need to study the History of Orthodox theology. The History of the Eastern Church and its thinking has been very largely neglected; or rather it has been taken for granted that the History of Orthodox theology finished with John of Damascus, and that since that time the Orthodox Church has been fossilized, so that what its theologians have been thinking about since the eighth century is not worth serious attention.

This has been falsified in common awareness by the resurgence of the Orthodox Church in the nineteenth and especially in the twentieth century. There are great treasures to which we have been blind. Even if some of the periods in the history are dull and unimpressive we still ought to know what was being thought in those periods, and to take account of the factors which threw the Orthodox Church on the defensive and made it difficult for it to deploy its own thinking. The History of Orthodox theology has not been fully surveyed, and a great deal remains still to be done, but we are fortunate in this volume to have an authoritative account of the theology from the seventh to the fourteenth century, and some indication of the lines for study in the later history.

Further, we need a new survey of the history of Roman Catholic theology since Trent. Too often both on the Catholic and Protestant side there has

been a progressive narrowing of the study of the history of theology.
Roman Catholics themselves have not fully explored the History of Roman
Catholic theology since Trent, understandably in some degree because the
seventeenth and eighteenth centuries in particular are not centuries they
would want to boast about. Catholic theology was on the defensive and
showed no great creative aspects. But in the nineteenth century were laid
the foundations of the revival of Catholic theology that has taken place in
the twentieth century, and at least from the end of the nineteenth century
we can trace the burgeoning of the thinking of men like Möhler and Newman. A detached history of Roman Catholic theology in these centuries
would benefit all students of Christian theology.

The history of Scandinavian Lutheran theology has not been written even
for Scandinavians themselves, and this is a field that could profitably be
explored.

The general history of Christian theology ought to take seriously the
history of American theology. Up to perhaps the end of the nineteenth
century, apart from some outstanding figures of whom it is not true,
American Christian theology appears to have been parasitic on Europe for
the main content of its thinking. Naturally it has developed this thinking
in relation to the demands of its own environment, and this has given it its
characteristic colouring. Nevertheless, even in its most highly gifted representatives it has been, in principle, dependent thinking. It is quite clear
that at the present time it is not so and developing in its own right. Even
so there are many aspects of the past history of American Christian theology
which are important and need to be noted even if they do not represent a
new creative advance. The place of American theology in the total perspective needs clearly to be explored, and freshly assessed.

One of the aspects of the history of Christian doctrine which has been
taken into account in this volume is the importance of the fifteenth century.
In this volume it has been placed in the context of the Reformation so that
the presentation of the Reformation shall take seriously the century and a
half which lies before it. This is part of the proper perspective in which the
Reformation is to be seen. The fifteenth century needs also to be seen as
late Medieval theology, and indeed it is in many ways the Medievalists
themselves who are exploring that century afresh. We really need a double
treatment of the fifteenth century, so that we can see it both as preparation
for the background to the Reformation and also as the late development of
the Medieval Period.

Lastly, when we come to the nineteenth and twentieth centuries the
whole development needs consideration. The study of theology in the
twentieth century depends upon having a workable perspective of what this
development has entailed. This is a difficult subject and it has not yet been
brought into common focus. It is certainly an important aspect of the
History of Christian Doctrine to see the Nineteenth Century and After as
the raising of the question how, in the context of the scientific universe,
and taking Christianity seriously as a historical phenomenon, just like any
other human part of history, we must still affirm God transcendent incarnate
in Christ.

4. QUESTIONS RAISED BY THE HISTORY OF CHRISTIAN THEOLOGY
(starting from the questions that Fisher himself raises)

(a) *Is theology possible?*

This is a perennial question. In Fisher's time it was the unknowable of Herbert Spencer which was the origin of the question for him. But every age has its own way of producing the question whether the activity of theology is possible and meaningful. Three questions seem to be involved.

(i) *Can we know the transcendent?* If the transcendent is in the very nature of the case beyond us, beyond the universe, beyond our knowledge and experience, how can we know it? No logical proof of the reality of the transcendent seems possible. Human beings who reflect on the problem seem to be divided into two groups, one of which would be perfectly content to say that there is no transcendent and no knowledge of it; the other group would say that having reflected on the problem they are compelled to affirm the reality of the transcendent. The compulsion that moves them is not primarily an emotional compulsion, in the sense that they affirm the transcendent because they have been brought up to do so, and it is part of their habit of life. It is rather their conviction that they affirm the transcendent because it is intellectually unsatisfying not to do so.

There is something intellectually unsatisfactory and unilluminating in *not* affirming that we are, through the very limitations of our human experience, able to see facets of that experience as pointers to what is beyond. The transcendent is that which we in no sense fully know, but which we can apprehend by paying close attention to what is involved and implied in our own human experience. If we are asked: 'Is this something which is due to the long dominance of the Christian faith in the life of mankind, and is it likely to fade away if the recession from the Christian faith continues?', our answer must be that it is no more likely that the recession should continue than that in a new way mankind should come to a new affirmation of Christian faith as true. In any case, the convinced Christian must continue to affirm in all circumstances his apprehension of the transcendent as a necessary condition of human life being fully human. For in the last resort the question cannot be decided on probabilities or on trends. It must be decided on apprehension of the truth.

(ii) *Are theological statements meaningful?* It is no use the theologians saying things in their private coteries if the terms they are using, in the way they are using them, amount to no more than a series of meaningless expressions. Two questions are relevant to the meaningfulness of theological statements.

One is the question of analogy. God, it has been claimed, is known in statements that are not univocal or equivocal but analogous. In univocal use terms are used in precisely the same sense, in equivocal use the same term is used but the meaning is utterly different. In analogous use the terms have a similarity of meaning which is not precisely the same. Now the question is: is there sufficient similarity between the way terms are used, both of God and man, is the gap between the meaning of the term as applied to God and the meaning of the term as applied to man sufficiently small for us to claim that there is genuine knowledge? This is a question of which there may be different opinions.

An illuminating positive use of analogy is to be found in the argument of Bishop Butler on the ignorance of man. Joseph Butler in his *Analogy of Religion* drew attention to factors within human experience that gave mankind confidence in the moral government of God. This was against the background of a vast ignorance that prevented man having anything like a full understanding of God's plan and purpose. The question of the meaningfulness of theological statements is the question whether we have sufficient awareness of the reality of God to give us practical confidence that we know him. Yet any such confidence must be held in the context of an ignorance of God so vast that we are constantly aware that we do not understand the full measure of his plan and purpose.

The other question which may be raised under this head is whether anything at all may be adduced to falsify belief in God. If a steadfastly believing Christian dies through a horrible and lingering experience of cancer in its most painful form, why does he not take this as a proof to him that God is not love? Why do not Christians take great experience of human suffering on a large scale caused by natural disaster or by the inhumanity of man to man (e.g. the murder of six million Jews in Germany) as a demonstration that God is not love? In sum, what *can* count as a crushing affliction to the belief that God is love? If the answer is nothing at all, is the statement that God is love really meaningful?

It is worth considering that the religious believer can adduce statements which, if true, though he does not believe that they are true, could be evidence that his belief is unfounded. Such statements would call in question the underlying foundation experiences that lie deeper than his explicit belief in God. For if the spirit of thankfulness, if the aversion to cruelty in one person's dealing with another, if the spirit of reverence, if the attitude of unselfishness, are meaningless or unworthy experiences, then it seems quite clear that the attempt to affirm the reality of God and the belief that God is love are quite unfounded. The believer thinks that nothing can in fact show this. But if it were shown it would be an empirical matter of fact.

(iii) A third question deals with the *nature of language* in relation to theology. Here Fisher calls attention to the perceptive work of Horace Bushnell in the nineteenth century. Bushnell's 'Preliminary Dissertation on the Nature of Language, as related to Thought and Spirit' in his *God in Christ* (1849) is relevant here. He raises the question of analogy which we have already mentioned, and also the crucial question of the 'cognitive' or 'non-cognitive' character of religious language.

Theological statements appear to give a true account of reality though they are statements about kinds of facts other than those investigated by the sciences. A number of contemporary philosophers, impressed by the difficulty of showing that statements about God are factual, have offered theories of religious language as non-cognitive. Such statements, they think, give the emotional setting for other statements and experiences. Philosophers or theologians who think in this way do not mean to rule theology out of court. Their intention is to give it a very different slant from that which it has traditionally had.

(b) *The relation of Christian theology to Faith and the Life of the Church*
Fisher starts from the faith of the individual believer. We shall start here from the faith of the Church. Some of the most remarkable statements on the nature of theology in relation to the church have come from Karl Barth. He says 'Dogmatics is a theological discipline. But theology is a function of the Church.' 'Dogmatics is the self-test which the Christian Church puts to herself in respect of the content of her peculiar language about God.'

But how does the Church test herself? By theology in respect of the content of her peculiar language about God. This takes place partly by the reflections of individual theologians – sometimes in lonely reflection (e.g. Anselm); sometimes in constant discussion with one another (e.g. the Cappadocian Fathers); properly also always in constant discussion with unbelieving thinkers; and partly by the corporate decisions of the Church.

This theological test of the language the Church uses about God is not the only way in which the Church needs to test the language it uses. But it is the test of the adequacy of that language to the Gospel which the Church seeks to proclaim, and to its meaningfulness and adequate articulation in the contemporary scene in the light of the historical discussion of the centuries.

What is the relation, then, of this process of theology to that Christian faith which is the response to the truth of the Christian Gospel? Fisher takes the view that 'the faith of the Christian disciple is not the product of science, but science is the intellectual apprehension of its contents'. In contemporary terms, this is to say, that faith is the first-order reality of which theology is the second-order reality. This means that theology should not be over-valued. It is not intrinsically a means for renewing the insight and vitality of faith. That must come from other sources. Only in special circumstances will the articulation of the intellectual content of faith have the result of invigorating faith itself.

It should be noted that the question whether the theologian must himself have this personal faith, is one that Fisher himself does not raise. The answer seems to be – not necessarily. It is natural for the theologian himself to be a man of faith; but where anyone combines with agnosticism or atheism an acute sensitivity and an intense interest in Christian theology, he may contribute as effectively as any other theologian to the intellectual articulation of the content of Christian faith. After all theology is intellectual articulation. A theologian must, however, be sufficiently sensitive to what he is articulating to be aware of its nature and content, and in many cases, the most natural and effective way to do this is through personal conviction.

(c) *The factors involved in formulating theological doctrine*
Fisher affirmed that three factors were involved in the formulation of Christian doctrines: the word, the spirit, the intellect; or scripture, experience, science. These are the factors by whose combined agency a gospel is

rendered into systematic expressions of doctrine. And he finds three distortions of the true use of these factors:

(i) 'There may be a servile reliance on inherited interpretations of scripture, or the adoption of meanings having no other ground than ecclesiastical prescription. The result is a traditionalism, which fails to penetrate to the core of scriptural teaching.'

(ii) 'There must be scope for the free activity of Christian feeling. When feeling, however, comes to be considered an immediate fountain of knowledge, the intellect is deprived of its rights, and the Bible sinks below its proper level.'

(iii) 'There must be as much scope for the free activity of the intellect in framing Christian doctrine as for Christian feeling. But a third species of perversion in the framing of doctrine arises from the exaggeration of the intellectual factor.'

On this the following comments may be made:

(i) Fisher's insistence on the gospel declared in the Scripture as the objective rule of Christian faith is rightly central. Yet the progress of the study of the literary forms and historical perspective used in Scripture to set forth the Gospel raises in an acute form the problem of distinguishing between that Gospel which is authoritative for Christians and the setting in which it is embedded.

Also we now understand that Scripture is rightly to be regarded as tradition, and that it is set in the midst of tradition. The precise determination of the authority of scripture as such, the precise determination of the authority of tradition other than scripture and the precise differentiation between scripture and tradition are questions to which the answers are not easily given.

In the actual course of historical theology there has been constant appeal to the authority of scripture. But this has operated in different ways. Quite often the appeal to scripture is not an appeal to the originating source of the particular theological conviction, but to confirmatory evidence for a conviction already reached.

Sometimes, however, the verbal form of the Bible has exercised a determining effect – many times beneficially in conserving an important insight that might otherwise have been minimized or lost; sometimes, however, with harmful effect, binding upon the Church either the meaning or a supposed translation of the meaning in a way that restricted insight into the nature of the Gospel. But, whatever the persisting difficulties in the appeal to the authority of the Gospel in scripture, the appeal must be made.

(ii) Feeling has its proper place in the formation of Christian theology as the response to more objective factors determining its process.

There are two main ways in which this has happened. The first comes from participation in the activity of worship. This has had both beneficial and harmful effects on the formulation of Christian theology. It has been beneficial in that it has saved theological formulation from becoming too arid and bound it closely to the centralities of Christian truth focussed in the experience of worship. It has had harmful effects where certain forms of devotion which have both met and fostered certain emotional needs have exercised a determining effect upon Christian theology, without being subject to the astringent criticism of responsible thinking.

(iii) Fisher was strongly hostile to a false rationalism in theology. There is, however, an opposite danger, that theology should be too pious, and rest content with the immediate utterances of Christian faith, and not grapple, with all the energy of mind available, with the task of expressing their truth in the intellectual climate of the day. The Christian theologian must not leave it to the agnostic or atheist to grapple manfully with difficult and pressing intellectual problems which threaten the very humanity of man.

There are, however, two types of intellectual activity, and the true functioning of the intellect in Christian theology comes from combining them in the right way.

These are: on the one hand, the native form of the ratiocinative intellect arguing with logical precision; on the other hand the mind open to all sources of apprehension in grasping what is real. These two may be called Understanding and Reason; but the distinction has been used in many periods in the history of Christian theology and the names have changed. Understanding has also been used for the richer form of the use of the intellect, and on the other hand, Reason has sometimes been used not for the higher form but for the use of the mind arguing precisely, logically and narrowly. It is, however, the richer form of the use of the intellect which should have the dominant place in the formulation of Christian theology, without denying the legitimate rights of the argumentative type. In the balanced use of the two types lies the truest insight.

(d) *Development and Upheaval in Theology*

The nineteenth century was a century that emphasized development. A notable contribution to the understanding of this was made by John Henry Newman in his Essay on Development written in 1845, which Fisher discusses in his Introduction. The twentieth century is much more a century of upheaval. Newman did a great service to both Catholic and Protestant theology in forcing upon the theologians a new consideration of the question of development and the fact that dogmatic propositions had not been the same from the beginning of the Christian era. Both tended to think in static terms and to discuss the matter in purely logical ways. The Reformers, having established the Bible as the source of authority, failed to give theological guidance as to how to deal with the developing tradition which the Reformation itself created.

The real question raised by Newman's own idea of development was the question of the idea from which he started: What is the character of the idea of Christianity which is developing? Agreement on this must take precedence over finding criteria of what developments are true or false. Whatever the importance of noticing development and making provision for it in our thinking, neither logical nor organic continuity determines whether a doctrinal statement or a doctrinal system is true. At every stage the question of truth and adequacy takes precedence over questions of consistency in development.

Discontinuity as well as development may have a place in our assessment of truth. The history of the Church is in many ways very disconcerting. We would not have supposed that certain developments which have come to stay would have taken place. Our theories of what God is doing with his Church must take account of how he has allowed the Church to live and change in the course of history. Organic development may mask a fundamental weakening or corruption of the fundamental idea. Periods of upheaval and drastic discontinuity may in fact exhibit a more fundamental continuity of faithfulness to the essential idea. Both organic development and radical discontinuity must be taken into account, with the consideration of truth and adequacy, in determining what is in fact true theology. True continuity is not incompatible with a Copernican revolution in many aspects. In the continuing discussion both conservative and radical theologians need patience with one another and a constant attempt to understand each other.

(e) *The Relation of the History of Christian Theology to General History and to Church History*

1. The distinction between the history involved in the history of Christian theology and that involved in the general history of mankind, is a distinction of content and not of method. Christian theology does not contract out of the general historical scene in order to have its proper characteristics given satisfactory treatment. In point of fact it is in the context of what was happening in that general history that some of the features of the history of Christian theology can be best understood.

The failure of theologians to be sensitive to what has been happening in the wider history of mankind militates against the satisfactoriness of their theology, just as the undue sensitiveness and subservience to what has been happening in general history may mean that their theology is less than satisfactory. Unless the historian seeking to understand the way that Christian theology has come to expression in history is really prepared both to set it in the context of the wider history of mankind, and also to accept the fact that he is pursuing a discipline which is governed by principles which are the same which general historians practise, he will do harm to his own craft.

2. What needs to be said specially about the relations of history of Christian theology to Church history is this: the history of Christian theology is in principle a hybrid discipline. That is to say it is both historical and theological. A satisfactory history of Christian theology will be equally competent and illuminating, both on the historical and the theological questions involved.

In practice this does not by any means always happen. It may be that the writer is primarily a historian. The historical setting, the historical preparation and outcome of the theology is most illuminatingly presented, but there is no corresponding insight as to what the theology meant and in this respect the history of Christian theology is defective.

Or, on the other hand, the author may be primarily a theologian. He does not consciously misrepresent history. He does not fall down on elementary historical facts. But his almost exclusive interest is to elucidate the theologically important character of the great theologians. He is insufficiently equipped technically to elucidate the historical setting in which they are given, the historical preparation for them on the part of lesser men, or the immediate historical consequences of this type of theology.

The ideal historian of Christian theology would be grounded deep in the truth of the Gospel and in Christian churchmanship, equally at home in the fields of history and of philosophy, and endowed with powerful gifts of exposition. How far the present volume measures up to this exacting standard is not for us to say.

(f) The Relation of the History of Christian Theology to Culture and Sociology
Paul Tillich has expressed in striking fashion the relation of his own three volumes of Systematic Theology to Culture as follows:

'A special characteristic of these three volumes . . . is the kind of language used in them and the way in which it is used. It deviates from the ordinary use of biblical language in systematic theology – that is, to support particularly assertions with appropriate biblical quotations. Not even the more satisfactory method of building a theological system on the foundations of a historical, critical, "biblical" theology is directly applied, although its influence is present in every part of the system. Instead, philosophical and psychological concepts are preferred, and references to sociological and scientific theories often appear. . . . Of course, I am not unaware of the danger that in this way the substance of the Christian message may be lost. Nevertheless, this danger must be risked, and once one has realized this, one must proceed in this direction. . . . Certainly, these three books would not have been written if I had not been convinced that the event in which Christianity was born has central significance for all mankind, both before and after the event. But the way in which this event can be understood and received changes with changing conditions in all periods of history. On the other hand, this work would not have come into existence either, if I had not tried during the larger part of my life to penetrate the meaning of the Christian Symbols which have been increasingly problematic within the cultural context of our time. Since the split between a faith unacceptable to culture and a culture unacceptable to faith was not possible for me, the only alternative was to attempt to interpret symbols of faith through expressions of our own culture.'

This passage from Paul Tillich provokes various reflections.
(i) The historian of Christian theology should be aware of the cultural context of the theologians and their propositions which he is investigating and recording. All theology is formulated in a cultural background.
(ii) Cultural factors have influenced the theology of theologians of the past in ways in which the theologians themselves have not always been aware.
(iii) Paul Tillich says that for himself a culture unacceptable to faith and

a faith unacceptable to culture constitute a split which is quite intolerable. The historian is, however, bound to ask whether this corresponds to the experience of the Church in history. Has not, in point of fact, the Christian faith and the theology of the Christian faith grown and grown strong in situations where there has been a split between the faith and the culture? Is the attempt to bridge over a split between faith and culture necessarily the best way of ensuring that the content of the Christian faith and the doctrines appropriate are in fact satisfactory? .

(iv) Another question which the historian will do well to be sensitive to, is whether theologians of the past have been unnecessarily insensitive to the culture in which they have been placed. Their theology may not have an adequate expression of Christian truth precisely because they were unaware of cultural factors in their own situation into which the formulation of Christian doctrine ought rightly to have been spoken.

(v) Paul Tillich has spoken of the danger that by using cultural symbols to express Christian truth, the substance of the Christian message may be lost. This is not the only danger. The danger is also that the message may be diluted and an unsatisfactory expression of the Christian message may be given. The historian is bound to investigate whether it has happened at any place in history that through over-sensitiveness to the culture, theology has not properly carried out its function of being properly aware and sensitive to its own dignity and the respect it desiderates from the culture in which it is set.

(vi) A special aspect of the relation of Christian theology to culture is presented by the sociology of religion. Of any theology it can be asked: what social background is the theologian unconsciously presupposing? When the theologian and his audience share a static background, the question is less important than when the theologian lives in a period of rapid social change. In the latter instance the theologian may be presupposing a social background that is two generations out of date.

The study of the sociology of religion has a salutary astringency for the study of Christian theology. It sets theology firmly in the social background of mankind as a whole, and calls attention to certain objectively ascertained factors of which the theologian may well prefer to be unaware, because they raise questions about the truth and relevance of the theology he is expounding.

It is important that the sociology of religion should, however, not be overvalued. It is one thing to call attention to social factors which consciously or unconsciously have affected the formulation of Christian theology. But such factors do not determine the question of its truth. If the social factor is made all-determining, it destroys confidence in any possibility of the existence of *truth*, even the truth that the social factor is all-determining. All it can do in fact is to make certain qualifications in the presentation of that truth. But this is an important service.

(g) *The Relation of the History of Christian Theology to Philosophy*

Whatever be the right relation of Christian theology to philosophy, their histories are very much entwined. The attitude of Christian theologians to

philosophy has covered a very wide range from almost total repudiation to almost total subservience.

Some theologians make a very sharp division between Christian theology and philosophy. What has the God of Abraham, Isaac and Jacob to do with the god of the philosophers? What has Athens to do with Jerusalem? This division is, however, not necessarily incompatible with the use of philosophical tools of thought in theology and rational processes of argument.

Many theologians will recognize that philosophy and Christian theology have an overlap of interest in the subjects, or some of the subjects, they discuss; and therefore it is incumbent on theologians to be aware both of contemporary philosophy and of the history of philosophy, and aware also of the way in which philosophy has, for better or worse, influenced the actual historical development. Some theologians make special use of a particular philosophy. Notable here is the use of Aristotelianism by St. Thomas Aquinas and in our own day the use of the philosophy of Martin Heidegger by Rudolf Bultmann.

On the other hand, some theologians affirm that Christian theology is compatible with any philosophy that does not deny any essential Christian truth, and that there is, on the other hand, no particular philosophy which can be called in a special way Christian. All philosophies which are not incompatible with the Christian truth may serve as useful allies and instruments of formulating Christian theology. Many theologians, perhaps most, have no fixed idea on the relation of Christian theology to philosophy but are concerned to see that in the product it is the Christian theology which controls the philosophy and not vice-versa.

In our own day a new question has arisen of the right and duty of the philosopher to scrutinize the meaningfulness of theological terms and the use the theologians make of them. However much theologians may be averse to letting their theology be controlled in any way by the philosophical enquiries of his own, or of his colleagues, there seems no escape from the fact that the philosopher has the right to judge whether or not the terms that the theologian is asking is meaningful.

(h) *The Relation of the History of Christian Theology to Doctrinal Criticism and Constructive Theology*

'Neither the historian of doctrine,' as has been said, 'nor the doctrinal critic can undertake his work in isolation from the other. Their methods are not mutually exclusive. The doctrinal critic requires a knowledge of the history of doctrine, and the historian of doctrine requires a knowledge of the presuppositions which he is using in making his historical inquiries, and some insight into the uses of language in making doctrinal statements. Each must learn from the other.'

The primary duty of the doctrinal critic is to pass judgments upon the truth and adequacy of any doctrinal statement or any doctrinal system. The primary duty of the constructive theologian is to make positive theological statements and submit them to the judgment of the Church. Both in doing their work have presuppositions which they bring to their study.

The historian of Christian theology will do his work less satisfactorily if he is not aware of the standards he himself would bring to use in doctrinal criticism and of his own interest and conception of what is the satisfactory doctrinal statement in his own contemporary setting. He cannot pursue his historical studies in isolation from the contemporary scene. That contemporary scene, whether he knows it or not, influences very greatly the questions which he asks of history. He brings the prejudices and presuppositions of his own time to his historical inquiries.

On the other hand, the doctrinal critic and the constructive theologian are influenced, whether they know it or not, by the historical theology of the past. They will do their work much better if they have a critical understanding of that history, and have a conscious rather than an unconscious grasp of how it influences them.

As they do their work in the contemporary scene, submitting it to the judgment of their fellows and to the judgment of the Church as a whole, they would also do well to look back into history and see what persons similar to themselves have been like, and the way in which doctrinal criticism and constructive theological statements given in the past have fared in the development of history.

A real sensitiveness to the way in which theological statements have been criticized, have often influenced many thinkers and then sometimes ceased to have that influence, is a salutary caution for those who propound theological statements as solutions to new problems. The study of history should not discourage theologians from making constructive statements. It should only cause them to be on their guard against over-confidence that their statements will in fact be accepted.

The work of the historian of Christian theology and that of the constructive theologian are inextricably bound together. Each is quite indispensable to the other. So we present this history not only as an attempt at a more satisfactory introduction to the history of the past, but also as a stimulating tool and resource for the task of the continuing present.

Christian Theology in the
Patristic Period

G. W. H. Lampe

Christian Theology in the
Patristic Period

G. W. H. LAMPE

I

THE APOSTOLIC FATHERS AND THE
SECOND-CENTURY MOVEMENTS

Christian doctrine had already undergone a long period of development by the time that the latest books in the canon of the New Testament had been written; and by that time, in all probability, a number of the writings known as the works of the 'Apostolic Fathers' had already appeared. There is an overlap in time between the New Testament and those writings which have traditionally been treated as though they were the products of a sub-apostolic age following after the 'New Testament period' in a clearly defined chronological succession. On the one hand, II Peter and probably other canonical writings are later in date than some at least of the Apostolic Fathers; on the other, it is conceivable that the *Didache* is very early indeed, perhaps dating from well within what is generally thought of as the New Testament period. From one point of view, then, it might be said that the Apostolic Fathers and some of the New Testament writings belong together as evidence for the history of doctrine at the end of the first century and the first half of the second. On the other hand, there can be little doubt that nearly all the canonical books do have an originality and freshness which is for the most part lacking in the Apostolic Fathers. These tend to be derivative; for although it is true that the New Testament canon has not yet emerged as such, yet the Gospels and the Pauline Epistles are regarded as authorities, the idea of an 'apostolic age' is developing, and Church leaders are looking to the traditions of the churches and to the forms of Church order which seem to safeguard the traditions handed down from the past, for protection against dangerous innovations and for guidance in the preservation of a supposed original and authentic deposit of truth.

The writings of the Apostolic Fathers are occasional pieces, evoked by contemporary needs. They do not include any works of systematic theology, and although they are of the greatest historical and literary interest, heightened by the fact that the first three-quarters of the second century is a period from which relatively little Christian literature has survived, they cannot be said to provide much important material for the history of Christian thought. On the whole these writers are content to reproduce ideas and language which were already traditional in the churches and familiar in the Gospels and Epistles. They do this, moreover, without for the most part seeming to be able to present to their readers the authentic gospel as we find it in the New Testament. We may feel some surprise, for instance, on finding that Clement of Rome in his letter to the church at Corinth cites the fourth 'Servant Song' from Isa. 53 and part of Ps. 22

only in order to draw the somewhat pedestrian and moralistic lesson that Jesus is an example of humility and therefore the congregation at Corinth should learn to abandon their factious pride and restore the presbyters whom they have unjustly deposed.[1] These writers have often been reproached, too, for their apparent failure to appreciate the Pauline doctrine of justification and grace; and, again, there is some truth in this criticism. The homily known as II Clement opens with a reminder of the sufferings of Christ 'for our sakes', but it continues in a quite unprecedented fashion by asking 'What recompense then shall we give to him?'; later it asserts that almsgiving is good, like repentance from sin; fasting is better than prayer, but almsgiving than both.[2] Nevertheless, it would be unfair to Clement of Rome, Ignatius, Hermas, Polycarp and the other writers of this period, to write them down as inferior Christians who introduced a kind of slump in the quality of the Church's preaching and teaching after the great achievements of the apostolic age. In the first place, the New Testament, with so large a proportion of its pages occupied by the Pauline and Johannine literature, probably gives a misleading picture of the thought of the primitive Church. It did not move at a consistently high level, followed by a sudden descent to a less elevated intellectual and spiritual plane of the Apostolic Fathers; it clearly followed a fairly consistent level, represented perhaps by Luke–Acts, the Pastoral Epistles and other New Testament writings, and also by the post-canonical literature, above which there stand out in lofty isolation the two great peaks of the Pauline and the Johannine writings. Secondly, it must be remembered that the themes with which these later authors had to deal were different from those which had occupied St. Paul. They do not have to deal with the question of the Law and grace in the same way at all, and much of their attention had to be focussed on the problems of moral conduct as these arose in the Christian communities, such as the disorder in the Corinthian congregation. It must not be forgotten, too, that for them the scriptures were absolutely authoritative, and that many apparent lapses in the direction of a Judaizing legalism, such as II Clement's remarks about almsgiving removing the burden of sin,[3] were directly derived from scriptural sources such as Tobit.

It is not because these writers are uninteresting or inferior that they present little of importance for the history of doctrine but rather because they do not set out to deal with the major aspects of Christian faith in any systematic way. There are, however, a number of passages which throw passing and incidental light on the development of Christian thought. Clement, for instance, speaks of God as 'Master of the universe';[4] he calls God 'Father' and links this appellation with God's creativity; he is 'Father and Creator of the whole world'.[5] This is an idea which adumbrates that combination of biblical and Platonist language about God which appears so strongly from the Greek Apologists onwards when scriptural phrases

[1] *1 Clem.* 16.
[2] *2 Clem.* 1, 16.
[3] *ib.* 16.
[4] *1 Clem.* 8.
[5] *ib.* 19.

about God's Fatherhood come to be glossed in terms of the 'Father and Maker of the universe' of the *Timaeus*. Stoicism is also exerting an influence, as in Clement's remarkable appeal to the orderliness and uniformity of nature, and so to the revelation through this of God's beneficent and sovereign rule, as a lesson in good order in the Christian society:[1] 'Seeing that we have this pattern, let us conform ourselves with all diligence to his will.'[2] A similar emphasis on the goodness of creation, though in a different context, appears in the *Didache* where, again, the idea that God is 'all-sovereign Master' is prominent.[3] The same thought is more fully developed by Hermas: 'God . . . who by his invisible and mighty power and by his great wisdom created the world and by his glorious purpose clothed his creation with beauty and by his strong word fixed the heaven and founded the earth upon the waters and by his own wisdom and providence formed his holy Church . . .',[4] a passage where even this unphilosophical writer is speaking of God's activity in terms familiar to Greek readers, such as 'providence' (*pronoia*), and naming those attributes of God which were soon to be hypostatized and identified with the pre-existent Christ – a process which had indeed already begun in the New Testament. It is not therefore surprising to find Hermas enunciating a doctrine of God in a quasi-credal form in the opening words of his *Mandates*. 'First of all,' he says, 'believe that God is one, even he who created all things and set them in order, and brought all things from non-existence into being, who comprehends all things, being alone incomprehensible.'[5]

The problem of relating these concepts of God to the Christian encounter with God in the person of Jesus Christ had not yet evoked any marked development in Trinitarian theology over and above the stages which this had reached in the New Testament writings. Clement uses Trinitarian language in his letter to the Corinthian church: 'Have we not one God and one Christ and one Spirit of grace, the Spirit that has been poured out on us?'[6] It is significant for the subsequent history of doctrine that what is said about the Spirit is directly related to the experience of the Christian life in the Church. For a long time to come what is said about God and Christ and their mutual relationship will be stated in terms of theological metaphysics, while what is said about the Spirit will be stated in the more direct and practical terms of 'grace', 'power', 'illumination', and prophetic and other charismatic gifts. A similar passage runs: 'For God lives, and Jesus Christ lives, and the Holy Spirit and the faith and hope of the elect. . . .'[7]

Ignatius uses similar Trinitarian language, exhorting the Magnesians to act 'by faith and by love, in the Son and Father and in the Spirit',[8] and working out an elaborate simile of the Church members as 'stones of a

[1] *ib.* 20.
[2] *ib.* 23.
[3] *Did.* 10.
[4] *vis.* 1.1.3.
[5] *mand.* 1.1.
[6] *1 Clem.* 46.
[7] *ib.* 58.
[8] *Magn.* 13.

temple, prepared for a building of God the Father hoisted up through the crane of Jesus Christ which is the Cross, and using for a rope the Holy Spirit'.[1] More important is his very direct ascription of deity to Christ as the Son and Word of God. 'The one God manifested himself through Jesus Christ his Son who is his Word that proceeded from silence.'[2] This is a remarkable concept of the Son as the revelation of the transcendent God. He is the uttered word of God because he is the divine purposive mind as expressed to men;[3] he is the mouth by which God has communicated with them.[4] Hence Christ is often called, simply, 'our God',[5] and Ignatius can speak, in terms which would seem extraordinarily paradoxical to the Greek world where the impassibility of the divine was held to be an axiomatic truth, of 'the passion of our God'.[6] Prayer to Christ is assumed as a natural expression of faith.[7]

The beginnings of Christology in these writers are still rudimentary. Ignatius merely sets the divine and human aspects of the person of Christ alongside each other, in terms which recall the foreshadowing of the later doctrine of the two natures in the opening words of St. Paul's Epistle to the Romans. Christ is 'one physician, of flesh and of spirit, generate and in-generate, God in man, true life in death, Son of Mary and Son of God, first passible and then impassible, Jesus Christ our Lord'.[8] According to the flesh he was of the seed of David, but he is both Son of man and Son of God.[9] The contrast between 'flesh' and 'spirit', which we shall notice more fully in later writings, is virtually synonymous with a contrast between 'humanity' and 'deity'. Thus Ignatius says that the risen Christ ate and drank with his disciples as one with them in the flesh though in the spirit he was united with the Father.[10] So far as the deity of Christ is concerned, Ignatius insists on his personal pre-existence, and, in the Johannine manner, on his con-tinuous existence with the Father: 'Christ, who came forth from one Father and is with one, and departed to one.'[11] Similar language to that of Ignatius is used by II Clement: 'The Lord who saved us, being first spirit, then became flesh and so called us.'[12] Christ is to be regarded as God.[13] For the writer of the *Epistle of Barnabas* Christ is the Son of God who was manifested in flesh in order to communicate his revelation to those who could not look at deity unveiled any more than men can look directly at the sun.[14] *Barnabas*

---

[1] *Eph.* 9.
[2] *Magn.* 8. (The variant reading 'eternal Word that did not proceed from silence' is probably a correction made in the interests of the later orthodox doctrine of the eternal generation of the Logos.)
[3] *Eph.* 3.
[4] *Rom.* 8.
[5] *Eph.* proem.; 18.
[6] *Rom.* 6.
[7] *Eph.* 20 and probably *Rom.* 4.
[8] *Eph.* 7.
[9] *ib.* 20.
[10] *Smyrn.* 3.
[11] *Magn.* 7.
[12] *2 Clem.* 9.
[13] *ib.* 1.
[14] *Barn.* 5.

also attributes the words 'Let us make man' (Gen. 1:26) to the Father's address to the pre-existent Son, conceived of as a distinct hypostasis. Although it is true that there is a common tendency among these writers to use the term 'spirit' somewhat vaguely to denote 'deity', the case is somewhat different with Hermas, for in the *Shepherd* he does appear to identify the Son or Word of God with the Holy Spirit, taking the latter to be the divine principle in the incarnate Christ: an identification which could be readily made under the influence of the Wisdom literature. Thus, 'the holy pre-existent Spirit which created the whole creation God made to dwell in flesh that he desired. This flesh therefore in which the Holy Spirit dwelt was subject to the Spirit . . . He chose this flesh as a partner with the Holy Spirit.'[1] Elsewhere Hermas speaks of the Holy Spirit as the Son of God;[2] but in this very imprecise writing it is hard to know how much developed content is being given to a term such as 'Holy Spirit'.

The contribution of the Apostolic Fathers to the interpretation of the work of Christ is not of any great significance. On the whole they are content to repeat traditional phraseology without doing much to elucidate it, and this is largely due to the fact that their allusions are mainly in the nature of *obiter dicta*. The greatest stress is usually laid on the work of Christ as the bringer to men of illumination, knowledge, truth and life, these ideas being probably connected with the baptismal catechesis, for much incidental light is thrown by these writers upon the central importance of baptism in the early community: the seal with which believers are marked out as God's people, the way of death to sin and demons and of rebirth to resurrection-life, the new white robe which must be preserved undefiled, the shield of Christ's soldier, the sacrament of the reception of the Holy Spirit.[3] For Ignatius, however, the death of Christ is linked with his own approaching martyrdom, and his thought is centred upon union with Christ in suffering; the hope is for life through the 'blood of God'.[4] *Barnabas* lays rather more stress on the sacrificial significance of Christ's death, as the antitype of the offering of Isaac, and also on the idea of cleansing from sin through the blood of Christ.[5] But these incidental allusions do not carry thought on this subject forward beyond the positions arrived at within the New Testament canon, except for the strong connection established by Ignatius between the redemptive death and resurrection of Christ and the Christian eucharist. The eucharist 'is the flesh of our Saviour Jesus Christ, which flesh suffered for our sins and which the Father raised up';[6] it is mystically interpreted as 'the bread of God which is the flesh of Christ who was of the seed of David' and 'his blood which is incorruptible love';[7] and it is, in a famous phrase, 'the medicine of immortality, the antidote that we should not die but live for ever in Jesus Christ'.[8]

[1] *sim.* 5.6.
[2] *ib.* 9.1.
[3] e.g., *2 Clem.* 7, 8; *Herm. sim.* 8.2; 8.6; 9.16; Ign. *Polyc.* 6; *Barn.* 11.
[4] *Eph.* 1
[5] *Barn.* 5.
[6] *Smyrn.* 6.
[7] *Rom.* 7.
[8] *Eph.* 20.

The pace of doctrinal formulation was quickened during the second century by the clash of conflicting systems which derived their beliefs in part, at least, from outside the main Christian tradition represented by the New Testament writings. Much of the advance in Christian self-understanding in the period which separates the Apostolic Fathers from the theologians of the third century was due to the need to examine and to evaluate, and often refute and replace with a more satisfactory theology, the ideas propagated by a series of teachers, many of whom visited or settled in Rome, which became the most lively centre of debate.

One of these systems of thought, Ebionism, had little importance, for it proved at an early date to be a dead-end and was significant in later times chiefly as an opprobrious tag to be fastened upon unpopular Christologies, such as those of Paul of Samosata or even, surprisingly, Arius. The Ebionites were a remnant of -Jewish Christianity, who, according to the third- and fourth-century accounts offered by Origen and Epiphanius,[1] interpreted Christ in terms of prophet and Messiah, continued to observe the Law, rejected St. Paul, believed that Christ's baptism meant the union of a heavenly being with a human Jesus, and were divided on the question of the virgin birth, the majority however affirming it. They were said to use as their authority only the Gospel according to the Hebrews, which Epiphanius believed to have been really a form of Matthew; and, according to Jerome,[2] they tried to be both Jews and Christians but succeeded in being neither.

Far more important as a catalyst in the formulation of Christian doctrine were the Gnostic movements of the second century. Gnosticism is a many-headed and many-sided phenomenon in ancient religion, with roots that go back into pre-Christian Hellenism, Judaism and oriental religion, and which therefore affected New Testament thought itself; but in the developed form in which it is proper to speak of Gnosticism as a coherent and recognizable pattern of belief, as opposed to a vaguer 'gnosis' or 'Gnostic tendencies', it belongs to the thought-world in which Hellenistic Judaism, Christianity, Greek theology and eastern influences were becoming fused together and producing a wide variety of systems of thought, through some very notable thinkers such as Valentinus, Basilides, and the authors of the Gnostic literature recently made known through the publication of the discoveries at Nag Hammadi.[3] The salient elements in these systems which make it possible, in spite of their variety, to speak of them collectively as 'Gnostic' are as follows. There is a general and predominant interest in cosmology as a road towards the solution of the problem of evil. This leads to an insistence on the transcendence and utter remoteness of the ultimate divine principle, between whom (or which, for this principle can be designated only by an abstraction such as 'Depth') and the universe there is postulated a series of emanations or aeons. The concept of these is linked

---

[1] Or. *Cels.* 2.1; 5.65; *comm. in Mt.* 16:12; Epiph. *haer.* 30.
[2] *ep.* 112.
[3] R. M. Grant: *Gnosticism and Early Christianity*; *Gnosticism – an Anthology*; R. McL. Wilson: *The Gnostic Problem*; Werner Foerster (ed.): *Gnosis* (Vol. I Patristic material, Vol. II Coptic and Mandaean sources).

with astronomy and the idea of a series of heavens with their respective planets. The totality of aeons, in the systems of Valentinus and Basilides, forms the pleroma, the world of the divine which is superterrestrial and spiritual. Through some error of 'fall' on the part of a heavenly aeon, variously pictured in Gnostic mythologies, the creation of the material world has come about. It is not the work of God, but is due to some cosmic catastrophe, and it is under the rule of a power hostile to the divine goodness. Nevertheless in man (or some men, for these systems tend to think of men as predetermined in their nature and only of an elite minority as capable of spiritual as opposed to physical and 'psychic' life), a spark or element of the divine pleroma has been preserved. The 'spiritual' man has something in him that is akin to God, though in this material world it is imprisoned and subject to ignorance and error and demonic oppression. Salvation is mediated by a saviour from the divine sphere who descends in order to impart the knowledge that brings release to the spiritual element in men. This knowledge is knowledge of the truth about oneself and one's situation in relation to the world and to one's heavenly origin. By this one can be assured of enlightenment and consequently of present liberation and future ascent to the pleroma when the body has been cast off at death.[1]

These systems are the main reason why Christian thought felt itself challenged in the century after the Apostolic Fathers at least as strongly in respect of its primary belief in God the Creator as of its faith in Christ. Hence the immense emphasis laid by early theologians on the goodness of God and the identity of the good God with the Creator of this material world. For another powerful attack on this faith was mounted by Marcion, whose conclusions were in many respects similar to those of the Gnostics though he arrived at them by a different approach. His starting-point, it is true, was, like theirs, the problem of evil; but he did not approach his attempt to solve it by way of cosmology. Nor did he share the usual Gnostic ideas that the soul is consubstantial with the divine, that salvation is by knowledge as opposed to faith, that men are predetermined to the categories of physical, psychical and spiritual, or that the work of the redeemer is to reintegrate the spirit of man with the divine element from which it came. The problem presents itself to him in terms of the Bible. The New Testament contradicts the Old. Hence there must be two gods, one being the god of the Old Testament, who is the creator and who stands in opposition to the true God. The Old Testament deity, who is just but not good, a deity of Law but not of Gospel, with his Christ, the Messiah promised in the Old Testament, is revealed as an enemy by the true Christ, the Christ of the good and loving God of the New Testament. For this revelation a true incarnation is both unnecessary (all that is needed is a divine messenger) and disgusting, for a divine redeemer from the evil world could not himself participate in materiality. The way of salvation is faith in Christ and in the true God whom he discloses, and purgation from the world of the hostile god by asceticism and renunciation. It is against the background of Gnosticism and Marcionism that we have to consider the Christian writings of the later second century.

[1] cf. Iren. *haer*, 1.5.1, 5; Heracleon ap. Or. *Jn.* 13.25.

II

THE GREEK APOLOGISTS

It would not be wholly untrue to say that systematic Christian theology begins with the work of the Greek Apologists of the second century. Unlike the occasional writings, evoked by situations arising within the Christian community, which have survived from the period of the 'Apostolic Fathers', the apologetic works of Aristides, Justin Martyr, Athenagoras, Tatian and Theophilus of Antioch, though differing considerably from one another in scope and length, have as their common object the defence of Christianity against the objections raised by intelligent contemporaries in the Greco-Roman world, especially the charge that Christians are 'atheists' and therefore a subversive influence. They seek, accordingly, to commend their faith in terms acceptable to the serious Greco-Roman enquirer, and this involves them in an attempt to examine and to articulate the fundamental beliefs which, as Christians, they profess. No such thorough attempt to analyse and interpret the significance of Christian faith had hitherto been made.

This does not mean that the Apologists were radical innovators in theology. The main lines of their defence of Christianity and their commendation of it to the world of their time (which for Justin, in his *Dialogue with Trypho*, included Judaism as well as the Hellenism to which most of these apologetic writings are directed) had already been adumbrated, more especially in the New Testament books themselves. A two-pronged apologetic is already sketched out in the Acts of the Apostles. To the Jewish world Christianity is there presented as the true Judaism: the authentic and predestined fulfilment of God's revelation to Israel, demonstrated as such by the prophetic scriptures of the Old Testament when these are rightly understood. The Gentile world is at the same time asked to recognize that Christianity is 'as old as the Creation'. Rightly understood, the realm of nature points to the Christian God, just as the prophets pointed to the climax of his work in the life, death and resurrection of Christ. Hence in the Acts of the Apostles Paul can be represented both as the ideal Pharisee who finds in Christianity the proper fulfilment of all that was good in his ancestral tradition[1] and can therefore appeal confidently to the Jewish scriptures to vindicate his belief, and also as the exponent of a philosophical monotheism who can appeal for confirmation of his preaching to the utterances of the Greek poets.[2] This double claim, that Christianity is the truth to which both the scriptures and the insights of the philosophers

[1] Acts 26:5ff.
[2] Acts 17:28.

directly lead, is a starting-point for the arguments of the Apologists; but they develop its implications and they provide it with a theological rationale. This was found in the idea that the divine Logos, the uttered and self-communicating reason of God, spoke through the prophets and was the subject of the theophanies recorded in the Old Testament in which men had found themselves encountered and addressed by the divine presence; and, at the same time, the Logos who is Christ is none other than the 'Reason' in which all men participate. Justin can thus adapt the Stoic theory of the immanent rationality by virtue of which the world is an ordered cosmos, and in harmony with which all wise and virtuous men must seek to live, so as to support his contention, not merely that Christianity is the proper fulfilment of the insights and aspirations of revealed (Hebraic) and natural (Greek philosophical) religion, but that all 'those who have lived "with Logos" are Christians even though they may have been considered to be "atheists", such as Socrates and Heraclitus among the Greeks and Abraham and Elijah among "barbarians" '.[1] The wording of this passage is itself a vivid illustration of the lengths to which the Apologists were prepared to go in translating an originally Palestinian-Jewish faith into terms intelligible to the world of sophisticated Hellenism.

This Logos is the 'seminal' or 'germinal' Logos which is implanted in men and enables them, albeit in incomplete and fragmentary fashion, to receive God's self-communication and to know something of him. Those who responded rightly to the potentialities for communion with God which had thus been built into their rational nature could be reckoned among Christians, so that 'whatever among all men has been well said belongs to us Christians'.[2] Because of this seed of the Logos implanted in all men the ethical precepts of Stoic philosophy are recognizably akin to the teachings of Christianity, so much so, in fact, that the demons who persecuted Christians have always tried to stir up hatred against those who live according to reason (i.e. Logos), including Heraclitus in the past and the Stoic philosopher Musonius, put to death in more recent times.[3] Nevertheless, the indwelling of the Logos in all good and wise men was only partial and fragmentary. The seed was there,[4] but it afforded only an indistinct and incomplete apprehension of the truth. Christianity brings men into an encounter with the actual source and ground of these partial apprehensions, for Christ is himself the Logos of God who is self-existent, uncreated and ineffable. He is the Logos of God, who became man for our sake and not only disclosed the truth which had been dimly discernible but also became a participant in our sufferings and brought us healing.[5] Justin lays most stress, however, on the work of the Logos as revealer. The partial character of the philosophers' discernment of the truth produced the inconsistencies and disputes which are inherent in their systems (a point which Tatian develops in a contemptuous attack on the philosophical schools). Christ, on

[1] *1 apol.* 46.
[2] *2 apol.* 13.
[3] *ib.* 8.
[4] *1 apol.* 32.
[5] *2 apol.* 13.

the other hand, is himself 'the whole Logos', or the 'Whole of what is rational', and the revelation which he has brought is not confined to an intellectual élite; it is embraced, to the point of martyrdom, by ordinary uneducated people.[1]

The identification of Christ with the divine Logos thus served to unite, and to give theological backing to, the old claim of Christianity to be faith in one who was both the glory of Israel and a light to the Gentiles. It had, however, more important functions to fulfil in this attempt to give a coherent and persuasive account of Christian belief. It served to bridge the gulf between God and the world; for God is unoriginate (or ingenerate: *agennetos*), nameless because indefinable and incomprehensible, unchangeable and eternal.[2] God, according to Greek theology, is everything which the finite world is not; it is variable, manifold, ever changing, subject in every part to the continuous process of coming into being, developing, decaying and ceasing to be, but God is absolutely simple, uncompounded, perfect and therefore incapable of any change but eternally constant and immutable, impassible, utterly remote from all process. Athenagoras contrasts the eternity of the unoriginate deity with the perishability and mutability of originate matter, and speaks of the great gulf which divides matter from God.[3] Theophilus uses similar language,[4] and these ideas are commonplace among all the theologians of this period. How, then, can God be related to the world of matter without himself being changed through being related to the sphere of change? It is this apparently insoluble problem which the Apologists, following lines already indicated in the Wisdom literature and in the New Testament, sought to overcome by means of the concept of the Logos.

God is the unchanging, invisible, sovereign Creator. Aristides speaks of him in this way at the beginning of his Apology, and Theophilus, attacking pagan idolatry, opens his own apologetic work[5] with a fine passage on the majesty and grandeur of God who is without beginning since he is uncreated, immutable since he is immortal, who cannot be described in terms of his essential being since he is incomprehensible, but only in terms of attributes. The biblical picture of the living God, active within his creation as well as transcending all things, is never forgotten by the Apologists. It is, in fact, combined by them in a remarkable fashion with the theology which they derive from the world of Greek thought. Thus they speak of God as Father, using the familiar New Testament image; but they tend like Clement (see above, p. 24) to associate his Fatherhood with creativity in a way that is foreign to the New Testament writings but has important precedents in Plato.[6] God is the Maker and Father of the universe;[7] he is Father inasmuch as he is Creator. Nevertheless God is concerned with his creatures and active in effecting their salvation in a way which is wholly in accordance with the

[1] *ib.* 10.
[2] *1 apol.* 14, 10, 61; *2 apol.* 6; *1 apol.* 13.
[3] Athenag. *leg.* 4.
[4] Thphl. *Autol.* 1.5.
[5] *ib.* 1.1ff.
[6] e.g. *Tim.* 28C, *Rep.* 506E.
[7] Just. *dial.* 7, 56, 60, etc.

biblical presentation of his work but which is by no means easy to reconcile with the philosophical presuppositions of the Apologists' own theology. Their solution of the difficulty is to assert that in the work of creation the Logos is God's instrument.

In their doctrine of creation the Apologists are, of course, taking up the thought both of the Johannine Prologue and of the Psalmist's 'By the word of the Lord were the heavens made' (Ps. 33:6), as well as the Wisdom-Word-Spirit theology of the Wisdom literature. They read these texts in the light of Platonic and Stoic thought, and especially of Philo's developed doctrine of the Logos as the mediator of divine creativity, providential care and revelation. This enables Philo to ascribe the creative activity of God and his immanence in the world of his creation, not, indeed, to another and inferior deity, still less to a divine power opposed, like Marcion's creator, to the true and supreme God (Justin is prepared to find Plato a useful ally against Marcion), but to one who, while not different from God, is distinguished from God the Father in 'number'. This distinction made it possible for early Christian theology to adopt the Hellenistic concepts of the divine, and indeed to employ them as presuppositions, without surrendering the essential Hebraic and Christian faith in God as creator, living God, saviour, and all else that belonged to the scriptural testimony. It also enabled the Apologists to ascribe the apparent localization of God and other anthropomorphic presentations of the divine activity in the Old Testament to one who is distinct from the Maker of the universe himself. Thus in a discussion of the exegesis of the story of the burning bush in his *Dialogue with Trypho*[1] Justin says that the appearance of God to Moses, declaring himself to be the God of Abraham, Isaac and Jacob, was not an appearance of the maker of the universe but rather of him who had appeared to Abraham and to Jacob in the theophanies recorded in their histories: that is, of the minister of the maker of all things, the Logos. No one with any sense, Justin continues, could suppose that the Maker and Father would leave the supracelestial sphere and become visible in a tiny bit of the world.

Plenty of scriptural texts were available to support the doctrine of the mediation of the Logos. Justin undertakes to prove to Trypho from the scriptures that he who appeared to Abraham and Jacob and Moses and is called by the biblical writer God is other than God the creator of the universe: 'other', as he immediately goes on to explain, in number but not in the intention with which he acts, for he has never done anything but that which the supreme God who made the world has himself willed to do.[2] Such a text as Gen. 19:24, 'The Lord rained upon Sodom and Gomorrah sulphur and fire from the Lord out of heaven', suggested that the Lord had a heavenly companion, also called 'the Lord'. Still more apt were passages such as Gen. 1:26 where, in saying 'Let us make . . .', God is apparently addressing this companion.[3] The existence of this ministering agent together with God the Father and Creator was proved even more clearly by the passages in which personified Wisdom speaks of being created to carry out

[1] *ib.* 60.
[2] *ib.* 57.
[3] *ib.* 62.

the work of God in the creation of the world; the most notable of these texts, one which was to have a long history in Trinitarian controversies, was Proverbs 8:22, 'The Lord created me as the beginning of his ways for his works. Before the ages he established me, in the beginning, before he made the earth . . .'.[1]

To the Apologists these scriptural evidences pointed to the distinction between the Creator and the mediating Logos and showed that this distinction had existed before all creation. God, indeed, was never without his Logos, for he could not be without reason; and the Apologists regard this relationship as having always implied real distinction. As Logos this 'other' is properly called 'Son', being Logos and 'firstborn' and 'power'.[2] Before Creation he was present with the Maker and Father, being begotten by him before everything and addressed by him (Gen. 1:26) before he acted as his agent in the making of the world.[3] Tatian offers a somewhat clearer picture than Justin of a first and second stage, as it were, in the existence of the Logos. From eternity the Logos was present with God, immanent in him as the creative reason may be said to be immanent in a man. It was, as it were, a potential capacity for creating, and at the moment of creation this was actualized; the Logos was put forth to be the agent of the making and sustaining of the whole created order.[4] This thought is developed by Athenagoras, who calls the Son God's Logos in idea and in actuality, describes him as 'mind and Logos' (meaning that he is God's reason both as immanent and as expressed), and points out that the Logos cannot be said to have been brought into existence, since God is eternally possessed of reason and always had his Logos in himself, but that for the purpose of Creation the Logos came forth to operate powerfully in an external relationship towards the creatures who were brought into being through him.[5] Theophilus expresses the same idea with the aid of language derived from Stoicism. He distinguishes between the two stages of the existence of the Logos, applying to the former stage the term *endiathetos* ('immanent') and to the latter *prophorikos* ('projected' or 'put forth'), saying that the Logos who has always been the mind and thought of God was begotten (and in this sense is the 'first-begotten of all creation') as the agent of Creation, continuing to consort with him inseparably, though as it were externally.[6]

This act of 'putting forth' or 'generation' by which the immanent divine reason comes to be distinguished as Son, and as the intermediary agent of the immutable Creator towards the world of coming into being and perishing, is purposive. It is by the Father's will that the Logos is 'generated' as the personal creative power of God. Justin tells Trypho[7] that God begat before all creatures a rational power out of himself which can, in scriptural language, be called the 'glory of the Lord' or 'Son' or 'Wisdom', or 'Angel' or 'God' or 'Lord and Word' or 'captain of the host' (this last being an

---

[1] *ib.* 129, etc.
[2] *1 apol.* 23.
[3] *2 apol.* 6, *dial.* 62.
[4] *orat.* 7.
[5] *leg.* 10.
[6] *Autol.* 2.22, cf. 2.10.
[7] *dial.* 61.

allusion to the theophany to Joshua (5:13) and an indication how closely related were the concepts of 'Logos' and 'angel', especially the angel Michael). All these appellations signify his function of ministering to the will of the Father and his being begotten by the Father's will. Later in the *Dialogue* Justin again insists, in order to emphasize the distinct existence of the Logos, that 'power was begotten from the Father by his power and will'.[1] This point receives similar emphasis in Tatian[2] and Theophilus. The latter pictures the Logos as God's counsellor before Creation began, being his mind and intelligence. Then, when God had determined to make the world, he begat this Logos 'externally projected' as the firstborn of all creation, and Theophilus is careful to point out that this emission of the immanent Logos did not mean that God was thereby deprived of Logos; rather, the Logos was externalized by the deliberate and purposeful act of the Father. The idea of this 'generation' is similar to Philo's conception of the Logos as first the plan or blueprint, as it were, for creation: the 'intelligible world' pre-existent in the mind of the Designer, which, when the Designer wills to translate his idea into concrete actuality, can be said to come forth and, as having an independent subsistence of its own, be termed the creative agent.[3]

In the period of the Arian controversy this insistence upon the generation of the Logos as a deliberately-willed act of the Father was to cause difficulty, for it then seemed to imply a degree of otherness and subordination which suggested a dangerously close relationship between the divine Logos and creatures. The Apologists, however, are simply anxious, like all pre-Nicene writers in the main Christian tradition, to express the need to clarify the distinction in God which their basic theology required.

Various attempts were made by these authors to state what they meant by the 'generation' of the Logos. Sometimes an analogy is drawn from the utterance of human speech, taking 'Logos' in the sense of 'communicating word'. 'When we utter a word,' says Justin, 'we beget a word, not by an act of division which would diminish the logos (i.e. reason) within us, but putting it forth without "abscission".'[4] The same illustration is used by Tatian and Theophilus, and by later theologians such as Tertullian, but it is deprecated by Irenaeus and Clement; it certainly suggests a different idea of the Logos, as God's communicating utterance, from that of a personal cosmic mediator which was what the Apologists required. Other analogies appeared more appropriate, especially that of fire. The picture of one fire, or torch, kindled from another served to establish the truth that the Logos is a distinct entity 'in number', but at the same time to show that the emission of the Logos is a distinct entity involves no such division or 'abscission' as would diminish the rationality of God.[5] This illustration, and that of the relation of the ray of light to the sun, a relation of identity and of distinction, are used by Justin to explain both that the begetting of the

[1] *ib.* 128.
[2] *orat.* 5.
[3] *opif. mund.* 4–5, *legg. alleg.* 1.8–9, etc.
[4] *dial.* 61.
[5] *ib.*, Tat. *orat.* 5.

Logos involves no division of the substance (*ousia*) of the Father and also that the distinction is numerical only.[1]

This is the other side of the Apologists' theological problem. If it was essential to make the distinction, it was also vitally important to preserve monotheism and avoid the possibility that the insistence on the mediating role of the Logos should not lead to a belief in two deities, such as might almost be suspected from Justin's statement that Christians hold the Son of God 'in second place' after the immutable and eternal God himself (though in fact Justin is here concerned only to demonstrate that it is not a 'crucified man' to whom this place is assigned but the actual Son).[2] It is in order to lay stress on the essential identity of the Logos with the Father that the biblical language of 'Son' or 'Child' is used of the Logos[3] and he is spoken of as 'offspring' by generation, as contrasted with 'creature'.[4]

Besides serving to unite God immanent with God transcendent and to bridge the gulf between the unchanging God and the created order, the concept of the Logos obviously helped to rebut the assertions of the pagan world that the object of Christian adoration was a man. Yet the Apologists made no important contribution to Christology. They assume an actual identity of the Logos and Jesus Christ. The Logos had been manifested in various forms in the Old Testament theophanies, such as the fire of the burning bush; but this Logos could be called, even in that pre-Christian context, Jesus the Christ, God's son and 'apostle',[5] and it is this same being who 'being formerly Logos, has now by God's will been made man for the sake of the race of men'. 'By God's Word Jesus Christ our Saviour possessed flesh and blood for our salvation.'[6] At one point Justin goes a little further and says that the whole rational principle of God became Christ, 'body and logos (or Logos) and soul'.[7] This may mean that Justin thinks of man as a being compounded of body, soul or life-principle, and rational mind, and that the Logos became man in this full sense. This is likely to be the right interpretation, though conceivably Justin could mean that the Logos became Christ, a man consisting of body, life-principle, and divine Logos which in him took the place of the human intellect. In any case, Justin believes that all men, in so far as they are genuinely rational, partake of, or live with, the Logos, and he is showing that whereas the indwelling of the Logos in all other men is partial, Christ is the totality of the Logos. But Justin unfortunately does not develop any theory of the relationship between the Incarnation and the participation of all rational men in the Logos. Nor do the Apologists contribute in any important way to the early Christian understanding of Christ's saving work.

In the thought of the Apologists the Holy Spirit plays a relatively indistinct role, as indeed might be expected from theologians who developed the doctrine of the Logos as they did. Usually the Spirit is characterized as

[1] *dial.* 128.
[2] *1 apol.* 13.
[3] *dial.* 105, 125.
[4] *1 apol.* 21, *dial.* 62.
[5] *1 apol.* 63.
[6] *ib.* 66.
[7] *2 apol.* 10.

'prophetic', and it is as the Spirit of prophecy and scriptural revelation that Justin declares that Christians honour the Spirit in the 'third rank' after the Creator and the Logos.[1] Whereas, however, Greek philosophy offered plenty of support for the Apologists' doctrine of the Logos, they found it hard to find points of contact between the biblical concepts of the Spirit and the theology of the Greek world. Justin, who believed that Plato had actually read the books of Moses, concludes that the obscure allusion to a 'third' which he found in pseudo-Plato, *epistle* 2, 312E, conceals a reference to the Spirit who moved over the waters at the Creation,[2] and he finds a perversion of the same idea of the Spirit's work in Creation expressed in the pagan practice of erecting statues of Kore at springs of water.[3] These far-fetched allusions, however, indicate that the Spirit played no important part in Justin's thought, and for the most part his references to the Spirit show that he was merely repeating the conventional language of Christian piety and liturgy, particularly in respect of the rite of baptism, administered in the name of the Father of the universe (this phrase is a striking example of Justin's assimilation of traditional Christian concepts to Greek theology), our saviour Jesus Christ, and the Holy Spirit.[4]

Tatian does indeed believe that the salvation of believers is the work of the divine Spirit. The human spirit is raised to the heavenly sphere by becoming united with the Spirit of God. This 'Spirit', however, is not distinguished from the Logos;[5] the long and ultimately self-defeating attempt of patristic theology to assign separate and distinct roles in creation and redemption to the Logos/Son and to the Holy Spirit had scarcely yet begun. Tatian and Athenagoras, like Justin, lay stress on the prophetic function of the Spirit, and the latter goes further than the other Apologists in attempting to picture the relation of the Spirit to God: the Spirit is an effluence (*aporrhoia*) from God, issuing from and returning to him like the sun's rays.[6] This analogy is derived from the Book of Wisdom, and could be employed either of the Son, as in the Epistle to the Hebrews, or of the Spirit with whom, as the Book of Wisdom itself suggested, the divine hypostatized Wisdom could equally be identified. Theophilus, in the first instance of the Christian use of the term 'Trinity' (*trias*), enumerates 'Father', 'Logos' and 'Wisdom'.[7] In fact it is always difficult, and in the last resort it proves to be impossible, to draw a real distinction between 'Logos' and 'Spirit', and the Apologists found it especially hard even to attempt to do this because of the very extensive use which they made of the concept of 'Logos'. The functions of each are interchangeable, so that Spirit and Logos can both be regarded as the source of the prophets' inspiration, and the Spirit who overshadowed Mary (Luke 1:35) is identified by Justin, as by other early theologians, with the Logos.[8]

---

[1] *1 apol.* 6, 13.
[2] *ib.* 60.
[3] *ib.* 64.
[4] *ib.* 61.
[5] Tat. *orat.* 7, 13.
[6] *ib.* 13; Athenag. *leg.* 7, 10.
[7] *Autol.* 2.15.
[8] *1 apol.* 33.

To some extent this apparent lack of definition in the Apologists' thought about the 'third' is due to the continuing use of the word 'spirit' in the sense of 'deity'. God is 'spirit', and the meaning of this term has to be carefully distinguished from the Stoic conception of a wholly immanent spirit pervading the cosmos: Christ, too, as divine, is 'spirit', and Theophilus speaks of the Logos as 'Spirit of God, Wisdom and Power of the Most High, who came down upon the prophets and through them spoke of the making of the world'.[1] This last passage shows how easily the use of 'spirit' as virtually synonymous with 'deity' passes over into a real identification of the Holy Spirit with the Logos, as we have already noticed in the case of Tatian. Despite these instances of seeming confusion, however, the achievement of the Apologists in laying the foundation of Trinitarian theology and enabling Christian faith to come to terms with Greek philosophical presuppositions was altogether remarkable. The defects of their theology, which gradually became apparent, were probably inevitable, given the nature of the task which they undertook, and are not the fault of the Apologists themselves in setting about that task in their particular fashion.

In contrast with the originality of their synthesis of biblical and philosophical ideas about God and creation the Apologists add little to the traditional Christian thought concerning man's sin and the meaning of salvation. Like all apologists in the Hellenistic world, Justin has to lay great stress on the freedom of the human will as against pagan notions of fate. This emphasis leads to an insistence upon divine judgement, rewards and punishments, and causes Justin to go out of his way to explain that the foreknowledge possessed by the prophets implies no doctrine of determinism but only that God foresees the course which men will freely choose.[2] Sin is thus due to man's misuse of freedom, but it is also to be ascribed to the malevolent tyranny of demons over the human race,[3] from which Christ set men free.[4] The main emphasis in the Apologists is upon the responsibility of man himself for the state of sin and servitude which has been his lot since the primary act of disobedience by Adam. In this connection it is interesting to observe that Theophilus interprets the primal condition of Adam as being childlike. Adam was capable of developing either for good or for ill; he might achieve immortality or incur mortality, and it was on account of his 'infantile' condition that God forbade him to eat of the tree of knowledge which would have been beyond his undeveloped capacities. The expulsion from paradise was in a sense remedial; it offered man the chance, through the divine gift of the Law, of freely repenting and so attaining to incorruptibility.[5]

Very little, however, is said by these authors about the nature of the redemptive work of Christ. There is fairly frequent repetition of stock New Testament themes, but these are not developed. There is also a fairly extensive typology of the Cross, the wood of which was, for instance,

[1] Athenag. *leg.* 16; Tat. *orat.* 4; *ib.* 7; Thphl. *Autol.* 2.10.
[2] *1 apol.* 43, 44, 61; *2 apol.* 7.
[3] *1 apol.* 5; *2 apol.* 5.
[4] *dial.* 41, 94.
[5] *Autol.* 2.24–27.

foreshadowed in the ark of Noah,[1] but there is little distinctive teaching about Christ's death; the work of the Logos in bringing men to salvation is chiefly to illuminate and instruct. Illumination, together with forgiveness of sins, is the chief effect of the baptismal washing which Justin is the first writer to describe in detail,[2] to which Theophilus adds a special emphasis on baptismal rebirth and recreation.[3] Where the soteriological significance of Christ's death, as opposed to the teaching function of the Logos, is most clearly brought out is in Justin's account of the Christian eucharist. In accordance with Christ's commandment the memorial of his Passion is made with bread and wine, realistically identified with his body and blood, and it is in the context of this commemoration that the worshippers offer their thanksgiving.[4]

The outcome of redemption is pictured, especially by Justin, in highly concrete terms. At this point the Apologists have to defend an Hebraic belief against the Hellenism which in so many aspects of their theology they were able to claim as an ally. They are greatly concerned to assert their faith in a physical resurrection, for the body as well as the soul must share in the future life for which man is intended by the Creator.[5] They are anxious to maintain the belief in man's creation by a decisive act of God in contrast to the Platonist view that the soul is inherently immortal, having pre-existed from eternity and being destined to live after death.[6] They also want to preserve the biblical idea of final judgement, reward and punishment, for which, indeed, they could cite Plato and the poets.[7] All this leads them to argue for a resurrection of the flesh, contending that this is no more miraculous than the manner of our conception and birth. Justin adds to this literalistic interpretation of New Testament eschatology the millenarian belief in an earthly reign of the saints with Christ which was, as Justin knew, rejected by many who were unquestionably good Christians, but which he believed to be necessitated by the Scriptural evidence.[8]

---

[1] *dial.* 138.

[2] *1 apol.* 61.

[3] *Autol.* 2.16.

[4] *1 apol.* 65, 66. It is on the whole improbable that Justin interpreted the word *poiein* (*do*) in the Words of Institution as meaning 'sacrifice': see *1 apol.* 66, *dial.* 41.

[5] Athenag. *res.* 18ff.

[6] Just. *dial.* 5.

[7] *1 apol.* 8; Thphl. *Autol.* 2.37–38.

[8] *dial.* 80.

III

MELITO AND IRENAEUS

Among the Greek Apologists there could be included Melito, bishop of Sardis in Asia, who wrote an apology, of which fragments survive, addressed to Marcus Aurelius. He must, however, have also been a prominent leader of the Church in Asia and a theologian of broad interests who exercised a considerable influence on the general development of Christian thought. During the last decade of the second century his name is mentioned by Polycrates, bishop of Ephesus, in a letter to Victor, bishop of Rome, as one of the 'great luminaries' in the firmament of Asian Christianity.[1] The context of this reference to Melito is the dispute between Rome and the churches of Asia over the date of Easter. This so-called 'Quartodeciman' controversy revolved round the question whether Easter should be observed at the actual time of the Passover, the preparatory fast thus ending on the fourteenth of the Jewish month Nisan, without regard to the day of the week on which this might fall, or whether the practice of commemorating the Resurrection on the first day of the week should be applied to the annual as well as the weekly festival of the Resurrection, and Easter be kept on the Sunday following the Passover time. In this quarrel Rome and most other churches followed the latter practice, which became universal. Asia, however, claimed to possess equally good apostolic authority for the former, and could point to the Johannine chronology of the Passion, and to St. Paul's identification of Christ with the Passover lamb, in support of its tradition.

The long list of Melito's writings includes what seems to have been the first systematic treatise on the Incarnation. Little of his large output survives apart from a homily on the Passover which is generally held to be authentic. It exhibits that elaborately rhetorical style for which, according to Jerome, Melito incurred the disapproval of Tertullian, whose theology he nevertheless seems to have influenced. This work is important as an example of typological exegesis and very possibly as a Christian version of the Jewish Passover *haggadah*; it certainly throws light on the early Christian interpretation of the Passover sacrifice and the Exodus as types of Christ's work of deliverance, his death as a sacrifice, and the Church as the people of the covenant. Much of the homily is written in the form of hymnody, and it ends with a quasi-credal ascription of praise to Christ as 'he who made the heaven and the earth . . . who is proclaimed through law and prophets,

[1] Eus. *h.e.* 5.24.2.

who was incarnate in a virgin, who was hung on a tree, who was buried . . . raised . . . and ascended, who sits at the right hand of the Father, who has power to judge and save, through whom the Father did his work from the beginning to eternity'.[1] Creation, the theophanies, and God's acts in the history of Israel are ascribed to Christ who is identified typologically not only with the sacrificial lamb of the Passover but with the righteous sufferers: murdered Abel, Isaac who was bound, Jacob the exile, Joseph who was sold, Moses who was exposed as an infant, persecuted David. Christ is himself the Law.[2] Like Ignatius, Melito glories in the paradox of the Incarnation: 'God was slain'.[3]

This strong emphasis on the pre-existence and the deity of Christ is balanced by an equal stress on the distinctness of his divinity and his humanity. Like Irenaeus, Melito calls the former 'God' and the latter 'the man'.[4] 'The Lamb,' he says, 'was buried as man and rose from the dead as God. He is father, inasmuch as he begets (*sc.* believers as sons of God), and Son, inasmuch as he is begotten';[5] 'he took upon himself the sufferings of him (i.e. man) who suffers, through a body capable of suffering, and destroyed the passions of the flesh, and by the Spirit that could not die (i.e. his divinity) he slew death the man-slayer'.[6] Indeed, if a fragment of Melito's treatise on the Incarnation is genuine (some have suspected it to emanate from a much later anti-Apollinarian source), he anticipated later theology in his emphasis on the two natures of Christ, for which, like Tertullian who spoke of two *substantiae* (essences or substances),[7] he uses the equivalent Greek term *ousiai*. Christ was at once God and perfect (i.e. complete) man. His human nature (*physis*) was real and no mere phantasm; it consisted of a soul as well as a body. Like Irenaeus, Tertullian, and in the fifth century the Antiochene theologians and Leo of Rome, Melito believed that the humanity and divinity of Christ operated almost independently of each other: in the thirty years preceding his baptism his humanity was revealed while the signs of his divinity were concealed; in the three years which followed it he disclosed his deity through working miracles.[8]

Melito thus seems to have gone considerably further in Christological speculation than the other Apologists. It is perhaps of some interest that he was a pioneer among Christian theologians in visiting Palestine, possibly as a pilgrim to the scenes of the Gospel, and ascertaining the Hebrew canon of scripture which he evidently regarded as an authoritative source of doctrine.[9] The curious assertion of Origen[10] that Melito was among those who thought of God so anthropomorphically as to believe him to have physical eyes, ears, feet and so on, may rest on a misunderstanding of the

[1] *pasch.* 104.
[2] *ib.* 82, 83, 87, 69, 9.
[3] *ib.* 96.
[4] *ib.* 5.
[5] *ib.* 8–9.
[6] *ib.* 66.
[7] *carn. Christ.* 18; *Prax.* 27.
[8] *frag.* 6 (Perler, *Sources chrétiennes* 123).
[9] Eus. *h.e.* 4.26.14.
[10] *sel. in Gen.* 1:26.

title of one of his books or possibly may have been inferred by Origen from what may well have been Melito's literalistic eschatology.

Irenaeus came from the same background, being a native of Smyrna, although he migrated to the West and became bishop of Lyons after the death of his predecessor, Pothinus, in the persecution of 177. He also was a prolific writer and of his work, too, relatively little survives, though far more than in the case of Melito. His chief writing, the treatise *Against Heresies*, is primarily directed against Valentinian Gnosticism in various forms, but, especially in the last three of its five books, it also contains much positive exposition of current orthodoxy. This is, in his view, based on the fourfold Gospel, which can be set over against the esoteric books which were claimed by the Gnostics as sources of teaching imparted secretly by the Lord to an inner group of privileged disciples, on the continuity of the succession of bishops in sees founded by apostles and the unbroken tradition of teaching which he believes to be guaranteed by the apostolic succession of bishops in the teaching chair of the local church, and on the rule of faith.

Irenaeus refers to the 'elders' in the Church who, with the succession to the episcopate, have received a sure gift of truth (*charisma veritatis certum*),[1] It seems improbable that, as has sometimes been suggested, Irenaeus means that the bishops who have taken up their office in due succession have been granted a special divine inspiration to teach the truth. The true faith is maintained, in his view, by the Church as a whole under the guidance of the Spirit; this is why he attaches so much importance to the witness to truth of the church at Rome, where not only is there to be found the one church of apostolic foundation in the West but also a doubly apostolic church founded by both the great apostles Peter and Paul, and where the truth may readily be ascertained because, as the capital city, Rome is the place where the whole Church is bound to meet together, the Church which consists of the faithful who, in every place, preserve the tradition that comes from the apostles.[2] It seems, then, that Irenaeus thinks of the bishops, the official teachers of the community, as being both the representatives and spokesmen, and also the authorized defenders, of the apostolic tradition of belief which, unlike the Gnostic traditions which are reserved for a privileged élite, constantly circulates among the whole Christian community and is preserved and purified by a process of comparison and interchange. If this is so, then the 'sure gift of truth' possessed by the bishops is probably not a special inspiration but the doctrinal tradition itself, which it is by no means inappropriate to call a *charisma*, a gift of the Spirit to the Church.

The rule of faith, or canon of truth, is the third of Irenaeus' norms of doctrine. He means by this (Irenaeus prefers the term 'canon of truth'; Tertullian calls the same thing the 'rule of faith') a summary of the teaching given in the churches. It is not a formal creed, but is more flexible in its wording and somewhat fuller in content. It resembles the outlines of the *kerygma*, or apostolic preaching, which modern scholars have extracted from

[1] *haer.* 4.26.2.
[2] *ib.* 3.24.1; 3.3.2.

the New Testament writings. One version begins with an allusion to the dispersion of the Church over the whole world and asserts that nevertheless it has received from the apostles and their disciples faith in one God, Father almighty, who made the heaven and earth and seas and all things in them; and in one Christ Jesus, the Son of God, incarnate for our salvation, and in the Holy Spirit who through the prophets proclaimed the dispositions made by God for salvation, the advents of Christ, his birth of the Virgin, his suffering, his rising from the dead, his incarnate ascension into the heavens, and his appearance from the heavens in the glory of the Father to 're-capitulate' all things and to raise up all flesh of all mankind, so that to Christ Jesus our Lord and God and Saviour and King, according to the good pleasure of the unseen Father, every knee may bow . . . and every tongue confess him and that he may give righteous judgment in all things, sending the spiritual forces of wickedness and the angels who have transgressed and the impious and unrighteous and lawless and blasphemous among men into eternal fire, and granting the gift of life and incorruptibility, and the promise of eternal glory, to the righteous and holy and those who have kept his commandments and persevered in his love, some from the beginning and some by the way of repentance.[1]

This is but one of a number of passages where Irenaeus quotes the 'canon of truth' at length. It represents a distillation of what the second-century church regarded as the central and essential burden of scripture. In its turn it could be used as a sort of key to the interpretation of scripture itself, and this was especially important at a time when the threat to traditional belief came not only from alleged secret and unwritten tradition handed down in esoteric groups and purporting to come from Christ and his disciples but also from distorted exegesis of the canonical books themselves. It was as true in antiquity as always that everyone with sufficient ingenuity can read whatever he pleases out of the Bible. The 'canon' which Irenaeus is so fond of producing as a main weapon of orthodoxy was a way of preventing this from being done and maintaining that no system could rightly claim scriptural authority if it contravened this essentially scriptural 'rule'.

Irenaeus applied his criteria of truth in the first instance to the confirmation of Christian faith in God as Creator. This lies at the heart of his teaching, since he develops his doctrine in reply to those who, like both the Gnostics and Marcion (from somewhat different presuppositions) wished to deny that the natural order is the work of God and to assert that in some sense salvation is to be understood as rescue from the natural, and evil, order. His starting-point, as he expressly states, is God the Creator (*demiurge*) who made heaven and earth and all things in them, and his object is to show that there is nothing above him or after him (that is, that there is no superior Power to the creator in a celestial hierarchy and no question of a good god intervening in history after another deity had created the material universe); and that he was not moved by anyone, but made all things by his own intent and freely, since he alone is God, the only Lord, only Creator, only Father, alone containing all things and causing

[1] *ib.* 1.10.1.

them to exist.[1] The alternative to the acceptance of belief in the one Creator is the chaos of polytheism; to maintain belief in a supreme Father but to ascribe creation to some other artificer or to angels is to imply that angels are more efficient than God, that God is negligent, or inferior or indifferent.[2] God is the artificer of all things, as the wise architect and supreme king; and the teaching of Christ shows that there is one Father and maker of the world, who is none other than the God proclaimed by the Law and the Prophets.[3] In accordance with this insistence on creation as the work of God, and God alone, Irenaeus strongly asserts the doctrine that God created out of nothing. Tatian had pointed out that God's creative act included the creation of the matter from which the world was made,[4] but Justin was not so clear on this point, and in certain passages[5] he seems to keep closely to the Platonic picture, characteristic of the notion of creation set out in the *Timaeus*, of all things being formed out of undifferentiated matter which itself was pre-existent. For Irenaeus, at any rate, nothing whatever is excepted from the universal truth that all things have been made by the will and power of God. Men cannot, indeed, make anything out of nothing; they require some already existing material for their work, but God himself supplied the material for his workmanship when as yet it had no existence.[6] The theme of creation is central in Irenaeus' thought, not only in argument against Gnostics and Marcion but also in his positive expositions of Christian faith; thus his *Demonstration of the Apostolic Preaching* begins with a declaration of belief in the uncreated and ingenerate God, the creator of all things, and points to God as the first cause from which all things in turn derive their being.

Irenaeus follows fairly closely the general line of the Apologists' attempt to reconcile the doctrines of creation and divine transcendence by means of a Logos theology. He does, however, introduce certain differences of emphasis. One, which is perhaps of no great significance since for him the two terms are plainly synonymous, is a tendency to use the word 'Son' as an equivalent for 'Logos' even when he is speaking of the eternal presence of the Word with the Father before his 'externalization' for the work of creation and redemption. He is anxious to make it clear that the Logos did not become Son of God by virtue of the Incarnation.[7] This may conceivably indicate a tendency to think less distinctly than the Apologists of two clearly distinguished stages in the existence of the Logos, corresponding to the terms *endiathetos* and *prophorikos*, and an inclination to think of the Logos or Son as being eternally 'with' God and extrapolated, rather than as God's internal reason 'coming forth'. Certainly, Irenaeus dislikes the analogy, so often used by the Apologists, from the utterance of human speech. This seems to him to assimilate the putting forth of the Logos much too closely to the temporal act of speaking and to obscure the truth that

---

[1] *ib.* 2.1.1.
[2] *ib.* 2.2.1.
[3] *ib.* 2.11.1.
[4] *orat.* 5.
[5] e.g., *1 apol.* 10.
[6] *haer.* 2.10.4.
[7] e.g., *ib.* 3.17.4.

God is himself mind and reason and that his word is absolutely identical with his reason.[1] He does not go so far as actually to repudiate the two-stage concept of the Logos as such, but he applies the text 'Who shall declare his generation?' (later to be greatly overworked during the Arian controversy) not only against the Gnostic inventors of genealogies of aeons but also against those more orthodox thinkers who venture to speculate about the generation of the Logos.[2]

It is through the Logos that God creates. Irenaeus, however, in contrast with the Apologists, links the Spirit with the Logos in his creative role. Not that he finds it easy to distinguish how Logos and Spirit respectively operate in the creative process. He can only suppose that the function of the former is to bring all things into being, and of the latter to bestow order and form on them.[3] It seems that in this rather awkward doctrine he is trying, as he consistently does, to remain faithful to the witness of scripture. Many passages, especially of the Wisdom literature, appear to identify the Spirit with Wisdom (a point which Theophilus had taken) and to assign Wisdom-Spirit a pre-eminently important role in creation; and it was not realized that such texts should be understood as parallel, and not complementary, to the notion of the creative work of the Logos. The association of Logos and Spirit in Irenaeus does, however, produce some interesting consequences. One is his idea that Logos and Spirit are the two creative hands of God, a thought which may have been arrived at through reflection on the 'moulding' of Adam in the light of 'Thy hands have made me' (Ps. 119:73). It was to his 'hands' that God said 'Let us make man'.[4] By these hands, which had created Adam, Enoch and Elijah were translated, and Irenaeus, in pointing this out, has the future resurrection of believers in view.[5] Irenaeus is always anxious to assert that it is the whole man, including his physical body, and not a part of him such as the rational soul alone, which was fashioned by God's hands and will be perfected hereafter.[6] This ingenious attempt to portray the co-operation of Logos and Spirit in the work of creation has the valuable effect of bringing the transcendent God more closely into touch with his world than less biblically-minded theologians than Irenaeus could easily imagine. It is God who acts; his hands are not independent agents simply carrying out his orders, but means through which he acts himself.

As in the theology of the Apologists, the Logos continues to be seen as the medium of God's self-revelation, particularly in the Old Testament theophanies in which the Logos was manifested to men. The revelatory function of the Logos is linked with his work in creation and in salvation. He is that hand of God which 'forms us from the beginning to the end, and makes us fit for life, and is present with the creature whom he has moulded and perfects it in accordance with the image and likeness of God'.[7] At the

---

[1] *ib.* 2.13.8; 2.28.5.
[2] *ib.* 2.28.5; 3.19.2.
[3] *dem.* 5; *haer.* 4.20.2ff.
[4] *haer.*-5.1.3.
[5] *ib.* 5.5.1.
[6] *ib.* 5.6.1.
[7] *ib.* 5.16.1.

Incarnation the Logos became manifest humanly, 'making himself like man and making man like himself, so that by his likeness to the Son man might become precious to the Father'. The Logos in whose image man had been made had formerly been invisible. When the Word of God was made flesh he displayed the true image by becoming that which was his image, and restored the likeness by making man like the invisible Father through the visible Word.[1] In this restoration the Spirit is again closely linked with the Logos, for the Spirit makes it possible to receive the revelation communicated by the Logos.[2]

Just as the doctrine of creation lies at the heart of Irenaeus' Trinitarian theology and supplies the motive for the progress which he made in that sphere, so also it is his concern with the re-creation of mankind which provides the driving-force for his Christology. He is interested primarily in soteriology: in the restoration of God's original Creation. He is also concerned to maintain the identity of the person of Jesus Christ with the eternal Son, as against the tendencies of the Gnostic systems and Marcion to separate the Christ from the human Jesus. These basic concerns are the source of the great strength of his Christology – the clarity with which he asserts the unity of the person of Christ who is the Logos, who in turn is the actual manifestation of God himself and not an inferior mediator, and who is also fully human with the same humanity which 'was created in the beginning and which is restored in him.

Irenaeus vigorously attacks those who divide Jesus from the Logos, or Jesus from the Christ, for scripture teaches one and the same Jesus Christ to whom the gates of heaven were opened by reason of his ascension in the flesh, and who will come in the same flesh in which he suffered, revealing the glory of the Father.[3] He expounds the idea, though he does not use the later terminology, of the two natures. In a way which almost anticipates the doctrine of the interchange of the properties of deity and manhood in Christ (*communicatio idiomatum*), he points out that the New Testament often uses the name 'Christ' (signifying a divine being, such as the heretics supposed to have descended upon the human Jesus) in contexts which in fact speak of his humanity, his humiliation, suffering and death. This serves to underline the truth that he is Son of God and Son of man; and the very name 'Christ' has a Trinitarian significance, since it speaks of one who anoints (the Father), one who is anointed (the Son), and an anointing (the Spirit).[4]

He is especially anxious to show that Christ's humanity is identical with our own.[5] It is on this truth that his whole soteriology hinges, for in his view the work of Christ would be valueless if he had not become what we are and so made it possible to 'recapitulate' Adam in himself. Since Irenaeus points out in this context that we are both body and soul, it is likely that he means to imply that in becoming man the Logos assumed both flesh and

---

[1] *ib.*
[2] *dem.* 7.
[3] *haer.* 3.16.8.
[4] *ib.* 3.18.3.
[5] *ib.* 3.22.1.

human soul. It would follow in any case from the general line of his argument that Irenaeus had a much clearer conception than most pre-Nicene theologians of the soteriological necessity of belief in the completeness of Christ's manhood as opposed to any idea that the Incarnation means a dressing up of the Logos in an outer garment of flesh. On the other hand, he finds difficulty in really maintaining the personal unity that he so earnestly wants to predicate of the Logos incarnate. Like Melito and all the other ancient theologians who worked with a 'two natures' Christology (in Irenaeus the idea of 'natures' is expressed by the terms 'the God . . . the man'), he can scarcely avoid giving the impression that he thinks of deity and manhood being alternatively switched on and off during the gospel events. 'Just as he was man so that he might be tempted, so he was Logos so that he might be glorified, the Logos remaining quiescent in the temptations, and in the crucifixion and death, but co-operating with the man (i.e. the human nature) in victory . . . and resurrection and ascension.'[1]

The purpose of the Incarnation was to repair the consequences of Adam's disobedience. Adam was created, according to Irenaeus, not as the glorious creature imagined by some Jewish and Christian thought, but as undeveloped and child-like.[2] He was given freedom of moral choice and a special gift, over and above the rationality which mirrored in him the Logos, which Irenaeus does not clearly specify but which is represented by the divine 'likeness'; this seems to be identical with possession of the Spirit. Adam should have advanced towards the realization of these potentialities, but he fell through disobedience. This fall did not merely affect the subsequent history of mankind. It actually was the fall of mankind as a whole, for Adam is an individual with a corporate significance; all men were in Adam when he disobeyed God: they and he are identical.[3]

This belief in the solidarity of the human race with Adam corresponds to the Christological emphasis on the one-ness of Christ with mankind. Christ is not, as Gnostics and others alleged, a heavenly being who descended from heaven and, remaining impassible, never became one with the human race; as the Logos who is always present with mankind, he was made one with his own creation and became flesh, gathering up or 'recapitulating' all things into himself. He 'recapitulates' man into himself, being the invisible made visible, the incomprehensible made comprehensible, the impassible made passible, the Logos made man.[4] This means that whereas all men had been, as it were, gathered up into Adam's disobedience, they have now been gathered up into Christ as the second Adam. In him they have been reconciled to God, having become, collectively, obedient unto death.[5] Thus the human race, summed up in Christ's humanity, regains what it had lost in Adam, that is, to be in the image and likeness of God: something which could be achieved neither by man in his sinful condition nor by a re-creation of the original Adam but only by the descent of the Son into the human

[1] *ib.* 3.19.3.
[2] *dem.* 12; *haer.* 4.38.1ff.
[3] *haer.* 5.16.3, etc.
[4] *ib.* 3.16.6.
[5] *ib.* 5.16.3 recalling Phil. 2:8.

state even to the point of death.[1] 'Recapitulation' has also another aspect. In becoming the collective 'Adam' of a restored humanity, Christ repeated and reversed the history of the first Adam. The essential element in this recapitulation is the reversal of Adam's disobedience by Christ's supreme obedience 'even unto death'. This is the heart of Irenaeus' whole theology, for the doctrine of recapitulation, to which his understanding of Creation and Incarnation leads up, has a profound ethical content: man is saved by being taken up into Christ's human obedience to the Father, and not simply by the fact of the Logos having assumed manhood. Irenaeus therefore delights in drawing out the parallel between the Adam story and the Christ story. The virgin birth of Christ, for instance, corresponds to the formation of Adam by a fresh act of creation. It could not be an exact parallel, for had the second Adam also been 'moulded' from the dust of the earth it would have been a new creation which would have been saved, and Adam's race would have remained unaffected. The birth from Mary thus presents a parallel with Adam's creation in that it is a new act of God and at the same time, so Irenaeus believes, it safeguards the continuity of Christ's humanity with Adam's, inasmuch as it is not newly created but is derived from Mary.[2] Another parallel, which was to have consequences which Irenaeus could scarcely foresee, was drawn between the disobedience of Eve when she listened to the serpent's voice and the obedience of Mary to the annunciation of the angel: the bonds which were tied by Eve's faithlessness were loosed by Mary's faith.[3]

Irenaeus' interpretation of Christ's work of salvation thus has at its centre the ideas of the restoration of man to the likeness of God through the Incarnation, and the incorporation of man into Christ's obedience. It is summed up briefly in the famous words, characteristic of patristic Christology and soteriology, '. . . who by reason of his immeasurable love became what we are, in order that he might make us what he is himself'; [4] and at rather greater length: 'The Lord redeems us by his own blood, and gives his life for our life and his flesh for our flesh, and pours out the Spirit of the Father to unite and bring into communion God and man, bringing down God to men through the Spirit and taking up man to God through his incarnation, and truly and actually bestows on us incorruptibility through communion with God'.[5]

The allusion to the blood of Christ is not merely a conventional piece of biblical phraseology, though Irenaeus, like all the ancient writers, uses a variety of scriptural images in interpreting the Cross. It is connected with his picture of man's salvation as a rescue operation from captivity. The devil holds man in bondage. Christ redeems him from the 'transgression and apostasy' in which the devil keeps him chained. This redemption is achieved by Christ's victory over the devil ('as by the defeat of a man our race went down into death, so by the victory of a man we may ascend to

[1] *haer.* 3.18.1.
[2] *ib.* 3.21.20–22.2.
[3] *ib.* 3.32.3–4.
[4] *ib.* 5 proem.
[5] *ib.* 5.1.1.

life'[1]), in which the Temptations play a vitally important role as the scene of the triumph of the second Adam's obedience.[2] Combined with this thought, however, is the interpretation of Christ's blood as a ransom paid to the devil for the release of his prisoners. This ransom is in accordance with the principle of justice; God's creation is saved from perishing, yet justice is safeguarded, and the devil is made to relinquish his victims by persuasion and not by an act of violence like that by which he had originally seized them.[3] Here, again, lie the seeds of unforeseen and unhappy theological developments: in this case the theory of the 'devil's rights'. Irenaeus, however, does no more than glance in that direction. His conception of the reconciling work of Christ is much more complex and profound than any theory of mere transaction. A good modern summary of it is afforded by Newman's well-known hymn, 'Praise to the Holiest in the height'.

It must, however, be admitted that although Irenaeus makes it perfectly clear that man is restored by Christ's recapitulation of Adam, he offers two different interpretations of this at the same time. As we have seen, he lays great emphasis on Christ's human obedience, culminating in his death, as the means by which Adam's disobedience is reversed and annulled. On the other hand, he also understands it as the union of humanity in the Incarnation with the incorruptibility and immortality of the Son of God, in whom what was mortal is swallowed up in immortality; so that in this sense 'he became what we are to make us what he is'.[4] Here, then, we find in Irenaeus that unresolved tension, so characteristic of Greek patristic theology, between salvation by sharing in Christ's human conquest of sin and salvation by participation in the nature of the divine Logos.

Man's perfection will come only after his resurrection, when he attains the incorruptibility that is given in the vision of God. Yet the words of Psalm 82:6, 'I said, you are gods', applies already to all Christians, for they have received the Spirit of adoption whereby we cry, 'Abba, Father'.[5] Their union with the incarnate Logos and with his Spirit is effected during this life through the operation of faith and love and through the sacraments. The transition of the individual believer from the old Adam to the new, from wearing the image of the earthly to wearing the image of the heavenly (1 Cor. 15:49), is effected in baptism. This signifies a washing from the old life of 'vanity' through belief in the name of the Lord and reception of his Spirit.[6] Baptism is the seal of eternal life and rebirth as sons of God.[7] The eucharist is an assurance of the hope of the resurrection of the body, a hope which belongs integrally to Irenaeus' theology of creation. 'How can they say that the flesh goes to corruption and does not participate in life, when it is nourished by the Lord's body and his blood? . . . We offer him his own, rightly proclaiming the fellowship and union of flesh and spirit. For as bread from the earth, receiving the invocation of God, is no longer ordinary

---

[1] *ib.* 5.21.1.
[2] *ib.* 5.21.2–3.
[3] *ib.* 5.1.1.
[4] *ib.* 4.38.3; 5 proem. See above p. 48.
[5] *ib.* 3.6.1.
[6] *ib.* 5.11.2.
[7] *dem.* 3.

bread, but thankoffering (eucharist), composed of two things, earthly and heavenly, so also our bodies which partake of the eucharist are no longer corruptible but have the hope of resurrection for ever.'[1] It is in line with his general insistence on belief in the creation of the material world by God himself that he uses the evidence of the eucharist to prove the value and significance of material objects. Christ took bread and wine and declared them to be his body and blood. It is therefore right to offer them as thanksgiving sacrifices, not as though God needed firstfruits and offerings from what he has created but 'in order that we may not be ourselves unfruitful and ungrateful'.[2]

In harmony, too, with his general doctrine of creation is Irenaeus' belief that the soul descends, like Christ, to an intermediate state (Hades) to await the resurrection of the body, with which, and not, as Gnostics believed, as a disembodied soul translated to heaven at the moment of death, it will ascend to God.[3] It is also characteristic that, like Justin, he should take a literalistic view of the hope of the new Jerusalem and the reign of the saints.[4]

[1] *haer.* 4.18.5.
[2] *ib.* 4.17.5.
[3] *ib.* 5.31.1–2.
[4] *ib.* 5.35–36.

IV

EARLY LATIN THEOLOGY:
TERTULLIAN AND NOVATIAN

The theology of Tertullian closely resembles that of Irenaeus in its main outline. Like the latter, Tertullian was largely concerned with the repudiation of heresies, including as the subjects of full-length treatises the teaching of the Gnostics Hermogenes (who maintained a dualist theory against the biblical doctrine of Creation) and Valentinus, and of Marcion against whom Tertullian produced the longest of his thirty or so surviving works. It is because of his preoccupation with controversy against what he judges to be dangerously syncretistic speculations that he adopts a vigorously hostile attitude towards Greek philosophy. This is to quite a large extent a position which he takes up for the sake of his polemics; he was deeply influenced himself by philosophy, and his debt to Stoicism in particular was great, causing him to hold a materialistic idea of the nature of the soul: it is a material substance, though of the most light and tenuous kind. Nevertheless, his attitude towards the dangers of philosophy and his rigid notions of the authority of ecclesiastical tradition differentiate Tertullian sharply from such theologians as the Apologists or Clement of Alexandria.

For Tertullian, as for Irenaeus, authority in matters of doctrine resides in the teaching of Christ which it was the task of the apostles whom he chose and sent out to impart to the nations. Everything must be understood by reference to its origin (itself a philosophical dictum), and the many churches scattered throughout the world can be traced back to the one from which they have all sprung: the church of the apostles. Tertullian, who did so much to establish the theological language of Latin-speaking Christianity, seems to be the coiner of the phrase 'the Apostolic Age'.[1] From a relatively early date the history of the primitive Church had been reconstructed in terms of a centrally directed, apostolically controlled, mission in which the original Twelve were the leaders and organizers and also the dominically commissioned teachers who imparted the orthodox faith, learned from Christ, to those whom they appointed in turn to rule the churches. This picture of the apostolic age, first sketched in Luke–Acts and 1 Clement, came rapidly to be elaborated during the second century as a defence against heretical innovations. Tertullian accepted it and explained it in even more formal and clear-cut statements than those of Irenaeus.

According to Tertullian, the norm of the correct apostolic doctrine is to be found in the living tradition handed down in the official teaching of the

[1] *praescr.* 32.

churches where the apostles preached and to which they addressed letters. The succession of authority is: the churches, the apostles, Christ, God.[1] This succession is maintained in those churches which can produce evidence of a pedigree of bishops from the present time to the apostolic founders, guaranteeing the maintenance of a succession of sound teaching. Tertullian's argument, however, tends to be circular, for even if an episcopal succession can be produced (or faked up) this is not enough in itself. Heretics may manage to do this, but their doctrine is shown up as false directly it is compared with the authentic apostolic teaching.[2] In the end Tertullian is claiming that what his church and the churches in communion with it recognize as orthodox is to be accepted as authoritative.[3] He will not allow heretics to appeal to scripture against this received tradition; indeed the argument of the whole treatise *De Praescriptione Haereticorum* (A Demurrer to the Heretics) is designed to forestall such an appeal by the argument that only those who stand in the right tradition, which is more ancient and therefore, as he thinks, true as contrasted with heretical innovations,[4] have the right to interpret scripture. The content of the authentic tradition is enshrined in the 'rule of faith' which his citations show to have summarized the main tenets of Christianity with considerable flexibility in detail.[5]

With this authoritarian concept of orthodoxy (he was impressed by the relation between faith and reason implied in the text, 'Unless you shall have believed you will not understand'),[6] it is not surprising that Tertullian professed to regard philosophy as a main source of heresy. 'Philosophical' heresy conflicts with Christian truth at certain points in particular: the wrath of God (as against Marcion's theology), creation out of nothing, the restoration in the resurrection of the same flesh in which death has taken place, and the virgin birth of Christ.[7] So, he argues, the characteristic ideas of Valentinus are derived from Platonism, Marcion's theology from Stoicism, and the influence of Aristotelian dialectic causes heretics and philosophers to ask the same questions about the problem of evil (Marcion's basic question), the origin of man, and 'whence is God?', all of which leads him to his famous rhetorical question, 'What has Athens to do with Jerusalem? What has the Academy in common with the Church, or what have the heretics with Christians?'[8]

Tertullian is greatly concerned with the need to defend the Christian idea of creation against dualism, and in doing this he follows similar arguments to those of Irenaeus. The material world is good; God would not make anything unworthy of himself. The Incarnation demonstrates God's love for his creation, and the sacramental use of water, oil, milk and honey, and bread shows that the God who is the Father of Christ does not reject the works of the Creator, as he would if, as Marcion supposes, the former

[1] *ib*. 20.21.
[2] *ib*. 32.
[3] *ib*.
[4] *Marc*. 4.5; 5.19.
[5] e.g., *Prax*. 2, *praescr*. 13.
[6] *Marc*. 4.20.
[7] *ib*. 5.19.
[8] *praescr*. 7.

stands in opposition to the latter.[1] Both scripture and natural religion are adduced as evidence for faith in the one God who is both Creator and the God of Jesus, the natural evidences including man's instinctive regard for the order and beauty of the world and also the innate faith in God evinced by the ordinary uneducated pagan's involuntary ejaculations of fear, praise, hope in *God* (he does not, in moments of strong tension, call upon the individual gods of polytheism).[2] Scripture is adduced at times in order to refute misunderstandings; for instance, the Pauline allusions, which might seem dualistic, to 'the rulers of this world' and 'the god of this world' are explained away: the former as referring to human authorities such as Herod, Pilate and the Roman Empire, the latter either by repunctuating the sentence so as to give an entirely different sense, or by identifying 'the god of this world' with the devil (but not with the creator).[3]

Tertullian realizes, however, that Marcion's dualism is ultimately rooted in the problem of evil. He therefore argues that man's fall does not impugn the goodness of God's creation. It was not due to God's impotence or malevolence, but solely to man's free will. Man is the author of sin. His soul is not a part of God's Spirit, which would involve God in sin, but is a created image of it. Isaiah (45:7) speaks of God creating evil, but this means only that God devises just punishments which, like the 'severity' of the surgeon, are intended for good. So, too, the Law is good and its apparent inconsistencies with the Gospel are to be explained by its having been adapted to the particular needs of the Israelites.[4] The Galatian dispute was about the one and the same God's Law and Gospel, not, as Marcion supposed, about two gods and two religions.[5] In the end dualism is incompatible with the Christian assurance that all things will be 'recapitulated' in Christ (Eph. 1); Marcion's God, invisible, remote, complacent, is a god of philosophers only; and Tertullian claims that 'if God is not One, he is not'.[6]

On another front, however, Tertullian has to fight against those who wished to understand the unity of God in a way which would make the deity an absolute monad, ruling out the distinctions within unity which seemed essential for bringing God into relation with the world and enabling deity to be ascribed to Christ. In antiquity this theology was termed 'monarchianism'. The modern distinction between 'modalist' and 'dynamic' monarchianism is rather confusing, since the latter term denotes 'adoptionism', which is a quite different form of unitarianism from the former, to which alone the term 'monarchianism' was originally applied. Monarchianism was intended as a simple way of expressing the essential beliefs that God is one and that Christ is God. Those who taught it believed that the subtleties of the Logos theology endangered both these truths; it could easily suggest that God is two, or three, and that though Christ is the Logos he could be inferior to the Father and not as fully God as he. Justin recognized

[1] *Marc.* 1.13–14.
[2] *test. anim.* 1–2.
[3] *Marc.* 5.6, 11.
[4] *ib.* 2.6–18.
[5] *ib.* 5.2.
[6] *ib.* 5.17; 2.27; 1.3.

that some Christians were prepared to admit a distinction between the Logos and the Father in name only; the Logos was an aspect of God's operation and not numerically distinct from him.[1] Noetus of Smyrna, according to the treatise against him by Hippolytus of Rome, Tertullian's contemporary, began from a literal interpretation of the Johannine text, 'I and the Father are one'. This meant that the one God, the Father, was incarnate as Jesus Christ, and was the subject of human experiences. To Noetus this was far from shocking. 'What have I done wrong,' he protested, 'in glorifying the one only God, who was born and suffered and died?'[2] He was anxious to de-personalize the biblical term 'Word'. If God is one without distinctions, then his word must be his spoken word; to allege that 'word' is 'Son' would be strange. When St. John speaks of the Word in the Fourth Gospel it must be borne in mind that there and in the Apocalypse he uses the term allegorically.[3]

Tertullian's opponent, Praxeas, held exactly the same position, and since it is not known who Praxeas was it is conceivable that he might be identical with Noetus or with one of those disciples of the latter who, according to Hippolytus, taught in Rome. He believed the Father and Son to be one and the same,[4] with the result that the one God who is impassible assumed passibility and experienced the life, death and resurrection. At the same time Praxeas had to account for the biblical language of 'Son'. He would not refer this to the Word, which must not be hypostatized, and therefore he used the term to refer to the man Jesus. The 'Spirit' or 'God' that operates in Jesus is the Father. Thus 'the Son suffers, the Father suffers with him'.[5] Had we a complete account of Noetus' theology we should probably find that he interpreted 'Son' similarly, for it is hard to see what else he could have done with that extremely frequent scriptural designation of Christ.

This is the theory which Tertullian attacked: one which, as stated by these proponents of it, laid itself immediately open to violent counter-attack from the horrified believers in the basic axioms of Greek theology. The same type of theology was apparently taught by Sabellius, who impressed Callistus, bishop of Rome, favourably but was himself attacked by Hippolytus.[6] As a bogeyman in the fourth-century controversies Sabellius exerted a much greater influence on theology than he ever had as a flesh-and-blood teacher; for this reason, it is hard to distinguish his doctrine from that of fourth-century theologians, such as Marcellus of Ancyra, whom their opponents labelled 'Sabellian'. It is likely, however, that for Sabellius 'God' meant essentially God the Father, while 'Son' and 'Holy Spirit' denoted aspects, perhaps successive, of this one God, relating to his work in redemption and sanctification respectively. In Sabellius' view, as apparently also in that of Callistus, there could be no hypostatic

[1] *dial.* 128.
[2] Hipp. *Noet.* 1.
[3] *ib.* 15.
[4] *Prax.* 5.
[5] *ib.* 7, 27, 29.
[6] Hipp. *haer.* 9.11.

distinctions in God; there is but one individual presentation (*prosopon*) of deity.[1]

Tertullian agrees that there is but one God, but this is to be understood with reference to the 'dispensation' or 'economy' (Tertullian uses the Greek word *oikonomia*, employed also by Hippolytus in this context) whereby there is a Son of the one God, his Word which proceeded forth from him through whom all things were made.[2] The meaning he gives to 'economy' is not wholly clear. The term, which means 'disposition' or 'arrangement', is very often used by the Fathers, including Irenaeus, to denote God's plan of creation and redemption, and it becomes a common synonym for the Incarnation. It may also mean the 'ordering' or 'organization' of a complex series or organism. Probably Tertullian intends it to mean that God's unity is subject to the disposition or 'deploying' of the single Godhead into Father and Son or Word (and Spirit) in accordance with the Father's intention to create. He goes on to state that unity of substance (i.e. essence) is preserved, 'while none the less is safeguarded the mystery of that "economy" which deploys the unity into trinity' (Tertullian introduces the actual Latin word, *trinitas*, corresponding to Theophilus' 'triad', into Christian literature), 'setting forth Father and Son and Spirit as three: three, however, not in quality but in sequence, not in substance but in aspect, not in power but in manifestation, yet of one substance and one quality and one power, seeing it is one God from whom those sequences and aspects and manifestations are apportioned out under the heading of the Father, the Son and the Holy Spirit'.[3] Here is a real attempt to say something about the relation between the diversity of the Godhead (in respect of its manifestation and operation) and its essential unity, and although Tertullian's terminology is difficult to interpret with precision it is clear that a great advance has been made in the development of Trinitarian theology.

In his scriptural exegesis Tertullian also took an important step towards the Trinitarian distinction between the three persons. Those texts which seemed to indicate that God was addressing a heavenly companion had long been used to prove the distinction between the Father and the hypostatized Logos. Tertullian introduced the Holy Spirit as a third participant in this divine dialogue. In Psalm 110:1 he assumes that the Holy Spirit is the speaker: 'Notice, too, the Spirit speaking as a third interlocutor about the Father and the Son, "The Lord said to my Lord" ' (i.e. the Holy Spirit's Lord). In Isaiah 53:1, again, the Spirit is addressing the Father concerning the Son: 'Lord, who has believed our report and to whom is the arm of the Lord (i.e. the Son) revealed?' 'So,' says Tertullian, 'in these texts the distinctness of the three is plainly set out, for there is the Spirit who makes the statement, the Father to whom he addresses it, and the Son who is the subject of it'.[4] Tertullian's recognition that despite this clear distinction between them the three are 'of one substance' paves the way for the Nicene formula.

---

[1] Epiphanius *haer.* 62.1ff.
[2] *Prax.* 2.
[3] *ib.*
[4] *ib.* 11.

In seeking to elucidate this 'economy' Tertullian is less successful. His opponent's attachment to the idea of 'monarchy' suggests to him an unfortunate analogy. Monarchy means sovereignty, and sovereignty can be exercised jointly by an emperor and a colleague, or it can be administered through provincial governors, while itself remaining one and indivisible.[1] This illustration is open to the retort that the 'economy' might seem to imply at the least an extreme subordination and at worst polytheism. In fact he can only try to defend himself by saying that if sovereignty does not cease to belong to one, and so to be a monarchy, because it is exercised by thousands of subordinate governors, how much less does God suffer division because, while they are partners in the essence of the Father, the Son and the Holy Spirit occupy second and third place. Other analogies, however, are better: 'God brought forth the Word as a root brings forth the shoot and the spring the river and the sun its beam. Each of these might aptly be termed a "son" or "offspring" of its parent source; but the shoot is not cut off from the root as a separate entity, nor the river from the spring. In each case there is a distinction without separation.' To bring the Holy Spirit within this series of analogies Tertullian proceeds to add a third member: the fruit to the shoot, an irrigation channel to the river, and the apex of light to the sunbeam. These may be taken as early attempts to say something about the 'procession' of the Holy Spirit.[2]

In trying to explain, rather than illustrate, the 'economy' Tertullian echoes the ideas of the Apologists. God was originally alone, in the sense that there was nothing external to himself. Yet properly speaking he was not alone, for he had with him his immanent reason, within himself. Here Tertullian has to explain the double meaning of 'Logos' as 'reason' and 'word', for he is at a disadvantage compared with the Greek writers in that he works with the Latin *sermo*. God's reason or word is identical with his Wisdom. Then, when the moment came for God to utter 'Let there be light' his Word came forth, and by this coming forth, or begetting, the Word became Son. The position, then, is that 'the Son is other than the Father, not by diversity but by distribution, not by division but by distinction, because the Father is not identical with the Son, they being actually numerically one and another. For the Father is the whole substance, while the Son is an outflow and assignment of the whole, as he himself professes, "My Father is greater than I" ... So also the Father is other than the Son as being greater than the Son, as he who begets is other than he who is begotten ... as he who makes is other than he through whom a thing is made.'[3] The subordinationism of this last passage, characteristic of Tertullian, is very general in pre-Nicene Trinitarian thought. The Godhead is one, but the substantial unity is compatible with a hierarchal ordering of the 'persons' within that unity, corresponding to the roles which they perform in the 'economy'. In line with this, too, is Tertullian's repetition of the old doctrine of the generation of the Word by the Father's will.[4]

[1] *ib.* 3.
[2] *ib.* 8.
[3] *ib.* 9.
[4] *ib.* 6.

It should be observed that Hippolytus was directing virtually the same arguments against the 'monarchianism' of Noetus at Rome. He begins with the primal one-ness of God: 'God being alone and having nothing contemporaneous with himself willed to create a world, which he made by thought, will and utterance . . . But although he was alone he was manifold, for he was not without reason or wisdom or power or counsel; but all were in him and he was the All.' For Creation God put forth the Logos: "When he willed, as he willed, he generated his Logos, through whom he made all things . . . for he constructs all things that he makes through his Word and Wisdom, creating by Word and setting in order by Wisdom.'[1] Here is a similar notion of a Trinitarian operation of God in Creation to that which was entertained by the Apologists.

The generation of the Logos means that he is thenceforth 'other'; but this does not imply two gods: the relationship is like that of light from light, water from spring and ray from the sun. There is one 'power' (by which Hippolytus, like Tertullian, virtually means 'deity in action'), which is from the Father. The All is Father, from whom is the power, the Logos; and this is Mind which, having come forth into the world was manifested as Son (or possibly, Servant) of God; all things are 'through him', but he alone is 'from the Father'.[2] Hippolytus repeats that this does not mean that he implies two gods, 'but one God: yet two "persons" (*prosopa*) by "economy" (that is, by virtue of the 'deployment' of God's creative Reason as effective Word), and thirdly the grace of the Holy Spirit'.[3] He tries to explain how the 'economy' requires this triadic structure; but, as his odd allusion to the 'grace' of the Spirit as 'third' indicates (assuming this to be the right reading of a confused text), he finds it hard to speak convincingly of the role of the Spirit. The 'economy' supports the unity of God, he claims, 'for there is one God, the Father commanding, the Son obeying, and the Holy Spirit giving understanding, the Father over all, the Son through all, and the Holy Spirit in all. The Jews knew the Father but not the Son, the disciples the Son but not in the Holy Spirit – otherwise they would not have denied him.'[4] All this leads Hippolytus on to quote the Trinitarian baptismal command of Mt. 28:19, and it seems probable that the attempt to produce a theology of the Spirit parallel to that which is expressed in terms of the economy of Father and Logos was undertaken chiefly with a view to taking account of the threefold structure of the credal interrogations of the candidates in the rite of baptism (described by Hippolytus in his *Apostolic Tradition*), the prominence of the Holy Spirit in the liturgy and theology of baptism, and the scriptural passages, such as the last verses of Matthew and the Johannine discourses, which lay behind the liturgical tradition. There was great pressure from the side of metaphysics for a dyadic theology; the presupposition of Greek religion required the Church to work along the lines of the Logos doctrine in order to reconcile divine transcendence with divine immanence, God in Christ with God in heaven. There was no such

[1] Hipp. *Noet.* 10.
[2] *ib.* 11.
[3] *ib.* 14.
[4] *ib.*

demand for a metaphysic of the Holy Spirit, and the natural language in which the Spirit was spoken of was that of Christian life and worship, individual and corporate. The attempt to bring the Spirit into the 'economy' of Creation produced a confusing mixture of language levels. Hence the awkward distinction between the creation and the 'ordering' of the universe; hence, too, the introduction into the metaphysical argument of the idea that if the disciples had known Christ 'in the Spirit' they would not have denied him. This latter thought belongs to the sphere of Christian witness, especially the witness of confessors and martyrs, and inspiration to know Christ and acknowledge him: and this, rather than the theory of the 'economy', is the area in which the language of 'Holy Spirit' is genuinely appropriate.

There is some difference of emphasis between Hippolytus and Tertullian in the use of the term 'Son'. For the latter it was appropriate to employ it in respect of the Logos as generated for Creation. Hippolytus, commenting on God's sending of the Son in the flesh (Rom. 8:3–4), says that the Logos is here termed 'Son' because he was about to become man. 'Son' is his new name of love for men; for without the flesh and in himself the Logos was not fully Son although he was fully 'Only-begotten Logos', nor could flesh subsist by itself without the Logos because it has its subsistence in the Logos; thus he was manifested (in the Incarnation) as one perfect Son of God.[1] Besides illustrating Hippolytus' view that the Sonship of the Logos begins with the Incarnation rather than the primal generation, this passage is Christologically significant. Christ is a unity; and the unity is located, as it were, in his being as the Logos. The flesh, by which Hippolytus means Christ's humanity as opposed to 'spirit' or deity, has its subsistence in the Logos. It has no independent existence as an hypostasis in itself, but exists simply in virtue of being the humanity of the Logos-Son. Here is an anticipation in some degree of the Alexandrian Christology of later times.

Tertullian, in somewhat different language, works out a more elaborate, but similar Christology. His first object is to refute the monarchian view held by Praxeas (as, according to Hippolytus, it was also by Callistus of Rome),[2] that it is proper to regard the humanity (flesh) of Christ as 'the Son' and his spirit or deity as 'the Father'.[3] Tertullian also uses this terminology, but for him, of course, 'spirit' means the divine Logos-Son. He wants to make it quite clear that the person of Christ is an indivisible unity: there is a true incarnation of the Son of God. The emphasis lies equally on both parts of this statement. Against Praxeas, it is the Son, distinct from the Father, who became man; against Marcion, the Son became fully man, and did not merely assume a human disguise. Tertullian therefore asserts the scandalous paradox of the Incarnation with the utmost possible vigour. The subject of the human experience of Christ, the subject, indeed, of the Incarnation, is none other than the Son. 'The Son of God was born; one is not ashamed to confess it, just because it is shameful. And the Son of God died; one can believe it, just because it is absurd. And he was

[1] *ib.* 15.
[2] *haer.* 9.12, 16–19.
[3] *Prax.* 27.

buried and rose; it is certain, just because it is impossible.'[1] That it is God the Son who lived and died is the essential truth on which Tertullian's soteriology depends; for, like Irenaeus, he interprets the work of Christ for salvation as an interchange of places with mankind: God lived with man, so that man might be able to live with God; God became small so that man might become great.[2]

He attempts to give a theological rationale of this basic belief. 'We must enquire how the Word became flesh: by being transformed into flesh, or by putting on flesh?'[3] It cannot be by transformation, for this would involve mutability on the part of the Word who is God; it might also imply a fusion, or confusion, of deity and manhood so as to produce what would be neither the one nor the other but a third entity different from either. It must therefore be by putting on flesh. There is no fusion; the Word remains God, the flesh remains man; he is Son of man and Son of God, each substance (that is, flesh or humanity and spirit or deity)[4] being distinct in its own proper nature (*proprietas*). Thus, Tertullian appropriately quotes Rom. 1:3–4: ' "Who was made of the seed of David"; here he will be man and Son of man: "Who was defined as Son of God according to the Spirit"; here he will be God and the Word, the Son of God. We observe a double quality (*status*), not confused but conjoined, in one person God and man, Jesus.' Quoting Jn. 3:6, Tertullian continues, 'Flesh does not become spirit, nor spirit flesh: evidently they can both be in one person. Of these Jesus is composed, of flesh as man, and of spirit as God.'[5] In this way Tertullian works out a doctrine of two 'essences' or 'substances' remaining unconfused and distinct, conjoined in one person. In the one person of the Word made flesh there is a two-fold quality, just as in his Trinitarian theology Tertullian pointed to a single quality (the three are one in *status*). The distinction between the two 'substances' is actual and not merely theoretical. The peculiar character (*proprietas*) of each remains unimpaired, so that the 'spirit' carried out its own activities in him, that is to say powers and works and signs, and the 'flesh' accomplished its own experiences, hungering, thirsting and weeping for Lazarus, and finally died.[6] This is a typical exposition of what came to be known as a 'two natures' Christology, clearly distinguishing humanity and deity, each of which operates what is appropriate to it, but less clear when it comes to trying to give an explanation of how one undivided person, and that the person of God the Word, can be the single subject of both these sharply differentiated sets of experiences. In the fifth century this first essay in Latin Christology was to become an unacknowledged source for the famous *Tome* ([dogmatic] treatise, see p. 140) of Leo.

A very important aspect of Tertullian's Christology is his insistence on the completeness of Christ's manhood. At times his language may suggest the contrary, as when he summarizes his Christology for a pagan audience:

[1] *carn. Christ.* 5.
[2] *Marc.* 2.27.
[3] *Prax.* 27.
[4] *carn Christ.* 18
[5] *Prax.* 27.
[6] *ib.*

God's Logos, like a ray of the sun, descended into the virgin, was formed as flesh in her womb, and was born as 'man mingled with God'. The 'flesh', informed by the 'spirit' was nourished, grew up . . . and is Christ.[1] But this is not the case. Tertullian believes that Christ's flesh did not even possess human distinction, let alone heavenly beauty; otherwise it could not have been despised and insulted. It was in fact subject to all human infirmities.[2] He is particularly clear in his conviction that the work of saving the whole man, soul and body, necessitated the assumption by the Word of a human soul: a point which was little understood by many early theologians.[3] Hence against Marcion and Valentinus he asserts the reality of Christ's birth. He did not simply appear as man without deriving actual humanity from Mary; and although Tertullian thinks the genuineness of Christ's manhood to be perfectly compatible with the virgin birth, for in his view the single parent is a sufficient source for genuine manhood, he nevertheless rejects the idea that Mary's virginity was preserved in giving birth as docetic in its implications.[4] This emphasis on the solidarity of Christ with the human race leads him into a discussion whether or not Christ's flesh was sinful. It could be argued that if his flesh were our flesh it must be sinful; and Tertullian does not in any way object to the premiss that our flesh is inherently sinful, for he insists more strongly than his predecessors on the participation of all men in Adam's sin, the uncleanness of all men until they cease to be in Adam and come to be in Christ, and the corruption passed on to them from Adam (a view which his traducianist theory of the soul, as inherited from parents along with the body, makes it all the easier for him to hold).[5] But he argues that the identical flesh which is by nature sinful in men was in Christ sinless; in making it his own he made it to be without sin. Sin is no more a necessary character of human nature than is birth by the ordinary process of generation: Adam was indubitably human but was not born by human generation. Christ was indubitably human, but neither born by human generation nor subject to the inheritance of sinfulness.[6]

Tertullian's contribution to soteriology is much less important. For the most part he repeats biblical language about the sacrificial nature of Christ's death, but although he speaks about the death more often than most earlier theologians had done, this is usually to prove the reality of Christ's flesh against docetism rather than to interpret the significance of the Cross for salvation. This is true of the well-known saying: 'Christ was sent to die (*mori missus*), and had necessarily to be born so that he might be able to die.'[7] The argument here is simply that the Incarnation must really involve the Word in human nature, unlike the appearance of angels in human shape. The same is true of the similar statement in his anti-Marcionite polemic, though there he does say rather more: 'Christ alone had to be born into flesh from flesh, so that he might give a new character to our birth by

[1] *apol.* 21.
[2] e.g., *carn. Christ.* 9.
[3] *ib.* 10ff.
[4] *ib.* 23.
[5] *res. carn.* 49; *anim.* 16, 39–41; *test. anim.* 3; *anim.* 27.
[6] *carn. Christ.* 16.
[7] *ib.* 6.

his birth, and so too abolish our death by his death, by rising in the flesh in which he was born that he might even be able to die.'[1] This 'Irenaean' interpretation of Christ's saving work is characteristic of the small amount of exposition which Tertullian devotes to the subject.

It is possibly surprising, though creditable to Tertullian's theological judgement, that he did not introduce into his interpretation of Christ's death the idea of 'satisfaction' which played a prominent part in his theory of penance. He was always greatly impressed by the seriousness of post-baptismal sin. In baptism the believer receives forgiveness of sins, regeneration, assurance of resurrection life, and the indwelling of the Holy Spirit (though the later chapters of his treatise on Baptism, seemingly in contradiction to his earlier insistence on the interaction of the Spirit and water, associate the coming of the Spirit with the post-baptismal laying-on of the hand by the bishop).[2] Here the believer comes within the scope of Christ's saving work. But this grace is retrospective rather than prospective, so far as forgiveness is concerned. The baptized person has been given a new start; but this cannot be repeated if he sins gravely after he has received it. This is why, since his idea of original sin does not imply a transmission of guilt as well as of defect, Tertullian thinks it dangerous to administer baptism to children.[3] It is true that in his earlier days Tertullian was prepared to follow the precedent of Hermas and allow that there could be a second penitence, that is to say one more after baptism: but never more.[4] It would seem that the sins in question were apostasy, murder and adultery; the first apparently continued to be thought unforgivable in the Church until Cyprian's policy established distinctions among those who had lapsed in the Decian persecution and laid down conditions for reconciliation varying with the gravity of the offence. Hippolytus,[5] who took a rigorist attitude, attacked Callistus for his readiness to readmit these serious offenders (but probably not apostates at this stage) and for his citation of the parable of the tares and the presence of clean and unclean animals in the ark as a warrant for his laxity.[6] Tertullian, in his Montanist period, having embraced an exclusive sectarian concept of the Church as a society of the morally righteous, which would be contaminated by the presence of sinners within its membership, violently attacked a bishop who presumed, like a heathen *pontifex maximus* (high priest) or a 'bishop of bishops', to remit, after the performance of penance, the sins of adultery and fornication (this lax innovator being either Agrippinus of Carthage or Callistus).[7] By that stage in his career Tertullian was sure that the Holy Spirit would be driven from the Church if grave sinners were not expelled.[8] Before he turned schismatic, however, he was prepared to speak more freely about the possibility of the post-baptismal sinner compensating for his offence and restoring his bap-

[1] *Marc.* 3.9.
[2] *bapt.* 1, 6, 8, 10.
[3] *ib.* 18.
[4] *paenit.* 7.
[5] *Dan.* 1.15.
[6] *haer.* 9.12, 22.
[7] *pudic.* 1.
[8] *ib.* 13.

tismal state of forgiveness by doing works of penance. In this way he makes satisfaction to God and restores the balance of debt. Later theology was to go further in this matter than Tertullian and apply the concept of satisfaction to the death of Christ.

Like Irenaeus, Tertullian holds a literalistic eschatology to be implied by his doctrine of creation. He therefore spends much time in asserting the truth of the resurrection of the flesh, and believes, like Irenaeus, in an intermediate state or *refrigerium* for the dead until the general resurrection.[1] Death in Adam was a bodily death; resurrection in Christ must be bodily. That 'flesh and blood cannot inherit the Kingdom' means only that the sinful works of the flesh cannot do so. St. Paul's allusion to baptism for the dead refers to the baptism of our bodies with a view to their resurrection from death.[2] These and many other arguments are deployed, especially against Marcion's denial of the value and goodness of the material creation. For the same reason, and also because of his Montanist inclinations (the original Montanists of Asia expected the descent of the new Jerusalem at Pepuza in Phrygia), Tertullian believes strongly in the millenarian reign on earth in the Jerusalem which is to come from heaven.[3] This strong belief in the early Church became discredited through its association with Montanism and because it came to be regarded as a naive piece of literalism. The movement in early third-century Rome of the *Alogi*, as their opponents called them (people without the Logos, or people without reason), and the Roman presbyter Gaius, against the Johannine literature sought to undermine the basic tenets of Montanism, millenarian eschatology and the doctrine of the age of the Paraclete, both of which were founded on the Gospel or the Apocalypse of St. John. It apparently had the effect of discrediting the old literalism; for Hippolytus, who was interested in apocalyptic and wrote both on Daniel and on the Antichrist, interpreted the thousand-year reign allegorically in a work against Gaius: it stands for a glorious spiritual reign of Christ.[4]

Trinitarian and Christological thinking of a generally similar kind to Tertullian's had established itself firmly in the West by the middle of the third century. At that time Novatian, probably before he led a very serious schism on the issue of Church discipline (he took a perfectionist view of the Church and consequently an ultra-rigorist attitude to grave sinners, particularly to those who apostatized in the Decian persecution), wrote his treatise *On the Trinity*, an exposition of the 'rule of truth' beginning with the ineffability and incomprehensibility of God, the supreme and unchangeable author of all good. Since God contains all things there could not be more than one God, one infinite being; and scriptural anthropomorphisms, which are parabolic, do not detract from the actual infinity and absolute simplicity of God. The second part of the rule of faith introduces Christ, 'our Lord God, but the Son of God'.[5] As Son of man he is genuinely human,

[1] *Marc.* 4.34.
[2] *ib.* 5.9, 10.
[3] *ib.* 3.24.
[4] *fr. c. Gaium.*
[5] *Trin.* 9.

not a docetic phantasm; but he is also fully God by reason of the mingling of the deity of the Word with humanity in the union.[1] Man and God (Tertullian's two 'substances') subsist in Christ together, manifested in weakness and power respectively; it is important to notice that Novatian does not speak of love in this context, for the general tendency to think of deity in terms of power, and of humanity in terms of infirmity such as hunger, thirst, suffering, and indeed almost in terms of animal nature and its experiences, increased the difficulty of the Christological problem. Such texts as 'glorify me with the glory which I had with thee before the world was' are taken by Novatian as proof that Christ as God existed substantially before the foundation of the world. It is not a matter of predestination in the counsels of God but of actual pre-existence.[2] Like Tertullian Novatian holds that the Word proceeded from the Father, but that this was before all creation.[3] The Word was begotten as Son, when the Father willed. This is a 'substantial' putting forth; the Word is a substance, not like a human word which is sound and not an entity. Yet he is always in the Father; his existence is timeless, since he is before time; and he is always in the Father since the Father would otherwise not be always Father. The Father, as such, is necessarily prior to the Son, and the Son is less, since his being is derived from the Father. This order or priority, arising from the derivation of the Son, safeguards monotheism, for, says Novatian, were the Son not begotten there would be two ingenerate beings, that is two gods; in fact, though he who was begotten is God, the derivation of his being shows that there is but one God. Further, the deity which the Father transmitted to the Son reverts back to the Father, 'turning back' to him by virtue of the community of substance between Father and Son.[4] This probably means, not that the Son will be reabsorbed into the Father when the 'economy' has been completed, though an allusion in this context to 1 Cor. 15:25ff. may point to that, but rather that the Godhead transmitted from Father to Son is reflected back, as it were, in a circular movement. If this should be Novatian's meaning, he is partly anticipating the later concept of *perichoresis* or mutual interpenetration (see p. 120).

Only one chapter of Novatian's book is devoted to the Holy Spirit, and it is significant that once again the theme changes at this point from theological metaphysics to a straightforward description of the operation of the Spirit: in prophecy, in the life and witness and worship of the Church, in bestowing new birth in the baptismal water, in sanctification, and in the maintenance of truth against false doctrines.[5]

[1] *ib.* 11.
[2] *ib.* 16.
[3] *ib.* 21.
[4] *ib.* 31.
[5] *ib.* 29.

V

THE ALEXANDRIAN THEOLOGIANS OF
THE THIRD CENTURY

In strong contrast with the Latin theology of the third century there stands the characteristic thought of the Alexandrian school whose earliest representative, apart from vague traditions concerning Pantaenus and other 'elders' to whom he was indebted, is Clement. Clement can, it is true, occasionally echo the ideas of Tertullian, making the 'canon of truth' or ecclesiastical tradition the norm for the interpretation of scripture, and holding that since the Logos himself has descended from heaven there is no need to run to Athens in pursuit of human wisdom.[1] Yet Clement's approach to the question of authority in religion is generally very different from Tertullian's. He concerns himself very little with the hierarchically organized Church and its successions of accredited teachers passing on the apostolic doctrine in the apostolic sees; and, so far from professing to regard Greek philosophy as a primary source of heresy, with which 'Jerusalem' has nothing in common, Clement, himself a very widely read scholar whose writings bristle with quotations from the classical poets and philosophers, welcomes it as a propaedeutic by which men's minds are trained to receive the full truth revealed by Christ. He is careful to explain that not every philosophy is simply to be accepted without more ado; the right philosophy is Platonism, and this chiefly because it teaches, or is consonant with, belief in monotheism, a doctrine of creation and the providential ordering of the universe.[2] Clement knows that some, indeed the majority, are afraid of Greek philosophy and run away from it as from a bogey;[3] but he argues with those who think that it is of the devil, reminding them that the devil can transform himself into an angel of light; if the devil prophesies as an angel of light what he says in that role must be true, and if he should utter philosophical truths they, too, are by no means thereby falsified. On the contrary, philosophy was divinely given to the Greeks as their own particular covenant, a fact that remains true even though the devil has sown tares among the wheat both of Christianity (heresies) and philosophy (atheistic and providence-denying systems such as Epicureanism).[4] It was given, in fact, to the Greeks as a preparation for the coming of Christ and the calling of the Christian community, just as the Law was given to the Jews for the same purpose.[5] The knowledge of truth gained by the philo-

---

[1] *str.* 7.16.94–95; *prot.* 11.112.
[2] *str.* 1.19.92.
[3] *ib.* 6.10.81.
[4] *ib.* 6.8.66–67.
[5] *ib.* 6.18.159; 1.5.28.

sophers was incomplete and partial,[1] yet, 'even if Greek philosophy does not grasp the greatness of the truth, and is still without strength to perform the Lord's commandments, yet it does nevertheless prepare the way for the supremely royal teaching'.[2] Clement, it is true, follows the conventional line of Christian apologetic in claiming that the Hebrew scriptures represent a far older philosophy than that of any Greek philosophical school,[3] and that the distinctive tenets of Platonism and some of those of Stoicism were borrowed from that source; and he puts this idea even more bluntly: the philosophers were plagiarists who 'stole' their ideas from Moses and the prophets.[4] Nevertheless, Clement is sincere in his belief that the universal Logos has provided philosophy as an introduction to the way of perfection through the teaching of Christ, and that this illustrates the fact that although there is one way of truth, yet many streams flow into it from different directions, as though into an ever-flowing river[5] – a sentiment which is rare enough among the early Christian writers to mark out Clement as a thinker of remarkable insight and breadth of sympathy.

Clement's writings, however, are very far from being systematic treatises. They consist of introductions to Christian faith and life, and miscellaneous reflections on these subjects, leading up to his conception of the ideal advanced believer: the 'Gnostic'. This 'Gnostic's' form of Christianity bears a considerable outward resemblance to that of the various Gnostic sects for it is highly intellectualized, knowledge is on the whole a higher stage of communion with God than faith, esoteric and unwritten tradition plays a not unimportant role in it, and salvation tends to be seen primarily in terms of illumination. On the other hand it differs essentially from the heretical gnosis in that the object of the 'Gnostic's' knowledge is quite differently conceived: God and the world and man's relationship to God and the world are by no means thought of in the same way.

In working towards his picture of the Christian 'Gnostic', or, as perhaps we should rather say, the 'gnostic Christian', Clement touches on many aspects of Christian thought, but makes few important contributions to the development of doctrine. His theological starting-point is the transcendence and ineffability of God. He quotes Plato:[6] 'To find the Father and Maker of this universe is a hard task, and it is impossible for one who has found him to tell of this to the multitude. For it can in no way be spoken of like the other objects of knowledge'; and he comments on this by means of an analogy with the ascent of Moses, alone and unaccompanied by the people, into the cloud 'where God was'. This signifies that God is invisible and ineffable, concealed from sight by the multitude's ignorance and disbelief. St. John's phrase 'the bosom of the Father' symbolizes the invisibility and ineffability of God, whom some call 'depth'. The first cause of all things is beyond all the logical categories of description; God transcends even the notions of 'the whole' or 'the one', and in calling God 'one', or 'good', or

---

[1] *ib.* 6.10.83; 6.18.160.
[2] *ib.* 1.16.80.
[3] *ib.* 1.21.101, etc.
[4] e.g., *ib.* 5.1.9–10.
[5] *ib.* 1.5.28–29.
[6] *Timaeus* 28C, a favourite citation with Christian writers.

'mind' or 'Father', or 'God', or 'Creator' or 'Lord' we are not applying to him an actual name but employing the best terms we can in our insoluble difficulty, so that our mind may have some basis to rest on. God, in fact, is inaccessible to every mode of human knowledge, and can be known only in so far as he discloses himself by grace through the Logos who is from him.[1] In himself God is 'one and beyond the one and above monad (oneness) itself, transcending present, past and future as "he who is" ';[2] but he is revealed by his Logos, the Son who is wisdom and knowledge and truth. He can express the inexpressible God. Into him as one entity all the powers of the spirit are gathered up into unity and comprised in the Son who comprehends the idea of each of the powers.[3] Clement's thought here is that the revelation of God is communicated through the Son or Logos who contains within himself the archetypal ideas. This conception recurs in Clement's allegorical exegesis of Gen. 22:3ff. On the third day, which stands for the illumination of the mind by the Word, 'the Teacher who rose on the third day', and also for the believer's illumination by the 'seal' of baptism, Abraham looked up and saw the place afar off; from afar, because the place is hard to reach, being God, whom Plato calls the place of the ideas.[4] So, too, Clement identifies the truth which, according to Jn. 14:6, is the Logos, with Plato's idea of truth; and the idea, Clement says, is God's thought or concept, that is, his Logos.[5] Thus the Logos is the mediator between the utterly transcendent One which is God, and the world of which he contains, as it were summed up in himself, the archetypes and the spiritual powers which motivate and govern it. The Spirit is the light of truth (the Logos being truth), true light without shadow, distributed without division to those who are sanctified through faith, bringing them knowledge of reality.[6] Thus Clement's Trinity is the traditional Christian triad of Father, Son and Holy Spirit reinterpreted along Platonist lines in terms of the communication, or 'broadening down', of God from the Unknown to the immanent illuminating Spirit who makes known to men's rational souls the truth revealed by the Logos, the bridge, as it were, by which the One passes over to the many. In many respects Clement's Trinity bears a close resemblance to the Neo-Platonist triad of the One, *Nous* (Mind) and the World Soul.

There is an inherent kinship between the Logos and the rational mind of man, existing by virtue of creation. God's Logos is his image, and the divine Logos is the authentic Son of his mind (*nous*), the archetypal light of light, and man is the image of the Logos. Man is *logikos*, possessing a mind (*nous*) which is made in the image and likeness of God.[7] Man's mind is thus an image of God's image,[8] and this fact serves Clement as a basis on which to build a natural theology. All men, and especially philosophers and poets, possess a kind of infused effluence of the divine, and to this is to be

[1] *str.* 5.12.78–82.
[2] *paed.* 1.8.71.
[3] *str.* 4.25.156.
[4] *ib.* 5.11.73.
[5] *ib.* 5.3.16.
[6] *ib.* 6.16. 138.
[7] *prot.* 10.98.
[8] *str.* 5.14.94.

ascribed their often involuntary testimony to the one eternal and ingenerate God.[1] This belief, similar to Justin's though more fully elaborated, does not conflict with the traditional doctrine that man is fallen and sinful. Sinlessness, which Clement is inclined to equate with the freedom from the passions (*apatheia*) which was the goal of Stoic ethics, belongs solely to the incarnate Logos, who alone is wholly free from passions;[2] man, on the other hand, was subjected to sickness, destruction and death.[3] Like his predecessors, Clement lays great stress on human free will, and regards the original condition of Adam as being childlikeness, with the possibility of development for good or ill. Where Clement differs from them is in seeking to identify the sin of Adam with sexuality, and thus to link original sin with 'pleasure', though it has to be observed that Clement denies Gnostic ideas concerning the inherent evil of sex and tries to confine his suggestion to the notion that intercourse was illicit, in the sense that it was not yet permitted by God when Adam fell, and that the fall therefore consisted in disobedience rather than sex as such.[4] Not that one can use the term 'original sin' without some qualification, for Clement is clear that a child which has done nothing cannot be reckoned to be under the curse of Adam but is free from sin.[5] It is something more like 'original passions', upsetting man's rational *apatheia*, which Clement thinks has been transmitted from Adam.

As regards the generation of the Logos, Clement lays stress upon the unity of the Logos with the Father. 'The Son is in the Father and the Father in the Son';[6] the Father is not without the Son, and to believe in the Son one must know the Father to whom the Son exists, and to know the Father one must believe in the Son because the Son of God teaches; the Father leads one on from faith to knowledge through the Son.[7] The Son is the timeless beginning, without beginning, of all creation;[8] he was the Father's counsellor before the foundation of the world, and Wisdom and Word before all the things that were made.[9] Yet it is not clear that Clement intends to propound the view that the generation of the Logos is itself eternal, as against the theory that had hitherto been current of a 'begetting' of the eternal and immanent reason of God for the purpose of creation. The allusions to the Logos being 'timeless' and 'without beginning' are compatible with the latter view, and in at least one place Clement speaks of the Logos 'coming forth'.[10] A fragment on I Jn. 1:1 preserved in a Latin version does certainly state the idea of eternal generation unequivocally, but the authenticity of this passage is uncertain.[11] He does undoubtedly hold

[1] *prot.* 6.68.
[2] *paed.* 1.2.4.
[3] *prot.* 11.114; *paed.* 1.9.83.
[4] *str.* 3.17.102–3; *prot.* 11.111.
[5] *str.* 3.16. 100; 4.25.160.
[6] *paed.* 1.7.53.
[7] *str.* 5.1.1.
[8] *ib.* 7.1.2.
[9] *ib.* 7.2.7.
[10] e.g., *ib.* 5.3.16.
[11] Potter p. 1009, *G.C.S.* vol. 3, p. 210.

a strong doctrine of the Logos as an actual hypostasis, not to be imagined to resemble a spoken word which has no concrete subsistence. 'The Logos of the Father of the universe', he says, 'is not the *logos prophorikos* (which Theophilus had asserted the Logos to have become by virtue of his being "put forth"), but the most manifest wisdom and goodness of God, an almighty and, in reality, divine power'.[1] He is also clear that the persons of the Trinity can be spoken of as distinct hypostases: 'One is the Father of the universe, one the Logos of the universe, and the Holy Spirit is one and the same everywhere.'[2]

In his Christology Clement follows lines of thought which were by now traditional: the Logos appeared to men, the one who was both God and man[3] and hence the mediator between God and man,[4] 'begetting himself' when he became flesh,[5] being born, suffering and dying in the flesh.[6] A somewhat docetic-sounding passage concerning the freedom of the incarnate Logos from human emotions and appetites is probably due less to any Christological motive than to Clement's ascetical preoccupation with the ideal of *apatheia*.[7] In soteriology, too, Clement offers little that is original. He concentrates attention chiefly on the revelatory work of the incarnate Logos, but he has some fine statements of the breadth of the love which has been extended to suffering and helpless mankind: 'He conformed himself to our weakness to enable us to gain his strength, offered himself like a sacrificial libation and gave himself as a ransom, and left to us a new covenant; he reveals God to man, causes corruption to cease, conquers death, reconciles disobedient sons to the Father: educates, admonishes, saves, guards, and promises the kingdom of heaven as the reward of discipleship.[8]

In his ideas about salvation it could be said that Clement 'realizes' the eschatology of Irenaeus. For both these writers the goal of salvation is the attainment of likeness to God, a likeness that transcends the natural relationship to God given to man in creation, for it is a participation in divine qualities, bestowed by pure grace. Irenaeus had identified the likeness with the indwelling of the Spirit in every believer, and held that its eschatological fulfilment would be incorruptibility in the resurrection life. Clement, however, identifies likeness or assimilation (*homoiosis*) to God with knowledge (*gnosis*), and his ideal 'gnostic', being a son of God by adoption, is a 'god' even in this life.[9] In his vision of Christian perfection *gnosis* is more prominent than incorruptibility, for Clement believes that the soul possesses a natural immortality; it was created with the gift of incorruptibility. Knowledge means assimilation, for patristic theology assumes as an axiom the philosophical principle that like is apprehended by like; knowledge both implies likeness between the knower and the known and also creates it. By

[1] *str.* 5.1.6.
[2] *paed.* 1.6.42.
[3] *prot.* 1.7.
[4] *paed.* 3.1.2.
[5] *str.* 5.3.16.
[6] *ib.* 6.15.127.
[7] *ib.* 6.9.71-2.
[8] *q.d.s.* 37; *prot.* 1.6.
[9] *str.* 7.16.

knowledge of God man is transformed into the likeness of God; indeed, knowledge of God is identical with union with God. In its intellectual aspect *gnosis* is assimilation to the divine through contemplation; morally it is assimilation to the divine through freedom from the passions (*apatheia*) and love (*agape*).

Since only the advanced Christian is able to receive true *gnosis*, Clement's hope of salvation is certainly élitist. It does not, however, represent a total transformation of the early Christian into a Platonist understanding of man's destiny. Assimilation to God means the closest communion with him, but it does not mean absorption into the One, nor the obliteration of the distinction between creature and creator; for Clement has no doubt that the soul belongs to the created order and is not to be identified with the divine. Further, although salvation is the fullness of *gnosis* (in the sense of contemplation) rather than deliverance from death and corruption, the resurrection of the body is maintained by Clement as part of the traditional Christian belief, although in his scheme of salvation it is really an anomaly. There is, too, the remarkable combination of freedom from the passions with love. This is often said to illustrate the difference between Christian *apatheia* and the 'detachment' cultivated in Stoicism. Yet it is not fully clear whether Clement's *agape* means the love of the soul for God alone, for which deliverance from the passions is the necessary preparation, or whether it also includes love of one's neighbour. Clement may here illustrate a tension within early Christian ideas of salvation; although every writer recognizes that the fruit of the Spirit is love, salvation, interpreted as the deification of the human soul (or of the human mixture of soul and body) tends in fact to be thought of as a solitary process of the perfecting of the individual.

Even so brief and selective a glance at Clement's theology illustrates some of the characteristic elements in the Alexandrian combination of biblical and Platonist religion. Origen approaches the problems of theology with similar presuppositions, but besides differing from Clement in being a systematic thinker, the first Christian to construct an integrated body of doctrine intended as a positive exposition of truth and not primarily as apologetics or polemics, he is also by far the most original theologian that the early Church produced: indeed, his is the most remarkable and interesting mind that we encounter during the whole patristic period up to Augustine.

Origen enters upon his work of theological construction fully aware that God is incomprehensible and beyond the scope of human thought. Man's reason, made the less keen through its embodiment in flesh and blood, can no more perceive the nature of God than a person whose eyes can scarcely bear the flicker of a lantern could gaze directly into the sun.[1] He recognizes, too, that his enquiry lies within two distinct fields, in one of which truth is given to the theologian on the authority of revelation whereas in the other problems remain unsolved and the way is open for original speculation; though such speculation uses scripture as the area of enquiry. The former is represented, generally speaking, by the beliefs enshrined in the rule of faith. They rest upon the authority of the apostolic preaching, handed down

[1] *princ.* 1.1.5.

in the Church's tradition derived from the apostles by succession. But while the unity of the operation of the Holy Spirit in the Old Testament prophets and the apostles of the New Testament, for example, is part of the authoritative preaching, the question whether the Spirit is begotten or unbegotten, or whether he should himself be reckoned as Son of God, is not. The soul's freedom, too, is laid down in the accepted doctrinal tradition in opposition to astrological fatalism; but questions about the origin of the soul have never been so decided. It is part of the Church's preaching that the world was created from a definite point of time and that it will in time be dissolved; it remains an open question what may have preceded this universe of ours and what may come after it.[1] This is how Origen's task presented itself to him as he began his major work *On First Principles* (*De Principiis*) which for the most past survives only in Latin translation somewhat tendentiously edited. Not that he observed the distinction with any great precision; he evidently feels it his duty not only to speculate where the questions seemed to be open but also to do a considerable amount of reinterpretation of the traditional teaching of the Church (the uniformity and definiteness of which he is in any case inclined to exaggerate in the passage just mentioned).

Like Clement, Origen regards philosophy as an ally in the quest for knowledge of God, provided always that it is the right kind of philosophy. Some philosophers, he observes, agree with Christianity in asserting divine creation, and some of them add that God created the world and governs it through his Logos; but philosophy is an enemy to Christianity when it assigns to matter or to the universe the same eternity that is rightly predicated of God and when it denies, or sets limits to, divine providence. Like Isaac and Abimelech, Christianity and philosophy are sometimes at peace, sometimes at war.[2]

The chief guide for Origen's great enterprise of theological exploration is scripture as interpreted according to certain vitally important principles which, he believes, afford the key to understanding what the Holy Spirit who inspired the scriptures seeks to communicate. The main principle is that the scriptures must not be read in their literal sense alone; they contain a deeper and inward significance, a 'spiritual' or 'inner' meaning, which lies, as it were, beneath the outward, that is to say the literal or historical sense. Origen complains bitterly that Jewish exegesis is absurdly pedestrian: the Jews interpret scripture according to the letter, not the Spirit. This would seem, superficially, to be a very ridiculous charge, for Jewish exegesis was far from literalistic and Origen himself was greatly indebted to it, deriving a very great deal of his allegorical interpretation from Philo and a substantial amount from rabbinic tradition (as, for example, in the symbolic meanings which he loves to find in Hebrew proper names, where his interpretations sometimes differ markedly from Philo's and are paralleled in rabbinic Judaism). What he means, however, is that Jewish exegesis naturally failed to interpret the Hebrew scriptures as books which, when their inner meaning had been discovered, were found to be books about

[1] *ib.* I *proem.* 1–7.
[2] *hom. 14.3 in Gen.*

Christ, and that it issued in actual observance of the precepts of the Law instead of treating these for the most part as symbolic of spiritual realities. He himself sets out a threefold method of exegesis, corresponding to the tripartite division of man into body, life-principle (*psyche*), and spirit, and scripturally warranted by the text, 'Write them down in a threefold way with counsel and knowledge' of Prov. 22:20. The bodily sense is the literal, the 'psychic' is the use of the text as a moral allegory for edification, such as St. Paul's use of Dt. 25:4 in I Cor. 9:9–10, and the spiritual sense discloses teaching about Christ, the gospel and the Church.[1]

Origen is not precisely or entirely consistent in his application of these principles. For the most part he is content to distinguish the outward or literal sense from the inner or spiritual. The latter may be typological, pointing to the correspondence between God's dealings with man in the Old Testament and in the New and so reading Christ and the Church out of the Old Testament, or allegorical, illustrating spiritual truths and moral lessons, on the lines made familiar by Philo. Sometimes Origen suggests that the literal sense is a necessary step towards the full meaning of a passage and that it must be taken seriously,[2] and at times, as in his homily on the story of the witch of Endor, he defends a strictly literal interpretation against the freer and more imaginative exegesis of others. But here the choice lies only between different versions of the 'outward' sense; no typological or allegorical meaning is in question, and for the most part he sits very loosely indeed to the plain meaning of the text, giving the impression that only a very naive and uninstructed Christian would pay any attention to it. In a number of cases, he claims, the literal sense is impossible, and it was never intended that it should be taken at its face value; in some of these a literal interpretation would be altogether shocking and unworthy of God (the story of Lot's daughters is an instance), and these examples serve as a reminder that what seems to be a descriptive account of 'marriages, procreation, wars and all sorts of histories really consists of types'.[3] Even in the narratives of the Gospels Origen finds a fertile field for allegorical interpretation. The text provides types or mysteries; that is, it points beyond itself to divine truths which it serves partly to mediate and partly to conceal. Origen's Platonism disposes him to see the 'letter' as an outward form, a husk which has to be cracked open and removed in order to reach the spiritual truth imprisoned within it. This means in practice that Origen's ingenious imagination has free scope; and he recognizes that to discern the authentic meaning of a passage is difficult and that exegesis must often be tentative. Hence he often indicates various alternative possibilities suggested by himself or by others.

Just as Origen's Platonism causes him to see the plain meaning of scripture as a kind of disguise in which the inner truth presents itself, so it makes him interpret the Christian sacraments along somewhat similar lines. This is especially true of his eucharist theology; with regard to baptism Origen tends to reproduce traditional teaching about union with Christ in

---

[1] *princ.* 4.2.1–17.
[2] *ib.* 4.2.5.
[3] *ib.* 4.2.2.

death and resurrection,[1] the descent of the Spirit on the believer,[2] and liberation from the tyranny of the devil,[3] and it is only occasionally that he suggests that the external rite is but an outward sign or symbol of a spiritual reality in comparison with which the sacrament as such is of small account.[4] In the case of the eucharist, however, this tendency comes out clearly. At times he uses 'realist' language about the eucharist elements, like all early Christian writers. Thus he says that we receive the Lord's body, and that by prayer the eucharistic gifts 'become a certain holy body'.[5] On the other hand he also shows that not only does he regard the bread and wine as outward and material signs pointing to an inner and spiritual reality, but that he interprets the 'body and blood of Christ' which they signify as being themselves symbolical of the life-giving truth which the Logos imparts. Hence it is the word which is spoken over it rather than the actual bread which benefits the recipient; the former, the prayer of faith, bestows spiritual discernment, the latter goes into the belly; so we do not lose any benefit merely by not partaking of the consecrated bread, nor do we receive any abundant benefit by merely eating it.[6] 'The bread which God the Logos proclaims to be his body is the word which feeds our souls . . . The drink which God the Logos proclaims to be his blood is the word . . . The body and blood of God the Logos can be nothing else but the word which nourishes and the word which makes glad the heart . . . The bread is the word of righteousness by eating which our souls are nourished; the drink is the word of the knowledge of Christ according to the mystery of his birth and passion.'[7] Origen is prepared to go so far as to maintain, in commenting on the story of the Last Supper: 'Let this bread and the cup be understood by the more simple people according to the more general acceptation of the eucharist; but by those who have been trained to a deeper understanding let it be interpreted as referring to the more divine promise, the promise of the nourishing word of truth.'[8]

This last passage illustrates Origen's tendency to treat both word (of scripture) and sacraments as, at best, visual aids for simpler folk, who depend upon the senses, as contrasted with those more advanced believers who have the capacity (the 'spiritual senses' which he enumerates at length in his *Dialogue with Heracleides*)[9] to grasp the spiritual truth communicated by the Logos. It also indicates how easy it was for Origen to come close to thinking that Jesus Christ is, in the last resort, a similar outward guise serving both to communicate (to earth-bound mortals) and in a measure to conceal the heavenly Logos, and how, without going to such extremes as that, he did certainly regard the purpose of the Incarnation as being primarily to reveal the Logos as *teacher* and revealer of the mysteries of God.

[1] *hom. 19.14 in Jer.*
[2] *hom. 22.27 in Lc.*
[3] *hom. 5.5 in Ex.*
[4] e.g., *Rom.* 5.8; *sel. in Ezech.* 16.9.
[5] e.g., *hom. 13.3 in Ex.*; *Cels.* 8.33.
[6] *comm. in Mt.* 11.14.
[7] *comm. ser. in Mt.* 85.
[8] *Jn.* 32.24.
[9] *dial.* 11-28.

Thus, when Celsus asserts that God is unattainable by reason Origen draws a distinction: God is certainly not attainable by the reason that is in us, but God is attainable by the Logos that was with God and was God, and is comprehended also by any man to whom the Logos reveals the Father.[1]

God is mind, and is simple, invisible and incorporeal; or rather, God is beyond being itself. This Platonist assertion[2] is required by the notion of participation; God 'is participated in, rather than participates; and he is participated in by those who possess the Spirit of God'. God therefore does not even participate in being (an assertion of Celsus with which Origen, subject to queries and qualification, agrees).[3] God is absolutely one and simple,[4] simple spiritual nature admitting of no superiority or inferiority in himself, but in every respect monad 'and as I might say "henad" ', being himself mind and the source from which the totality of spiritual and intellectual nature is derived. Yet God[5] may be known by natural theology: not directly, any more than the sun can be seen directly, but only by inference from the brilliance of its rays shining on to windows; but the design of the universe and the works of providence serve like the sun's rays, and thus enable us to infer the Father of the universe from the beauty and order of the created world.[6]

This presupposes the creative and revelatory work of the Logos; and Origen's version of the Logos doctrine, which is both interesting and important for its effect upon the subsequent development of theology, is motivated and controlled by a strong cosmological interest derived from the Platonist background of his thought. Like Clement, Origen thinks of the Godhead as subsisting at different levels; there is, so to speak, a broadening down of deity from the apex of the divine hierarchy where the Father is the source, himself participating in no higher stage of divine being, from which deity at every level is derived, and descending in an order of participation and of functional subordination through Logos and Spirit to the archetypal ideas which are contained in the Logos, and so by the process of derivation to all spiritual and rational beings, the *logikoi* who, in so far as they participate in the Logos, may properly be called 'gods'. Origen's cosmology, in the light of which his more specific doctrine of the relation of the Logos to the Father has to be understood, requires him to believe that God must always have a universe related to himself. God is unchanging; his attributes do not cease to be exercised; and the beneficence of the Creator and his providential care, which are his eternal qualities and operations, could not become inactive. Nor could God be said to be omnipotent if he had no object upon which to exercise his sovereign power. It follows that there has been a created world (not necessarily this particular world) from all eternity and that there will be a created world of some kind for ever.[7] This does not mean that the universe is a second uncreated principle alongside God. On the

[1] *Cels.* 6.65.
[2] *ib.* 7.38 (Plato *Rep.* 509B).
[3] *Cels.* 6.64.
[4] *Jn.* 1.20.
[5] *princ.* 1.1.6.
[6] *ib.*
[7] *ib.* 1.4.3–4; 1.2.10.

contrary, it, or possibly a succession of universes, exists by virtue of the divine creativity and providence, continually exercised towards it. It is contingent and wholly dependent, but linked with the Creator through his direct image, the Logos, the rational creation which has been created as 'images of the image',[1] and the descending order of participation in, and communion with, the transcendent Father.

It follows from this unchanging pattern of relations that the primary and archetypal relation, that between the Father and the Logos, should be eternal. It is thus in this wider context of the eternal relations between God and the rational (*logikos*) creation that Origen's belief in the eternal generation of the Logos has to be seen. Unlike the Apologists and Tertullian who envisaged two stages in the existence of the Logos, first as the reason conceived within the mind of God and then as the expressed reason or uttered Word, Origen holds the 'external' relationship to be without beginning. To assert a beginning, that is to say to imagine a stage when the Logos had not yet been generated, is impossible: it would imply either that God had been unable to do what afterwards he did, or that he was unwilling to do it.[2] The generation is eternal and sempiternal, like the generation of brightness from light.[3] Origen does indeed call the Logos a 'creature', and 'firstborn of all creation'; but this is because he is using scriptural terminology (he quotes the standard proof-text for the Logos or Wisdom as a creature, Prov. 8:22), and in the same short passage, a fragment of the original Greek, he points out that since God is light (I Jn. 1:5) he can never have been without the emission of light, the 'brightness of his glory' (Heb. 1:3), and so there 'was never when he (Wisdom–Logos, the image of God) was not'.[4] Thus Origen denies one of the main thesis of Arius in advance, and he uses the same argument elsewhere when he says that just as light can never exist without producing its effulgence, so Wisdom, being an effulgence of everlasting light (Wisd. 7:26) is eternally generated. The Saviour is Wisdom and is therefore generated eternally by the Father; and the believer who possesses the Spirit of adoption is by God's action able to become an eternally generated son of God in Christ.[5]

As regards the manner of this generation, Origen employs the old analogy of 'light from light' many times.[6] He points out that it is not to be likened to any corporeal process; it involves neither creation from non-existence nor a division of the divine substance; but it is like the emergence of will from mind.[7] As such, it is an act of the Father's will,[8] but not a single act for the purpose of the 'economy', but a continuous exercise of will. This point seems to differentiate Origen's idea of the generation of the Logos from the Plotinian theory of the relation of *Nous* (Mind) to the One, which in other respects it closely resembles. *Nous* is continuously generated from

[1] *Jn.* 2.3.
[2] *princ.* 1.2.2.
[3] *ib.* 1.2.4.
[4] *ib.* 4.4.1.
[5] *hom. 9.4 in Jer.*
[6] e.g., *princ.* 1.2.7.
[7] *ib.* 1.2.6; 4.4.1.
[8] *ib.*

the One, just as the World Soul is continually generated from *Nous*, but not by the purposeful will of the One. Origen is careful to explain that in calling the Son Wisdom he does not mean to imply that he is a mere abstraction; on the contrary, he subsists substantially, and when he is termed Word, and such texts as Ps. 45:2 are applied to him, it must be remembered that they do not imply that the Logos is like a verbally uttered word, for Logos is a figurative term like 'vine' or 'door' and must not be taken literally. The fact that the term 'Son' is conjoined with it should save 'Logos' from being misunderstood.[1]

Origen tries in various ways to describe the unity between the Father and the Logos. It can be interpreted in terms of identity of operation, on the lines of Jn. 5:19; what the Father does, the Son does. As the mirror of God the divine Wisdom reflects the acts of God, but this does not mean that the Father's acts are copied by the Son, as a pupil copies a master, nor that the Son imitates in the earthly sphere what the Father does in the heavenly, but that the Son's work is not *like*, but actually *is*, the Father's.[2] Or it can be presented through an analogy with the union of man and wife as one flesh, and of the believer with Christ as one spirit: the Saviour in his relation to the Father is neither one flesh nor one spirit, but – what is superior to both flesh and spirit – one God.[3] In any case, what Origen wants to do is to avoid the monarchian error of abolishing the Son, and so in effect preventing the Father from being Father, and at the same time to avoid denying Christ's divinity.[4] What has been said above, however, concerning the generation of the Logos is enough to show that Origen recognizes a substantial unity, and when, reverting once again to the idea of the effulgence of God's glory, he takes the allusions in Wisd. 7:25–26 (breath of God's power and effulgence of glory) as showing that an effulgence or a breath are consubstantial (*homoousios*, of the same essence) with that of which they are the effluence or breath, there is no reason to doubt the authenticity in his writing of the technical term which was soon to acquire immense importance.[5]

Nevertheless Origen is most anxious to emphasize the distinction between Father and Logos. He wants to refute the monarchian view which would make no distinction in 'number' between them but postulate a unity not only of substance but of individual existence, so denying that the individuality of the Son is other than that of the Father.[6] He knows that people are afraid of the implication that there could be two gods, but he insists that Father and Son differ from each other in hypostasis, that is, in their substance as individual entities or persons.[7] The Father is absolutely God; this the Johannine Prologue acknowledges by prefixing the definite article, *ho theos* ('The God'), whereas the Logos is not God absolutely (*autotheos*) and the article is not prefixed when he is called 'God' any more than it would

---

[1] *ib.* 1.2.2; *Jn.* 1.24ff.
[2] *princ.* 1.2.12.
[3] *dial.* 3.
[4] *ib.* 4.
[5] *fr. in Heb.* (Migne *PG.* 14.1308).
[6] *Jn.* 2.2; 10.37.
[7] *ib.*; cf. 2.10.

be in the case of other deified beings. The Son is first of *theoi* (gods), above all others as being 'the Lord the God of Gods'. The others, saints and all 'deified' creatures, derive their divinity from him; they are copies of the archetype. But he is the archetype, the model of all copies; only, his own deity is derived from the fountain-head, the Father, and he is the archetype because he is always with the Father and eternally beholds the 'depth' of the Father's being.[1] Two points stand out here: the Logos is God by derivation and so, despite being substantially one with the Father, he stands, as it were, at a lower level in the hierarchy, as mediator between the Father whom he mirrors and all creatures who derive their relation to God through him; and his derivation of deity from the Father is pictured in Platonist terms as a continual process of contemplation.

In his Commentary on John, Origen discusses at length the various meanings which should be attached to the words *'logos'* and *'theos'* in different contexts, showing how these can be arranged in hierarchical order. This illustrates clearly how he conceives of deity being, as it were, eternally broadened down through a series of relationships (of communication and participation) from the apex or fountain-head to the rational creation at the base of the pyramid. It throws particular light on his theory of the intermediary, and mediating, status of the Logos between the Father and the many creatures who are *logikoi* and can rightly be termed *theoi*. As the logos in the *logikoi* is to the Logos who was in the beginning with God and is God, so the Logos who was in the beginning with God and is God is to the Father himself. As the true and absolute God (*autotheos*) is to the image and the images of the image, so the absolute Logos (*autologos*) is to the logos in every man; for, as God is the source of deity (and thus the Son is not *autotheos*), so the Son is the source of logos in the rational creation (and thus no angel or man could be *autologos*).[2] For these reasons Origen wants to lay the greatest possible stress on the distinct hypostatic existence of Father and Son, to the extent of using such a phrase as 'second God',[3] and of declaring the Son to be other than the Father in respect of *ousia* (substance or essence), although if this were his meaning it would contradict his other statements mentioned above and it may well be that, since the technical terminology had not yet acquired precision, Origen intends only to say that the Son is distinct in his individual personal subsistence.[4]

Thus the Logos, in Origen's scheme as in that of Philo, occupies an intermediate position. He is the line of communication whereby the transcendent God can be comprehended, for 'since . . . God is mind, or transcends mind and being, and is simple and invisible and incorporeal, he is not comprehended by any being other than that made in the image of that mind'.[5] He is also the actual connecting link between uncreated deity and created nature, standing himself midway between these.[6] This link is provided by the fact that he contains in himself the *logoi*, that is the

[1] *ib.* 2.2, 10.
[2] *ib.* 2.3.
[3] *Cels.* 5.39; cf. *dial.* 4.
[4] *or.* 15.1.
[5] *Cels.* 7.38.
[6] *ib.* 3.34.

rational principles or (Platonic) ideas, of all creatures;[1] thus, whereas the Father is absolute unity the Son contains in himself the many.[2] This manifold character of the Logos expresses itself in the variety of *epinoiai* (ideas or notions presented by different aspects) in which the Son is manifested. These, according to Origen, account for the many different titles, descriptions and metaphors applied to Jesus in the New Testament, some of which had already been predicated of the Logos by Philo: 'firstborn from the dead', 'shepherd', 'light', 'resurrection', 'way', 'truth', 'life', 'door', 'vine', 'bread', and so on. These terms indicate that he was not manifested to everyone in the same way; the Logos adapted his self-revelation to the capacities of those whom he encountered; thus chosen disciples were shown his glory as transfigured, but the crowds could not see him in that state and after the Resurrection he was not seen by them in any mode at all. Origen speculates on whether, but for the fall of man, the Logos would have revealed himself under any aspects besides wisdom, word, life and truth. Certainly he would not have been needed as physician, shepherd or redeemer, and, a most important point for understanding Origen's outlook, it would be a most blessed state of affairs if believers did not now need to know the Logos in these capacities.[3]

With this theory of the mediating position of the Logos is linked Origen's understanding of his high-priestly office. The imagery of the Epistle to the Hebrews and the underlying typological interpretation of the Pentateuch is used to teach a doctrine of the mediation of the Logos between the Christian believer and God as the object of his faith and worship. Hence prayer must not be addressed to any creature, nor even to Christ, but only to the God and Father of the universe. It is, in fact, a sin to pray to Christ; but prayer must not, on the other hand, be made to the Father without the mediation of the 'high priest'.[4]

It is not precisely clear just where Origen conceives the Logos or the Spirit as standing on the descending scale, as it were, of deity. He can say that the Saviour and the Spirit transcend all creatures, not in degree only but in kind, but that they are in their turn as far transcended by the Father as they themselves transcend all creatures. The Son is above all angelic hierarchies, but he is nothing in comparison with the Father; he is not the effulgence of God himself but of God's light and glory, a mirror reflecting whatever the Father does.[5] Elsewhere, on the other hand, he asserts that the fact that the Logos is the image of God's goodness (Wisd. 7:26) places him higher above all inferior beings than the Father, by the fact of being absolute goodness, is placed above him.[6] The Holy Spirit, Origen recognizes, is, like the Logos, an individual substantial entity and not an abstraction. The Spirit is not an energy, or force, of God, but an active substance, represented in scripture as acting personally;[7] and such is the authority and

[1] *ib.* 5.39.
[2] *Jn.* 1.20.
[3] *Cels.* 2.64; *Jn.* 1.20ff.
[4] *or.* 15.1.
[5] cf. *Jn.* 13.25.
[6] *comm. in Mt.* 15.10.
[7] *fr. 37 in Jn.*

dignity of the Spirit, revealed in scripture, that in the Trinitarian formula of baptism the name of the Spirit is joined with those of Father and Son. The Spirit operated in the Creation, and scripture nowhere calls him a creature; various texts witness to his deity, such as Isa. 6:3 where the cherubim represent the Son and the Spirit, and Hab. 3:3 (LXX) where the 'two living creatures' have the same meaning. In the Spirit the Son's revelation of the Father is received, but it is not through the Son but directly that the Spirit himself knows the Father. He is eternal, as one of the eternal Trinity.[1] On the other hand (and it may well be that the theology of *De Principiis* has been 'tidied up' at this point) the *Commentary on John* discusses whether the Spirit is included in the 'all things' which came into being through the Son or whether the Spirit is ingenerate. Since Origen maintains that there are three hypostases, since the Spirit is not an insubstantial 'energy', and that there is but one ingenerate principle, he concludes that the Spirit is the chief and highest in rank of all things that came into being through the Son; that is why he is not himself termed 'Son', and thus it would appear that he is wise, rational, righteous, and so on, through participation in the Son's *epinoiai*.[2] Thus Origen's Trinity is pluralistically and hierarchically conceived, and the distinctions of hypostases pass over into distinctions of functions, for the operation of the Father is towards the entire universe, that of the Son is more restricted, being directed only to the rational creation, and that of the Holy Spirit still more limited, being confined to those who are holy.[3] Yet it marks a great change from earlier Christian thinking, for Origen's Trinity is, generally speaking, conceived of as the eternal mode of God's being, and in no way as determined or evoked by the needs of the 'economy'.

Origen's Christology similarly displays his profundity as a Christian thinker and at the same time the difficulty of reinterpreting the Christian tradition so as to harmonize with his philosophical presuppositions. His theory of the world of created *logikoi* enabled him to advance a highly original explanation of the union of deity and manhood in Christ. The Christological problem is to try to understand how the power of the divine majesty, the Word and Wisdom by which all things were created, can have existed within the limitations of the man who appeared in Judaea, how the Wisdom of God entered the womb and was born and cried like an infant, and suffered a shameful death. In some aspects he is manifested as a divine being, in others as human.[4] The answer given by Origen is that whereas all rational creatures had the opportunity of participation in the Logos, every soul fell away through the wrong exercise of its free will except that soul which adhered to him inseparably and was made to be 'one spirit' with him. This soul, totally receptive of the Logos, is the medium through which the divine nature was able to unite itself with material flesh and as such to be born as God-man; this soul united with the Logos, together with the flesh which it assumed, is rightly termed Son of God, power of God, Christ and

---

[1] *princ.* 1.3.1–5.
[2] *Jn.* 2.10.
[3] *princ.* 1.3.5.
[4] *ib.* 2.6.2.

wisdom of God; and the Son of God is correspondingly termed Jesus Christ and Son of man. Here is an interesting anticipation of the idea of the interchange of divine and human properties (*communicatio idiomatum*, see p. 123).[1] The union of the soul of Christ with the divine Logos is described as a union of adoration and participation, but it results in as close and indissoluble a fusing together of the divine and the human as that which takes place between iron and fire when the metal becomes red-hot – a simile which was to recur many times in later Christology.[2] In this remarkable way Origen is able to posit a bridge between the divine and the human and to make the union of God and man something real, at a far deeper level than that of a divine being clothing himself with flesh.

On the other hand, he runs into difficulty when he tries to claim uniqueness for this union. When St. Paul said that 'he who is joined to the Lord is one spirit', he was referring to all believers. The soul, with the flesh, which has come to be at one with the Logos has done so 'in a higher and more divine way';[3] but what this means is not clearly stated except that this soul was sinless. Origen also finds it necessary to point out that the union does not mean that the divine Logos is circumscribed by humanity: the Logos does not cease to exist outside the soul and body of Jesus; his descent from heaven is not a movement in space and does not involve his heavenly throne being left empty.[4]

Christ is God and man: human and divine nature begin to come together in him so that by communion with deity human nature may be deified (in believers who live the life which he taught, as well as in Jesus himself).[5] The Logos remains unmoved in his deity; he remains Logos in essence, and suffers nothing of the experience of the body or the soul. But 'sometimes he comes down to the level of him who is unable to look upon the radiance and brilliance of the deity and becomes as it were flesh . . . until he who has accepted him in this form is gradually lifted up by the Logos and can look even upon, so to speak, his absolute form'.[6] Thus the human emotions reflected in such texts as 'now is my soul troubled' are not to be ascribed to the Logos but to the human soul.[7] The two natures with their respective properties are always clearly distinguished, sometimes as 'man' and 'God'.[8] Yet scripture does not present Christ as two but as one;[9] he was a 'composite being';[10] his human soul and body were raised to the divine level not only by communion but by union and intermixture, so that even the mortal quality of his body was changed into an ethereal and divine quality.[11] For the Logos is the directing principle of the incarnate life, and the 'divine' sayings ascribed to Jesus, such as 'I am the living bread', are the very

[1] *ib.* 2.6.3–4.
[2] *ib.* 2.6.6.
[3] *Cels.* 2.9; *princ.* 4.4.4.
[4] *Cels.* 2.9; 4.5; 4.12.
[5] *ib.* 3.28.
[6] *ib.* 4.15.
[7] *princ.* 4.4.4.
[8] *Jn.* 10.6; 1.28.
[9] *ib.* 1.28.
[10] *Cels.* 1.66.
[11] *ib.* 3.41.

words of the Logos.[1] Origen somehow conceives of the Logos as it were
discarding and apportioning the elements of his human nature at his death:
his body to the grave, his soul to Hades, his spirit resigned to the Father
from whom he reclaims it in the ascension of which he spoke to Mary in the
garden;[2] and he thinks that at the Resurrection Jesus was in an intermediate state between the corporeality of the earthly body and the condition of a disembodied soul.[3] These and similar ideas clearly indicate that
although his theory of the human soul of Christ gave him an opportunity to
avoid many of the difficulties inherent in Christologies which worked only
with the concepts of Logos on the one hand and flesh on the other, he still
failed to take the humanity with complete seriousness. This was because
his Platonism caused him to take the Incarnation itself insufficiently
seriously; it tended to seem to him in the last resort rather like a concession
made by the Logos to those weaker human beings who could not bear to
receive his direct revelation of himself unveiled. This idea seems to underlie
his simile of the statue so huge as to fill the whole world, which therefore
cannot serve its purpose of making known its subject since no one can see
it properly; only when a miniature copy has been made, adjusted to the
capacity of human observers, can the grandeur of God be conveyed to
them.[4] So in the Incarnation Origen tends to see the divine Logos cut down
to human size rather than exalted in the glory of self-giving love.

This tendency is reflected to some extent in his treatment of the redemptive work of Christ, which is primarily seen as the revelatory activity of the
Logos illuminating men's minds, bringing them out of darkness into light,
and enabling them through participation in himself to share in his transformed humanity and be exalted in him to fellowship with God. The human
life and death are thus thought of primarily as channels of illumination. At
the same time there are many passages in Origen where the traditional
images of sacrifice, ransom, expiation and the defeat of the devil are
introduced and explained. For instance, after carefully explaining that it
was a man who died for the people (Jn. 11:50) and that the Truth, Wisdom,
Peace and Righteousness is not a man, that the Logos did not die, since
God's image is not subject to death, and that it was Jesus as man who died,
Origen goes on to say that this man, the purest of living beings, was able to
bear the sin of the world, taking it upon himself and destroying and annul-
ling it, since he knew no sin and thus could become an expiation, a sacrifice
offered to avert demonic wrath, for the whole world.[5] Similarly, Origen
tells Celsus that Christ's death is like that of those righteous men who are
believed by the pagans to have died voluntarily for the community to avert
by expiation the activities of evil demons who would otherwise have
brought plague or famine. Jesus died to destroy the ruler of demons who
held all men's souls in bondage.[6] His death has not only offered an example
of how to die for the sake of religion but begun the overthrow of the devil's

[1] *ib.* 2.9.
[2] *dial.* 6ff.
[3] *Cels.* 2.62.
[4] *princ.* 1.2.8.
[5] *Jn.* 28.18.
[6] *Cels.* 1.31.

dominion; the proof is the number of people who have been freed from the devil and enabled to devote themselves to God and to progress in spiritual life.[1] Origen does in fact lay as much emphasis on Christ's death and resurrection as on the defeat of the devil,[2] only adding to the ideas of his predecessors the notion that Christ offered his life to the devil as a ransom in exchange for man, and that the devil, having exceeded his rights in seeking to hold the one who was sinless, was deprived of his prey by the resurrection.[3] This theory of a kind of treaty or commercial bargain, however, plays but a very small part in Origen's thought.

The situation which the work of Christ remedied is seen very differently by Origen from the way in which it had previously been understood. His belief in the pre-existence of rational souls means that the fall of man is transferred from the 'historical' setting of Eden to a supra-mundane sphere. The Adam story is much used by him, but he treats it, in the last resort, as a parable or a Platonic myth. God created rational creatures as pure spirit; they were therefore equal and alike, there being no cause for diversity among them. They were endowed with free will and had the opportunity either of making progress in communion with God or of falling away. Origen is most insistent on the freedom of the human will. Any kind of predestinarian language, including much in the scriptures that he finds himself obliged to explain away, seems to him to encourage pagan fatalism and Gnostic determinism. Thus the fact that all souls, except that which the Logos was to unite with himself, fell away was due solely to their misuse of their freedom. Through this alienation from God the soul, which was by origin pure spirit, has become 'refrigerated' into *psyche* (which Origen fancifully derives from the root of *psychros*, 'cold'). Those supra-human intelligences that fell became demons; the human souls entered the material world as a place of punishment, or, rather, of corrective training,[4] for Origen holds that life in this visible world is really all part of purgatory, continuous with that process of purification and education which awaits the soul after death, and it is as a training-ground that the soul, embodied as a human being, must use its mortal life. The clothing of souls with flesh for this purpose is mythically portrayed in the 'coats of skin' which God made for Adam and Eve. Origen compares this myth with that of the soul's loss of its wings in Plato's *Phaedrus*; they denote both the corporeal character of man's life on earth and also the diversity which this entails.[5]

In one sense the believer has already been saved through Christ's offering of himself as a propitiatory sacrifice to avert God's wrath and his rescue of mankind from the devil who had gained the mastery over him through sin.[6] But this is only the beginning of the process of salvation. Indeed, to know Christ as redeemer is only a rudimentary form of faith, suitable for the simpler Christian.[7] God's will for the soul is its transformation into the

---

[1] *ib.* 7.17.
[2] e.g., *comm. in Mt.* 12.40; *Jn.* 6.55ff.
[3] *comm. in Mt.* 16.8.
[4] *princ.* 2.9.1–6; 1.8.1.
[5] *Cels.* 4.40; *princ.* 2.1.4.
[6] *Rom.* 3.8; *hom. 24.1 in Num.*; *comm. in Mt.* 16.8; *Rom.* 2.13.
[7] *Jn.* 2.3.

divine image through knowledge of himself, that is, its deification. Deification is attained through following the Logos as teacher,[1] and the advanced Christian participates in the Logos not merely through having been created as a rational being (*logikos*), but by becoming fit, through purification and through rising above all material things, to receive the divine gift of perfect knowledge of God.[2] This is no less than a sharing in that contemplation of the Father through which the Logos himself derives his eternal deity.[3] The Logos is thus the archetype of all the 'gods' of Psalm 82:6, who are souls deified by the vision of God and formed into the likeness of their archetype. Thus purification, according to Origen's ascetic teaching which greatly influenced the monastic movement, passes over into contemplation or knowledge which is unitive; so by union with God the 'cold' soul is 're-heated'. The end of salvation is contemplation of the Father which requires no intermediary. Not only is the incarnate Christ left behind, as it were, in the progress towards deification, but in the end the Logos himself; for, as Paul stated, the Logos will hand over his kingdom to the Father and God will be all in all.[4]

This end will be achieved through a continuing process of purgation and illumination after death. The fire that awaits sinners destroys evil, but it is also purificatory and, like all God's chastisements, ultimately remedial.[5] Men will be assigned their due place in this process by divine judgement. In scripture the judgement is pictured as a vast assize, but Origen recognizes that this must be understood symbolically. It means that through the full illumination of all men everywhere by the manifestation (not a spatial 'second coming') of the Logos they will know themselves as they really are, acknowledge his authority, and, in a sense, judge themselves.[6] Between death and the judgement there is an intermediate state, a training course, varying in duration with the needs of the individual soul. It is conceived of in a strikingly academic fashion as 'a place of erudition and, as one might say, a lecture-hall and school of souls'.[7]

The end of God's purpose for his creation must resemble the beginning. Diversity must return into unity. The distinction between good and evil will disappear, for all will be uniformly good, and it will be as though the tree of the knowledge of good and evil had not been discovered. In Origen's view, it must be remembered, evil is purely negative; there are degrees of being and that which fully and perfectly is (*to on*) is the good (*to agathon*).[8] God will be all in all, and this means that the rational mind, purified from wickedness and cleansed from faults, will feel, think, and hold to nothing but God: God will be the mode and measure of its every thought and act.[9] This is what is meant by the Pauline idea of the subjection of every enemy

[1] *Cels.* 3.28.
[2] *ib.* 6.13.
[3] *Jn.* 2.2.
[4] *ib.* 20.7.
[5] *princ.* 2.10.4; *Cels.* 5.15; *hom. 1.2 in Ezech.*
[6] *comm. ser. in Mt.* 70.
[7] *princ.* 2.11.6.
[8] *Jn.* 2.7.
[9] *princ.* 1.6.1–4; 3.6.1–3.

to Christ and the handing over of the kingdom to God. The clear implication, though it is nowhere stated explicitly, is that the demonic enemies and the devil will be won over by persuasion and illumination to the knowledge, and therefore to the likeness, of God; for God's reign is established by persuasion and not coercion, and in the end there will be no creature left to defy his will.

For Origen salvation is thus a complex process of *re*-deification, a return to the beginning. For this reason the ultimate goal involves no abolition of the original distinction between uncreated God and created spirits. It may be partly in order to emphasise this distinction that Origen makes room in his eschatology for a resurrection of the body. Of course, he follows St. Paul in believing that the resurrection of the body (a term which, unlike Tertullian, he prefers to 'resurrection of the flesh') cannot mean that the soul will be involved with flesh and blood and their accompanying passions; it denotes the putting on of a spiritual body, a body fitted to minister to a soul so intimately united with God as to have become 'one spirit' with him: 'a better garment for the purer, ethereal and heavenly regions'.[1] In the sixth century Origen was anathematized for propounding the belief that the resurrection body would be spherical.[2] This is not stated in his extant works, though like Plato (Tim. 33B) and others he thought celestial beings possessed this perfect shape. There was enough, in any case, in his original eschatology to excite the fury of traditionalists.

The hope of a literal resurrection of the flesh had very naturally been upheld by Tertullian, since he believed that the soul, as well as the body, is a material object. It was polemically defended against Origenism by the violently anti-Origenist bishop of Olympus, Methodius.[3] It seems, however, to be an anomaly when salvation is interpreted as deification, for it was agreed on all sides that God is not corporeal. There seem to have been three main reasons why, despite Origen's teaching, belief in physical resurrection was tenaciously retained. It was part of the tradition, though St. Paul's 'spiritual body' represents a very different concept from Tertullian's *resurrectio carnis*. It was a safeguard against any tendency to suppose that salvation means the loss of personal and individual identity through a Neoplatonist absorption into the One; though this was in fact adequately secured by the acknowledged distinction between creator and creature and by the recognition that although the soul belongs to the spiritual world (*kosmos noetos*) it is, nevertheless, not a part of God but one of his creatures. It was also, and more importantly, a defence against Gnostic and Manichaean depreciation of the physical world and its creator. Unless the body was to share in the soul's salvation the way seemed open to treat it, and the material world to which it belongs, as lying outside the scope of divine creation and providence. The argument seems to turn in the end on the assumption that value is proportionate to duration. This is not self-evident, and if life in the body is, as most Christians and not Origen alone believed, a course of training for the soul's life in the spiritual dimension, it might

---

[1] *ib.* 2.10.3; 3.6.6; *Cels.* 7.32.
[2] Justinian *adv. Or.* (Migne *P.G.* 86.973) *anath.* 5; cf. Or. *or.* 31.
[3] See below, p. 91 .

seem unnecessary that the body should accompany the soul there just as it would be unnecessary for a butterfly to take to the air with caterpillar's feet and hairs. Had the writers who argued about this subject believed that the union of soul and body is totally indissoluble, or that body was actually to be converted into soul, the position would have been different; but although some held that in this life body and soul are only theoretically separable (others thought that the soul enjoys an independent life of its own in dreams), and although some inclined towards an Aristotelian rather than a Platonist view of the soul, they agreed in fact that body and soul were two entities and that they were separated by death.

VI

EASTERN THEOLOGY FROM ORIGEN
TO THE COUNCIL OF NICAEA

As the first fully worked out and coherent system of Christian doctrine, and as a strikingly original attempt to grapple with some of the major problems presented by the task of expressing Christian faith intelligibly in a world of thought conditioned by Greek philosophy, Origen's work had a profound effect. Some of his more startling innovations provoked vigorous opposition and were generally rejected, but his Trinitarian theology with its pluralistically and hierarchically conceived system of relationships between the divine hypostases provided the framework for the development of theology in the Greek-speaking Church and ensured that in the East, at any rate, monarchianism and any attempt to deny the hypostatic otherness of the Logos from the Father would be seen as the main heretical enemy by conservative- and orthodox-minded Christians. The chief fear would be of Sabellianism (see p. 54).

Dionysius, bishop of Alexandria, one of the ablest of the followers of Origen in his Trinitarian theology (though in his extant writings he does not acknowledge his debt to him), encountered this Sabellian bogey among the bishops of Pentapolis in Libya and wrote a letter to them protesting against the Sabellian identification of the incarnate deity with the Father. A complaint was then made against him by certain of its recipients to Dionysius, bishop of Rome, who, according to Athanasius, wrote a letter in condemnation both of Sabellianism and also of the alleged opinions of his Alexandrian namesake who was supposed to have anticipated Arius in declaring the Son to be alien in essence to the Father and to be included among his creatures. In reply Dionysius set out his defence at length, and, since the alleged Arianism of his predecessor was highly embarrassing to Athanasius, the latter devoted a book to an examination of this controversy, putting the opinions of Dionysius in the best possible light and defending his statements.

Dionysius was alleged to have held the view that God was not always Father; there was not always a Son. God was without the Logos and the Son was not before he was begotten: there was 'when he was not'; 'for he is not eternal, but came into being later'.[1] Thus according to Athanasius the accusers of Dionysius believed him to have taught the same doctrine as Arius. They also said that he failed to speak of the Father when naming the Son and vice-versa, and divided, separated, and postulated a distance between the Father and the Son.[2] They further charged him with including

---

[1] Ath. *sent. Dion.* 14.
[2] *ib.* 16.

the Son among the things which have come into being, that is, of making him a creature, and denying that he is of the same essence or substance (*homoousios*) with the Father; and they supported this last allegation with illustrations which he was said to have used: the Son is alien to the Father in respect of essence (*ousia*) just as the vinegrower is to the vine and the boat-builder to the boat.[1] The letter which this evoked from Dionysius of Rome contained a head-on attack upon those who divide, cut up and destroy the monarchy of God proclaimed by the Church into three powers and separated hypostases and three deities. This is as bad as its opposite error, Sabellianism, for these people preach a kind of tritheism, dividing the divine monad into three separated and alien hypostases. The Trinity is proclaimed in the scriptures, but not three gods.

Scripture likewise attests the generation of the Son, but not his creation or formation; for this would imply that he was not eternal, whereas if he is Logos and wisdom and power he must be eternal, for God could never be without these essential attributes. Those who hold such an opinion mistake the meaning of Prov. 8:22, which may have led them astray: 'created' does not mean the same thing as 'made' (as Deut. 32:6 (LXX) shows), and the scriptures never speak of the Son having come into being although they say much about his generation. Therefore, the 'wonderful and divine monad is not to be divided into three hypostases, nor is the excellence of the Lord to be diminished by the use of the term "making" (instead of "begetting")'. The Roman bishop ends by citing 'I and the Father are one' and 'I am in the Father and the Father in me' and declares that both the divine Trinity and the holy proclamation of 'monarchy' are to be preserved.[2]

If the Alexandrian's self-defence against this attack is to be credited, and it is hard to believe that he had ever adopted a theology which anticipated Arius rather than reflected Origen, Dionysius of Rome had been misinformed. At the same time his reaction to what he had been told is important, for it illustrates the different climate of thought in which Eastern theology was developing after Origen from that which still prevailed in the Latin West. In the days of Praxeas, Noetus and other 'monarchians', the West, and Rome in particular (where bishops like Callistus and his predecessor Zephyrinus seem to have reacted sharply against the pluralistic Logos theology of Hippolytus) had as it were been inoculated with a large dose of theological monism – plain and scriptural rather than subtly philosophical. It made Western theologians, on the whole, highly resistant to the Arian epidemic; it also made them very deaf for a considerable period to what the pluralist theology of the Origenist tradition was saying. Hence the indignation of Dionysius against the idea of a division of the monad into three hypostases, separated and alien from one another, indistinguishable from three gods, and against the notion of the Son as a creature. This reaction would not have been greatly different even if there had been no confusion over terminology, as there probably was: '*hypostasis*', which to the Alexandrian corresponded to Tertullian's *persona* and meant an individually distinct entity, might easily be assumed by the Roman to denote *substantia*,

[1] *ib.* 18; 4.
[2] Ath. *decr.* 26.

of which it was etymologically the equivalent, and to mean the essential reality of deity: to speak of three 'substances' would be to speak of three deities. Conversely, the Roman bishop's extreme stress on the absolute unity of the deity evidently looked dangerously Sabellian to those who stood in the Alexandrian tradition.

The treatise which Dionysius of Alexandria issued in defence of his views complained that he had been misrepresented, and that he had been understood as attributing to the Logos what in fact ought to be taken as referring to Christ's humanity.[1] He admitted that certain of his similes had been unfortunate, such as those of the vinegrower and the vine and the boat and the builder. Yet he had no intention of denying that Christ is *homoousios* with the Father, although he had to point out that the term itself is unscriptural; he accepts it, and adduces another of his similes to show that he has affirmed what the term denotes. This is the analogy of parents and children. They are homogeneous; the only respect in which they are 'other' is that the parents are not the children, and this otherness is a necessary condition for there being either parents or children. Other similar illustrations had been of homogeneous objects: seed or root and plant, river and spring, and so on. He also spoke of the Son as light kindled from light.[2] These analogies, says Athanasius, plainly indicate that he never shared the beliefs of Arius. He believed that 'Father' eternally implies 'Son', that the Son is derived from the Father's substance and not created out of nothing, that eternal light could never have been without its radiance, and so on.[3] The Father, the Son and the Spirit are indivisible: 'we broaden out the monad into the Trinity indivisibly, and again we sum up the Trinity in the monad without diminution'.[4]

Another conflict between the dominant Origenist theology of the later third century and a form of monarchian belief is to be seen in the condemnation in 268 of the teaching of Paul of Samosata by a council of Origenist bishops at Antioch. The Christology of Paul followed the general lines of the 'adoptionist' teaching which had been current among various theologians since early in the century. Novatian ascribed the motive of this type of Christology to a concern for strict monotheism against the doctrine of two gods apparently implied by the orthodox belief that the Father and the Son are alike God, but distinct from one another;[5] and this motive was behind monarchianism as well as adoptionist Christology. Hence in modern times the latter has been given the name 'dynamic monarchianism'; but these two theologies are by no means the same. Adoptionism resembling that of Paul of Samosata was taught at Rome before the end of the second century by Theodotus of Byzantium, a tanner, and Theodotus of Rome, a banker, and subsequently by Artemon. It substituted for the identification of Christ with the actual divine entity of the Logos or Son incarnate the belief that Christ was a man uniquely inspired, and therefore divinized, by the

[1] *sent. Dion.* 14.
[2] *ib.* 18.
[3] *ib.* 18–22.
[4] *ib.* 17.
[5] *Trin.* 30.

Spirit. What was meant by the divinization of Jesus appears to have varied as between these theologians, some thinking that he had actually been elevated to deity, others that he remained a Spirit-possessed man, or one whom the Word uniquely indwelt.

In this kind of theology the Word lacks personal subsistence. The relation between Christ and God is conceived in terms of inspiration rather than incarnation, and in this context 'Logos' means the uttered word of God rather than an intermediary divine being or a second divine principle derived from and reflecting the first. 'Logos' thus tends to signify the 'Word of the Lord' which came to the prophets and, in a fuller measure and in a permanent relationship, came upon the man Jesus. Paul naturally emphasized the unique degree of Christ's participation in the Word: 'Wisdom does not dwell thus in any other. Wisdom was in the prophets . . . but was in Christ as in a temple.'[1] The simile of the temple or shrine indwelt by the divine Logos was to play an important part in later Christology; Paul, however, was understood to mean, and this was probably correct, that the Wisdom or Word dwelt in Christ as an impersonal divine influence, animating and motivating him, and not as a substantial and personal presence. It was united with him, not substantially but after the manner of a quality.[2] It is at this point that Paul's humanist Christology does make some contact with Sabellian, or 'modalist' monarchianism; for like the latter, but having arrived at this point by a different route, it dispensed with the hypostatic distinctions in the Godhead that were made by current Trinitarian orthodoxy. If 'Logos' denotes an impersonal communication from God, without individual subsistence, then God is one person and the Trinitarian distinctions refer only to abstractions except in so far as the traditional terms Son and Spirit may be used with reference to the man Jesus and to the grace of God in the Church (which is how Paul is said to have used them by Pseudo-Leontius of Byzantium in the sixth century).[3]

Paul's opponents, according to a fourth-century source, contended that the Logos is a substantial entity, an *ousia* and not merely a power or influence.[4] It may have been in response to this that Paul made use of the term *homoousios*. Conflicting accounts of his reasons for doing this are given by Athanasius and Basil on the one hand, and Hilary on the other.[5] According to the former account Paul used the term in an argument on these lines: 'if Christ was not a man who became deified, then, according to you, he must have been consubstantial with the Father. But this would imply three entities: Father, Son and the antecedent 'stuff' (deity) of which they are: just as in the case of two coins of the same substance there are three entities, the two coins and the metal from which they are struck. Thus your doctrine postulates a divine substance anterior to the persons of the Godhead, which would be absurd'. Hilary, on the other hand, says that Paul used the term in his own theology, to signify that Father and Son are

---

[1] de Riedmatten, *Les Actes du Procès de Paul de Samosate, fr.* 6.
[2] *ib.* 29.
[3] *de sectis* 3.3.
[4] Epiphanius *haer.* 73.12.
[5] Ath. *syn.* 45; Bas. *ep.* 52.1; Hil. *syn.* 81.

numerically identical; God is a solitary monad. This would mean that Paul, denying a personal subsistence to the Word, reduced it to a divine 'utterance', in no way constituting a distinct hypostasis, and thus in no way incompatible with an extreme monistic conception of God. The Word in this sense is certainly of the same essence with the Father. Not only by reason of antecedent probability, but because Hilary seems to have had reliable evidence whereas Athanasius and Basil were confused by fourth-century arguments relating to the post-Nicene situation, Hilary's account should probably be preferred.

The council of Antioch, led by Malchion, a philosopher, repudiated the *homoousion* in this sense. It is unlikely that they formally condemned the use of the term as such. Had they done so, their action would have greatly embarrassed the West which had very recently insisted on the theological importance of accepting it in the correspondence between the Dionysii. It would also have presented a serious obstacle to the adoption of the term in the creed of Nicaea, whereas in fact the question of what had happened at Antioch in 268 began to be canvassed by the opponents of the *homoousion* only in the middle of the fourth century (it is possible but not very likely that the events at Antioch had been forgotten in detail by 325 even though Paul was well remembered as a theological bogey). The council also rejected Paul's Christological assertion of the separateness of the Word from the man Jesus whom the Word inspired or indwelt. He had argued that 'the Logos was greater than Christ; for Christ became great through Wisdom. The Logos is from above; Jesus Christ is a man from here. Mary did not bear the Logos for Mary was not before the ages . . . but she bore a man like us, but greater in all respects since he was from Holy Spirit'.[1] Wisdom and its 'temple' are two different things.[2] The council insisted, against all this, that the substantial Logos was substantially united with the man, not by participation or discipleship but by the actual substance of the Logos being substantiated in a body.[3] They explained this union without recourse to Origen's ingenious doctrine of the soul of Christ. This was one of those speculative elements in Origen's system which generally failed to win approval, and from the time of Paul of Samosata onwards to postulate a human soul in Christ tended to suggest to many people that a dichotomy was being made between the divine Logos and the man Jesus, that a substantial union of deity and manhood centred in the divine person of the Logos was being denied, and that therefore what was generally believed to be the essential category of incarnation was being interpreted so as to bring it dangerously near to the category of inspiration. The Council of Antioch in fact asserted that the union is between the Logos and human flesh. The Logos assumes flesh; and just as every man is a composite being, of flesh and soul, so Wisdom was in Christ's human body like the soul in ours.[4] God the Logos is in him what the 'inner man' is in us.[5]

---

[1] de Riedmatten, *fr.* 26.
[2] *ib.* 14.
[3] *ib.* 36; 33.
[4] *ib.* 36.
[5] *ib.* 30.

This reinterpretation of Origen had most important consequences. The problem of the unity of the person of Christ – how one who was God and man could properly be said to be one person: how two distinct natures each operating in its own sphere could unite in a single person – was solved quite neatly, but at the cost of reducing Christ's humanity to bodily nature alone: almost of reducing it from human nature to animal nature. Eusebius, Arius, Athanasius, representatives of very different sides in the Arian conflict, all held this Christology, and its inherently unsatisfactory character was not widely recognized until Apollinarius made the idea, that in Christ the Logos takes the place of the human rational soul in all other men, the centre of his theological system and provoked a reaction which caused it to be, at least in theory, abandoned. Origen's disciple Pamphilus of Caesarea and later Eustathius of Antioch are among the most notable of the few who perceived the Christological and soteriological difficulties inherent in the apparently straightforward theory of a union between the Logos and human flesh; and it is significant that in his defence of Origen Pamphilus felt bound to admit that many were offended because Origen had maintained that Christ had assumed a human soul, and to point out in his defence that at least the idea was scriptural (e.g. Mt. 26:38, Jn. 10:18, 12:27).[1]

Methodius, bishop of Olympus, a leading opponent of Origen's theology at the turn of the century, exemplifies the typical Christology of this period. There are, it is true, some peculiar elements in his thought. He carries the typology of Adam-Christ so far as to deny that it is typology at all: Christ actually is Adam, and it was proper that the first-born and first-begotten of God, the divine Wisdom, should become man by being mingled with the first-created and first-born of men.[2] Hence Methodius develops the Irenaean parallel between the mode of Christ's birth and that of Adam's creation.[3] He is following a more general tradition when he speaks of Christ as a man filled with unmixed and perfect deity, God contained in man,[4] and of his humanity as 'the man whom he assumed, enthroned at the right hand of the Almighty'.[5] The Logos made a body which he united with deity[6] so that it could become the instrument of the devil's defeat through Christ's death. The 'heavenly man' wore the form of flesh that was the same as ours, and, though he was not man, he became man in order that by his death and resurrection all might be made alive in him and attain to the resurrection of that same flesh.[7] The Lord raised to heaven the flesh that he wore as a glorious garment.[8] Such passages are typical of the 'Word-flesh' Christology which had become widespread. It is not out of harmony with this idea of the person of Christ that his saving work should be understood primarily in terms of a victory over the devil, won less, perhaps, by Christ's human

[1] *apol. Or.* 24.
[2] *symp.* 3.4.
[3] *ib.*
[4] *ib.*
[5] *ib.* 7.9.
[6] *Porph.* 1.
[7] *res.* 2.18.
[8] *symp.* 7.8.

obedience than by the inability of the devil to subject the immortal being of the Logos to death, the fruit of victory being the exaltation of human flesh to the divine level and the consequent transformation in Christ of the mortal into incorruptibility and the passible into impassibility.[1] In its turn, this conception of redemption (from mortality rather than sin) is associated with two other features of Methodius' thought: a very strong emphasis on the virtue of asceticism, and in particular of virginity, for the attainment of incorruptibility, and an extreme antipathy to Origen's ideas about the spiritual body and the life to come. For Methodius these ideas are tantamount to a denial of resurrection. He insists on the literal and physical character of the resurrection of believers, which must be similar to that of Christ, and on the fact that it is this present flesh which is to be raised to immortality.[2] This eschatology which is linked with a literalistic interpretation of the new Jerusalem,[3] is supported by a prosaic exegesis of scriptural texts, such as his discussion of the significance for the resurrection body of Mt. 8:12; the risen body must possess teeth if it is to be able to gnash them.[4]

Eusebius of Caesarea, who was believed in 325 to be sympathetic enough to Arius to warrant his being placed under a kind of suspended sentence of excommunication by a council held at Antioch which rejected Arianism, and who had to clear himself of this charge later in that year at Nicaea, was in fact a representative of the Origenist tradition who pushed certain aspects of Origen's system to extreme lengths. He was certainly not an Arian, but the pluralism and subordinationism of his Trinitarian theology made him highly uneasy with what he regarded as the dangerously monistic tendency of the beliefs of Arius' opponents. He begins his *History of the Church* with a revealing summary of what he holds to be the essential faith by which the Church lives. In Christ there are two modes of being: one is like the head of a body, since he is conceived of as God, the other like its feet, since he assumed human nature with passions like ours. As Logos he was the first and only begotten of God, before all creatures, the minister of the Father's will, the second cause, after the Father, of the universe, who has received from the Father deity and power and honour. The Father rules universally by his sovereign will; the Logos, holding the second place, carries out the Father's commands. He appeared to men in the biblical theophanies, for 'reason does not permit that the uncreated and immutable essence of God should be changed into the form of a man'. What, then, should the Lord be called (since he may not be termed the first cause of the universe) but the pre-existent Logos? He is the power and wisdom of the Father, entrusted with the second place in the kingdom: an essence living and subsisting before the world, which ministered to the Father in the making of all created things.[5]

God alone is ingenerate and without beginning. He transcends the beginning of all things, is superior to any designation whatsoever, and is ineffable,

---

[1] *Porph.* passim; *res.* 3.23.
[2] *res.* 3.3–6; 3.12–14; 3.16.
[3] *symp.* 9.1ff.
[4] *res.* 1.24.
[5] *h.e.* 1.2.

inconceivable, the first principle of all things, the one sole God from whom and for the sake of whom all things are. He created by reason of his own goodness, for his will could not but be good; and he created, not out of nothing (for Eusebius holds that non-being could not be the origin of anything, and non-being could not be the cause of anything's subsistence) but by putting forth as a kind of material and substance for the creating of the universe his own will and power.[1] The Father, the indivisible monad, is the one first principle. The Son, begotten from him, is not without beginning nor ingenerate; otherwise there would be two principles and two gods. He was begotten of the Father and has the Father as his origin and principle.[2] His first-born Wisdom is absolute Mind and Logos and Wisdom (*autonous, autologos, autosophia*), the good offspring of the good Father, the steersman at the helm of the creation of the universe. He is begotten deity, the unique image of the ineffable God, who is in and through everything as a living law and principle.[3] He must be unique, for there can be no more than the one effulgence of any one light; and to be the exact image he must not only reflect the Father's substance but his numerical unity, that is, he must be perfectly one without multiplicity. Not that Eusebius likes the traditional analogy of the effulgence or ray and the light, for the light emits its radiance of necessity; there is nothing purposive about this, whereas the Father begets the Logos by an act of will[4]. Thus the Father is prior to the Son, as ingenerate to generate; and although Eusebius does not want to adopt Arianism he finds it impossible to think that the Son can be of the substance of the Father. The reason is that this would imply some kind of 'passion' (that is, alteration) and division in the substance of deity. For him the alternative possibility, that the Son is equally of the divine essence by virtue of co-existing with the Father from eternity, is ruled out since it would imply that there are two ingenerate first principles.[5] Hence Eusebius has to explain 'I and the Father are one' by taking it to mean 'one in glory', for the Son participates in the Father's glory which the Father imparts to him and which he in turn passes on to his disciples, following the pattern of the Father's benevolence. Eusebius cannot allow that the Logos and the Father are one single hypostasis.[6] Here, then, is an extreme presentation of the concept of a broadening down of deity so as to subsist at different levels in hierarchical order. The fact that Origen's theory of eternal generation has been discarded, which would probably have seemed to Eusebius to be the natural concomitant of dropping the theory of the eternity of a created world, makes this theology look superficially very like Arianism; but that was by no means its intention.

In Christology, Eusebius is a representative of the theory of the union of the Logos with flesh. This becomes especially clear in his discussion of the death of Christ and his resignation of the Spirit to the Father and the body

[1] *d.e.* 4.1.
[2] *e.th.* 2.6.
[3] *d.e.* 4.2.
[4] *ib.* 4.3.
[5] *ib.* 5.1.20.
[6] *e.th.* 3.19.

to the tomb.[1] The demonic enemies of Christ are pictured, in a remarkable exegesis of Ps. 22, as circling round the Cross like vultures or beasts of prey ready to seize their spoil, thinking that nothing was 'tabernacling' in the body of Jesus other than a human soul like other men's.[2] It would be unfair to say that in his ideas about the Logos and the work of Christ he is so much concerned with cosmology as to have little interest left (unlike Athanasius) for soteriology. He has in fact much to say about the saving work of Christ, listing a number of reasons for his death, revelatory, sacrificial, relating to the defeat of the devil and so on, and he has a fine exposition of Psalm 41 in which he discusses how Christ makes our sins his own in order to heal them.[3]

A different approach, though one which was also derived from Origen, is seen in the letters of Alexander, bishop of Alexandria, one to his namesake bishop of Thessalonica and another an encyclical, sent after Arius had attacked his teaching. Alexander asserted the existence of the Logos as a distinct hypostasis, co-eternal with the Father since the Father could not ever not have been Father; hence his generation is without beginning. The 'nature' or 'hypostasis' of the Logos is intermediary, standing between God and the created order, and the Logos and the Father are two entities. These cannot be separated from one another, but 'I and the Father are one' is not to be taken in the sense of a single hypostasis.[4] Alexander's system is Origenistic in its emphasis on the Logos as an independent hypostasis and on the mediating status and function of the Logos. It also appears to reproduce Origen's theology in its assertion that the generation of the Logos is an eternal relationship, but this has been detached from Origen's complementary theory of an eternal relationship between Father, Logos and created universe, so that 'eternal generation' as understood by Alexander and Athanasius is very different from the same phrase as used by Origen.

Alexander's statements of his belief had been evoked by the protest of Arius at what he conceived to be the erroneous teaching propounded by the official leadership of his church (he was one of Alexander's presbyters at Alexandria). The theology of Arius might appear superficially to reflect the Origenist tradition as exemplified by Eusebius of Caesarea, and in fact to be based upon a repetition in a more extreme form of the pluralistic and subordinationist Trinitarian doctrine characteristic of Dionysius of Alexandria in his less guarded utterances. This, however, would be misleading. His ideas follow from certain important presuppositions which were different from those of Origen and his followers, and Arius himself was to a considerable extent an original thinker. It is, in fact, notoriously difficult to try to trace a pedigree for the characteristic tenets of Arianism. In his own letter to Eusebius of Nicomedia, his most important ally among contemporary bishops,[5] Arius claimed to be Eusebius' 'co-Lucianist', which appears to mean that both were disciples of Lucian of Antioch, a renowned scholar

[1] *d.e.* 3.4; 4.12.
[2] *ib.* 10.8.74.
[3] *ib.* 10.1; cf. 4.12 and the exposition of Ps. 22 at 10.8.
[4] *ep. Alex.* 26; *ep. encycl.* 13; *ep. Alex.* 52, 45, 15, 38.
[5] Epiphanius *haer.* 69.6.

and a martyr in the last persecution in 312. Alexander traces the error of Arius back through Lucian to Paul of Samosata and thence to Artemon and the Ebionites;[1] but this would link Arius with the so-called dynamic-monarchian tradition or unitarianism, and although Arius is often mis-understood as having simply denied the deity of Christ he was far from asserting, in the ordinary modern fashion, that Jesus was a mere man (and therefore not God). On the contrary, Arius maintained that Jesus was God, and not fully man; but that he was *created* God. There is no reason to doubt that Arius and Eusebius were connected with Lucian; but whether Lucian stood in any sort of succession to Paul of Samosata is much more doubtful. It may be that Alexander was simply picking on the damaging fact that the theology of Arius placed the gulf which divides God from his creatures between the Father and the Son, whereas what was now traditional ortho-doxy placed it between the Holy Spirit and the highest of created beings, and that, in order to find a convenient stick of propaganda with which to beat Arius, Alexander was suggesting that this was where Paul's theology had also placed that crucial gulf: in this case between the monadic God (including his immanent and anhypostatic Word) and his creatures (of whom the man Jesus was one). If so, the connection of Arius with that unitarian tradition consists simply in the fact that in one particular respect they could be said to arrive at similar results by opposite routes.

Arius rejected the Origenistic theory of one and the same divine essence broadening down, as it were, so as to subsist at different, hierarchically graded levels. Consequently he repudiated the idea that the Logos occupies an intermediate position, in the sense that the Logos is a second divine principle perfectly reflecting the transcendent Father and transmitting to the world of creatures the image by which alone the Father can be known and described. In their dislike of a second divine principle intermediate in status and subordinate in function the Arians and the theology of Athana-sius and Nicene orthodoxy have more in common than they have with Origen. In their opposite ways both parties are concerned to express in the sharpest possible terms the fundamental distinction between the absolute God and all that is not absolute God. Nicaea took the Logos out of any conceivable intermediate position by bringing the belief that he is of the same essence as the ingenerate Father into the Creed and giving it central theological importance: what the Father is, that the Son is, and no less. The Logos is set firmly on the side of absolute deity. Arius, on the other hand, also setting out to affirm the same total dichotomy between the ultimate source of all things and everything which is derived from it, did so in the opposite way by assigning the Logos to the creatures' side of the gulf which separates them from absolute deity. Like all else that is not the one ultimate source, the Logos is created out of nothing; for in Arius' system there is no descending scale of hierarchically graded divine being; all that is not the absolute monad belongs to the scale of creaturely being. Thus according to the Nicene theology there is no possibility of a divine principle which is 'second' in any but a numerical sense; in essence it must be one with the first principle. According to Arius, on the other hand, there cannot

[1] *ep. Alex.* 35.

be a second principle which is divine in any but a nominal or honorific sense.

The divine essence is simple and indivisible; it cannot be shared, for this would imply that the substance of deity suffers division. Hence the participation of the Son in the Father is not a participation in his essence but a participation in grace. The Son receives from the Father and transmits or reflects what he receives, but what he receives is not substance; rather he receives and reflects in somewhat the kind of way in which an icon might be said to participate in, imitate and transmit the virtue of its original. The Father communicates his attributes to the Son by an act of grace, and it is by virtue of this that it is possible to predicate divine attributes of the Son. At the root of much of this thinking there lies Arius' conviction that there can be no more than one unoriginated and self-existent principle. The quality of being *agennetos*, which strictly means 'unbegotten' but was used by Arius synonymously with *agenetos* (unoriginated), belongs to the Father alone. The Son must therefore belong to the created order, as the highest and most excellent of all creatures but different in essence from God.

Arius makes many of his points clear in his letter, appealing for support, to Eusebius of Nicomedia.[1] The Father and the Son do not co-exist from eternity as two unoriginate principles, and the Father is, contrary to the teaching of Alexander, both conceptually and temporally anterior to the Son. The Son is not unoriginate (for that would imply two gods), nor a part of the unoriginate deity; he came into existence by a deliberate act of the Father's will before time and ages, but not by an eternal act of generation: he was not before he was begotten, a term which for Arius is not to be differentiated from 'created'.[2] Arius complains that his party is being persecuted at Alexandria because they assert that the Son has a beginning whereas God is without beginning, and for their belief that, since he is not a part of God by a division of the divine substance, he is created, like all other creatures, out of nothing.

A careful statement of their beliefs was sent by Arius and his supporters to Alexander,[3] claiming that theirs was the traditional faith. It acknowledges one God, alone ingenerate, alone eternal, alone without beginning, alone true, immortal, wise, good, powerful, who is unchangeable and immutable, who begat the only-begotten Son before all time, through whom he made the ages and the universe, begetting not in appearance but in reality, and causing him to subsist by his own will as a perfect, unchangeable and immutable creature of God, 'but not as one of the creatures'; an offspring, 'but not as one of those things that are begotten': not a projection, as the Valentinians would teach, nor a consubstantial part of the Father as the Manichaeans would affirm, nor one who is both Son and Father as Sabellius asserted; nor was he who was prior (i.e. the Father) afterwards begotten or made subsequently to become Son; but he was created by God's will before times and ages, receiving his being from the Father. In giving him the inheritance of all things the Father did not deprive himself of what

[1] Epiph. *haer.* 69.6.
[2] cf. Ath. *Ar.* 1.5, 9.
[3] Ath. *syn.* 16.

he possesses ingenerately in himself, for he is the source of all things. Thus there are three hypostases. God as the cause of all things is solely without beginning. The Son, begotten timelessly and created and established before the ages, was not before he was begotten. For he is not eternal or co-eternal or co-unoriginate with the Father. Nor does he co-exist with the Father as a correlative term, as some affirm, thereby introducing two ingenerate principles. If the divine substance were divided, the Father would be divisible and mutable, and would, as the incorporeal God, suffer what pertains to a corporeal being.

The argument from correlative terms which Arius here rejects is the assertion that in the case of God 'Father' implies 'Son' and since he is eternally Father there must be an eternal Son: God's relations being necessary and permanent and not accidental and temporary. This was rejected by the Arians on the ground that, according to the same argument, since God is Creator there must eternally be creatures and it would be as impossible to say of them as of the Son, 'They were not before they were begotten (or created)'.[1] The Arians had a point here, and Athanasius in reply had to lay great stress on the difference between 'generation' and 'creation' (as in the Nicene clause: 'begotten not made') and on the difference between the Father-Son relationship and the external and contingent relationship of creator-creature. The Arians, however, with their insistence that the generation of the Son was by an act of will, were extremely averse to any idea which might suggest that the Son, or the universe, was necessary to God.

Arius' *Thalia*, a compendium of his theology, largely in verse, meant for popular consumption, dwells on the point that God was originally alone, and became Father only when the Logos had been created from nothing. The implication which Arius drew was that the Father had his own Wisdom by which the Son was made, and that the Son is Logos and Wisdom by grace only.[2] Nor is the Son authentically God; he only participates in deity by grace.[3] Hence the Son does not comprehend God in his infinity, but only in so far as divine grace has granted him a revelation.[4] The conclusion is that the Son is 'alien and dissimilar in all respects to the Father's substance and individual being'.[5]

A consequence of this theory is that the Son, unlike the Father, is mutable, though made morally perfect by grace given to him by the Father in accordance with his foreknowledge of the excellent way in which the Son would exercise his free will.[6] This theory enabled Arius to account for the episodes such as the Temptations which always presented grave difficulty for theologies which tried to combine a full doctrine of Christ's deity with a Christology that took little or no account of a human soul and will in Christ. For Arius held a Christology of this type, as is clear from Athanasius' arguments with the Arians over the passages in the Gospels implying

[1] Ath. *Ar.* 1.29.
[2] *ib.* 1.5.
[3] *ib.* 1.6.
[4] Ath. *ep. Aeg. et. Lib.* 12
[5] *Ar.* 1.6.
[6] *ib.* 1.5.

Christ's ignorance or weakness;[1] and this is borne out by Eustathius of Antioch's telling criticism of Arian Christology: that it attributes mutability to the deity ('spirit') of Christ and thereby supports their theory that this deity could not be begotten from a nature that is immutable.[2] At a later stage in the Arian controversy the creed of Eudoxius of Constantinople (360) makes the point clearly: '. . . incarnate, not made man; for he did not assume a human soul, but became flesh in order that through flesh as through a veil he might be made known to us as God; not two natures, since he was not a complete man but instead of a soul God in flesh; the whole one nature by composition'.[3]

The controversy which these opinions evoked was the main business which Constantine required the 'First Ecumenical Council' (though in fact it was almost entirely an Eastern Council) to settle. The formula of Nicaea was an uncompromising rejection of Arianism. Its anathemas condemned the Arian tenets: 'There was when he was not', 'He was not before he was begotten', 'He was created out of nothing', 'He is of a different hypostasis or substance' (these terms being here treated as synonyms), 'He is created, mutable and changeable'. The Creed itself asserts that the Son is of the substance of the Father, begotten not made, *homoousios* with the Father. Thus the Council effectively ruled out Arius' solution to the problem of the relation of the Son to the Father, and declared that the Son was God, as being in essence what the Father is. This was in line with Western theology, and the insertion of the *homoousion* into the creed, apparently on the insistence of the emperor himself, may have suggested to some Eastern theologians, such as Eustathius and Marcellus of Ancyra, the possibility that it could lend itself to a highly monistic interpretation; but it was accepted at the time by the large majority of conservative Origenists in the East as a means of defeating Arius, and at that time few wanted to be Arian. For this reason Eusebius of Caesarea subscribed to the formula of Nicaea, and in this he was typical of much Eastern opinion, even though he had doubts, which, as he informed his church in a letter after the council, he believed had been satisfactorily met, about the possible implications of the *homoousion*: doubts, that is, concerning the possibility of the term being misunderstood, as Arius had interpreted it, to mean that the divine substance had been divided and God subjected to mutation.[4] Yet, having for the time being ruled out Arianism, the Council had in fact only rung up the curtain on a long debate between those who had accepted the negative implications of Nicaea while remaining suspicious lest its positive teaching might lead to the Origenists' bogey of Sabellianism, and those who were prepared to accept this creed and make the interpretation of its assertions the basis of their Trinitarian thinking. Nicaea was thus not the end but the beginning of the fourth-century controversy.

[1] *ib.* 3.26.
[2] *fr.* 15.
[3] Hahn, *Bibliothek der Symbole*, p. 261.
[4] Eus. *ep. Caes.* 5ff. See below, p. 98f.

VII

THE DEVELOPMENT OF TRINITARIAN THEOLOGY
AFTER THE COUNCIL OF NICAEA

The purpose of the formula of Nicaea was mainly negative. The Council was concerned to refute the teaching of Arius and to make unequivocally clear its denial of the assertion that the Son is different in essence from the Father. The terms in which it expressed this denial were necessarily those in which the Arian party had framed its assertions. Eusebius, bishop of Nicomedia, the most important and influential of the supporters of Arius, had declared in a letter which was read at Nicaea that if uncreatedness is predicated of the Son this is tantamount to saying that he is *homoousios* with the Father – a proposition which Eusebius held to be self-evidently absurd. It was because the Arians had taken the initiative in throwing the *homoousion* into the ring that their opponents were forced to take up the challenge and insert it into the creed. The intention was not that the term should become a battle-cry for the orthodox, but that the inclusion of it should put teeth into the creed of Nicaea as an anti-Arian document, making it impossible for any who actually held Arius' doctrine to accept it. As Ambrose, who recounts the facts about Eusebius' letter puts it, the Council cut off the head of the Arians' heresy with the sword which the Arians themselves had been the first to draw.[1]

What precise positive meaning might be assigned to the term to which the Council gave such central importance was not defined. Apart from its negative significance as a denial of Arianism it was a dangerous word. It could be attacked, as Ambrose goes on to explain, as being unscriptural and as implying a Sabellian identity of Father and Son as a Godhead without personal distinctions.[2] Athanasius and other defenders of Nicaea had to show that though the word itself is not found in Scripture, its insertion into the creed was designed to safeguard the truths implicit in the biblical revelation; Ambrose also points out, less satisfactorily, that *ousia* itself can be considered a scriptural word since other compounds of it, though admittedly not *homoousios*, are to be found in the Bible. Ambrose, like Athanasius and others, replies to the charge of Sabellianism that the *homoousion* actually implies distinction: one thing can be said to be consubstantial only with another, not with itself.[3] Eusebius of Caesarea thought it necessary to write a letter to his diocese explaining why he had endorsed the creed which included so suspicious a term, and in it he shows that his

---

[1] Ambrose *fid.* 3.15.125.
[2] *ib.* 126–7.
[3] *ib.*

main fear was lest it should be given a materialistic interpretation and be understood to imply that the divine essence is not absolutely simple but capable of division. So he reassures his people that ' "consubstantial" signifies that the Son is of the Father', but not as being 'part of the Father's nature' or 'part of his substance'; it does not imply 'division of substance nor abscission nor any change or diminution in the power of the Father'.[1] Eusebius himself gave a minimizing interpretation to the Nicene creed's explanation of 'only-begotten', 'that is, from the substance of the Father'. He took it to mean only that the Son does not resemble in any respect the creatures which he has made, but that to the Father who begat him he is in all points perfectly similar.[2] More disingenuously, Eusebius defended the Council's condemnation of the assertion that 'before he was begotten he had no existence' on the ground that everyone agrees that he was Son of God before he was *born according to the flesh* (a proposition from which Arius himself would not have dissented), and his acceptance of the creed's implicit teaching of the eternity of the son on the ground that (as he claims Constantine explained it) the Son was potentially in the Father, without being begotten, before he was begotten in actuality.[3]

'In all points perfectly similar', 'like in all respects', are phrases which represent the way in which not only Eusebius but the majority of thinkers in the Origenistic East were either to interpret the Nicene *homoousion*, or else to replace it with other formulations, for a long time after 325. At the time all but a tiny Arian minority accepted the *homoousion* in order to rule out the Arian assertions, and they understood it to mean that the Son is not different in essence or nature from the Father but is of the same essence or nature (i.e. homogeneous) with him. It is likely that some of them would go further and recognize that when it is applied to the persons of the Godhead 'homogeneity' must involve actual identity of substance: monotheism requires no less. This was probably the case with Constantine's adviser Ossius, bishop of Cordova, and the few other representatives of the West at Nicaea; Latin theology had spoken of 'one substance' since Tertullian's time. It was certainly true of those Eastern leaders whose idea of God was monistic, as opposed to the pluralism of the Origenist tradition, and who therefore tended to think in terms of an impersonal Logos, divine Reason immanent in God from eternity and projected as divine Word for the purpose of the 'economy' (and thus identical in essence with the Father), rather than of a Son personally subsisting. These conclusions, however, as the letter of Eusebius to Caesarea plainly shows, were not drawn by the Council of Nicaea itself. It had asserted that the Son is God in the full sense: the word 'God' means the same when Christians say that the Son is God as it does when they say that the Father is God. There is no difference in essence, since the Son is 'true God of true God'. The Council had not proceeded to attempt any explanation of the divine unity: to indicate how its assertion of 'consubstantiality' may be compatible with belief (a) that there is one God only and not two equal and homogeneous Gods, and (b)

[1] Eusebius *ep. Caes.* (Socrates *h.e.* 1.8; Theodoret *h.e.* 1.12).
[2] *ib.*
[3] *ib.*

that the Father and the Son who are of one essence and not distinct in essence are nevertheless distinct as Father and Son and not identical in a Sabellian sense. Thus, far from settling the problem of Unity and Trinity, the Council of Nicaea raised it in a sharper form; and behind the Trinitarian question there lay the problem of Christology: what does it mean for Christians to say that Jesus Christ is God when the word 'God' carries the full weight of meaning involved in the Nicene *homoousion*?

The problem was complicated, and the controversy exacerbated, by the fact that among those who understood the formula to imply identity of substance were monistic theologians who stood, in some respects at least, close to the tradition of Paul of Samosata and who represented the type of thinking which, since the controversy between the Dionysii and the Council of Antioch of 268, had been most abhorrent to the 'central' majority of orthodox Eastern Christians for whom a clear distinction of persons and the assertion of three hypostases was all-important. Among these theologians were Eustathius, bishop of Antioch, and Marcellus, bishop of Ancyra. The former was the first episcopal victim of what was in fact not so much a reaction against the Nicene definition as a movement by the majority of those who had subscribed to it on the understanding that it should be interpreted in a loose anti-Arian sense such as was given to it by Eusebius of Caesarea. He was deposed by a council at Antioch in 331 on the doctrinal ground of Sabellianism. Socrates, it is true, took this incident as an illustration in his *Ecclesiastical History* of the misunderstandings and confusions which arose over the *homoousion*: a fight in the dark in which, while objectors to the term accused its supporters of being Sabellian subverters of the hypostatic existence of the Son and advocates of it accused its opponents of being polytheists, all were really agreed that the Son is a distinct hypostasis and that there is one God in a Trinity of persons.[1] Nevertheless, it seems that Eustathius was vulnerable to the Eusebian attack and not simply a victim of misunderstanding. He was in a sense an old-fashioned theologian, sometimes echoing the ideas of his second-century countryman, Theophilus. The Son, who is Word, Wisdom, and Spirit (by which is probably meant 'divine being') is God's power put forth, or 'begotten', as his externally directed activity; Eustathius seems not to regard this Son as a distinct hypostasis subsisting personally from eternity.[2] This 'anhypostatic' conception of the Logos enabled Eustathius to point out the deficiencies of Arianism from a new angle. Recognizing that the Arian assertion of the possibility and mutability of the Logos was bound up with their denial of a human soul in Christ,[3] he maintained the full reality of the 'man' assumed by, anointed with, borne by, or indwelt by, the Logos or Spirit of God.[4] The human soul, rather than a personal Logos who had 'come down from heaven' is the centre of the personality of Christ, and this soul is also the meeting-point of the human and the divine, living with the Word and God,[5] and

[1] *h.e.* 1.23.

[2] cf. *hom. in Prov. 8:22*; (Spanneut, *Recherches sur les Ecrits d'Eustathe d'Antioche* Lille. 1948, pp. 102, 104); *fr. in Pss. (ib.* p. 106).

[3] *fr.* 15. See above, p. 97.

[4] *frr.* 9, 19, 24, 41–45, 47.

[5] *fr.* 17.

inseparably united with the indwelling divine Spirit. By reverting to this older type of Christology Eustathius was able to assert both the unity of God and the full humanity of Christ more uninhibitedly than his Origenist contemporaries, to cut the roots of Arianism, and to anticipate the Antiochene Christology of a century later, though at the cost, as it would seem to Alexandrian theologians, of positing a 'moral' or 'psychological' rather than 'hypostatic' union between God and man in Christ.

Although he was a primary target for the attack mounted against those who seemed to be undermining the traditional Eastern belief in three hypostases, Eustathius was always regarded by those who upheld the positive implications of Nicaea as a hero. Athanasius mentions him as a 'confessor and orthodox man', a victim of pro-Arian plotting.[1] A more embarrassing adherent of the same 'Nicene' party was Marcellus, bishop of Ancyra, who was deposed like Eustathius on the ground of Sabellian monarchianism but somewhat rashly included with Athanasius and Asclepas, bishop of Gaza, in the vindication of deposed Eastern bishops (Eustathius having probably died before this) announced in 343 by the Western Council of Sardica.[2] Marcellus, whose teaching is preserved mainly in the citations contained in two works directed against him by Eusebius of Caesarea, reacted most vigorously against the denial of the divine unity which he found in the Arian theologians such as Eusebius of Nicomedia, Narcissus of Neronias and Asterius the Sophist, especially the last-named against whom his championship of the *homoousion* was chiefly directed, and which he also saw in the pluralistic Trinitarian doctrine of Eusebius of Caesarea. The beliefs that the Father is 'one' and the Logos 'another', that the unity between Father and Son is a union of wills, that the Logos can be termed 'second God', that he is a creature, and that it is proper to speak of two, or three, *ousiai*,[3] were countered by Marcellus with a monistic theology which confirmed the worst fears of those who suspected Sabellianism in the Nicene formula but which in fact, like that of Eustathius, was akin, not so much to Sabellianism as to second-century orthodoxy of the type represented by Theophilus of Antioch.

Marcellus reverted, in fact, to the idea of deity as pure monad (a concept which he held to be supported by such texts as 'I am the first and the last and beside me there is no God'), as opposed to the idea of a distinction of hypostases which for him amounted to ditheism.[4] In this one God, the Father, the Logos subsisted as immanent reason until, when the purpose of God to create the world required it, the Logos came forth as an active operation of God by which creation was carried out.[5] The Father and the Logos are not two *ousiai*, two entities, or two powers, for the Logos is the power and wisdom of God, inseparable from him and one and the same with him.[6] The 'coming forth' of the Logos is not a 'generation of the Son' but an extension or broadening out, of the indivisible monad into triad, for the

[1] *fug.* 3.
[2] Theodoret *h.e.* 2.8.
[3] Marcellus *fr.* 3 ap. Eus. *Marcell.* 1.4; *fr.* 63, *fr.* 33, *fr.* 71, ap. eund.
[4] id. *fr.* 67 ap. Eus. *eccl. theol.* 2.19.
[5] id. *fr.* 54 ap. eund. 3.3.
[6] id. *frr.* 72, 63, ap. Eus. *Marcell.* 1.4; *fr.* 64 ap. eund. 2.2.

'procession' of the Logos is parallel to the 'procession' of the Holy Spirit (Marcellus uses the same term in each case). Marcellus claims, indeed, that his 'dynamic' concept of both Logos and Spirit, taken with his insistence on the absolute unity of the divine monad, enables him to make sense of the fact that St. John ascribes the procession of the Spirit to the Father as its source and yet at the same time says that the Spirit will 'take of mine', i.e. of what pertains to the Logos. These statements, he maintains, become contradictory if Son and Spirit are conceived of as distinct hypostases.[1] For the economy of salvation the Logos has indwelt the man whom he assumed, indwelling as a power rather than as a person, enabling the assumed man, who is fallen man, to be raised to God's right hand and reign as king. This kingdom is temporary, for it will cease when the economy is completed in the subjugation of every enemy to his authority: an idea for which Marcellus naturally finds evidence in I Cor. 15:24–28. When that consummation has been achieved there will be no need for the economy, in which the Logos can be said to have assumed the form of a servant, to continue; the Logos reigns eternally because God reigns and his Logos is immanent in him, and when the economy of salvation has been wound up the Logos will no longer be projected externally but will, as it were, be withdrawn once again into the inner being of the monad.[2]

The idea that Christ's kingdom is not eternal was naturally fastened upon by Marcellus' opponents; but it was perfectly possible for the Council of Sardica to reply that he did not affirm, as they represented, that the origin of the divine Logos was dated from Mary's conception or that his kingdom would have no end; on the contrary, he wrote that his kingdom (i.e. in the sense of the reign of God's immanent Reason) had had no beginning and would have no end.[3] More important in his theology is his firm adherence to the notion of 'Logos' as the expression or utterance of the mind of God. It is analogous to the human word which cannot be separated as a distinct hypostasis, or even power, from the person who utters it, but is distinguishable only as an activity of that person.[4] This makes it possible for Marcellus to follow traditional exegesis in taking it to be the Logos who addressed Moses in the burning bush. The Logos spoke to him, but only as the organ, as it were, of the Father: the Father said 'I am' through his Logos,[5] as it might be through the agency of a tongue. Further, the fact that he does distinguish the Logos as the divine revelatory activity enables him to differentiate his theology from that of Sabellius who, according to him, simply denied that 'Logos' refers to anything except the Father and asserted that the content of the words 'Logos' and 'Father' is absolutely identical.[6] Important, too, is his consequent interpretation of the divinity of Christ in dynamic terms; the hypostasis or person of Christ is the man whom the Logos or Power of God has assumed and indwells and who is thereby Son of God. The notion of an end to the Incarnation (or rather, the

[1] *fr.* 60 ap. *eccl. theol.* 3.4.
[2] *fr.* 104 ap *Marcell.* 2.4; *fr.* 108 ap. *eccl. theol.* 3.10.
[3] Thdt. *h.e.* 2.8.
[4] Marcell. *fr.* 55 ap. *Eus.* Marcell. 2.2.
[5] id. *fr.* 56 ap. eund.
[6] *fr.* 38 ap. *eccl. theol.* 1.15.

'economy' of the assumption of the man by the Logos), though it raises its own great difficulties, was at least a bold attempt to deal with the Trinitarian and Christological problems at the point where they seem, even if only superficially, to be most acute: namely, in respect of the post-Ascension state of the incarnate Son of God.

It was these last aspects of his teaching which made Marcellus an obvious target for attack by the opponents of the *homoousion*, especially in the light of the further development of his Christology in an adoptionist sense by Photinus, bishop of Sirmium. Having made a profession of faith in a form which a comparison with the baptismal creed in Hippolytus' *Apostolic Tradition* and with the evidence in Rufinus' *Exposition of the Apostolic Creed* shows to have been the creed of the Roman church itself,[1] he was accepted by a local synod under Julius, bishop of Rome, in or about 340 and never explicitly disowned by the Western leaders. Eastern councils, however, formally anathematized him, linking his name with those of Sabellius and Paul of Samosata (in the third creed of Antioch of 341) and with Photinus as well as Paul of Samosata (in the fourth creed of Antioch, 341, and the creed of Antioch of 345).[2] The first of these creeds also insists on the hypostatic existence of the Logos, the second and third on the eternity of Christ's reign and heavenly session, and the third on the doctrine that the Son exists from before the ages as the companion addressed by God in the words 'Let us make man . . .' and is not to be thought of as the immanent Logos which became externalized (Logos *endiathetos* and *prophorikos*).

The series of creeds produced by these councils, by the council at Philippopolis in 343 to which the Eastern bishops withdrew after refusing to associate with the Western supporters of Athanasius and Marcellus at Sardica, and by the first council of Sirmium in 351, represent, on the whole, an attempt to steer a middle course. They avoid the characteristic statements of the Nicene formula, speak of the Son as the exact image of the Father's deity, and of the Father, Son and Holy Spirit as being three in hypostasis but one in harmony,[3] and anathematize the distinctively Arian formulae[4] concerning the creation of the Logos out of nothing and there having been (a time) when he was not. At the same time they condemn the tenets of Marcellus such as the reduction of the idea of the 'Son' to that of a temporary extension of the divine substance[5] and the belief that the son of Mary was only a man;[6] they also repeatedly assert the vital importance of the belief that the Son's generation is by the will of the Father.[7] Arianism and Sabellianism are thus ruled out, without any desire to endorse the specifically Nicene doctrine. Nor was the key word *homoousios* employed in the statement of faith contained in the encyclical letter of the Western

---

[1] Marcell. ap. Epiphanium *haer.* 72 (Hahn, *Bibliothek der Symbole*, p. 22).

[2] Ath. *syn.* 24 (Hahn, p. 186); *ib.* 25 (p. 187); *ib.* 26 (p. 194).

[3] Second ('Lucianic') Creed of Antioch (341) ap. Athn. *syn.* 23 (Hahn, pp. 185–6).

[4] *ib.*; also Fourth Creed of Antioch (341), Creed of Philippopolis ap. Hilarium *syn.* 34 (Hahn, p. 191), Creed of Antioch (345), Creed of Sirmium (351) ap. Ath. *syn.* 27 (Hahn, p. 197).

[5] Creed of Sirmium (351) anathemas 6 & 7.

[6] *ib.* anathema 9.

[7] Creed of Philippopolis, Antioch (345) and Sirmium (351), anathema 25.

council of Sardica which approved the teaching of Athanasius. This formula treats 'hypostasis' as synonymous with 'substance' (*ousia*) and affirms one hypostasis or substance of Father, Son and Holy Spirit. The unity of Father and Son is not like the sonship towards God enjoyed by the regenerate, for it is a one-ness of hypostasis. The Father is greater than the Son, not because of any difference of hypostasis but simply because the word 'Father' is greater than the word 'Son'. The Son is eternal, without beginning or end.[1] This statement thus goes further than Nicaea in a positive affirmation of the divine unity and in rejecting the subordinationism characteristic of the Origenist tradition.

The theological working out of the 'Nicene' theology represented by the Sardican statement was the great achievement of Athanasius. His thought is centred upon a few major theological principles. One of these is a clear idea of divine creativity. The Arian view, that creation is a two-stage process in which the Son is first created as an intermediary being by whom all other creatures will subsequently be made, is refuted by Athanasius on the ground that no such intermediary is necessary. God himself can and does create by his mere fiat. Were it necessary that a mediator should be interposed between God and the creation of the world, it would also seem that another mediator would be required for the creation of the first mediator, and so on infinitely. On the other hand, if, as Scripture asserts, God continues himself to create along with, and by the agency of, his Word, it is absurd to suppose that a created intermediary was necessary in the first place. The doctrine of creation thus offers no support for any attempt to relegate the Son to a status inferior to that of deity in the fullest sense.[2]

While holding that the relation between God and the created universe offers no reason for assigning the Logos to the created sphere, Athanasius denies the Origenistic principle that deity subsists at different levels. The essence of God, which is one and the same in the Father and the Son, is not communicated or extended to any lower order of being. It is true that Athanasius describes the divine essence as 'productive' or 'fruitful',[3] but this does not mean that it is extensible beyond the Logos; it means that God is essentially creative, and the argument of Athanasius is that since God creates through the Logos, and since without the Logos he would not possess creative energy, God's creativity implies the essential unity of the Father and the Logos/Son. Thus Athanasius allows no place for an hierarchical subordination within the divine being; and in this respect his aim is similar to that of Arius, though whereas Arius avoided any 'broadening down' of deity by placing the Son among the creatures Athanasius follows the opposite course of asserting that the Son and the Father are one and the same substance. There is no difference of *ousia*. The deity of Father and Son is actually identical; 'the deity of the Father is that of the Son',[4] the being of the Father is proper to the Son, and he is of the same nature as the

[1] Theodoret *h.e.* 2.8; Hahn, pp. 188ff.
[2] Ath. *Ar.* 2.24–29.
[3] *ib.* 2.2.
[4] *ib.* 1.61.

Father, but of another essence and another kind from all creatures.[1] The nature of Father and Son is one; the Son as offspring, is different from the Father: as God he is the same. Father and Son are one in the identity of the one deity; hence whatever is predicated of God is predicated interchangeably of the Father and the Son. The old simile of the sun and its ray is adduced as an illustration: there are not two lights, but the one light of the sun which shines in the ray.[2] The idea of the eternal generation of the Logos is, of course, entirely dissociated from its Origenistic framework of thought. It no longer has any connexion with a relationship subsisting between God and his creation; on the contrary, it serves to emphasize the absolute uniqueness of the relation of Son to Father. It is also used in refutation of an Arian argument that if the Son is co-eternal with the Father he should be termed brother rather than son, and to show, too, that the idea of 'generation' does not imply either a temporal priority of the Father or any kind of deficiency in the Father which had to be made good. 'Generation' must not be interpreted anthropomorphically.[3]

The Arians attempted, according to Athanasius, to disguise their teaching that the Logos is a creature by wrapping it up in the time-honoured assertion that he is begotten by an act of the Father's will. This traditional doctrine had been originally intended to safeguard the hypostatic distinction of Father and Son against Gnostic ideas of emanation and monarchian notions of numerical unity. It had now become incompatible with Athanasius' doctrine of the total otherness of the Logos from all created being and the absolute identity of substance of Father and Son. He accordingly cleared up a frustrating dilemma by refusing to accept the alternatives: voluntary begetting or involuntary (i.e. under constraint or contrary to the divine will). The Son is begotten, not by the Father's deliberate intention but by reason of his nature. God cannot not beget the Son, just as he cannot not be good. In neither case is God subject to necessity, other than the necessity of his own nature, nor can his actions be termed involuntary.[4] Athanasius also clarified the long-standing obscurity about the usage of the terms *agenetos* and *agennetos*, which should strictly speaking denote 'unoriginated' and 'unbegotten' respectively, but which had constantly been confused. It is an indication of the extent of this confusion that in the passage where Athanasius deals most explicitly with this question the manuscripts vary greatly in their spelling of these key words. The Arians were asking whether there is one *ageneton* principle or two. Athanasius replies that if they really mean 'unoriginated' then the Son must be so described; if they mean 'unbegotten' then the Father alone can be so called. But the Son's being begotten (being *gennetos* or a *gennema*) does not make him *genetos* in the sense of being originated or created; on the contrary, if he were this he could not be the perfect image of the unoriginate Father; he would, rather, belong to, and reflect, the order of created being.[5] The

[1] *ib.* 1.58.
[2] *ib.* 3.4.
[3] *ib.* 1.14; cf. *decr.* 20.
[4] *Ar.* 3.59–67.
[5] *ib.* 1.3.

term *agenetos* should not, according to Athanasius, be used in discourse about the relation between the Father and the Son, for the Son is the eternal Logos of, and subsisting with, the unoriginate Father, but it is appropriate only with reference to the relation between God and creatures.[1]

Besides his doctrine of creation which caused him to react so vigorously against any notion of an intermediate being, at once created and creative, between God and the world, Athanasius' soteriology was a powerful motive in the working out of his Trinitarian theology. The Saviour must be none other than God. He could not be an intermediary. Not only was God the creator of man in the beginning; it was as a participant in the divine Logos, enabled by this participation to contemplate God, that man was enabled to rise above his natural condition of mortality and enjoy undying blessedness as one who bore the stamp of the divine image. The Fall meant man's loss of blessedness; transgression led on to a state of steadily increasing corruption, the natural end of which would be man's total dissolution. Only the Creator could re-create fallen man; redemption involved the restoration of the divine image in man, for which, as for an almost obliterated portrait, the presence of the original 'sitter' was required; it involved the return of corrupt human nature to the state of incorruptibility; and, since God had decreed total death as the penalty for transgression, it necessitated the preservation of God's self-consistency (which forbade the simple revocation of the sentence by an act of forgiveness) without the frustration of his creative purpose which would be brought about by the annihilation of the creature to whom he had granted participation in his own Logos.[2] Only he who is the Father's Logos, transcending the whole creation, 'was capable of re-creating all things, suffering for all men, and acting as advocate for all men with the Father'.[3] Athanasius also understands salvation in terms of divinization, and he holds that, since divinization means participation in God, only one who is essentially God can bestow it. It may be questioned whether this argument was cogent, since the 'divinization' of man did not mean for Athanasius that man was to become one with God in the sense in which he believed that the Son was one with the Father. Deification is virtually identified with adoption into sonship;[4] we are made sons by adoption and grace, participating in the Spirit that is the earnest of deification. 'We are sons, but not as the Son, and gods, but not as he is God.'[5] It may seem that there is no reason why the participation in God, through grace, of a created being should not be effected by an Arian Logos who is himself a created being participating in deity by grace. Athanasius, however, is sure that one who is himself deified cannot deify; no one can make others participate in what he himself possesses only by participation and not in his own right, for it is not his to bestow but it belongs to another, and he enjoys possession of it only by grace which is sufficient for himself alone.[6]

[1] *decr.* 28–32.
[2] *inc.* 4–16.
[3] *ib.* 7.
[4] *Ar.* 1.39.
[5] *ib.* 3.20; *inc. et c. Ar.* 9.
[6] *syn.* 51

Similar considerations played a great part in Athanasius' thought about the being of the Holy Spirit. It is in the middle of the fourth century that the question of the relation of the Spirit to the Father and the Son becomes a theological issue. The Nicene formula had been content with a third article in the form, 'And in the Holy Spirit', without explanation. The *Catechetical Lectures* of Cyril of Jerusalem in or about 348 affirm the divinity of the Spirit in contrast with the Arian teaching that the Spirit is the highest of the creatures that have, as the Origenist tradition understood Jn. 1:3 to state, been brought into being through the Logos.[1] Athanasius, however, was compelled to attempt a more thorough treatment of this subject, for not only did the creaturely status of the Spirit follow from the Arian doctrine of the Logos, but belief in it was also propagated by some who did not profess Arianism in respect of the Son. Athanasius addressed a series of letters on the subject to Serapion, bishop of Thmuis, who was concerned about the Egyptian Christians known to Athanasius as 'Tropici', this name probably referring to the *tropoi* or 'figures' by which they read their doctrine out of certain biblical texts, such as Am. 4:13 (misunderstood as alluding to the creation, not of 'wind' but of 'Spirit'), which they interpreted as evidence that the Spirit is among the created angels of God.[2] Athanasius attacks this view, using as a primary argument the Spirit's work as life-giver and sanctifier: the Spirit makes men participate in God, but only one who is God, and not one who is himself a participant by grace, can effect such participation; creatures are recipients of life and sanctification: the Spirit is the giver of them; therefore the Spirit is not a creature; the Spirit deifies, and therefore cannot be a recipient of deification like a creature.[3] To support this argument Athanasius asserts that Scripture shows that the Spirit is Spirit of God and Spirit of the Son; the Son is wisdom and truth, the Spirit is the Spirit of wisdom and truth.[4] The Spirit's operation is inseparable from that of the Father and the Son, and the relationship between Father and Son must subsist also between the Son, and so also the Father, and the Spirit.[5] A somewhat less convincing argument takes belief in the Trinity as a datum; if the Trinity is eternal and unchanging, as all would agree, neither the Son nor the Spirit can have been created.[6] The Spirit is therefore not a creature, but one with Father and Son in the deity of the Trinity, and *homoousios* with God.[7]

The developed Trinitarian doctrine which Athanasius thus constructed on the foundation of the anti-Arian formula of Nicaea involved him in acute Christological difficulty. He was committed to the belief that the Son's deity is the Father's, that the 'form of God' (Phil. 2:6) means nothing less than that the being of the Son is the fulness of the Father's deity, and that the Son is 'complete God'.[8] Eustathius and Marcellus could affirm all this

[1] *Catech.* 8.5; 4.16; 16.8, 3, 23; 6.6.
[2] Ath. *Serap.* 1.21; 1.3, 10, 11.
[3] *ib.* 1.22–24.
[4] *ib.* 1–26.
[5] *ib.* 3.1–5.
[6] *ib.* 3.7.
[7] *ib.* 1.21, 27.
[8] *Ar.* 3.6.

and yet, by interpreting 'incarnation' in terms of an indwelling of the fullness of God within the human personality of the 'assumed man', safeguard the humanity of Christ against docetism. Athanasius, however, was typically Alexandrian in his Christology; there is, certainly, an indwelling of the Logos, but it is an indwelling in a fleshly body;[1] the idea that the Logos entered into a holy man ('as into one of the prophets', he adds) means, for him, a division of the one Person into a human Christ, on the one hand, and a divine Logos on the other; it is as shocking as the opposite notion that the fleshly body is *homoousios* with the deity of the Logos and that it was the deity, *homoousios* with the Father, and not rather the created flesh, which underwent the human experience and suffered.[2] Any idea that the Logos entered into 'a man from Mary' is ruled out on the ground that the Incarnation is then no longer unique, that the uniqueness of the Resurrection and the need for a miraculous birth become, alike, inexplicable, and that Christ's death would not be the death of the Logos in the sense that it was the death of the flesh which he had taken and made personally his own flesh; it would be the death of a man associated with the Logos, and therefore, on Athanasius' principles, it could not be a saving death.[3] Athanasius therefore has to combine his assertion of the total deity of the Son with the Alexandrian insistence that the subject of the experiences recorded in the Gospels is the Son. A personal being who was in the fullest sense God came down from heaven; the Logos became flesh.

One aspect of his Christology is thus clear enough. The Logos gives life and light to all things; he causes the world to be an ordered *cosmos*; it is at his providential bidding that the stars move, birds fly, trees grow, plants come up.[4] The Incarnation did not deprive the universe of the omnipresent Logos. On the contrary, he continued, while in a fleshly body, to be immanent in all things and transcendent over all things, for the body imposed no limitation;[5] rather, it was made the instrument of the Logos who had so appropriated it as to make it his own.[6] It is thus the Logos who is the personal subject of the Gospel story.

On the other side, Athanasius' Christology is much less definite. He finds it, as we should expect, extremely hard to maintain the reality of the human experiences of which the Logos was the subject. For the Arians it was not difficult to attribute hunger, thirst, sorrow, and ignorance (of the last day) to the Logos, nor to avoid embarrassment at the texts which spoke of his inferiority to the Father; these were all the very passages which supported the thesis that the Logos is created and mutable. Athanasius has to explain them otherwise, and he tries to do so by ascribing all human weakness and suffering to the flesh. Because the Logos had condescended to make human flesh his own he could be said to appropriate its experiences, including those of ignorance and fear, and speak of them as his own. As Logos he knew the day and the hour; as Logos he could not pray that the

[1] *inc.* 8, 9, 20.
[2] *Epict.* 2.
[3] *ib.* 10–11; cf. *Adelph.* 3.
[4] *gent.* 44.
[5] *inc.* 17.
[6] *ib.* 8, 18; *Ar.* 3.35.

cup might pass from him; but as the Logos who had assumed human flesh he could as it were come down to the level of flesh, for the edification and salvation of men, and take its weaknesses on himself.[1] This Christology clearly verges on the docetic. Athanasius increased the difficulty for himself by operating, like Arius, with two concepts; the divine Logos and the human flesh. He does not bring a human rational soul into his Christological scheme, and such of the human experiences as cannot be ascribed to the flesh have therefore to be explained away. The question has been much discussed whether at a late stage in his development Athanasius changed his view on this matter. When the formal and explicit denial by Apollinarius of a human soul in Christ was becoming a question of public controversy, Athanasius' council at Alexandria in 362 declared that the Saviour's body did not lack 'soul', 'sense', or 'mind'. Since the idea of a human mind or rational soul in Christ continued to play no positive role in Athanasius' Christology, it has been plausibly argued that this statement means simply that the human body was not inanimate, but animated by the Logos, the Logos being its mind. Apollinarius certainly explained the council's declaration in this sense, but it is an interpretation which strains the sense of the statement, which goes on: 'it was impossible, since the Lord became man for us, that his body should be without mind, nor was it the salvation of the body alone but also of the soul which was effected in the Logos himself'[2] – words which are paralleled in the Epistle to Epictetus: 'our salvation is not a fantasy, nor was it the salvation of the body alone, but of the whole man, soul and body, that took place in the Logos himself.'[3] The latter point would not be met by Apollinarius' interpretation of the council's words: indeed, it stands in contradiction to Apollinarius' soteriology. It seems likely that Apollinarius was trying to explain the declaration away; it conflicted with his own idea that Christ's body was a 'temple' of the Logos, prefigured by Solomon's temple which was without soul, mind or will. So it may be that Athanasius came formally to acknowledge the completeness of Christ's manhood, though without developing the implications of this. In any case, he stretched the meaning of 'flesh' far enough to ascribe to it a will.[4]

From 350 onwards, when Constantius reigned as sole emperor (the Western Nicene party having until then enjoyed the support of Constans), the explicitly Arianizing party had the active backing of the secular authority. The formula produced by the second council of Sirmium in 357 (called by Hilary the 'blasphemy of Sirmium') affirms the Trinity, citing the baptismal formula of Mt. 28:19 which for Athanasius had been a proof of the *homoousion*, but insists on the 'two persons' of Father and Son and strongly emphasizes the inferiority and subordination of the latter to the former; at the same time it deprecates speculation concerning the divine substance and, in particular, the use of the terms *homoousion* and *homoiou-*

---

[1] see the long discussion in *Ar.* 3.34–57.
[2] *tom. ad Ant.* 7; cf. Apollinarius *ep. Diocaes.* 2 and *fr.* 2 (Lietzmann, *Apollinaris von Laodicea und seine Schule*, pp. 256, 204).
[3] *Epict.* 7.
[4] *decr.* 31.

sion (of like substance).[1] Some were prepared to acknowledge, simply, that the Son is like the Father, while refusing to discuss the question of substance, and this point of view was embodied in the creeds of the councils of Nice in Thrace in 359, Seleucia and Ariminum in the same year (the Western bishops for the most part subscribing under imperial pressure), and Constantinople in 360. A much more positive and extreme Arian theology was worked out by Aetius, Eunomius and others, asserting the unlikeness in substance of the Son to the Father, though likeness could be predicated of their operations since the Son participated by grace in the operation of the Father.[2] The creed of Eudoxius, bishop of Constantinople, reflects the outlook of this 'Anomoean' (*anomoios*, 'unlike') party, in its assertion that the one God, the Father, is alone ingenerate, that the Son is the first and chief of creatures, and that he was made flesh, but not man, since he took flesh without a human soul.[3]

In reaction against this movement those who, without inclining at all to Arianism, had opposed the Nicene formula through fear of 'Sabellianism' drew closer to the position of Athanasius. They acknowledged that, as Cyril, bishop of Jerusalem, stated in his exposition of the baptismal creed, the Son is God begotten of God, like his begetter in all respects.[4] He, and those who shared his views, were always anxious to preserve the distinctness between the Father and the Son: to deny the concept of 'Son-Fatherhood';[5] but they ascribed the unity of the Son with the Father not merely to an identity of will or operation but to a common deity.[6] From this position it was no long step to the declaration of the council of Ancyra (358), led by Basil, the bishop of that city: that the Son, who is an *ousia* (here denoting 'individual entity' or 'person') and not an impersonal divine activity (as Marcellus believed), is like the Father in respect of substance. This council anathematized the *homoousion*, associating this with *tautoousion* 'identical in substance', or, if *ousia* retains the meaning indicated above, 'identical as an individual entity'), but it opened up the possibility, which the council of Sirmium had rejected, of speaking of *homoiousion*.[7]

This term became characteristic of the theology of Basil of Ancyra, George, bishop of Laodicea, and others who, while still anxious not to compromise the distinctness of the two hypostases, were moving nearer to the Nicene position in the face of the developed Arianism of the 'Anomoeans'. A formula drawn up in 359 by George of Laodicea asserted likeness in substance between the Father and Son as distinct hypostases and identity of deity.[8] At about this time Athanasius explicitly recognized that this party shared his own view, differing only in respect of their hesitation over the actual term *homoousion*; if they were content to acknowledge that the Son is both 'of like substance' with the Father and

[1] Hilary *syn.* 11 (Hahn, p. 200).
[2] Eunomius *apol.* 24, 26.
[3] Hahn, p. 261; see above, p. 97.
[4] *catech.* 4.7.
[5] *ib.* 11.16.
[6] *ib.*
[7] Epiphanius *haer.* 73.2ff. (Hahn, pp. 201–4).
[8] *ib.* 73.12ff.

of the Father's substance, they were in agreement with what the *homoousion* was intended to signify.[1] The fact that Athanasius himself took care to dispel misunderstandings helped towards a *rapprochement*. If two objects are consubstantial, he explained, this does not mean that they must be collaterally derived from a third substance anterior to them both; the one may be derived simply from the other and yet be consubstantial with it.[2] He could also equate 'consubstantial' with 'of the same nature', and say that as men we are *homoousioi* with one another.[3] He continued, indeed, to maintain that *homoiousios* was inappropriate to one who is by nature, and not by participation, God. For a natural identity *homoousios* is the proper term.[4] Hilary of Poitiers, however, who was involved in the Eastern controversies while in exile from his diocese from 356 to 359, was ready to concede the propriety of either term: *homoousion* as safeguarding the identity of essence which 'likeness in respect of essence' implied, and *homoiousion* as preserving the distinctness of the hypostases which were acknowledged as being identical in essence.[5] Further, the important council held by Athanasius at Alexandria in 362 did much to clarify the identity of outlook which subsisted between those who used the theological terms in different sense and were therefore suspicious of one another's jargon. Some spoke of 'three hypostases'; but by this they did not, it was now acknowledged, mean three different *ousiai* in the sense of three principles or three Gods. Others spoke of 'one hypostasis', but it was now clear that by this they meant one *ousia*: that the Son is of the Father's substance and possesses one and the same divine nature with him. They did not intend to deny the distinction of Father, Son and Holy Spirit or to affirm that either the Son or the Spirit is not an individually subsisting entity.[6]

With this clarification the post-Nicene debate could resolve itself into a straight argument between a fully developed Trinitarian theology on the one hand and sheer Arianism on the other. The final steps towards such a Trinitarian theology were taken by the 'Cappadocian Fathers', that is, Basil of Caesarea, his brother Gregory of Nyssa and their associate Gregory of Nazianzus, and to a lesser degree by Didymus of Alexandria and Evagrius Ponticus. The argument with Arianism, as this was carried on in the treatises of Basil, Gregory of Nyssa and Didymus against Eunomius, for example, was largely a matter of developing the lines of thought already laid down by Athanasius. In one field, however, the issue was still undecided: the question of the deity of the Holy Spirit. As late as the delivery of his *Theological Orations* (*Orations* 27–31), probably in 380, Gregory of Nazianzus complains that the subject is hard, and that some regard the Spirit as a divine operation, some as a creature, others as God, while others again either take up an agnostic position on the ground that Scripture gives no clear guidance here, or make a broad hierarchical distinction

[1] Ath. *syn.* 41.
[2] *ib.* 51.
[3] *Serap.* 2.3.
[4] *syn.* 53.
[5] Hilary *syn.* 84ff.
[6] Ath. *tom. ad Ant.* 5–6.

between the Spirit and the Father and Son.[1] A few years earlier Eustathius
of Sebaste, one of the group which had held the Council of Ancyra in 358,
had emerged as the leader of a party of *Pneumatomachoi*, 'fighters against
the Spirit'.[2] The historian Socrates associates with this party Macedonius,
bishop of Constantinople, after his deposition in favour of the Arian
Eudoxius, and gives them the alternative name, 'Macedonians'.[3] Socrates,
and also Didymus,[4] indicate that they refused positively to speak of the
Spirit as a creature, but that they could not acknowledge him to be God.
One of the difficulties was the lack of positive Scriptural teaching, and
Gregory Nazianzen, admitting this, has to contend that it was not until
after man had assimilated the revelation of the Son that God could reveal,
after the close of the period of the Canon, the truth about the being of the
Spirit.[5] There was also the difficulty of explaining the relation of the Spirit
to the Father and the Son in such a way as to avoid a duplication of
'begotten' deity, that is, an assertion of two Sons who are brothers, or a
duplication of the unbegotten principle, that is, two Fathers.[6] In the background, less explicitly stated, was the more serious problem that the Logos
doctrine had already served to give an account of God transcendent and
God immanent and it was difficult to find an adequate theological place for
a third Person.

The argument of the Cappadocians starts from the scriptural testimony
to the work of the Spirit and the parallel witness of Christian worship and
devotion in the formula of baptism, the traditional doxology, and the
experience of the Spirit's work of sanctification. This line of argument is
developed most fully in Basil's treatise *On the Holy Spirit*, the conclusion
of which is that the Spirit cannot possibly be reckoned among creatures,
for he operates what is proper to God and is reckoned with, and not below,
the Father and Son in the regular worship of Christians. Further, the Nicene
formula was extremely terse about the Spirit, but only because no controversy had then arisen under this head; it is now right, says Basil, to affirm
that the Spirit, who is glorified with the Father and the Son, is holy by
nature, just as the Father is holy and the Son is holy, that he must not be
separated from the Father and the Son, but that this does not mean that
we should assert either that he is ingenerate, which the Father alone is, or
that he is generate, which the Son alone is. We are to maintain that he
'proceeds' from the Father, and in this way is of the Father without being
created; for the Holy Spirit is not to be included among the created
'ministering spirits'[7] – in refutation of an ancient tendency to include the
Holy Spirit among the angels, or at least, as Anomoean theology was doing,[8]
to link the hierarchical ordering of Son and Holy Spirit directly and, as it

[1] Gr. Naz. *or.* 31.2–5.
[2] Bas. *ep.* 263.3.
[3] Socr. *h.e.* 2.45.
[4] Didym. *Trin.* 2.8.
[5] Gr. Naz. *or.* 31.24–27.
[6] *ib.* 31.7; Didym. *Trin.* 2.5.
[7] Bas. *ep.* 125.
[8] e.g., *Homily* 2.15ff. of the Anomoean Homilies published by J. Liébart (*Sources chrétiennes* 146).

were, without a break with an hierarchical order of angels. Since the Spirit has not himself received sanctification and life, but is holy and life-giving by nature, he can impart these gifts; he is therefore not to be separated from the Trinity but is, as God, consubstantial with the Father.[1]

Gregory of Nyssa makes a significant addition to Basil's statement about the 'procession' of the Spirit. The Spirit is derived from the Father and is also 'of the Son'; he proceeds from the Father through the Son, like a third light kindled through the medium of a second light from a first light.[2] This language is important in view of later controversies arising from the Western adoption of the doctrine of the 'double procession' of the Spirit from the Father and the Son. At this stage, however, no clear-cut distinction as between East and West had yet arisen on this issue; Gregory's formulation represents the subsequent doctrine of the East, but although adumbrations of the theory of double procession may be discerned in Hilary they are also present in the Eastern theologian Epiphanius. To distinguish 'procession' from 'generation' sufficed as a verbal weapon to repel Pneumatomachian attacks. It was impossible, however, to give any meaningful content to the distinction. The Johannine concept of a 'proceeding' of the Spirit from the Father was never intended to be understood with reference to the internal relations of the person of the Godhead to one another and it did not lend itself to transference to this quite different sphere of thought.

The Cappadocians' positive task was to explain and define the orthodox theology which had emerged from the long controversy. The old confusion in terminology over the meaning of *ousia* and *hypostasis* which had exercised Athanasius' council at Alexandria in 362 had to be cleared up. *Hypostasis* was now defined as denoting a particular existent. It is related to the term *ousia*, which denotes a universal essence, as the proper name 'Paul' is to the generic word 'man'.[3] *Ousia* denotes the universal being in which every existing particular has a share; *hypostasis* denotes the particular which is differentiated by its individual properties. Thus the oneness of deity is affirmed in the assertion that the Son is of the same *ousia* as the Father, while by calling him, and each of the other two, an *hypostasis* the distinction between Father, Son and Holy Spirit is preserved.[4] In this way unity is safeguarded by the acknowledgment of the single Godhead and the distinction of 'persons' (*prosopa*: i.e. 'individual presentations') is maintained by the recognition of the distinctive properties of each.[5]

This equation of *ousia* and *hypostasis* with universal and particular could obviously lend itself to a tritheistic interpretation. The analogy often drawn by the Cappadocians with three particular men who are one by virtue of the common manhood of which they all partake could readily suggest that there are three Gods who are one because they all share a common deity. But in fact the Cappadocians insist most emphatically on the absolute oneness of God. There is a total identity of nature or substance.[6]

---

[1] Bas. *ep.* 159; Gr. Naz. *or.* 31.10.

[2] Gr. Nyss. *Maced.* 2, 6, 10, 12.

[3] Gr. Nyss. (Pseudo-Bas) *ep.* 38.3.

[4] Bas. *ep.* 214.4.

[5] *ep.* 236.6.

[6] Gr. Naz. *or.* 42.15; 30.20.

This makes it actually impossible to say that the Son is either unlike or like the Father.[1] It is manifested in, and acknowledgment of it is necessitated by, the absolute identity of the operations of the three persons. There is one activity; therefore one and the same nature.[2] The three men in the analogy are distinguished by variety of operation; in the Trinity there is but one single operation.[3] Indeed, his Platonist insistence on the reality, and the priority, of universals leads Gregory of Nyssa to think that, so far from understanding the 'manhood' of the three 'men' as merely an abstract concept, it might be possible to speak of them, and indeed of all men, as 'one man'.[4] This extreme emphasis on unity leads to great caution in applying the concept of number to the 'persons' at all. Each hypostasis can be mentioned severally, but though we enumerate them together this does not imply polytheism; for the numbers (one Father, one Son, one Holy Spirit) cannot be added up. They are individually, as distinct *prosopa*, one, one and one; but in respect of being God they are one and not three. It is possible to say that the Father is one and the Son is one; but not that they are 'one and one' to make two Gods. A king and his picture do not add up to two kings; the honour paid to the image passes through it to the original. And what the picture is by way of imitation the Son is by nature; the image is not constituted in his case by community of form but by common deity.[5] God is one in the sense that he is absolutely incomposite.[6] Hence Evagrius replies to accusations of tritheism by saying that God is one, not in number but in nature.[7] The conclusion is that undifferentiated deity subsists in distinct persons.[8]

In the last resort the difficulty involved in this theology is less that of avoiding tritheism as of assigning any content to the distinction of the hypostases. There is no difference in their activity; one and the same activity is predicated of the one deity. Yet the course of theological speculation which culminated in the full Trinitarian doctrine had been embarked on in the beginning largely with the object of making it possible to predicate distinctions of operation without denying the principle of monotheism. Here was an insoluble problem. The Cappadocians try to assign peculiar properties to the several hypostases; but Basil's attempt to ascribe to them Fatherhood, Sonship and sanctification, respectively, is unsatisfactory.[9] 'Sanctification' is an activity, whereas Fatherhood and Sonship are modes of subsistence; and, if there is one and the same operation of the Godhead as such, it is useless to attempt to distinguish any one hypostasis by assigning to it a specific activity such as sanctification. In the end the only possible distinctions were in a sense tautologous: that which distinguishes the Father is that he is Father, the Son that he is Son, the

---

[1] Evagr. (Pseudo-Bas.) *ep.* 8.3.
[2] Gr. Nyss. (Pseudo-Bas.) *ep.* 189.6.
[3] Gr. Nyss. *quod non sint tres dii* (*PG*. 45.125).
[4] *ib.* (120).
[5] Bas. *Spir.* 18.44, 45.
[6] Gr. Naz. *ep.* 243.
[7] Evagr. (Ps.–Bas.) *ep.* 8.2.
[8] Gr. Naz. *or.* 31.14.
[9] *ep.* 236.6.

Spirit that he is the Spirit of the Father and the Son; or, which is the same thing, that the distinctive property of the Father is unbegottenness, of the Son begottenness, of the Spirit procession.[1] Thus it came to be recognized that the distinct properties of the three are their modes of subsistence or modes of relationship;[2] yet, when it had to be admitted that no explanation could be given of the difference between the modes of subsistence of the Son and the Spirit,[3] it might well seem that abstract speculation had lost contact with reality. The one case in which Greek theology was able to give solid content to a hypostatic distinction was its insistence that the Father alone is the principle and fountain-head of deity, which is imparted by him to the Son and the Spirit: a continuing vestige of the hierarchical Trinity of pre-Nicene theology.

The victory of Nicene orthodoxy over Arianism was sealed by the expanded creed traditionally designated 'Nicene' in service-books such as the Book of Common Prayer. This creed is often known as the 'Niceno-Constantinopolitan Creed', for the Council of Chalcedon in 451, when endorsing it, referred to it as the creed of the 'hundred and fifty Fathers', that is, of the so-called Second Ecumenical Council (which was in fact an Eastern synod only), assembled at Constantinople by the orthodox emperor Theodosius I in 381. Those parts of this creed which relate to belief in the Father and the Son are generally similar to the creed of 325, though with certain notable differences. Whereas, however, the 'third article' of the creed of Nicaea contained nothing more than the bare assertion, 'and (we believe) in the Holy Spirit', in this later creed that article is greatly expanded and reflects the developed theology of Athanasius and the Cappadocians, at least to the extent of ascribing to the Holy Spirit divine operations and affirming that he is worshipped and glorified together with the Father and the Son. It does not, however, proceed from speaking about the Spirit's operation and his dignity to speaking about his being, and in this creed the *homoousion* of the Spirit is not explicitly asserted.

What indirect connection this creed has with the council of 381 is very obscure. The traditional belief that it is that council's official revision and expansion of the creed of Nicaea is improbable in view of the difference between the Christological sections of the two creeds, the silence about this creed before the Council of Chalcedon, and the possibility that the virtually identical creed contained in Epiphanius' treatise *Ancoratus* may have been in existence before 381. Having, however, received ecumenical endorsement at Chalcedon, it superseded the creed of 325 as the norm of 'Nicene' orthodoxy and as the standard Eastern baptismal creed.

Meanwhile, in the West, the orthodox attack on Arianism had taken a fresh and interesting form in the writings of Victorinus Afer, the professional philosopher whose dramatic conversion to Christianity in about 355 made a profound impression on Augustine when the story of it was recounted to him as he was approaching a similar decision. His books, *Against Arius* and *On the Generation of the Divine Word*, with three theological hymns, are

---

[1] Gr. Naz. *or.* 25.16; 29.2.
[2] Amphilochius *fr.* 15.
[3] Gr. Naz. *or.* 31.8.

extremely difficult; Jerome thought them unintelligible to non-experts. Their approach to the problem, however, is original, for Victorinus attempts to construct a Trinitarian theology out of Neoplatonist presuppositions modified by Christian insights. He finds an analogy to the modes of being of the Godhead in the inner life of the soul, which is a real reflection of the Trinity. In the soul Victorinus discerns three modes: being, living, and understanding. Undifferentiated being receives form by living and comes, in 'understanding', to knowledge of itself (self-consciousness).[1] These modes correspond to the sequence: substance, form, and concept. So in the Trinity the Father is pure undifferentiated being. Victorinus occasionally follows Plotinus in refusing to attribute being to God because God is beyond (transcending) being itself;[2] but usually he diverges at this point from the Neoplatonist outlook and rejects its negative theology. The Son is form or life, categorized being, the Father made knowable. He is the self-revelation of the Father,[3] for which Victorinus used the ancient image of the Word emerging from silence.[4] The Son is the express image of the Father and there is mutual knowledge between Father and Son, knowledge being an active desire for an object and thus to be identified with will. The Spirit is related to the Son as self-consciousness is to life. In the Spirit the divine being which is self-revealed in the Son knows (and wills, or actively desires) itself. The Spirit is the communication of the Word,[5] and the link of mutual understanding between the Father and the Son.[6] There is thus within the Godhead an eternal movement, as it were, outwards in self-revelation (*progressio*) and returning back (*regressus*) into its source.[7] The Spirit unites the Father and the Son by reuniting the Father's self-revelation with himself. This process does not mean that there is mutability in God. Victorinus is original in holding that God is unchangeably dynamic. God's essence is motion;[8] generation and creation belong inherently to his being.[9] 'God the Father', says a modern expositor of Victorinus' system, 'is essentially a stupendous virtuality, brimming with Life and Power, but as yet undetermined or defined by Form or Thought.'[10] It follows that Victorinus understands the *homoousion* in terms of identity of activity. There is one movement, one operation. God is one being, one life, one understanding.[11] God exists in a threefold manner;[12] and each of the three modes is identical with the divine essence and with all the divine attributes, for God does not possess attributes: he *is* his attributes and they are his being.[13]

Victorinus anticipated in a number of important respects the more fully

[1] Victorinus *adv. Ar.* 1.32, 62.
[2] *ib.* 4.23.
[3] *ib.* 3.7; 4.20.
[4] *ib.* 1.13.
[5] *ib.* 3.16.
[6] *ib.* 1.60.
[7] *hymn.* 1.
[8] *adv. Ar.* 1.43.
[9] *gen. verb.* 29.
[10] Paul Henry, *JTS* NS. 1.1 (1950), p. 50.
[11] *adv. Ar.* 3.4, 17.
[12] *ib.* 2.4.
[13] *ib.* 1.4.

developed Trinitarian theology of Augustine. Augustine's thought on this subject is worked out in a vast number of passages in the great library of his writings, but it is concentrated especially in his fifteen books *On the Trinity* which represent his thinking during a period of twenty years in the middle of his episcopate (399–419). Augustine, too, starts from the one-ness of the divine essence and tries to work from this basic presupposition towards a rational statement of the Trinitarian theology which he accepts as an unquestioned datum. He, too, believes that theology can speak intelligibly, though of course only in the consciousness that it is dabbling on the edge of an unfathomable mystery, about the internal structure of deity as distinct from that self-disclosure of God in the 'economy' which had been the chief concern of the Eastern and earlier Western theologians. He, too, holds that each person of the Godhead is identical with the divine essence, so that the fact that Christ is 'the wisdom of God' according to St. Paul does not mean that the Father is wise only because he is the begetter of the Son who is Wisdom. The Father is wise; the Son is the expression of this.[1] For Augustine, as for Victorinus, everything in God is the single divine essence. Augustine, too, develops greatly the approach to an understanding of the relations within God by the analogy of the inward operations of the soul.

Augustine's object is to show 'that the Trinity is the one and only and true God, and how Father, Son and Holy Spirit are rightly believed to be of one and the same substance or essence'.[2] It is the Trinity itself which is God. The three are strictly identical in essence, and are not consubstantial in the sense of participating in a generic unity;[3] indeed, Augustine does not use the term 'consubstantial' and he thinks that even to employ 'substance' with reference to God is strictly incorrect, since it should properly be used of mutable and composite entities, subjects which possess attributes, whereas God is absolutely simple and *is* his attributes. He prefers to use 'essence'.[4] There is thus absolute equality in the Godhead. Whereas it is broadly true to say that earlier Trinitarian theology had conceived of an hierarchically ordered deity of three, related to each other in a vertical descending order of derivation, as it were, Augustine substitutes for the image of a vertical line an equilateral triangle, any one of whose three points may be uppermost: the whole triangle is God. 'The Father, the Son and the Holy Spirit are one and the same substance in indivisible equality.'[5] Hence whatever is ascribed to God in himself is also ascribed to each of the three severally: thus the Father is almighty, the Son is almighty, and the Holy Spirit is almighty, but yet there are not three 'almighties' but one 'almighty'.[6] The Father is perfect, the Son perfect, and the Spirit perfect; but this does not mean that God is greater than each of them severally, for Father, Son and Spirit are one perfect God. The unity of Son with Father

[1] Aug. *Trin.* 6.1–3.
[2] *ib.* 1.4.
[3] Jo. *tract.* 39.2ff.
[4] *Trin.* 7.10.
[5] *ib.* 1.7.
[6] *ib.* 5.9.

and Spirit with Father and Son does not mean that God is a kind of sum total of three.[1]

This does not imply that there are no distinctions; it says in Jn. 10:30, 'I and the Father *are* (not '*is*') one'. But in acknowledging that there are three Augustine finds it very hard to answer the question, 'Three what?' The Greek formula, 'one *ousia*, three *hypostaseis*' will not go literally into Latin, for this would produce 'one *essentia*, three *substantiae*'. Latin theology had therefore grown accustomed to speak of three *personae*. But Augustine does not like this term, and thinks it should be used, not for what it positively says, but simply to avoid having nothing to say at all.[2] He wants above all to safeguard the one-ness of will and operation, and, although neither *prosopon* in Greek nor *persona* in Latin possessed the psychological connotations of our 'person', but signified only a distinct individual entity, he seems to have feared that to lay positive emphasis on the term *persona* might compromise the truth that Father, Son and Spirit are inseparable and operate inseparably.[3] There is one will and an inseparable operation.[4] This principle causes some difficulty in relation to the scriptural theophanies. They are not to be ascribed exclusively to the Son, as in earlier Trinitarian thought, but may be attributed either to any one of the three or to God the Trinity, always with the proviso that the nature or substance or essence, or whatever term may be used to speak of what God actually is in himself, cannot be made visible physically.[5]

To convey some idea of what may be meant by Trinity in identity Augustine seeks images of the Trinity in the structure of the soul. Since man is made in the image of God, he must in some degree reflect the Trinity; even the physical or 'outward' man which perishes (II Cor. 4:16) discloses a certain representation of the Trinity which is to be found in the relation between the perceiving subject, the perceived object, and the perception which links them, or between the object perceived, the perception of it, and the voluntary direction of the mind towards what is perceived;[6] analogies in which Augustine had been partly anticipated by Victorinus.[7] Within the soul are to be discerned the analogies of memory, understanding and will and of the mind, its self-knowledge and its self-love;[8] an extension of the latter gives the triad, memory, knowledge and love, in respect of the soul's awareness of God.[9] The last two of these analogies are a development of the idea of a triad of loving subject, loved object and the love which joins them.[10] This last, however, is not in itself of great importance in Augustine's own thought; although it has been used as a foundation for the idea of a 'social Trinity' this does not correspond with Augustine's own theology,

---

[1] *ib.* 6.9.
[2] *ib.* 5.10.
[3] *ib.* 1.7.
[4] *ib.* 2.9.
[5] *ib.* 2.12–34.
[6] *ib.* 11.1ff.
[7] *adv. Ar.* 1.40.
[8] *Trin.* 10.18; 9.8.
[9] *ib.* 14.11ff.
[10] *ib.* 9.2.

which is too monistic to allow of such a concept: God's love and knowledge, in this context, are knowledge and love of himself, not love subsisting between 'persons' in the modern sense of the word. Further, Augustine is well aware that these analogies are no more than very dim adumbrations of the reality. The activities or faculties of the mind or soul are not identical with its essence, as the three are identical with the divine essence.[1] In God there is one activity, which is not the case with the human faculties, and the Trinity which is a triad of persons is more indivisible than the trinity in the soul which is only one person.[2]

Augustine is faced with what is really an impossible task: to explain what the distinctions between the three really are. He tries to answer this question by pointing out that the distinctions between Father, Son and Spirit are not substantial (which would imply tritheism), nor accidental (for with God there are no accidents), but relational.[3] The Father is called Father only in relation to the Son, and so on. The 'persons' are real and eternally subsisting *relations*. Further, because 'Son' denotes a relation of 'begottenness' it is appropriate to ascribe certain operations, namely, those of the incarnate life, to the Son, even though the 'economy' was the work of the whole Trinity inasmuch as the three co-operated in a single operation.[4] The procession of the Spirit is distinguished from the begetting of the Son by being an identical relation to the Father and to the Son whereas the generation of the Son is a relation to the Father only.[5] He is the Spirit of both, but this does not imply that there are two sources of the Spirit for he proceeds from both by one and the same operation.[6]

Augustine's Trinitarian theology found formal expression in the so-called 'Athanasian Creed',[7] a didactic composition which gained a place in the West among the authoritative credal formulations. Its authorship is uncertain but its place of origin is in all probability southern France and its date seems likely to be the fifth century. 'The Catholic Faith,' it declares, 'is this: that we worship one God in Trinity and Trinity in Unity, neither confusing the persons nor dividing the substance.' There is one deity of Father, Son and Holy Spirit, equal glory, co-eternal majesty. The attributes of each of the three are identical, for there is, for example, one uncreated and not three uncreated: the attributes are of *God*. Hence, while each person is to be acknowledged as God and Lord, there are not three Gods or three Lords. The distinctions are relational: the Father is not made, created or begotten; the Son is of the Father alone, not made nor created but begotten; the Spirit is of the Father and the Son, not made nor created nor begotten but proceeding. 'And in this Trinity nothing is prior or posterior, nothing greater or less, but all three persons are co-eternal and co-equal', so that 'Unity is to be worshipped in Trinity and Trinity in Unity'. Here is a concise statement of Augustinian doctrine, with its immense emphasis on

[1] *ib.* 15.7.
[2] *ib.* 15.43.
[3] *ib.* 5.6ff.
[4] *ib.* 2.2ff.
[5] *ib.* 1.7; 5.15; 15.47.
[6] *ib.* 15.46–47.
[7] Hahn, pp. 175–7.

the divine unity, on the relational nature of the distinctions of 'persons' and the consequent equality of the Father, Son and Spirit, and on the double procession of the Spirit. This last doctrine became characteristic of Western theology. It was formally affirmed in the profession of faith made by the Visigothic king Reccared and his bishops in their reception into Catholic orthodoxy from Arianism at the third council of Toledo in 589,[1] and from that time the *Filioque* clause ('proceeding from the Father *and the Son*') was added to the Nicene-Constantinopolitan Creed as used in Spain, where in accordance with an enactment of the same council it was introduced into the eucharistic liturgy. By the end of the eighth century the liturgical use of the Creed with this unecumenical addition had established itself in France and in the eleventh century it was finally adopted at Rome.

Later developments in Trinitarian theology in the East may be mentioned very briefly. Under the influence of the Christianized Neoplatonism of the sixth-century 'Dionysius the Areopagite' and Maximus the Confessor, his seventh-century commentator, the standard orthodoxy of the Greek world, as it was expounded by John of Damascus in the eighth century, laid great emphasis on the Neoplatonist principle that God is beyond all the positive attributes which may be conceived, and is beyond being itself. God's essence is unknowable, for it transcends all categories of affirmative theology; hence to speak of his essence is to say what God is not rather than what he is.[2] Within this general bracket, as it were, of 'negative theology' Trinitarian doctrine asserts the one-ness of the divine substance in three *hypostases* or *prosopa*, which are modes of the being of the one substance.[3] These modes are conceived as 'ingeneracy, generation and procession' or 'Fatherhood, Sonship and procession', so that the distinction of persons is a distinction of relations;[4] in no other respect is there any difference, and the three are inseparable, subsisting and operating within one another by a mutual interpenetration (*perichoresis*) yet without loss of relational distinctness.[5] At the same time John of Damascus continues to assert, in the Eastern tradition, that the Father is the fountainhead and cause of the Son and the Spirit,[6] and the Spirit proceeds from the Father as originator through the Son as co-operating intermediary[7] – though how 'procession' differs from 'generation' John, like all other theologians, admits that he cannot tell.[8]

[1] Hahn, p. 232; Mansi *Concilia*, vol. 9, p. 977.
[2] John of Damascus *fid. orth*, 1.4.
[3] *ib.* 1.8.
[4] *ib.*
[5] *ib.* 1.14.
[6] *ib.* 1.7–8; 2.12.
[7] *ib.* 1.12.
[8] *ib.* 1.8.

VIII

THE CHRISTOLOGICAL CONTROVERSIES

In this brief survey the problem of the relation between Trinitarian distinctions and the unity of God has been discussed for convenience's sake in isolation from the problem of the relation between deity and manhood in the person of Christ. In the actual development of Christian thought, however, these two problems were always interconnected. Christological speculation, which we traced in its relation to Trinitarian theology down to Athanasius, did not stand still while the later stages of the Trinitarian development were being worked out. On the contrary, the emergence of the Nicene position as the dominant theology brought the problem of Christology out into the open and introduced a century of vigorous Christological controversy which continued in the East for a further two hundred and thirty years and resulted in schisms between 'Orthodox' and 'Monophysite' Christians that have not yet been healed.

The Nicene faith rested ultimately on the soteriological convictions that it is through Christ that we are saved, and that salvation could not be effected by one who was less than God in the fullest possible sense of 'God'. As we have seen in considering the thought of Athanasius, that faith rested on the application to soteriology of the principle, accepted as an unexamined axiom, that what is received through participation, or as a gift, and is not possessed naturally as an inherent property cannot be passed on to others; it is sufficient for the recipient alone. Hence the conclusion was drawn that Christ cannot be the saviour of mankind unless he is consubstantial with God the Father in respect of deity, and that neither an Arian Logos nor a Macedonian Holy Spirit can give life or sanctify.

Yet, just because it grew out of soteriology, the Nicene faith in fact made the Christological problem insoluble. The Christ of the Alexandrian theologians is men's saviour because he is the consubstantial Logos who, being unchangeable (*atreptos*), is able to save because he cannot succumb to sin and death. His divine power overcomes the weakness and sin of humanity, and, himself remaining unchanged and impassible, he unites manhood to deity and raises it as an offering to the Father.[1] The Alexandrian Christology made it possible to affirm an incarnation of the Nicene Logos, but it did so at the cost of denying the full reality of that incarnation; the Logos of Athanasius and Cyril conquers temptation automatically. On the other side the Antiochene theologians also implicitly deny the full reality of the incarnation that they profess to preach, but for the opposite reason:

[1] Cf. Cyril *Heb.* (Migne *P.G.* 74.985–8).

namely, in order to safeguard the full reality of the saviour's humanity. By his participation in the actual and complete nature of the human race Christ, according to the Antiochenes, effects its salvation. In asserting this, however, they have to pay the necessary price of denying a real incarnation of the Nicene Logos by separating the 'assumed man' from the impassible 'God the Word'. Throughout the controversy the Christology of both sides was determined by soteriology, but a Christological impasse was unavoidable in the last resort so long as soteriology clung to both of its axiomatic assumptions: the impassibility of God and the hypostatic subsistence of the Nicene Logos as the consubstantial God the Son.

Christians generally were agreed that they wanted to affirm that 'in Christ God was reconciling the world to himself'; that Jesus Christ is the Logos incarnate, yet that he was moved by human emotions, was affected by human weakness, and if he was not actually subject to ignorance he at least spoke as though he were – as the Gospels indicated with embarrassing clarity; that he died, as the central affirmations of Christian faith proclaimed; that it is possible neither to affirm with naive monarchianism that God is passible, nor to deny with Arianism that the Logos is absolute God. All wanted to affirm that Christ's divine actions, such as miracles, and his human experiences, such as sorrow, suffering and death, were to be attributed to a single personal subject, the Logos incarnate. The problem was how these affirmations were to be made without contradiction and without reducing the force of any of them. The controversy was between those who sought a solution by ascribing the weaknesses and suffering, and the human experiences generally, to the man whom the Logos assumed and indwelt, and those who attempted to maintain that in some sense they are the human experiences of God the Logos, yet without predicating passibility of deity as such.

In addition to the conviction that only one who is personally and substantially God can be men's saviour, certain other deeply held beliefs and presuppositions were focal points in this controversy. They included the presuppositions of Hellenistic theology which caused the limitations and suffering of the incarnate Logos to be seen as humiliations, experiences which, far from revealing the nature of God, are alien to it and paradoxical; the determination to safeguard the absolute uniqueness of the Incarnation and at the same time to interpret man's salvation in terms of deification; and the growing 'realism' of eucharistic theology which, maintaining that the bread is ontologically the flesh of Christ, has to go on to assert either that if this flesh is not the actual flesh of the Logos himself it cannot be deifying, or that if this flesh is not consubstantial with our own human flesh it may be potentially deifying but cannot deify us.

Athanasius had attempted to maintain that the Logos was the subject of genuine human experiences without ceasing to be eternally the subject of divine activity. His Christology was carried further, indeed to extreme lengths with all its logical consequences drawn out, by Apollinarius, bishop of Laodicea, in teaching which began soon after the middle of the fourth century, became a matter of public discussion at Athanasius' council at Alexandria in 362, and a subject of acute controversy in the succeeding decade. His theory of the union of the divine and the human in Christ is apparently clear-cut and simple, as Christology can be when it approaches the problem from the divine side, as it were, and reasons from what is conceived to be the nature of the Logos who came down from heaven.

Apollinarius believed that Jesus Christ is, simply, the divine Logos. The eternal Son and the Jesus who walked in Galilee is (not 'are') one and the same unchanging person. Certainly, the figure described in the Gospels is a human figure; but the ruling principle which determines that figure's every thought, word and action is the Logos. It is his flesh which is human, and this flesh the Logos has appropriated to himself so as to make it the flesh of the Logos, the flesh of the unchanging divine person. It is united with the Logos in such a way as in no respect to alter, add to, or diminish the divine nature, though the assumption and appropriation of human flesh so as to make it actually his own involves a voluntary self-limitation in respect of the operation of the Logos in and through a body. There is no place in this union for a human soul, for this would imply a certain duality in the one person. This, in turn, means that the flesh is moved by the Logos and not by human reason and will; and since an essential characteristic of the human will is that it is variable and liable to move either with or against the will of God, Christ, possessing no human freedom of moral choice, is sinless in the sense of being by nature incapable of sinning. The flesh, Apollinarius points out, is not a complete living creature by itself, but is moved by some agency external to itself; Christ's flesh became appropriated by, and united to, the Logos as its own ruling principle, so that the experiences proper to it, such as suffering, became those of the Logos, while the divine activity proper to the Logos became that of the flesh. Here is the idea, which played a great role in later Christology, of the interchange of properties (*communicatio idiomatum*). It is, according to Apollinarius, a real interchange, possible because the flesh has become God's flesh, and so is now a living creature since it is united with the divine in such a way as to be one nature with it.[1] In a famous passage, later adopted by Cyril of Alexandria under the impression that it was the work of Athanasius (under whose name, together with those of Julius of Rome and Gregory Thaumaturgus of Cappadocia, much of Apollinarius' surviving work was preserved), he says that the same is Son of God and God according to the Spirit, and Son of Man according to the flesh (here using Rom. 1:3–4, a favourite text of the opposing, Antiochene tradition); but, he continues, the one Son is not two natures, one to be worshipped and one not, but 'one incarnate nature of God the Word, worshipped together with his flesh with one worship'. There are not two sons, the one being true God and worshipped as such, the other a man derived from Mary and not worshipped, but by grace made to be son of God in the sense in which men may become sons of God; but there is the one Son of God who is from God, and it is the same and not another who was born, according to the flesh, of Mary. He who was born of Mary was Son of God by nature, not by grace and participation, and was man only in respect of the flesh derived from Mary. According to the flesh he died, while remaining impassible and immutable in respect of his deity; he

[1] *fr.* 107 (Lietzmann, *Apollinaris von Laodicea und seine Schule*, p. 232).

ascended into heaven in so far as his flesh, the flesh of the Logos, was exalted, while being eternally omnipresent and uncircumscribed.[1]

The union of humanity and deity is comparable with that of soul and body in man; deity and flesh remain unconfused, but form one entity.[2] This means that just as a man is a single nature, so is Christ; hence it is possible to say that the Son of Man came down from heaven and that the Son of God was born of a woman.[3] There is a one-ness of nature (*henosis physike*) of flesh and Logos; there is 'one nature, one hypostasis, one operation, one person (*prosopon*), the same wholly God and wholly man'.[4] Christ's body is God's body, and not consubstantial with man's body if that implies that, like the latter, it is a 'body of death' needing to receive the gift of life; for in fact it is a 'body of life'.[5]

This last point is explained by Apollinarius as follows. The Incarnation means, not that Christ is man, but that he is 'as man' (cf. Phil. 2:8); hence, strictly speaking, he is not consubstantial with man.[6] On the other hand, in respect of his flesh alone he is consubstantial with man; or rather, his flesh is not consubstantial with God but with our flesh, for it did not come down from heaven but was assumed by the Logos who did come down from heaven.[7] In making this assertion Apollinarius is repudiating the suggestion of his opponents that he maintained that Christ's flesh was by origin divine ('from heaven'), a misunderstanding of the sense in which he affirmed that the flesh is the flesh of the divine Logos. It was not by nature that the flesh was divine, but by its union with the Logos[8] which makes it possible to say that Christ with his flesh is consubstantial with God and that the flesh, being the flesh of the one who is consubstantial with God, can be called God.[9] Apollinarius claims that he never wishes to affirm that the Saviour's flesh is from heaven, nor that the flesh as flesh is consubstantial with God, since as flesh it is not God, but inasmuch as it has been united with deity so as to be one *prosopon* it is God.[10] Hence, as he frequently reiterates, the flesh is worshipped inasmuch as it is one *prosopon* and one living being with the Logos.[11]

In a summary of his doctrine Apollinarius recognizes that Christ is both God and man; otherwise he would be no mediator between God and man, nor would he act sometimes in a divine way, as in saving the world, and sometimes in a human way, as in dying in order to save it. But a man 'energized' by God is not God: a body joined to God is God. Christ is God; he is therefore not a man energized by God but a body united with God. If what was born of Mary was a temple of God (Apollinarius here uses the analogy which was often employed by Athanasius as well as by Antiochene theologians), the

[1] *ep. Jov.* 1–2 (p. 251f.).
[2] *fr.* 129 (p. 239).
[3] *ep. Dion.* 1.4–5 (p. 258).
[4] *fr.* 148 (p. 247); *fid. et inc.* 6 (p. 198f.).
[5] *fr.* 116 (p. 235).
[6] *fr.* 45 (p. 214).
[7] *fr.* 163 (p. 255).
[8] *fr.* 160 (p. 254).
[9] *fr.* 153 (p. 248).
[10] *ep. Dion.* 2 (p. 262).
[11] *fr.* 85 (p. 225); cf. *un.* 2 (p. 186).

miracle of his virgin birth would be unnecessary, for men may be temples of God without any such birth. If Christ's nature were the same as ours his humanity would be the 'old man', a 'living soul' (I Cor. 15:45) and not a 'life-giving spirit'. But Christ gives life and is life-giving spirit; therefore he does not share our nature.[1] This last point is of great importance for Apollinarius' idea of man's need for a wholly divine saviour, and for the soteriological arguments which were soon advanced against his Christology. It is connected with the belief that there can be no place for a human rational soul in Christ, and hence no mutable will. If Christ is, simply, God incarnate, his flesh is directly and absolutely controlled by God and unassailable by the passions which belong to human beings.[2] In the view of Apollinarius the divine operation supplies the place of the human soul and mind. There cannot be two intellectual and volitional principles co-existing in Christ, for if there were then at least in theory there could be conflict between them. The Logos, then, did not assume a soul, but simply a body which, as the temple of the Logos, was foreshadowed by Solomon's temple which lacked soul, mind and will.[3] The language which he uses here corresponds to that which the Council of Alexandria repudiated, and may point to the likelihood that Athanasius was prepared in 362 to acknowledge a human rational soul in Christ even though the concept had been alien to his own Christology and continued to play no positive part in it. What had tended to be an unexamined assumption of both Athanasius and Arius had now been brought out into the open by Apollinarius and made a basic theological principle. If the Logos did not indwell Christ as a holy man, in the way in which he dwelt in the prophets, then, according to Apollinarius, he became flesh, not assuming a human rational mind which would be mutable and liable to be led captive by evil thoughts, but a mind that was divine, heavenly and immutable.[4] For Apollinarius to say that the Logos 'assumed' a heavenly mind is odd; for the Logos, according to him, *is* that mind[5] or takes the place of a mind. He is, in fact, at this point trying to explain, or explain away, the language of the Council of Alexandria and probably finding it difficult to harmonize it with his own Christology.[6]

From all this it follows that Christ's flesh is the source of divinization to those who partake of it; it is saving and life-giving because deity belongs inherently and essentially to it.[7] It was, however, precisely in respect of its soteriological weakness that the teaching of Apollinarius was most vigorously attacked. Origen had pointed out long ago that if the Logos did not assume complete manhood the whole man is not saved.[8] The same point was driven home by the Cappadocians, especially in the Irenaean argument used by Gregory Nazianzen that Christ would not be the new Adam unless he assumed Adam's nature in its completeness (an answer to Apollinarius' fear

[1] *anac.* 17–24 (pp. 244–245).
[2] *kata meros pistis* 30 (p. 178).
[3] *fr.* 2 (p. 204).
[4] *ep. Diocaes.* 2. (p. 256).
[5] *fr.* 155 (p. 249).
[6] See above, p. 109.
[7] *fr.* 155 (p. 249); *fr.* 116 (p. 235).
[8] Or. *dial.* p. 136.

that if Christ's nature were not different from ours he would be merely the 'old man'),[1] and in his well-known phrase, 'What has not been assumed remains unhealed'.[2] Indeed, it was of supreme importance that the human rational soul should have been assumed, for this is the seat of sin and the original agent of Adam's disobedience.[3] Didymus makes the same point, that Christ's soul is effective in the salvation of our soul just*as his body, *homoousion* with ours, is in the salvation of the body.[4] Belief in salvation through Christ requires the recognition that God united to himself a human soul capable of sinning; otherwise, that is, if, as Apollinarius thought, Christ was different in essence from men in respect of the most important element in the human make-up, the humanity of Christ would be reduced to the animal level.[5] Gregory of Nyssa, who makes this last point, goes on to claim that Apollinarius is worse than Arius: Arius lowered the nature of the uncreated Son to the level of the created angels; Apollinarius reduces Christ to the level of the fleshly. Here Gregory is being unfair; Apollinarius would reply that he was exalting fleshly nature to the divine level, not degrading God to the level of flesh. Gregory himself, however, wants to say the same thing, in different language: there is a 'mixture' of God with human nature, which is like the sun shining in darkness and dissolving it; God has taken our nature with its pollution and is not himself defiled by this but cleanses it.[6] The really important principle for soteriology, according to Gregory, is that in Christ there should be genuine freedom of the will,[7] and that salvation should have been brought to man's soul through the union of the human soul with deity in Christ.[8]

In his positive and non-polemical teaching, Gregory of Nyssa seeks to return to the historical evidence of the Gospels as the real ground for the belief that in Christ deity is 'mixed with' manhood. The manner of the Incarnation is an impenetrable mystery, like the 'how' of Creation; but the Gospels show that Christ both experienced the limitations proper to man and also transcended them and acted, within his human existence, with divine power.[9] This power was conjoined with love, in such a way that it was precisely in the humiliation of the incarnate life that it was most wonderfully manifested. Gregory has here, in his hands as it were, the material for constructing a much more satisfactory Christology than the aridly metaphysical arguments about the union of two real and actual universals, deity and humanity, in a single *prosopon*. Unfortunately he does not develop the thought that divine power is a power of love and that it is most fully demonstrated in self-giving. Rather, he works out the thought that the deity was concealed under a veil of manhood so as to deceive the devil and induce him to accept the humanity as a ransom for sinners and thus to find

[1] Gr. Naz. *or.* 30.5.
[2] *ep.* 101.7.
[3] *ib.* 101.11.
[4] Didym. *Ps.* 70:23.
[5] Gr. Nyss. *Apoll.* 23.
[6] *ib.* 26.
[7] *ib.* 45.
[8] *ib.* 55.
[9] *or. catech.* 11–13.

himself caught, in the act of snatching a prey to which he had no right, on the fish-hook of deity.[1] It should, however, be added in fairness that Gregory dwells more fully on other aspects of Christ's saving work, especially the healing and cleansing of man's disease and corruption,[2] and that the deception of the devil is itself remedial since in the end the devil, too, will be brought within the scope of the purifying and saving efficacy of the Incarnation.[3] Gregory also lays emphasis on the fact that the presence of deity in human nature through the Incarnation is different, indeed, in mode, but nevertheless parallel to, its continual immanent presence in all things. God is 'mingled' with us inasmuch as he contains and sustains the entire natural order in himself; in the Incarnation he was 'mixed' with our nature in order that by this mixture with the divine it might be deified. Thus the union of God and man in Christ is related to the indwelling of the divine in everything, clothing itself with it and embracing it, and Christology is harmonized with Neoplatonist thought concerning the world soul.[4] Gregory is anxious to safeguard the distinction of the divine and human natures. Each operates in its own sphere: human nature did not bring Lazarus to life, nor did the 'impassible power' weep for him. Yet because of the union of the natures both sets of experiences were common to each and can be predicated of either.[5] For Gregory's basic concern with soteriology it is essential to affirm both the completeness and the distinctness of Christ's manhood and the absolute indivisibility of its union with God by which humanity is exalted and deified.

Gregory of Nazianzus lays similar stress on the wholeness of the natures and their indissoluble union. The Logos forms for himself a complete mortal nature, an equivalent exchange for the whole man, Adam, who had died; the divine cannot directly unite with flesh, and the human soul and mind, as the image of God, constitutes an intermediary link through which, as being akin to itself, deity can consort with flesh so that what deifies and what is deified can become one God.[6] This interesting revival of Origen's speculations about the mediating role of the human soul in Christ was not developed further by Gregory. Although the assumption by the Logos of complete manhood is important in his anti-Apollinarian argument, he does not pursue its implications in his own Christology. For the most part he is content to affirm that the Logos is united inseparably with 'the man' whom he assumed for our salvation, so that Christ is at once passible in flesh and impassible in deity, earthly and heavenly, comprehensible and incomprehensible. By this union, one and the same person being complete man and God, the whole man who fell under sin is re-created.[7] Gregory recognizes two natures, God and man; but there are not two Sons or two Gods any more than the duality of a man's soul and body implies that there are two men. The natures are distinct: they are 'one thing and another thing'; but

---

[1] *ib.* 21–24.
[2] See below, p. 151.
[3] *or. catech.* 24–29.
[4] *ib.* 24.
[5] *Eun.* 5 (*PG*, 45.705).
[6] Gr. Naz. *carm.* 1.10.54–61.
[7] *ep.* 101.

there are not two distinct persons ('one personal entity and another personal entity').[1]

The union is 'substantial' ('according to *ousia*'). Hence, to deny that Mary is 'God-bearer' (*theotokos*) is to deny Christ's divinity.[2] This title was intended to express a Christological rather than a Mariological truth. It was meant to assert that, although deity as such is impassible, the humanity which was properly the subject of the experience of human birth was totally appropriated by deity; Mary was not, therefore, the mother of a man indwelt by God, but of one who was personally and essentially God. It had been used, with no controversial intention, by Origen,[3] and by the pre-Nicene bishops of Alexandria, Peter and Alexander.[4] It appears in the Greek text of Hippolytus' treatise on the *Blessing of Jacob*,[5] but is probably a later interpolation there. Eusebius used it frequently, as did Apollinarius and the Cappadocians. In the Nestorian controversy it was to become a focal point and touchstone of Christology.

Apollinarianism was rejected by a council held under Damasus, bishop of Rome, in 377 and subsequent councils in the East. The Cappadocians had tried to maintain a Christology on the Alexandrian lines without excluding the human soul from the humanity assumed by the Logos, but the real alternative to the basic assumptions on which Apollinarius had proceeded towards his extreme solution of the problem was provided by the Antiochene theologians who, in reaction against Apollinarianism, developed elements in the old tradition which had been exemplified by Eustathius.

This reply to the Alexandrian Christology found expression in the work of Diodore, bishop of Tarsus, and his pupil, Theodore of Mopsuestia. Of the former's writings (he died in about 394) little remains. It is clear, however, that he reacted sharply against the idea of deity and humanity being combined in one hypostasis.[6] This would suggest to him that God and man were conflated so as to be neither one nor the other. Accordingly, he drew so clear-cut a distinction between the divine and the human in Christ that it tended to suggest a virtual separation of the two. Thus he interpreted the saying of Christ about blasphemy against the Son of Man on the one hand and against the Holy Spirit on the other as stating a contrast between blasphemy against the man (Jesus) and blasphemy against the deity who dwelt in the man as in a temple.[7] The one is the son of David, the other the Son of God.[8] In a similar fashion Diodore interprets Matt. 22:41ff. to mean that Christ as man is David's son, whereas Christ as the Logos is David's Lord. On the other hand, because David's son is the temple of God the Logos, the title 'Lord', which belongs by nature to the Logos, is bestowed on David's son by grace. 'The one born of Mary is by nature David's son,

---

[1] *ib.*

[2] *ib.* cf. *or.* 43.38.

[3] *sel. in Dt.* 22:23; *hom. 7 in Lc.*

[4] Peter of Alexandria, *fr.* (*PG.* 18.517); Alexander, *ep. Alex.* 12.

[5] Hipp. *ben. Jac.* 1.

[6] Brière, *Rev. de l'Orient chrétien* 30 (1946), *fr.* 26.

[7] Abramowski, *ZNTW.* 42 (1949), *fr.* 20.

[8] *ib. fr.* 42.

but by grace the son of God'.[1] Hence, although Diodore holds that the 'one worship' on which Apollinarius laid so much emphasis implies blasphemy, since it presupposes that humanity and deity are one and the same in essence, he allows that 'we worship the temple because of the one who dwells in it'.[2] Thus in Diodore's Christology the *communicatio idiomatum* is an interchange of honour, grace and worship, not of nature. The difficult question for this type of Christology is to define the uniqueness of the Incarnation. Diodore's answer is that in Christ, unlike the prophets, the indwelling of the Logos was complete and permanent.[3]

Diodore's terminology can at first sight give a misleading impression of his typically Antiochene attempt to start from the basic assumption of the duality of deity and manhood in Christ and to work towards a personal unity of the divine Son with the 'assumed man'. This is because in speaking of the human nature his usage varies between 'man' and 'flesh'. Indeed, 'flesh' is his more usual term for Christ's humanity. The fact that he can equate 'the flesh' with 'the man born of Mary', ascribe the cry of dereliction on the Cross to the 'flesh', and state, in expounding Luke 2:52, that 'the flesh' increased in wisdom through the gradual impartation of wisdom to it by the Logos, shows clearly that he intends 'flesh' to be synonymous with 'man'.[4] Theodore of Mopsuestia, it may be observed, points out the comprehensive range of meaning which 'flesh' can carry in the letters of Paul.[5]

A more impressive exposition of this line of thought was furnished by Theodore of Mopsuestia, enough of whose work survives to enable his polemical theology to be compared with his biblical commentaries and, in his *Catechetical Homilies*, his explanation of the Faith to candidates for baptism. He offers a radically different alternative to Apollinarianism. Whereas the Cappadocians had been content, on the whole, to point out the soteriological weakness involved in the denial of a rational soul in Christ, Theodore challenges the soteriological foundation of the whole Alexandrian theology. This was the principle that only the divine can deify, and therefore the flesh of Christ must be divine flesh: the flesh of God. Theodore substitutes a different principle: salvation is through participation in the humanity of Christ, which, it is essential to believe, was the same as our manhood and not, therefore, a human nature which, whether or not it be formally acknowledged as possessing a rational soul, was naturally and necessarily controlled and motivated by the Logos. This humanity of Christ was joined to deity and it is thereby glorified and deified, but it was the assumed and glorified human soul which was the scene of the defeat of the devil and the victory over sin. The idea of a genuinely human victory is central to Theodore's Christology, and the soul of Christ is thus for him not merely a theological construction but a religious concept of primary importance. This means that he cannot ascribe the actions of Christ simply and directly to the Logos; the saving work of Christ in self-giving and in the

[1] Brière, *frr.* 21, 3, 30.
[2] Sev. Ant. *orat.* 3.25.
[3] Abramowski *fr.* 35ff.
[4] Brière *frr.* 12, 36ff.
[5] Thdr. Mops. *Rom.* 7:5.

conquest of temptation is, throughout, an act of the human will. Hence Theodore thinks of the union of deity and humanity as a moral union consisting of total harmony of will, a union of mutual love, of the response of the human soul to the 'good pleasure' or 'favour' of God. The union is so complete that there is one person of Christ, not two. The one person, furthermore, is the person, or concrete presentation as an individual entity, of the conjoined divine and human natures. It is not, as in Alexandrian Christology, the one person of the Logos which has, in addition to its own 'natural' divine nature, assumed a human nature which has no person or hypostasis of its own, but is, simply, the human nature of the divine person.

In his *Catechetical Homilies* Theodore declares that it was not merely a human body that was assumed, but a complete man of body and soul.[1] It is the limitations of the human soul which bring about the weaknesses of human physical life; the flesh of God, according to the Apollinarian understanding of this, would not suffer weakness or defects, for these are not inherent in flesh as such. Hence God, the Logos, cannot be to Christ's flesh what the rational soul is to the flesh of ordinary men. If that were so, Christ either did not suffer the 'fleshy' weaknesses which the Gospels tell us he suffered, or he pretended or appeared to do so.[2] If, however, the human soul was the direct controlling principle of the human flesh, then the problem had to be faced concerning the natural liability of the human soul to sin. Apollinarius had secured the absolute immutability of Christ's will by postulating as the seat of his will the Logos and not a rational soul. Theodore is equally clear that Christ was totally sinless, but he ascribes this to divine grace operating on the human soul and making it in fact immutable.[3]

Theodore naturally shows no hesitation in speaking of the humanity of Christ as the 'man assumed'.[4] He can therefore answer the crucial question, whether Mary is 'man-bearer' (*anthropotokos*) or 'God-bearer' (*theotokos*), with the reply: 'both'. She is the former by nature and the latter by relation: that is, she is 'man-bearer' inasmuch as he who was born of her was man, and 'God-bearer' inasmuch as God was in the man who was born, not naturally (so as to be circumscribed) but according to the voluntarily assumed relationship. The question whether God or a man was crucified is answered along the same lines.[5] So, too, with the embarrassing text, Lk. 2:52: there was a genuine advance of Jesus in wisdom as well as in stature, to a greater degree than was possible for any other men, because the Logos, foreseeing his future excellence, united himself with him from his conception and co-operated with his progress.[6] This indwelling is illustrated, as we should expect, by the old simile of the temple.[7] It is not an indwelling 'according to substance' (*ousia*), for this would mean either that God's indwelling in Christ was no more than an instance of his universal presence,

[1] *catech.* 5.19.
[2] *ib.* 5.9ff.
[3] *ib.* 5.19.
[4] *catech.* 8.5, 13; *inc.* 7, 15.
[5] *inc.* 15.
[6] *ib.* 7.
[7] e.g., *catech.* 8.5.

or else that God's substantial presence was circumscribed and localized in Jesus Christ. Nor is it only an indwelling 'according to good pleasure' (*eudokia*), the good will of God towards those who respond to his graciousness. This is the mode in which God dwells in the saints. But in the case of Christ it is indwelling 'as in a Son'. This means that it involves a union of the whole assumed man with the Logos, a preparation of the man by the Logos for full participation in the sonship which belongs to the Logos by nature, and a completeness and permanence of union which affects a single concrete presentation (*prosopon*) of the two who have been so united.[1] For, although Theodore says that the form of God, the one who assumes, is God, while the form of a servant, the one who is assumed, is man,[2] and distinguishes the 'true' Son who is Son by nature from the one who truly shares in the same Sonship by union with him, he disallows any talk of two Sons. One Son alone is to be acknowledged, and both the distinction of the natures and the unity of the *prosopon* are to be safeguarded.[3] There must be neither confusion of natures nor division of the person.[4] Just as a man and his wife are said to be one flesh, so we might say that 'they are no longer two *prosopa* but one', not thereby saying anything detrimental to the duality of the divine and human natures, each in itself perfect; each nature has in itself its own concrete subsistence and is an hypostasis, an entity with its own individual external presentation (*prosopon*); but there is one external presentation (*prosopon*) of the two conjoined.[5]

Much in Theodore's Christology represents an advance towards a more satisfactory theory. It has the great merit of ascribing genuine soteriological significance to Christ's manhood and of avoiding the Alexandrian necessity of explaining away much, including some of the most central and vitally important elements, in the Gospel narratives. It could not fail, however, to be condemned by theologians of the opposing school as deficient in respect of the unity of Christ's person, and so also of the uniqueness of the Incarnation. Theodore's biblical exegesis certainly lent colour to the charge of dividing the unity, for if the Alexandrians had difficulty in making the Logos the sole and unique subject of all that Christ experienced, Theodore found himself in the awkward situation of having to attribute some experiences and some words of Christ to the Logos and others to the 'assumed man'. To Alexandrians a union 'according to good pleasure' was not enough to differentiate Jesus from a prophet or saint – though the fact that Theodore liked to speak of the union as a 'conjunction' (*synapheia*) could not properly be held against him (as it often has been) on the ground that it denotes a loose association rather than a union; on the contrary, Apollinarius uses the term himself (it can signify any degree of unity from association to fusion), while Theodore is perfectly content to make almost equal use of what has wrongly been regarded as the stronger term *henosis*.

The controversy did not come to a head until the Antiochene theologian,

[1] *inc.* 7.
[2] *catech.* 8.13.
[3] *inc.* 12.
[4] *ib.* 5.
[5] *ib.* 8.

Nestorius, had succeeded to the patriarchate of Constantinople in 428, the year of Theodore's death. It did so, not because the views of Nestorius differed in any significant respect from those of Theodore but because his ecclesiastical position gave them mass publicity and enabled his formidable opponent, Cyril, patriarch of Alexandria, to pursue his political aim of hounding Nestorius out of his see by denouncing him as a heretic. Cyril's theological opposition to the Antiochene Christology was genuine; it is clearly expressed in biblical commentaries written before the controversy with Nestorius broke out. His refusal to make the slightest concession to Nestorius' point of view or to try to understand what Nestorius wanted to say was motivated by inter-patriarchal rivalry rather than theological concern. His success in reaching agreement with the Antiochene leaders, once Nestorius had been removed, on a basis of mutual explanation and willingness to listen, is sufficient evidence of this.

Like Theodore, Nestorius emphasized most clearly the distinction between the deity and the manhood. The Son of David and the Son of God are two distinct natures; and for Nestorius 'nature' (*physis*) stands for an objective reality with, of necessity, its own concrete presentation *ad extra*, its *prosopon*. This point, on which he does not differ from Theodore although he labours it much more, is made clear in his long defence of his position, the *Book of Heracleides*.[1] Hence he explains that it was not God as such who was born or was buried in the grave, but since God was in the one who was assumed, the one assumed may be called God by virtue of his union with God who assumed him.[2] The Logos, says Nestorius, was God, united with man and dwelling in him; and he tries to support this with a far-fetched exegesis of Mt. 2:13: the angel told Joseph to take the 'child' and his mother, not the 'God' and his mother.[3] In his view the Nicene creed indicates the duality of natures. It expresses belief in 'one Lord Jesus Christ'; 'Christ' signifies both natures, and the creed, by not saying 'We believe in one God the Word', safeguards the orthodox against the idea that the subject of the credal affirmations that he was crucified and buried is the deity.[4] Any failure to maintain this duality, he believed, led to the mutable Logos of Arianism or the incompletely human Christ of Apollinarius. It also meant the denial of the truth concerning redemption, through failure to acknowledge that it was as authentic man that Christ experienced temptation and suffering and won the victory.[5]

His fear of confusing the natures led Nestorius, like Theodore, to be very reluctant to allow Mary to be called *theotokos*. In his case, however, the protest was public and brusquely controversial, his follower Dorotheus of Marcianopolis anathematizing, in a service at which Nestorius was seated on his episcopal throne, any who used this term which was evidently becoming dear to popular piety, and Anastasius, a priest whom Nestorius had brought with him from Antioch, preaching against the practice on the

---

[1] Nest. *Heracl.* 304, 442. On the interpolations in this work see L. Abramowski, *Untersuchungen zum Liber Heraclidis* (Louvain, 1963).

[2] *fr.* C. 9 (Loofs, *Nestoriana*).

[3] *fr.* C. 11.

[4] *fr.* C. 17.

[5] *Heracl.* 132ff.

ground that Mary was a human being, and God cannot be born of a human being.[1] Nestorius held that the term contradicted the 'without mother' of Heb. 7:3; Mary did not bear deity, for 'that which is born of the flesh is flesh', nor did a creature bear the uncreate or the creator; Mary bore a man who was the instrument of deity.[2] If Mary is truly the mother, then the offspring is manhood, not deity (for no mother can bear what is not consubstantial with herself); if what was born was God the Word and not a human nature then Mary was not his mother.[3] Nestorius would prefer to call Mary the 'God-receiver' (*theodochos*), reserving the description 'God-bearer' for the Father in respect of the generation of the Logos.[4] He would, alternatively, approve of 'Christ-bearer' (*Christotokos*), since 'Christ' designates the union of the two natures;[5] and he would even be willing to concede the use of *theotokos* (which does in fact occur in the second of three homilies on the Temptations ascribed to him) on the understanding that it does not signify that deity was born of Mary but that the union of manhood with deity from the moment of Christ's conception makes this title permissible by the 'interchange of properties'.[6] In any other sense than this, *theotokos* is heretical, recalling the errors of Arius, Eunomius and Apollinarius,[7] and leaves the Christian bereft of argument against pagan 'mothers of gods'.[8] Nestorius also observes that the Nicene creed said nothing about Mary as 'God-bearer'.[9]

Nestorius is as emphatic as Theodore that there is a true union of the two natures. If the human were not conjoined with the Logos, Christianity would be a cult of a human being. As it is, however, 'we maintain the conjunction of natures without confusion; we acknowledge God in man, we reverence the man who, by reason of the conjunction with God is the object of joint adoration with God Almighty'.[10] Christ is not mere man, but man and God together; hence, Nestorius says, 'I separate the natures but I unite the worship'.[11] There are not two Sons; the Logos was Son by nature from eternity, and the 'form of a servant' receives the status of Son by being assumed by the Logos.[12] There are not, therefore, two persons but one who is, in respect of nature and not of status, twofold.[13] The error of Paul of Samosata is to be repudiated, for he denied the complete and permanent ontic unity of Christ's humanity with God.[14] This union is not hypostatic or 'natural', but voluntary and personal. It is a union in one *prosopon*, for there is one concrete external presentation of the natures that are thus

[1] Cyr. *ep.* 11; Socr. *h.e.* 7.32.
[2] Nest. *fr.* C. 9.
[3] *fr.* C. 8.
[4] *fr.* C. 10.
[5] *fr.* A. 6; C. 10.
[6] *fr.* A. 7; cf. *hom. in Matt.* 4:6 (Nau, *Nestorius, Livre d'Héraclide*, p. 345).
[7] *ib.*; *fr.* C. 10.
[8] *fr.* C. 9.
[9] *fr.* A. 1.
[10] *fr.* C. 8.
[11] *fr.* C. 9.
[12] *fr.* C. 10.
[13] *fr.* C. 12.
[14] *fr.* C. 18; *Heracl.* 67ff.

united, and this is Christ. The *prosopon* of deity conjoined with manhood is Christ; so that, although the *prosopon* of each nature remains separate from the other, there is, as it were, an over-arching *prosopon* (the concrete reality of Christ) which embraces both.[1] Within the *prosopon* of union there is an interchange of properties (*communicatio idiomatum*) in the sense that the properties of either nature can equally be predicated of Christ, the single external presentation of the two.[2] This interchange is involved in the 'unifying of the worship' on which Nestorius laid such emphasis; it does not imply that there is an actual exchange of attributes between deity and manhood.

Cyril represents the opposite side of the Christological dispute. One might imagine Cyril and Nestorius contemplating the Christmas scene. Neither wishes to withold worship from the Christ-child: on the contrary, both reverence him as Son of God. Nestorius, however, insists that in doing this he must at the same time repudiate any idea that God has been born as a baby and that God is in a cradle: as he actually put it, 'I deny that God is two months or three months old'.[3] On the other hand, Cyril insists equally strongly that the baby in the cradle is God. By this, Cyril means that the one being, the person of the eternal Logos, is the subject of the human experience. It is as incarnate, or in human nature, that the Logos is born, suffers and undergoes the weaknesses of human life; but it is the same Logos who was previously discarnate, and none other, who experiences humanly. Cyril thus maintains the tradition of Athanasius and other Alexandrian theologians. The union of deity and humanity is a union in the person of the Logos and not in Nestorius' 'Christ' who is the *prosopon* of the assumed-man-conjoined-to-the-Logos. The latter theory seemed to Cyril to mean that Christ is an inspired man, not truly God but a man united to God and given divine status.[4]

Cyril's basic principle of Christology is summed up in the Apollinarian phrase which he adopted, believing it to be Athanasian: 'one incarnate nature of God the Word'.[5] By 'nature' (*physis*) Cyril means virtually the same as 'hypostasis'; there is one individual entity who became incarnate, and this is the Logos. Cyril does not follow Appollinarius in denying the completeness of the humanity; the Logos united to himself hypostatically flesh 'ensouled with a rational soul'.[6] The soteriological objection to Apollinarianism had settled this question. Cyril wants, rather, to affirm the belief which Apollinarius aimed at expressing, that the subject of the human experience is none other than the eternal Logos. He wants to do this without denying the completeness of the manhood and yet at the same time without opening the door in the slightest degree to the idea that the Incarnation means the indwelling of a man by the Logos. He does it by denying that the humanity, which is complete, has any independent existence. It is not a mere abstraction. On the contrary, it is a real (Platonic) universal, so that

[1] *Heracl.* 212, 219.
[2] *ib.* 289, 331, 343.
[3] Cyr. *ep.* 23.
[4] *adv. Nest.* proem.
[5] *ib.*; *ep.* 40.
[6] *ep. Nest.* 1; *adv. Nest.* 2 proem.

on the lines of Cyril's Christology it is right to say that Christ is 'man' but not 'a man', and that the humanity is 'impersonal' in the sense that it has no concrete subsistence of its own, but is hypostatized in the hypostasis of the Logos. After the 'hypostatic' or 'natural' union there is, as there has always been from eternity, the Logos who is by nature God; there is no one other than the self-same divine Logos who is now also by nature man. The human nature subsists only in the hypostasis of the divine Logos; it has no hypostatic existence by itself.[1] The Logos was and is always in 'the form of God', but over and above this he took the 'form of a servant' which he did not previously possess.[2] This is why Cyril finds the name 'Emmanuel' peculiarly significant for Christology and constantly uses it in order to show that the historical figure of the Gospels is none other than 'God with us'. Mary is therefore 'God-bearer' because the humanity born of her is humanity hypostatically united with deity from conception; and the Antiochenes are wrong in worshipping the manhood along with the deity: there is but one undivided worship of Emmanuel.[3] There is, too, an actual, and not merely conceptual, interchange of properties, the flesh receiving the glory of the Logos and the Logos making the experiences of the flesh his own.[4] This principle was obviously important for Cyril's soteriology. The work of Christ must be the work of God incarnate,[5] and the flesh of Christ must be flesh which God has made his own, or, rather, it must actually be God's flesh, to which the life-giving energy of God has been imparted like coals energized by fire. Otherwise, says Cyril, the eucharistic body would be a man's and not God's, and (reversing Nestorius' contention that Christ spoke of eating the flesh of the Son of Man, not of God) those who supposed Christ to be talking about the literal and cannibalistic eating of a man's flesh would have been right.[6]

Cyril does not deny the duality of the divine and the human. Christ is 'from two', and the two are distinct 'objects'.[7] In the union the two are neither confused nor changed,[8] but the union, so far from being a conjunction 'according to good pleasure', is like the union of soul and body in man or the union of fire and coal in a red-hot lump.[9] The distinction of natures is thus always theoretical, for they are in fact indivisible, though Cyril comes close to making an exception to this at the crucial point of the suffering of Christ. The Logos, he says, 'suffered impassibly', or 'was impassible in the suffering body'.[10] On the analogy of the fire and coal it could be said that the fire is not itself affected if the red-hot coal is poked, even though the constituent elements in the lump are only theoretically distinguishable. On the analogy of soul and body it could be said that the

[1] *apol. Thdt. (PG. 76.401); ep. Nest.* 3.
[2] *adv. Nest.* 5.2.
[3] *ib.* 2.10.
[4] *inc. unigen. (PG. 75.1241).*
[5] *adv. Nest.* 3.2; 4.4.
[6] *ib.* 4.5.
[7] *ep.* 45; *apol. Thdt. (PG. 76.396).*
[8] *ep.* 45, 46; *quod un. Chr. (PG. 75. 1292).*
[9] *adv. Nest.* 2 proem.; *schol. inc.* 9; *ep.* 46.
[10] *ep.* 45; *adv. Nest.* 5.4.

former is not directly affected in itself by a physical blow. But the weakness of the Christological tradition of Athanasius, and Alexandria generally, becomes apparent again in Cyril at this point; the presuppositions, that the subject of the Gospel record is the Logos and that deity is impassible, can be reconciled only by ascribing suffering exclusively to the flesh. Hence Cyril's treatment of Gethsemane and the Temptations is inadequate.

Cyril established his case against Nestorius by letters which secured the support of Celestine, bishop of Rome, and treatises which gained him the backing of Theodosius II and the imperial family. After a synod at Rome at which Celestine condemned the teaching of Nestorius, Cyril sent his third letter to Nestorius containing anathemas which he was to accept. These assert Cyril's doctrine in its most polemical form. Mary is God-bearer because she bore in a fleshly manner the Word of God made flesh. The Logos was united with flesh hypostatically, and with his flesh is one Christ, the same God and man. After the union the hypostases (for Cyril, as was stated above, the terms hypostasis and nature are virtually synonymous and interchangeable) are not to be divided on the supposition that there is a conjunction between them in respect of status or authority or power and not, rather, a coming together in a natural union. The statements made about Christ in Scripture are not to be apportioned between two persons (*prosopa*) or hypostases and assigned to a man conceived of apart from the Logos, or *vice versa*, respectively. There is no question of Christ being an inspired man and not truly God the Logos who is Son by nature and who became flesh; nor is the Logos the God or master of Christ, but rather one and the same who is God and man. Nor, again, is Jesus a man energized by the Word and thereby glorified, as though he were distinct from the Logos. The joint worship of the 'assumed man' with the Logos is condemned, as is the idea that Christ was glorified and empowered by the Spirit as by a power which was alien to himself and not his own Spirit; and it is the Logos incarnate who is our high priest, and not a man separate from the Logos, his sacrifice being entirely for our sake and not for himself. So, too, his flesh is life-giving as being the flesh of the Logos who gives life universally. The last of the twelve anathemas condemns any denial that the Logos suffered in flesh and rose from the dead as being himself life and, as God, life-giving.[1]

This was the Christology endorsed by the Council of Ephesus of 431, the Third Ecumenical Council, although the anathemas themselves, which were read to the council, did not receive, like Cyril's second letter to Nestorius, formal recognition as an authoritative document of the Faith. This assembly, which condemned Nestorius in his absence, was a small body of Cyril's supporters and the representatives of Celestine of Rome. The bishops of the Antiochene party, led by John of Antioch, arrived late and held a separate council which repudiated the anathemas and ineffectively deposed Cyril. The views of this group are best represented by the writings of Theodoret, bishop of Cyrrhus, against whose attack upon his position Cyril wrote an extended defence of the anathemas. Theodoret follows the traditional Antiochene line of thought. He strongly emphasizes the distinction of the natures, the one which assumed and the other which was

[1] *ep. Nest.* 3.

assumed, and objects to the confusion between them suggested by Cyril's theory of a real interchange of properties.[1] He preferred to call Mary both 'man-bearer' and 'God-bearer', not employing the one term without the other, but he was prepared to accept the latter title in the sense, not that God was born in his own nature but that Mary bore the man who was united to God who created him.[2] Theodoret wished, too, for the sake of soteriology, to lay stress on the human activity of the assumed man.[3] He followed the Antiochene tradition in seeking to safeguard the voluntary character of the union and to understand it in terms of divine initiative and human response, and hence he found difficulty in Cyril's 'hypostatic' and 'natural' union.[4] On the other hand, he strongly asserted the union of the natures in a single *prosopon*, which he came to identify with hypostasis and to envisage as the actual concrete being, the Logos, rather than, in Nestorius' manner, as a *prosopon* of united *prosopa*.[5]

Theodoret's view was expressed in an official letter, which he probably composed, from John of Antioch's council at Ephesus to the emperor in August, 431. This states that Christ is perfect God and perfect man, of rational soul and body, begotten before the ages in respect of deity and the same born of Mary in respect of manhood, consubstantial with the Father in respect of deity and consubstantial with us in respect of manhood. 'For a union of two natures took place; wherefore we acknowledge one Christ, one Son, one Lord. According to this conception of the unconfused union we acknowledge the Holy Virgin as God-bearer, because God the Word became flesh and was made man and from his actual conception united with himself the temple which he took from her.' The New Testament statements about Christ may be applied either indiscriminately to the one person (*prosopon*) or else separately to the divinity and humanity respectively in view of the duality of natures.

After Cyril, in a letter to Acacius, bishop of Beroea, had somewhat modified his more extreme statements, at least to the extent of explaining that he intended no confusion of deity and humanity,[6] this Antiochene document became in substance the basis of agreement between Cyril and the party of John of Antioch and Theodoret. This had become possible through the deposition and subsequent exile of Nestorius, and through Cyril's willingness, once that objective had been gained, to explain his position and interpret the substance of the anathemas less offensively. Accepted by Cyril and John in correspondence between each other,[7] this document is generally known as the Formula of Union of 433. It marks a great step forward in the long controversy. Terminology was improved, and the precision given to 'person' and 'nature' helped to dispel the apprehensions caused by Cyril's formula of 'one nature incarnate'. The duality of natures was maintained, but it was balanced by strong emphasis

---

[1] *Thdt. eran.* 2; *reprehens. anath.* 4.
[2] *ep.* 151; *inc.* 35; Cyr. *apol. Thdt.* 1.
[3] *inc.* 20.
[4] *reprehens. anath.* 3.
[5] *eran.* 3; *ep.* 145.
[6] Cyr. *ep.* 33.
[7] Cyr. *epp.* 38, 39 (Hahn, p. 215).

on the fact that it was 'the same' eternal Logos who was born of Mary. Thus the chief tenets of Antioch (the distinctness of deity and humanity) and Alexandria (the Logos as the personal subject of the human experience) were alike secured. The term *theotokos* was formally approved, in a sense in which it would create no difficulty for Antiochene Christology. The double *homoousion* anticipated the definition of Chalcedon.

The formula of 433 and the reaction to it offer in fact a preview of what was to happen at Chalcedon and afterwards. Like the definition of 451, the formula appears to satisfy the principal theological concerns of both sides; like it, however, it soon ran into opposition. This came from both wings, but, as might be expected from its Antiochene provenance, the formula was attacked most bitterly by the upholders of Cyril's Christology in its most intransigent form. This renewed opposition was expressed moderately by Proclus, the new patriarch of Constantinople, in the *Tome* in which, in 435, he briefed the Armenian Christians on the current situation, attacking the Antiochene position as this had been propounded by Theodore of Mopsuestia. It was stirred up in a much more extreme form by Dioscorus, who succeeded Cyril at Alexandria in 444 and regarded any retreat from the formula of 'one nature' as a betrayal of the Alexandrian tradition of orthodoxy. Theodoret had to complain to Dioscorus in 447 that he had been misrepresented by disaffected visitors to Alexandria, apparently coming from Antioch, as teaching a division of Christ into two Sons; but as the only witnesses to his orthodoxy whom he cited were successive bishops of Antioch including John's successor, Domnus, who was shortly to be deposed by the party of Dioscorus, the Alexandrian patriarch was unimpressed.[1] In his dialogue, *Eranistes* (Collector), Theodoret attacks a 'one nature' Christology which involved the notion that the human nature had been absorbed into the divine and, though not absolutely abolished, merged in the essence of deity.[2] This represents, in all probability, the view of Eutyches, the head of a monastery near Constantinople, who was accused by Eusebius of Dorylaeum before a local council presided over by Proclus' successor, Flavian, in 448, the charge being heresy of the Apollinarian type.

Eutyches' actual views are somewhat obscure. His statements tended to be ambiguous and he was inclined to modify or retract them under pressure. It is, however, fairly clear that he denied two natures in Christ and affirmed one nature of God incarnate and made man.[3] 'Nature' seems to be used here in its Cyrilline sense, for Eutyches was willing to acknowledge that Christ was God and man ('He who is eternally perfect God, the same was also made perfect man for our salvation');[4] and he even agreed that Christ is 'of two natures' in the sense that deity and manhood can be theoretically distinguished as the constituent elements, as it were, though after the union there is but one 'nature' in the sense of a single concrete entity.[5] Leo of Rome pours scorn on this idea: it is as foolish to affirm two natures before

---

[1] Thdt. *ep.* 83.
[2] *eran.* proem; *ib.* 2.
[3] Council of Constantinople, 448 (Schwartz, *Acta Conciliorum Oecumenicorum* 2.1, p. 159.
[4] Eutyches *ep. Leon.* (Hahn, p. 319).
[5] Leo *tom.* 6.

the union (when the Logos subsisted in the divine nature only) as to deny two natures after the union (when, *ex hypothesi*, the divine nature had taken humanity into union with itself); but he does so by taking Eutyches' statement literally and naively, whereas Eutyches probably meant by 'acknowledging Christ to be of two natures before the union' much the same as Cyril meant by saying that the natures could be distinguished, though only conceptually. Worse in the opinion of his critics was his statement that the flesh of Christ is not consubstantial with ours, though when pressed on this point he was prepared to concede it – reluctantly, however, because he held that since the flesh is the flesh of the Logos it can scarcely be said to be a man's flesh, which is what 'consubstantial with ours' would seem to imply.[1] He was suspected, almost inevitably, of suggesting that the flesh of Christ was 'from heaven', but, like Apollinarius and for the same reason, had no difficulty in denying any such belief.[2] Leo evidently thought that the views of Eutyches amounted to an unsophisticated docetism. In fact, however, they look like the Christology of Cyril in his most uncompromising mood pushed to extreme lengths. This was certainly how they appeared to Dioscorus.

Eutyches was condemned by Flavian's council which also adopted a profession of faith subsequently embodied in a letter from Flavian to the emperor Theodosius. This largely repeats the Formula of Union, but continues with further explanations. It acknowledges Christ 'from two natures' (this being probably the authentic text rather than 'in two natures') 'after the incarnation, in one hypostasis and one *prosopon*, one Christ, one Son, one Lord'. In the sense that Christ is one and the same, though of the two natures, this document does not quarrel with the formula 'one incarnate and "made human" nature of God the Word', and thus upholds the legitimacy of Cyril's position; at the same time it anathematizes those who affirm two Sons or two hypostases or two prosopa, and names Nestorius as one of these heretics.[3] This credal statement is important for the further clarification that it brought to terminology. The unity of Christ's person is now defined in terms of one hypostasis or prosopon, the two being synonymous and meaning 'concrete individual being' or 'person'; and Cyril's 'one nature' is allowed because it is defined as meaning the same, in effect, as 'one hypostasis or prosopon'. 'Hypostasis' thus ceased to be used for the 'natures' in the strict sense, i.e. the humanity and the deity of Christ; hence, even though Cyril had spoken of two hypostases, meaning natures, this usage, with all the confusion that it entails, is now ruled out.

After his condemnation Eutyches protested his orthodoxy to Leo, bishop of Rome, but Flavian informed Leo at length concerning his own, and his council's, view of the matter, and Leo was not disposed to listen to Eutyches. Instead, he wrote a reply to Flavian, the *Tome* ([dogmatic] treatise), which was intended to be communicated to the council which Dioscorus and Eutyches persuaded the emperor Theodosius to summon at Ephesus in 449. This council was controlled by Dioscorus, who refused to

[1] cf. Council of Constantinople (448) (*A.C.O.* 2.1, p. 142).
[2] Eutych. *ep. Leon.*
[3] Flavian *ep. Thds.* (Hahn, p. 320).

allow Leo's envoys to read the *Tome*. Eutyches was reinstated, Flavian deposed (and physically assaulted, so that he died soon afterwards), and the Antiochene leaders also deposed, including Theodoret from Cyrrhus and Domnus from Antioch. This council, described by Leo as *latrocinium* ('robber-synod' or 'brigandage'),[1] set up the decisions of Ephesus, 431, without the formula of 433, as the standard of orthodoxy against the line taken by Rome.

Rome's position, as set out in Leo's *Tome*, contributed to the dispute little, if anything, new. It is a reaffirmation of traditional Western Christology as originally worked out by Tertullian, and Leo borrows some of his most significant passages from previous Western writers, Tertullian and Gaudentius of Brescia. The *Tome* asserts the doctrine of the one person and the two natures. It was 'the same' only-begotten eternal Son who was born of Mary, and the birth in time neither diminishes from nor adds to the eternal generation.[2] The distinctive character of each nature remained unimpaired, and, coming together in one person, an inviolable nature was united to a passible nature, so that one and the same Jesus Christ was capable of death in the one nature and incapable of death in the other. In the whole and perfect nature of true humanity true God was born, complete in what belonged to him, complete in what belonged to us.[3] The Son of God descending from heaven and yet not leaving the glory of the Father, was born miraculously; but the miracle does not mean that his human nature is unlike ours. God is not changed, nor is manhood absorbed. Each 'form' operates what is proper to it in communion with the other, the Word performing what belongs to the Word and the flesh what pertains to the flesh.[4] Thus it is proper to the human nature to weep for Lazarus and to the divine to raise him from the dead. But, having so strongly emphasized the distinction of natures as to ascribe different sayings of Jesus to each – 'I and the Father are one' to the divinity and 'My Father is greater than I' to the humanity – Leo abruptly applies the (conceptual) interchange of properties in order to maintain the unity of the one person. We can say that it was the Son of Man who came down from heaven and that it was the Son of God who was crucified and buried.[5] Leo thus restates, rather in the manner of the formula of 433, the chief principles to be upheld: the eternal Son as the subject of the human experiences and the duality of the divine and human natures; but he lays such stress on the latter as justly to alarm those who followed the Alexandrian approach. If he does not, as they suspected, divide the one Christ despite all his assurances concerning the identity of the Gospel figure with the eternal Son, he can fairly be accused of splitting the personality. Although he maintains the personal unity by means of the artificial device of the interchange of properties in Christological discourse, his ideas, derived from Tertullian, that each nature operates in its own sphere, albeit with the concurrence of the other, so that

[1] Leo *ep.* 95.
[2] *tom.* 2.
[3] *ib.* 3.
[4] *ib.* 4.
[5] *ib.* 4, 5.

Christ acts now divinely and now humanly, suggests the throwing of a switch and the turning on of one nature and turning off of the other.

The first opportunity to decide the conflict between Leo and Dioscorus came with the death of the latter's sympathizer, Theodosius II, in 450. Marcian, the new emperor, supported the other side and acceded to the requests of Leo and Theodoret for a council, which met at Chalcedon in 451. This, the Fourth Ecumenical Council, reaffirmed the creeds of Nicaea and 'Constantinople' (see above p. 115) and the authoritative character, as statements of the Faith against Nestorius and Eutyches respectively, of Cyril's second and third letters to Nestorius and Leo's *Tome*. It added a further Christological definition, closely resembling the formula of 433, Flavian's statement of 448 and, in substance, Leo's *Tome*.

This Definition acknowledges 'Christ as one and the same Son, the same perfect in deity, the same perfect in humanity, truly God and truly man, the same consisting of a rational soul and a body, consubstantial with the Father in respect of deity, the same consubstantial with us in respect of humanity, like us in all things save sin; begotten of the Father before the ages in respect of the deity, the same . . . born of the Virgin Mary the God-bearer in respect of the humanity, one and the same Christ, Son, Lord, Only-begotten, to be acknowledged in' (or possibly 'from', though it is likely that 'from' may have been amended at the Council to 'in') 'two natures without confusion, without change, without division, without separation; the distinction of natures being in no way abolished because of the union, but the characteristic property of each nature being preserved and concurring into one *prosopon* and *hypostasis*, not as though Christ were separated or divided into two persons, but one and the same Son and only-begotten God, Word, Lord, Jesus Christ'.[1]

Granted the presupposition with which the Council operated, that the basic Christian belief in the divinity of Christ must be expressed theologically in terms of one and the same entity, God the Logos, coming down from heaven and assuming human nature, Chalcedon offered as satisfactory a formulation as was possible. The presupposition had been established by the whole trend of Christological thinking during the previous centuries and above all by the Alexandrian theology. Chalcedon succeeded in combining with this the Antiochene principle that the humanity is real, distinct, and identical with the manhood of Adam, thus safeguarding the truth of man's salvation.

The Antiochene and Western tone of the Definition was clear enough. Nestorius was able to greet Leo's *Tome* as an irreproachable statement of the Faith,[2] and although an imperial edict early in 452 optimistically declared that the Council had finally closed the controversy the situation was not unlike that which prevailed after Nicaea: a credal statement had been adopted which commanded the powerful support of Rome and the West and was enforceable through imperial sanctions, but which failed to allay Eastern misgivings. Dioscorus had been deposed, but devotion to the actual language as well as the essential doctrine of Cyril continued to be

<hr>

[1] *Symb. Chalc.* (Hahn, pp. 166-7).
[2] Nest. *Heracl.* 298.

extremely strong, especially in Egypt (as the murder of Dioscorus' Chalcedonian successor, Proterius, showed), and despite Leo's explanations of the dualistic passages in the *Tome*, especially the assurance that all Christ's actions, whether naturally human or divine, are to be referred to a single personal subject,[1] it was widely supposed that Chalcedon had in effect repudiated Cyril and his achievement at Ephesus in 431. The long struggle between different parties after Nicaea was therefore paralleled by a see-saw contest between Chalcedonians and various kinds of monophysites in most of the Eastern sees, apart from Constantinople, between 452 and the death in 578 of Jacob Baradaeus, bishop of Edessa, who organized independent schismatic (Jacobite) churches under their own leaders.

During the earlier part of this period the main stream of monophysite thought is represented by Egyptian leaders such as Timothy Aelurus, the successor of Proterius at Alexandria, who, after deposition and restoration, instigated the publication in 476 of the 'Encyclical' of the usurping emperor Basiliscus which reversed the hitherto pro-Chalcedonian policy of the secular authority. This theology is virtually that of Cyril with very little modification, and the battle-ground for the struggle between its supporters and the Chalcedonians was less theological than political. The question was whether Chalcedon and its associated statements of faith were or were not to be regarded as having binding authority. Basiliscus' *Encyclical* rejected Chalcedon and Leo's *Tome* as having 'disturbed the unity and order of the holy churches'.[2] In line with this ultra-Cyrilline Christology was the addition, ascribed to Peter Fullo, patriarch of Antioch, twice deposed and restored between 470 and 488, of the words 'who was crucified for us' to the *Trisagion* hymn: 'Holy God, Holy Mighty, Holy Immortal'.[3] This caused much offence because the threefold 'Holy' was referred at Constantinople to the Trinity and not, as Peter Fullo intended, to Christ alone. More important was the attempt by the emperor Zeno, at the prompting of Acacius, patriarch of Constantinople, in 482, to reconcile the Egyptian church. Zeno's *Henotikon* ('unifying instrument') shows the growing tendency to explain away or whittle away the Chalcedonian formulation in order to conciliate those in the Cyrilline tradition. It anathematizes Eutyches as well as Nestorius, but it receives Cyril's twelve anathemas as authoritative, ascribes both the miracles and the sufferings of Christ to a single person, and denies that the birth from Mary produced another Son besides the Logos, which would have meant an expansion of Trinity into quaternity. It anathematizes those who have ever expressed contrary opinions 'whether at Chalcedon or at any other synod whatever'.[4] This attempt at a rather weak compromise led to the thirty-five years 'Acacian schism' between Constantinople and Rome but did not heal the Eastern divisions.

The principal theologian among the monophysites of the sixth century was Severus, patriarch of Antioch from 512 to his deposition on the acces-

[1] Leo *ep.* 124.
[2] Evagrius *h.e.* 3.4.
[3] Theodore Lector *h.e.* 1.20; cf. Evagrius *h.e.* 3.44.
[4] Evagr. *h.e.* 3.14.

sion of the Chalcedonian emperor Justin in 518. His Christology was practically no more than a repetition of Cyril's, and it is thus monophysite in phraseology rather than in substance. It is an interesting example of the extent to which the 'monophysite' – 'Chalcedonian' struggle was really only a sham fight so far as theology was concerned. It was a bitter and often murderous conflict, but the reality of it was political and cultural, not theological. Severus and others were content to man the entrenched positions that had been occupied in 431 without attempting to break out of them and advance. He is himself devoted to the old terminology with all its ambiguities. For him 'hypostasis' and 'nature', and indeed 'person', all mean a concrete individual entity. So in Christ there is one nature: 'out of two', certainly, but two natures united hypostatically are one nature.[1] There is no confusion of deity and humanity. In Christ there is not one *ousia* but two, brought together in a synthesis, by which is meant a union which is neither a conjunction of separate objects nor a fusion but a union in which the one element is dependent for its existence on the other.[2] When pressed, Severus is in fact ready to admit two natures, but, like Cyril, he insists that they can be distinguished only theoretically.[3] Unlike Eutyches, Severus has no hesitation in affirming the double consubstantiality of Christ's deity with God and of his humanity with ourselves. Where Severus did make a distinct contribution was in his insistence, against Leo's theory that each nature operates what is proper to it, that since the incarnate Logos is the subject of all activities, divine and human, there is one operation only; this is characterized as one divine/human operation or 'theandric energy'.[4]

The accession of Justinian brought the reconciliation of Constantinople with Rome on the basis of Chalcedon, but much effort was devoted to interpreting and glossing Chalcedon in a Cyrilline sense to win over those who, like Severus, would recognize nothing but the 'one incarnate nature of God the Word'. Justinian succeeded in getting agreement with both Rome and the Severans to a condemnation of any who denied that 'Jesus Christ . . . who was crucified is one of the holy and consubstantial Trinity'.[5]

Meanwhile a more thorough attempt had been made to explain the two sides to each other. The work of Leontius, a monk of Constantinople known as Leontius of Byzantium, and his namesake of Jerusalem who seems to have worked at about the same time (the former died in or about 543), served to clarify the terminology further and to add a finishing touch to the Cyrilline Christology while seeking to demonstrate that Ephesus and Chalcedon had not contradicted one another. Working on the basis of the Aristotelian categories, Leontius of Byzantium defined the terms *ousia*, nature, hypostasis, and so on. He pointed out that an hypostasis is a species or nature individuated; it is an independently subsisting entity. There cannot actually be an 'anhypostatic' nature, that is, a nature which is not

---

[1] Anastasius Sinaita *hod.* (*PG.* 89.148, 304).
[2] Leontius of Jerusalem *monoph.* (*PG.* 86. 1848).
[3] Eustathius Monachus *ep.* (*PG.* 86.908, 921, 936).
[4] *ib.* (*PG.* 86.924–5); Diekamp, *Doctrina Patrum*, p. 309f.
[5] *Codex Justiniani* 1.1.6.

individuated so as to be, concretely, the nature of a particular object.[1] An anhypostatized nature would be an abstraction, and for this reason Leontius disliked Severus' insistence that the natures of Christ have a distinct existence only in theory.[2] The human nature of Christ is not a mere abstraction, a nature anhypostatized. Nor is it an hypostasis, for it has no independent existence; it does not subsist in, or as, a human hypostasis. It is, rather, *en*hypostatized. It has its hypostasis *in* the Logos; the human nature is individuated as the nature, not of a human being but of the Logos.[3] This development in terminology served to clarify Cyril's meaning; it states what is meant by the 'impersonal' humanity of Christ. It also helped to show, on the one hand, that a duality of natures need not entail a duality of persons, and, on the other, that to accept the single hypostasis does not necessitate speaking of one nature. Leontius upholds the Chalcedonian formula and speaks of two natures in one person or hypostasis, but, provided that the sense in which the terms are used is properly understood, he does not disallow the 'one incarnate nature of the Word' nor 'natural union'.[4]

Part of the policy of reconciling Severan monophysites to the Chalcedonian definition was the repudiation of the 'Three Chapters', the person and writings of Theodore of Mopsuestia, the writings of Theodoret on the controversy between Cyril and the Antiochenes, and the letter of Ibas, bishop of Edessa, to the Persian bishop Maris, on the same subject, written in or about 433. This was virtually to reverse the verdict of Chalcedon in favour of that of Dioscorus' 'Robber-Synod', and, despite a condemnation of the 'Three Chapters' contained in Justinian's *Confession of Faith* issued in 551, the assent to this of the West, represented by Pope Vigilius, was only obtained with great difficulty after a general council at Constantinople in 553 (the Fifth Ecumenical Council) had pronounced against them. The Council also repeated in substance anathemas which had been attached to Justinian's confession. These sum up the contemporary Christological orthodoxy, asserting the hypostatic or 'synthetic' union and allowing the phrases, 'from two natures' (as well as 'in two natures') and 'one incarnate nature' provided these are recognized as asserting unity of person and not confusion of natures or essences.[5]

None of these essays in restatement succeeded in unifying the Church. A more determined effort was made in the following century. This was the adoption by Sergius, patriarch of Constantinople, and the emperor Heraclius of Severus' theory of one operation in Christ. This meant that even though the two natures may be distinguished in theory there is but one divine-human activity. This implies one will, and although it was only during the course of the controversy that attention came to be focussed specifically on the question of one or two wills the teaching of Sergius and his supporters is known as 'Monothelitism', the doctrine of a single will. A reunion was

---

[1] Leontius of Byzantium, *Nest. et Eut.* (*PG.* 86.1280–1).
[2] *arg. Sev.* (*PG.* 86.1929ff.).
[3] *ib.* (1944); *Nest. et Eut.* (1277).
[4] *id. cap. Sev.* (1905); *arg. Sev.* (1929).
[5] Hahn, pp. 168ff.

achieved in 633 in Egypt between Cyrus, appointed patriarch of Alexandria by Heraclius with this object in view, and Severan monophysites. The formula of agreement was a statement of the usual Cyrilline Christology in an extreme and uncompromising form (for instance, glossing *theotokos* by 'conceiving and bearing God the Word made flesh') with a declaration that 'the same one Christ and Son operates the activities which befit God and the human activities in one "theandric operation" ', for which phrase 'Dionysius the Areopagite' is given the credit (Severus having probably derived it from him).[1]

Monothelitism was opposed by Sophronius, patriarch of Jerusalem, in a long synodical letter sent to Honorius of Rome as well as to Sergius and others.[2] He reasserts Leo's view that each nature operates what is proper to it, and argues that since a nature is distinguishable only by its operation the assertion of one operation must lead to confusion of the natures. The 'one theandric operation' is implausibly explained as referring only to activity which simultaneously involved both natures. There are two operations, but one person is the operating subject of both. A much fuller defence of the duality of operations and of wills was worked out by Maximus the Confessor. His main point is that 'operation' belongs to a nature and not to a person. If this were not so, three distinct operations, including wills, would have to be ascribed to God who is three persons.[3] The one 'theandric operation' is explained either on Sophronius' lines or as expressing the interchange of properties and the mutual interpenetration of the natures in their operations.[4] There are two wills, for in Christ there is the 'natural will' belonging to deity and the 'natural will' belonging to humanity; Christ does not share the deliberate or purposive will of ordinary men, for this rationally calculating, as opposed to intuitive, will is inherently bound up with ignorance and sin.[5] There are thus two wills, but in no sense a split personality, for the union of natures implies that the deified human will is always freely in perfect agreement with the divine.[6]

The 'Ecthesis' (Exposition), a document drawn up by Sergius and issued by the emperor in 638, obtained general support for a time, including that of Pope Honorius. It asserts one personal subject of both the divine and the human acts, but deprecates the affirmation of either one or two operations, for fear of either monophysitism or else a division of the one person which would be worse than Nestorianism (for though Nestorius postulated two Sons he never asserted two wills). It affirms one will in the sense that the 'rationally ensouled flesh' of Christ never acted independently of, and in opposition to, the dictates of the Logos.[7] This moderate statement was soon rejected by the West which remained loyal to Chalcedonian Christology and reaffirmed it at Pope Martin's Lateran Council of 649 which even rejected the somewhat desperate attempt of the emperor Constans II in

[1] *ib.* p. 338f.
[2] *PG.* 87.3148ff.; Hahn, pp. 340ff.
[3] Max. *ep. Anast.* (*PG.* 90.152); *Pyrr.* (*PG.* 91.289).
[4] *schol. epp. Dion. Ar.* (*PG.* 4.530ff.); *opusc.* (*PG.* 91.100); *Pyrr* (*PG.* 91.289).
[5] *Pyrr.* (308).
[6] *opusc.* (*PG.* 91.30ff.).
[7] Hahn, p. 343f.

648 to settle the controversy by repealing the *Ecthesis* and issuing, in the *Typus* (Decree), a declaration that discussion of the will or wills of Christ should cease. Changes in the political situation enabled a Chalcedonian reaction to take place in the East which resulted in the reaffirmation of the Chalcedonian formula by the Council of Constantinople of 681, the Sixth Ecumenical Council. A further clause was added which affirmed two natural operations and wills, without separation, change, division or confusion, the two natural wills not being mutually opposed but the human will being subject to the divine.[1]

The Cyrilline-Severan doctrine was by no means the only form which monophysitism took after Chalcedon. This was a genuine attempt to maintain the Christology of Ephesus without the concessions that Leo and Chalcedon seemed to have made towards the position of Theodore and Nestorius; but other kinds of monophysite speculation tried in various ways to suggest that in the Incarnation human nature had been virtually absorbed into the divine. They may be called extreme types of Eutychianism. Among these were the idea of Julian of Halicarnassus, who was opposed by Severus, that because of the hypostatic union Christ's body had been removed from the sphere of physical laws and exempted both from all suffering except that which the Word willed to endure, working a miracle to make this possible, and also from all possibility of corruption.[2] This theory, known as 'Aphthartodocetism', rests on an extension of the traditional argument used against Arianism: that only a fully divine Christ can save mankind. Corruptible flesh can be raised to incorruptibility only by a Saviour who is absolutely without the possibility of corruption. This is a striking instance of the real weakness of that whole argument as it had been used against Paul of Samosata or Arius. Another type of monophysitism was the flat denial òf any distinction of natures after the union, as in the teaching of Niobe of Alexandria. These variations are of no great importance, though they represent a line of thought which exercised some influence on the Iconoclastic movement in the eighth century. The fierceness and the long duration of the iconoclastic controversy were due more to political than to theological reasons. It was a struggle between the emperor and the army on one side and conservative nobles on the other, and between bishops and monks. There were, however, certain Christological implications in the dispute. A very ancient line of Christian tradition, looking back to the Second Commandment and the biblical hatred of idolatry, strongly disapproved of the use of images, especially representations of God and Christ; the true image of God is Christ the Logos; the presence of the saints is portrayed spiritually, not physically, in their writings and in their virtues.[3] On the other hand, the use and veneration of images of Christ, his Mother and the saints developed rapidly, especially from the late fourth century onwards, alongside the earlier practice of depicting Christian themes by

---

[1] *ib.* pp. 172ff.

[2] Leont. Byz. *Nest. et Eut.* (*PG*. 86.1329ff.).

[3] e.g., Clem. *prot.* 4.62, *str.* 7.5; *Acts of John* 27; Epiph. *ep.* (*PG*. 43.390f.); Or. *Cels.* 8.17; Chrys. *hom. in Ps. 145:2*; Theodotus of Ancyra cited at the Second Council of Nicaea (787) *act.* 6.

means of symbols and Old Testament types. In place of the Hebrew prophets' view that the veneration of a religious image was nothing more than the worship of wood or stone, Christians generally came to share the attitude of the emperor Julian: 'We do not say that the statues of the emperors are mere wood and stone and bronze, nor that they are the emperors themselves, but that they are images of the emperors. He therefore who loves the emperor delights to see the emperor's statue.'[1] Christians felt the same delight in seeing Christ and the saints portrayed, though there continued to be agreement that no image can be made of the incorporeal, invisible and infinite deity itself.[2]

The attack launched by the emperor Leo III in the years following 726 against images of Christ in human form, as opposed to Christological symbols such as the lamb,[3] and images of Mary, the saints and angels, culminated in the decisions of the iconoclastic council assembled at Constantinople by Constantine V Copronymus in 754. This council anathematized the making, setting up and veneration of images as contrary to God's commandments and the dogmas of the Fathers. It condemned any attempt to portray the indivisible hypostatic union of the nature of God the Word with flesh, asserting that the portrayal of Christ implies either a Nestorian separation of the humanity from the divinity or a monophysite confusion of uncircumscribed deity with manhood. Man alone is the earthly image of God, and the only proper image of Christ is the eucharistic bread and wine.

The Second Council of Nicaea in 787 (the Seventh Ecumenical Council), made possible by the empress Irene's reversal of imperial policy, ordered the setting up of images of Christ, the *Theotokos*, angels and saints. The reasons advanced by the council in justification of their decision are those which had been put forward during the controversy by John of Damascus and other opponents of the iconoclasts. Against the Christological objections to icons it is argued that a picture of Christ no more involves a separation of the humanity from the divinity than a portrait of an ordinary man implies a separation of his body from his soul, and that if a picture implies an apparent circumscription of deity the same is equally true of the actual infant in the manger.

At the same time the Council endorsed the anti-iconoclastic writers' insistence that the Second Commandment is not meant to be taken in a strictly literal sense, for veneration is not in fact paid to the image itself but to its subject; and Basil's assertion that 'the honour paid to the image passes through to the original'[4] is taken out of its proper Trinitarian context and invoked in support of this principle. The purpose of an icon is therefore to put the worshipper in mind of, and stir up his devotion towards, its prototype. If, however, the icon is to be regarded in this way as an outward visual aid to devotion, and the devotion is really paid to the original – it may be to Christ – it seems somewhat inconsistent that at the same time

---

[1] Julian *fr. ep.* (294C).
[2] Jo. D. *imag.* 2.7; 3.16.
[3] cf. canon 82 of the Council in Trullo (692).
[4] See above, p. 114.

veneration is carefully defined as *proskynesis*, the reverential honour which, in another context, is paid to the human person of the emperor, and distinguished from the absolute worship (*latria*) that is due to God alone.[1] A more positive understanding of the function of the icon, which has continued to exercise an immense influence on the devotion and the theology of the Eastern churches, is to be found in the view of John of Damascus and others that the icon is not merely an aid to devotion but a channel of divine grace, parallel in some degree to the sacraments.[2]

---

[1] Jo. D. *imag.* 1.4; *fid. orth.* 4.15, 16.
[2] Jo. D. *imag.* 1.19.

IX

SALVATION, SIN AND GRACE

In our discussion of individual theologians and in our survey of the Christological controversies we have touched on various aspects of patristic thought about man's salvation. There are two central ideas, repeatedly expressed by the writers of this period, to which all those aspects are related and in the light of which they have to be understood. The first of these is the concept of 'deification' or 'divinization' (we use these terms as synonyms) as the goal of salvation and as the process by which the blessings of salvation, the fruit of Christ's saving work, may be progressively experienced by the believer during this present life. The second is the interpretation of the saving work of Christ as an 'exchange of places' by which the Logos/Son took upon himself, or entered into, the human state in order to enable sinful, alienated and perishing human beings to enter, through incorporation into himself, the state of sonship towards God.

'Sonship towards God' is in fact virtually equivalent to what is generally denoted by 'deification' in patristic theology; for 'deification' or 'likeness to God' (*homoiosis theoi*) means the operation of sanctifying grace, already experienced by believers who are indwelt by the Spirit and enjoy communion with God as sons of a Father, but to be brought to its complete realization only in the final consummation. The most direct, and indeed startling, expression of the idea of deification in the New Testament is the characterization of believers as 'partakers of the divine nature (*physis*)' in 2 Pet. 1:4; but the usual scriptural basis of the patristic development of this idea is the Pauline teaching on adoptive sonship towards God and the re-creation of believers in the likeness of the Son of God. This transformation and renewal involves the replacement of human mortality by incorruptibility and immortal life.

This understanding of salvation was also deeply rooted in the Platonist tradition. According to Plato the aim of the soul must be to flee from the world and become, so far as is possible, assimilated to God.[1] In the myth in the *Phaedrus* the lover and his beloved jointly re-grow their souls' lost wings through participating in their particular god, 'in so far as a man can partake of a god', and the philosophical souls follow and participate in Zeus.[2] So for Plotinus man's aim is not simply to become free from sin but to 'be a god', one of the gods who follow the First God (i.e. Plato's Zeus or the Good). It is to the gods that man should strive to become assimilated,

---

[1] Plato *Theaet.* 176b; cf. *Phaed.* 82ab, *Phaedr.* 248a, *Rep.* 10.613a.

[2] *Phaedr.* 253a.

and not to good men, for likeness to good men is the likeness to each other of two pictures of the same subject, whereas likeness to the gods is likeness to the original model.[1] Christian thinkers, with their doctrine of the re-fashioning of man in the likeness of the Logos, the exact image of God, and with Psalm 82:6 as their proof-text for the divine purpose of transforming men into 'gods', could readily assimilate the biblical to the Platonist tradition – always with the proviso that deification is God's work of grace and not an achievement of the philosophical soul.

As we have seen, Irenaeus believed that Psalm 82:6 is already being fulfilled for Christians who possess the 'Spirit of adoption', though final perfection must await the incorruptibility that will come through the eschatological vision of God.[2] Theophilus of Antioch, too, held that if Adam had used the gift of freedom rightly he would have gained the reward of immortality and become a god.[3] It is especially characteristic of Alexandrian theology to associate man's deification with illumination and *gnosis*. Thus Clement asserts that man is deified by illumination and the teaching of the Logos; being baptized we are illuminated, being illuminated we are made sons, being made sons we are perfected, being perfected we are made immortal in fulfilment of Psalm 82:6; the knowledge of God gives incorruptibility, and this is to partake of divinity; the 'gnostic' can already become a god, one of those of whom it is said 'You are gods and all sons of the Most High'.[4] For Origen, as we have seen, salvation means deification or re-deification.[5] In his exegesis of Psalm 82:6 he ingeniously associates with that well-worn proof-text the words of Psalm 116:11, so as to read out of the scriptures the Platonic idea of the flight of the soul into the divine likeness: 'I said in my ecstasy, Every man is a liar' means that we ought to escape from being men and hasten to become gods; and it means, too, that those who are not liars but who stand on the truth, the rock of Exodus 33:21 which is Christ, are not men but the 'gods' of Psalm 82:6.[6] The deification of man through the 'interchange of places' between the Logos and mankind is also the central theme in Athanasius' understanding of salvation: 'He became man that we might be deified, and he revealed himself through a body that we might receive an idea of the invisible Father, and he himself endured insult from men that we might inherit incorruptibility'. 'He assumed the created and human body in order that, having as creator renewed it, he might deify it in himself and thus bring us into the kingdom of heaven according to God's likeness.[7] Cyril of Alexandria repeats these themes: if God, he says, has become man, man has become a god; and this is possible because the deification of man is in Christ.[8]

The contribution of Gregory of Nyssa to this understanding of salvation is particularly important. Unlike Origen who held that man was created in

---

[1] Plotinus *Ennead.* 1.2.6–7.
[2] See above, p. 49.
[3] *Autol.* 2.27.
[4] *prot.* 11.114; *paed.* 1.5.26; *str.* 5.10.63; *ib.* 4.23.149; see also above, p. 68.
[5] See above, p. 82.
[6] *Jn.* 29.27, 29.
[7] *inc.* 54; *Ar.* 2.70; see also above, p. 106.
[8] *Rom.* 9.3; *thes.* 23 (229B).

the beginning as pure spirit, Gregory believed that man was from the first a synthesis of soul and body. The first creation of the ideal man prefigured his ultimate state of blessedness; his reason reflected the beauty of God, but his upright posture indicated the dignity of his bodily nature which had received immortality as a special gift, his soul possessing it by nature.[1] The 'coats of skin' with which God clothed Adam and Eve are, therefore, not, as for Origen, man's physical body, but rather his animal nature and especially his sexuality.[2] The final restoration (*apocatastasis*) is thus not a return of man's soul to pure spirit, as Origen had held, but a return of all things, including man, to their original condition. The whole creation in a sense participates in God, for everything is a 'substantiation' of God's will: 'the divine will became the matter and substance of created things'.[3] Man, however, has the special function and responsibility of mediating the spiritual to the material, for man is a bridge between the worlds of spirit and matter, the intelligible realm (*kosmos noetos*) and the sensible realm (*kosmos aisthetos*). He is a microcosm of each of the two worlds, created to enjoy God through his spiritual nature and to enjoy the world at the same time through the senses which belong to that world.[4]

Gregory is here using an idea which had its roots in Plato and had been developed by Philo; the thought that man, as a microcosm, is intended by God to link mortal creatures with immortal, rational with irrational, is also expressed in the treatise *On the Nature of Man* by the fourth century Christian writer Nemesius of Emesa.[5] The link between the two worlds is formed, according to Gregory, when man's rational mind reflects the divine beauty, which it contemplates, to nature and thus brings form and order to what would otherwise be formless matter. When, however, this harmony is broken by man's reason ceasing to contemplate God and thereby become assimilated to the divine goodness, this process is thrown into reverse. The formlessness of matter corrupts the beauty of nature, and this in turn further distorts the capacity of the reason to reflect the divine.[6]

For the soul this 'fall' does not mean extinction, for it is created immortal, but it means spiritual death, the separation of the soul from God, the source of the goodness that is true life. Through the Incarnation, however – the mingling of divine nature with human – Christ's humanity was deified. This deification opens the way for all men to participate in divinity through conversion, renunciation of sin, moral effort and the sacraments; in baptism the soul is united to God, the eucharist is the principle of life for the body. Freedom from the passions (*apatheia*) restores harmony to soul and body, and when the predetermined number of souls has been attained man will be changed 'in the twinkling of an eye, at the last trump' into the state of perfect *apatheia*.[7]

[1] *or. catech.* 5; *hom. opif.* 7–8.
[2] *anim. et res.* (PG. 46.148Cff.); cf. *virg.* 12.
[3] *or. catech.* 24; *hom. in 1 Cor. 15:28*.
[4] *hom. opif.* 2.
[5] cf. Plato *Timaeus* 81A, D; Philo *q.r.d.h.* 155; *Nemesius nat. hom.* 1 (PG. 40.525A, 529B, 532Cff.).
[6] *hom. opif.* 12.
[7] *perf.* 8.1; *or. catech.* 37.

This is not, according to Gregory, a static condition of blessedness. The soul will be active, sharing the divine activity of love (divine love being essentially self-knowledge, since God is perfect beauty and the beautiful is absolutely lovable).[1] Gregory, however, goes further than this in his 'dynamic' idea of salvation. To participate in divine virtues is a journey into infinity.[2] Not only is there progress in perfection, but human perfection, unlike the static perfection of God, consists in progress. This does not mean that human aspirations are to be eternally frustrated. On the contrary, this idea of a progressive heaven rests on the belief that on this journey there can be no point of arrival, for the journey has no end. True fulfilment, and therefore ultimate salvation, consists in an eternal progress into that which must lie eternally beyond man, since man is a creature.[3]

This realization that deification is an infinite progress follows logically from the acknowledgment that the Psalmist's 'gods and sons of the Most High' are not consubstantial with uncreated deity. Their deification is not 'according to substance' for they never lose their creaturely status – a truth which is expressly stated in different ways by Eusebius, Athanasius, Maximus the Confessor and John of Damascus.[4] Deification is always the work of God, an operation of the Spirit or a gift of grace.[5] No theologian emphasizes this more plainly than the Christianized Neoplatonist 'Dionysius the Areopagite'. Having defined deification in the Platonic manner as 'assimilation to, and union with, God so far as this is attainable' and stated that the means towards it is contemplation,[6] he quotes Jn. 1:12 to show that this likeness to God through union with him has been made possible because God has given us the power to become his children.[7] Deification, which can also be understood as the imitation of God, is his own gift, a gift of grace proceeding from the one who alone is God by nature and not by grace.[8]

This teaching is echoed in the seventh century by Dionysius' expositor Maximus the Confessor. Deification, which consists in the knowledge of God, love and peace[9] cannot be effected by any natural power of our own; we can but experience it through grace as a supernatural gift, for nothing created can deify: it belongs to the grace of God alone to bestow deification on created beings in due proportion.[10] Its ultimate source is God's love and goodness,[11] and it crowns his work of creation: God is the author both of being and of well being, creator by nature of the being of all that is, and author by grace of the deification of his creatures. Echoing the language of 2 Peter, the Book of Wisdom and 1 John, Maximus declares that God has 'made us to become partakers of divine nature and sharers in his own

[1] *anim. et res.* (PG. 46.93B–97A).
[2] *v. Mos.* 1.7–8.
[3] *hom. in Cant.* 12.
[4] Eus. *e.th.* 3.18; Ath. *inc. et c. Ar.* 9; Max. *cap.* 1.62; Jo. D. *fid. orth.* 2.12.
[5] cf. Origen *hom. 6.5 in Ex.*; Didymus *Trin.* 2.25; Cyril *Jn.* 1.10 (105C).
[6] *e.h.* 1.3.
[7] *ib.* 2.2.1.
[8] *ep.* 2; *e.h.* i.4.
[9] *myst.* (PG. 91.680C).
[10] *cap.* 1.75; cf. *opusc.* (PG. 91.33C); *ambig.* (PG. 91.1237B); *qu. Thal.* 22.
[11] *ep.* 2 (PG. 91.393B); *ep.* 9 (PG. 91.445C).

eternity and to appear like him through that deification by grace' which is the goal of all creation.[1] The ground of this is the interchange of deity and humanity in the Incarnation, by which human nature was deified, man becoming God in so far as God became man. This is the assurance that 'he who became man without sin will deify human nature without transmuting it into deity'.[2] Maximus seems at one point to go further than this and to envisage a kind of continuing incarnation of God in the deification of believers, or at any rate a continuing extension of the reciprocal interchange between deity and manhood by which man is made God and God appears as man: a reciprocal 'hominization' of God and 'divinization' of man through God's lovingkindness (*philanthropia*) on the one hand and man's response of virtuous conduct on the other.[3]

Like Gregory of Nyssa, Maximus emphasizes man's role as a participant in two realms[4] and the consequent cosmic implications of his salvation. Man is intended to become the mediating link or bridge to span the divisions between male and female, paradise and the world of men, heaven and earth, the 'intelligible' and 'sensible' realms of being, God and his creation. He comes to perform his proper function in so far as he attains freedom from the passions, cultivates a holy way of life which abolishes the difference between this world and paradise, imitates the life and the knowledge of the angels, and enters into union with God.[5]

Our examples of this concept of man's salvation have so far been drawn from Greek writers, but it is by no means absent from Latin theology. Tertullian, for instance, points out that scripture does not hesitate to call men who have become sons of God through faith 'gods', though he interprets this eschatologically: men are not yet gods nor are they yet in heaven.[6] Ambrose, again, echoes traditional teaching when he says that knowledge of the Logos brings us participation in divine nature, and at the same time draws the contrast between the 'gods' of Psalm 82:6, who are the saints, and Christ who is not, like them, a man who received 'the inspiration of deity' (i.e. a Spirit-inspired man).[7] Augustine makes much use of the idea of deification which he equates with sonship towards God. Justification implies deification, because by justifying men God makes them his sons; if we have been made sons of God (Jn. 1:12) we have also been made gods, not through a natural begetting but through the grace of adoption.[8] To become gods means that believers live 'according to God' and not 'according to the flesh', and it is through loving God that they are made into gods. This love must include the human neighbour, for if a human being denies humanity to a fellow man God will deny him divinity, that is to say the immortality by which he makes men gods.[9]

---

[1] *cap.* 4.32; *ep.* 24 (*PG.* 91.609C).
[2] *cap.* 1.62; cf. *ambig.* (*PG.* 91.1113B).
[3] *ep.* 2 (*PG.* 91.401B).
[4] *myst.* 7.
[5] *ambig.* (*PG.* 91.1304D–1313B; cf. 1193C–1196B).
[6] *Prax.* 13; *res. carn.* 49.
[7] *ep.* 29, 3, 14; *fid.* 5.1.23.
[8] *enarr. in Ps.* 49.2.
[9] *civ. Dei* 14.4.2; *serm.* 121.1; *serm.* 259.3.

The ground of deification, once again, is the Incarnation. 'God', says Augustine, 'wishes to make you a god, not by nature like him whom he begat, but by his gift and adoption. For as he through humanity became partaker of your mortality, so through exaltation he makes you partaker of his immortality.'[1] In the Incarnation the 'human divinity' and the 'divine humanity' of Christ mediate between divinity in itself and humanity in itself.[2] Augustine repeats more often, perhaps, than any of the Greek theologians, the theme of the 'interchange of places'. 'The Word', he says, 'became what we are that we might attain what we are not. For we are not God; but we can see God with the mind and interior eye of the heart.' 'To make those who were men "gods", he who was God was made man.' 'The divinity of the Son became partaker of our mortality, that we might be partakers of his immortality.' 'For you he who was Son of God became son of man, so that you who were sons of men might be made sons of God'; so, Augustine concludes, 'do not think it impossible to become sons of God; for you he who was Son of God became son of man.'[3]

Augustine finds support for his teaching on deification in other texts besides Psalm 82:6. Like Origen, he introduces Psalm 116:11: 'All men are liars if they are not sons of the Most High. If you are sons of God, redeemed by the Saviour's grace, purchased by his precious blood, reborn by water and the Spirit, predestined to the inheritance of heaven as sons of God, then you are gods.'[4] 'God is the great king above all gods' (Psalm 95:3) because he is above all men whom he has willed to make into gods by grace and not by nature; that is, all who believe in him, to whom he gave power to become sons of God.[5] Matthew 16:23 shows Christ blaming Peter because he thinks as men think. 'What then', asks Augustine, 'does he want to make us to be, if he blames us because we are men? The answer is given in Psalm 82:6: "I said, you are gods".'[6]

Salvation, according to Augustine, is the renewal of man in the image of God. The human soul is not a part of God; otherwise it would be wholly immutable and incorruptible, but this is not so: man's defects and infirmity cannot be simply ascribed to the body. It is in a sense, however, immortal because, although it dies when it is alienated from communion with God, it does not actually cease to be. The image of God is not wholly abolished (Augustine cites Psalm 39:7, reading 'Man walks in God's image'); but man's nature is vitiated.[7] Man's creation in God's image does not mean that even if he had not sinned he would have been equal and coeternal with God; the likeness of God in man cannot even be compared with the original. It means that if he had used his freewill to obey God he would have been for ever blessed and immortal; but God created man in the foreknowledge that he would sin, but foreknowing also that from his progeny there would come saints seeking not their own, but giving glory to their creator, who by

[1] *serm.* 166.4.
[2] *serm.* 47.12.21.
[3] *serm.* 117.15; *serm.* 1.92.1; *serm.* 117.10; *serm.* 121.5; *serm.* 119.5.
[4] *serm.* 81.6.
[5] *enarr. in Ps.* 94.6.
[6] *serm.* 76.2.3.
[7] *Trin.* 14.4.6.

worshipping him and being freed from corruption would deserve to live for ever in blessedness with the angels.[1] This is the renewal of the image, which man himself cannot achieve; he can de-form it, but only the artificer who made it can re-form it. It is renewed through the love of God and participation in him, and will be perfectly restored through the vision of God in the post-resurrection life. 'God hates you as you are, in order to make you what you are not yet. You will be what he is'; but Augustine hastens to add that this means that we shall be God's image in the sense in which a man's reflection in a mirror is his image inasmuch as it is *like* him, not in the sense in which a man's son is his image inasmuch as he *is* actually what his father is 'according to substance'.[2] Participation in God is beatitude, for God is himself the beatitude 'in whom and by whom and through whom all that is blessed is blessed'; salvation, according to Augustine, is therefore 'fruition', the perfect enjoyment of God.[3]

It was not until Augustine's time that the relation of divine grace, to which every Christian ascribed the salvation of man, to the freedom of the human will became a subject of controversy. It had been of some peripheral importance in connection with Apollinarian ideas about the consequences of admitting a human rational soul in Christ, but it had not been thought out in any systematic way by the earlier Christian writers. Predestination tended to be treated as a dangerous concept, and the Pauline passages which suggested it were something of an embarrassment which patristic commentators, such as Origen and Chrysostom in particular, sought to explain in terms which would not impugn the freedom of the human will to take the initiative in repentance and faith. This freedom was of central importance in the Christian apologetic against pagan fatalism and the influence of astrology, and in the orthodox repudiation of Gnostic determinism, especially, from the middle of the third century onwards, in its Manichaean form. According to this the world, including man except in so far as he may become aware that he has in his inner being a particle of the divine and may thus be saved out of the world, lies in the realm of darkness to which by its nature and origin it inescapably belongs.

This general insistence on the freedom of the will was accompanied by a parallel emphasis on the moral law. The Pauline teaching that Christ is the end of the law was generally interpreted as meaning that Christ is the law's goal, the end, in that sense, to which the moral law of the Old Testament (from which the ceremonial law was distinguished, Christ being indeed the 'end' of this in the other sense of the word, since its significance was typological and not literal) had always been directed. This moral law was held by Christian apologists to be in essence a universal law of nature, capable of being apprehended in some degree by the Gentile world, so that Christian preachers could appeal to the ethical teaching of the philosophers and Christian ethics could be stated in traditional classical forms, as in the adaptation by Ambrose in his *De Officiis Ministrorum* of the Stoicism of Cicero's *De Officiis*. God required men to keep his commandments and do

[1] *de. Gen. ad litt. lib. imperf.* 16.61; *serm.* 24.3; *serm.* 278.2; *catech. rud.* 18.30.
[2] *serm.* 43.3.4; *Trin.* 14.14.18; 14.18.24; *serm.* 8.8.9.
[3] *c. Faust.* 20.5; *soliloq.* 1.1.3; *beat. vit.* 4.33; *lib. arbitr.* 2.13.36.

good works. The believer who had sinned after baptism was required to perform good works by way of compensation. It could not be supposed that men were inherently incapable of directing their wills to the fulfilment of God's demands. Further, since Christ's teaching could be construed as offering a special reward for fuller self-sacrifice than was required of the ordinary run of believers, it was generally held that a life of perfection, the 'evangelical' or 'angelic' life, was possible for those who possessed heroic sanctity. Since deification, the ultimate goal of blessedness, involved freedom from the passions, the 'evangelical counsels' were identified with asceticism and increasingly from the earlier part of the fourth century onwards with the monastic movement and communal withdrawal from the world.

This view was not accepted everywhere. From Jerome's polemic *Against Jovinian* it appears that Jovinian held that the grace of baptism implies that all the baptized are equally and communally the temple of the Spirit; after the Judgement all will enjoy equal blessedness rather than rewards proportionate to their achievements. For the most part, however, the way to blessedness was understood within the monastic system as the ascent of a ladder of perfection towards the fullness of contemplation, and, for the ordinary believer, as a life of faith and works which merited reward from God. It is true that in commenting on Paul many theologians taught that we are justified 'by faith alone'. The actual phrase occurs in Basil, Chrysostom, Ambrose, and others, including (surprisingly, at first sight) Pelagius himself. The framework of reference for *sola fide* is different, however, from what it was to be in the Reformation controversies. It is concerned with conversion and acceptance of the Christian Faith, and is especially associated with the justifying grace of baptism. Thus free will and man's ability to repent and to win the rewards of obedience to God's commandments were generally assumed in early Christian thought.

This does not mean that there was little appreciation of man's sin or God's grace. From Ignatius and Melito onwards[1] grace is seen as the distinctive characteristic of the Christian dispensation as contrasted with pre-Christian legalism. It is acknowledged to be the necessary source of all virtues in the present life, the means by which sin and the devil are overcome, and, as we have seen, the ground and the agency of ultimate deification. The idea that grace is indefectible, however, was associated with Gnostic determinism.[2] Grace was seen as altogether compatible with human free will;[3] prevenient grace may be acknowledged, but man's effort must co-operate with grace in the Christian life. Chrysostom can even preach that man's effort has to take the initiative, so that grace is in some measure a response of God to man.[4] The grace of forgiveness is freely given in baptism, but constant effort is required if it is to be preserved intact. Grace is divine assistance, enabling, strengthening and inspiring men in good works. It does not simply take over when human effort fails; still less does it

---

[1] Ign. *Magn.* 8.1; Mel. *pass.* 2.11.
[2] Iren. *haer.* 1.6.4; Heracleon ap. Or. *Jn.* 13.10.
[3] e.g., Chrysostom *hom 11.1 in Act.*; *hom. 45.1 in Matt.*
[4] *hom. 1.5 in 2 Cor. 4:13.*

render effort superfluous, but at every point it co-operates with the rightly-motivated human will.

The reality of sin was also recognized. Athanasius' view of original sin is typical of Eastern theology. Adam turned from the contemplation of the Logos, which was a supernaturally given possibility for him, conferring immortality, and lapsed into an ever-worsening entanglement with the material world and idolatry, thus plunging the human race into corruption and causing the defacement and virtual obliteration of the divine image in man.[1] Thus Athanasius has a very clear picture of the involvement of all men in the Fall, and of the subjection of all men, in consequence, to sinfulness and death. This does not mean that all possibility of obedience to God has been lost, for some men may have altogether avoided actual sin,[2] and, since the effect of the Fall is thought of so largely in terms of corruption, and salvation in terms of the restoration of immortality, the question whether guilt is actually transmitted to each individual because of Adam's sin is not raised in its later form. Athanasius thinks of the reversion of man to corruption as the execution of God's sentence of death against dis-obedience; all men are therefore, but for the vicarious payment of their penalty by Christ, under sentence of death as part of a doomed humanity; but it can scarcely be said that each man bears a burden of actual guilt. The Cappadocians and Antiochenes follow similar lines of thought. The idea of an inheritance of actual guilt is expressly repudiated through the assertion that infants are born free from sin.[3] The freedom of the will is strongly affirmed against Manichaeism, and the Fall and its continuing consequences was the result of man's free choice of evil.[4] All men are involved in these consequences, which include moral infirmity and bias towards sin, and the progressive disintegration of mankind, individually and socially. According to Antiochene exegesis the divine image in man consists in his domination over creation, and this has not been lost by the Fall; the divine likeness consists in man's freedom to control his passions, and it is this which has been impaired.

Western thought was not markedly different. Tertullian, as we have seen,[5] did not interpret the corruption of Adam's progeny as involving the trans-mission of actual guilt, and regarded the baptism of children as dangerous. At about the same time, however, and also in Africa, the idea that un-baptized children are doomed to torment found expression in the martyr Perpetua's vision of Dinocrates, her brother who had died as a child;[6] and Cyprian differs in this respect from his 'master', Tertullian, in permitting no delay in the baptism of new-born infants, for they have contracted the contagion of death by their birth, on account of Adam's sin.[7] Ambrose

[1] *gent.* 3; *inc.* 4ff.

[2] *Ar.* 3.33.

[3] Gr. Naz. or *40.23*; Gr. Nyss. *de infantibus qui praemature moriuntur*; Chrys. *hom. 28.3 in Matt.*

[4] Bas. *hom.* 9.7; Gr. Nyss. *or. catech.* 7; Chrys. *hom. 20.3 in Gen.*

[5] See above, p. 61.

[6] *M. Perp.* 4.

[7] *ep.* 64.5.

believed strongly in the solidarity of all men with, or rather in, Adam,[1] and he interestingly defines Adam's transgression as his attempt to gain equality with God, an idea that was perhaps expressed in Phil. 2:6; he also maintains that the washing-away of original sin is sacramentally effected in the feet-washing which was part of the Milanese rite of initiation, whereas baptism cleanses from actual sin.[2] Yet Ambrose ascribes to infant baptism the positive effect of the opening of the kingdom of heaven to the baptized rather than the negative result of cleansing from inherited sin.[3] He does, however, think that original sin, meaning by this a sinful propensity rather than actual culpability for sin, is transmitted by physical generation – a disastrous notion which could easily be read out of Psalm 51:5.[4] Here Ambrose anticipates the thought of Augustine, and another vitally important aspect of this was foreshadowed by the exegesis of the commentator 'Ambrosiaster' on the text Romans 5:12, where 'inasmuch as all sinned' was represented in the Old Latin version by 'in whom all sinned'. This was taken to mean that in Adam all men sinned 'as in a lump'; all are therefore sinners, born in sin.

This idea was at the centre of the Pelagian controversy. The conflict between Augustine himself and Pelagius with his supporters Celestius and Julian of Eclanum (who championed Pelagianism in the later stages of the controversy) began gradually. Augustine began to involve himself in it when he heard that some were teaching that infants receive sanctification in Christ through baptism, but not forgiveness of sins, that is to say, of original sin.[5] Pelagius had reacted against the apparent denigration of free will which, as he thought, was implied in Augustine's prayer in his *Confessions*, 'Give what thou dost command, and command what thou dost will'.[6] Pelagius' own views were not notably different at the outset from most traditional theology, especially in the East, but the teaching of himself and his associates became more sharply defined and in some respect exaggerated under the pressure of the controversy which reached its acute stage after Pelagius' work *On Nature* had been answered in 415 by Augustine's *On Nature and Grace*.

Pelagius was concerned, especially in his *Exposition of the Epistles of Paul*, to refute the Christological heresies and also any tendency in respect of the doctrines of sin and grace towards the Manichaeism which Augustine had himself professed as a young man, and against the orthodox view of creation which, he held, must include human free will and the possibility for every man of genuine moral struggle and progress. He believed that, if the goodness of the Creator were not to be denied with the Manichaeans, man must be a creature endowed with reason and conscience and the capacity to follow reason and obey conscience. He is capable by nature of turning in either direction, with a genuine capacity for good and evil. There could be no sense in speaking of man's virtue if he did not possess freedom of

[1] e.g., *excess. fratr. Satyr.* 2.6.
[2] *myst.* 32; *sacr.* 3.1.5ff.
[3] *Abr.* 2.79.
[4] *apol. proph. Dav.* 56.
[5] *pecc. merit.* 3.6.12.
[6] *conf.* 10.40; *persev.* 53.

deliberate choice; our nature is not bound to a necessity either of sinning or of immutable goodness.[1] It is thus at least theoretically possible that a man might not sin. This is involved in the reality of the freedom to move in either direction. It is a possibility which, as being bound up with authentic free will, is a gift of God. Freedom itself is not attained by the exercise of free choice, and it must therefore be recognized as a built-in constituent of human nature (indeed, the central constituent which distinguishes man from other creatures), and thus a gift of grace. It is, in fact, a gift of a quality which is one of the attributes of God, though Pelagius does not clearly distinguish the necessary reservations which should be made in transferring the concept of freedom from the idea of God to that of human freedom to sin or not to sin.[2]

It is thus to what one may call the grace of creation that man owes his basic freedom as a moral agent. By the grace of redemption he is freely forgiven in conversion and baptism. Through the reconciliation effected by Christ's sacrificial death[3] men are accepted by God, being justified by faith alone.[4] Grace enables men to live without sin and to carry out 'the more easily what they are commanded to do through their free will'.[5] Pelagius can speak, like Augustine, of grace as divine assistance, but he thinks of this assistance chiefly in terms of the teaching of God and the revelation both of God's will and of the rewards promised to those who do good. Grace enlightens the understanding and stirs the will towards a longing for God.[6] As a modern exponent of Pelagius expresses it: 'We might capture Pelagius' whole teaching on the grace of Christ as "help" in a single formula: Christ by the example of his life, by his commandments, and by his teaching concerning man and God has brought the final revelation of that "way" for man which leads to life and in doing so has brought "help" sufficient to overcome the power of sinful habit'.[7] Pelagius thinks of grace as bestowed in the basic conditions and the external framework, as it were, of the Christian life, rather than as a power infused into the soul of the Christian. It lays out the race-track, as one might say, round which the believer has to run his course, provides signs and directions to assist him to follow the right way, and gives him exhortation and encouragement as through a coach's megaphone; it does not act, as the Greek theologians had supposed, like an auxiliary engine on a racing cyclist's machine, nor, as Augustine believed, as the machine itself, or, rather, as the rider's actual legs, lungs and heart.

It was not, therefore, an entirely fair criticism of Pelagius when Jerome accused him of inconsistency in saying that a man can achieve sinlessness through his own efforts and at the same time maintaining that he can do nothing without grace.[8] Pelagius did not mean by 'grace' what Jerome and

[1] Pelag. *ep. Dem.* 2ff.
[2] Aug. *nat. et grat.* 53; 59.
[3] Pelag. *exp. epp. Paul* 33.10; 320.12.
[4] *ib.* 9.15; 34.20; 346.6ff.
[5] Aug. *grat. Chr.* 5; 30.
[6] *ib.* 8; 11.
[7] R. F. Evans, *Pelagius: Inquiries and Reappraisals* (A & C Black, 1968), p. 111.
[8] Jerome *ep.* 133.

Augustine meant by it; he believed that freedom to obey or disobey God's law (and in his insistence on this freedom he owed much to the teaching of Origen, brought to the West in the Latin translations of Rufinus of Aquileia) was itself given to men by grace. So, too, the Law of Moses is itself a means of grace and a manifestation of grace. The moral precepts of the Law reinforced the law of nature which had been man's guide between Adam and Moses, and enabled him to obey God and merit his rewards. If the Law did not provide justification this was because men, by their free choice, failed to keep it.[1] Scripture as a whole is the source of law and so of grace to show men how to live well and encourage them to do so.[2] Aided by grace, in this sense, those who have come to faith may live righteously, by which Pelagius means without sinning. For faith, if genuine, produces works of righteousness.[3]

Adam, according to Pelagius, committed the primal transgression and thus sin came into the world, not by transmission but because men followed Adam's example and imitated his disobedience.[4] Sin is always in Pelagius' view a matter of concrete acts of wrong-doing; and since wrong-doing takes place through the exercise of free choice it cannot be an inevitable element in the make-up of every man, nor can any man be held guilty of sin unless he has consciously willed it.[5] The soul, furthermore, is created anew for each individual and is not derived by inheritance from progenitors; there cannot therefore be original sin in the sense of transmitted bias, let alone culpability, since sin resides in the soul and not the body. Pelagius thus denies Ambrosiaster's interpretation of 'in whom all sinned'.[6] Pelagius therefore argues that every child is born, so far as his individual soul is concerned, as a fresh creation of God and therefore good. If a child were to inherit original sin, then the child of baptized parents ought, by the same argument, to inherit original righteousness in the sense, at least, of a bias towards good. By a similar argument Pelagius argues that if those who have not actually sinned are guilty of Adam's sin, then those who have not believed in Christ are in a state of salvation through Christ's righteousness.[7]

Pelagius accordingly holds that baptized infants inherit the Kingdom of God, but that those who die unbaptized are not doomed to perdition; sin is not a 'substance' but consists in freely chosen action, and cannot as it were enter into human nature and permanently debilitate it.[8] This does not mean that Pelagius takes an excessively optimistic view of man's actual capacity to avoid sin. On the contrary, he thinks of a cumulative intensification of the grip of sin upon the human race. Individual acts of sin build up into social sin, and thus men find themselves enslaved to the habit of sin. In this sense one could almost say that Pelagius holds a doctrine of original sin, for sin as social habit imposes a kind of necessity of sinning on the individual

---

[1] *exp. epp. Paul.* 57.18ff.; 246.19; *ep. Dem.* 8.
[2] *ep. Dem.* 9.
[3] *virg.* 6; *exp. epp. Paul.* 34.9–19; 37.1.
[4] *exp. epp. Paul.* 45.11ff.; Aug. *nat. et grat.* 10.
[5] Aug. *nat. et grat.* 21; 33ff.; 8; 10; 13; 54.
[6] *ib.* 21; *exp. epp. Paul.* 47.7ff.
[7] Aug. *pecc. orig.* 14; *gest. Pelag.* 2.
[8] *nat. et grat.* 10; 21.

despite the fact that he started life free from a sinful inheritance. Indeed, the sinful habit is so strong that the Law was rendered incapable of setting men free from it and needed to be replaced by the new law of Christ.[1] Men are themselves responsible for this state of affairs since virtually all men contribute to this accumulation of social habit. Nevertheless, both before and after Moses there have been a few saints who have lived without sin.[2] On predestination Pelagius said relatively little; in so far as he makes use of the idea at all it is that God has determined the relation of reward to moral effort and that those whose conversion is foreknown by God are recipients of grace.[3]

The teaching of Pelagius' supporter Celestius is represented in a summary form by his theses which a council at Carthage condemned in 411 or early in 412. According to these, Adam was created mortal, and would have died whether or not he sinned; his sin injured himself alone and not the entire human race; infants are in the same state as Adam was in his condition of original righteousness before he sinned; the whole human race neither dies through Adam's death nor rises through Christ's resurrection; the Law, no less than the Gospel, can provide a way into the kingdom of heaven; even before the advent of Christ there were some sinless men.[4] The first of these propositions was again anathematized at Carthage in 418, but by avoiding the implications of that relationship between mortality and original sin which was generally assumed as axiomatic it could have eased the theological problem of sin aud redemption.

Celestius seems to have differed from Pelagius in his view concerning the state of infants; the latter held that since infants cannot exercise rational moral choice they cannot be said to share the original condition of Adam.[5] The moral teaching of Celestius included a requirement that the rich must renounce their property on receiving baptism; otherwise their good deeds would not be credited to them and they could not inherit the Kingdom.[6] This may possibly have been a reason for the intervention of the secular power to exile Pelagius and Celestius in 418.

Despite the condemnation of Celestius at Carthage, a council at Diospolis in Palestine in 415 vindicated the Pelagian position against Western accusations, greatly to the indignation of Jerome at Bethlehem. The African Church leaders, however, obtained a condemnation of it from Pope Innocent in 416, but his successor, Zosimus, reversed this verdict. After the intervention of the emperor Honorius, however, and a further condemnation by a large council at Carthage in 418, Zosimus adhered to the view of the African Church. At Ephesus in 431 Pelagianism was condemned in the persons of Celestius and his associates, though this was largely due to the alleged connection of these Western heretics with the party of Nestorius, Julian of Eclanum having been received by Theodore of Mopsuestia.[7]

---

[1] *ep. Dem.* 8; Aug. *grat. Chr.* 43; *exp. epp. Paul.* 59.13.
[2] *ep. Dem.* 6; 8.
[3] *exp. epp. Paul.* 68.23ff.; 69.7ff.
[4] Aug. *pecc. orig.* 2ff.; Marius Mercator *commonit. Caelest.* 1.
[5] Aug. *pecc. orig.* 13; 16.
[6] *ib.* 12; cf. *de divitiis* (Migne, *PL.* suppl. 1.1380) possibly by Celestius.
[7] Schwartz *A.C.O.* 1.1.3, p. 9.

The council of 418, besides condemning the theory of Adam's mortality, anathematized the view that infants ought not immediately to be baptized (Pelagius in fact attempted rather illogically to maintain the practice of infant baptism within his theological system), and that they are not baptized for a genuine remission of sin, that is to say, original sin which they have contracted through physical generation. It condemned the idea of limbo, John 3:5 being taken to mean that salvation is literally impossible for the unbaptized. It rejected the reference of justifying grace to the remission of past sins and not also to assistance against the committing of sins in the future, and also the Pelagian understanding of grace as enlightenment rather than power to do what we know we ought to do. The council also repudiated the somewhat unfortunate statement of Pelagius that grace enables man to do more easily what he is commanded to do by the exercise of free will, and attacked the notion of the possibility of sinlessness and the implied corollary that 'Forgive us our trespasses' might occasionally be prayed vicariously for others rather than for the saintly user of the prayer.[1]

All these anathemas represent the Augustinian position against Pelagius. According to Augustine all men have sinned in Adam. The Fall was the consequence of Adam's misuse of free will which had been granted to him as the means by which he might obey God and be deterred from sinning, and by which he might make even further progress in the state of original righteousness. All Adam's progeny has been contaminated by Adam's sin, not by voluntarily following his example but by being in Adam 'as in a root'; it is therefore under the divine sentence of death and damnation, doomed to carry its burden of original sin to the appointed end which is eternal punishment with the rebellious angels. Indeed, the process of generation itself, involving carnal desire, is both an extension of, and also a kind of penalty for, the primal sin of Adam which is concupiscence. Mankind, rooted in Adam, is thus a 'condemned lump'.[2]

By 'concupiscence' Augustine meant desire for that which is opposed to God, and hence self-centred desire which seeks another object of attraction and devotion in the place of God. Unfortunately, he regarded sexual desire as a primary and obvious expression of concupiscence, and laid himself open to the powerful attack of Julian of Eclanum against what the latter regarded as Augustine's Manichaean association of the transmission of original sin with physical generation.[3] However much he might protest that he did not intend to denigrate marriage, Augustine always regarded sexual desire as irrational and a token of man's fallen condition. He had held this view long before the Pelagian controversy began, and it is fully expressed in his early anti-Manichaean writings. For the Manichaeans it was procreation which was especially abhorrent, since it perpetuated the involvement of spirit with matter – the imprisonment of the divine element in man within a fleshly body. This notion that procreation is a worse sin than sexual intercourse aroused Augustine's strong objections, causing him to make the disastrously revealing statement that unless sexual intercourse within marriage is

---

[1] Hahn, pp. 213–15.
[2] *enchir.* 8–9.
[3] *c. duas epp. Pelag.* 9ff.

directed towards procreation it is a form of prostitution: the wife is then joined to a man for the purpose of gratifying his lust in return for certain benefits. He also committed himself to the belief that God's will allows carnal desire to be released from the control of reason in sexual intercourse only for the purpose of propagating children.[1] In his early works, indeed, Augustine thought that Genesis 1:27–28 should not be interpreted literally;[2] later, however, he acknowledged that sexuality existed in man's state of original righteousness, but held that it was then totally subject to reason.[3]

Augustine's views on this subject were neither original nor surprising. The sexual morality of the Roman Empire was generally low and Christianity did little to improve this, for, apart from the high estimate of marriage implied by the teaching of Jesus on divorce and his grounding of marriage in God's original creation of man (Genesis 2:24), Christianity was considerably inferior to Judaism in its theological understanding of sex. As early as the writing of Paul's first letter to them there were evidently many Corinthian Christians who regarded sexual intercourse as sinful, and Paul's apparently compromising attitude towards their views, as expressed in 1 Corinthians 7:1, gave encouragement to the exaltation of virginity which became a strongly marked feature of almost all Christian preaching and teaching in the patristic period. Indeed, in much popular literature, such as the Apocryphal Acts, the apostolic mission is presented almost as though it were primarily an anti-sex movement. Admittedly, much of this literature is more or less heavily tinged with Gnosticism, but writers of a very different intellectual calibre, such as Clement,[4] do not differ significantly from Augustine in their attitude. Although the pressure of Manichaean heresy compelled orthodox writers of the fourth century to uphold the legitimacy of Christian marriage, and the ascetic movement launched in the later decades of that century by Priscillian of Avila was condemned because, among other false beliefs, the Priscillianists held that such marriage was 'exsecrable',[5] the immensely high spiritual value placed on virginity[6] and the identification of the ascetic and monastic vocation with the 'angelic life' resulted in a very general consensus that human sexuality, if not actually evil (which no orthodox theologian could directly assert) was certainly regrettable. Jerome's opponent, Jovinian, was one of the few explicit opponents of this general view, teaching that marriage is not inferior to celibacy. Jerome's attack on this doctrine was so fierce as to make the theological distinction between his own view of marriage and that of Manichaeism appear to be very finely drawn; in its turn, Jerome's denigration of marriage in his *Against Jovinian* aroused the alarm of an unnamed monk at Rome who was probably Pelagius,[7] then, as later in the controversy with Augustine, intensely suspicious of any tendency towards a Manichaean rejection of the orthodox doctrine of creation.

---

[1] *de moribus Manich.* 18.65; *c. Faust.* 22.30; cf. *de bono conjug.* 6.

[2] *de Gen. c. Manich.* 1.19; 2.11.

[3] *de Gen. ad. litt.* 9; 10; *civ. Dei* 14.21, 24; *c. duas epp. Pelag.* 1.17.

[4] See above, p. 67.

[5] First Council of Toledo (400) *anath.* 15 (Hahn, p. 212).

[6] e.g., in the treatises *On Virginity* of Basil of Ancyra and Gregory of Nyssa.

[7] Jerome *ep.* 50.

According to Augustine, 'from the time when "through one man sin entered into the world, and through sin death, and so death passed on into all men, in whom all sinned", the whole lump of perdition became the possession of the one who causes perdition. No one, therefore, either has been freed, or is being freed, or will be freed from this state except by the grace of the Redeemer.'[1] Augustine relied greatly on this text (Romans 5:12). He attacked Julian of Eclanum as a reckless innovator for translating the Latin *in quo* in the sense of 'inasmuch as'.[2] He himself usually associated it with I Corinthians 15:22 ('As in Adam all die'),[3] and used it to prove that all men are sinners, not through imitating Adam but by actually participating in him, just as they are saved through participation in Christ's grace and not by imitating him. He does, however, offer an alternative interpretation of *in quo*: '(the sin) in which all sinned'. It then signifies that besides the actual sins of each individual all alike are guilty of having sinned in the primal sin.[4]

Augustine finds his idea of original sin in such scriptural passages as Psalm 51:5 as well as in Romans 5:12, and he believes it to be confirmed by the practice of infant baptism. To the Pelagians infant baptism was an established practice which they were not concerned to repudiate – Celestius maintained that he always said infants needed baptism and ought to be baptized; what more, he asked, could anyone ask?[5] – but it was apt to be a theological embarrassment. For Augustine it was a welcome piece of evidence for the truth of his theology. Although infant baptism had become the general practice it was in some degree a rite searching for a theological rationale. Augustine formulated a rationale and read this back out of the rite. This was especially easy in so far as the Church had never evolved a baptismal rite specifically designed for infants, but applied to them the service for adult converts including the exorcisms and the renunciation of the devil. If, he argues, all this is to be taken seriously (which he never doubts), the sin from which infants are really rescued in baptism must be 'original sin through which they are captives in the devil's power'.[6]

It is no mere bias towards sin which is transmitted to Adam's offspring but the actual guilt of sin. Indeed, it may be said to be primarily guilt, because this is what the grace of baptism removes. The inheritance of sin, that is, of evil disposition or regrettable limitation, remains after baptism, but the guilt attaching to these is put away. Here Augustine had to meet a difficult Pelagian argument: if concupiscence is the essence of sin and if it is inherent in sex, why does it obviously remain in the baptized, since they continue to beget children, and is not abolished in baptism? Alternatively, if sexual concupiscence is not a sin in a baptized parent, why is it a sin in his child (unless baptized)? Augustine maintains that guilt is remitted in baptism, but concupiscence remains, though without the imputation of guilt. Ignorance is a great source of evil: baptism does not cure it, and

[1] *grat. Chr. et pecc.* 2.34.
[2] *c. Jul.* 6.24.75.
[3] *c. Faust.* 22.78; *pecc. merit.* 1.8.8; 3.11.19.
[4] *pecc. merit.* 1.11.
[5] *pecc. orig.* 4.3.
[6] *nupt. et concup.* 1.22.

ignorance of God's will, such as that with which Paul reproached the baptized Corinthians, remains; but it is not imputed as sin. Concupiscence, admittedly, is a much greater evil; but though it persists in Christians it is no longer imputed as sin and it will gradually be overcome by progress in sanctification, by growth in more and more fervent charity: it is diminished day by day in those who are advanced in the spiritual life and in continence, and 'especially as old age comes on'.[1] Augustine cannot say that procreation ought to cease among the baptized. He was already too vulnerable to the Pelagian accusation that he was still at heart a Manichaean. He has to affirm that in itself it is good, being ordained by the Creator; but he goes so far as to follow Ambrose (so he claims) in supposing that the conception of Christ without human intercourse freed him from the chain of original sin.[2] All others except Christ were in Adam when he sinned through his free choice and so vitiated human nature.[3]

Augustine claims that against the Manichaeans he acknowledges the goodness of marriage and the legitimacy of procreation; but at the same time he says unequivocally that sexual desire, though not actually imputed as sin to the regenerate, is an element in human nature which sin has introduced. In itself it is shameful, though, since he cannot deny that procreation is a work of God, he allows that it can have a 'good use' for that purpose only.[4] It is both the daughter and the mother of sin; it is therefore the means by which original sin is transmitted and continues to hold captive all who are not reborn in Christ who was born without concupiscence.[5] This close relationship of sex to the primal sin is a topic to which Augustine returns again and again. This is because his identification of concupiscence to a large extent with sexual desire underlies his picture of the universality of sin, its hereditary transmission, and the powerlessness of man to break free from it. It is also because it was here that his opponents found the weakest point in his theological system where his hold on the orthodox doctrine of creation was uncertain. It would have been far more satisfactory for his arguments and for the value of his theology if he had concentrated his attention less on the sexual aspect of concupiscence and more on the broader understanding of sin which he shows in discussing the nature of Adam's transgression itself. This was the sin of pride, and pride means the abandonment of God in order to please oneself, and thus the surrender to the temptation to 'be as gods' (Gen. 3:5).[6]

The Fall means that mankind has sunk far below the level of weakness and insensibility that characterizes the human infant. The further back an arrow is pulled on a bow, the greater its velocity in the opposite direction when it is released; man has fallen into a state where his natural condition is bondage to sin and inevitable death.[7] This does not imply that free will has been lost. Augustine is quite clear that human action is not determined;

---

[1] *ib.* 1.28–30; *c. Jul.* 6.49–50.
[2] *nupt. et concup.* 2.15.
[3] *op. imperf. c. Jul.* 4.104.
[4] *nupt. et concup.* 2.36.
[5] *ib.* 1.27.
[6] *civ. Dei.* 14.13.
[7] *ib.* 13.3.

one can choose freely between different options. The Pelagians, however, he thinks, do not realize that while free choice is possible freedom has been lost. Freedom means freedom from sin and freedom for righteousness. It is experienced in, and consists of, serving God in living the life of free sons of God.[1] In the fallen state man can choose, but he cannot enjoy liberty, for he is in bondage to sin and his every choice, his exercise of free will, takes place within, as it were, a bracket governed by the sign of sin.[2] He is under the necessity of sinning.[3] It follows that no one can pray 'Forgive us our trespasses' except in the straightforward sense of the words.[4] It also follows, according to Augustine's logic, that since infants receive the *exsufflatio* before baptism they must be at that stage possessed by the devil; otherwise, if there were no devil to expel the rite would presumably be directed against God the Creator – a frightful blasphemy. Therefore, if not rescued by baptism, the infant will necessarily go with the devil into eternal fire.[5] He was, however, prepared to modify his strict logic by admitting that the punishment of those who had added no actual sin to their original inheritance would be 'the most gentle of all'.[6]

Freedom, in Augustine's sense, can come only through grace. Grace is not, as Pelagius affirmed, given merely in the conditions laid down by God for living good lives and in the laws and other aids to the good life which he provides, but it is the internal operation of the Holy Spirit[7] which makes possible both the exercise of the will and the accomplishment of good actions. God does not only give us the possibility of doing good but operates in us the willing and doing.[8] God 'prepares man's good will in order that it may be helped, and helps it when he has prepared it. He "prevents" the unwilling man so as to make him will, and when he does so will God accompanies him with his aid so that his will may not be ineffective.' Grace does not merely teach men what to do, but enables them to do it.[9] It wins victory for them in the inward conflict between flesh and spirit, and is thus different in its operation in them from what it was in Adam, for whom grace gave the possibility of not sinning if he remained in his pristine beatitude. This state, in turn, must be distinguished from the final state of the saved in heaven for whom there will be no possibility of sinning. Adam had the assistance without which he could not persevere in blessedness through the exercise of free will. Those who are elected to salvation receive the assistance which actually enables them to persevere: the distinction is between 'assistance without which something cannot be attained' (*adiutorium sine quo non* . . .) and 'assistance by which something can be attained' (*adiutorium quo* . . .).[10] Thus Augustine lays down the classifications of

---

[1] *c. duas epp. Pelag.* 1.5.
[2] cf. *perf. just. hom.* 9.
[3] *op. imperf. c. Jul.* 1.106.
[4] *c. duas epp. Pelag.* 4.27ff.
[5] *op. imperf. c. Jul.* 3.199.
[6] *enchir.* 23.
[7] cf. *ib.* 11.
[8] *grat. Chr.* 24–26.
[9] *enchir.* 9; *grat. Chr.* 36–37.
[10] *corrept. et grat.* 29–34.

grace: prevenient, co-operating, sufficient, efficient. The relation between the operation of grace and human freedom is that the irresistible will of God operates in and through human wills, not by over-riding them but by moving them from within so that they come to be instruments of God's will.[1] This is how prevenient grace works.[2]

Here we approach the problem of predestination. Some men are brought to salvation. This is not through their merits but by grace, because they are freely justified in the blood of the second Adam. Those who are chosen out of the 'lump of perdition' have been predestined from before the foundation of the world without regard for any merits on their side.[3] Predestination signifies the foreknowledge of God and the fore-ordaining of the means by which those who are to be saved will be saved. It is by God's just judgment that the rest are left in the 'lump of perdition' and either not given an opportunity to believe or, if they are given it, they are without the ability to take advantage of it. No one can come to Christ unless it be given him, and it is given to those who have been chosen in him before the foundation of the world. Those who are elect can respond to the gospel; the rest, whether they hear it or not, cannot act upon it. Perseverance is thus a gift; it cannot be meritorious, for it is given by grace to those who are pre-destined. Yet this does not make preaching unnecessary; on the contrary, it is the elect alone who can respond and so make it possible for the preaching to take effect.[4] Everything from initial conversion to final perseverance is God's gift according to the 'election of grace'.[5] Hence the question why of two infants, equally bound by original sin, one is taken and one left, or of two unbelieving adults one is called to conversion and the other not, or why of two believers one is given final perseverance and the other not, can only be left to the inscrutable judgment of God. All that we can know is that the one was among the predestined and the other not.[6] The number of the elect, again, is a mystery, but Augustine believes that it is in the end to be equated with the number of the fallen angels.[7] This presents difficulties in view of the assertion of 1 Tim. 2:4 that God wills all men to be saved. Augustine's way of getting round this text is to interpret it to mean either that no man can be saved unless God wills it (and so it is right to pray that God wills the salvation of any individual person), or that in those elected to salvation all sorts and conditions of men are included, from kings to beggars, wise men to fools: so that the text really means that God wills the salvation of all the predestined.[8]

This attempt to push the logic of grace to extremes provoked a consider-able reaction in the West, especially in the developing stronghold of monasticism in southern France. The ascetical theology of the Eastern desert fathers, which was held up as a model for the West by Cassian,

[1] *ib.* 45.
[2] *enchir.* 9.
[3] *corrept. et grat.* 12–17.
[4] *persev.* 35–37.
[5] *ib.* 47–49.
[6] *ib.* 21ff.; *tract. in Jn.* 43.13; 110.2.
[7] *civ. Dei* 22.1; *enchir.* 9.
[8] *enchir.* 27; *corrept. et grat.* 44.

Vincent of Lerinum and others, rested on a concept of grace which allowed genuine scope for moral effort and meritorious progress and interpreted the operation of grace in terms of assistance. Augustine's belief that the initial turning of a man to God, the beginning of conversion, is a gift of prevenient grace and is not initiated by the human will, was sharply questioned by Prosper, a strong Augustinian in other respects, and by Cassian and others of the party called in modern times 'Semi-Pelagians'.[1] This was a vital point, one of those on which the Augustinian idea of pre-destination depended. Another was the interpretation of I Tim. 2:4, which was challenged by both these writers, Cassian holding that it must be taken literally: that if God wills the salvation of all men the loss of any must be contrary to his will, in the sense that it is due to their own sin. Predestina-tion, therefore, can be accepted only in the greatly reduced sense that God foresees the merits of the elect and the demerits of the lost, or rather that God elects those whom he foresees as meriting salvation.[2] Cassian also held that Augustine had over-stated the depravity of fallen man, who can recognize God's will, though he needs grace to enable him to do it.[3]

So far as the West was concerned (the East was very little affected by Augustine's teaching; thus predestination was denied by John of Damascus),[4] it was an essentially Augustinian view which prevailed, despite the fact that such a theologian as Vincent regarded it as a dangerous innovation and in this context had formulated his famous 'canon' of tradition: that which is believed always, everywhere, and by all men.[5] This theology was summed up by the Second Council of Orange in 529. The main headings include the belief that by the Fall man was totally changed for the worse, in soul as well as body, and that Adam's sin was transmitted to the entire race. The initial movement of faith, the will to conversion, is entirely a gift of grace; there can be no response to the gospel without the illumina-tion and inspiration of the Spirit. In every good work and in all good intention it is God who acts and wills; our evil intentions and deeds, on the other hand, are our own, for lying and sin are all that we can claim as our own achievement. Grace is necessary for all men without exception; there is no merit, and, in particular, no reward for merits preceding the operation of grace, because nothing good or meritorious can be done without grace.

Only in one respect does the Council's doctrine markedly differ from Augustine's. This is in its avoidance of any direct reference to predestination except in the condemnation of the idea that any men are actually pre-destined to evil by God's power. In two of the Council's clauses, however, we catch a glimpse of the elements of genuine religious truth which lie at the heart of Augustine's understanding of grace, distorted as they often were by his terrible conception of sin: God loves us as we shall be through his gift of grace and not as we now are through our own deserving. To love God is a gift given by God who loves although he is unloved. He loves us

---

[1] Prosper ap. Aug. *ep.* 225.5–6; Cassian *coll.* 13.8.4; 13.11.1.
[2] Prosper ap. Aug. *ep.* 225.4; 226.7; Cassian *coll.* 13.7.
[3] Cassian *coll.* 13.13.
[4] Jo. D. *fid. orth.* 2.30.
[5] Vincent *commonit.* 2.

although we are not pleasing to him, so that there may come to be in us that through which we shall be pleasing to him; for the Spirit, whom we love together with the Father and the Son, pours out in our hearts the love of the Father and the Son.[1]

---

[1] Council of Orange (529) *cap itula* (Hahn, pp. 220–227).

X

THE CHURCH AND THE SACRAMENTS

The teaching of the Christian writers of the second and early third centuries about the Church and the Sacraments has already been briefly noticed. So far as Western theology is concerned, the most important figure in this field is Cyprian. As bishop of Carthage during the Decian persecution and its aftermath, he had to work out a theory of the nature of the Church, the limits of its membership, its unity and its discipline which could meet the stresses caused by numerous apostasies of Christians under persecution, and the consequent recriminations and disunity after peace had been restored and quarrels about, and between, the 'resistance' and the 'collaborators' had begun to cause disruption and to lead to the schism which ensued. Cyprian was an administrator rather than a speculative thinker, and his ecclesiology was hammered out in response to the practical problems which he had to solve.

Cyprian's main concern was to preserve the Church's unity, threatened by the conflict between three parties. There were some who shared the outlook of Tertullian and held that grave sinners, especially apostates, could not be reconciled to the Church during their lifetime, some who held, like some of the confessors who had suffered in the persecution and their admirers, that the granting or withholding of pardon to the lapsed was a privilege of those who, as martyr-witnesses, had proved themselves to be Spirit-possessed saints, and some who, like Cyprian, believed it to be the duty of the bishop to examine each case on its merits and prescribe appropriate penitential discipline. In trying to assert his episcopal authority in respect of penitential discipline Cyprian took care to work in close co-operation with Church leaders elsewhere, especially with Cornelius, the bishop who, after the cessation of the persecution, was elected to fill the long-vacant see of Rome. It was at Rome that Novatian started his break-away movement, having been consecrated to the bishopric in due form by neighbouring bishops, but after Cornelius had been properly elected. The issue in this schism was the treatment of post-baptismal sin. Novatian's followers held that penitential discipline leading to restoration to communion in the end, perhaps only when the offender is on his death-bed, cannot be made available for mortal sin such as apostasy; the Church has no power to reconcile such sinners, and if it does do so it becomes corrupted so that its ministry and sacraments become invalidated: for those from whom the Spirit has departed cannot in their turn impart spiritual blessing. Their view was thus similar to the rigorism of Hippolytus in his controversy

with Callistus, and virtually identical with the position of Tertullian in his
De Pudicitia.

Cyprian, with the main body of the Church in Africa and elsewhere, held
that the Church cannot be restricted in its membership to the morally
perfect. In this age it is bound to be a mixed society of good and bad. It
can, of course, seek to insure itself to some extent by selecting its applicants
for membership carefully. As the rules for the admission and testing of
catechumens in the *Apostolic Tradition* of Hippolytus strikingly show,
anxiety to recruit worthy members had led to baptism becoming more like
a reward for virtuous conduct, administered after a long period of probation,
than the actual beginning of Christian life which it had apparently been in
the first century. Nevertheless, the Church will contain tares as well as
wheat; like the ark, it will house unclean as well as clean inmates; and in
this age it not possible to separate them, for at best this can lead only to
more and more sectarian subdivision in the quest for a visible remnant
which will be manifestly the genuinely holy Church, and at worst to an
attempt to perform the impossible task of discovering and judging hidden
motives and secret sins.

The third-century controversy about post-baptismal sin ended with the
triumph of the view that the Church may grant reconciliation sooner or
later to all sinners who have given adequate tokens and pledges of repentance. Only in Africa did the sectarian ideal of total visible holiness in this
present age remain a really powerful influence. The controversy had, however, produced the first schism which did not involve controversy about the
fundamentals of belief in God, and thus it confronted theologians with the
need to mark out the limits of the true Church since these were not now
necessarily coterminous with the boundary between recognized orthodoxies
and heresies. This became especially necessary when Novatianists made
their own converts to Christianity and the question arose whether, if these
later wished to join the majority Church, they had to be baptized (or, as
Novatianists would see it, rebaptized). Cyprian held uncompromisingly to
the strict view that there is no salvation and no Christianity outside the
visible Church. Whoever separates himself from the Church and is joined to
an adulteress cuts himself off from the Church's promises. He who leaves
Christ's Church cannot attain Christ's rewards. He is an alien, 'profane', an
enemy. He cannot have God for Father who has not the Church for mother.
Whoever is outside the Church can no more escape than anyone could who
stayed outside the ark of Noah: 'he who is not with me is against me'.[1] He
who is outside the Church of Christ, whoever and whatever he may be, is
not a Christian.[2] It follows that outside the Church there is no baptism,
nor any other gift of grace. Cyprian, following the general outlook of the
time, held that confession under persecution and martyrdom were the
highest goal of Christian discipleship. If the catechumen suffered martyrdom
his death was equivalent to baptism, for it was a literal, and not merely
figurative, dying with Christ to rise with him. But for a 'heretic' martyrdom
profited nothing, since 'there is not salvation outside the Church'. How

[1] Cypr. *un. eccl.* 6.
[2] *ep.* 55.24.

much less, asks Cyprian, could a man profit from schismatic baptism? To be 'dipped' in a cave and hide-out of brigands with the contagion of adulterous water not only does not remove a person's former sins but adds to them new and more serious ones.[1] The Holy Spirit does not operate in sacraments outside the Church; prayer is not heard and the eucharistic offering is not consecrated where there is no Holy Spirit.[2] Schismatic ordinations are therefore profane; they are conferred by false bishops and antichrists, and the ministries of people so ordained consist in offering false and sacrilegious sacrifices against the one divine altar. Cyprian therefore directs that if schismatic clergy return to the fold they shall be reconciled as laymen, and 'not allowed to retain the arms which they used against us as rebels'.[3] Those who have been 'baptized' by schismatics must therefore be baptized on entering the Church. Only within it is there Christ's authentic sacrament.

The criterion of 'within' or 'outside' the Church is not doctrinal but organizational. Irenaeus and Tertullian had seen the continuity of bishops in their sees in succession to apostolic founders as a primary guarantee of true doctrine. Cyprian saw in this succession the guarantee that the societies over which they preside are true parts of the authentic Church of Christ. The Church is based upon, and depends upon for the ordered process of its life, the episcopal succession. It is governed by the bishops in its every act. This means that, although the episcopate itself is 'constitutional', in the sense that the Church consists of bishops, presbyterate, and laity who attend and assent, the limits of the Church are defined by communion with those bishops who can show that they stand in apostolic succession, which means succession in office, and not simply succession by consecration (which Novatian possessed equally with Cornelius).[4] The bishop is the key to the unity of the Church: there is one God, Christ is the one Lord, there is one Holy Spirit, one bishop in the (local) Catholic Church;[5] and schism arises when there is failure to recognize in the Church one priest and one judge deputizing for Christ.[6] Thus the bishop is in the Church and the Church in the bishop, and whoever is not in communion with the bishop is outside the Church.[7] For the bishop is not merely the bond of unity in the local congregation. He is a member of a collegiate body: the episcopate is one corporate holding, as it were, in which each individual bishop holds his share.[8] It thus serves to bind together, and define the boundaries of, the Church which is diffused throughout the world.[9]

Yet although the episcopate is corporate Cyprian finds it important to trace the bishop's office as the source and guarantee of unity, not only to the corporate body of the apostles but within this to a single individual

[1] *ep.* 73.21.
[2] *ep.* 65.4.
[3] *ep.* 72.2.
[4] *ep.* 33.1.
[5] *ep.* 49.2.
[6] *ep.* 59.5.
[7] *ep.* 66.8.
[8] *un. eccl.* 5.
[9] *ep.* 55.24.

person. Christ, he says, founded the Church on one man, Peter, and, although all the apostles were given equal authority to his, Christ arranged that the origin of the Church's unity should begin from one man, so as to demonstrate that the Church is one.[1] This idea finds support in other passages where Cyprian speaks of the episcopate in relation to Christ's commission to Peter.[2] Its meaning is, however, substantially altered in a variant version which affirms, indeed, that the power bestowed on all the apostles was equal, but that Christ established 'one chair', the chair of Peter on which the Church was founded. No one can claim to be in the Church who deserts the chair of Peter, and primacy was given to Peter in order that the Church might be shown to be one. It is likely that Cyprian may have seen the focussing of the unity of the apostles on Peter as paralleled by a focussing of the unity of the episcopate on the person of the bishop of Rome as 'primus'. If he did, then, on the assumption that the variant version is in fact Cyprian's work, he may have written it at or about the time of the schism of Novatian in order to support the episcopal authority in Rome, and deleted it in a revised edition of the treatise *On the Unity of the Catholic Church* after his dispute with Stephen of Rome over schismatical baptism. If so, an important step had been taken towards the establishment of the primacy of the see of Rome, not merely on the ground that the church at Rome was the church of the capital city of the world but on the Petrine claim. The possibility, however, that this variant text is a product of much later times, designed to give support to the Petrine claims, ought not perhaps to be dismissed so readily as it has been by modern scholars in reaction against earlier Protestant anxiety to reject it as a 'forgery'. More important, in any case, is the fact that in Cyprian's ecclesiology the episcopal succession has become more than the symbol of unity and pledge of the continuity of the Church's life and doctrine; it is now the foundation on which the Church itself rests, and the continuing life and ministry of the Church is made to depend upon it.

Cyprian's theory of the Church had the great merit of 'wholeness' and consistency. The Christian community was seen as the sphere of the operation of the Holy Spirit; in its life Christ was embodied and re-presented; its mission and worship was the framework or context of the sacraments, and these could not be conceived as possessing any significance, or indeed as existing at all, outside that living human situation. Unfortunately, what was gained by tying the sacraments so firmly into the wholeness of the Church's life was lost by defining the boundaries of the Church so narrowly by reference to the historic episcopate. For this meant that schismatics like Novatian, who fully shared in the life, thought and worship of the Christian community, had to be treated as non-Christians.

This attitude was opposed by Stephen, bishop of Rome, in respect of the question of those baptized in schism who wished to join the majority church. On Cyprian's principle, these people had never been baptized at all and must be received into the Church as though they were heathen converts. Stephen, also claiming the authority of traditional practice, held that they

[1] *ep.* 55.24.
[2] *un. eccl.* 4.

had been baptized, and that since baptism is essentially unrepeatable, they should be admitted with the laying-on of hands. The precise meaning of this rite was left undefined, except that it was regarded as an efficacious sign of the coming of the Holy Spirit on those to whom it was administered. It resembled the laying-on of hands in the reconciliation of penitents, and this may have been, in part at least, the intended meaning: the restoration of the Spirit to those who had been outside the Church, the sphere of the Spirit. On the other hand, the baptismal rite known to Tertullian had included the laying of the bishop's hand on the newly baptized, as a sign of the coming of the Spirit, and during the third century it is clear that there was an increasing tendency to regard the post-baptismal rite, whether of chrismation or, in the West, the imposition of hands, or both, as the sacramental sign of the gift of the Spirit. The common occurrence of clinical baptism, when the sick person would be baptized privately and receive the post-baptismal rite from the bishop at a later date, if he had recovered,[1] contributed towards the separation of what later became known as Confirmation from the rite of baptism proper, and also towards the tendency to exalt it at the expense of baptism which could even be reduced to a kind of purificatory rite of cleansing in preparation for the reception of the positive sacrament of 'Spirit-baptism'. This tendency was especially marked in the baptismal doctrine of the treatise *On Rebaptism* which dates from this controversy and represents Stephen's point of view. Baptism in water is there treated as an incomplete sacrament; it is of lesser importance than the laying-on of hands. and it is the latter which is the sacrament of the Spirit and of the promise of salvation.[2] It seems probable, then, that the development of this tendency, which was contrary to Cyprian's general insistence on the unity of the initiatory rite,[3] contributed to the willingness of Stephen's party to recognize baptism outside the Church so long as the laying-on of hands was administered to those who had received such baptism by the legitimate bishop on their reception into the Church.

Stephen's attitude prevailed in the West (in the East the criterion for the recognition or otherwise of baptism administered in schism was the degree of Trinitarian orthodoxy in the sect concerned) and came to be adopted even in Africa by the Catholic (as opposed to Donatist) Church: in 314 it was endorsed, against the Donatists, by the Council of Arles. How it was possible to combine a Cyprianic theory of the frontiers of the Church with a recognition, to the extent of believing it to be unrepeatable, of baptism administered outside them, was left undefined until fourth-century Catholicism in Africa had to justify its practice against the Donatists.

The Donatist ecclesiology was similar to the Novatianist, although strictly theological considerations were to some extent subordinated to the social, cultural, economic and political factors which contributed to the rise of the movement and gave it its remarkable strength and staying-power. It assumed that the true Church must be visibly holy, and that those who had offered less than total resistance to the demands of Diocletian's

---

[1] e.g., *ep.* 33.1; 66.8.
[2] *rebapt.* 5–6; 11; cf. Cornelius ap. Eus. *h.e.* 6.43.15.
[3] Cypr. *ep.* 63.8; 69.13; but cf. 73.9.

persecuting officials, especially those who had handed over copies of the Scriptures, must be rigorously excluded from membership. In particular, clergy who were guilty of this would, if allowed to remain in the Church, pass on the pollution; their ministrations would be valueless, their ordinations would perpetuate a succession of false priests. In the eyes of the Donatists the 'Catholics' were a schismatic and contaminated body. Its members must therefore be (re)baptized on joining the (Donatist) true Church. Against their teaching Optatus, bishop of Milevum, argued in about 367 that the Church must be a mixed society of good and evil (here following Cyprian against those who claimed to be Cyprianic); unity and universality characterize the Church as much as outward holiness; and baptism is God's rather than the Church's, so that the character of the administrant is relatively unimportant.[1]

Augustine developed this last idea in his long polemic against the Donatists. The Church's unity is central in his theology. It is grounded in the identity between the Church and Christ, for the community and its Lord are the members and the head, and together are a single organism or person.[2] The solidarity between the head and the members is maintained by the Spirit,[3] and the manifestation of the Spirit is love. Love is therefore the essential characteristic of the Church,[4] and although Augustine shares Cyprian's organizational definition of the Church's visible structure and boundaries he thinks of the inward operation of love as the real distinguishing mark of the Church which separates it from the rest of mankind. Schism is the negation of love, so that where there is schism there is no love and therefore no genuine Church.[5] Unfortunately, Augustine could not say that where there is no love there is schism; for his definition of the Church is determined in the last resort by the nature of its structure, and so he has first to identify schism by means of external criteria and only then begin to interpret the nature of schism in terms of the inward quality of lovelessness. This, however, enables him to say that what a person baptized in schism lacks is, precisely, love. He has been genuinely baptized, for the sacraments are not the Church's but Christ's. His baptism is real and unrepeatable. It is 'valid'. On the other hand, until he is admitted into the Church where love, the operation of the Spirit, is present, his baptism cannot become 'efficacious'. It is like a frozen credit, from which no profit can be derived until entry into the Church with the laying-on of hands releases its grace.[6] Thus, in his anxiety to devise an eirenic theory to encourage Donatists towards reunion, he broke through the narrowness of Cyprian's practice at the expense of losing the 'wholeness' of Cyprian's theory. The sacraments are given a validity of their own outside the framework of the Church's actual life, and they are depersonalized. Instead of being essentially means of grace, in the sense of channels of God's gracious approach to man, they come to be thought of mechanically and impersonally. A means of personal

[1] Optatus 2.20; 2.1ff.; 3.2; 5.4ff.
[2] *enarr. in Ps.* 30.4; *enarr. in Ps.* 127.3.
[3] *serm.* 267.4; 268.2.
[4] *enarr. 2 in Ps.* 32.21; *Trin.* 15.33ff.
[5] *ep.* 61.2; *serm.* 265.7.
[6] *bapt.* 1.18; 4.1; 4.24; 5.9; 6.1, 7; 7.87; *serm. ad Caes.* 6.

graciousness cannot be 'valid' in the sense of being the genuine article, and yet not 'efficacious'; Augustine's idea of baptism is closer to the notion of a cheque which can be stopped until, in different circumstances, the drawer chooses to unstop it.

Augustine regards the visible Church as a mixed society of good and bad, but he is less satisfied than some of his predecessors to stop when he has said this. He realizes that sin within the organized Church is a problem, and he tries to solve it by distinguishing nominal members from the real Church which is the society of the righteous. He does not imitate the Donatists in trying actually to sort out the one group from the other; the authentically holy Church is known only to God.[1] This belief in what is virtually the idea of an invisible Church only partly coterminous with the visible institution is in harmony with Augustine's idea of the relationship of Church and State to the earthly and heavenly 'cities', the realms of God and of evil. The Donatists held that the Church, as the holy society of God's people, must be in a constant state of war against the secular power, whether this be a persecuting heathen empire (which to the Donatists is almost the natural and proper relationship of Church to State) or a persecuting, self-styled Catholic, Christian one. Most Churchmen from Eusebius to Optatus and on to Augustine's contemporaries had held that the Christian empire, embracing the Church, was virtually a mirror of the Kingdom of God with the emperor as God's vice-gerent. Augustine, on the other hand, believed that neither was the Church an embodiment of the Kingdom of God nor was the State simply to be identified with the earthly or anti-Christian 'city': still less was the State to be thought of as forming, with the Church, a kind of approximation to God's Kingdom. In both Church and State there are elements of both realms; and the Church contains members who belong to the evil sphere just as outside the Church there are those who belong to the heavenly. This thought finds much clearer and sharper definition in Augustine's doctrine of predestination, which prevents him from accepting the naive sectarian concept of the visibly righteous Church and also forces him in theory to revise the Cyprianic doctrine, which he himself professed, that outside the Church there is no salvation; the logic of predestinarianism makes it impossible for him to deny that there may be salvation for some who are now outside the Church.[2]

Later Latin theology added little to Augustine's ecclesiology apart from the full development of the Petrine theory of the Roman see, carried out by the late fourth-century bishops of Rome and their successors and formulated most clearly by Leo.[3] In the East the doctrine of the Church was never itself a focal point of controversy and there was less reason for definition; essentially, the Greek Fathers' conception of the Church is expressed in the thought of the incorporation of believers in the deified humanity of Christ, especially through participation in the eucharist.

Eucharistic theology had developed in the meanwhile in two principal directions. The idea of the eucharistic rite, and so, by transference, of the

[1] *bapt.* 5.38; 6.3; *civ. Dei* 10.6.
[2] *corrept. et grat.* 39ff.; *bapt.* 5.38.
[3] Leo *ep.* 14.11.

offered bread and wine themselves, as a sacrifice of thanksgiving tended to give way to the belief that the eucharistic sacrifice was a propitiatory or expiatory sacrifice. The belief that the elements received in Communion are the body and blood of Christ in the sense that they are the effective sign, 'type', 'figure', 'representation', of Christ's body and blood, identified therewith by prophetic symbolism, tended to give way, especially in the East, to the belief that the identification is substantial and involves actual change.

Both these developments are often traced in origin to Cyprian, and this is partly, but not entirely, true. The tendencies which we have just mentioned co-existed in the Church before his time, and we have already touched upon some early examples of this. An instance of the varied ways in which the eucharist was understood to be a Christian sacrifice can be seen in the different forms in which a favourite proof-test was applied to it. This was the reference in Malachi 1:11 to a 'pure offering'. The Didache refers this to the self-offering of believers in the eucharistic liturgy.[1] Justin finds Malachi's prophecy fulfilled in the eucharistic offering of bread and wine in thanksgiving.[2] Tertullian understands it to refer to the liturgical offering of praise and prayer.[3] As we have already noticed in discussing Justin and Irenaeus, what would in later times be described as a 'realist' conception of the eucharistic presence of the body and blood of Christ characterizes the thought of both those writers,[4] and the same is true of Tertullian.[5] In calling the eucharist *'oblatio'* and *'sacrificium'*, as he does many times, Tertullian is using traditional language which goes back to Clement of Rome's reference to 'offering the gifts';[6] but he adds a fresh nuance to this language when, anticipating Cyprian, he speaks of the celebrant as the 'priest' (*sacerdos*).[7] Hippolytus appears to go further, and actually to understand the eucharistic sacrifice as propitiatory rather than as a thankoffering, when, in the *Apostolic Tradition*, prayer is made that the bishop 'may unceasingly propitiate thy countenance and offer to thee the gifts of thy holy Church'.[8] The Latin treatise *De Aleatoribus* ('Concerning Dice-Throwers'), probably of the third century, speaks of the eucharist as the sacrifice of Christ.[9]

When Cyprian speaks of offering sacrifices for the martyrs on their anniversaries,[10] his language might readily suggest that he regards the eucharist as a propitiatory sacrifice for the living and the dead. The context, however, which speaks of the martyrs having already won their 'palms and crowns', indicates that the sacrifice is still regarded as a thanksgiving in which the martyrs' passion is linked in commemoration with the Passion of Christ which is the theme of every eucharist. In a better-known passage,

[1] *Did.* 14.1-2.
[2] *dial.* 41.1-3; 117.1-5; cf. *1 apol.* 65-67.
[3] *Marc.* 3.22.6; 4.1.8.
[4] Just. *1 apol.* 65-67; Iren. *haer.* 5.2.2-3.
[5] *Marc.* 4.40.3; 5.8.3.
[6] *1 Clem.* 44.4.
[7] *exhort. cast.* 11.
[8] *ap. trad.* 3.
[9] *de aleatoribus* 4, 5, 8.
[10] Cypr. *ep.* 39.3.

Cyprian declares that 'the Lord's Passion is the sacrifice which we offer'.[1] The language here is somewhat novel; but, again, the context equates the 'offering of the Lord's Passion' with 'making mention of his Passion in all our sacrifices', and 'offering the cup in commemoration of the Lord and his Passion'. It is therefore probable that the sacrifice is still thank-offering, *eucharist* in the strict meaning of the term. Cyprian also uses strongly 'realistic' language about the eucharistic Presence: 'we drink the blood of Christ'.[2] At the same time, however, as he maintains with such apparent literalness that the wine is Christ's blood he affirms that the water mixed with the wine in the chalice is the Church, the people of Christ. He has evidently not ceased to think, like his predecessors, in dynamic-representational terms.

Nevertheless, the impact of such ways of speaking about eucharistic sacrifice and such realism in speaking of the elements made itself strongly felt in relation to the Ministry. The growing tendency to assimilate the central concepts in Christian worship to the ideas of sacrificial worship in the Old Testament led to a profound, if subtle, change in the Christian understanding of priesthood, as the ministry of bishops, presbyters and deacons came to be virtually identified with that of high-priest, priests and levites and the teaching of the Old Testament about the ancient hierarchy came to be applied without hesitation or qualification to the Christian hierarchy. This tendency, apparent already in Hippolytus, was certainly strengthened and developed by Cyprian, as a study of his use of Old Testament terms when speaking of the Ministry and his application of Old Testament texts to his theory of the Church readily reveals.

The two lines of development which have been mentioned become steadily more apparent in the fourth century. Origen, in working out the correspondence between the Old Testament sacrifices and the eucharist, had already suggested that the eucharistic commemoration of Christ's death has a propitiatory value, and thus supersedes the old sacrifices.[3] In the eucharistic prayer of Sarapion the offering of the elements is a 'likeness' of Christ's death and the prayer asks that the sacrifice may propitiate God.[4] These tendencies are most marked in the *Catecheses* of Cyril of Jerusalem, where intercession for the dead (rather than, as probably in Cyprian, thanksgiving for them) is related to the setting forth of the 'holy and most awful sacrifice'.[5] Cyril continued to use the terminology of 'figure' or 'type' which had been used by the third-century *Didascalia* which spoke of 'the likeness of the royal body of Christ',[6] and by Eusebius for whom the bread is a symbol of Christ's body and the eucharist a celebration of the memorial of Christ's sacrifice and the memorial of his body and blood.[7] Yet he also speaks of a change effected in the elements by consecration and likens this to the

---

[1] *ep.* 63.17.
[2] *ep.* 63.15.
[3] *hom. 13.3–4 in Lev.*
[4] *euchol.* 13.
[5] *catech.* 23.8–9 (perhaps later than Cyril himself).
[6] 26.
[7] *d.e.* 8.1.80; 1.10.28, 38; 1.10.18.

miracle at Cana.[1] This 'conversion' is believed to be effected, not by the whole action of eucharistic thanksgiving (which in early Christian thought is held to be consecratory of that for which, or over which, God is thanked), but in response to the invocation of the Holy Spirit or the recitation of the words of Institution.[2] Chrysostom, too, combines the 'realism' of speaking about 'a holy and awful sacrifice' in which 'Christ is set before you slain' with the more precise theology of his explanation that 'we do not offer another sacrifice (i.e. other than Christ's), but the same; or rather, we make a memorial of the sacrifice'.[3] Ambrose develops a strongly propitiatory doctrine of eucharistic sacrifice in relation to Christ's heavenly intercession, and echoes the 'conversionist' language of the Cappadocians in speaking of a transformation of the elements, of their character being changed, and of their nature being altered by Christ's word and the 'mystery of holy prayer'.[4]

It is in the light of this teaching that the strength of the explicit or unspoken eucharistic presuppositions in the Christological controversy can be appreciated. Hence Cyril of Alexandria wishes to repudiate the traditional language of 'figure' and to replace symbolism with an uncompromising assertion that the elements are transformed into Christ's body and blood,[5] while Theodoret, in the interests of his argument against Eutychianism, is equally anxious to deny the idea of a 'conversion' of symbol into body.[6] In the later stages of Greek theology, however, the duality of symbol and reality is firmly rejected. According to John of Damascus bread and wine are changed into the body and blood which are the body and blood of God the Word, in such a way as to be no more two entities but one and the same. They must not on any account be regarded as a figure of the Lord's body and blood but as actually being this by virtue of a hypostatic union of two natures, the nature of bread and the divine nature.[7] This understanding of the eucharistic presence is connected with the belief that reception of the Lord's body is the sacramental means of the grace of deification, as Gregory of Nazianzus and 'Dionysius the Areopagite' had taught.[8]

On the other hand, Western eucharistic theology remained much less uniform, and besides the 'realism' of Ambrose the ancient tradition of 'symbolism' continued and received clearer definition in the thought of Augustine. Augustine's eucharistic doctrine, like his ecclesiology, is centred upon his fundamental belief in the identity of the Church with Christ, in the sense that the body with its divine head forms a single personal entity. The Church, symbolized by the eucharistic loaf composed of many grains, is consecrated in the eucharistic offering to be Christ's sacrifice;[9] the Church

---

[1] *catech.* 22.2–3 (also perhaps of later date).

[2] *ib.* 23.7; Chrys. *sac.* 3.4; Gr. Nyss. *or. catech.* 37; Chrys. *prod. Jud.* 1.6; Ambr. *myst.* 9.54 *sacr.* 4.4.14.

[3] Chrys. *prod. Jud.* 2.6; *sac.* 3.4; 6.4; *hom. 17.3 in Heb.*

[4] Ambr. *enarr. in Ps.* 38.25; *fid.* 4.10.124; *myst.* 9.52; cf. Gr. Nyss. *or. catech.* 37.

[5] Cyr. *Mt.* 26.26.

[6] Thdt. *eran.* 1.

[7] *fid. orth.* 4.13.

[8] Gr. Naz. *or.* 25.2; Dion. Ar. *e.h.* 6.3.5.

[9] *ep.* 54.2.

offers itself in union with its head, or, rather, Christ offers it in himself. To communicate is therefore synonymous with 'to offer'.[1] Christ's oblation of himself is commemorated in the eucharistic thank-offering, of which an essential element is the self-offering of the Church; and the daily remembrance of Christ's benefits with thanksgiving may be called a daily immolation of Christ, since the sacrament, because of its resemblance to that which it signifies, may rightly be given the name which properly belongs to the reality signified.[2] Augustine, who often follows the older practice of applying the term 'sacrifice' to the entire eucharistic liturgy instead of, as was increasingly the case in the contemporary East, to the consecrated elements, is also traditionalist in his general avoidance of the tendency to interpret the eucharistic sacrifice in terms of propitiation rather than thanksgiving. With this understanding of sacrifice there goes a sharp distinction between the outward sign and the spiritual reality. What is physically perceived is the bread and the cup; the body and blood of Christ are apprehended by faith. The bread and wine of the Last Supper were a 'figure' of Christ's body and blood; so, too, the eucharistic bread is Christ, but it is the heart, not the throat, which must be prepared to feed upon that which is the object of faith and not sight.[3] The sacrament signifies Christ; and it also signifies his body, the Church. What is placed on the altar, Augustine tells his congregation, is the mystery of ourselves. It is one bread, compacted of many grains. Wine is made from many grapes: the sacramental mystery of unity requires us to maintain the bond of peace. 'Be what you see, and receive what you are.' Thus the Augustinian theology of the sacraments, and especially of the eucharist, and the contrast between his dynamic symbolism and the almost literalistic realism of much that was said on this theme by other theologians, particularly in the East, already foreshadowed the controversies of the ninth and the eleventh centuries.

[1] *enarr. in Ps.* 75.15; *ep.* 187.20–21; *ep.* 98–9.
[2] *serm.* 272; *enarr. in Ps.* 3.1; *serm.* 112.4–5.
[3] *serm.* 272.

Christian Theology in the East
600-1453

Kallistos Ware

Christian Theology in the East
600–1453

KALLISTOS WARE

I

THE GENERAL CHARACTER OF BYZANTINE THEOLOGY

The history of eastern Christendom is marked by a deep sense of continuity with the past. In twentieth-century Istanbul the residence of the Greek Orthodox Patriarch is still called *Rum Patrikhanesi*, the 'Roman Patriarchate', while the Greeks of the city continue to call themselves *Romaioi* or 'Romans'. Behind this somewhat unexpected way of speaking there lies an historical fact of great significance. In the west the Roman Empire collapsed under the pressure of barbarian invasions in the fifth century, and the medieval society which slowly emerged from the ruins, while it had many links with the past, was fundamentally different from what had gone before. But in the east there was no such sudden break. The Roman Empire survived in the east for a thousand years longer than in the west: despite the profound economic, political, and social changes which it underwent, above all in the seventh and eleventh centuries, despite its progressive decline in size and in material resources, it yet remained – right up to the capture of Constantinople by the Turks in 1453 – essentially the same Empire as that over which Augustus had ruled at the moment of Christ's birth. Anyone who studies Byzantine theology must keep this fact constantly in mind. Historians distinguish for convenience between the 'Byzantine' and the 'Roman' Empire: but there is no clear line of demarcation between the two, and the one is a continuation of the other.

This element of continuity with the past is apparent in all branches of Byzantine civilization: in literature and philosophy, in political thought and law, and not least in theology. The Byzantines knew no 'Middle Ages' in the western sense: their approach to theology remained basically Patristic, and they continued to argue and theologize in much the same fashion as the Early Fathers. Categories of thought in the medieval west were radically altered, from the twelfth century onwards, by the great synthesis of philosophy and theology which we know as 'Scholasticism'. In Byzantium, by contrast, there was nothing comparable to this Scholastic 'revolution'. A western Christian around the year 1350 might read and honour the writings of the ancient Church, but the words of the Fathers came to him as a distant voice from the past: between him and them there was a profound cultural separation. But for an eastern Christian around 1350 the Fathers were members of the same world – elder brothers and in a vital sense contemporaries. The 'Age of the Fathers' in eastern Christendom does not come to a close with the Council of Chalcedon in the fifth century, nor yet with the meeting of the last Ecumenical Council in the eighth, but it extends without interruption until 1453; and even today – despite heavy borrowings from the Roman Catholic and Protestant west during the seventeenth and following centuries – Eastern Orthodoxy remains basically Patristic in outlook.

'Innovation I abominate above all things', remarked Emperor Julian the Apostate (361–3): and, pagan though he was, he here expressed a characteristically Byzantine attitude. The Byzantine approach to Christian doctrine is perhaps best summed up in the one word *paradosis* – 'tradition', or more literally, 'that which is handed down'. The Byzantine saw himself as heir to a rich Christian inheritance from the past, which it was his duty and privilege to transmit unimpaired to future generations. This attitude of mind is clearly evident in the dogmatic decree of the seventh and last Ecumenical Council (Nicaea, 787). 'We take away nothing and we add nothing', the assembled bishops stated, 'but we preserve without diminution all that pertains to the Catholic Church . . . We keep without change or innovation all the ecclesiastical traditions that have been handed down to us, whether written or unwritten.' The same reverence for tradition is displayed by the leading theologian of the eighth century, St. John of Damascus (+ c. 749). 'We beseech the people of God, the holy nation, to hold fast to the traditions of the Church', he writes. 'The taking away of any part of the traditions, however small, like the removal of stones from a building, quickly brings down the whole structure in ruins' (*On icons*, I: P.G. xciv. 1284A). St. Theodore the Studite (759–826) based his entire reform of the monastic life on the one principle that a monk must follow exactly what is prescribed in the tradition of the Fathers: 'You shall not transgress the laws and rules of the Holy Fathers . . . but in everything that you do or say, have as your witness either the words of Scripture or the custom of the Fathers' (*Testament*: P.G. xcix. 1820C). Six and a half centuries later, at the Council of Florence (1439) St. Mark of Ephesus displayed a precisely similar hostility to innovation. Opposing the western addition of the *filioque*[1] to the Nicene Creed or 'symbol of the faith', he observed: 'This symbol, this noble heritage of our fathers, we demand back from you. Restore it then as you received it. It may not be enlarged; it may not be diminished. It has been closed and sealed, and such as dare to innovate in its regard are cast out, and those who fashion another in its stead are laid under penalty.' (Quoted in J. Gill, *The Council of Florence*, Cambridge, 1959, p. 163. On Byzantine loyalty to tradition see especially J. Pelikan, *The Christian Tradition, 2. The Spirit of Eastern Christendom (600–1700)*, Chicago, 1974, the opening chapter.)

Reverence for tradition, however, can easily degenerate into stagnation and formalism; and this was what tended to happen in Byzantium. All too many Byzantines of the later period are mere compilers of what others have said before – protagonists of a narrow 'theology of repetition' which does no more than reiterate the accepted formulae of the past. Under such conditions the 'appeal to the Fathers' became simply an external appeal to

[1] On the *filioque*, see pp. 203ff. The Nicene Creed, for the Byzantines, meant the one adopted at the Council of Constantinople in 381.

'authorities' and 'proof texts'. But it should not be assumed – as is some-times done – that the whole of Greek theology after St. John of Damascus was of this type. Alongside the 'school of repetition' there were also religious thinkers of genuine originality – men such as St. Symeon the New Theologian (949–1022) or St. Gregory Palamas (1296–1359), who understood tradition in living and dynamic terms, as an *immediate* awareness of the presence of the Holy Spirit, which spoke formerly to the Fathers and which now speaks in just the same way to us. The continuity of the Eastern Roman Empire, at its best, was always a developing and creative continu-ity, in which conservatism was mixed with change.

In the history of Greek theology from 325 to 1453, four main periods may be distinguished:

(i) 325–381: from the first to the second Ecumenical Council. Doctrinal discussion in this period is concerned above all with the dogma of the Trinity – with 'theology' in the narrower Greek sense of the term.

(ii) 431–681: from the third to the sixth Ecumenical Council. The primary centre of interest moves from the Trinity to the doctrine of Christ. These are the Christological centuries *par excellence*.

(iii) 726–843: the iconoclast controversy. The dispute involves both the *making* and the *veneration* of images. Is it legitimate to make icons or pictorial representations of the Saviour, His Mother, and the saints? And if so, may these icons be treated with veneration and liturgical honours?

(iv) 858–1453: from the accession of Patriarch Photius until the fall of the Empire. These years are dominated by two main developments:

(a) Negatively, by a growing estrangement between the Greek east and the Latin west. This gives birth to a vast body of polemical writing, often superficial and unattractively aggressive in tone, but some of it raising issues of genuine principle.

(b) Positively, by a greatly deepened understanding of mystical theology. What does a man experience at the higher levels of inner prayer? How far can he attain 'deification' and union face to face with God, even in this present life? What, in other words, are the ultimate potentialities of man's nature, and what is implied in the fullness of his salvation?

Such is the general pattern of doctrinal development in the Christian east: from Trinitarian theology and Christology, in the earlier centuries, to 'anthropology' (the doctrine of man) and soteriology (the doctrine of salvation) in the age that follows.

As regards the last three of these four periods, there are certain wide-spread misconceptions that it is necessary to avoid. First, in connection with the second period, it is often tacitly assumed that all important discussion about the nature of Christ came to an abrupt end in the middle of the fifth century. But students of Patristic doctrine who stop short at 451 have heard less than half the story. Chalcedon must be seen, not as a final conclusion, but as a stage in a far more extended process of discussion; and the terms of its definition can be properly understood only in the light of the two subsequent Ecumenical Councils held at Constantinople in 553 and 680–1.

In the second place, it is a mistake to dismiss the iconoclast controversy as an argument simply about the nature of Christian art – a dispute, that is, about aesthetics, and therefore of no more than peripheral interest for the history of doctrine. On the contrary, the dispute raises problems of a fundamentally theological nature concerning the character of God's creation and of man's place within the created order. Matters of Christology are also involved, and so the iconoclast controversy must be seen in part as a continuation of the earlier debates about the person of Christ.

Thirdly, the developments in Byzantine mystical theology should not be relegated to the sphere of 'devotion' and religious psychology, and treated as lying outside the scope of the historian of dogma. The Christian east has always refused to acknowledge any separation or sharply drawn contrast between mysticism and theology, between spirituality and dogma. As Evagrius of Pontus (†399) expressed it, 'If you are a theologian, you will pray in truth: and if you pray in truth, you are a theologian' (*On prayer*, 60: P.G. lxxix. 1180B). All theology must be mystical – something based, as St. Symeon the New Theologian insisted, upon prayer and personal experience: otherwise it becomes an arid intellectual exercise. Equally, all mysticism must be theological: otherwise it becomes subjective, arbitrary, and heretical. Mystical theology, as the Byzantines conceived it, is an attempt to understand, through a personal experience of the Spirit, what it is that God has accomplished in saving and redeeming man; and as such it is something fundamentally doctrinal. In the words of a modern Russian theologian, Vladimir Lossky (1903–58), 'Far from being mutually opposed, theology and mysticism support and complete each other. One is impossible without the other . . . It is not by chance that the tradition of the Eastern Church has reserved the name of "theologian" peculiarly for three sacred writers of whom the first is St. John, most "mystical" of the four Evangelists; the second St. Gregory Nazianzen, writer of contemplative poetry; and the third St. Symeon, called "the New Theologian", the singer of union with God' (*The Mystical Theology of the Eastern Church*, London, 1957, pp. 8–9).

With such an understanding as this of the connection between theology and mysticism, the mystical tradition of the later Byzantine world can be viewed as an extension and completion of the earlier discussions about the Trinity and the Incarnation. 'God became man that we might become God', said St. Athanasius (*On the Incarnation*, 54). The doctrinal controversies from the fourth to the eighth century concentrated more especially on the first half of this sentence, 'God became man'. Byzantine religious thought in the 11th and 14th centuries worked out the full implications of the second half, 'that we might become God'. There is thus an integral link between Greek theologians in the earlier and in the later period: the two groups complement each other, and throughout the whole course of Christian doctrine in the east from 312 until 1453 there may be discerned an essential continuity.

II

THE SEVENTH CENTURY. THE MONOTHELETES;
ST. MAXIMUS THE CONFESSOR

The Christological disputes of the fifth and sixth centuries continued in the Christian east during the century that followed. The centre of discussion was no longer the word 'nature' (*physis*), but the terms 'energy' (*energeia*) and 'will' (*thelema*). Does the Incarnate Christ have two energies or one, two wills or one?

The political background must not be forgotten. From the emperor's point of view, the Council of Chalcedon left much to be desired. Since Constantine's day, a primary objective in imperial religious policy had been to preserve unity in the Church. When the emperor summoned an Ecumenical Council, he expected the bishops to bring an end to controversy and divisions, and to find some formula of union which the whole Church, or at any rate an overwhelming majority, would be ready to accept. Here Chalcedon had not proved an unqualified success, for its decisions were fiercely rejected by a substantial portion of the emperor's Christian subjects, above all in Egypt and Syria, who looked upon the Chalcedonian definition as a betrayal of the tradition of St. Cyril of Alexandria.

Egypt was the granary of Constantinople, and the Syrian frontier was vitally important in the struggle against the Persian Empire. It was a matter of deep concern to the imperial administration to ensure the loyalty of these two provinces. Successive emperors, therefore, not regarding the Chalcedonian 'settlement' as final, searched persistently for some new formula which might reconcile their anti-Chalcedonian subjects. One such effort at conciliation was Zeno's *Henotikon* (482). A more subtle venture was made during the reign of Justinian by the fifth Ecumenical Council (553), which sought to reinterpret the decisions of Chalcedon in terms of Cyril's Christology. But the Christians of Egypt and Syria remained substantially unsatisfied.

Early in the seventh century yet another attempt was made to conciliate the 'monophysites'. Patriarch Sergius I of Constantinople (610–38) suggested, by way of compromise, that although the Incarnate Christ has two natures, there is in Him only one operation or 'energy'. In 633 a union on this basis was effected with the 'monophysites' of Egypt. The 'one energy' formula was opposed, however, by St. Sophronius, Patriarch of Jerusalem (634–8). Sergius therefore modified his terminology, though not his basic standpoint: abandoning all reference to the term 'energy', from 634 onwards he maintained that Christ has only one will – the view known as Monotheletism. This Monothelete theory was supported not only by

Emperor Heraclius (610–41) at Constantinople, but equally by Pope Honorius I (625–38) at Rome, who had in fact originally suggested the Monothelete formula. In 638 Heraclius promulgated as an imperial edict the *Ekthesis* or 'Exposition' which Sergius had written, and this document was approved by synods held at Constantinople in 638 and 639.

But the victory of Monotheletism proved short-lived. Honorius' successors at Rome repudiated the *Ekthesis*, and the Monothelete position was condemned at the Synod of the Lateran in 649 and by a further council at Rome in 679. In Africa and the east it was strenuously opposed by St. Maximus the Confessor (c. 580–662), who suffered imprisonment and exile for his beliefs, eventually dying as a result of ill-treatment. Maximus was by no means a fanatic over questions of theology: for him, what mattered in Christology was content, not the words used to express it. He considered it legitimate to speak, not only of two 'natures' in Christ, but also of 'one nature': it all depends how the word *physis* is understood (*Letter* 12: P.G. xci. 477B; *Letter* 18: P.G. xci. 588B). He believed equally that the formula 'one energy' was capable of an orthodox interpretation (*Disputation with Pyrrhus*: P.G. xci. 344BC). When Sophronius and he opposed the theology of Sergius, it was not from any desire to contend about words, but because they believed that Monotheletism undermined the fullness and integrity of Christ's manhood. Human nature without a human will, so they felt, is an unreal abstraction. Christ is no longer genuinely man, for his manhood has been made into a mere *organon*, an instrument or tool without real power of free choice – a puppet show of passive attributes, worked from outside by the divinity of the Word.

Monotheletism, seen from this point of view, was a revival of the heresy of Apollinarius. Where Apollinarius denied Christ a human soul, distinct from the indwelling Logos, Sergius denied Him a human will, distinct from the divine will. The effect in either case is the same: the scheme of salvation is endangered. As St. Gregory of Nazianzus had insisted, 'Not assumed means not healed'. Christ's human will, like His human soul, is vital for soteriology: for the part of us that requires to be redeemed and healed is above all else our power of free will and moral choice. What we see in Christ – so Maximus argued – is precisely a human will, truly free, yet continuing in unwavering obedience to the divine will: and it is in virtue of this voluntary submission on Christ's part that we men are saved and are enabled to make our own will freely obedient to that of God.

The teaching of St. Maximus triumphed after his death and was confirmed by the sixth Ecumenical Council at Constantinople (680–1). In its dogmatic decree the council proclaimed that our Lord Jesus Christ has not only two natures but 'two natural wills and two natural energies, without separation, without change, without division, and without confusion . . . The two natural wills are not opposed to each other . . . but His human will follows His divine and almighty will, not opposing it nor struggling against it, but rather being in obedience to it.' Among the supporters of Monotheletism whom the council condemned by name were Patriarch Sergius and Pope Honorius.

When the 250 years of Christological controversy are viewed as a whole, there may be observed an alternating movement as of a pendulum. Ephesus affirmed the unity of Christ's person, Chalcedon the diversity of His two natures. The fifth Ecumenical Council confirmed the work of Ephesus; the sixth in its turn reasserted the principles of Chalcedon, proclaiming that, just as the Incarnate Logos has two natures, so He is endowed with two energies and two wills. For a balanced understanding of Christology, all four Councils must be taken into account, and each interpreted with reference to the rest.

The third Council of Constantinople in 680–1 marked the end of an era in Christological discussion, much as the first Council of Constantinople, exactly three centuries before, had marked the end of an era in Trinitarian controversy. After 681 there was no further attempt within the Byzantine Empire to dilute or modify the 'two nature' teaching of Chalcedon. The reason was in part political: the newly-established power of Islam, in the decade following the death of the Prophet in 632, had seized the non-Chalcedonian centres of Syria and Egypt, which lay henceforward outside the limits of Byzantine rule. The diplomatic motive which had led the emperors to search for a doctrinal compromise now existed no longer.

But were the emperors in fact so very wrong to look for a compromise? Perhaps the theological differences between Chalcedonians and non-Chalcedonians were never insuperable. Severus of Antioch and Maximus the Confessor, while using different terminologies, were substantially agreed on matters of fundamental doctrine. A solution might well have been found but for the presence of non-theological factors. In the course of controversy subtle doctrinal formulae inevitably developed into popular slogans. The theological arguments that lay behind the formulae must have been understood by very few; but the slogans, once adopted, became symbols of an intense party loyalty. By the end of the sixth century, the division between 'Chalcedonians' and 'non-Chalcedonians' was reinforced by increasing tension between the central authorities at Constantinople and the centrifugal forces of Egyptian and Syrian nationalism. Part of the reason why the native Christians of Egypt and Syria rejected Chalcedon with such fierceness was that in their eyes the Council constituted the symbol of a foreign Greek domination which they bitterly resented.

Today, with such political factors eliminated, the two sides have begun to draw closer together. At the conclusion of an unofficial consultation held at Aarhus in Denmark during 1964, delegates from the two traditions – Eastern Orthodox ('dyophysite') and Oriental Orthodox ('monophysite') – declared in an agreed statement: 'We recognize in each other the one orthodox faith of the Church . . . On the essence of the Christological dogma we found ourselves in full agreement. Through the different terminologies used by each side, we saw the same truth expressed . . . Both sides found themselves fundamentally following the Christological teaching of the one undivided Church as expressed by St. Cyril.' Three years later, at a meeting in Bristol, the two groups made a similar joint declaration, alluding more specifically to the Monothelete controversy: 'Both [sides] affirm the dynamic permanence of the Godhead and the Manhood, with all their natural properties and faculties, in the one Christ. Those who speak in terms of "two" do not thereby divide or separate. Those who speak in terms of "one" do not thereby commingle or confuse . . . All of us agree that the human will is neither absorbed nor suppressed by the divine will in the Incarnate Logos, nor are they contrary one to the other.'

If such agreement can be achieved in the twentieth century, why could it not have been achieved in the seventh? Neither side has radically changed its teaching during the interval. What made *rapprochement* impossible in the past was not primarily theology, but the political climate and the prevailing spirit of mutual intolerance.

III

THE ICONOCLAST CONTROVERSY

For nearly 120 years, from 726 until 843, the Byzantine world was shaken by the long dispute concerning icons. By 'icon' or image is meant, in this context, a religious picture representing the Saviour, His Mother, or one of the angels or the saints. Statuary is extremely rare in the art of eastern Christendom, and so the 'icons' involved in the Byzantine controversy during the eighth and ninth centuries were almost exclusively two-dimensional: portable paintings on panels, most usually of wood, or else pictures on walls, executed in mosaic and fresco. The 'iconoclasts' or icon-smashers insisted that such pictures had no rightful place in Christian churches or homes; the 'iconodules' or 'iconophiles' – the venerators or lovers of icons – held that they were legitimate and even necessary.

It was only by slow degrees that the use of icons became established in the Church. Reacting against their pagan environment, the first Christians were anxious to stress above all the exclusively *spiritual* character of their worship, and they sought to avoid anything that might savour of idolatry: 'God is a Spirit, and they that worship Him must worship Him in spirit and in truth' (John 4:24). Early Christian art – as found, for example, in the Roman catacombs – showed a certain reluctance to portray Christ directly, and He was most often represented in symbolical form, as the Good Shepherd, as Orpheus with his lyre, or the like. With the conversion of Constantine and the progressive disappearance of paganism, the Church grew less hesitant in its employment of art, and by A.D. 400 it had become an accepted practice to represent our Lord not just through symbols but directly. At this date, however, there is as yet no evidence to suggest that the pictures in church were venerated or honoured with any outward expressions of devotion. They were not at this period objects of cult, but their purpose was decorative and instructional.

Even in this restricted form, however, the use of icons aroused protests on the part of certain fourth-century writers, in particular Eusebius of Caesarea (†339), whose objections are to be found in his letter to Constantia Augusta, the sister of Emperor Constantine. Eusebius argued that an icon must necessarily represent the 'historical' image of Christ, the 'form' of His humiliation; this, however, has been superseded, since Christ's humanity has been assumed into divine glory and now exists in a state which cannot possibly be depicted in paint and colour. A painted icon of Christ, he concluded, is therefore both unnecessary and misleading. Behind this line of thought may be detected a typically Origenist tendency to undermine the full historical significance of the Incarnation. Objections to the use of icons seem also to have been made by that fierce anti-Origenist, St. Epiphanius of Salamis (c. 315–403): but there is some doubt whether the works on this subject attributed to him are in fact authentic.

The first type of icon to receive veneration was not religious but secular – the portrait of the emperor. This was regarded as an extension of the imperial presence, and the honours that were shown to the emperor in person were also rendered to his icon. Incense and candles were burnt in front of it, and as a mark of respect men bowed themselves before it to the ground, such prostration being normally described by the term *proskynesis*. This cult of the imperial image dates back to pagan times: with the conversion of the emperor to Christianity it was readily accepted by Christians, nor was any objection raised on the part of the ecclesiastical authorities.

If men paid such respect as this to the image of the earthly ruler, should they not show equal reverence to the image of Christ the heavenly King? It was an obvious and natural inference, but it was not an inference that was made at once. In fact, *proskynesis* was shown towards the relics of the saints and the Cross before it began to be shown towards the icon of Christ. Not until the period following Justinian – during the years 550–650 – did the veneration of icons in churches and private homes become widely accepted in the devotional life of eastern Christians. By the years 650–700 the first attempts were made by Christian writers to provide a doctrinal basis for this growing cult of icons and to formulate a Christian theology of art. Of particular interest is a work, surviving only in fragments, by Leontius of Neapolis (in Cyprus), rebutting Jewish criticisms.

The veneration of icons was not accepted everywhere without opposition. In the late sixth century protests were made at distant geographical extremes, in both instances outside the bounds of the Byzantine Empire – to the west in Marseilles, and to the east in Armenia. Somewhat more than a century later a far more extensive and thorough-going attack on icons was launched, this time within the Empire itself. The ensuing controversy falls into two main periods: the first phase, 726–80; and the revival of iconoclasm, 815–42.

Emperor Leo III the Isaurian (717–41) began the campaign against icons in 726. His initial measures provoked a violent riot among the people of Constantinople and a rebellion in Greece, thus indicating the popular support which the icons enjoyed, at any rate in some areas. Leo attempted to win over to his side Pope Gregory II of Rome and Patriarch Germanus of Constantinople, in both cases without success. In 730 Leo held a *silentium* – a mixed council of clergy and laity – in his palace at Constantinople, and an edict was issued demanding the destruction of all images, whether in places of worship or in private houses.

Some three years before Leo III initiated his attack on icons, about the year 723 the Mohammedan Caliph of Damascus, Yezid II, issued a decree ordering the destruction of all images in his realm. There is some evidence that he was acting under Jewish influence. Later apologists for the icons, anxious to discredit Leo, nicknamed him 'the Saracenizer' and suggested that he was attempting to introduce Jewish and Islamic notions into the Christian Church. While it is not impossible that Leo was to some extent inspired by Yezid's example, there is in fact no proof of any explicit link between Islam and Byzantine iconoclasm. Leo seems rather to have been acting under the influence of certain bishops from Phrygia in Asia Minor, most notably Constantine of Nacoleia and Thomas of Claudiopolis. One thing, at any rate, is abundantly clear: iconoclasm cannot simply be explained away as an importation from non-Christian sources, but it was a movement that enjoyed strong support *within* the Christian community. Fathers such as Eusebius and Epiphanius, as already noted, could be cited in favour of the iconoclast standpoint; and the cult of icons which grew up from the middle of the sixth century onwards was by no means universal throughout the Byzantine world at the start of the eighth. If the icons were highly popular in certain circles – at Constantinople, above all among the lower classes, and also in Greece and in most monasteries – they were viewed with far greater reserve by many Christians in Asia Minor.

The attack on icons reached its height under Leo's son, Constantine V (741–75). In his personal views Constantine went far beyond the normal iconoclast position: his Christology was markedly monophysite in tendency, and he is said to have condemned not only the veneration of icons, but equally that of relics and also the practice, already long accepted in the Church, of invoking the intercession of the saints. In 754 Constantine summoned a synod at Hieria, an imperial palace close to Chalcedon; this assembly was attended by 338 bishops, and was regarded by its own members, though not by subsequent centuries, as the seventh Ecumenical Council. The bishops at Hieria renewed the condemnation of icons, but declined to endorse the emperor's monophysite theories concerning Christ's person. They specifically defended the invocation of the Mother of God and the saints: the saints were to be venerated, but not their images. In his persecution of the iconophiles, Constantine treated the monks with particular savagery, for it was in the monasteries that the chief defenders of the icons were to be found.

The iconoclast emperors were not opposed to all art as such, but simply to the representation of the human form in religious pictures. They were very far from insisting that church interiors should be left unadorned, with bare walls in stark and Puritan simplicity. On the contrary, they encouraged rich schemes of decoration – but a decoration consisting only of foliage, ornamental scrolls, birds, flowers, and musical instruments, from which the human figure was excluded: their opponents scornfully accused them of making the church into 'a greengrocer's stall and a bird cage'. The iconoclasts allowed the Cross to be depicted and also venerated, but they did not permit any figure to be shown hanging upon it. What they feared, among other things, was the infiltration of paganism and idolatry into the Christian community. They were archaists and reactionaries rather than innovators; their aim was to preserve, or rather to revive, the older tradition of Christian art which relied upon symbolic *motifs* and did not portray our Lord directly. In their secular and domestic art the iconoclast rulers permitted the human form to appear, though never that of Christ. While excluding all veneration of the icon of Christ, they insisted upon the display and veneration of portraits of the reigning emperor.

On the theological level the leading champion of icons was St. John of Damascus. He was a subject of the Arabs, not of the Byzantine Empire, and this gave him a freedom of action which otherwise he would probably not have enjoyed. In the years 727–33, when he composed his three orations in defence of the holy icons, he was still a layman, a civil servant under the Caliph of Damascus. Though small in compass, his three orations provided at the very outset of the controversy the main doctrinal arguments on which the iconodules were to rely. Written for the most part in simple and scriptural language, they are aimed at the ordinary believer as well as the scholar and specialist. Subsequently John entered the monastery of St. Sabas close to Jerusalem, and here he composed his main work, *The Fount of Knowledge*, a comprehensive survey of philosophy and theology, in which he attempted to gather together in a single synthesis the teaching of earlier Fathers. [The most important section of this work is Part III *On the Orthodox Faith*.] The work quickly came to constitute a standard textbook of orthodoxy for the Byzantine world. Its influence extended also to the west: translated into Latin in the twelfth century, it was used by Peter Lombard, and formed one of the chief sources for the *Summa Theologica* of Thomas Aquinas. But in his theological method Aquinas differs from John in making a far heavier use of philosophical categories.

In 780 Empress Irene brought the persecution of the iconodules to an end, and seven years later the veneration of icons was formally proclaimed at the second Council of Nicaea, the seventh of the Ecumenical Councils, and the last to be recognized as such by Eastern Orthodoxy. Meeting under the presidency of Patriarch Tarasius, this council reversed the decision of Hieria, and it decreed that icons were to be displayed and venerated in all churches. But an appreciable proportion of Christians in the Byzantine Empire still remained iconoclast in conviction, and Emperor Leo V (813–20) revived the policy of Leo III. A synod, held at St. Sophia in Constantinople during 815, deposed Patriarch Nicephorus, a supporter of the icons, and cancelled the decrees of 787, reaffirming those proclaimed at Hieria. But the campaign against icons in this second period (815–42) proved less fierce than under Leo III and Constantine V. While *proskynesis* of icons was prohibited, pictures of Christ and the saints on the upper walls of churches were often left undisturbed. It was the cult of icons, rather than their mere presence, which was attacked; pictures which were inaccessible were ignored, for they could not easily be venerated. The leading spokesmen for the iconodule viewpoint during the second phase were St. Theodore (759–826), abbot of the monastery of Studios at Constantinople, and the deposed Patriarch, St. Nicephorus († c. 828). Of the two, Theodore displays the greater originality as a writer. More abstract and philosophical in approach than St. John of Damascus, he seeks to explain the nature of the icon in terms of Aristotelian thought.

Once more it was a woman, Empress Theodora, who brought the attack on icons to an end. In 842 the persecution ceased, and in the following year a Council at Constantinople renewed the decrees of 787. This time the return of the icons proved definitive: by the middle of the ninth century iconoclasm had clearly lost most of its popular support, and although it lingered on for another generation or more in parts of the Empire, it was no longer a force seriously to be reckoned with. The restoration of icons in 842–3 became known in later years as the 'Triumph of Orthodoxy', and it is still commemorated annually at a special service on the first Sunday in Lent. After 787 no new Ecumenical Council was assembled; the events of 842–3 were seen as setting the seal upon the Seven Councils that had gone before, and henceforward in many circles within the Byzantine Church the idea gained ground that 'orthodoxy' was now to be viewed as an integral and completed whole, a single unity to which nothing could be added and from which nothing could be taken away. Naturally this encouraged the 'theology of repetition' to which reference has already been made; but, as we have emphasized, this type of uncreative theology, although widespread, was not representative of Byzantine religious thought as a whole.

The attitude of the west during the iconoclast controversy was ambiguous. The Papacy, from Gregory II onwards, supported the iconodule cause, and Hadrian I (772–95) accepted the decisions of the seventh Ecumenical Council. But further to the north, in the now powerful kingdom of the Franks, Charlemagne repudiated the decrees of 787. For this there were various reasons, not all of them theological. Political relations at this time were strained between Charlemagne and Byzantium; furthermore, he knew of the acts of 787 only through an inaccurate Latin translation, which made it appear that the Council of Nicaea was advocating idolatry – not merely the veneration but the *worship* of icons. Apart, however, from political tensions and linguistic misunderstandings, Charlemagne and his religious advisers also disagreed with the decisions of Nicaea on specifically doctrinal grounds. In their opinion the Councils of 754 and 787 were both at fault – Hieria in advocating the destruction of icons, and Nicaea in advocating their veneration. According to Charlemagne, icons could be displayed in churches, but were not to be assigned *proskynesis*: his standpoint was neither iconoclast nor iconodule, but intermediate between the two. This intermediate position was upheld at the Synod of Frankfurt in 794, and at the later Synod of Paris in 825. Anxious to maintain good relations with the Franks, Hadrian and his successors at Rome made no protest against the decisions of Frankfurt, but themselves refrained from disowning the decrees of 787. It was not until the eleventh century that the authority of the seventh Ecumenical Council became generally accepted throughout the west.

The controversy about icons, in common with almost all controversies in the history of the Church, was never exclusively doctrinal. Social, political, and economic problems were also involved, and these non-theological factors served greatly to prolong and embitter the dispute. Secular and theological issues are so closely intertwined that it is virtually impossible to determine with precision their relative importance and influence.

On the theological level, the first point that calls for consideration is the *question of idolatry*. The iconophiles, so their opponents believed, were ascribing to created and material objects the worship that properly is due to God alone. A modern reader naturally tends to assume that this was the main argument on the iconoclast side. As a matter of historical fact, however, this question of alleged idolatry did not figure at all prominently in the iconoclast case. The point was mentioned, but not especially emphasized, at the Council of 754; the later Council of 815 speaks of it scarcely at all. The iconoclasts were in fact far more interested in the Christological issue; and to this we shall shortly turn.

The iconophiles, or at any rate the more moderate among them, were not by any means blind to the latent danger of idolatry in the popular manifestations of the icon cult. But they believed that, if properly understood, this cult was in no sense idolatrous. A distinction must be drawn, so they argued, between (i) *latreia*, which signifies worship or adoration in the full sense, and which is to be rendered only to the three Persons of the Holy Trinity; and (ii) *timē*, which connotes 'honour' or 'veneration' of a strictly qualified kind. When we make obeisance (*proskynesis*) to the invisible God, it is an expression of *latreia*; but when we make obeisance to the icons in church – or, for that matter, to the emperor or the local governor – we are ascribing to them, not *latreia*, but the *timē* which is their due. As the Council of Nicaea stated in its dogmatic decree, icons are to receive 'not the worship (*latreia*) that is due to God alone', but merely 'honourable veneration (*timetikē proskynesis*) . . . such as is given to the sign of the precious and lifegiving Cross, to the Book of the Holy Gospels, and to other holy objects', for example, relics. The reference here to the Cross is deliberate, for (as we have seen) the iconoclasts permitted the veneration of the Cross.

This *proskynesis* of icons is constantly described by iconophiles as *schetichē* or 'relative': an icon is honoured, not because of what it is in itself – wood and plaster, paint and coloured stones – but because of the *relation* which it bears to the person depicted. In St. Basil the Great's words, often repeated during the course of the controversy, 'The honour shown to the icon is ascribed to the prototype' (*On the Holy Spirit*, 18: P.G. xxxii. 149C).[1] The icon, in other words, is not an idol but a symbol. As Leontius of Neapolis put it, some years before the start of the iconoclast dispute: 'When the two beams of the Cross are joined together, I adore the emblem because of Christ who was crucified on the Cross; but if the beams are separated, I throw them away and burn them . . . We do not make obeisance to the nature of wood, but we revere and do obeisance to Him who was crucified on the Cross' (P.G. xciv. 1384CD).

The iconophiles laid especial emphasis upon this notion of 'relative' or 'relational' veneration, because (as they saw it) the iconoclast party had misunderstood what an icon really is. The iconoclasts considered that an icon is somehow 'consubstantial' – identical in essence (*ousia*) – with its original; and so they argued that the only true icon of Christ is the bread and wine of the eucharist. The iconophiles, following St. John of Damascus (*On icons*, III. 18: P.G. xciv. 1337C–1344A), differentiated between three distinct kinds of icon: 'natural' (*physikē*), 'by imitation' (*mimetikē*), and 'artistic' (*technikē*):

(i) Christ is the 'natural' icon of the Father (Colossians 1:15); and in this

---

[1] In its original context, this phrase was not used by St. Basil with reference to painted icons.

case there is complete identity of essence between the prototype (God the Father) and the icon (God the Son).

(ii) Man is God's icon 'by imitation', for he is made 'according to the image and likeness of God' (Genesis 1:26); but man is not identical in essence with his Creator.

(iii) The images displayed in church are 'artistic' icons, and here again there is no identity in essence with the original; for the *ousia* of the original is a living person, spirit, soul, and body, whereas the *ousia* of the image is mosaic, fresco, wood, and paint.

As for the holy gifts at the eucharist, so the 787 Council insisted, these cannot rightly be described as an 'icon of Christ' in either the second or the third of the above three senses, for after consecration they are 'the very Body and the very Blood of Christ', not just an icon of His Body and Blood.

The iconoclasts appealed in the second place to the *evidence of Scripture*, and in particular to the Old Testament prohibition against images (Exodus 20:4; Deut. 4:14–19, 5:7–8). To this the iconodules replied that such a prohibition was necessary in Old Testament times, because the invisible God had not as yet been revealed in the flesh. But the Incarnation has entirely altered the situation, rendering possible a representational religious art. Material images, St. John of Damascus argued, can be made of Him who took a material body: 'Of old God the incorporeal and uncircumscribed was not depicted at all. But now that God has appeared in the flesh and dwelt among men, I make an icon of God, in so far as He can be seen . . . The Old Israel did not see God; but we behold with unveiled faces the glory of the Lord as in a mirror (2 Corinthians 3:18)' (*On icons*, I.16: P.G. xciv. 1245A, 1248B).

In the third instance, the iconoclasts advanced what is usually termed the '*ethical' argument*: this was employed in particular at the Council of 815. We should represent Christ and the saints, so the iconoclasts urged, not through wood and paint, but by our lives; instead of setting our reliance on material reproductions, we ought to imitate the virtues of Christ and so transform ourselves into living icons. It is indeed essential, so the iconodules replied, to become living icons of Christ; but this does not signify that all use of painted icons is necessarily excluded. A living icon is incomparably the more precious, but a painted icon has also its value. One of the chief functions of a painted icon is precisely to act as a vivid reminder of the life of Christ and the saints, and so to inspire us to imitate them. Thus the 'ethical' argument of the iconoclasts, so far from constituting an objection against images, is a strong reason in their favour.

The iconophiles attached great importance to this didactic function of iconography, to the rôle of icons as a reminder and a source of moral inspiration. Man does not learn about God through the written word alone, but through many other forms of revelation, most notably through the visual image. A picture may move his heart when words do not. Icons serve as the Bible of the unlettered: 'What the Scripture is to those who can read,' said John of Damascus, 'the icon is to the illiterate' (*On icons*, I. 17: P.G. xciv. 1248C). In this way the holy images are closely parallel to the Gospel: icons are the Gospel made visible, just as the Gospel is a verbal icon, and the Council of 787 therefore proclaimed that both the icons and the Book of the Gospels should be venerated *in the same way*. Icons form a part of the tradition of the Church: a man has only to enter a place of Christian worship to see unfolded before him in iconography all the mysteries of the Catholic faith.

In the fourth place, the iconoclasts invoked the *question of Christology*, and it was upon this that the discussions at Hieria and Nicaea chiefly concentrated. Most theologians on either side evidently regarded this as the crucial point at issue. The iconoclasts put their argument in the form of a dilemma:

either Christ is represented simply as a man: in that case His human nature is separated from His divine nature – which is Nestorianism;

or else Christ is represented as both God and man at once: in that case an attempt is made to depict the invisible Godhead, and at the same time the two natures are merged and confused – which is Monophysitism.

The iconophiles for their part denied the underlying assumption on which this dilemma was based. The iconoclast argument takes it for granted that an icon of Christ must depict either the human nature alone or else both natures together. What an icon depicts, however, is not the *natures* of Christ, but His *person* or *hypostasis*: it shows neither the human nor the divine nature, nor both natures together, but Christ Himself, the indivisible person of the God-Man (*Theanthropos*). When we make an ordinary portrait of a living person, we represent only his outward appearance – the body alone, not the soul – but this is sufficient to constitute a true portrait of the person concerned. We do not thereby introduce an illicit separation of his body from his soul, nor yet a meaningless confusion between the two. The same is true of an icon of Christ. It depicts neither His divinity nor yet His human soul, but it is still a true likeness and image of His person.

Turning the tables on their opponents, the iconophiles argued that it was in fact the iconoclast standpoint, and not their own, which was monophysite. The Chalcedonian Definition lays down that each of Christ's natures retains its distinctive characteristics in a union without confusion. Now one among the distinctive characteristics of our Lord's humanity is precisely the property of being visible; and what is visible can be depicted. The iconoclasts, by suggesting that Christ cannot be depicted because He is God as well as man, imply in effect that in the hypostatic union the human nature loses its characteristic properties and is swallowed up in the divinity; and this is Monophysitism.

In theological controversy it is a standard practice for one side to accuse the other of various past heresies, long since condemned. But in this instance the allegation of monophysite tendencies is not simply an empty insult, but raises a point of fundamental significance for the understanding of the whole controversy. The defenders of the icons saw in iconoclasm a tendency to detract from the full reality of Christ's human nature. As St. Theodore of Studios expressed it, the iconoclast refusal to depict the incarnate Saviour implies that 'Christ came upon earth merely in outward seeming and appearance' (*Antirrheticus*, II. 48: P.G. xcix. 389D). 'In reality they deny that Christ became man,' he maintains, 'even though they affirm it in words. For if He is man, He can be depicted: it is a primary character-istic of man to be capable of depiction. If, however, He cannot be depicted, then He is not man but lacks flesh' (*Letters*, II. 21: P.G. xcix. 1184D).

In the course of its history the Church has witnessed a long series of doctrinal deviations which, in one way or another, have served to under-miné the fullness of the Incarnation: Docetism, Origenism, Apollinarianism, Monophysitism (at any rate in its Eutychian form), Monotheletism. Icono-clasm, so its critics believed, was yet another example of this same trend. It is in such a sense as this that the charge of Monophysitism must be understood. Taken literally, it is certainly untrue. The monophysite theories of Constantine V were not endorsed at Hieria, while the non-Chalcedonian Churches, such as the Coptic and the Ethiopian, are most certainly not iconoclast. But in a deeper sense there is justice in the accusation. When the Council of Chalcedon condemned Eutyches, and when the second Council of Nicaea condemned the iconoclasts, both alike were concerned in the last resort to defend the same thing – the entire and unimpaired reality of Christ's flesh-taking. Icons, as the Council of 787 put it, are a 'guarantee that the incarnation of God the Word is true and not illusory'. When St. John of Damascus and St. Theodore of Studios opposed iconoclasm, their primary concern was not to defend a theory of religious art, but to safeguard the right faith in the Incarnation.

But St. John and St. Theodore were concerned to defend something else as well. Icons, in their belief, serve not only to protect the true doctrine of the Incarnation, but equally to ensure a correct attitude towards the material creation. The iconoclasts are sometimes accused by their opponents of being Manichaeans. If understood literally, this charge is even less justified than that of Monophysitism; and yet, like the charge of Mono-physitism, it contains a certain vital truth. Of course the iconoclasts believed in principle that all creation is God's handiwork, and therefore intrinsically good. But how far did they work out in practice the full consequences of this belief? Behind their repudiation of icons, does there not lurk a crypto-Manichaean attitude, a disposition to underestimate the spiritual potentialities of matter? In making religious art something purely decorative and symbolic, in excluding all devotion towards the holy images, they did not allow properly for the fact that material wood and paint can serve as a channel of grace, a means whereby the worshipper is brought into living and immediate contact with the spiritual presence of God and his saints.

As St. John of Damascus protests, the iconoclasts 'desire to be above the body', and they 'say that we should be linked to God only with our mind'. Whereas the Council of Hieria saw in the cult of icons nothing but the 'grovelling and materialistic worship of created things', John for his part insists on the reverence which should rightly be shown towards the material order. 'I do not worship matter,' he says, 'but I worship the Creator of matter, who for my sake became material and accepted to dwell in matter, who through matter effected my salvation. I will not cease from reverencing matter, through which my salvation came to pass . . . Do not insult matter: for it is not without honour. Nothing is to be despised that God has made. That is a Manichaean error' (*On icons*, I. 16: P.G. xciv. 1245AC).

By taking a material body at the Incarnation, God has made manifest the spiritual value of material flesh, and thus of the material creation in general: as St. John of Damascus claims, 'The Word made flesh has deified the flesh' (*On icons*, I. 21: P.G. xciv. 1253B). If human flesh can be redeemed and made a vehicle of the Spirit, then so – though in a different way – can wood and paint. St. Theodore of Studios went so far as to state, 'It would not be wrong to say that the Godhead is present in an icon . . . not in virtue of a natural union (for the icon is not deified flesh), but in virtue of a relative participation: for the icon shares in the grace and honour that belong to God' (*Antirrheticus*, I. 12: P.G. xcix. 344BC). The icon of Christ the God-Man is not merely a reminder, bringing the absent Saviour into our thoughts: it is an actual point of meeting between ourselves and Him, filled with supernatural grace and making the power of God truly present among us. As the Council of 787 stated, icons 'make us share in a certain sanctification'. While clearly on a different level from the consecrated elements at the eucharist, the icon is none the less sacramental: it is a visible sign conveying invisible grace. No doubt behind this understanding of icons there is a certain influence of the Platonic Theory of Ideas or Forms; but it is possible to expound the iconophile viewpoint – as John of Damascus in fact expounded it – purely in Scriptural terms, and without invoking Platonism.

The icon painter is performing a task of the utmost spiritual significance. He takes paint and a panel of wood, in which God's glory is already present, as it is present in all creation. Then by means of line and colour he renders that glory present in a manner incomparably more splendid and explicit. He acts as the priest of creation, transfiguring it and making it articulate in praise of God. 'Through heaven and earth and sea, through wood and stone', writes Leontius of Neapolis, '. . . I render obeisance and honour to the one Creator and Master and Maker of all. For the creation does not venerate the Creator through itself directly; but it is through me that the heavens declare the glory of God, through me the moon offers homage to God, through me the stars ascribe glory to Him, through me the waters, rain, and dew, with the whole of creation, worship and glorify Him' (P.G. xciii. 1604AB). The artist is a creator after the image of God the eternal Creator: in the words of Theodore, 'The fact that man was made in the image and likeness of God shows that there is something divine in the making of icons' (*Antirrheticus*, III. iii. 5: P.G. xcix. 420A).

These were some of the more profound issues involved in the dispute. The iconophile partly valued icons as a means of instruction, as the 'Bible of the unlettered'; but it valued them far more because they safeguarded the visible and material reality of the Incarnation, and because they manifested the spiritual potentialities of the material order. It was not merely the didactic and aesthetic significance of the icon that the iconophiles were anxious to defend, but something more fundamental: the true doctrine of the Word made flesh, and the right understanding of God's creation and of man's place within the creation.[1]

---

[1] The works of St. John of Damascus should now be consulted in the critical edition of B. Kotter (3 vols. so far, Berlin/New York, 1969–75).

IV

CONSTANTINOPLE AND ROME
(858–1439)

At the close of the iconoclast controversy in 842–3, the future outlook
for Christian unity must have seemed definitely encouraging. During the
controversy itself, the throne of Constantinople had been occupied over
long periods by an iconoclast patriarch not in communion with the Papacy,
and relations between Rome and Byzantium had been severely strained;
but now peace was at length restored. Unfortunately it was not to last. In
858, fifteen years after the 'Triumph of Orthodoxy', St. Photius became
Patriarch of Constantinople. He was the most eminent scholar of his day,
an outstanding influence in the ninth-century revival of learning at
Byzantium; but he has been chiefly remembered by posterity for the unhappy dispute which broke out during his reign between Constantinople
and the Papacy. It was an ill-omened and disastrous quarrel, not so much
in its immediate results – since communion between east and west was
quickly re-established – but in its long-term effects: for Photius brought
into the open a doctrinal question which was to remain an enduring source
of difficulty throughout the centuries that followed.

In the schism between Greek east and Latin west, as in earlier religious
disputes, the strictly doctrinal issues were closely linked with non-theological matters. In the past this was not always fully recognized by
historians and controversialists. They tended to approach the schism from
a narrowly ecclesiastical standpoint, concentrating their attention chiefly
upon two incidents: the controversy between Pope Nicolas I and Patriarch
Photius during 858–67, and the exchange of anathemas between Cardinal
Humbert of Silva Candida, legate of Pope Leo IX, and Patriarch Michael
Cerularius in 1054. It is today generally agreed that these two incidents,
although important, cannot be treated in isolation, but must be seen as
part of a much wider development. The separation between Byzantium and
Rome was conditioned by many factors, secular as well as dogmatic; it was
by no means a sudden and simple event, accomplished everywhere at once,
but was a gradual and intricate process, whose distant origins extend far
back much earlier than the ninth or the eleventh century, and whose final
completion should perhaps be placed as late as the eighteenth.

Long before any open and permanent schism had been formally established, east and west had been growing steadily apart – not so much
specifically in the field of doctrine, but more broadly in their general
historical situation. Had it not been for the fact of this pre-existing
estrangement, the subsequent doctrinal disputes would never have proved
so explosive. The two halves of Christendom drifted into schism, mainly

because Christians on either side had already become *strangers* to each other. This is not to say that no point of doctrine was involved in the separation; but the difficulties were never exclusively doctrinal.

How did this gradual estrangement come about? At the time of our Lord, the Mediterranean world as a whole was held together by the all-embracing social and political unity of the Roman Empire. Whether they were 'eastern' or 'western', Greek or Latin, men acknowledged the same emperor, obeyed substantially the same laws, and shared in the same intellectual formation and cultural background. All this was of incalculable benefit to the Early Church in its missionary expansion and its internal organization, and it helped to maintain the visible oneness of the Christian community.

But from the fourth century onwards this political and cultural unity was progressively undermined. In 330 Constantine founded a new capital, Constantinople, in addition to the Old Rome in Italy, and thereby unwittingly he sowed the seeds of future ecclesiastical rivalry between the Popes of the Old Rome and the Patriarchs of the New. Then in 406–7 the Rhine frontier collapsed and the western half of the Empire was engulfed by the barbarians. Christians in east and west now found themselves in radically different situations, and this meant that they developed in divergent ways, socially, culturally, and politically. During the late sixth and the seventh centuries east and west were still further isolated from one another by the Avar and Slav invasions of the Balkan peninsula: Illyricum, which once had served as a bridge, now became a barrier between Byzantium and the Latin world. Shortly afterwards the Arabs gained control over much of the Mediterranean, thus rendering travel by sea incomparably more hazardous. Personal contacts now grew far less frequent. In the earlier period educated men were normally bilingual, but from the start of the sixth century there were few Greeks who knew Latin, and fewer Latins who knew Greek. Mutual isolation led inevitably to prejudice, ignorance, and hostility. Neither side really understood how the other lived and thought and felt; neither could easily enter into the other's viewpoint and see it from within.

In the days of Basil the Great and Augustine, there had been but a single Christian civilization in east and west. Four centuries later, by the time of Photius and Alcuin, this cultural unity had been critically impaired. Charlemagne made notable efforts to restore learning in the west, but this Carolingian revival was marked by an unfortunate anti-Byzantine bias. The process of disintegration is still more clearly evident in the later Middle Ages, with the rise of Scholasticism in the west. Educated Christians of the thirteenth century no longer shared – as they had done in the Early Church – a single civilization, a common 'universe of discourse'.

In consequence of the barbarian invasions, the Church in the west came to occupy a position within the framework of society markedly different from that of the Byzantine Church. In the west the Papacy was for much of the time the one guarantee of stability and continuity in a world of disorder; and as a result immense authority, political as well as spiritual, became concentrated in the person of the Pope. In the east, by contrast, there was a strong secular head, the emperor, to uphold the civilized order and to enforce law, while behind the emperor stood a powerful lay civil service. Only on rare occasions was the Patriarch of Constantinople required to assume the political rôle which habitually fell to the lot of the Pope. Even though the Byzantine Church was capable on occasion of defying the emperor, under normal conditions he wielded an influence over ecclesiastical affairs such as few if any western rulers ever acquired.

In the west the only effective education to survive through the Dark Ages was ecclesiastical – given by the clergy and intended for the clergy. But in Byzantium there was always a tradition of lay scholarship, above all within the civil service; and many laymen, including several emperors, took a lively and intelligent interest in theology. A number of the most celebrated Patriarchs – for example, Tarasius (784–806), who presided at the seventh Ecumenical Council; Nicephorus I (806–15), opponent of iconoclasm; and Photius himself (858–67, 877–86) – were drawn from the ranks of the civil service, and were still laymen at the time of their election. Such appointments were virtually unthinkable in the medieval west. Byzantine Christendom was less clericalist than that of the west, less centralized and less rigidly institutionalized; the laity always counted for more. These differences in the social situation of Greek and Latin Christianity could not but affect men's understanding of doctrine, and in particular their approach to ecclesiology.

Such are a few among the broader factors which must be taken into account when considering the schism, and more especially when discussing the incidents of Photius and Cerularius. The dispute between Patriarch Photius and Pope Nicolas I was not initially concerned with any matter of dogma. The two came into conflict, and eventually broke off communion with one another, because Nicolas found himself unable to recognize Photius' appointment as Patriarch. A second point of difficulty was the question of Bulgaria, which was turning towards Christianity at this very time, and which both Rome and Constantinople were anxious to include in their own sphere of jurisdiction. From the very beginning of the dispute, however, there was a serious doctrinal question lurking in the background, even if it was not made clearly explicit: the nature of Papal primacy. Nicolas, as his actions indicated, laid claim to a universal supremacy over the whole Church, eastern as well as western: Photius, and the Byzantines in general, were willing to treat Rome as a court of final appeal, but they resented the direct intervention of the Pope in the internal affairs of the Eastern Patriarchates. This problem of Papal authority was more than a matter of canon law, of jurisdiction and ecclesiastical organization: it involved – even though few if any on either side clearly realized it at the time – fundamental questions concerning the character of Christ's Church on earth.

In 867 a further theological question was raised – this time not by implication, as with the Papal claims, but openly. Photius accused the west of heresy because it believed in the double procession of the Holy Spirit – from the Son as well as the Father – and because it had inserted the word *filioque* ('and from the Son') into the text of the Creed. Alongside the *filioque*, certain lesser points of difference also figured prominently in the controversy: the Greeks and Latins followed divergent rules of fasting; married clergy were an accepted institution in the east, whereas the Latins preferred clerical celibacy; and the Latins objected to the Greek practice whereby the sacrament of chrismation (confirmation) is administered by a priest.

By the summer of 867 the conflict between Nicolas and Photius had come to assume menacing proportions, but in fact no lasting breach ensued. In that same year Nicolas died and Photius was deposed – for political, not ecclesiastical, reasons. Communion was now restored between Constantinople and Rome, and it continued unbroken during Photius' second period of office as Patriarch (877–86). Pope John VIII (872–82) did not attempt to impose his authority in the east as Nicolas had done; and Photius on his side refrained from pressing the question of the *filioque*. It used to be thought that there was a second 'Photian schism', but historically this is now acknowledged to be a fiction: Photius died in full eucharistic fellowship with the Papacy. If the conflict between Photius and Nicolas is important, this is not because it led immediately to a permanent schism (which it did not), but because it outlined all too exactly the pattern which subsequent controversy was to follow, and because it brought the vexed question of the *filioque* into the open for the first time. Byzantines of a later period, in their polemic against Rome, constantly referred back to the arguments which Photius had originally advanced in 867.

The dispute in 1054 between Humbert and Cerularius was dominated by a matter of relatively minor importance: the Greeks objected to the Latin practice of using 'azymes' or unleavened bread in the eucharist, and they argued that leavened bread alone constituted the proper matter of the sacrament. Attempts were made on both sides to reach an understanding, but without success. Cardinal Humbert, who had been sent to Constantinople as Papal legate, eventually laid an excommunication against Patriarch Cerularius on the altar of St. Sophia, and the Patriarch and his synod retorted by excommunicating Humbert. These mutual anathemas, which were eventually revoked on December 7th, 1965, were long regarded by historians as constituting the 'final breach' between Orthodoxy and Rome, the definitive consummation of the schism. But this is to attribute to them an altogether exaggerated importance. Humbert directed his excommunication, not against the Byzantine Church as such, but against Cerularius personally; and Cerularius in his turn was careful not to anathematize the Pope, but only Humbert and his companions, whom he declined to regard as accredited spokesmen for the Church of Rome. Humbert was in fact exceeding his powers when he issued the bull, for the Pope whom he represented had already been dead for three months; and it seems probable that Humbert had already received news of the death. What is chiefly striking about the incident of 1054 is the degree to which both sides concentrated on subsidiary issues, of no real dogmatic importance. The *filioque* question, although mentioned, was not emphasized in the discussions; and while the problem of Papal authority underlay the entire conflict, it was not raised directly.

Before long the excommunications exchanged between Humbert and

Cerularius were largely forgotten, both at Byzantium and Rome. Psychologically, other events of a less specifically ecclesiastical character had a far greater effect in creating a division between eastern and western Christendom: the seizure of Byzantine possessions in South Italy and Sicily by the Normans in the eleventh century (it was this, indeed, which precipitated the conflict of 1054); the commercial expansion of Venice, Genoa, and other Italian maritime cities in the eastern Mediterranean; and, most serious of all, the Crusades, culminating in the deplorable sack of Constantinople in 1204. From this time onwards most Byzantines felt a deep hostility and indignation against the Latin west; and if the beginning of the schism is to be dated to any particular moment, then the year 1204 is certainly less misleading than 1054.

There were sporadic attempts at reconciliation throughout the later Byzantine period. Two reunion councils were held, at Lyons in 1274 and at Ferrara and Florence in 1438–9. On both occasions an agreement was reached, the Greek delegates accepting without substantial modification the terms of union upon which the Latins insisted. The union effected at Lyons was primarily political; at Florence, on the other hand, there were prolonged and searching doctrinal discussions, covering the *filioque*, the Papal claims, and also the question of azymes, purgatory, and the blessedness of the saints. Both unions proved little more than agreements on paper, and were rejected by the overwhelming majority of eastern Christendom.

We spoke earlier of the isolation and mutual ignorance prevailing between east and west. But it should not be imagined that there was no theological contact at all, except on such rare occasions as the Council of Florence. During the later Byzantine period, on the contrary, there was a notable series of Greek scholars who took a constructive interest in western theology. Maximus Planudes (1260–1310) translated Augustine's work *On the Trinity* into Greek, and Demetrius Cydones (c. 1324–1397/8) made translations of further writings by Augustine, along with Anselm's treatise *On the Procession of the Holy Spirit*. The most notable achievement of Cydones, however, was to provide a Greek version of the *Summa contra Gentiles* and the *Summa Theologica* by Thomas Aquinas; and during the later fourteenth century Thomism became almost fashionable at the Byzantine court. Another translator and enthusiastic admirer of Aquinas was George Scholarios (c. 1405–c. 1472), also known by his monastic name Gennadius. Scholarios was the last great theologian of the Byzantine period, and the first Patriarch of Constantinople under the Turks. A number of those who studied Latin theology – for example, Demetrius Cydones – were also advocates of union with Rome. Scholarios, by contrast, although he had at first supported the Union of Florence, subsequently became the leader of the anti-unionist party; yet to the end of his life he retained his enthusiasm for the works of Aquinas.

From the middle of the fourteenth century, therefore, there was available in Greek translation a substantial *corpus* of Latin theological literature. The Greeks had a better first-hand knowledge of Thomism than the Latins had of Palamism:[1] for while the east knew about Thomas Aquinas through

[1] On the theological views of St. Gregory Palamas, see pp. 219ff.

his own writings, the west knew about Gregory Palamas predominantly through the writings of his enemies.

Taking into account the various non-theological factors – the different historical situations in east and west, the mutual ignorance, the friction caused by Normans and by Crusaders – the question naturally arises: what theological 'residue' still remains in the controversy between Greeks and Latins? Was the schism really due to a primary and fundamental discrepancy in doctrine, to a basic contradiction between two quite opposite approaches to the Christian faith? Or were minor points of disagreement exaggerated beyond all due measure because of political antagonism and ecclesiastical rivalry?

Without doubt, in much of the polemic on either side there is a disturbing failure to distinguish between matters of fundamental principle and secondary issues. Questions of fasting, clerical celibacy, azymes, and the like, while not necessarily as trivial as they may at first appear, clearly do not involve any point of basic theology. Such matters caused bitterness out of all proportion to their real importance, mainly because of bigotry, narrow-mindedness, and mutual isolation. Cut off as they were from each other, Latins and Greeks each came to regard their own distinctive customs and liturgical observances as alone legitimate, and it was all too easy for them to confuse differences of ritual with differences of doctrine. Not that such confusion was universal: at the end of the eleventh century a Byzantine writer such as Theophylact of Bulgaria dismissed the dispute about azymes as relatively insignificant, and insisted that the only genuinely dogmatic question at issue between east and west was the *filioque*.[1] The Council of Florence also made a firm distinction between matters of faith, where agreement was essential, and matters of custom and liturgical tradition, where diversity could be permitted.

More serious doctrinally than the questions mentioned above was the problem of purgatory. This was not raised in the time of Photius or Cerularius – at that period the medieval western teaching on the state of the departed had not been developed so explicitly – but it was debated in some detail at Florence. Yet even here there was no question of a direct collision between opposed theologies. It was a matter, rather, of unequal doctrinal development: the Latins sought to define and analyse, where the Greeks preferred to limit themselves to the language of the Early Church, and otherwise (for the most part) to preserve a reverent agnosticism. Thus while the Latins spoke of a 'third place' called purgatory, in which souls undergo expiatory punishment, the Greeks spoke only of heaven and hell; and while the Latins applied juridical concepts to the next world, the Greeks on the whole refrained from asking precisely how prayers and offerings assist the dead. But both sides agreed that it is the Christian's duty to pray

[2] Even in the matter of the *filioque* Theophylact was surprisingly eirenic, and he sought to transfer the whole controversy from the dogmatic to the linguistic level. The basic problem, in his view, was the poverty of the Latin language, which possessed only the one word *procedere* where Greek possessed three or four terms: as a result the Latins were unable to distinguish with precision between the different types of relationship within the Trinity. In this way Theophylact refrained from accusing the west of downright error in doctrine.

for those who have fallen asleep, and that the faithful are helped by such intercessions.

There are, however, at least two points in the controversy that cannot be so easily dismissed: the *filioque* and the Papal claims. And in the background, more intangible yet none the less important, there is a third question: the differing attitudes in east and west towards the nature of theology.

To the majority of Christians today, the *filioque* controversy appears remote and unreal, and it is often asserted that the only serious obstacle to reunion between Orthodoxy and Rome is the question of the Papacy. The Byzantines saw things differently: in their eyes, it was the *filioque* that constituted the crucial point at stake. It is significant that the Council of Florence spent eight months debating the *filioque*, and rather less than two weeks discussing the Papal claims. Why was such decisive weight attached to the procession of the Holy Spirit?

In the *filioque* dispute, two main questions arise, the first ultimately ecclesiological in character, the second more specifically Trinitarian:

(i) Should the *filioque* be in the Creed?

(ii) Is the doctrine of the *filioque* true?

(i) So far as the first question is concerned, it is agreed by all that the *filioque* is an addition. The Creed, as adopted at the Council of Constantinople in 381 and reaffirmed at that of Chalcedon in 451, stated that the Spirit 'proceeds from the Father', and such is the form still used in the east. At a later date the west inserted the clause, 'and the Son' (*filioque*), so that the text ran, 'who proceeds from the Father *and the Son*'. This addition, so it seems, first appeared in Spain during the sixth century, where it was intended as a safeguard against Arianism; it spread subsequently to France and Germany, being finally adopted at Rome around the beginning of the eleventh century. The *filioque* was retained by the Churches of the Reformation, forming part of the inheritance which Protestants accepted without question from the western Middle Ages. From an Orthodox point of view, the Reformers went wrong in this as in a number of other matters, not because they were too radical, but because they were not radical enough.

Granted that the *filioque* is an addition, is it to be considered a *legitimate* addition? Even if the doctrine expressed by the *filioque* is in fact true, it does not therefore follow that the clause should be inserted in the Creed; for there are many true doctrines which are not included in the symbol of the faith. The question at issue is somewhat different: can the text of the Creed be altered, and if so, by whom? According to the standard eastern view, upheld by St. Mark of Ephesus at the Council of Florence, all alterations to the text of the Creed were formally forbidden by the Council of Ephesus in 431. Other Orthodox adopt a more moderate position: they admit in principle the possibility of revising the Creed – in 381 the Council of Constantinople made many changes to the original Nicene Creed of 325 – but they maintain that, since the Creed is the common possession of the universal Church, such revisions can only be made by an Ecumenical Council speaking in the name of the Church as a whole. The Creed, then, cannot be altered by a part of the Church acting in isolation, as the west acted when it inserted the *filioque* without consulting the east.

This question of the addition to the Creed is therefore closely bound up with the subject of the Papal claims, to be discussed shortly. It is true that the addition of the *filioque* was not made initially by Rome, but by Spain and the north; but once Rome had in fact accepted the insertion, the authority claimed in its support was naturally that of the Pope. The addition of the *filioque*, then, raises a problem of ecclesiology: does the Pope stand higher than the Ecumenical Councils, and has he the right to revise and modify on his own authority what they have formally decreed? Admittedly, the western addition of the *filioque* was ratified at Lyons and Florence, and therefore in the eyes of the west it now possesses conciliar as well as Papal sanctions: but the Orthodox east does not recognize either of these councils as ecumenical.

(ii) Far more intricate than the question of the addition of the *filioque* is the problem of the truth of the *filioque* doctrine as such. Two main standpoints may here be differentiated, the one more 'liberal' and the other more 'rigorist'. According to the 'liberal' view, the Greek and the Latin doctrines on the procession of the Holy Spirit may both alike be regarded as theologically defensible. The Greeks affirm that the Spirit proceeds from the Father *through* the Son, the Latins that He proceeds from the Father and *from* the Son; but when applied to the relationship between Son and Spirit, these two prepositions 'through' and 'from' amount to the same thing. This, in broad outline, was the view adopted by the Greeks who signed the act of union at Florence. It is a view also held by many Orthodox at the present time, who regard the matter of Papal authority as the one difference of fundamental doctrinal importance between the two Churches.

This 'liberal' position, in its most widely accepted form, can be expounded somewhat as follows. Both parties were at fault in the *filioque* controversy, because both failed to allow sufficiently for the possibility of a *plurality of theologies*. There are many different approaches to the mystery of the Holy Trinity, and no single approach can exhaust the full meaning of that mystery. The approach of Augustine or Anselm is not that of the Cappadocians, but both approaches have a rightful place in the fullness of Christian thought. The doctrine of the double procession of the Holy Spirit is legitimate and even necessary, within the framework accepted by the west; but, within the framework assumed by Photius and the east, such a doctrine has no real meaning. Both west and east, therefore, went astray in the dispute, because both assumed that their own theological framework was the only one which could rightly be employed. The Latins were wrong at Lyons, and to a lesser degree at Florence, because they forced the Greeks to accept a statement on the procession of the Spirit which was framed in uncompromisingly western categories; the Greeks from Photius onwards were wrong because they treated the western approach as necessarily heretical.

According to the 'liberal' view, then, the *filioque* controversy was based in large measure upon a confusion. Both parties for the most part failed to appreciate that what they were arguing about was a matter not of conflicting dogmas, but simply of differing *theologoumena* or theological stand-points: and whereas all Christians must be at one on questions of dogma, within this unity of faith there is room for a rich diversity of theo-logical approaches. The doctrine of the *filioque*, then, is to be seen as a *theologoumenon*, acceptable in western but not in Greek Trinitarian theology.

This way of looking at the controversy, however, is vehemently contested by the 'rigorist' party. According to the standard Orthodox view, as upheld by St. Photius in the ninth century, by St. Mark of Ephesus in the fifteenth, and by recent Orthodox theologians such as Vladimir Lossky, the *filioque* question raises genuine problems of a dogmatic nature, and it cannot be relegated to the level of *theologoumena*. Admittedly, the arguments involved are often obscure and complicated, but this is true of almost any dispute concerning Trinitarian theology. Since the doctrine of the Holy Trinity is at the very heart of all Christian thought and life, a small and seemingly insignificant variation in Trinitarian teaching can have far-reaching consequences. The *filioque* doctrine, many 'rigorists' believe, has in fact led the west to underestimate the rôle of the Holy Spirit in the world and has produced a distortion in the Latin doctrine of the Church. Since this 'rigorist' position will strike many contemporary Christians, whether Roman Catholic or Protestant, as unduly narrow and bigoted, it is important to understand the arguments which the stricter party among the Orthodox have advanced in support of their views.

When Photius and others maintained that the Spirit proceeds from the Father alone, in their minds they distinguished clearly between the 'eternal procession' and the 'temporal mission' of the Spirit. The Nicene Creed differentiates plainly between the 'eternal generation' of the Son – His birth from the Father 'before all ages' – and His Incarnation or birth from the Blessed Virgin Mary at a particular moment in time. A distinction must likewise be drawn between the 'eternal procession' of the Spirit – which is something that concerns the inner life of the Godhead, and takes place outside time – and the 'temporal mission', the sending of the Spirit to the world, which concerns the manifestation and activity of the Holy Trinity outside itself and within time. When Greeks and Latins argued about the *filioque*, they were not arguing about the sending of the Spirit to the world, for over this there was no conflict between them: both sides agreed that the Spirit is sent by the Son. Where they disagreed was over the procession, that is, over the eternal relationships existing within the Trinity. The term 'proceed' (in Greek, *ekporeuesthai*; in Latin, *procedere*) is to be understood throughout as denoting the hypostatic origin of the Spirit, the eternal source from which He derives His being.

In the *filioque* controversy the Greeks took as their starting-point the Trinitarian theology of the Cappadocians. The Father is the 'source of Godhead' (*pegaia theotēs*); He alone may properly be termed 'cause' (*aition*) or 'principle' (*archē*) within the Trinity. Accordingly it is possible to speak of the 'monarchy' of the Father; and it is this quality of being the *aition* and *archē* that constitutes the distinctive characteristic of the Father. In contrast to the Father the two remaining members of the Trinity are both 'caused' (*aitiata*). The second and third persons are distinguished from one another by the different mode of their origin: the Son is begotten by the Father, the Spirit proceeds from the Father. This is sufficient to mark the distinction between them.

Such was the Trinitarian theology which St. Photius took as his basis, when he maintained that there is a temporal mission of the Spirit from both Father and Son, but an eternal procession of the Spirit from the Father alone. As St. John of Damascus expressed it, 'We do not speak of the Spirit as from the Son, although we do call Him the Spirit of the Son' (*On the Orthodox Faith*, I. 8: P.G. xciv. 832B). Within such a Trinitarian framework as this, it is not easy to find a meaningful place for the doctrine of the double procession.

While Photius did not attempt to establish an eternal relationship between Son and Spirit – apart from the respective relationship of each to the Father – certain later Byzantine theologians sought to carry the question a little further. In an effort to bridge the gulf with the west, Gregory of Cyprus, Patriarch of Constantinople (1283–9), followed by St. Gregory Palamas (1296–1359), maintained that not only is the Spirit sent by the Son into the world but there is also, within the inner life of the Trinity, an 'eternal manifestation' (*aïdios ekphansis*) of the Spirit by the Son. In this sense of 'eternal manifestation', so they argued, the Spirit may correctly be said to proceed 'through' (*dia*) or even 'from' (*ek*) the Son. But the two Gregories were careful to distinguish this 'manifestation' from 'procession' in the strict sense. 'Manifestation', as they understood it, did not signify a relationship of hypostatic origin: so far as the origin of the Spirit was concerned, they agreed with Photius that He proceeds from the Father alone.

Between the Trinitarian doctrine of the two Gregories and that of the west there is perhaps no basic contradiction, so long as the western teaching is presented in its more ancient form, as expounded, for example, by Augustine. According to Augustine, the Spirit proceeds 'principally' (*principaliter*) from the Father, and from the Son only in a secondary and derivative sense. Is this 'secondary and derivative sense' of procession wholly different from the 'eternal manifestation' accepted by the two Gregories? In Augustine's teaching the 'monarchy' of the Father is still preserved, since the Father remains the only ultimate 'source' and *arche* of the Godhead. There is a considerable difference between this earlier western view and the later Scholastic doctrine, as upheld by the west at Lyons and Florence, whereby the Spirit proceeds from Father and Son 'as from one principle', *tanquam ex* (or *ab*) *uno principio*. This Scholastic theory, in contrast to that of Augustine, no longer affirms a personal principle of unity in the Godhead; the source of unity is now the divine essence, and the Cappadocian notion of the Father's 'monarchy' is abandoned. The difference in teaching between Augustine and the Scholastics is probably greater than that between Augustine and the Cappadocians. If we take as our standard of western Trinitarian teaching, not Lyons and Florence, but Augustine's work *On the Trinity*, then it is far easier to treat the *filioque* question as a matter of alternative *theologoumena* and not a dogmatic conflict. Despite their avowed aim to promote Christian unity, the Councils of Lyons and Florence served rather to crystallize western teaching on the Trinity in a Scholastic form that the east was bound to find uncongenial.

Against the Latin doctrine of the *filioque*, Photius advanced three main arguments:

(i) The *filioque* implies that there are two 'causes' or 'principles' in the Godhead, thus introducing a 'Manichaean' division into the doctrine of the Trinity and so leading to ditheism.

(ii) Supporters of the *filioque* understand the Trinity in terms of a Neoplatonic 'scale of being': Father, Son, and Holy Spirit are ranged in a descending order, the Spirit being one degree further removed from the Father than is the Son.

(iii) If the Latins deny that there are two principles in the Trinity [see point (i)], then in seeking to avoid the stigma of ditheism they fall into a type of 'semi-Sabellianism'. For they affirm that Father and Son, in their relation to the Spirit, are to be regarded as a single cause and *archē*. What is properly the distinctive characteristic of the Father – that of acting as the sole source within the Trinity – is thus ascribed to the Son as well; and in this way the Latins, like Sabellius, merge and confuse the persons.

The first of these three arguments is the least serious, for both at Lyons and Florence it was most carefully stated that there are not two *archai* within the Trinity but only one, because the Spirit proceeds from the Father and the Son 'as from one principle'. The second argument is more weighty, and in one form or another it has continued to be used by the 'rigorist' party up to the present day. The third is perhaps the most serious of all: Photius only mentions it briefly in his letter of 867, but it is developed at length in the *Mystagogia*, a work of his old age written after 883, when he had come to possess a far closer knowledge of Latin theology.

Combining the second and third arguments of Photius, we may state the 'rigorist' case as follows. The Latins, while affirming the divinity of the Spirit, have failed to appreciate sufficiently His distinct personality. As a result of the *filioque*, they have tended to treat the Spirit as a function and instrument of the Son, and not as a sovereign and co-equal hypostasis in His own right. This has meant that inadequate attention is paid in western thought to the work of the Spirit in the world, in the life of the Church, in the daily experience of each Christian. The living and immediate presence of the Spirit has been too much forgotten, and so the Pope has come to be regarded as the 'vicar' of an *absent* Christ, while the Church has come to be understood predominantly in terms of earthly power and jurisdiction, and not in terms of divine grace and of a free and direct encounter with God in the Spirit.

The *filioque*, so the 'rigorists' maintain, is a symptom of a wider defect in Latin Trinitarian thought. The west has overemphasized the unity of substance within the Trinity, and has not underlined adequately the distinction between the persons. In medieval Scholastic theology God is envisaged too little in concrete and personalist terms, and too much as an abstract essence in which various relationships are distinguished. The Thomist view, whereby 'the person is the relation' (*persona est relatio*), has led to an impoverishment in the western understanding of the personal nature of God.

The greatest care must of course be taken to hedge about these general charges with the necessary qualifications. They do not apply in the same measure to every writer without exception in the medieval west. If the followers of Thomas Aquinas can with some justification be accused of allowing the common essence within the Trinity to overshadow the three persons, such a criticism is far less applicable to (for example) Richard of St. Victor (†1173).

Compared with the *filioque* controversy, the dispute about the Papal claims involves issues that are comparatively clear and straightforward. The Byzantines believed that the highest visible authority in the Church was the Ecumenical Council; and next to the Council they honoured the 'pentarchy' or system of five Patriarchates – in order of precedence, Rome, Constantinople, Alexandria, Antioch, and Jerusalem. Until the disagreement over the *filioque*, they looked on Rome as constituting, more clearly than any other apostolic see, the norm of doctrinal orthodoxy. But the Pope, in their view, had no right to decide disputed questions of doctrine by himself: this could only be done through a *consensus* of all five Patriarchs, or if necessary through the convening of a council representing the Church as a whole. The Byzantines acknowledged the Pope as senior hierarch in the Church and at times they seem to have ascribed to him – although the evidence is often ambiguous – something more definite than a mere primacy of honour; but they never attributed to him an unlimited supremacy of power and universal jurisdiction, such as Nicolas I and many of his successors claimed. As Bessarion, Archbishop of Nicaea and later Cardinal, expressed it at the Council of Florence, before he acceded to the full Roman position: 'Indeed, we are not ignorant of the rights and privileges of the Roman Church; but we know also the limits set to these privileges . . . No matter how great the Roman Church is, it is notwithstanding less than an Ecumenical Council and the universal Church '(quoted in J. Gill, *Personalities of the Council of Florence and Other Essays*, Oxford, 1964, p. 267).

Up to the tenth century, appeals from the east to Rome were an accepted, though never a very common, practice. St. Athanasius and St. John Chrysostom had both made notable appeals to Rome in the earlier period. During the iconoclast controversy St. Theodore of Studios recommended the emperor to consult Rome: 'If there is anything in the Patriarch's reply about which you feel doubt or disbelief . . . you may ask·the Elder Rome for clarification, as has been the practice from the beginning according to inherited tradition' (*Letters*, II. 86: P.G. xcix. 1332A). In 861 St. Photius willingly submitted the disputed question of his appointment as Patriarch to the arbitration of a council over which the Papal legates presided. But the Byzantines felt free to reject a Roman decision when they disagreed with it: this happened, for example, in 906 when Pope Sergius III gave a ruling in favour of fourth marriages, which was not accepted at Constantinople. 'Rome was a convenient court of reference, an umpire at a distance from the capital, but in no serious sense a juridical superior of the

Patriarchate' (G. Every, *The Byzantine Patriarchate*, London, 1962, p. 168).

The Byzantines believed that it was by no means impossible for the Pope to err in matters of the faith; and most of them considered that he had in fact done so over the *filioque*. In such a situation he forfeited his position of primacy. 'As long as the Pope observes due order and remains in the truth,' stated Nilus Cabasilas, Archbishop of Thessalonica (†1363), 'he preserves the first place which belongs to him by right; he is the head of the Church and supreme pontiff, the successor of Peter and of all the apostles; all must obey him and treat him with complete respect. But if he departs from the truth and refuses to return to it, he deserves condemnation' (*On the Primacy of the Pope*: P.G. cxlix. 728D–729A).

Underlying these two matters of the *filioque* and the Papal claims, there is a third point of variance, far less precise and definite. East and west, at any rate during the later Byzantine period, had different ideas about the nature of theology, about the way in which religious thinking should be carried on, and in particular about the place of juridical categories and of logical inference in an exposition of the faith.

To take in order these two questions of legalism and rationalism: eastern Christians have long felt, in the first place, that Latin theology is too juridical, too much influenced by the notions of Roman law. In the words of a recent Orthodox writer, 'One of the features which distinguishes our theology from that of the Catholics is this – it does not look at things legalistically, but in terms of God's grace' (Alexander Elchaninov, *The Diary of a Russian Priest*, London, 1967, p. 54). It is this legalistic approach, so Eastern Orthodoxy believes, which has led the west to misunderstand the true nature of Papal primacy: Rome attempted to turn her 'presidency of love' (St. Ignatius of Antioch's phrase) into a juridical supremacy of power and outward authority. The same question of juridical concepts also lies behind the dispute about purgatory: where the medieval west thought predominantly in legalistic terms, of an established measure of punishment which man must undergo either in this life or the next, the east thought rather in terms of the soul's capacity to enjoy the vision and glory of God. Juridical concepts form the basis likewise of the Latin doctrine of indulgences and the treasury of merits, and also of the medieval doctrine of the atonement, from Anselm's treatise *Cur Deus Homo* (*Why did God become man?*) onwards. In all these matters, it is not so much this or that specific point in the Latin teaching to which the east objects: it is the general approach and manner of posing the question which Orthodoxy finds unacceptable. The Greek east has always been reluctant to speak about the nature of the Church, the redemption of man, or the communion of saints in this strongly juridical way.

The Greeks felt, in the second place, that Latin Scholastic theology had become altogether too rationalistic and philosophical, too much dependent on purely human methods of argument. Despite its heavy debt to the philosophers, Greek theology never used philosophical forms of thought as unreservedly as did Aquinas and the Schoolmen. Since the fourteenth century, if not before, many Orthodox have seen, in this western rationalizing tendency, a root cause of the schism between east and west. In the words of a Russian writer of the last century, Ivan Kireevsky, 'Rome preferred the abstract syllogism to sacred tradition, which is the expression of the common mind of the whole Christian world, and in which that world coheres as a living and indissoluble unity. This exaltation of the syllogism over tradition was in fact the sole basis for the rise of a separate and independent Rome . . . Rome left the Church because she desired to introduce into the faith new dogmas, unknown to sacred tradition, dogmas which were by nature the accidental products of western logic' (*Polnoe Sobranie Sochinenii*, Vol. I, Moscow, 1911, p. 226). Kireevsky has here stated – albeit in a somewhat stark and oversimplified form – a view which many eastern Christians share.

The Greeks' reserve towards 'western logic', and their appeal to 'sacred tradition' rather than the 'abstract syllogism', are clearly seen at the Council of Florence. When the Latins invoked the authority of Aristotle, an eastern delegate exclaimed impatiently, 'What about Aristotle, Aristotle? A fig for your fine Aristotle!' And when asked whose authority he recognized, he replied, 'St. Peter, St. Paul, St. Basil, Gregory the Theologian; a fig for your Aristotle, Aristotle' (J. Gill, *The Council of Florence*, p. 227). The Greeks, as we have already emphasized, had never ceased to theologize in the Patristic fashion: their criterion was always 'Holy Tradition' – the Fathers and the Councils – and they remained profoundly suspicious of the syllogistic reasoning in which the Latin Scholastics delighted. Even the humanist Bessarion wrote: 'The words of the Fathers by themselves alone are enough to solve every doubt and to persuade every soul. It was not syllogisms or probabilities or arguments that convinced me, but the bare words of the Fathers' (*Letter to Alexios Lascaris*, P.G. clxi. 360B: in Gill, *The Council of Florence*, p. 227).

In Greek eyes, Latin religious thought was altogether too confident, and insufficiently sensitive to the limitations of religious language. The Latins, so the Byzantines felt, had attempted to make theology too 'scientific' and philosophical, as if the realities with which it deals were accessible to ordinary human reasoning; whereas theology should be above all else 'mystical', for it is concerned with a mystery that surpasses all scientific reasoning and human understanding. There was of course no lack of mystical writers in the west during the later Middle Ages, but between them and the theology of the Schools there was normally a great gulf set; and it was precisely this that made the Byzantines uneasy. In Latin Scholastic theology, so it seemed to the Byzantines, everything was cut down to size, analysed and classified according to man-made categories: the sense of mystery was lost.

What is here involved, of course, is not a precise and sharply distinguished conflict in dogma between east and west, but rather a difference in emphasis and broader attitude; nor is it easy to summarize that difference without distorting its true nature. Nevertheless, a difference in approach to theology does certainly exist – a difference which colours the whole range of religious thought and which undoubtedly contributed to the separation.

No one today disputes the important part played, in the evolution of the schism, by cultural, political, and personal factors. Yet when full account has also been taken of the *filioque* controversy, of the disagreement about Papal authority, and of the differing attitudes towards the nature of theology, it becomes clear that the schism has also a spiritual and doctrinal aspect. Even if the doctrinal divergences were never as great as most Byzantines imagined, yet they existed and cannot be ignored.

V

MYSTICAL THEOLOGY: ST. SYMEON THE NEW THEOLOGIAN AND THE HESYCHASTS

It was during the fourteenth century – precisely at a time when, in the west, the gulf was widening between the mystics and the theologians – that the Byzantine tradition of mystical theology came to its fullest development. But the foundations of this tradition had already been laid long before, by Origen in the third century and by St. Gregory of Nyssa and Evagrius of Pontus in the fourth. Other writers who exercised a decisive influence on Byzantine mystical theology were the unknown author of the Macarian Homilies (late fourth–early fifth century), St. Diadochus of Photike (mid fifth century), St. 'Dionysius Areopagita' (late fifth–early sixth century), St. Maximus the Confessor, and St. Isaac of Nineveh, also known as Isaac the Syrian (late seventh century).

In this developing tradition, three points are of especial significance.

(1) First, Greek spiritual writers laid great emphasis upon the 'otherness' of God. Reacting strongly against Eunomius, who claimed that the divine essence is as comprehensible to man as it is to God Himself, the Cappadocians insisted upon the radical unknowability of God. At the most, St. Gregory of Nyssa argued, we can be aware of God's *presence*, but never of His *essence*. 'The true knowledge and the true vision of what we seek,' he wrote, 'consist precisely in this – in not seeing: for what we seek transcends all knowledge, and is everywhere cut off from us by the darkness of incomprehensibility' (*On the life of Moses*, P.G. xliv. 377A: ed. Jaeger-Musurillo, p. 87). The mystical vision of God is a vision not only of His immanence but of His transcendence and infinity: at the very moment when we are brought face to face with God, we realize as we never did before how profoundly He is still hidden from us.

Holding as they did this notion of the unknowability of God, the Greek Fathers, in common with many religious thinkers of the present day, were sharply conscious of the limitations of theological discourse. 'No theological expression,' said St. Basil the Great, 'can adequately express the meaning of the speaker . . . Our intellect is weak, and our tongue is weaker still' (*Letter* 7: P.G. xxxii. 345A). The Christian faith is fundamentally a mystery, and our doctrinal formulations are no more than signposts on a path of initiation. In this connection, St. Dionysius distinguished two contrasting methods of theology: the way of affirmation (cataphatic or affirmative theology) and the way of negation (apophatic or negative theology). Cataphatic theology consists in saying what God *is*: that He exists, that He is good, wise, loving, and the like. Such statements are true as far as they go, but they fall far short of expressing the full reality of God; for

God is not an object that 'exists' in the same way as other objects, nor is He 'good', 'wise', and 'loving' exactly in our sense of these terms. Cataphatic theology is therefore gravely insufficient, and must always be corrected by the use of apophatic approach. Every time we make an affirmative statement about God, we must also make a corresponding negative statement, 'for God is neither being . . . nor deity nor goodness nor spirit, as we know these things' (Dionysius, *Mystical Theology*, 5: P.G. iii. 1047A). The way of negation is definitely superior to the way of affirmation: since God is fundamentally unknowable, we come closer to the truth when saying what He is *not* than when saying what He is. Nor is this all. Apophatic theology, by its rejection of human images and concepts, enables man's mind to transcend its normal modes of reasoning, and to attain an unmediated experience of God on a level beyond all words and thought. So apophaticism is not merely negative, but forms a prelude to mystical union. This brings us to the second point.

(2) Alongside the emphasis upon the transcendence and otherness of God, Greek mystical theology insists also upon the possibility of a real and unmediated union with the deity. To describe this union, Greek writers – in common with mystics of many other traditions, both Christian and non-Christian – use two symbols, contrasting but not contradictory: the symbol of *darkness* and the symbol of *light*. Gregory of Nyssa and Dionysius are the chief 'darkness mystics' of the Christian East: Gregory refers, as we have seen, to the 'darkness of incomprehensibility', while Dionysius speaks of 'entering into the truly mystical darkness of unknowing' (*Mystical Theology*, 1: P.G. iii. 1001A). Most Greek writers, however, are 'mystics of light': Origen, Evagrius, and the Macarian Homilies, and at a later date Symeon the New Theologian and Gregory Palamas, all belong to the 'school' of light. The difference between the two 'schools' of light and darkness must not, of course, be exaggerated: the divine darkness of which Gregory and Dionysius speak is a 'radiant' or 'dazzling' darkness, due not to the absence but to the superabundance of light.

(3) On the practical level, Greek spiritual writers recommend one way of prayer above all others, as a means of approach to the unknowable yet ever-present God: the continual recitation of the Jesus Prayer, 'Lord Jesus Christ, Son of God, have mercy upon me' (this is the standard formula, but there are a number of variants). A 'spirituality of the Name of Jesus' is already apparent in the writings of Diadochus; what we have termed the 'standard formula' is first found in a text of the sixth or seventh century, the Life of Abba Philemon. In the course of time – certainly not later than the thirteenth century, and perhaps considerably earlier – a 'physical method' was recommended, as an aid to concentration when reciting the prayer: head bowed, chin resting on the chest, eyes fixed on the place of the heart, and breathing carefully regulated. This bodily technique never constituted an essential and primary element in the recitation of the Jesus Prayer, but was regarded simply as a useful accessory.

Such are the three themes which predominate in the Greek mystical tradition: a stress on the unknowability of God, and on apophatic theology; a belief in the possibility of direct union with God, this experience being envisaged sometimes as an entry into divine darkness, but more often as a vision of divine light; and a widespread employment of the Jesus Prayer, at times accompanied by the 'physical method'. It is the second of these three themes that is particularly evident in the writings of St. Symeon the New Theologian. More emphatically, perhaps, than any other Byzantine writer, he insisted upon the need for an unmediated awareness of the Holy Spirit, a direct union with God. 'Mystical experience', in his eyes, was not reserved for a privileged elite, but should be the conscious goal of all Christians alike.

Like the author of the Macarian Homilies, Symeon is emphatically a 'mystic of light'. The theme of 'immaterial light', of 'uncreated and invisible fire', recurs unceasingly throughout his works. The divine and uncreated light, as Symeon understood it, is not merely symbolical and imaginary, but an existent reality; though immaterial, it is not just inward and intellectual, but something which a man may on occasion perceive through his bodily eyes. Here, for example, is a description of the vision which Symeon received as a young man, before he had become a monk. He speaks of himself in the third person: 'While he was standing one night and saying the prayer, "God be merciful to me a sinner" – more with his mind than with his lips – a divine splendour suddenly appeared in abundance from above and filled the whole place. When this happened, the young man was no longer aware, but forgot, whether he was in a house or under a roof: for he saw nothing but light on every side, and he did not even know if he was standing on the ground. Yet he was not in any fear of falling, for he did not think at all about the world, nor about any of the cares which normally absorb men's attention while they are in the body. But he was wholly united with immaterial light and, so it seemed, he had himself become light. Then he forgot all the world, and was filled with tears and unutterable joy and exultation' (*Catechesis* 22: edited by B. Krivocheine, *Sources chrétiennes*, vol. 104, p. 372).

But, vitally important though the vision of the divine and uncreated light is in Symeon's teaching, he does not regard it as the supreme end of the mystical experience. What matters primarily is not the vision of light in itself, but He who appears and speaks to us in the light. It is not enough simply to behold the light; we must also meet Christ face to face within the light. We must hear Him speak and in our turn reply, 'as a friend talking with his friend', to use Symeon's phrase. In contrast to certain authors in the Greek mystical tradition, such as Evagrius, Symeon is always strongly Christocentric. Unlike Evagrius once more, he is also profoundly sacramental in outlook, and underlines the cardinal importance of the eucharist. The mystical life, for Symeon, is life in Christ and life in the sacraments.

Along with earlier Greek authors, Symeon envisages the ultimate aim of the Christian life in terms of *theosis* or 'deification'. Quoting a saying of St. Gregory of Nazianzus, he writes: 'God is joined in unity with those who are god and is known by them' (*Theological, Gnostic, and Practical Chapters*, III. 21: edited by J. Darrouzès, *Sources chrétiennes*, vol. 51, p. 86). Like can only be known by like: if man is truly to know God, he must himself become a 'created god' – he must strive to become by grace what God is by nature.

The tradition of mystical theology, of which Symeon is such an outstanding representative, came to full development with the Hesychast movement of the fourteenth century. Between Symeon and the fourteenth-century Hesychasts there is one obvious point of contrast: Symeon nowhere speaks of the Jesus Prayer, whereas in later Hesychast spirituality the invocation of the Name occupies a central place. The term 'Hesychast' denotes in general anyone who desires *hesychia*, that is, inward quiet or stillness: a Hesychast, then, is one who withdraws from worldly distractions and seeks God through wordless prayer. In practice, however, the term is normally employed in a more restricted sense, being used to describe a group of Byzantine writers in the fourteenth century, and their followers in more recent times. Within this group two figures are of special importance: St. Gregory of Sinai (1255–1346) and St. Gregory Palamas. The former was primarily a spiritual director, giving advice about the practice of prayer; the latter was more explicitly a theologian, and it was his achievement to provide a firm dogmatic basis for Hesychasm, which he integrated within the system of Christian doctrine as a whole.

This task Palamas undertook in response to a specific challenge. During 1337 and the years following, the whole mystical tradition, which has been outlined above, came under violent attack from a learned Greek, Barlaam the Calabrian. Although by origin from Italy, Barlaam was not at the outset particularly Papalist or pro-Latin: he regarded himself as a faithful son of the Orthodox Church, but he was at the same time a 'humanist' in approach, deeply imbued with that new spirit already abroad in the west, which was soon to lead to the Italian renaissance. In his intellectual outlook he was a Nominalist and an anti-Thomist.[1] He owed much to the writings of Dionysius, but interpreted them in a one-sided fashion. Advocating a type of 'Christian agnosticism', he pressed the traditional doctrine of divine transcendence to extremes.

His attack on the Hesychasts comprised two main points:

(i) Since God can only be known indirectly (so he argued), the Hesychasts are wrong to claim a direct experience of the deity and an immediate union with Him. The light which they behold in prayer, so far from being divine and uncreated, is merely a created light.

(ii) The physical method of prayer employed by the Hesychasts is grossly superstitious: they are *omphalopsychoi*, people who believe that the soul resides in the navel.

In both cases, Barlaam was attacking what he felt to be the *materialism* of the Hesychasts: their claim to see the divine light – that is, God Himself – through their physical eyes; and their claim to harness the body in the work of prayer. The issues which Barlaam raised have an interest far beyond the immediate context of the Hesychast controversy, and questions of an all-embracing significance are evidently involved: In what way is God revealed? How can He be known? What is the relation of creature to Creator?

What was St. Gregory's answer? As regards the first point in Barlaam's attack, Palamas agreed with his opponent that God is by nature unknow-

---

[1] Such is the view of J. Meyendorff in his major work, *A Study of Gregory Palamas*. But Barlaam's philosophical background requires further study.

able. No less than Barlaam, he was a convinced upholder of the Greek apophatic tradition, and he honoured the Dionysian writings, which – in common with all Byzantine and western writers of this period – he considered to be the work of St. Paul's disciple (Acts 17:34). In typically Dionysian language, Palamas speaks of the deity as 'superessential' (*hyperousios*) and 'more than God' (*hypertheos*), and he underlines the radical distinction between creature and Creator: 'How can we come close to God? By drawing near to His nature? But no single thing of all that is created has or ever will have even the slightest communion with the supreme nature, or nearness to it' (*Chapters*, 78: P.G. cl. 1176C). While many western theologians have characterized God as 'pure being', in Gregory's view neither this nor any other mental category can properly be applied to the Godhead. 'He is being and not being,' Gregory writes; 'He is everywhere and nowhere; He has many names and cannot be named; He is both in perpetual movement and immovable; He is absolutely everything and nothing of that which is' (*Apology*: quoted in J. Meyendorff, *A Study of Gregory Palamas*, London, 1964, p. 209).

Thus far there is agreement between Barlaam and Gregory: God is unknowable. But while Barlaam stopped short at the divine unknowability, Gregory went a step further. To maintain that all our knowledge of God is merely indirect and symbolical, so Gregory argued, is to reduce the Christian believer to the level of the pagan Greek philosopher; it is to take no account of the Incarnation, of the Church and the sacraments. The coming of Christ on earth and the sending of the Spirit at Pentecost have entirely transformed the relationship between God and man. This is a point of crucial significance for Gregory, and he returns to it repeatedly. The 'unknown' and 'hidden' God, without ceasing to be unknown and hidden, has at the same time revealed Himself in Christ Jesus His Son; and through the Holy Spirit all men may experience that self-revelation directly and immediately. As members of Christ's Body through baptism, as communicants in His flesh and blood through the eucharist, we come to enjoy an intimate and unmediated relation with God such as is not accessible to the pagan thinker. Barlaam's notion of the knowledge of God is fundamentally Neoplatonist; Gregory's notion, like that of St. Symeon the New Theologian, is Christocentric and sacramental.

God, then, is radically transcendent yet truly immanent; He is the 'wholly other', yet man can meet Him face to face; He is infinitely remote, yet closer to us than our own soul. In St. Paul's phrase, God is both 'unknown yet well known' (2 Corinthians 6:9). As St. Gregory Palamas put it, 'The saints possess knowledge of God, but they possess it in an incomprehensible fashion' (*Triads in defence of the Holy Hesychasts*, I. 3. 17: edited by J. Meyendorff, Louvain, 1959, vol. I, p. 145). To safeguard the two aspects of this saving paradox, Gregory differentiated between the *essence* and the *energies* of God. The essence signifies God as He is in Himself; the energies signify God in His activity towards the creation. The divine essence, so Gregory believed, is known to none save the three persons of the Trinity: it is unknown both to angels and to men, and will necessarily remain unknown, not only in this present age but in the age to come. But

God's energies fill all the world, and all who so desire may participate in them. These energies are divine and uncreated: they are not something that exists apart from God, not a gift that He bestows, but they are God Himself in action. God, then, is *essentially* unknowable, but *existentially* revealed through the energies or free acts of His omnipotence. This contrast between the essence and the energies of God was not invented by Gregory, but taken over by him from earlier Greek Fathers, in particular the Cappadocians; Gregory, however, imparted to the distinction a prominence and a precision which it did not before possess. Gregory's aim in insisting upon this distinction was to allow a true 'deification' while excluding any taint of pantheism. 'God,' he wrote, 'remains wholly within Himself and yet dwells in His entirety within us, granting us to share, not in His own nature, but in His own glory and brightness' (*Triads*, I. 3. 23: Meyendorff, vol. I, p. 159). We participate in God, but we cannot appropriate Him; God possesses us, but we can never possess Him. If we knew God's essence in the same way that He knows ours, then we should ourselves *be* God in the literal sense. But in fact this does not happen; however closely linked we are with God, He still remains God and we remain man. 'Deification' signifies that we become 'gods' by grace and by status, but never by nature: as St. John of Damascus expressed it, man 'is deified by sharing in the divine illumination, but he is not changed into the divine essence' (*On the Orthodox Faith*, II. 12: P.G. xciv. 924A). There is a true union, but no fusion or absorption.

This distinction between the divine essence and the divine energies, as expounded by St. Gregory Palamas, has never been accepted in western theology. Latin writers have usually judged Palamism on the evidence of Gregory's opponents, and so they have frequently failed to appreciate the real character of his teaching. They have also tended to interpret him according to the criteria of Thomism, without allowing sufficiently for the fact that Gregory's terms of reference are very different from those assumed in western Scholasticism. The main western criticism of Palamism is that the distinction between essence and energies overthrows the simplicity of God, making Him into a kind of composite being. In Gregory's view, however, the energies are most emphatically not a part or subdivision of God – still less, an emanation or inferior divinity – but the very God Himself in His entirety. 'Each power or energy is God Himself,' Gregory insisted (*Letter to Gabras*: in Meyendorff, *A Study of Gregory Palamas*, p. 214); 'God is wholly present in each of His divine energies' (*Triads*, III, 2. 7, Meyendorff, vol. II, p. 657). There is, then, no division in the Godhead and no destruction of the divine simplicity, for the one God is fully and indivisibly present in each of the energies, just as He is fully present in each of the three persons, and fully present in His single essence.

When the medieval west misunderstood Gregory's teaching on the energies of God, this was partly because it started primarily from the idea of God as essence, whereas Gregory, in common with earlier Greek Fathers, started primarily from the idea of God as personal. (The same difference in approach, as we have seen, was involved in the *filioque* controversy.[1]) On the assumptions of western Scholasticism, therefore, a distinction between

[1] See p. 211.

essence and energies inevitably seemed to impair the simplicity of the Godhead. But on Gregory's presuppositions, this danger is avoided. God remains single, simple, and unique, because He is not just an essence but personal: the multiplicity of energies and the indivisible essence are both alike ascribed to the selfsame Triune subject, to the single, living, and personal God.

The divine energies are in no sense an intermediary between God and man; on the contrary, the Christian who participates in the energies of God is actually meeting God *face to face*, so far as this is possible for man. In relation to man, the energies are often designated by the term 'grace' (*charis*). 'Grace', in other words, is not just a gift of God, a 'thing' which He bestows on His creature. It is more than this: it is God Himself in confrontation with man – all the fullness of the divine presence and the divine life, as communicated to humanity. In this way Gregory excluded any magical and mechanistic understanding of salvation. God saves man directly by His own divine energies. Saving grace is not something created, to be stored quantitatively through sacramental acts and indulgences, to be dispensed and manipulated by the ecclesiastical hierarchy. Saving grace is always sovereign, uncreated, and free.

These uncreated energies, which from one point of view are termed 'grace', may with equal truth be described in terms of divine light. Barlaam was wrong, so Gregory argued, to conclude that the light beheld by the Hesychasts in prayer is nothing but a created and physical light. On the contrary, this light is the energies of God; and so it is not created but uncreated, not physical but non-material (*aülon*) and 'intelligible' (*noeron*). Though it is not physical, the saints sometimes see it through their physical eyes; but in such a case their senses must first be transformed by divine grace, for they do not perceive the uncreated light by virtue of their normal powers of perception, but through the power of the Holy Spirit that dwells and acts within them. In order to be capable of the vision of God, the body and its faculties must first be transfigured and made spiritual.

According to Gregory, this light which is manifested to the Hesychasts is identical with the light which shone from Christ at His transfiguration on Mount Tabor, and which will shine from Him likewise at His second coming on the Last Day. 'Is it not evident,' he asks, 'that there is but one and the same divine light: that which the apostles saw on Tabor, which purified souls behold even now, and which is the reality of the eternal good things to come?' (*Triads*, I. 3. 43: Meyendorff, vol. I, p. 205). The vision of the divine light is eschatological, and he who sees it is sharing already in the glory of the future age.

There remains Barlaam's second ground of attack, against the 'physical method' employed by the Hesychasts. In itself this method was of secondary importance, and could have been abandoned by the Hesychasts without involving any major reorientation in their spirituality. But Palamas realized that behind Barlaam's challenge there lay a question of basic significance for the Christian doctrine of man: and therefore he defended the bodily techniques, not primarily for themselves, but because of the deeper principle involved. As Palamas recognized, Barlaam held a fundamentally

Platonist doctrine of man. The Calabrian saw man as a soul imprisoned in a body, and for this reason he affirmed a knowledge of God through the intellect alone, to the exclusion of man's material nature; that was why he found the physical techniques so scandalous. In opposition to Barlaam's Platonizing doctrine, Gregory expounded an anthropology that was thoroughly scriptural. He insisted that man is a single whole, a unity of soul and body together; it is not just man's soul, he believed, but the *whole* man that is created in the image of God. In Romans 7:24, as Gregory points out, it is not our material nature as such which St. Paul condemns, but 'the body of this death': the body in itself is not evil, but only our 'bodily thoughts' (*Triads*, I. 2. 1: Meyendorff, vol. I, p. 77). At His Incarnation Christ took not only a human soul but a human body, and so He has 'made the *flesh* an inexhaustible source of sanctification' (*Homily* 16: P.G. cli. 193B). In the eucharist we do not simply feed on Christ with our minds, but we actually eat His Body and drink His Blood: in this way our flesh is made holy by His flesh and it shares in His divine life.

Gregory, then, affirms a doctrine of total sanctification: the whole of man, body as well as soul, is to be redeemed and transfigured. 'The flesh also is transformed; it is raised on high together with the soul, and together with the soul it enjoys communion with God, becoming itself the possession and dwelling-place of God' (*Triads*, I. 2. 9: Meyendorff, vol. I, p. 93). Man's body is not an enemy, but a partner and collaborator with his soul. If this is true of the Christian life in general, it is also true of Christian prayer. When we pray, our body is not to be regarded as something indifferent or antagonistic – a lump of matter to be ignored, an obstacle to be overcome. On the contrary, the body too can share in the ascent to God's presence. The physical technique of the Hesychasts is therefore based upon a genuinely Christian and Biblical understanding of human nature.

True to this doctrine of man's total sanctification, Gregory insists (as we have noted) that the vision of divine light, although in itself spiritual, can be seen through man's bodily eyes. Not only do the saints gaze upon the light, but they are themselves filled with light – in their souls *and in their bodies*. To see the glory of God is also to share in it and to be transfigured by it. This bodily transfiguration will be accomplished in its fullness only at the resurrection of the body at the Last Day; but the first-fruits of that final glorification can be experienced even now. Here, as elsewhere, St. Gregory adheres to an inaugurated eschatology. 'If in the age to come,' he writes, 'the body will share with the soul in unspeakable blessings, it must certainly share in them, as far as possible, even now' (*Tome of the Holy Mountain*: P.G. cl. 1233C). So it may happen that even in this present life the bodies of the saints shine with divine glory, as Christ's body shone on Mount Tabor. St. Symeon the New Theologian hints at this, in a passage already quoted:[1] 'He was wholly united with immaterial light and, so it seemed, *he had himself become light.*' St. Gregory Palamas speaks in similar terms: 'He who has received the divine energy . . . is wholly as light' (*Homily* 53: edited by S. Oikonomos, Athens, 1861, p. 177).

Such were the primary themes in the thought of Palamas. God is un-

[1] See p. 218.

knowable in His essence, but revealed through His divine energies; and man can participate in these energies – which are God Himself – not only in the age to come, but here and now. The energies are experienced above all in the form of divine light. Since man is a single unity of body and soul, the body shares in the work of prayer and in the vision of God: the saints behold the uncreated light through their bodily eyes, and themselves shine bodily with the light that they behold. In this response of Palamas to Barlaam's double challenge, it is at once evident how close is the link subsisting between spirituality and dogma. Gregory was concerned to defend certain ways of prayer, a particular tradition of mystical experience; but he was fighting also for a proper understanding of human nature and of man's total salvation in Christ.

The theology of Palamas – in particular, his distinction between essence and energies and his doctrine concerning the divine light – was confirmed at a series of councils held in Constantinople during 1341, 1347, and 1351. Although Barlaam abandoned the struggle in 1341 and returned to the west, Gregory's views still encountered fierce opposition at Byzantium, his leading adversaries after 1341 being Gregory Akindynos, and subsequently the scholar and historian Nicephorus Gregoras. Whereas Barlaam had stood primarily for a 'humanist' approach, Akindynos was a representative of the traditionalist 'theology of repetition'. Akindynos, unlike Barlaam, did not attack the methods of prayer in use among the Hesychasts, but solely the distinction between essence and energies. Palamas was thus fighting on two fronts. Faced by the philosophical Nominalism and the doctrinal agnosticism of Barlaam, he championed the mystical realism of the Greek monastic world; faced by the narrow conservatism of Akindynos, he insisted upon the need for a living theology – for a creative understanding of tradition, rather than a mechanical traditionalism. Although the synods which confirmed the Palamite teaching were local and not general, they have come to enjoy an authority in the Orthodox East that is second only to that of the Seven Ecumenical Councils themselves.

Among the friends and supporters of the Hesychasts, one of the most gifted and attractive is Nicolas Cabasilas (1322/3–c. 1380), a nephew of Nilus Cabasilas, Archbishop of Thessalonica.[1] Nicolas, so far as is known, never became either priest or monk, but was a layman, serving at the court and in the civil service. Although the Byzantine mystical tradition flourished above all in monastic circles, it was never limited exclusively to hermits or members of religious communities; but its influence extended also to the laity, as the example of Nicolas indicates. Indeed, Symeon the New Theologian insisted explicitly that the full mystical experience is accessible to all alike – to married men and women, living in the midst of society, as well as to the anchorite and the recluse. In the same way, St. Gregory of Sinai – while living himself in strict withdrawal – instructed one of his spiritual children, Isidore, to postpone his monastic profession and to return for a time into the world, so that he could serve as guide and example to lay people who sought to practise inner prayer. And in a text attributed to St. Gregory Palamas it is stated: 'Let no one think, my

[1] See p. 213.

brother Christians, that only priests and monks need to pray without ceasing, and not laymen. No, no: every Christian without exception ought to dwell always in prayer' (*Philokalia*, vol. v, Athens, 1963, p. 107).

The Hesychast vocation, then, is a path open potentially to everyone. Faithful to this understanding of Heyschasm, Nicolas Cabasilas strove to translate the mystical theology of Palamas into concrete and practical terms, more readily intelligible to ordinary Christians. He did this primarily by showing how the entire life of the Christian is centred upon the sacraments: in the words and ceremonial actions of the Liturgy and other offices, all the inner reality of mystical prayer is summed up and made outwardly manifest. In Nicolas Cabasilas the liturgical theology of Byzantium attained its finest flowering.[1] Another notable exponent of Byzantine liturgical theology was Symeon of Thessalonica (†1429).

As a typical example of Cabasilas' way of thinking, we may take his simple yet penetrating statement on the nature of the eucharistic sacrifice: 'What are the teachings of our faith concerning sacrifice? In the first place, that this sacrifice is not a mere figure or symbol but a true sacrifice; secondly, that it is not the bread which is sacrificed, but the very Body of Christ; thirdly, that the Lamb of God was sacrificed once only, for all time . . . Now it is clear that, under these conditions, it is not necessary that there should be numerous oblations of the Lord's Body. Since the sacrifice consists, not in the real and bloody immolation of the Lamb, but in the transformation of the bread into the sacrificed Lamb, it is obvious that the transformation takes place without the bloody immolation. Thus, though that which is changed is many, and the transformation takes place many times, yet nothing prevents the reality into which it is transformed from being one and the same thing always – a single Body, and the unique sacrifice of that Body' (*A Commentary on the Divine Liturgy*, translated by J. M. Hussey and P. A. McNulty, London, 1960, pp. 81–2).

The works of Cabasilas, above all his treatise *On Life in Christ*, show how closely mysticism and the sacramental life were linked together in the Hesychast *milieu*. Gregory of Sinai, Palamas and Cabasilas, like Symeon the New Theologian before them, did not in any way advocate a mystical ideal that was sub-Christian or individualist. Their teaching was firmly based upon the person of the Lord Jesus Christ, upon the corporate life of the Church, and the communal receiving of the sacraments.

St. Gregory Palamas and the other leaders of the Hesychast movement constitute a striking proof that Byzantine religious thought retained its vitality until the very end of the Empire. The history of Christian doctrine in the east does not cease with the Council of Chalcedon in 451, nor yet with the last Ecumenical Council in 787. If the flame of theology burnt sometimes less brightly, at no point before 1453 was it ever entirely extinguished: and particularly during the fourteenth century, on the eve of the final collapse of Byzantine power, it shone once again as brilliantly as ever. It is a moving thing to observe how Byzantium made what is perhaps its greatest contribution to Christian civilization, not at a time of outward prosperity, but in the midst of material weakness and distress.

[1] See further J. Meyendorff, *Byzantine Theology*, London, 1975, chapter 16.

The Middle Ages
604-1350

David Knowles

The Middle Ages
604–1350

DAVID KNOWLES

INTRODUCTORY

The development of western theology in the long period of more than seven hundred years between the death of Pope Gregory I and the death of William of Ockham was for long a neglected historical topic. In part this was due to the comparative scarcity of great theologians and great theological controversies between the centuries of patristic and conciliar brilliance, during which theological writings and discussions were the principal intellectual achievement of the Christian Empire, and the early modern period of ferment and controversy during which confessional differences rent western Europe and were a major interest alike of statesmen and of the newly literate and religiously active lower middle class in every country. In part, however, it is certainly due directly to the basic conviction of the Reformers, that for a thousand years Christian teaching had been deformed and obscured by ever greater accretions of error and superstition, and that it was necessary to rediscover the pure faith of the apostolic, or at least of the patristic age. This conviction, which was both an effect and a cause of the appearance and growth of critical scholarship, influenced the conservative or Catholic party also, and 'scholastic' theology gave way in many places to 'positive' historical and scriptural studies.

It is undeniable that the Middle Ages gave birth to relatively few theologians worthy of being joined to the great company of those who flourished between the age of Origen and that of John Chrysostom in the east, and Tertullian and Leo the Great in the west. Between the seventh ecumenical council (787) and the council of Constance in 1414 there were no epoch-making conciliar debates. Nevertheless, even in our narrower period, which begins after the death of Gregory the Great and ends before the emergence of Wyclif, theological discussions and definitions took place that have deeply influenced all subsequent ages in the Roman church and have left their mark also, if only of reaction, upon the other churches of Christendom. They should not, indeed they cannot, be ignored by the historian, for they were the frame of great historical changes, and it is not for the historian to reject any opinion as a deviation from revealed truth, though he may assess modifications of traditional teaching and deviations from orthodoxy.

The somewhat arbitrary choice of the death of Gregory I is defensible, for that great pope's active life was passed at a moment of crisis in the west, and Gregory himself, like other great figures of the sixth century, looks both backward and forward. He is the last great figure in the procession of Latin fathers, while in his government of the city of Rome and his missionary energy he is the harbinger of the half religious, half secular papal monarchy of the Middle Ages. In his writings, also, there is the double thread. On the one hand he uses and does not fear to adapt the teaching of Augustine and other great men of the past, while on the other hand he shows an unmistakable lack of theological profundity and of stylistic distinction when compared with a Leo or a Jerome, and his *Dialogues* show all the characteristics of a medieval, rather than of a classical, mentality. Similarly, the middle years of the fourteenth century mark a real watershed in the intellectual life of the church, when the marriage between philosophy and theology has broken up and the whole fabric of ecclesiastical thought and government is under critical attack.

Within our long period we can make several divisions, which do not exactly correspond to those usually made in general or political history:

I. There is, first, the period of about 150 years in which the church of Rome is still involved in the controversies and developments of the eastern church.

II. Next comes the age of the Carolingian theological writers, and then the Photian age in the eastern church, followed by more than a century of stagnation and ending almost at the millennial year.

III. This is followed in turn by the intellectual revival, which in the theological field saw the emergence, for the first time for more than four centuries, of individual minds of eminence, culminating in the careers of Anselm, Abelard and Bernard.

IV. Overlapping this is the first great age of the organized schools, beginning with the cathedral schools of Chartres, Laon, Liège and elsewhere, and continuing in the masters of the Sentences and the nascent universities.

V. Next, there is the great age of scholastic theology, particularly at Paris and Oxford, but also in many other universities and schools, in all of which the same methods and interests prevailed.

VI. Finally, there is a period of change, in which the scholastic synthesis is dissolved by the New Logic.

I

FROM GREGORY THE GREAT TO CHARLEMAGNE.
ROME AND CONSTANTINOPLE

1. *The Monothelete controversy*

For more than 150 years after the death of Gregory the Great central and southern Italy from Venice southward along the Adriatic and from Bologna southwards through Rome, was nominally still part of the Empire, though only once after A.D. 600 did an emperor of Constantinople set foot in the duchy of Rome. While the north-eastern region formed a province or exarchate based on Ravenna, the central and southern part of the peninsula west of the Apennines fell gradually under the control of the papacy. In the duchy of Rome itself the pope, like other bishops in the western part of the empire, became the effective civil governor when the imperial government failed to protect or to assist, and the popes by gifts or inheritance became large landowners throughout central and southern Italy and Sicily. When the emperor and pope, as we shall see, were at odds, the people of Rome and the neighbourhood supported their familiar protector, and thus the pope, by an accident of history big with consequences, acquired the status of a temporal monarch in the 'patrimony of St. Peter' which, when the emperor lost control of the exarchate of Ravenna, was joined by the coastal region from Ravenna to Ancona. During all this period the pope remained nominally a subject of the emperor and in imperial theory and practice he was bound to submit his election to Constantinople for ratification. On the other hand, the patriarch of Constantinople recognized a primacy in the Roman see, and each new patriarch informed the pope of his election and orthodoxy. It was therefore natural in this period that the Roman church should share in the controversies of the eastern church, which were in fact often referred to it for decision.

The first of these was the dispute that was ultimately known as the Monothelete controversy.

The great Christological disputes of the fifth century had issued in a clear assertion of the twofold nature and single personality of Christ, and in the statement that the Son of God had taken to himself a human nature which retained all its qualities and powers. This agreement had not fully covered areas which in some cases were regions of dissidence or uneasy assent on either side, as it were, of the central orthodoxy. On the one hand the Nestorians, more definitely unorthodox than the alleged author of their belief, held fast to the two natures without a clear enunciation of the single personality. Christ, the whole Christ, had in some mysterious way been united to the divine nature without a clear definition of personal union. Nestorianism retained its hold on parts of Syria. On the other hand, Monophysitism in its most characteristic form maintained that Christ's human nature had been entirely absorbed in the divine. This was in origin an Alexandrian opinion, and the church in Egypt remained Monophysite in sympathy, and its teaching spread also to Syria and Armenia.

When, early in the seventh century, the emperor Heraclius (610–641) was engaged in repelling the Persian invaders, his enemies received considerable support from the Monophysites, who hoped to remain in greater security under Persian government. Heraclius therefore attempted to restore unity to the east and attract dissident Christians to his rule, by finding a formula that would satisfy both orthodox and monophysite opinion. His close ally Sergius, patriarch of Constantinople, seconded his efforts. There had been previous discussions as to whether, in the face of the decree of the council of Chalcedon, it was still possible to say, in view of the hypostatic or 'personal' union of the two natures, that in Christ there was only one principle of operation (ἐνέργεια). Sergius and Heraclius adopted this opinion, and held it out as a basis of agreement with the Monophysites. Cyrus, patriarch of Alexandria, and Anastasius, patriarch of Antioch, accepted this, and a general agreement seemed to be within sight. It was challenged by two Egyptian monks, Sophronius, who became almost immediately patriarch of Jerusalem, and Maximus (580–662), celebrated later as the Confessor. Sophronius circulated his teaching to Rome and the other patriarchs: it was that two natures demanded two separate 'operations', both directed by a single personality. Meanwhile Sergius had written to Pope Honorius (625–38) and others, deprecating the assertion of either one or two 'energies' in Christ, as adding a new precision to Chalcedon which would alienate one or other of the two bodies of opinion. He therefore asked for the pope's approval to the proposition that Christ, the Word made Man, had only a single principle of activity, and that there was no conflict of will in Christ.

Honorius, who was not an expert theologian and who saw the practical need for unity, agreed that there was no conflict of will in Christ, and that it was the business of philosophers, not of religious teachers, to decide whether there were one or two 'operations'. By this time the formal opposition of Sophronius, setting out the doctrine of two wills in Christ, had reached Sergius, who in consequence changed his terminology. He consequently prepared a dogmatic statement for the emperor Heraclius to publish – the celebrated *Ecthesis* of 638. In this the emperor and his patriarch deprecated the assertion of either a single or a double operation in Christ, but to silence the opinion of Sophronius the document ended by asserting that there was in Christ only a single will.

Hitherto the popular, and perhaps also the theological, mind had been confused by the manipulation of scriptural and conciliar texts alongside of technical philosophical terms such as nature and person. Sophronius, and still more Maximus, helped to clarify the matter by showing that personality added nothing to a nature beyond giving it existence and the power to act; all the faculties are within a nature, and although the person is said to act and suffer, this is because the existing person is regarded as a compound of nature and personality. In the case of Christ, where two natures are united in one personality, the human nature is absolutely complete in itself with will, reason, etc., but it is actualized by a divine person. In other words, the Word does not either absorb the human nature or use it merely as an instrument. Christ's human nature has all the faculties and powers, including the will, which is not of itself subordinated to the divine will, but is freely directed to compliance with it. There are therefore two wills in Christ, in whom the human will is indissolubly (though freely) united with the divine will in virtue of the grace of the hypostatic union.

Pope Honorius died in 638. Two years later Pope John IV, at a council held in Rome, condemned the doctrine of a single will in Christ, now known as the monothelete heresy. The emperor Heraclius died a few weeks later, and the pope wrote to his sons who succeeded him a letter which, after endeavouring to justify the action of Honorius, set out what was ultimately to be held as the orthodox doctrine. Shortly afterwards the Arab conquest of Armenia and Egypt weakened and isolated the monothelete party both within and without the new boundaries of Christendom.

Disagreement nevertheless continued to appear between successive popes on the one hand, and emperors and patriarchs of Constantinople, on the other. The patriarch Paul was excommunicated by Pope Theodore in 647, while the patriarch persuaded the emperor Constans II to abolish the *Ecthesis* and to publish the *Typos* ('Rule') in which he reiterated the earlier prohibition of all discussion as to the wills and energies of Christ. This came too late to be effective, and in 649 Pope Martin I held a synod at the Lateran attended by 500 bishops. Here, after a discussion, the two wills of Christ were proclaimed in a reiteration of the creed of Chalcedon, to which an addition was made for this express purpose, together with an anathema of the *Ecthesis*, *Typos* and erring patriarchs of Constantinople. This was accepted without demur in the west, where the issue had never been controversial, but the emperor Constans II caused the pope to be seized and brought for trial to Constantinople, allegedly for anti-imperial treason. He was brutally treated and exiled to the Crimea, where he died. Maximus the Confessor, seized in Rome along with the pope, was tortured and exiled. A period of confusion followed, in which the imminent danger of attack from the Arabs, and a widespread revulsion at the treatment of Martin and Maximus, prevented further disunion. Finally, when the siege of Constantinople (674–8) had ended, Pope Agatho held a council in Rome in 680 which reiterated the decisions of 649, and delegates carried a dogmatic letter to Constantinople where the emperor Constantine IV had convoked a council, recognized as the Sixth Ecumenical. In this, after long discussion, the decisions of previous Roman councils were reaffirmed, and the doctrine of two wills in Christ was proclaimed, with anathemas for the erring patriarchs, to whom was added the name of Honorius. Pope Leo II accepted both the decisions and the anathemas.

This was the end of the heresy as a controversy dividing the churches, though it continued to smoulder for some years and was part of the background of the great controversy over images. It was also the end of the long theological dialogue in which the doctrine of Christian Christology was hammered out, to assert at once the divine personality and the complete human nature of Jesus Christ. The monothelete issue had its importance as the last attempt to impose upon Christendom what may be called a series of pseudo-supernatural conceptions of the divine Redeemer. All of these might superficially have simplified the intellectual problems of the believer, or at least the believer in an age which readily admitted the possibility of demiurges and theophanies and degrees of divinity. But it would not only have debased or destroyed the simple, original, evangelical belief that the son of Mary was also the Son of God, but would have presented future ages, more rationalistic and naturalistic in their outlook, with insuperable difficulties of scriptural and theological definition. The doctrine of the Incarnation necessarily remained, and still remains, a mystery, for it expresses the greatest and most sublime creative work of a transcendent, infinite, incomprehensible deity, but once granted belief in an omnipotent divine Being, the Incarnation can be expressed in terms that do not violate the dignity and truth either of God or of man, and that display, even to the unbeliever, an alliance between God and human nature which, if its reality is granted, appears as a marvel of wisdom and love.

General histories sometimes convey the impression that all theological and administrative ability disappeared from the Roman church with the death of Gregory I. This was not so, and the stages of the monothelete controversy show that bishops of Rome still disposed of theological resources and were able to rally, for discussion and decision, considerable members from the episcopate of Italy, the Mediterranean islands and the coasts of the Adriatic. Historians of liturgy, music and architecture show that the seventh and early eighth centuries were something of a golden age, in which Greek influences, side by side with Roman traditions, enriched the life of the church. It was in this age that Greek Marial devotion introduced several new festivals into the Roman calendar, including the Assumption, which originally celebrated the passing of the soul of the Virgin into God's presence, without express assertion of a corporeal assumption. This close connection with Greek thought and liturgy was to be seen in the history of the Iconoclast controversy, in which the pope of Rome still showed his ecumenical influence, though the political consequences of the struggle were to have a critical effect upon the relations of East and West.

2. *The Iconoclast controversy*

This disastrous affair, which is often treated as a self-contained episode in Byzantine history, was in fact a mixture of doctrinal, sociological, political and personal issues. The doctrinal issue was long-standing, important and twofold. As is well known, the making and still more the cult of images and pictures of the divinity or of any sacred object or person was strictly forbidden to the people of Israel. The prohibition was not carried over into the New Testament, and from very early times painted and (later) sculptural and other representations of the cross, of Christ, and of incidents in the gospel made their appearance, and despite the opposition of a few rigid 'puritanical' writers, such as Eusebius of Caesarea, and certain churches, the custom spread and was accepted in both east and west. Later the cult made its appearance; that is, marks of honour, private and liturgical, were paid to the cross and to pictures and statues of Christ, his Mother and the saints. This again met with opposition but received the theological justification that became traditional. In the western church at this time extravagance and superstition were rare, but in the east, and particularly in Constantinople and its hinterland, and in the monasteries of the Empire, the reverence and cult shown to ikons (images) were often excessive and superstitious. This would not, however, have occasioned violent political upheaval, which was originally entirely due to the action of the emperor Leo III the Isaurian, whose leadership and military genius had recently rescued the empire and the City from the attacks of the Arabs. In 726 he prohibited the cult of images and decreed their total destruction. The causes of this drastic action are still uncertain. The emperor was a Syrian by birth, and the inborn eastern repugnance to representational art in religion, the influence of Old Testament and Muslim prohibitions, the monophysite dislike of any honour paid to the humanity of Christ and the divine motherhood of Mary, may all have had a share in Leo's action. In any case, a violent persecution ensued which disrupted the life of the empire for more than a century, though with intervals of peace. Popes Gregory II (715–31) and Gregory III (731–41) protested strongly, and the latter held a council of 93 bishops in 731 at which the accepted traditional doctrine was reiterated with anathemas. This provoked direct action by the emperor, who confiscated the papal estates in Sicily and south Italy and attached to Constantinople the Balkan peninsula and Greece, hitherto considered as lying within the western patriarchate. Finally, in 754 a council of eastern bishops held near Chalcedon condemned the manufacture, possession and veneration of images. This, however, did not reflect the great mass of sentiment in the Byzantine church, and thirty years later the empress Irene, a supporter of images (an 'iconodule' as opposed to an 'iconoclast'), in consultation with Pope Adrian I arranged a council at Nicaea, the Seventh Ecumenical (787), which pronounced the lawfulness and value of images and distinguished between the honour and cult (*dulia*) due to them and the adoration (*latria*) due to God alone. This settlement was reversed for a while (813–43) but finally re-established solemnly and permanently.

Meanwhile the controversy had brought about unpredictable consequences in the west. We are not concerned with political or papal history as such, but it may be well to recall that the papacy, which had by the force of events succeeded to the dominion of central Italy when the emperors lost their grip on the west, had later been driven by attacks from the invading Lombards to solicit the aid of the rulers of Frankland (roughly modern France, Belgium and the Rhineland), Pippin and his son Charles. As a result this son, Charlemagne, whose sphere of rule had extended into north Italy, came to exercise a certain control over the papacy and to regard himself as a divinely appointed ruler of the people of God, responsible for their beliefs and morals, leaving the pope as ultimate authority. Meanwhile Charlemagne had gathered round him at his court at Aachen a number of able and active theological writers, among whom were the Spaniard

Theodulf, bishop of Orleans and the Anglo-Saxon Alcuin of York (730–804).
Compared with their activity the papal curia, which had suffered at the
hands of both Byzantines and Lombards, was comparatively inactive. This
permitted a series of controversies in which the imperial theologians,
supported by Charlemagne, acted without reference and sometimes in
opposition to papal policy. Iconoclasm was one such matter. The Frankish
and Germanic west was hostile both in politics and religion to the Byzantine
church, and had no sympathy with the excessive part played by ikons in its
liturgy and devotional life. Charlemagne himself was smarting under a
serious rebuff from the empress Irene. At this moment he received (788)
from the pope a very faulty Latin translation of the acts of the council of
Nicaea, which seemed to authorize adoration (in the theological sense) of
images. The king called on his theologians for a refutation, and Theodulf
and Alcuin produced the long and celebrated Caroline Books (*Libri
Carolini*), in which even relative worship – that is, worship given externally
to the image and internally to the person or mystery represented – was
declared unlawful. Such worship, it was argued, would in any case be beyond
the intelligence of most Christians. Candles and incense burnt before images
were prohibited, though the artistic representation of persons and events
was permitted. Pope Hadrian, surprised at this, wrote to Charles explaining
the faults of translation and reiterating the traditional doctrine of the
council, but this would seem to have had little immediate effect upon the
king and his advisers, and the church of Frankland stood by the position of
Alcuin until the Fourth Council of Constantinople (869) reiterated the
decisions of Nicaea taken a century earlier.

3. *The Spanish Adoptionists*

This was not the first excursion of Alcuin and his allies into theological
controversy. He had previously undertaken to controvert what was given
the name of Spanish 'Adoptionism'. On an earlier page of the present book
mention has been made of the Christological heresy named Adoptionism,
which taught that Jesus was adopted as his son by God the Father at his
baptism. This had been recognized at once as unorthodox, but several of the
Latin fathers had been at pains to distinguish between the divine and the
human natures in Christ, and to emphasize that while the Son had been
God from eternity, the divine Person had taken to himself or 'assumed' in
time a complete human nature (*homo assumptus*) at the first moment of its
coming into being in the Virgin's womb. They went on to state that by this
action of the Son human nature, as realized in all other human beings, had
through union with Christ been received into adopted sonship by God. As
in the monothelete controversy, orthodoxy could be preserved only by those
who could distinguish both in word and thought between human nature as
a concept, and an individual human nature personified.

This may help to explain the occurrence in the Spanish Mozarabic liturgy
of several ancient formulas, among them allusions to the assumption by
the Person of the Word of a human nature, which was described as
'adoption'. This may explain the convocation of a council by Elipandus,
archbishop of Toledo in Spain, when he was called upon to act against one

Migetius. Migetius was alleged to have taught that Jesus was one of the three Persons of the Trinity – a permissible expression if carefully explained, but not a desirable one for general use. The council, criticizing Migetius, asserted that the Son of Man was the adopted son of God as distinguished from him who was the Son of God by nature. He was 'at once son of man and Son of God, adopted son in his humanity, not adopted in his divinity'. This statement also, like that of Migetius, would seem to be patient of an orthodox explanation, but it was seized upon by the abbot Beatus, the well-known commentator on the Apocalypse, who delated Elipandus to Pope Hadrian I as an heretic.

Hadrian replied with a careful theological explanation, condemning the expression 'adopted son' as used of Christ, whereupon Elipandus referred the matter for judgement to his suffragan Felix of Urgel, a town recently recaptured from Islam by the Franks. Felix approved of the expression, whereupon he was delated to Charlemagne and summoned first to Regensburg and then to Rome, duly recanting his opinions to king and pope. Meanwhile the Spanish bishops, in full agreement with Elipandus, had replied to Beatus, standing firmly by the expression 'adopted son', which they probably understood as 'adopted human nature', and applied to Charlemagne for support. Charlemagne in turn applied to Pope Hadrian, who sent a second and firmer letter to Spain, reiterating his condemnation under anathema. At the same time Charlemagne, at the great council of all the bishops of his realm at Frankfurt (794), in which the question of images had been discussed, secured a condemnation of the phrase 'adopted son' and provided, through Alcuin, a long and powerful refutation. This did not end the matter, for Elipandus and Alcuin continued the controversy which disappeared, unresolved, into the darkness which covers Spanish history from the end of the eighth to the middle of the eleventh century. The Adoptionist issue, like some other and earlier Christological disputes, was probably caused by confused thinking on the part of all parties in Spain, only to be fanned by a lack of sympathetic understanding on the part of Alcuin.

4. *The Filioque controversy*

Meanwhile another dispute was looming up which was to have more fatal consequences. This was the first appearance of the difference of opinion in east and west on the Procession of the Holy Ghost.

The so-called Nicene creed in its original and traditional form asserted the procession of the Holy Ghost from the Father, and no more, but during the sixth century the words 'and from the Son' (*Filioque*) had been added in Spain, perhaps as a precaution against any remaining traces of Arianism, and in 589 the council of Toledo had embodied it in its profession of faith, whence it had passed to the churches of Gaul. Theologically speaking, it was to Latin minds no more than a corollary of the Nicene definition of the consubstantiality of the Father and Son. Nevertheless, it was unquestionably an addition, unauthorized by Council or Pope, to the sacrosanct formula which had been canonized repeatedly and publicly, and an addition which in fact enshrined a way of expressing the mystery that was unmistakably western; the eastern church preferred to say that the Spirit proceeded from the Father by way of the Son.

In the event, the phrase was included in the creed as recited and sung in the liturgy throughout Gaul, and specifically in the royal chapel at Aachen. In the strained political situation which had given both birth and bitterness to the Caroline books, the *Filioque* issue was placed on the carpet gratuitously enough, at the command of Charlemagne, at the council of Friuli (796) by Alcuin and his associates, and the Greek position was condemned. Not content with this, Theodulf of Orleans, a Spaniard by birth, returned to the charge, and the double procession was affirmed as of faith at a council at Aachen (809). A petition was sent to Pope Leo III demanding that he should approve this decision and insert the phrase in the creed, to be chanted at Mass. The pope approved the doctrine, but expressed displeasure at the insertion of the phrase in the creed, and refused to adopt this usage himself. So the matter rested for some sixty years.

5. *The development of the discipline of Penance*

While in the west both the liturgical development and the theological issues were the result of contacts with the eastern church, a development of great importance for the personal religious life of Christendom was taking place at the western periphery of Europe. The history of what came to be recognized as the sacrament of penance is one of the strangest, as also one of the darkest, chapters in the development of doctrine and devotional practice. When the clarity of the words of Christ when bestowing power on his apostles to forgive sins (John 20:23) is recalled, it must seem strange to the historian that the exercise of this power, apart from such rites as baptism and anointing, which derived their efficacy from other dominical institutions, was so long in achieving definition. While the practice of punitive excommunication and remission of sentence is apostolic, that of penitential segregation following upon the confession of serious fault, and itself followed by formal reconciliation, is slow to appear, and when it appears, is for long and of set purpose extremely limited in its application. The celebrated controversies of the days of Origen and Tertullian as to the irremediable character of certain sins and the unrepeatable nature of public penance, strike the modern mind as out of harmony with the spirit of Christ, while on the other hand the restriction of attention to a few sins, such as homicide, adultery and apostasy, would seem to show an unreality of moral outlook which is out of harmony with the teaching of Christ and St. Paul. Yet all the scanty evidence goes to show that for the first four centuries of the church's existence the only official exercise of the power of the keys was the yearly assignment of penance and the subsequent public reconciliation by the bishop at the end of Lent. The rare adumbrations of later discipline such as the permission of private confession preceding public penance, and the delegation of the penancing and absolution by the bishop to priests, had no wide influence. When Christians, from being a people apart, living under disabilities and persecutions, and therefore remaining few and fervent, became a vast multitude of varying degrees of piety and mediocrity, the old discipline was clearly inapplicable, but for several centuries no revolutionary change was made and the public Lenten penance and absolution seem to have continued, as did the similar discipline of the catechumenate, as a public liturgical ceremony which became more and more vestigial.

Meanwhile the fervent were finding satisfaction in the new movement of monasticism. In this the relationship of elder and spiritual father to disciple and novice gave birth to spiritual direction and to the confession of daily faults to the abbot or master. This was often accompanied by the imposition of a penance and a prayer for the penitent's forgiveness on the part of the abbot, and thus the elements of the modern practice of confession were assembling. As monasticism spread westwards from Egypt, matter for a knowledge of the principles of what are now called moral and mystical theology was accumulating. This teaching was given form and currency by the writings of Cassian and the Rule of St. Benedict, but the confession of 'venial' faults and shortcomings was made to the abbot or spiritual father as such, with no thought of 'sacramental' absolution. A similar development took place in the Greek church, with monks as its leaders, and it was among them that regular private confession was in time introduced.

In the west, the great change took place in the Celtic monasteries of the sixth century. The tribal monasteries outside the jurisdiction of a diocesan bishop ruled out the possibility of the ancient penitential discipline, and the frequent presence of a bishop and several priests in the monasteries seems to have given rise quite naturally to frequent auricular confession, and very soon a type of document appeared, known as the penitential, in which all common varieties of sin were enumerated, together with the appropriate penance.

Very soon the practice spread to all, monks, clerics, and layfolk, and was carried by the Celtic emigrants and missionaries wherever they went, from Iona to Luxeuil. It passed into Northumbria by way of the missionaries from Iona and elsewhere, and was widely adopted by the Anglo-Saxon church after the Whitby meeting. Archbishop Theodore, who as a Greek monk would have been familiar with the eastern practice, formally accepted confession for layfolk, and his decisions were embodied by a disciple in the so-called Penitential that bears his name. Bede (674–735) and archbishop Egbert approved the custom and it was carried by Willibrord and Boniface to Frisia and Germany. For some time there was no evolution of discipline in Rome and south Gaul, though the public penance of Lent was rare apart from a few cities, and penance for heinous crime was presumably a private matter between penitent and bishop, a reconciliation in public (*in foro externo*) rather than an absolution in private (*in foro interno*). Among the bishops and liturgists at the court of Charlemagne and his son, Louis the Pious, there was an antiquarian attempt to revive public penance, at least for grave sins, but this was clearly impracticable in the large dioceses and scattered communities of rural areas, and gradually the new practice became universal. In monasteries a weekly or daily confession became common; Chrodegang of Metz inserted it in his rule for clerics, while in the tenth century confession before communion at the four great feasts of the year became common for layfolk. In time, the practice spread down to southern Gaul and Italy. The decree on making confession (*Omnis utriusque sexus*) of Chapter 21 of the Fourth Lateran Council (1215) did no more than canonize common usage.

Auricular and frequent confession gave an impetus to moral teaching and spiritual direction all over Europe, and hearing confessions and solving problems of conscience became one of the most important of a priest's pastoral tasks. Thus the Celtic and Anglo-Saxon churches gave to western Europe and in course of time to the world-wide Catholic church one of the most important elements of its sacramental and ascetical life. Yet the fact that private, frequent confession had come in, so to say, by the back door, left the practice without full theological expression, and, as we shall see, discussions on the worth and conditions of sacramental absolution continued for more than two centuries.

6. *Indulgences*

Closely allied in origin, though totally different in its theology, is the history of indulgences. It was the traditional teaching, supported by universal Christian sentiment, that even after a serious fault had been committed the penance imposed or performed might not have fully 'satisfied' for the sin, or, in modern phraseology, might not have fully reintegrated the personality in the fullness of faith and love. This was less obvious in public penance and in the early penitentials, where the penalties imposed were often both lengthy and severe, but the universal tendency in later centuries to soften discipline gave rise to uneasiness, while the common practice of commuting or dispensing from severe penances (e.g. the substituting of almsgiving for severe fasting) was itself a tacit assertion of the power of the church to give an 'indulgence'. In the tenth century the bishops of southern France and northern Spain are found assigning a remissive value to pilgrimages, especially that to the shrine of St. James at Compostela, quite apart from their knowledge of the sins of individuals, and the passage from the commutation of a penance to its remission was accomplished when the reward of remission was attached to the fulfilment of fixed conditions, and when it was announced that the accomplishment of a particular act or prayer was the equivalent, in remissive terms, of so many days or years of penance. Hence the phrases such as 'forty days of true indulgence', which were often mistaken to signify a shortening of the term of punishment after death. A landmark in the extension of the practice came when an indulgence was held out as an enticement to fight for the faith on crusade in Spain or in the East, and it received unparalleled advertisement by the offer of a 'plenary' (i.e. total) remission of temporal penalties to crusaders by Urban II in 1095. From that time the public proclamation of papal indulgences became common, and it was natural that popes should take steps to prevent inflation of the currency, if the metaphor be allowed, by forbidding bishops to give more than a relatively small remission of forty days, and indulgences for long remained occasional. It was this that gave significance to the plenary indulgence which St. Francis of Assisi secured for his Porziuncola chapel, or that which later popes attached to the devotions of pilgrims throughout the Roman jubilee year.

The theological basis of an indulgence is to be found in the power of Christ's representatives on earth to direct the intercessory merit of the Church, regarded as the mystical and holy Body of Christ, to the needs of particular persons, or, in other words, to apply to individuals the treasures of love and self-sacrifice amassed by Christ, his mother and all the saints. It does not remit the guilt of sin, indeed it presupposes a soul restored to active membership of the church by repentance and absolution; it is concerned solely with the deficit of sufficient practical and remedial satisfaction for past sins already remitted; but popes, bishops and preachers cannot be acquitted of having often used ambiguous or incorrect terms, and layfolk and even clerics were often persuaded that a plenary indulgence remitted both guilt and punishment for sins, and that the length of time specified represented a remission of time spent by the soul in Purgatory. Indeed, the uninstructed faithful from the eleventh century onwards were often confused in mind and regarded indulgences in a legalistic and mechanistic way as providing passports to heaven, an illusion which encouraged and was stimulated by all kinds of unworthy and sacrilegious traffic.

II

FROM CHARLEMAGNE TO THE ELEVENTH CENTURY

1. *The first Eucharistic debate*

The theological writings during Charlemagne's lifetime were the work of official spokesmen of the king or emperor, and in particular Alcuin and Theodulf, attacking supposed errors which threatened to contaminate Frankland, such as Adoptionism, or which were part of the stock-in-trade of controversialists and diplomats in the eastern and western courts. In the following generation, when capacity for theological writing was diffused more widely, the debates took place between individuals or groups of the clergy of Francia or Germany, and usually ended without a final or official doctrinal pronouncement.

The first of these concerned the manner of Christ's presence in the consecrated elements of the Eucharist, and is of interest as bringing up some of the problems, and of the solutions to those problems, that were to occupy the minds of theologians for many centuries at a later date. It was opened almost unwittingly by Paschasius Radbert (d. 860), later abbot of Corbie in Picardy, who composed c. 831–3 a long treatise on the Eucharist for the monks of Corvey, the German daughter-house of the French abbey. This treatise, a few years later, was touched up and presented to the emperor Charles the Bald. Throughout this work he insisted on the reality of the presence of Christ behind the veil of appearances. It is the body of Christ, born of the Virgin and sacrificed on the cross, that is now offered again as victim. So far Radbert was no more than expressing clearly, not to say starkly, the doctrine that had developed in the west, deriving particularly from the writings of St. John Chrysostom and St. Ambrose, but he went on to describe the body of Christ as if spatially existent in miniature in the host, and as present by a miraculous transformation or creation. This presentation of the matter came as a shock to those who had been nurtured on St. Augustine and who regarded the Eucharist as a mystery and as an effective symbol both of the presence of Christ and of the unity of the faithful. Rabanus Maurus (784–856), 'the schoolmaster of Germany', replied that in his view the presence of Christ was primarily something realized by the recipient when united with the Lord in the sacrament. The strife became general. Gottschalk, whom we shall meet later, raged from his prison against Radbert, while objecting also to the symbolic expressions of Rabanus; for him, the presence of the Lord was objective, even if mysterious in its manner. Ratramnus (d. 868), like Radbert a monk of Corbie, commissioned by the Emperor to give his views, attacked Radbert, holding the presence of Christ to be spiritual, indeed, but real, as was also the reception of the Body and Blood of Christ. Radbert replied more than once, insisting on the real presence ('this is my body') while disclaiming any intention of supposing a corporeal presence. The body and blood of Christ are there, but we cannot define the manner of their presence. With this, the controversy faded away, to be revived more than two centuries later, when the presentation of Radbert in the main prevailed. Ratramnus, for his part, as a would-be faithful Augustinian, may have helped to influence Aelfric in England in the late tenth century, and was excavated as a medieval forerunner by some theologians of the Reformation.

2. *Predestination*

The second controversy, which was more prolonged and into which all the leading theologians of the age were drawn, concerned predestination and was initiated by Gottschalk. This unfortunate man (d. 868–9), originally a monastic oblate at Fulda and the protégé of its abbot, Rabanus Maurus, obtained release from the monastic life and became a priest, only to spend the rest of his life in a succession of controversies and imprisonments. Saturating himself with the teaching of St. Augustine, he began to hold and to broadcast in northern Italy an extreme version of that doctor's teaching on predestination. All are predestined, either to glory or to damnation. Alerted by the bishop of Verona, Rabanus Maurus moved to the attack of his erstwhile pupil. Failing perhaps to see the real problem, he attributed all eternal consequences for men to God's foreknowledge: seeing the good actions of the just and the misuse of grace by the evil he allots the fitting reward to each. Rabanus ignored altogether the kernel of Augustine's problem, which was the accepted existence of a human race immersed in sin, original and personal. Gottschalk in reply asserted this with ruthless clarity. Man in original sin could do no good without grace, God's free gift. Not all men are saved; hence God did not will the salvation of all; Christ died only for the predestined. Rabanus passed this treatise on to archbishop Hincmar of Rheims (d. 882), and Gottschalk was scourged and imprisoned (848); undeterred, he continued to publish his opinions which were in fact almost identical with Augustine's harshest utterances. Hincmar replied, mainly in the manner of Rabanus, and stressing that Christ died for all men, but Ratramnus, a friend of Gottschalk and a strong Augustinian, opposed him, as did also Lupus of Ferrières, holding fast to the Augustinian presentation of the human race as a *massa damnata*. Hincmar, facing defeat, appealed to the Irish Dionysian theologian, John Erigena (c. 810–c. 877), who replied in a basically Augustinian sense, but as a Neoplatonist refused to admit the existence of evil or the possibility of the divine simplicity issuing alternative decrees of predestination. This produced widespread dissatisfaction, and a kind of theological 'free-for-all' ensued, in which Hincmar took most of the punishment. Councils regional and royal succeeded one another, and that of Quierzy (853) marked something of an epoch with its four celebrated decrees of an anti-Augustinian tenor, viz.:

(1) There is only one predestination, that of the elect, and this does not depend upon God's foresight of their merits. In the case of the lost,

the divine foresight sees that some will remain in original sin, and that others, who are now in grace, will fall from grace.

(2) Man's liberty, lost by original sin, is restored by grace.

(3) God wishes the salvation of all.

(4) Christ suffered for all.

Thus when controversy had raged for some fifteen years the question of predestination remained finally unsettled. Bishops and theologians had disagreed, as they had disagreed in the fifth and were again to disagree in the sixteenth and seventeenth centuries in their interpretation and acceptance of Augustine, and in the different emphasis they attached to the sovereignty of God, to human liberty and to the breadth of the redemptive will of Christ.

3. *The breach between East and West*

The most important happening in the medieval centuries from the ecumenical standpoint was undoubtedly the separation of the eastern and western churches. It was a long process, and the year 1054, often regarded as the decisive date, is no more than a useful indication of the moment in autumn when a wintry day reminds us that the year is dying. The deepest causes of that division were not primarily or strictly theological. Rather, they were sociological and political, differences of life, race and outlook, aggravated by repeated intemperance, obstinacy and pride of office in the leaders on both sides, and irreconcilable in practice owing to the physical and linguistic chasm between the Christian peoples, who were entirely ignorant of the catastrophe that threatened. It was only in the later stages of the quarrel that liturgical and theological differences were inflated so as to become seemingly insurmountable barriers.

The eastern church, despite charges of heterodoxy bandied backwards and forwards at times of tension, was never regarded as formally and irrevocably heretical by the Roman church. The shoe, indeed, was on the other foot. The sole purely theological issue, the procession of the Holy Spirit from Father and Son (*Filioque*) was, as we have seen, due to an arbitrary, if *bona fide*, addition to the Nicene creed by the Spanish church, adopted by Charlemagne largely for reasons of state, deprecated for long by the papacy, and only officially embodied in the western creed when the eastern church hardened its opposition into a charge of heresy. The west never officially condemned the east as heretical on this point, and indeed the eastern church did no more than abide by a hallowed formula; to this day the Orthodox church, from the Roman point of view, is in schism, not in heresy. The east, on the other hand, accused the west of heresy with growing insistence, and when in later centuries, for whatever reasons, a temporary union was achieved, the Greeks did no more than allow that the western formula, if understood rightly, was not heretical. Moreover, although the jeers of historians from Gibbon downwards at the futility of the controversy show ignorance of genuine theological difficulties, there have not been wanting eminent theologians on either side who have allowed that several of the ancient Greek fathers used language patient of the western interpretation, and that, when all is said and done, the difference between the two beliefs, at least until the days of Photius, was one of expression rather than of substance.

As for the other chief points of controversy many, such as the celibacy of the priesthood, the use of unleavened bread, the date of Easter, and the like, are patently inessential to the faith. The real divergence on the matter of divorce is in part a survival from the long ages when even the western church as a whole had not yet made a precise definition in the matter, and in part due to the contamination of old eastern practice by ancient Roman law. The western Mariology and teaching on purgatory, which the modern eastern church repudiates, are in fact descended (whether legitimately or not does not affect the historical fact) from seeds of tradition or cult which are found in the later patristic age in both eastern and western authors.

There remains the one great dispute, important for its far-reaching practical implications as well as for its theological content, on papal supremacy and doctrinal authority. Basically, here also a series of large-scale political and demographical changes, added to a gradual move on both sides away from the common outlook of the pre-Constantinian or pre-Justinian churches, have resulted, again on both sides, in a theory of church government and doctrinal control bearing little apparent resemblance to that held throughout Christendom in sub-apostolic days. Even later, in the fourth century, the ecumenical church was taken by all to consist of four or five cultural and political areas governed by a 'patriarch' who exercised little more than a supervisory role over the bishops within his area. Of these patriarchs one, the Roman patriarch of the west, had in the eyes of all an acknowledged if ill-defined primacy. The ultimate source of unity was the general council at which the bishop of Rome was accepted as having rights of precedence and initiative. This unwritten constitution was rendered void by three great political changes – the conquest of all the eastern patri-archates save Constantinople by the Muslims; the close political and ecclesiastical union between the eastern emperor and the patriarch of Constantinople; and the rise to a monarchical position of the papacy in a newly converted continent, when the papacy itself had been hardened by its struggle for independence from lay control and from the eastern and western empires. As the centuries passed, the eastern church, hand-in-glove with the imperial government, became a missionary, apostolic force in Russia and the Balkans, while the western church under the stress of its own contest with the Empire and moral relaxation, became a tightly disciplined, legalistic body, in which the clergy were the masters under a monarchic pontiff who claimed rights in the political sphere as well as in the spiritual realm. As a result a seemingly unbridgeable gulf opened between an organized and centralized church, looking to Rome for its doctrinal and functional well-being, and a church which for long was closely associated with the imperial government and later, owing to political catastrophe, lost external coherence as well as the essential elements (patriarchs and general councils) of its original ecclesiology.

III

THE AGE OF REVIVAL AND REFORM,
1000–1150

In the history of the church, this age is chiefly remarkable for the successful reassertion of papal supremacy within the western church which now, as a closely-knit hierarchy under papal control, became a separate 'estate' from the laity and developed its claim to guide, and under certain circumstances to dictate to and to depose secular rulers. Of this nothing will be said in these pages, partly because the theology, as distinct from the political and canonical developments, of the papal claims received little or no theological elaboration in the period and partly because the subject is one of extreme complexity in which political thought and legal theory occupy more space than theology.

1. *The second Eucharistic controversy*

The first theological controversy of the new age was eucharistic, and is inseparably linked with the name of Berengarius (d. 1088), the archdeacon of Angers and former pupil of Fulbert of Chartres. He was by predilection a dialectician and a strong advocate of the use of logical and rational argument in theology, and his unorthodox opinions on the Eucharist were probably inspired by his conception of the powers of logic rather than by theological difficulties, though he may well have taken his theological opinions from Ratramnus, and ultimately from Augustine. His opponent Lanfranc (c. 1010–89), then teaching at Bec, likewise found support in Carolingian writings and followed Paschasius Radbert. Berengarius was excommunicated in a Roman synod in 1050, and after imprisonment professed the current orthodox teaching. He continued nevertheless to put out his old opinion, denying any change of 'nature' or 'essence' in the consecrated elements, and asserting Christ's presence to be merely conceptual (*intellectuale*). This called forth Lanfranc's *On the body and blood of the Lord*, which asserted as orthodox and defined in precise terms the change of substance from bread and wine to the 'essence' of the Lord's body while the 'appearance' (*species*) remained without change. Berengarius answered in his *On the Lord's Supper* that the change which occurred was purely spiritual and refused to admit that the material bread and wine were replaced by the body and blood of Christ. A profession of orthodoxy was once more required of him at Rome in 1079, though he probably remained at heart of his old opinion. Despite his chequered career, he remained an active and respected teacher of dialectic till his death. Probably his difficulties, as some modern critics have suggested, were grammatical rather than theological, and were based on the intimate connection which he held to exist between a word and the thing of which it is the expression. Words to him were things on another plane and it was therefore impossible for the bread in the priest's hand (*hoc*) to be (*est*) at the same moment the body of Christ (*corpus meum*). Nevertheless, Lanfranc did no more than maintain what had long become the accepted teaching of the western church, that the bread was *changed into* the body of Christ, and he used the new dialectic to express this in set terms for the first time. His presentation was accepted as orthodox and adequate, and the term transubstantiation, though not in fact employed by Lanfranc (it was probably a coinage of Peter Damian) came into common use and was ultimately given the highest sanction by Innocent III and the Fourth Lateran Council. It was indeed a clear statement in the current philosophical vocabulary, that of Boethius, of what the ordinary reflecting literate Christian in western Europe believed. Thus the Berengarian programme, which was essentially an attempt to present a mystery in terms of dialectic, was countered by confining the orthodox theologian to a philosophical terminology.

The advantage of the term 'transubstantiation' was that it asserted without compromise or confusion the 'real' presence of Christ, both physical and spiritual, in the sacred elements. The disadvantage, in addition to that of defining a mystery by a philosophical term which might some day cease to be significant for some minds, was that it gave a handle to crude and materialistic imaginations about the host as merely veiling a physical body. This could be countered by an elaborate metaphysical analysis of substance and accident, but it remained a danger on the lower levels of mental and spiritual competence. On the other hand, it certainly encouraged devotion to the reserved sacrament as providing Christ's presence in a church, and to processions and blessings in which the host was revered as Christ. The Eucharistic hymns of Aquinas, in particular the 'O hidden God, devoutly I adore thee' (*Adoro Te devote, latens Deitas*) expressed this to perfection. Moreover, by emphasizing the presence of the Incarnate Son, Jesus, son also of Mary, upon the altar it helped to strengthen the tendency, long present in the west, to regard the Mass primarily as a sacrificial act of the priest for and on behalf of the laity, and thus to obscure other aspects of the Eucharist, dear to the Greek and Latin Fathers, as the offering of the mystical body of sanctified humanity to the Father as God by Christ the Head of the Church, and thus the principal means of uniting the faithful in and into Christ's mystical body.

2. *Anselm of Bec and Canterbury*

If Lanfranc is the first medieval theologian to use dialectic in controversy and definition, Anselm of Bec and Canterbury (1033–1109) is the first to use the reasoning mind with the specifically scholastic purpose of penetrating revealed truth. His celebrated *mot d'ordre*, his programmatic phrase, *fides quaerens intellectum*, faith seeking to understand, reverses the Berengarian aim. While the dialectician aimed at reducing theology to logic or meta-physics, Anselm hoped to advance in theological insight by means of intellectual enquiry directed by a mind illuminated by God. In the realm of speculative theology, which he was the first medieval thinker to inhabit, he is chiefly remembered for the cause he assigned for the Incarnation, the answer to the question he had asked: *Cur Deus homo?* Why did God become man?

Christian thought had given several replies to this question and to the consequent one: how was man redeemed? Many Greek fathers had seen in the Incarnation, taken by itself, the basic redemption of the human race. The uniting of a human nature to the divine in the Person of the Son elevated the whole human race to a supernatural destiny. Others, and especially the early Latin fathers, saw in the Passion and death of Christ the sole and sufficient agency of redemption. Sin, disobedience and lack of love were redeemed by the obedience and love of Christ.

St. Leo the Great gave to the west a classic expression of this (cf. his Letter 28 to Flavian, Archbishop of Constantinople, commonly called 'the Tome', e.g. 'And this nativity [of the Only Begotten] which took place in time took nothing from, and added nothing to that divine and eternal birth, but expended itself wholly on the restoration of man who had been deceived: in order that he might both vanquish death and overthrow by his strength the Devil who possessed the power of death. For we should not now be able to overcome the author of sin and death unless He took our nature on Him and made it his own, whom neither sin could pollute nor death retain').

Mankind lay under the dominion of sin; no mere man could give due satisfaction to God – or in other words submerge man's failing in an ocean of love. Nor could God, as God. But a divine Person who had assumed human nature could do so. Concurrently with these two opinions, another stream of tradition regarded man as the slave of the devil, irredeemable save by the payment to his master of a death that was wholly unmerited. This was the so-called 'ransom' theory, of which an alternative took the form of regarding the death of Christ, the just man, brought about by diabolical malice in ignorance of Christ's divinity, as having transgressed the limits of the devil's just claim to sinful humanity. These two last opinions, especially the former, which Augustine had regarded with favour, had become very general in the west since the sixth century. Anselm's presentation was a fuller version of the familiar argument of St. Leo. Only a sinless man who was also God could satisfy for man's sin, which had in it an infinite quality as being an offence against an infinite Being. Anselm thus firmly rejected the ransom theory and the supposition that the powers of darkness had rights.

Besides *Cur Deus homo* Anselm composed treatises on Predestination and Free Will, on the Trinity and on the Procession of the Holy Ghost from Father and Son. He made it his boast that he departed not at all from the teaching of Augustine, and the claim is justified in so far as he made no great advances from Augustine's position, or even from his phraseology, but Anselm's style and method are consistently clear and luminous, lacking both the frequent lapses into flatness, and the rhetorical colours and inimitable flashes of sublimity of his model. The treatise on the Holy Ghost was read to the fathers of the council of Bari, and used in their pronouncements against the teaching of the eastern church.

Beyond and above all these writings, Anselm's fame throughout the centuries rests principally upon his so-called 'ontological' argument for the existence of God propounded in his *Proslogion*. This argument, which has had the singular fortune to be attacked by Aquinas and Kant, and accepted in the main by Bonaventure, Scotus, Descartes, Leibniz and Hegel, cannot be discussed in full here. Thinkers of the modern world are still as divided as were Anselm's contemporaries. Is it a logical fallacy, an illicit transference from the realm of ideas to that of existent being? Is it an endeavour to rationalize a mystical experience? Or is it not so much an argument in logical form as a true and cogent intuition, that once the reality of being and existence is perceived by the mind, the metaphysical necessity of infinite existent being is already present in the mind's consciousness?

The originality of Anselm as a thinker is unquestioned. To pass from Berengarius and Lanfranc to him, and then to pass again to John of Salisbury or Gilbert de la Porrée, is to step for a moment out of the Middle Ages and enter the presence of one who, like Plato and Aristotle, transcends his age and remains for all time as a thinker and as a person. Though his debt to Augustine is immense, he is no more a second Augustine than Augustine is a second Plotinus. He stands alone in his age, and has no followers approaching to his stature. Though he is in a sense the father of scholastic theology, in another sense his formula of thought died with him; Boethius, not Aristotle, was his unacknowledged master. His method is, like that of Socrates, to follow where the argument of reason leads, and his limpid monologue succeeds as none had done since Plato, in giving the illusion of complete spontaneity, with the additional narcotic of personal charm. He does not employ the techniques of analysis and dialectical opposition; that was yet to come. Whereas the scholastics of the thirteenth century, from Albert onwards, use the findings of reason as a foundation and buttress of revealed truth, Anselm first accepts the truth (*fides*) and then penetrates it with the reason, spiritually enlightened (*intellectus*). It remained for another generation to decide whether Anselm, in the fresh dawn of Europe's adolescence, gave to reason powers and rights beyond its due.

3. *Abelard*

The peer of Anselm in mental power, and a contrast in all else, Abelard (1079–1142) is primarily a thinker rather than a theologian. Contrary to earlier opinion, recent scholarship has considered his influence on medieval theology to have been greater than that of Anselm. Whereas the latter lives for us because he illuminates familiar truths, Abelard used his great critical powers and lucid mind to clear away mist and rubble with which his predecessors had obscured truth. Both lived in a climate of exhilaration in the powers of reason, but whereas Anselm held that human intelligence could go far in its understanding of divine truth, Abelard came near to subjecting that truth to rational criticism and analysis.

Abelard turned to theology only in 1121, as a new world to conquer.

Neither by training nor by cast of mind was he a theologian according to the classical definition of Aquinas, as one who contemplates divine truth and imparts to others what he has seen. His attitude was that of one who uses his powers of reasoning to explain the faith as far as possible in rational terms, and to perfect its expression so as to remove what is illogical or unacceptable. Nevertheless, his acute and fearless mind left a greater mark on theological method than did any other before Aquinas, and in several respects he pointed the way that was to be followed by all in a later age.

Abelard's first important work in this field was his *Christian Theology*, composed to meet the demand of his pupils for a comprehensive survey of Christian teaching that should include an explanation of difficult points. Abelard's reply, by its name and by its content, gave a new meaning, which was to become universal, to the word theology. Hitherto used according to its etymology for the knowledge of God (as in 'mystical' and 'natural' theology), it now signified the discipline concerned with the Christian doctrine in its fulness, including the whole of faith and morals.

On his way through Christian doctrine, Abelard used the methods of the schools of logic and dialectic of which he had been a consummate master. The new dialectic found in the doctrine of the Trinity, with its use of the strictly defined terms 'nature' and 'person', and its apparent relevance to the problem of universals (three Persons, one God) an irresistible attraction and pitfall. Roscelin, who allowed only a verbal reality to universal terms, applied this teaching to the divinity, and became at least verbally unorthodox by admitting the existence of three divine beings. Abelard, in reaction, regarded the names of the divine Persons as little more than attributes or appropriations – Power, Wisdom and Love – of a single God. He trod on dangerous ground also when he touched the central point of Christology. Concerned to safeguard the transcendence of the Divinity, Abelard regarded the human nature of Christ as 'nothing' (*nihil*) to the divine Person. This opinion was adopted by Roland Bandinelli, by Peter Lombard, and in part by Gilbert de la Porrée, and spread widely in France and later in Germany. Later, Bandinelli, by now Pope Alexander III, after twice forbidding discussion for or against this opinion, finally (1177) condemned it. On another topic of Christology, the doctrine of Redemption, Abelard was equally daring. He reacted against the legal or forensic implications of both the 'ransom' and the 'adequate satisfaction' interpretations of the Incarnation and Passion. His views were to some degree changeable, but for a considerable time at least he regarded as sufficient the 'exemplary' purpose of the Incarnation, as being necessary to instruct and stimulate mankind in the perfect love of God. On this view the Passion of Christ was the supreme example of self-abandonment in Christ's unhesitating championship of truth against error. This view had a supporter in Peter Lombard, though he gave equal value to the 'ransom' opinion.

Abelard reacted also against the current Augustinian conception of original sin as implying a physical weakness, almost a moral disease of mind and will, manifested in concupiscence. In his view it was simply a penalty, the loss of a title to eternal beatitude. Grace in consequence became an assistance rather than an essential, physical enablement for meritorious action. Here he was opposed by St. Bernard, who repeated the traditional view in his treatise on grace, but both Bernard and Abelard left the manner of action of grace undefined, to await further clarification from Aquinas.

In another field, that of ethics and the analysis of good and evil actions, Abelard's influence was strong and beneficent. In the countries of the west, gradually converted and without any higher education or culture, the Christian life was regarded as the accomplishment of the ten commandments and those of Christ and the Church, and it was common (as it has always been common among those without either human or spiritual discernment) to regard as sinful any breach of a commandment (e.g. that of fasting on certain days) under any conditions and even through ignorance and forgetfulness. Abelard in his *Scito te ipsum* (Know thyself) declared the necessity of full knowledge, advertence and intention before moral guilt could be imputed, and thereby proclaimed the rights and responsibility of the individual conscience. A man acted rightly if he did what his conscience bade him do here and now, and his will and intention to do right was the significant criterion. Abelard would have made his own in an ethical sense Hamlet's words: 'There's nothing either good or bad, but thinking makes it so'. He does not seem to have realized fully the deeper psychology of an act: that what we think now is largely conditioned by past thoughts and actions. When he used the words of Christ: 'Father, forgive them, for they know not what they do', to prove the innocence of those who crucified Christ, his readers felt that he had concealed the force of the second word. They needed forgiveness, for the gospel narrative itself shows them as gratuitously cruel and brutal, and therefore prone to evil, even if they did not, in the circumstances, incur the guilt of killing the Son of God. Without such reservations, the door is open to moral relativism or, in the medieval context, to nominalist ethics – that good and bad are words of no meaning; merely signs by which we denote the arbitrary commands and prohibitions of God. Nevertheless, Abelard's doctrine was in itself sound, and it gradually passed into common currency.

In addition to these and other doctrinal novelties and aberrations, Abelard's approach to theology inevitably roused hostility in conservative quarters for two reasons. His reverence for the philosophy of the ancients, such as Cicero, of whom he had little firsthand knowledge, was very great. He regarded them as harbingers of Christianity, and saw in the resemblances to Christian teaching in their works a divine adumbration of revealed truth. Even the Trinity, he held, had been dimly perceived by them. This attitude fell in with his exaggeration of the powers of the human mind in its use of dialectic, which could, so he maintained, demonstrate and explain the mysteries of the faith. Here we touch upon what was to opponents such as Bernard the basic error of Abelard. He approached the truths of the faith not primarily as rich veins of precious metal to be excavated, refined and moulded by reverent thought, or as depths to be scanned with patience and humility, but as verbal formulae to be explained and extended and used as major and minor in a syllogistic argument. Such an attitude and such deductions, proposed brilliantly to generations of eager students, rapidly became deformed and exaggerated, and critics and enemies, as always in the history of the church, delated to authority expressions and even opinions which could be deduced from his words, but which he himself had not held. As for Abelard himself, it seems clear that he wished always to follow the teaching of the church. His condemnations at Soissons and Sens, and the attacks of Bernard and others on his authentic or reputed teaching, had their effect in silencing his followers and diminishing the copies of his works, but many of his opinions won their way in generations to come.

4. *The problem of reordination*

A theological issue of great practical significance, long debated in the past, recurred to exercise minds in the eleventh and twelfth centuries. This was the reordination of heretical, schismatic and otherwise irregular clergy before admission or re-admission to the exercise of their orders. The matter was controversial owing to the lack of precision in defining the nature and effects of the various sacraments, and a failure to recognize seven, and only seven, sacraments as distinguished from other customary rites such as the ceremonial washing of feet. In particular, the teaching, later to become classical, of the indelible 'character' bestowed on the soul by the sacraments of baptism, confirmation and holy orders had not yet been explicitly formulated. In the early church, both eastern and western, a long and often acrimonious controversy had been carried on as to the necessity of rebaptizing heretics and schismatics. St. Cyprian was the protagonist of the rebaptizers in Africa, but the decision of the church, as expressed by Rome, went against him. This decision, diffused by the writings of St. Augustine, was final and became universal, but the problem of reordination was a longer business. St. Augustine defended what was later to become the official doctrine, but others, shocked at the supposition that the sacred powers of the priesthood should survive a lapse into heresy or apostasy, or be unaffected by excommunication, demanded reordination on repentance. Roman practice failed to show consistency; there was some confusion between the powers of holy orders and those of jurisdiction, and this affected the pronouncement of Innocent I, that no one could give what he did not possess, which was quoted for centuries by the reordainers.

The difficulty presented itself frequently between the seventh and twelfth centuries owing to the wide and ill-defined conception of heresy then current. Thus in England after the council of Whitby there was a debate concerning the orders of the clergy who held to Celtic practices, and archbishop Theodore, with memories of current practice in the east and at Rome, introduced reordination. It was maintained by archbishop Egbert of York and appeared as normal in insular penitentials. A century later it was a useful excuse for retaliation in the feuds, scandals and irregular elections at Rome, and nullification of orders and compulsory reordination of opponents by victorious partisans was common, as e.g., after the antipope Constantine II (767–9) and pope Formosus (891–6). Between these two occasions, the issue of the most vexatious of all the tussles of archbishop Hincmar of Rheims hung upon the status of the clerks ordained by his rival Ebbo after his irregular resumption of office as bishop.

The reform movement of the eleventh century brought the question into full daylight. Simony (the act of buying or selling ecclesiastical office, from Simon Magus, *Acts* 8:18–19) and incontinence in a priest or bishop were 'heresies' to be fought with every canonical weapon. Were those found guilty of those faults, and as such excommunicated, any longer priests or bishops? If so, one granted the transmission of orders and all means of sanctification to heretics and backsliders, and now that the fight for reform was engaged all over Europe, this would be to put the enemy on an equality with the children of light. In the general clash of politics and personalities the principal theologians differed among themselves and popes acted inconsistently. Peter Damian, whose teaching ultimately triumphed and won for him the title of doctor of the church, and the canonist Cardinal Deusdedit, were against reordination, while the extremist Cardinal Humbert and the canonist Anselm of Lucca, later pope as Alexander II, were for it. Leo IX, Gregory VII and Urban II were inconsistent in practice. In an age of theological development and pamphlet warfare all kinds of procedural solutions were proposed. One school was for obliging reconciled heretics to submit to a new laying-on of hands, though the anointing and other ceremonies could be omitted. Another school took the complicated view that ordination 'within the church' remained valid (that is, a bishop who had fallen into 'heresy' still retained episcopal orders and could validly ordain), while ordinations 'without the church' were invalid (that is, a priest or bishop ordained by an orthodox bishop turned heretic could not himself ordain or consecrate). The question had not received theological settlement when Gratian and Peter Lombard compiled their manuals in the mid-twelfth century, but in practice reordination was becoming rare, and it was finally eliminated by the precisions effected by the theologians of the late twelfth and early thirteenth century on the matter of sacramental 'character'.

5. *The influence of Bernard*

Strange as it would have seemed to earlier generations, to say nothing of contemporaries in the twelfth century, modern historians of medieval thought and theology often go near to forgetting St. Bernard. While he dominates the political and spiritual life of the age, it is true that as regards the evolution of the scholastic method and the development of theology he might never have existed, save as a persecutor of those who sought new ways. Yet he had a unique position in the mental life of the times, a position in this respect alone not unlike that held by Newman a century ago. Read by all men in monastic and ecclesiastical circles, and immensely influential with individuals, Bernard's treatises influenced Abelard and Gilbert de la Porrée no more than Newman's essay on the development of doctrine influenced the European theologians who were about to create neo-Thomism in the late nineteenth century. Bernard indeed was the last of the fathers; when all around him was changing, he continued to compose as monuments of his genius the meditative monographs of a kind that had been the vehicle for all western theology from the days of Augustine to the eleventh century. Here was no *sic et non*, no anthology of authorities, no dialectic. Bernard treated the old questions, such as grace, predestination, the Incarnation and the rest, with broad traditional arguments and his own incomparable rhetoric. He was widely read, but by monks and churchmen rather than by masters in the schools, and when a century later he became an 'authority', he was cited as the fathers were cited, and like them, his opinions counted for much in the long run, though his influence was perhaps at its greatest in the border country between devotional writing and formal theology. In his lifetime he was known in the schools as the watch-dog of tradition and the repressor of originality and the advance-guard. Modern research which has been kind to Abelard and Gilbert has set Bernard in a truer light, as a conservative indeed, but also as a theologian of spiritual depth. While Bernard failed to see that the mind of a Europe attaining its mental majority must use disciplines and discuss problems that to him seemed trivial, Abelard was more concerned with the intellectual superstructure of theological thought than in its rich doctrinal foundation, and regarding theology as a province in which the reason and a particular dialectical method could explore and explain. When the final balance of influence is calculated, it may well be that Bernard did what he alone of his age could have done. He 'contained' the new dialectic at a moment when it might have washed away all landmarks, and ensured that theology should remain a matter of traditional faith rather than of mental gymnastics.

6. *The Virgin Mary*

During the medieval centuries considerable development took place in the discussion of the privileged position of the Virgin Mary in the Christian economy, and this can be traced more conveniently in a separate section than if it is parcelled out chronologically. Her physical virginity before, during and after the birth of her Son, the justice of her title as Mother of God and Second Eve, her fulness of grace implying absolute sinlessness throughout life, were elements of the faith received from the patristic age. At the beginning of our period liturgical commemoration of her was almost entirely restricted to the group of festivals around Christmas, including the Circumcision, the Epiphany and the presentation of the child Jesus in the temple – which she shared with her son. Later, as we have seen, largely owing to the series of Greek popes from southern Italy, and the influx of eastern Christians driven from their homes by Persian and Muslim invaders, a further group developed, including the Annunciation (25 March), the Birthday (8 September) and the Assumption (15 August). The last-named feast became a principal landmark of the summer liturgy, and the bodily assumption into 'heaven', though not to be defined by Rome for thirteen centuries, was commonly accepted in the west, largely through eastern traditions, and was never seriously questioned, though some of the apocryphal documents purporting to describe it were treated with suspicion. Both the liturgy and the iconography of the great cathedrals of France are evidence of its universal acceptance, and from the eleventh century onwards devotion to Mary, hitherto pictured in art as the regal Mother holding her Son for the homage of worshippers, was now directed to the maiden of the Annunciation or the advocate by the judgment seat.

The matter of her sinless conception, the question, that is, of the preservation of her soul from the stain of original sin from the first moment of its existence, had not been debated before the eleventh century. It had been implicitly held in the eastern church as a consequence of Mary's absolute fulness of grace, and of her position as second Eve, repairing by her faith and innocence what the first woman had lost, but the east had never shared with the west its preoccupation with the problems of grace and evil, and western expositions of devotion to Mary, as in the writings of St. Ambrose, had always maintained a great sobriety of language.

Meanwhile the feast of the conception of Mary had become common in the eastern church and its outposts in south Italy. At the end of the tenth century monks from Greek Basilian monasteries in the south moved northwards, founding abbeys such as Grotta Ferrata in the Alban hills and SS. Alexius and Sabas on the outskirts of Rome, and it was doubtless from this source, by way of pilgrims or exiles from the east, that the liturgical celebration of the feast of the Conception reached some Old English monasteries, among them the Canterbury and Winchester houses and Worcester. This feast, celebrated on 8 or 9 December, did not commemorate the Immaculate Conception as it was later understood. It had been instituted in the east on the analogy of that celebrating the marvellous conception and sanctification of John the Baptist as related by St. Luke, and it rested on a similar, but legendary, account of the miraculous conception of Mary by her mother, and the accompanying sanctification of Mary's soul. It did not rest upon, or itself express, a precise doctrinal basis, and was celebrated without any direct account being taken of original sin. The feast was suppressed at the Norman Conquest along with other Old English liturgical practices, but was reintroduced early in the twelfth century by abbot Anselm, nephew and namesake of the archbishop of Canterbury, who had been abbot of St. Sabas in Rome before becoming abbot of Bury St. Edmund's in 1121. Shortly before this the writings of St. Anselm had laid stress on Mary's absolute purity from sin, and the archbishop's confidant and biographer, Eadmer, wrote a treatise in defence of the reintroduced feast. In this, he provided the first western theological statement on the Immaculate Conception – that is, that the soul of Mary never incurred the stain of original sin – based on Greek sources and what is called the argument of suitability. Though frequently quoted later, this had no wide effect at the time, for attention was diverted by the well-known attack of St. Bernard upon the liturgical celebrations of the Conception by the canons of Lyons, a church with a long tradition of connections with eastern devotion.

This began a theological controversy that lasted for more than two centuries. St. Bernard, whose intense devotion to the Mother of God was well known, took exception to what was to him a novel doctrine. Not only did it infringe the universal law of original sin in the children of Adam, but it seemed to Bernard unfitting in itself. He, with his contemporaries, understood the term conception in an active sense, and accepting the ruling Augustinian opinion that original sin was transmitted by an act induced by concupiscence, maintained that this act and its effect were in a sense sinful and certainly not a suitable object for a cult. Thenceforward the issue was controversial, and even when it was agreed that the word conception was used in a passive, not an active sense (i.e. that it referred to Mary, not to her mother) and that original sin was not transmitted by any act of man, there still remained the theological problem. All human beings need the redemptive merit of Christ, because they are born in original sin. But if Mary had no guilt, not even of original sin, how could she need or receive redemption? In the thirteenth century Aquinas cleared the issue by his teaching that original sin consisted essentially in the absence of grace, not in the quasi-physical transmission of a sinful quality; but after more than one change of opinion during his career, reflected in his writings, he finally decided against immaculate conception, while admitting that Mary was sanctified the moment after her soul had been created. It was left to Scotus to solve the difficulty caused by the need for redemption by teaching that Mary was preserved from original sin by the foreseen merits of Christ. This indeed is the ordinary explanation given by theologians of all personal grace received by the chosen people and others before the Passion of Christ; the only difference in the case of Mary is that the grace was bestowed before there was any (original) sin to remove.

IV

THE FIRST CENTURY OF SCHOLASTIC THEOLOGY,
c. 1050–*c.* 1200

1. *Theological education, 600–1160*

Before considering the development of teaching and method in theology in the twelfth and thirteenth centuries it is essential to realize the religious, social and educational background. From the epoch of Gregory I to that of Gregory VII (say, from 600 to 1050) western Christendom was a long and narrow territory stretching from the British Isles to Sicily and from the eastern border of Austria to the Pyrenees. Within the period it had been constricted by the Muslim occupation of Spain (711), and extended from time to time northward and eastward of Frankland and Germany by conquests which did not, before the eleventh century, add any real cultural or spiritual force to the west. Within all this area, with the partial exception of some northern and central Italian cities, no public lay education existed, still less any higher education, whether secular or theological. Speaking generally, only the monks and a majority of the higher clergy were fully literate; many of the bishops were in fact monks, and the higher administration of the country was largely carried out by clerics, many of them bishops and some monks. At the opening of our period such theological and spiritual writing and teaching as there was came from bishops and the higher clergy of their entourage, but the seventh century saw a decrease in episcopal activity and a growth of literacy in the monasteries, and these last became and remained for three hundred years the principal reservoirs of learning. Charlemagne indeed endeavoured to extend education by republishing old decrees which made the establishment of a school at each cathedral obligatory, but these decrees had little immediate effect. In consequence, almost every theological writer between the two great Gregories was a monk.

In both monasteries and episcopal schools (where they existed) the education, a ghost of the old Roman rhetorical training, was grammatical and literary, enabling a pupil to read classical and patristic Latin and write both in the quasi-classical style for literary and liturgical purposes, and in less classical Latin for administrative and diplomatic use. The purpose of education, as expressed by theorists such as Alcuin, was to enable the pupil to read and understand the Scriptures, and the crown of the course was the thorough study of the Bible and the commentaries of the fathers thereon. In addition there were the other writings of the fathers among whom Augustine held unrivalled pride of place, followed at a long distance by Gregory the Great, Leo the Great and Jerome and such writers as

Prosper and Hilary of Poitiers. In addition, the larger cathedrals and some monastic libraries would have copies of the acts of councils, extracts of canon law, papal letters and, in due course, copies of Charlemagne's voluminous capitularies and the writings of such European figures as Bede and Alcuin. Mention of these two names will remind us that in some chosen places in Europe – Jarrow, York, Tours, Poitiers, Aachen and the north Italian cities – an able scholar had at hand a considerable quantity of material for study, and the bulk of the literature available grew as the decades passed, especially during the century 780–880 covering the so-called Carolingian renaissance. During that epoch, indeed, an attempt was made by Alcuin and others to create an educational system, but the troubles of the time were against the movements, and the only permanent result was a rise in the quality of the best monastic literature. But while the renaissance lasted it gave rise, as we have seen, to a number of theological controversies in which the leaders, from Alcuin to Hincmar, showed a wide knowledge of Augustine and later Latin writers, and an ability to marshal their evidence from Scripture and tradition. If evidence were needed of the high degree of technical competence present in the Frankish empire, it could be found in the productions of the group, wherever it may have been situated, that composed the various documents known as the 'false decretals' and their companions.

With the liquidation of the Carolingian empire all evidence of theological training, apart from the informal teaching of the monastery, is absent for more than a century. The revival, when it came, was part of the wider rebirth of all intellectual activities known as the renaissance of the twelfth (more accurately of the eleventh) century. Its forum was the cathedral school, which rose slowly from elementary obscurity into efficient maturity, aided by the contemporary emergence of the individual teacher of dialectic who might be either a permanent member of the cathedral staff, or a free-lance moving from place to place and often taking his pupils with him. While the early masters of the revival were dialecticians, of which class Berengarius, Roscelin and Abelard were members, the discipline aided the rise of theologians also, among whom Lanfranc and his disciple Anselm were preeminent. These two, and Abelard also, were monks, but the typical masters of the age were the heads of the cathedral schools such as Chartres, Rheims, Laon and Paris. In these the central influence was that of the Chancellor or, by delegation, the master of the schools. Chartres in particular, for a century between Fulbert and Gilbert de la Porrée, developed a curriculum of grammar, dialectic and scripture in which the last-named developed into a doctrinal study.

The method of teaching on the higher levels of the course was by lectures on the Bible and its official gloss or commentary, and towards the end of the eleventh century the practice began for masters to compose Sentences or Flores, that is, collections of texts from the Scripture or councils bearing upon a particular point of doctrine. Of a large group of masters who were composing ordered arrays of texts of this kind Ansellus (or Anselmus) of Laon was the most distinguished in the early twelfth century. By a natural development these Sentences came to include a number of opinions or judgments on the theological issues and the term *sententia* gradually shifted its reference from the authority to the commentator; from denoting a selection of authoritative passages it became a collection of pronouncements or opinions of a teaching master. Finally, as *Sententiae* multiplied attempts were made to consolidate or harmonize their conclusions in *Summae sententiarum* (handbooks of doctrine).

Hitherto dialectic and theology had been two separate disciplines, and although men such as Berengarius, Roscelin and the young Abelard had made use of theological propositions regarding the Trinity or the Eucharist as matter for dialectical analysis, while conversely theologians such as Lanfranc and Anselm had used dialectic as a technique for investigating theological truth, there was, until about 1100, a very clear distinction between the schools and masters of dialectic and those of 'the sacred page', as the Bible when studied came to be called. Abelard, always an innovator, did more than any other man to effect what would be currently called a 'break-through'. In early life he had used the Trinity as matter for dialectic, and soon afterwards he had adopted from the canonists the technique of methodical doubt or, as it came to be called from one of his treatises, the method of *Sic et non* (as we should say, the method of pros and cons). But the true moment of fusion came after he had turned from dialectic to theology, when he answered the demand of his pupils to give them a picture of the whole field of doctrine, to explain its difficult parts and to give rational arguments in it support.

Meanwhile two other minds of great distinction were at work. At the newly-founded abbey of St. Victor at Paris, a canon of the house named Hugh was accomplishing in a discursive, Augustinian fashion, a summary of the whole economy of creation, redemption and sanctification, while Gilbert de la Porrée, bishop of Poitiers, who like Abelard was a dialectician, but a Platonist and a patristic scholar to boot, was translating revealed truth into his own vocabulary and language. Since many students passed through more than one school, the streams of Abelardian criticism, Victorine contemplation, and Platonic exemplarism were beginning to merge in the later *Summae Sententiarum*.

Concurrently, the study of canon law was developing on similar lines. The collections of earlier times had at first been haphazard, and then increasingly 'loaded' in the days of the investiture controversy, and finally more comprehensive and orderly under Ivo of Chartres and others. The canonists, however, were stimulated by the civilians or Roman lawyers, who from *c.* 1100 had a classical text, the Digest of Justinian, to attract their commentaries. The canonists too felt an urgent need for a text-book, and the need was met by a Camaldolese monk Gratian who, *c.* 1140, produced his *Concordia discordantium canonum*, a 'resolution of conflicting decrees', in which he combined the advantages of the *Summae sententiarum* and methodical doubt. Gratian's achievement in the field of canon law and its immediate success may have been the impulse that produced a similar union of methods in theology. Peter the Lombard, who may himself have been a pupil of Abelard, and who was now a master at Paris, published *c.* 1150 what came to be known as *The Four Books of the Sentences*, in which the whole content of Jewish and Christian revelation, and the economy of the Christian life, were set out. As in Gratian's *Concordia*, so in the Lombard's *Sentences* the framework of contradictory texts and ultimate resolution was derived from Abelard's *Sic et non*. It became at once the sole and sufficient text-book for students of theology; it invited comment and soon became the text to which masters added their criticisms, explanations and additions. For more than four centuries it was the regular duty of the young bachelor in theology to read the *Sentences* as *baccalaureus sententiarius*, and the writing of a commentary on the Sentences was the inevitable prelude to a successful career as master. Bonaventure, Aquinas, Duns Scotus and William of Ockham were only the most celebrated names in a great army.

During the twelfth century the academical teaching of theology took shape. In the new universities, whether student-universities as at Bologna, or master-universities as at Paris, the Arts course formed the first stage, in which logic and dialectic were studied with ever-increasing elaboration, and were fortified in the thirteenth century by increasing doses of Aristotelian philosophy. Concurrently the framework of a university in the modern sense of the word grew up – faculties, examinations and degrees, set books and lectures, Chancellor and regent masters. The course of theology, like those of medicine and canon law, began after the bachelor's degree in arts had been taken, and was elaborate and lengthy, and in practice relatively few proceeded to the mastership or what later became the doctorate in divinity. Officially, the course in arts was confined to the techniques of thought and argument, logic and dialectic, and all questions connected with theology were banned, such as the immortality of the soul; but in practice philosophy in all its various branches, including psychology and the origins of the world, was often introduced. Conversely, the technique and methodology of logic and dialectic were carried over into theology. Topics which Plato treated in dialogue form and Aristotle in a treatise were now fed into the process of dialectic, and all spoken and written teaching was expressed in syllogisms and disputation. Thus the whole of the *Summa Theologiae* of St. Thomas is built up of multitudinous articles cast in *sic et non* form, often opening with a question, such as: 'Does God exist?' (*Utrum Deus sit?*), and even the apparently continuous and often lengthy statement in which Aquinas gives judgment can usually be broken down into an elaborate syllogism. Academic exercises and a master's monographs were alike 'disputations'. The whole of scholastic theology was conditioned by its logical and dialectical basis, and though in the golden age the greatest masters – Alexander of Hales, Albert, Bonaventure and Thomas – subordinated their method to the fabric of speculative or spiritual truth which they built upon it, the purely logical and dialectical elements, reinforced to some extent by mathematics in England, reasserted their potency in the fourteenth century, and the essence of theological truth was neglected for the brilliance of the mental exercise.

Yet however true this may be, the formal method in the thirteenth century must not be allowed to conceal from us the deep theological wisdom of the greatest masters. Above and beyond their scholastic method and their philosophical background a Bonaventure or an Aquinas, and lesser men as well, were theologians of the first order. They were steeped in the Scriptures more thoroughly than many modern divines, and their personal lives of apostolic ministry, private prayer and constant reflection on the truths of the Christian faith gave them a spiritual insight and wisdom which enabled them to look upon details and conclusions as the outward expression of spiritual realities. Whereas some of the masters of logic and dialectic subordinated doctrinal pronouncements to technical manipulation, the great masters of theology penetrated and absorbed the reality of the Incarnation by a kind of natural sympathy with the mystery and the divine Person – a connaturality, to use their own word. Here, rather than in new dogmatic or credal affirmations, lies the significance of the scholastics.

2. *Canon Law and the Sacraments*

In the middle years of the twelfth century an epoch in the history of western theology was ending. For a century great men had succeeded one another – Lanfranc, Anselm, Abelard, Bernard, Gilbert de la Porrée – and a series of controversies had led to important treatises and declarations. The monastic centuries ended with the death of Bernard, the cathedral schools were losing ground to the nascent universities, and with Gratian and Peter Lombard the novel critical methods and the disputed opinions of yesterday became matter for the text-book and the lecture-hall. The fifty years that followed appear as a kind of interlunary twilight. In thought and theology there is no great name of the first rank between Bernard and Gilbert, on the one hand, and Alexander of Hales and Robert Grosseteste on the other. Yet it was not a stagnant age. If there were no supreme thinkers, there were hosts of masters and a growing number of text-books, and the framework of university life was rapidly assembling, while unobserved in Spain and Sicily the translators of Aristotle – Avicenna, Averroes and Maimonides – were preparing the new material for the scholastics of the golden age. Moreover, it was a century of law. The lawyers, both canonists and civilians, had found their text-books, organized their universities, and risen to great place in the church fifty years or more before the schools of Paris reached maturity.

Historians of theology and canon law have not always appreciated the very considerable influence of the canonists in the development of doctrinal expression. In every field of Christian worship and discipline, practice, the outward manifestation of common conviction, has always run ahead of theory and definition. The established way of acting as well as the established form of prayer may create the established formulae of belief. If this had always been so, it became far more evident in an age when papal decisions, often based on a mixture of law and practice, became at once firm precedents and definitions of doctrine. The sacraments, for example, and in particular the discipline of penance and holy orders, had been constantly topics for legislation and papal decision, and the tradition thus established had been expressed or modified by canonists in their ordinary task of presenting and explaining the law.

It was in the realm of sacramental theology that the twelfth century saw undoubted progress. Hitherto in the west, as in the east to the present day, Baptism and the Eucharist had stood pre-eminent as rites conveying particular gifts of grace. The anointing and laying on of hands at confirmation, holy orders and the visitation of the sick were also generally regarded as 'sacraments' of divine institution, but the double ambiguity of the word sacrament, both verbal (either 'mystery' or 'bestowal of sanctification') and in its loose application to any established practice of devotion, long hindered an attempt at rigid classification. This was achieved at length by the discussions of Hugh of St. Victor and the Lombard, as was also the distinction between the words by which the grace is bestowed and the material which the minister uses. The exclusive number seven, however, was not defined as a matter of faith until the appearance of the creed or confession approved for the Greeks in 1439. The two sacraments not mentioned above, Penance and Matrimony, were long in entering the final list partly because of their intractibility in complying with definitions and analysis, but chiefly because of the long development of penance and the existence of matrimony in other legal systems and with other social customs, both before and after the foundation of the church by Christ.

As we have seen, the practice and virtual obligation of auricular confession for all, and its frequent use by the devout, were well established in the west before 1100, but the theology was still fluid. Was confession to a priest merely a dispensation from the regime of public penance and re-admission to communion by the bishop? Were the powers of the priest merely delegated, or did the bishop simply give permission for the priest to use powers bestowed on him at his ordination? Did the priest absolve from sin, or merely declare the sin to have been remitted, or simply pray for its remission? What disposition was needed in the penitent? If he were fully contrite what more could absolution give? If not, how could it give anything? Can forgiveness be obtained without confession and, if not, what obligation of confession exists? Some of these questions were settled by practice and law before the theologians had answered them satisfactorily, but the Lombard was able to set out formally the three constituent elements, of confession, contrition and satisfaction.

The nature of the contrition required and the direct effect of absolution were topics to be discussed for many centuries to come. In practice the decree *Omnis utriusque sexus* (cf. p. 240 above), making an annual confession to the parish priest the condition of full membership of the church, was the final and universal establishment of a primary duty for those with the care of souls. One of its results was to multiply manuals intended to help the physician of souls; another was to make the new orders of friars coadjutors and rivals of the secular clergy in their most intimate relationships with their flock.

Matrimony, though more simple in its theology and performance, was to remain the most complicated in administration. Custom and scriptural authority, old and new, had erected a forest of obstacles based on relationship, natural and spiritual, and on status, social custom and personal engagement, while the church had never, in the first millennium of her existence, imposed an absolute obligation of the presence of a priest for lawfulness or validity. As the medieval centuries passed, the impediments of relationship were rationalized and the obligation of receiving the blessing of the church strengthened, but it was not till the days of the council of Trent that the clandestine marriage was pronounced invalid, and the ceremony of betrothal was deprived of obligations and consequences almost as solemn as those of matrimony.

3. *Heresy*

Heresy is a 'loaded' word, and when used by theologians it implies falsehood of doctrine as opposed to orthodox truth. The historian as such does not consider the truth or falsehood of opinions, but their relationship to the official teaching of the church concerned. Regarded thus, heresy may be merely an extravagant, temporary aberration, or it may be the seed from which a separate and abiding body of Christians take their growth. A heresy, therefore, may be very relevant to a history of theology.

Writers in the past have often regarded the 'ages of faith' as an epoch when orthodoxy was universal and heresy rare and uninfluential. Recently, however, it has been recognized that for a century or more (1150–1250) organized heresy was rife in the western church, and presented a serious challenge to authority, both lay and ecclesiastical.

In the early pages of this study we noted the last of the great Christological controversies, that on the single will of Christ. Like its predecessors, it was a theological dispute, albeit rising out of political circumstances, and one in which highly placed and reputedly orthodox ecclesiastics were divided in opinion, and which was finally decided by conciliar and papal decree. The subsequent controversy over the honour to be paid to images was of a different kind, but this too was a dispute between parties who in other respects were orthodox Christians. From that time, for more than two centuries in the west, there was no division of opinion worthy of the name of heresy, and until the end of the eleventh century the rare appearances of heterodoxy (excluding the so-called heresies of simony and Nicolaism) were isolated outbreaks of antinomian, reformist or illuminist disturbances which were usually suppressed with violence and ease by popular reaction or authority. (Nicolaism means clerical incontinence – its derivation is unknown.)

Early in the twelfth century these revolts became more serious. They were at first mainly directed against targets, such as the simoniacal and worldly clergy, at which contemporary Gregorian reformers also were aiming, and some historians have seen in these revolutionaries the extreme 'left wing' of an orthodox reform. Arnold of Brescia, for example, a preacher of poverty and a denouncer of slovenly clergy, was finally hanged (1155), not as a heretic, but as an incorrigible agitator. But there was in most of these movements, as in that of Peter de Bruis (d. c. 1140), an attack on sacerdotal and sacramental religion.

At about the middle of the century a far more formidable foe to orthodoxy appeared. This was the gradual but ultimately massive infiltration of the Bogomil heresy from the Balkans. This, originally derived from Manichaeism in the east, grew strong in Constantinople and passed through

Bulgaria and Bosnia along the trade-routes. By about 1140 its adherents were to be found in populous districts all over western Europe: at Cologne, at Rheims, in Lombardy and central Italy, and above all in southern France, in the wealthy and cultured society of Languedoc around Toulouse and Carcassonne. It became known as Catharism from the name Cathari (='the pure') given to the proved adepts of the sect.

Catharism was not so much a heresy as a new, anti-Christian religion, a kind of shadow-church, and it was this that made it appear sinister to contemporaries. It was a dualistic religion in which the principle of good, the creator of the world of spirit, was opposed by the principle of evil, creator of the world of matter. Souls, fragments of spirit, were enmeshed in material bodies, and in consequence marriage was evil, and the ideal life was one of chastity, austerity and vegetarian food. This was in practice attempted by a few only, the leaders and priests of the sect, who gave their name to the whole body. When established in Europe the Catharists used a liturgy which imitated the Eucharist, and set up a hierarchy of ordained ministers similar to that of the church. They held that Christ was the highest of the angels, adopted by God as his son, and that the body of the Lord and his death were appearances only. The strong ties of a united, charitable and quasi-secret organization, with active leaders and a high ideal of austerity which was attained by a few and admired by many, won its way largely through the contrast it provided to the rich, ignorant and unhelpful bishops and priests of the Catholic south of France. When repeated efforts of the neighbouring bishops and later of preachers commissioned by the papacy had failed, and when political motives and intrigues mingled with religious stresses, Innocent III made a twofold attempt to overcome the Albigensians, as they were called from Albi, one of their strongholds. He encouraged missions and preachers, whose central figure came to be St. Dominic, and by means of a crusade from central France brought force to bear under Simon de Montfort. The crusaders, with reputations stained by pillage and massacre, were eventually successful, and the remains of Catharism were gradually obliterated by the Inquisition reorganized for the purpose. Catharism ceased to exist as a rival to the Catholic church, though at a cost of much misery and the debasement of ecclesiastical humanity and justice.

Meanwhile, a wholly different movement had sprung up at Lyons and elsewhere and developed in the cities which lay at the foot of the Alpine highlands from south Germany to northern Lombardy. This was made up of several groups, of which the Waldenses, named after Waldo, a merchant of Lyons, were the chief. All preached, in varying measure and detail, a life of poverty in common, with Bible-reading and prayer, and in general a reference for individual piety rather than sacramental and sacerdotal religion. They were the first organized appearance of the simple, congregational 'nonconformity' that was to spread here and there in Europe during the Middle Ages, and to attain revolutionary stature under Wyclif in England and John Hus in Bohemia. It developed ultimately into a group of churches forming the left wing of the Protestant Reformation.

Waldo and many of his followers, and the bulk of some other bodies such as the 'Humiliati' and Poor Catholics, remained in intention orthodox, and some groups were confirmed as religious companies by Innocent III. Others, denying the Real Presence in the Eucharist and any doctrinal authority in the Pope and bishops, drifted gradually into heresy. They too were harassed by the Inquisition, but they were more difficult to distinguish from orthodoxy, and they continued to live permanently and quietly, some of them Catholics or near-Catholics, coming into prominence here and there, as in Bohemia in the late fourteenth century. In Piedmont the Waldenses, the true proto-Protestants, continued to exist. Taken as a whole, they are remarkable as proposing a programme which contains almost all the features of the early sixteenth-century Reformers apart from those peculiar to Luther and Calvin.

In the last century of our period (1250–1350) there was little organized and militant heresy in Europe. In south Germany and the Rhineland there were a few antinomian sects that might seem to foreshadow the Anabaptists, and the *béguinages* in the cities there and in the Low Countries were often but usually unjustly accused of heresy. The most notorious disturbers of the peace were the groups of Franciscans, soon known as the Spirituals, who campaigned for the literal observance of the rule of St. Francis and later brought upon themselves the charge of heresy as well as schism for their obstinate adherence to the opinion that Christ had owned no property on earth and that all clergy, as well as all friars, were bound to absolute poverty on pain of losing their jurisdiction in the church.

V

THE GOLDEN AGE OF SCHOLASTICISM

1. *Theological education, 1160–1300*

In order to understand the character of the theology of the schools in the thirteenth century, to appreciate their achievement and to assess their limitations, it is necessary to glance at the evolution of theological study and academic practice between the age of Peter Lombard and that of Duns Scotus.

While the Lombard was teaching and writing at Paris the university, which for almost four centuries was to be the intellectual centre of Europe, was coming into being. In 1100 all higher education, save that in law, was confined to the cathedral schools, and in particular to those of France north and west of the Loire and including those of southern Flanders – Orleans, Chartres, Paris, Laon, Rheims, Tournai, Liège – in particular. Paris was only one, and not the most famous, of a large group. But Paris had three schools, that of the cathedral on the island in the Seine, that of the abbey of St. Victor, and that of the Mont Sainte Geneviève, and the dazzling genius of Abelard on the Mount, and the steadier flame of Hugh at St. Victor's, attracted crowds to Paris, and the city, a political and social capital already famed for its beauty and hospitality, had advantages shared by no other. Consequently, by 1150 the arts school, an essential preparation for a career in theology, law and medicine, was the most flourishing in northern Europe. Nevertheless, the university as an organization was more than fifty years in developing, and the society or 'guild' or 'university' of masters did not come into existence before the last decade of the century and was not fully recognized till 1215. Long before that time the large student population had overflowed from the Island to the left bank of the Seine, the Latin quarter of later days.

In Abelard's day no formal qualification was needed for a teacher. He could set up school outside the cathedral precinct and teach what he wished, to students who came of their own choice and were bound by no examinations. Gradually the organization developed. The society or university of masters controlled recruitment to their body and imposed an oath of obedience to its statutes. The title of master, hitherto given as an honorific to all distinguished teachers, was restricted to one who, as pupil of an existing master, had qualified by examination in certain subjects after a fixed course of study. When this evolution was complete the essential elements of a modern university – matriculation, terms of residence, syllabus, examination and degree, distinction of faculties and government by all graduates or by regent masters – were in existence.

The first course, to be taken by all, was that in arts. In the distant past this had been the education of the late Roman empire in the seven liberal arts. In the monasteries and cathedral schools of the early Middle Ages the philosophical and mathematical parts of this education had been reduced to a minimum, and attention had been given almost solely to the literary discipline of grammar and rhetoric, which entailed the reading of classical authors and composition in Latin. At the scholastic revival of the early eleventh century dialectic had begun to assume supreme importance and logic was the crown of a career in the schools. By 1150 the literary arts had been relegated to the 'grammar' schools which were preparatory to the university course, and the 'arts' course, which lasted for six years, was almost entirely occupied with logic, dialectic and the techniques of disputation, though in some schools a kind of 'advanced level' in grammar was part of the course. The mastership in arts could not be attained before the age of twenty, and the newly-admitted master had then to teach in the arts school at Paris for at least two years. Then he could, if he so decided, begin his course in theology, but many masters in arts began this after several more years of teaching, for while the course in theology lasted for eight years, no one could attain the dignity of master (later doctor) of holy writ (*pagina sacra*) under the age of thirty-four. Of the eight years' course five were spent as a student, three as a bachelor of theology. It was indeed a long and exacting preparation which made demands upon the moral and material resources of candidates, and it was inevitable that the wastage or 'fall-out' rate was very high. It was one of the principal faults of medieval university education that there was no adequate theological course available for those who looked no higher than a useful pastoral life on a parish.

Another peculiarity of the developed educational system was the ambiguous position of philosophy proper – epistemology, metaphysics, ethics and psychology. For reasons which are beyond our present scope, Plato's dialogues were virtually unknown in western Europe before the fifteenth century, while the works of Aristotle, beginning with a long series of logical works, became progressively familiar to the schools and universities over a long period of two centuries, 1050–1250, and, as they became available, became and remained the basic text-books of all secondary education. When the purely philosophical works were received at Paris, from about 1200 onwards, all topics in them that bordered upon theology, such as the immortality of the soul, freewill, the origins of the world, and such, were banned to the arts school. This ban soon proved impossible to maintain, for it was inevitable that arts masters should wish to read and to teach the whole Aristotelian corpus as it became available. On the other hand, both Aristotle and the Arabic commentators whose works came along with his, were unorthodox by any Christian standards on several points, such as the nature of the soul, its origin, and the determinist outlook of both Aristotle and his commentators. It was this tension that brought the great cleavage of the last decades of the thirteenth century between the masters in arts, who followed Aristotle 'right or wrong' when he conflicted with the truths of the faith, and the theologians. These latter were also divided among themselves between those who, with Albert the Great and Thomas Aquinas, used Aristotle as a base of their thought and explained or eliminated his theological errors, and those who, with Bonaventure and the Franciscans in general, distrusted Aristotle and, after unsuccessful attempts to make a viable philosophy out of Augustine's writings, turned with Duns Scotus to a new and original system.

What has just been said will help to explain why the theological system of the late Middle Ages is called 'scholastic'. It was not only created and elaborated in the schools, whereas earlier and later theology often had its origin in monastic cloisters and the studies and books of individuals such as Erasmus, Calvin, Luther and others, but it used throughout the technique of the arts school, the technique of logic and disputation, which became and long remained the instrument of all acquisition and imparting of knowledge.

2. *Philosophy and theology*

To the element of logic and dialectic was added, in the thirteenth century, a strictly philosophical complement when the ethics, metaphysics and psychology of Aristotle became known. The use of a complete body of philosophy was a godsend to the arts faculty, hitherto confined to the technique of thought rather than to thought itself, and to whom any theological topic was forbidden ground. The initial prohibition of Aristotle by the provincial synod of Sens in 1210, by the papal legate Robert de Courson in 1215 and by the pope in 1231 have often given rise to misunderstanding. These decrees applied only to Paris (Oxford was not covered) and to teachers (private reading was not forbidden) and to the arts school (not to the theologians), and was due to the known or suspected unorthodoxy of some of the Philosopher's teaching, e.g., on the eternity of the world and the nature of the soul. It was not in fact enforceable and was ignored twenty years after the first condemnation. Meanwhile the theologians, all past masters in dialectic, were using philosophical arguments more and more to defend and explain revealed doctrine.

This leaven of philosophy that permeates the mass of doctrine is characteristic of thirteenth-century theology. In this, the age of Aquinas differs from that of Anselm and Abelard. Both those thinkers used logic and dialectic in their analysis and explanation of religious truth, and accepted from their distant predecessors, as part of tradition, certain principles or assumptions derived ultimately from Plato. But neither of them had even the beginnings of a system, and the later Platonizers, such as Gilbert de la Porrée, applied philosophical (or semantic) principles to this or that particular teaching. The twelfth century, in fact, was not in possession of any system inherited from the past, and made no attempt to construct one. In the thirteenth century all this was changed. By 1200 a large part of the philosophical, as distinct from the logical, thought of Aristotle had been translated from the Arabic and had reached Paris, and by 1250 the complete corpus of the only tolerably complete ancient system of philosophy was available in adequate Latin form. To almost all medieval minds it was axiomatic that the human mind could attain to truth in its contact with the world 'outside' itself – that it could, in other words, express the nature of things rationally and truthfully. Philosophy, therefore, was a natural and certain grasp of the created universe which gave a firm base for theology, God's revealed truth. Moreover, the strong medieval reverence for the wisdom of ancient times, the existing familiarity with the technical Aristotelian machinery of thought, and the clarity and cohesion of Aristotle's teaching, combined to prejudice minds in its favour. So, in the first half of the thirteenth century, there was a gradual assimilation of Aristotle which became complete and programmatic with Albert the Great and his pupil Aquinas, as also, though this is outside our sphere, with the leading masters of the arts school.

The supremacy of Aristotle was only gradually and never universally acknowledged. While the climate of thought at Paris and Oxford impelled all theologians to the use of philosophy as a handmaid of theology, many were apprehensive of Aristotle as a pagan whose conception of God as Creator and Provider, and of the immortal soul and its destiny, left much to be desired. The Franciscan masters in particular, who early rose to eminence at Paris and Oxford, regarded theology not so much as a science, as a way to God, a directory of the spiritual life. In this they were adapting their Franciscan ideals to the outlook of St. Augustine. Augustine, it must never be forgotten, had been for eight hundred years the doctor and theologian *par excellence*, accepted and imitated by all. He was not primarily a philosopher, but he owed much to Platonic thought, and throughout his life and writings he accepted what he took to be Plato's, but which was largely in fact Plotinus's, explanation of the universe as the true 'One'. In particular, the 'exemplarism' of both Augustine and the medieval Franciscan school, which regarded all creation as reflecting the divine Mind and its ideas, was a Christianizing of the Platonic 'ideas' and of the emanation of all things from the 'One' in Plotinus. Similarly, the Augustinian explanation of knowledge as the 'divine illumination of the intellect' – an irradiation of truth in the form of ideas and moral principles from the Word of God – is a Christianized version of the Neoplatonic illumination of soul by the divine Mind. The latter teaching, in particular, so different from the prosaic, empirical, almost mechanical Aristotelian explanation, was the shibboleth of traditionalist orthodoxy. There was therefore a clash of minds between those who claimed to follow the old ways and those who regarded Aristotle as the exponent of right reason. Hitherto there had been no schools or 'parties' of theology; henceforth there was to be a succession of schools – traditionalist 'Augustinian', Thomist, Scotist, Ockhamist and the rest, in agreement as to the fundamental truths of the faith, but differing widely in their explanations and in the conclusions drawn from them. On one point, however, all were for the rest of our period agreed. A theologian must have a background of philosophical thought.

3. *Bonaventure and Albert the Great*

This is not the place for an account of the developments and varieties of presentation in the thirteenth century. Such space as is available must be given principally to Aquinas. His voluminous output, and the overall consistence of his account of Christian doctrine, to say nothing of the qualities that earned for him in his lifetime the title of 'our common master' at Paris (*communis doctor*), and that have put him in a place apart in modern times – all these demand that some account should be given of him. Second only to Aquinas in influence and genius, St. Bonaventure, his 'opposite number' among the Franciscans and in some ways his opponent, must receive at least a short notice.

Bonaventure (1221–74), though an exact contemporary, was even more precocious in talent than Thomas, and left the academic life for ever when called to be general of his order at the age of thirty-six. Consequently he seems to be of an older generation in his career as in his thought, though he lived to know, and to controvert, some of the later work of Aquinas, for his reputation and high office gave him an audience at Paris whenever he wished. A saint as well as a Franciscan, he regarded theology as a spiritual rather than an intellectual pursuit, a way of life rather than a science. In his most familiar and characteristic work, the *Journey of the Mind to God* (*Itinerarium mentis ad Deum*) he translates into a way of life St. Augustine's conception of a Christian education, a progress from human knowledge by way of scriptural and theological learning to mystical knowledge and ecstatic union with God. Holding with Augustine that God and the soul are the only topics of interest to the theologian, he writes chiefly in all his works – in his commentary on the Lombard and in his discussion of Genesis – of God's nature, of the angelic choirs, and of the creation of man, his soul and his spiritual gifts. With Augustine he holds that God is directly, though darkly and intuitionally, perceptible to the human intellect, and therefore known with innate knowledge before all else. With Augustine also (and with Plato) he regards the soul as a metaphysical substance living a life of its own here below, 'within' the body, not forming with it a single human nature. The senses pass on to the soul the impressions they have received from outside, but the soul judges of their nature and of truth by the divine illumination of the intellect that has already been described.

Bonaventure was the first to present a comprehensive scheme of Christian doctrine resting upon an explicitly formulated outlook on the universe, on the metaphysical constitution of beings, and the process of cognition in the senses, mind and soul. All this is informed by a spirit of balanced fervour and 'unction' unequalled in the work of any other master save Hugh of St. Victor. This, together with his official position and the holiness of his life, make him the standard-bearer of the Franciscan theologians, and when, after his death, differences crystallized into rival systems, his work, supplemented by that of John Pecham, the friar-archbishop of Canterbury, became the basis of the 'Augustinian' as opposed to the 'Aristotelian' theologians, and the resulting amalgam was given further philosophical and theological reinforcement by Duns Scotus, to go down the centuries as the only orthodox rival to Thomism.

Bonaventure used Aristotle in many places, when it seemed that his was the most helpful explanation of a particular point, but he was not fully an Aristotelian, and in fact expressed distrust of purely human wisdom. The theologian responsible for integrating Aristotle into the Christian outlook, and also for giving philosophy – and principally Aristotelian philosophy –

an autonomous value as the basis of certain natural truth accessible to all men, was the German Dominican Albert (?1206–80). Almost as learned, as versatile and as prolific as the Philosopher himself, he recognized that of all systems then known that of Aristotle, with its unique combination of empiricism and idealism, common sense and abstract thought, was the most viable and the most 'rational' to serve as a basis for theology. It was indeed for him pure natural truth, as distinct from the supernatural truth of revelation. He therefore set himself to translate and comment upon the whole Aristotelian corpus, and practically completed his task. Yet in another phase of his long career, he did much the same service for the pseudo-Denis, then still held to be St. Paul's convert Areopagite, and therefore enjoying quasi-apostolic authority. The actual writer of the works of 'Denis' was probably a Christian Neoplatonist of c. 500, but this was suspected by no one in the thirteenth century, and Denis held, in the realm of mystical theology and angelology, a comparable place to that of Aristotle in natural philosophy. Albert was a wide and sympathetic thinker, but not an original one, and he made no attempt to extend or correct Aristotle so as to make his system fully capable of integration into Christian thought. That task was carried through by his pupil and friend Thomas Aquinas.

4. *Thomas Aquinas*

Thomas Aquinas (1225–74) owes his title of prince of the scholastics to a combination of qualities. On the level of philosophy it was he who took the decisive step of accepting in principle the need for a complete and ordered system of rational thought as a foundation and instrument for subsequent theological construction, and in building this edifice with Aristotle as his guide.

Nevertheless, he did not only depart from the Philosopher on numerous points where Aristotle's teaching was incompatible with Christian truth, but he altered the emphasis and shifted the centre of gravity so as to construct what was in effect a new and original system in which all created, finite being appeared as the work and reflection of a simple, uncreated, personal Being, God, and in which all lines of being and potency descended from God, while all activities of all beings serve to obey and glorify him. The centre of all thought is found in the word spoken by God to Moses: 'I am who I am.' He thus reverses the Aristotelian outlook. While the Philosopher gives all his attention to the universe perceptible by the senses, and finds above it only a First Cause, a Prime Mover, Aquinas regards above all the infinitely rich Being of God, Three in One, the source of all being, goodness, life, love and truth, of whom the sun, source of all material energy, is a type in the physical realm.

On the level of theology he appears as a thinker who, above all others, ordered the whole complex of the Christian revelation, as his contemporaries saw it, to the smallest detail, and who brought to this task an unparalleled capacity for preserving unity in multiplicity and for infusing spiritual wisdom into every subject he touched. No great theologian has been more familiar with Scripture and tradition, yet no great theologian, save perhaps

St. Augustine, has given more pregnant and original illustration to the truths of faith.

One of his greatest achievements was the delimitation of natural and supernatural. The writers of the Old and New Testaments, and Christ himself in his utterances, had viewed human life in terms of good and evil, flesh and spirit, service of God and service of self. It was an existential outlook and as such went home to the bosoms of all men, and although Christ himself, and his apostles in their letters, had always asserted the necessity and gratuity of a new and heavenly life for those who were to be saved, they had not found occasion to make any distinction between human nature as such and sinful human nature, or between the divine help that enabled Peter to walk upon the waters and the divine life that comes, for example, at baptism. St. Augustine, who gave so much of its character to western theology, was even more fully 'existential' in describing human life in terms of the Christian life with its mingled good and evil, self-love and God-given love, nature and grace. Though Augustine was so precise and assured as to the total inability of a human being to rise from his low estate and to perform morally good works without the assistance of grace, the human being Augustine considers is either the unbaptized creature, intrinsically sinful, or the baptized and believing Christian. Moreover, the neoplatonist philosophy, which lay behind his outlook on the world, allowed no place for any being that was not in some sense an emanation from the principle of good, and to some degree a spiritual being. In other words, neither as a Christian nor as a philosopher did Augustine draw a clear line between the creature of God in its natural condition and the creature elevated to the life of Christ in God by grace.

Anselm inherited this outlook, as did the long series of Augustinian theologians from Hugh of St. Victor to Bonaventure, while Abelard, who was not an Augustinian, had a totally inadequate conception of the life of grace. It was only when Aristotle's writings, especially the Ethics, became familiar, that the picture emerged of a man, without the Christian faith, and without the Christian sense of moral evil, with no conception of divine assistance or an eternal destiny of life or death, seeking after ethical goodness with a hierarchy of natural, human virtues. This impelled Aquinas to seek for a clear distinction between human life with its natural faculties and virtues and ends, and the life of regenerate man with habitual grace and a life of God-given virtues. In lieu of Augustine's single life of evil rescued by grace, Aquinas reckons with three lives – that of the human being as such in his 'pure nature'; that of fallen and sinful human nature; and that of redeemed and spiritually endowed man. By so doing he can assess both the dignity and the fallibility of human nature as such, and the nobility of the Christian life which is the germ of eternal life, and a real initial participation in the divine life of Christ. The very reality and nobility of this participation implies a share in its supernatural quality which, so far from implying spectacular or miraculous experiences, implies rather an absolute transcendence of human powers of perception and feeling.

Holding as he did with Aristotle and the general agreement of mankind and human practice that man's mind, working upon sense-perceptions of the universe external to itself, can recognize in it order and causality, Aquinas held also that the mind could attain to a firm rational certainty of a First Cause possessing, in an eminent degree, the powers of intelligence and outgoing benevolence that are potentially present in a human being. Thus he rejected the Anselmian argument, that the intuition of being implied, in the ultimate resort, its existence in the fullest grade of perfection; Aquinas based his own argument on the realization that to accept the existence of any being that is not the cause of its own existence implies the existence of a supreme being who has no cause outside himself, but is the cause of all existing things. From this it followed that the supreme being possessed, in an eminent, inconceivable degree, all the perfections and endowments recognizable in the universe, as also supreme dominion and provident care of all.

With this rational outline as a preparation, the historical fact of God's revelation of himself and of his gifts and promises provided those who accepted it with the uncovenanted gift of the new light of faith, by which God is accepted not as the end of a process of reasoning, but from the outset as the infinitely rich Source of Being. 'I am who I am'; loving Father; co-equal Son and Word; and Love personified, from whom descends all light and life to mankind.

We are not here concerned with the content of the Christian revelation, but with the theological presentation characteristic to Aquinas. As regards the existence of God, he dismisses the theory of innate ideas, and also the Anselmian argument, as we have seen. His own celebrated five proofs, which derive ultimately from Greek philosophy, are various forms of the argument from causality or origin. As for the soul, we have no direct knowledge of its essence, but experience of its activity, the reflex argument, is sufficient. Its immortality is proved primarily by the Platonic argument of its simplicity as spirit, which has no parts and therefore cannot be destroyed, but Aquinas is aware of such other arguments as the natural desire for happiness and the need for some sanction for good and evil actions.

As regards the Incarnation, Aquinas bases himself upon the words of the Creed (which epitomizes scriptural and apostolic teaching) that the primary cause of the appearance of a divine person in human form was to redeem man from sin and to give him eternal life by a share, through adoption, in his own true sonship of God, by means of his obedience even unto death. The 'exemplary' interpretation, that the Word became flesh to instruct us by teaching and example, though true, was secondary to the principal end. St. Thomas therefore held that without sin there would have been no Incarnation: in the wisdom and loving-kindness of God, Adam's fall was a happy mishap (*felix culpa*). The profound and moving teaching of Scotus, that the Son took human nature because by no other means could perfect love be given to God by his creation, and that therefore the Incarnation would have taken place even had there been no sin, would have failed to satisfy Aquinas, primarily because precise revelation is our only guide to God's purposes, but also because the opinion of Scotus would not only make the Incarnation historically irrelevant (since mankind would have been elevated to divine sonship in the divine plan irrespective of the Fall of man and the Resurrection of Christ) but would also deprive us of the supreme example of God's power to bring greater good out of evil.

In dealing with the Trinity, Aquinas developed the teaching of the Greek fathers and Augustine and Hilary. The three divine Persons in one divine Nature are 'subsistent relationships'; that is, the single, simple Godhead, which in all its relations with creatures acts as One, is distinct within its simplicity by the relationships of paternity and sonship and 'spiration' which are at once real as individual personalities within the Godhead, and yet exist to our minds only in so far as they are relationships.

As regards the Fall and its consequences, Aquinas was the first to distinguish clearly between the natural being of man, without either sin or grace, and man as we know him to have been from revelation and experience. The first man, according to Aquinas, was endowed after creation with grace, that is, with a supernatural knowledge and love of God. The Fall was possible because a finite creature, endowed with freewill, has always within himself an element of imperfection. Though never compelled to fail he is incapable by himself of always succeeding, and in the case of the first man the powerful suggestion to evil came from a spiritual agency outside himself. In Aquinas' view original sin differs widely from personal guilt, and in fact is called sin only by analogy; thus unbaptized infants fail indeed to attain to the beatific vision, but have no personal punishment or suffering. The motions of concupiscence, the rebellious physical desires, are a part of the result of original sin, but not in themselves sinful, still less original sin itself. On this point Aquinas firmly opposed Augustine. But besides the loss of grace, or immortality, and of a title to eternal beatitude, the total aversion of Adam from God left in his progeny the egoism of pride, together with weakness of will and (to a lesser extent) darkness of mind. These can be healed only by a more than natural strength and light, that is, by divine grace. Aquinas explained the difficult matter of the transmission of original sin by emphasizing the position of the First Man as head and representative of the whole human race, as Christ was to be of redeemed and glorified humanity, and he used the analogy of the sympathy between the head and other members of the human body.

The Israelites received sanctifying grace through the gift of faith in God and his revelation, and in a Messiah who was to come. Christians receive in baptism or at conversion from sin the faith and love of Christ whom they now recognize as God. This 'sanctifying' grace establishes in the soul the adoptive sonship of God, gives to it supernatural light and power, and enables it to merit, by free obedience, greater grace and ultimately the vision of God. But human nature, in itself, is not evil; grace ennobles nature, it does not destroy it.

In his treatment of grace Aquinas followed Augustine, as modified by the decrees of the second council of Orange (529) and Roman pronouncements. Man when without grace cannot merit internal, sanctifying grace by any action, though he may be disposed to receive it by 'external' graces such as, e.g. the preaching of a missionary. He is free to accept or to reject grace, but in the case of acceptance the act, though free, is essentially due to the impulse of grace, whereas rejection, or non-acceptance, is due to man's own deficiency. Aquinas repeats more than once the words of Isaiah (xxvi 12): 'Thou hast wrought all our works in us', and of Hosea (xiii 9): 'O Israel, thou hast destroyed thyself; but in me is thine help.'

As regards the mystery of salvation and election to heavenly glory, Aquinas, following St. Paul and St. Augustine, gives primary and final place to the foreknowledge of God. The elect, chosen from eternity, are saved by the omnipotent decree of God, that is, by predestination. The lost, of whose number we have no knowledge whatsoever, are foreseen from all eternity as failing through their own deficiency. Aquinas studiously avoids the 'double predestination' that appears in some utterances of Augustine. The reconciliation of God's foreknowledge and decree with man's freedom is made by the assertion that God's infinite power can effect with infallible certainty both that an action shall take place and that it shall be a free action. God indeed wishes the salvation of all men and Christ died for all men, but man can freely refuse the gift of God, and God permits this failure which he has foreseen but has not decreed. Free-will can at any moment fail to accept, but if no obstacle is placed the first grace gives birth to the second. In other words, in the way of salvation every grace that is not freely refused is in fact efficacious. Aquinas, following St. Augustine, is insistent that grace is effective within the soul as an act of God's controlling power. It is an instance of the general truth that all positive action is in the ultimate resort the work of God. Aquinas's attitude to grace has therefore no similarity with later conceptions of saving grace as a superior attraction (save in a purely descriptive sense) or as solely a providential collocation of circumstances. It is the action, infallible yet sweet, of God within the soul, producing the action and by means of his omnipotence, producing it freely. St. Thomas nowhere uses the phrase 'physical premotion' which was later to be a Thomist shibboleth but it is, properly understood, a fair comment on his teaching.

Besides the graces common to every soul predestined to receive supernatural enablement and light, there are certain important kinds of grace peculiar to the visible church of Christ, known as the sacraments. Aquinas and his contemporaries inherited the findings of more than a century of debate and themselves gave classic formulation to the doctrines of the sacraments. The seven – and only seven – sacraments, each with its 'matter' and 'form', of which three – baptism, confirmation and order – impress an eternal character upon the soul, were by now part of the common belief of the church. In Aquinas's system Penance had assumed the shape which it still holds in the Roman Catholic church, consisting of a detailed confession, contrition (or sorrow) which includes a serious resolve of amendment, and satisfaction, that is, the performance of an enjoined task of prayer, penance or almsgiving. In the matter of contrition, Aquinas held that 'imperfect' contrition (usually known as attrition), that is, detestation of sin as incurring the divine sentence of punishment, is a sufficient disposition for absolution.

In the matter of the Eucharist Aquinas added precision to the common teaching that, while the substance (a metaphysical, not a physical term) of the elements was changed, the accidents or species remained, by holding that the accidents perceived by the senses 'inhered in the basic accident of quantity'. As is well known, St. Thomas gave a remarkable statement both of his beliefs and of his piety and devotion to the Real Presence in the sequence and hymns he composed for the office of the newly instituted feast of Corpus Christi. The hymn *Adoro Te devote*, now recognized as certainly by him, is in the same vein.

The distinguishing mark of sacramental as opposed to other forms and means of grace is its connection with an external act and in some cases with an external medium, such as water or oil. The seven sacraments were considered to be means instituted by Christ himself as a permanent and essential feature of the Christian life, and part of the public and social activity of the church. For all save two of the sacraments priestly or episcopal ministration was necessary, and the remaining two (baptism and matrimony) became, the one immediately and the other belatedly, peculiarly 'social occasions', normally requiring the presence of a priest. In all these save matrimony the main lines of theology and discipline were settled in practice and law in the twelfth century, but were given full theological treatment by Aquinas and others.

A further property of sacramental grace, suiting the visible, public nature of its occurrence, was its certainty. Whereas the bestowal of sanctifying grace in the individual case is normally not only inapprehensible but also unsusceptible of observation or record, with the sacraments the performance of the correct act with the suitable inward disposition gives certainty of the reception of sacramental grace, *ex opere operato* (by virtue of the act duly performed) as the later phrase went. This transaction, so often seen as something mechanical, is in the mind of Aquinas and his contemporaries governed by a spiritual condition on the part of the recipient which is necessary for its fulfilment. For the reception of four of the sacraments, called 'sacraments of the living' (that is, living already in grace), the soul, if it is to receive actual sacramental grace, must be right in its relationship to God. Otherwise, for so long as the hindrance to grace exists, the grace remains inoperant. For the others – baptism, penance and anointing – the recipient, if not an infant, must at least not be in a state of positive aversion from God, and normally explicit sorrow for sin is required. Moreover, the familiar axiom, that the quality of a gift is determined by the capacity of the recipient, holds good here as in other circumstances. Grace cannot be measured, but a careless, thoughtless recipient is by his own fault barring the way to the inflowing of God. By definition he is not wholly averse, but he may, by his habitual or actual love of things in this world, be refusing to accept the invitation to advance in the love of God.

Not the least important part of the Thomist system is his detailed treatment of the endowment of the Christian soul for the service of God. In this he discovered four levels of virtuous and meritorious activity. Defining virtue as a habit rendering right action not only possible but in a sense 'second nature', he took as his basis from Greek philosophy the four 'cardinal' virtues of prudence, justice, fortitude and temperance as the norms of a good, rational human life. The Christian is raised to a higher level by his new knowledge and love of God, for which he is indebted to the 'theological' virtues of faith, hope (or trust) and charity (love). As however the Christian is, by his reception of the gospel teaching, committed to higher standards of life than is the 'natural' man, he needs a special assistance of God, which he receives in a more refined form of the cardinal virtues, by which, for example, prudence is no longer merely a right judgment in human relationships and activities, but is right judgment in preferring the teaching of Christ and the service of God to all purely human convenience or custom. Above this again is the service of one made perfect in the Christian life, in which he no longer acts by reasoning or deliberation, but by inspiration and a sense of sympathy with the words and actions of Christ. For this life there are the Gifts of the Holy Spirit – wisdom, understanding, knowledge, counsel, fortitude, piety and the fear of God – given to the soul in a special way at Confirmation, and enabling the strong servant of Christ to act without argument or effort as he sees his Master acting and willing him to act.

This hierarchy of habits and actions, so schematic and artificial at the first glance, is in fact, like so much of scholastic thought which is based on Greek philosophy, merely a formal analysis and exposition of familiar experience. This is brought out very clearly in Aquinas's account of the exercise of the virtuous habits. The human virtues imply simply a rational choice and a greater or lesser amount of moral effort. They do not differ in the manner of their action from a physical exercise such as throwing a ball at an object, and a 'habit' can be acquired by a series of acts. The theological virtues and the 'infused' moral virtues need a God-given capacity and a God-given light and strength, but these helps, which are unfelt and recognized only by their effects, elicit actions which are the outcome of reasoning and effort. The Gifts of the Holy Spirit, on the other hand, in a properly disposed subject, bestow both the capacity to act and the act itself, that is, they bestow knowledge and accomplish acts in a soul capable and willing of accepting the gift of God. In other words, while in the case of the virtues, once they are infused, the divine action cooperates in and with the human agent, in the case of the Gifts, the divine action operates in and without any effort on the part of the recipient. 'For as many as are led by the Spirit of God, they are the sons of God.' Or, as Tennyson wrote:

> 'Our wills are ours, we know not how,
> Our wills are ours, to make them thine.'

It is not surprising therefore that St. Thomas sees the Gifts of the Holy Spirit in action in the lives of Christians made perfect and drawn to the mystical life. In common with all major scholastic theologians, who in this do but echo the unanimous opinion of medieval Christendom, he held that the Christian life could and should be a steady and gradual progress in virtue, achieved by God's grace in a soul that offers no hindrance and trustfully consents to the inspiration to follow all Christ's commands and counsels, with the inevitable sacrifices and hardships they may seem to entail. He held also, again in accordance with tradition, that certain 'states' of life are, considered in the abstract, more 'perfect' than others, as implying an acceptance of ideals and aims beyond that of obeying the explicit commands of God and of the earthly representatives of God, the rulers of his church. Thus the dedicated state of virginity and celibacy, in both men and women, is a higher vocation in itself than marriage; that of an ordained minister of religion is higher than that of a layman, as being devoted essentially to the direct service of God; that of the vowed religious higher than that of a cleric, as being that of one solemnly pledged to obedience, chastity and the lack of ownership of material property, and pledged implicitly to aim always at the perfect service of Christ. These grades, however, though valid in the abstract when all other things are equal, are not in fact and existentially the ultimate criterion of excellence; this consists solely in the degree of the love of God manifested in thought, word and deed by the individual Christian. Thus in the concrete a married man may be far holier than a bishop, but in such a case the one is living with a more intense devotion to God than his 'state' demands, whereas the other is failing to live up to the obligations he has voluntarily undertaken.

Aquinas, again in accordance with universal western tradition, divided the Christian life, according to its essential character in the individual, into active and contemplative, the latter being the nobler of the two. In his treatment of this point, he was not always successful in avoiding an ambiguity of long standing which had its origin in antiquity and has persisted to the present day. Greek philosophy in the age of Aristotle divided the use of human faculties into the active way, i.e., the doing or making of something by means of visible action, or implying the use of external means, and the contemplative way, i.e., the purely intra-mental activity of reflection and reasoning upon the nature and purpose of the universe of spirit and matter. The latter was pronounced to be the nobler occupation for which all others were but a preparation. This terminology was taken over by Plotinus and later thinkers in the Greek tradition, but with a strictly ethical and religious slant – the active life was the exercise of virtue in relation to persons and things, the contemplative life was the absorption of the mind in a gradual ascent from all things to the One, who was also the supreme Good. By an easy transition, St. Augustine, in this as in other matters profoundly influential, Christianized the two terms with subtle changes. The active life was the life of Christian virtue; the contemplative life, found in its fulness only in the after-life of the Beatific Vision, was found also but rarely in Christian experience as a momentary enlightenment which was seen by the recipient as a glimpse of uncreated light, as of God himself.

Henceforward there was ambiguity. The active life was the life of common Christianity, lay and clerical, devoted to charitable and apostolic work. The contemplative life was that of hermits and monks and nuns in general, whose principal occupation was prayer and meditation (reading and reflection) on the truths of the faith. At the same time on a deeper internal plane the active life was that of good actions performed consciously and voluntarily, with the help of grace. Contemplation was the rare reception of knowledge and vision such as was known by experience to occur in persons of unusually holy life. Neither St. Thomas nor any of his contemporaries fully avoided this ambiguity. With all theologians St. Thomas was agreed on the superiority of the contemplative life, and on the conviction that contemplation was the highest spiritual experience of the soul, but it is often extremely difficult to be certain whether in a given place contemplation means for him devout meditation of a mind enlightened by grace, or the reception of inexpressible, incommunicable knowledge and love of God in a way recognized to be supernatural, i.e., beyond the natural powers. Throughout his writings, however, and again in harmony with a tradition as old as the Greek fathers, he regards the seven Gifts of the Holy Spirit as a species of supernatural agency more direct and simple than that given in the Christian life to all. This agency does not merely work in and with the human mind and will, but it moves the powers, which do no more than give their consent, to a higher form of activity than they are capable of by themselves. From this it is only a step – and that step was soon taken – to equate the inward contemplative life with the mystical life and to define it as the infusion of love and knowledge by means of the Gifts of the Holy Spirit, taking the form of directly 'operant' grace, as distinct from the active life of the virtues brought into play by 'cooperant' grace. In either case the grace is 'supernatural' and as such inapprehensible by the senses and faculties, but in the case of 'operant' grace of this special kind the soul (though not the senses or reason) is conscious that it is receiving a love and knowledge that it cannot express. This account of the contemplative life is not proposed explicitly by St. Thomas, but it can be found in its component factors in scattered sentences and phrases, and it has always been accepted by Thomists.

VI

THE LATER SCHOLASTICS

THE BREAKDOWN OF THE THOMIST SYNTHESIS

1. *The condemnations of 1270 and 1277. Duns Scotus*

When Bonaventure and Thomas took their doctor's degree together in 1257 there was indeed a rivalry between the two leading orders of friars, but theologians had not yet irrevocably split into groups of warring partisans. Aquinas, indeed, then and later had aroused criticism as well as interest by his thorough-going acceptance of Aristotelian philosophy, suitably processed, as the steel framework of his system. In particular his adoption of Aristotelian epistemology, to the exclusion of divine illumination, and of Aristotle's definition of the soul as the 'form' of the body, which seemed to some less reconcilable with Christian tradition than the Platonic view, aroused hostility among the traditionalists. But a fatal crisis and confrontation might have been avoided but for the appearance in the arts school of a frankly heterodox interpretation of Aristotle, which placed in full daylight his doctrine of the eternity of the world (thus leaving no place for creation), the absence of any clear declaration of the immortality of the soul, and a rigid order in the universe which, when it touched upon the human soul, came near to moral determinism. A series of these and other propositions was condemned by Bishop Tempier of Paris in 1270. No Thomis thesis was included in the condemnation, but there was a general feeling that the escape was a narrow one. St. Thomas died in 1274, and in 1277, on the third anniversary of his death, when he was no longer there to answer, a second and more extensive batch of propositions, including several of his philosophical theses, were condemned in what was a general onslaught on Arabic-Aristotelian positions. The slur on Aquinas was removed fifty years later by Pope John XXII, but the condemnation of 1277 was, and was accepted at Paris as being, a warning against Aristotelian thought and in particular against the Philosopher's inadequate conception of God, of the human soul and of the universe as an eternal being developing inevitably in all its parts. Henceforth, the followers of Aquinas became a school, and for long a small school, while philosophy, at least in the theological faculty, moved away from Aristotle.

In the event this meant that the achievement of St. Thomas in constructing a system in which nature and grace, human knowledge and revelation, human reason and infused knowledge, interlocked to construct a Christian system of divine government, remained isolated as the teaching of a school and had no influence on the climate of the period that immediately followed.

In Etienne Gilson's familiar words: 'after a brief honeymoon, theology and philosophy feel that their marriage was a mistake'. But Gilson elsewhere finely applied to Aquinas the words of the Psalmist (Ps. ci 19 vulgate): 'These things shall be written in a generation other than our own, and a people yet to be created shall praise the Lord'.

The age of the great synthesis of philosophy and theology ceased suddenly, and in the twenty years that followed masters of a lesser calibre followed Bonaventure or Thomas, or chose what appealed to them from this master or the other. Then, at the end of the century, the Franciscan school was immeasurably strengthened by John Duns the Scot (c. 1266–1308) born in the Border county of Roxburghshire, and teacher first at Oxford and then at Paris and Cologne. The philosophy of Scotus, the 'subtle doctor', is not easy to comprehend or to propound, and no attempt will be made here to perform either feat. It is however important to realize its significance, apart from any consideration of its worth. In the first place, with Plato unknown and Aristotle virtually condemned, the way of tradition could no longer be followed. Imperceptibly, a long epoch had ended. Hitherto all thinkers from Augustine onwards had regarded it as axiomatic that the great ones of the past, Plato or Aristotle, Plotinus or Avicenna, had discovered one aspect at least of the ultimate truth of things. All that remained to be done was to get at his exact meaning, to bring his teaching up to date in a Christian context. It could then be taught like Euclid. That attitude had been driven off the field, at least for the time, by the scandals that Aristotelian learning had caused. Secondly, with Scotus there had appeared a master who was prepared to re-think large tracts of abstract philosophy with new concepts and new terms. In this he was the first of the moderns, to be followed by numerous imitators. Theologically he is of importance also in two respects. First (to develop Gilson's metaphor) he began the formal divorce proceedings between faith and reason, natural philosophy and supernatural revelation. He accepted indeed the Aristotelian account of knowledge, as the mind working upon the data provided by the senses, while at the same time he emphasized, in this opposing Augustine, the infinity and unattainability of God by the human mind. He would not admit either the Anselmian proof, nor the Bonaventuran innate intuition, nor the Thomist argument from causality. No proof could run from creator to creature, from finite to infinite. Duns's own proof for the existence of God was a stronger version of that of Anselm, and postulated God's infinity, and of an infinite being the mind can form no concept. Secondly, Duns, a Franciscan with something of the spirit of St. Francis and the Augustinian theologians, reacted against the alleged determinism of Aristotle and emphasized the primacy of the will. Whereas for Aquinas the will is a blind faculty, determined in general by the good but dependent upon the mind for its direction in each particular choice, for Scotus love is the ultimate source of God's action, and the ultimate law for man. Love is the only command. Acts are good simply because they are commanded by God, the supreme Love, not because they are good in themselves. Absolutely speaking God is free; the will of God and not his mind or law has the last word. This way of thinking led to the well-known difference between Thomist and Scotist as to the necessity of the Incarnation.

Duns was not a sceptic, but he refused to accept either the Aristotelian conception of nature, which implied the Thomist nature-grace opposition and subordination, or the Augustinian fusion of the spheres of nature and grace. This, added to his acceptance of a conceptual (that is, an intellectual) grasp of the individual prior to the abstraction of the essence of a being, marked the parting of the ways with Aquinas. Nevertheless Duns was a true theologian, with a spiritual outlook. He died young, and while many of his opinions are clear, it is not always known what were his arguments for holding them. His system as he left it was not complete, but it was extended by his successors and became for some two centuries after his death, more widely held than that of St. Thomas. They differed on many points of importance. One such, the ultimate cause of the Incarnation, has been mentioned. Another was the nature of grace, which Duns held to be directly, in its form of Charity (or Love), the 'pouring forth of the Holy Spirit' himself in the soul. Yet another difference, as we have seen, concerned the Immaculate Conception of the Blessed Virgin. It was natural that the Franciscans should use to the full the only mind and the only coherent system that could stand up against the Thomist synthesis. Duns's genius lay in criticism, St. Thomas's in constructive power, but the credal differences between the two were less important than their twofold witness to the traditional body of teaching which they had inherited.

2. *The Rhineland Neoplatonists*

While the strict Thomist teaching was suffering something of an eclipse at Paris and Oxford, a new school of Dominican theology was coming into being in the Rhineland. Cologne, though not the seat of a university for almost a century after the death of Aquinas, had been from early times one of the international centres (*studia generalia*) of the Dominicans, and equally the seat of a great Franciscan school. Albert, Thomas and Duns had all taught here. When Albert was regent and later prior provincial he had given a great deal of attention to the study of the writings of the pseudo-Areopagite, as we have seen, and a succession of pupils culminating in the great Master Eckhart created a school of eminence and influence. Eckhart (1260–1327), in modern times, was for long regarded as primarily a mystical writer, in whom some found the first dawn of the movement that ultimately issued in Lutheran teaching. More recently, it has been shown that in all his writings Eckhart has a firm basis of Thomist technique and theology, though he certainly used this as a vehicle for a description of the universe and of human life in Neoplatonic terms, with the ecstatic union as the crown of the spiritual life and the mystical life as the goal of Christian endeavour. Eckhart, fundamentally orthodox and willing to submit to the teaching of the church if shown to be deviating from it, was condemned after his death for propositions that were at least verbally unorthodox and pantheistic, and scholars are still in disagreement as to whether he was a mystic speaking in Neoplatonic form, or a Dionysian theologian putting his teaching into mystical phraseology. Whatever the truth may be, Eckhart had a very great influence. His disciples John Tauler and Henry Suso 'screened' his system, eliminating unorthodox and Dionysian elements while retaining his mystical bent. Both Tauler and Suso were mystical writers rather than theologians, and in the realms of pure theology the Rhineland school had little importance, but the combination of Thomist principles with mystical teaching, which was followed in practice by numerous saintly disciples, of whom Ruysbroeck was the most celebrated, was of supreme importance in mystical theology. On the one hand it extended the traditional teaching, found in Aquinas but not applied by him to the experience of the spiritual life, while on the other hand it strengthened and gave technical and adequate theological explanation to the experiences and writings of the mystics themselves. By routes hitherto unmapped, it spread to England and was reproduced by the group known as the English mystics, and later still the writings of Tauler and others penetrated to Spain where they were absorbed by the early Spanish mystical writers of the sixteenth century and served as an auxiliary to the teaching of St John of the Cross and others, and thus became a principal current in the main stream of Roman Catholic mystical theology.

3. *William of Ockham* (c. 1285–1347)

Meanwhile at Paris and Oxford theology became steadily more eclectic and monographic, with an interest in the individual both as an object of cognition and as a preoccupation in the choice of topics for consideration. Predestination, after an interval of many centuries, became once more a burning object of controversy, with a cognate interest in freewill, the divine prescience of free acts in the future, and the fate of the unbaptized infant and the 'good pagan' outside the church. Then, shortly before 1320, another thinker of genius appeared at Oxford, the Franciscan friar William of Ockham. Unlike Duns, with whose thought he had throughout his work something of a love-hate relationship, Ockham was first and foremost a logician, claiming to stand to Aristotle in that domain as Aquinas had stood in the higher levels of speculative philosophy, a devoted but not blind admirer and amplifier. His system was a blend of Aristotle with the complicated new logic of the Oxford school, and it became a formidable weapon when he proceeded to expound his new epistemology and became the founder of the new Nominalism. [*See note at the end of the chapter.*] This, in its explanation of the process of acquiring knowledge, abandoned the way of intellectual abstraction and of any mental form or idea of universal or generic application. He eliminated also the Scotist doctrine of an intellectual apprehension, by way of intuition, of the individual. Extending Scotus, and applying the principle that runs through all his thought and was afterwards known as 'Ockham's razor', that all unnecessary notional entities should be suppressed, he held that the individual, the singular entity, is alone knowable, but this knowledge is wholly intuitional, not expressible in a concept, as Duns had thought. The mind does not abstract an essence from things, as Aristotle and St. Thomas had held, because there is no evidence either of the mental process of abstraction, or of the existence of an essence to be abstracted. Words such as 'man', 'rose' and the rest, are not universal terms about which we can philosophize; they are merely signs which we attach to the mental image and memory of our intuition of an individual, and have no more metaphysical connection with the objects to which they are applied than has a natural exclamation of pleasure or pain. They are purely a mental reaction. Metaphysical philosophy therefore is not a process of real knowledge and understanding, but a shifting about in our mind of mental symbols, as it were a shifting of ciphers or tickets. So far the system of Ockham might seem merely a matter of technique. When he proceeded further, however, the consequences became apparent. None of the so-called truths of natural religion can be proved – neither the existence of God nor his attributes nor the existence and immortality of the soul. All these and much else are held, and must be held, by faith alone. Hence, knowing nothing of God by our natural powers, but believing in his transcendence and omnipotence by faith, we cannot predict or define his action or lay down any limits either to his powers or to his ways of acting. Ethics depend upon revelation; God might have made a different or even a contradictory list of commandments. God is absolutely free to reward whom he will without precedent merit. No preparation or disposition is needed for any grace or for final salvation. Grace as a quality or force, and all the traditional virtues, are superfluous. Charity, as Scotus said, is the Holy Spirit, God's Gift. Nothing else is required. All else can be cut out. We know from Scripture how we may expect God to act, and may frame our lives accordingly; but it is merely a revealed probability. Ockham was not a philosophical sceptic; he held that the universe existed and that the human mind had intuitional knowledge of its detailed parts; but this was the only knowledge available or possible. The cause-and-effect sequence was an illusion; we know the sequence in time between one event or appearance and another, and we know no more. If Aristotelian philosophy has been flippantly described as the exposition in philosophical terms of what we all hold, or 'dazzling glimpses of the obvious', the thought of Ockham might be characterized as the exposition in set terms of the mental outlook of an uneducated man before he has begun to put his thought into words.

Ockham was delated by an Oxford master to the Curia at Avignon, whither he went to defend himself, but before the long-delayed and mild censure was pronounced he had disappeared to join the schismatic Franciscans and the Emperor in their opposition to Pope John XXII. He had not yet proceeded master in theology at Oxford, and his remaining years were spent in propounding revolutionary theses concerning the papacy and the church. He died c. 1349 unreconciled to the papacy. He was never a regent master in the schools, but his logical and dialectical work remained, and it spread like oil over Europe. It was the instrument that gave what was, for the time being, the final blow to the traditional synthesis of philosophy and theology. Philosophy was reduced to logic, broadly understood, and theology to a study of the Bible and the preaching of revealed truth.

Ockhamism or Nominalism spread widely and rapidly and for more than a century was to influence all thought to a greater or less degree. Only one powerful voice was raised against William of Ockham in his lifetime, that of his fellow Oxonian Thomas Bradwardine (c. 1290–1349), later for a few months archbishop of Canterbury. Bradwardine was chiefly concerned with Ockham's exaltation of the divine and human freewill, which was one of the legacies from Scotus that he had exploited, and with his reduction of grace to no more than an arbitrary relationship of a man to God. If grace did not exist as a force or entity, man's 'good' acts were his own work. Therefore Ockham could be labelled with the name of the only heresy that was familiar to all western medieval writers, that of Pelagius. Bradwardine therefore entitled his work *The Cause of God against the Pelagians*.

Ockham, an object of distrust among Catholic theologians since the Council of Trent, has found powerful apologists in recent years among both his fellow-Franciscans and those brought up in a philosophical climate not unlike his own. Undoubtedly much criticism in the past has been ill-informed and parrot-talk, and the thought of the fourteenth century has rightly received some of the attention that it deserved. Reaction, however, may go too far. It is reasonably urged in defence of Ockham that he was a logician, and not a theologian, and that there was little or nothing in his writings in early life (which alone are the issue here), or in those of his principal followers, contrary to Catholic belief as formally defined by creeds and councils before or during his lifetime. The first statement is formally correct. Ockham never touched theology as such. But to hold his position and follow his method was in fact tantamount to abandoning all use of the reason in explaining or defending revealed truth. No doubt in every age many are prepared to accept a body of religious teaching without any desire to criticize or analyse its meaning and credentials, and in the fourteenth century such a position was perhaps almost universal, but this would be an impossible position in a sophisticated and largely unbelieving world. The second statement is also formally correct, save perhaps in the single but important matter of grace, where Bradwardine was justified in the title of his work. But the Christian faith, the gospel message, had not yet been solemnly defined in all its amplitude, and there were many beliefs, held by all true Christians, and inmost convictions, which were jettisoned by Ockham's logic, such as, e.g., the direct enlightenment and strengthening of the reason and will by God, and the ability of the created mind to rise from a consideration of the creatures to a natural conviction of the existence and goodness of a creator. These, if not defined in Ockham's day, could scarcely be denied without a real mutilation of the Christian faith.

4. *Scholasticism in retrospect*

We have now reached what is generally agreed to have been the end of an epoch in thought and theology. During the preceding two centuries, and particularly between 1200 and 1300, the body of Christian theology, in the shape in which it was available to the schools of the west, had been ordered, analysed, explained and extended, and supported by traditional philosophy, more fully than ever before. The legacy of the western masters – Anselm, Bernard, Bonaventure, Thomas – has been carried over almost entirely into its currect teaching by the Roman Catholic church, and has deeply influenced in various ways all subsequent Christian theology, even that which has been ready to reject many of its most characteristic parts. No serious and well-informed theologian would today deny this achievement.

Yet at the same time the constructive force in theology had ceased by the end of the fourteenth century, and an era of criticism and, in a sense, of destruction had followed, which was to continue until an altogether new situation of revolution and controversy supervened. Why did scholasticism cease to be a pregnant and constructive force? Setting aside all deeper spiritual reasons which are unseen, and also the historically ceaseless ebb and flow, action and reaction, of human thought in all mental activities, we may perhaps point to two major causes.

The first is, that for three centuries before 1350, the basic instrument and pursuit of secondary and advanced education and scholarship was logic, and this secured the prizes of the academic and ecclesiastical world, and turned all its endeavours towards the critical, formal exercises of a technique, the technique of disputation, rather than towards the exposition of many-sided reality or the intuitional deepening of spiritual knowledge.

The second is that the essential aim of the Aristotelian logic and epistemology is the attainment of abstract truth. To Aquinas, as to Aristotle, the abstract truth, the essential definition, the general proposition, are more valuable, more real, higher in degree than the knowledge and experience and intuition of the individual mind and its individual object. Methodically, as was later proved by its enemies, this starved all hope of progress in scientific knowledge of material things. It has also the grave defect that when syllogism led to syllogism, the slightest verbal or technical falsity if overlooked could vitiate what appeared to be a faultless chain of argument. It has always been a fault in neo-scholastic thinkers that they regard the tenth syllogism in a series of deductions from an admitted principle to have the same weight as the first. Both these characteristics tended to lead both philosophers and theologians further and further away from life and practical reality into a world of ideas and conclusions. Medieval thought and medieval theology also ran ultimately into the doldrums because they lost touch the one with the world of things and men, the other with the living Christ of the gospel, present still in his body, the church, in its saints, its teachers and its daily life.

Note to p. 283: 'the founder of the new Nominalism'.

Since Dom David Knowles wrote his script, a clear distinction has been drawn between William of Ockham's own teaching and Ockhamism or Nominalism which followed but distorted his teaching. What Ockham himself did was to turn away from the exploration of what was metaphysically possible, and confine knowledge to what could be known naturally from experience, or inferred from what was believed. Evidence and meaning for universals must be derived from the knowledge of individuals. He stressed the contingency of all creation in the light of God's omnipotence; though in that context he accepted the regularity of nature and the constancy of moral terms. He himself held to a balance between nature and supernature which his successors did not. *Ed.*

Christian Doctrine from 1350 to the Eve of the Reformation

E. Gordon Rupp

Christian Doctrine from 1350 to the Eve of the Reformation

E. Gordon Rupp

The century and a half preceding the Reformation baffles the historian of doctrine. There is still a dearth of monographs, so that comparative studies abound in contradictory judgments. The view of the period as one of disintegration and decline has been modified, if not shattered by modern scholars. Yet it is true that the days of the great syntheses, of Thomas and Bonaventura, of Scotus and Ockham are over, and a late fourteenth-century 'Summa' is more like a modern 'Collected Papers' than an attempt to hold together the body of revealed and natural theology. The word 'eclectic' which crops up in many descriptions of the first half of the period, like Josef Lortz's 'Unklarheit' of the second, are words of warning rather than description, but they point to the danger of rigid labels, since Nominalists and Realists are alike affected by cross-currents, by Augustinian or Dionysian revivals. And in the fifteenth century we have to take account of a return to orthodoxy, as in the neo-Thomism of Totting of Oyta or above all Johannes Capreolus.

When we turn to England, Dr. Leff's words are apt: 'the intellectual life of the period is everywhere largely veiled in mists: but in England the obscurity is near to fog.' This applies in a special degree to Wyclif studies, and he still awaits a competent theological re-assessment in the light of modern scholastic studies which tend either to ignore him or walk round him as a kind of 'rogue elephant'.

JOHN WYCLIF (c. 1330–84) was very Oxford of very Oxford. He raised the prestige of its great school of theology to new heights before plunging it to disaster. He emerged from that Merton-Balliol axis with its proud pedigree of intellectual enterprise. He stood in the dominant Augustinian-Platonic tradition of Grosseteste, Fitz Ralph and Bradwardine (itself a warning against the too facile judgment that Wyclif has no mystical element in his thought). It was also a tradition with close affinities with mathematics and with science, and in this too, Wyclif ardently shared.(The notion that it is Nominalism which nurtured modern science ignores not only the medieval Oxford tradition but the Platonists of Florence and Cambridge in later days.) His training in the years before he took his D.D. (1372) showed a formidable concentration on logic, philosophy and Biblical study. It is a pity that we know little of the corrosive and sceptical Nominalism in Oxford against which Wyclif vehemently reacted, and for which he found the antidote in a thoroughgoing realism which made

coherent for him his view of the universe, of the nature of man, of the
relation of time and eternity, and of the nature and authority of Holy
Scripture. If it involved him in trouble in the realm of sacramental theology,
it smoothed for him (as for Calvin later) his rationale of Predestination.
But if his theology was affected, it was not controlled by his metaphysics;
neither logic, philosophy nor political involvements account for his theology.

Like Gerson, with whom he has more affinities than usually credited, he
deemed it was a glorious thing to be a theologian, for though he believed
that in some sense, all Christians have a theological vocation, he believed
also in the special authority of the trained scholastic ('pure theologis oportet
credere ad interpretandum scripturas secundum vivaces rationes et testi-
monia sanctorum, quia illi erunt boni judices in propria facultate' – 'One
must trust implicitly in the theologians if one is to interpret the Scriptures
in a living and meaningful way and in accordance with the testimony of the
saints; for the theologians will prove to be good judges in their own sphere.'
De officio Regis, 70.1.15). His tedious argumentation is in the manner of the
age – the spiral repetitions, the wrestling with a point like a dog with a bone;
but there is a sturdy rationality and a logical concentration which set him
and his contemporaries many points above the sixteenth-century humanists
and reformers. He was deeply imbedded in tradition, and we must not let
his emphasis on the authority of Holy Scripture blind us to the extent to
which his most daring arguments are clinched with an appeal to the words
of Chrysostom, Grosseteste or Bradwardine. Needless to say, for him
Augustine is the great master, but in his discussions of the great Christological and Trinitarian themes it is to Anselm and Aquinas that he turns. And
for all his Platonism, he quotes Aristotle as often as does a Gerson or a Biel.

The mass of his writings would have brought no more than local notoriety
had he not attacked first the religious and then the mendicant orders, and
many of the charges of error and heresy would not have been brought apart
from this enmity, as they are certainly not sustained by the generally
inferior arguments of Cunningham in his life-time, or the wild charges which
Netter of Walden felt free to make long after his death. His treatise on the
Trinity is learned but unremarkable. His tract on the Incarnation stresses
the humanity of Christ, though apart from its beautiful exordium it does
not perhaps quite merit Bernard Manning's eulogy of it (Camb. Med. Hist.
VII (1932), pp. 486ff.). More impressive is his *De divinis mandatis*, an exposition of the Commandments. While drawing heavily upon moral
theologians of the preceding century it centres God's laws in the commands
of Christ and in the commands of love, set within a 'theologia viatoris'
('pilgrim-theology') and a doctrine of the beatific vision which is in the
finest tradition of Augustine and Bernard.

His knowledge of Canon law and his astonishing use of history has
surprised some commentators, but it is something he shared with an age
which had to tackle problems of Papal and conciliar authority, and with
those who were involved in the latest round of the long struggle in England
between the crown and the claims of the spiritual power. None of Wyclif's
themes was invented by him. The abuses of the Church, which for him
centred in its involvement with wealth, with power and with violence,

had been the subject of protest by saints, moralists and satirists for centuries. The drastic remedy of disendowment had behind it a century and a half of debate about the question of apostolic poverty, the more immediately controversial views of Fitz Ralph about 'dominion' and an appeal to the temporal power to redress the balance of a greedy clericalism. When in his theoretical arguments on behalf of the Crown, Wyclif appeals to English history, he is in an important pedigree going back through the 'Anonymous' of York to the Anglo-Saxon church, as it looks forward to Matthew Parker and Lord Burghley.

That in mid-life, like Walter Birley before him and Jean Gerson after him, he should become involved in power politics and the affairs of Princes, by no means contradicts his fierce antagonism to 'Caesarean clergy' who neglect their spiritual vocation to do work better done by laymen, for it was as a 'peritus', a professional theologian, that he acted as King's Servant, went on an embassy and prepared long memoranda. Nothing shows this more clearly than the fact that at the end of his vast disquisitions on 'Divine and Civil Dominion' he rests his theological case, and pleads that it is entirely for the temporal power to decide when, how and where these arguments should be practically applied.

It was from Wyclif's discussion of practical applications of 'dominion' (*De Civili Dominio*, Bk. I, cap. xxxv) that the propositions condemned at Rome were taken. But he grounded his main argument in Augustine and Fitz Ralph. Dominion is the direct relationship of God with all men, and therefore rooted in grace. Where grace is vitiated by sin, true dominion ceases to exist. But the abstract discussion of the state of man in the time of his innocency does not deny him the use of possessions in this fallen world. And Wyclif does not desert Augustine for the Donatists, as do others of his contemporaries, and hold that continuance in mortal sin might lead to the deprivation of clergy of their spiritual and temporal possessions.

Though in an ancient usage he speaks of the Gospel as 'Christ's law', and though in his teaching, which has room for merit, there is no premonition of 'sola fide', he is not a legalist (the same cannot be said of later Lollardy). For him all God's demands are summed up in the deeds and speech (*virtute sermonis* – the 'power of the Word') of God's Son, and in the commands of love of God and neighbour. Here are the norms of God's commandments which are neither many nor grievous, but which have been multiplied and complicated by the commands of men (this is the gravamen of his attacks on Roman civil law and Canon law).

The background of all this is Wyclif's view of Holy Scripture which is Christologically orientated. It is sad that reputable scholars (Smalley, Leff) can use the grossly anachronistic word 'fundamentalist' to describe Wyclif's view of the plenary inspiration of Scripture. For his doctrine of the relation between God, time and eternity is not an eccentric deviation based on Augustinian and neo-Platonic conceptions, but the view that God, to whom past, present and future are one, can fill each moment and each word with power (*virtute sermonis*). Like St. Thomas he searches under the merely literal (cf. his frequent disparagement of what is written on the skins of animals or in parchments) or the allegorically mystical, for the authentic meaning. There is here a doctrine of hermeneutic which should be of interest to students of Bultmann, Barth and Ebeling. Scripture is for him the supreme norm, and this is more and more emphatically stated in his later works. But I believe that Père de Vooght is correct as against Fr. Hurley and that Wyclif by no means discards the authority of the Fathers and Doctors of the Church. Like John Wesley he had become *homo unius libri* (a man of one book), but like him he draws on all learning and sound tradition for the elucidation of Scripture.

The year 1378 is the watershed of Wyclif's career. Then it became plain that John of Gaunt and his party had no hope of carrying through a drastic disendowment of the English Church. It was also the year of the Great Schism, which confirmed Wyclif's worst forebodings. He abandoned an earlier acceptance of the papal primacy in face of this dire proof that the Church had so far fallen from its primitive simplicity that its Head had become the emblem of Anti-Christ. There followed his retirement to Lutterworth and a stream of bitter polemic. He had now only one weapon left, his words: and these he used with a poignant and perhaps pathological vehemence which made him the Milton of the fourteenth century, the Kierkegaard of the later Middle Ages.

He now attacked the doctrine of transubstantiation, about which he had long had philosophical difficulties, and put forward his own not more clear doctrine of the 'remanence' of bread and wine, and of a sacramental presence. The attack may be the measure of his political disillusion, for his royal patrons would not dare associate themselves with heresy of this order, even if they understood it. But if his doctrine expresses his honest conviction, it is also likely that, with the later Lollards, he saw in the power of the priest to make and offer Christ, the fateful mystique which overawed the laity. We must not exaggerate: Wyclif would not have used the opprobrious epithets beloved of the later Lollards. He was devoted to the eucharist, and his last seizure fell on him at Mass.

His diatribes were related also to his doctrine of the Church. Like Gerson, but unlike Sir Thomas More, he knew that any definition of its nature must be complex and many-sided, but with Augustine he turned for its primary meaning to those called and chosen in Christ to be saved, the *universitas praedestinorum* (totality of the predestined). For the reprobate he used the guarded phrase of Bradwardine – the *praesciti* or 'fore-known' (which seems to leave open the question of salvation *ante merita praevisa* or 'foreseen merits') and like Augustine his view of Church history is dualistic. There has been conflict and tension in the story of the People of God from the time of Cain and Abel. This is the serious point of what otherwise would seem mere abuse – his description of the lavish buildings of the mendicants as 'Caim's Castles' (Caim is not only an anagram of the four mendicant orders but a medieval variant on Cain e.g. in the mosaics at Monreale). That is, they belong to the false church, to the accursed succession from the violent one, the usurper, the one whose vain worship is to be rejected.

We can understand how in his lectures and disputations he could tickle the groundlings and infuriate the learned, for he has an almost casual way of turning from abstruse dialectic to withering denunciation, not erroneous or heretical, but certainly offensive to pious ears, at a time when the rule of faith was becoming more and more rigidly conceived.

In one sense his programme was more revolutionary (dare one say than modern so-called 'Christian Marxists' or the 'Liberation' theologians?) than that of the Reformation. He seems to have believed that really drastic economic action carried through by political power, by disendowing the Church, might deflate its swollen structure and turn it back to better ways, to its original character as a congregation of the faithful who by goodness and love might win the loyalty of men.

It has often been pointed out how much of Wyclif's programme was carried out by the English crown, one hundred and fifty years later. The secular arm did indeed reject papal authority and all its complex implications (though it is interesting to find Cranmer, Ridley and Matthew Parker defending the 'patrimony of Christ' against the laity). And article 28 of the 39 articles put Wyclif's point exactly when it declared that 'transubstantiation cannot be proved by holy scripture, but is repugnant to the plain words of scripture, overthroweth the nature of a sacrament and hath given occasion to many superstitions'.

The cause of Wyclif in Oxford was ruthlessly repressed: his writings were proscribed, and, in England, almost totally destroyed. In an age when Oxford dons had not taken to the idea of martyrdom (would the Methodist Holy Club or the Newmannites have done more?) for the opinions of their leaders, his disciples foresook him and fled to preferments. Only a simplistic version – often a caricature of his teaching, survived amid the many spuria and dubia of his so-called 'English works'. However attenuated may be his responsibility for the Wyclif Bible and for the Lollard preachers, it was from his circle and from no other that they came. The modern historical study of Wyclif has problems still to solve. The serious re-assessment of his theology can hardly be said to have begun.

Yet it was not in England that this very English theologian found what Kierkegaard would have called 'his lovers' but in the middle of Europe, in Bohemia, where the accident of a royal wedding opened an ideas-route, where his views came at a timely and critical moment in Bohemian history, and were not so much a blood-transfusion as an organic transplant. The causes of this deep impact are complex and have been bedevilled by national and cultural controversy and by Marxist views. Certainly there had been in Bohemia a long-continuing attack on the abuses of the Church and on the wealth and privilege of the clergy. The young Czech theologians were in revolt against those Nominalist traditions so powerful in Paris and in Germany, and they found in Wyclif's philosophic realism a congenial and exciting weapon. One consequence of the dispersal of the so-called 'German Nation' from the Charles University of Prague was to spread angry anti-Wycliffite phobia among German Universities, an element of fateful influence at the Council of Constance.

JOHN HUS (1369–1415) was as thorough a Czech as Wyclif an Englishman. Not in the same class as Wyclif as a philosopher and theologian, he was none the less learned, and with the status of a *Sententiarius* came to a position of eminence.

When first the philosophical writings of Wyclif and then (at the turn of the century) his theological treatises reached Prague, Hus was but one of a number of scholars who became devoted expositors of Wycliffian realism – though there were others, like Stanislav and Palĕc, who outwent him in uncritical acceptance of the master's ideas, and who later were to become dangerous foes. Hus was a great preacher, of passion and burning sincerity, and found in the Bethlehem chapel an apt vehicle for the propagation of his concern for preaching and pastoral care, and a deadly invective against the sins of the clergy. For him many of these abuses centred in simony, about which he wrote his most devastating treatise. In an age of manuscripts there were problems of communicating programmes which only printing would solve, but one by-product was the not always happy custom of scholars of incorporating innumerable passages from their own (Gerson and Wyclif both were prone to this) and other people's writings.

Though there are difficulties about any statistical assessment of the amount of Wyclif which Hus incorporated into his own work (one has always to allow for a great amount in both writers directed to English or Bohemian conditions), the proportion of Wyclif in Hus is high. But he is never naive or uncritical; and with a discretion sometimes under-rated, Hus again and again drew back from apparent consequences of Wycliffite ideas, though always – and this it was that got him into endless trouble – he put the best interpretation on Wyclif's ideas and defended him against misunderstanding. Hus's *De Ecclesia* is an illustration of this. Heavily indebted to Wyclif in its first part, preoccupied with his own defence in the second, he produced his own version of their common Augustinian tradition. For him too the Church is primarily the *universitas Praedestinatorum* and the unsaved the *Praesciti*, while for him too the false church is described in apocalyptic terms as Anti-Christ. But as with Wyclif, his overall picture of the lamentable state of the church, and the revolutionary corollaries of his attack, dangerously affronted such by no means uncritical statesmen as D'Ailly and Gerson. Into the tragic ending of the Hus story we may not enter. It was perhaps naive of Hus to think that he would be allowed to address the Council of Constance on equal terms with his opponents, even if he was ignorant of the extent to which the verdict against him was predetermined before his arrival.

Nor did he perhaps realize how alarmingly rigid were the inquisitorial procedures for dealing with one vehemently suspect. Certainly Hus, imprisoned despite his safe-conduct, and a sick man, found himself confronting a raging and hostile assembly in one of the most shameful moments in the history of religion. But with honest obstinacy he refused to avow ideas which he had never held, in particular the 'remanence' eucharistic teaching of Wyclif (see p. 292), while he insisted on putting the best interpretation on words of Wyclif which authority had already condemned. Far more than any verbal transfusions from Wyclif's works, his relation to the dead Englishman is poignantly shown in his defence of the integrity of Wyclif. Whether any recantation could have saved him must be doubted, but if he had thrown Wyclif overboard the task of the authorities would have been made more difficult. But the death of Hus and of his ebullient colleague Jerome of Prague was not the end, but the beginning. A movement a hundred times more powerful than Lollardy emerged, involving all classes of the Bohemian people, rooted in deep anti-clerical, anti-Papal and anti-Imperial sentiments which turned the Hussite movements into the most formidable schism and the most deeply-biting challenge to the authority of the Western church in the centuries before the Reformation.

Two leading figures in the University of Paris dominated the thought of the Council. Peter D'Ailly (1350–1420) was a follower of Ockham in philosophic matters, and much of his energies went into the immensely intricate problems of conciliar reform; but he had great width of intellectual interests and made notable studies in astrology, geography and other sciences, which were treated with reserve and suspicion by his gifted friend, disciple and successor, the great Jean Gerson.

JOHN GERSON (1363–1429) – 'Doctor Christianissimus' (but he took a leading part in the impeachment of Hus) was the son of a farmer and sufficiently low-born to have something of a complex about aristocracy. He became Chancellor of the University of Paris, himself a great Doctor in Theology, and he rated highly his office as a theologian and his University's role in France ('Filia Regis' – 'daughter of the King'). He held some Nominalist doctrines – the concern for the untrammeled liberty of God – 'God does not will certain actions because they are good, but they are good because he wills them' – and therefore he attacked realists who thought of the moral law as autonomous. He delivered smashing blows at the sectarianism of the schools, the bitterly warring factions, the preoccupation with hair-splitting speculation in an age of moral and spiritual disorder. His famous lectures against 'curiositas' and 'singularitas' took as their text the moralistic themes of repentance and conversion. He specially attacked the 'formalizantes' among the Scotists. Yet he himself was more and more drawn to spiritual theology, to the tradition of the Victorines, of Albert the Great and above all, Bonaventura, and came more and more to insist on the importance of the life of contemplation. Though he opposed the realist Platonists, he became more and more devoted to the teaching of Dionysius the Areopagite (who after all was St. Denis of France!). In his stress on the need for practical reform, his distrust of abstract speculation, he turned more and more to the thought of pastoral renewal and the need for the education of youth, and above all the reform of preaching. By the time of the Council of Constance he had won eminence as a statesman, as servant of the King and of the Duke of Burgundy and as the preacher of many notable set-piece orations before court and university. He accepted the Papal primacy but upheld the doctrine of the supremacy of a General Council, and had reservations about the practicability of reform of the Church from the top downwards, looking for renewal rather in the dioceses and parishes.

His obsessive antagonism to the doctrine of violence and assassination put forward by John Petit led to a calamitous breach with his patron, the

Duke of Burgundy, which barred his return to Paris after the council, and in Austria and in Lyons he devoted the rest of his life to a career of preaching, teaching and pastoral care and a great literary activity which included scores of works of moral theology and edification deeply influential on succeeding generations, not least on the young Luther. Like the authors of the 'Modern Devotion', he helped set the note of pietism in the coming age when inward religion and the care of conscience would be major theological concerns. His was the aristocracy of the self-made man: if he taunted theologians he could be brutal about the untutored laity, and he believed that the use of the Scriptures should almost entirely be confined to the clergy. But equally firmly he rejected the view that only the institutionally 'religious' could find evangelical perfection. His famous tract addressed to his five sisters ('The Mountain of Contemplation') attempted to dissuade them from the miserable estate of matrimony, but set before them a life of contemplation and action leading to ever higher states of faith, hope and love. Further at this time, as Père Combes has shown, he did not go, but in his later writings he turned more and more to the theme of union with God. His controversy with the Flemish mystic Ruysbroeck may have rested on misunderstanding, for it seems that Ruysbroeck did not pantheistically blur the line between creator and creature. His loyalty to Bonaventura and Dionysius prevented him from divorcing mystical from speculative theology, and in fact his views of salvation, of the sacraments and of the church seem to be held within a hierarchical and Dionysian view of the chain of being. With true insight he saw that reform must begin with a new and unspoiled generation and therefore with education, and he himself conducted experiments of which he wrote an interesting rationale. But it was his concern with conscience which marked him as a precursor of later attitudes, and it is no accident that he is almost the only fifteenth-century theologian still quoted by the English Puritans. His little tracts on *Nocturnal Pollutions* and on *Pusillanimity* were best-sellers. The period has been called by one historian 'the century of Gerson', and he influenced not only Catholics but Protestants in the age to come. There are interesting resemblances between his preaching and that of the next great French preacher, John Calvin.

The emphasis on edification, on moral renewal, on Christianity as a way of life and a vision of God, as indeed the life of God in the soul of man, a life of renunciation and of the search for perfection, not out of but in the world – this mood was reflected and in part stimulated by the movement in Holland which has become known as 'the Modern Devotion'. The origin and import of the term is not clear. Certainly there was little up-to-date or innovating about the mind and temper of its founder.

GERHARD GROOTE (1340–84) who was a man of learning and indeed more than a bit of a bookworm, was by training more of a lawyer than a divine, and a man with not very wide horizons, as his curious letter discouraging a young man from going as missionary to Islam reveals. But he was a man of discipline for whom contemplation and the good life were paramount, and he became the spiritual director of groups of devout laymen and women. Since new orders had been forbidden in 1215 and there had long existed in Holland sodalities of men and women who had lived on the verge of orthodoxy. Groote's 'Brothers and Sisters of the Common Life', living in community without taking vows, and with a minimum of clerical direction, were bound to arouse suspicion and antagonism. But assisted by Florentius Radewyn (1350–1400) a devotee, co-adjutor and eventually his successor, the movement grew rapidly. The emphasis was on the life of meditation and contemplation, interspersed with manual labour which at first took the form of copying books and manuscripts.

As in other movements which had begun with the laity, a clerical element became indispensable, and this centred in the Augustinian Canons, beginning at Windesheim. The relation of the movement to education has, it seems, been misconceived. Not until the last half of the fifteenth century did the Brethren found schools or take a direct part in education. Rather they established hostels, a little like modern chaplaincies in University Halls of Residence, where they exercised spiritual supervision of adolescents – an invaluable supplement to the teaching of the civic schools. The movement gradually infiltrated south, via Munster in Westphalia, and by mid-fifteenth century had penetrated South Germany, where Gabriel Biel was its best-known adherent. By the end of a century-and-a-half most currents of renewal seem to silt up, and we could do with a fuller knowledge of what happened to the 'Modern Devotion' at its latter end (but see R. R. Post, *The Modern Devotion*, 1968, ch. 15). Certainly the movement contributed to the reform of the church, not in a spectacular way but by refreshing its life at the roots.

Like English Puritanism it had its own brand of edifying literature, letters, diaries and spiritual biographies; and it produced a small but important number of spiritual exercises, Christocentric in devotion.

Among these were the *Devota Exercitia Passionis* of Dirk of Hexen (1457), the *De spiritualibus ascensionibus* of Zerbold von Zutphen, and Jan Mombaer's *Rosetum exercitiorum spiritualium et sacrarum meditationum* (1494) a work with lingering influence on both Catholic (Ignatius Loyola) and Protestant (Joseph Hall and Richard Baxter) spirituality. But the one classic which gives the full flavour of the movement is the *Imitation of Christ* of Thomas à Kempis. This work came to exist in 700 MS Sin a few years, has been translated into 95 languages and in 3000 editions. Its great virtues are obvious: it is short and succinct, and its lapidary sentences and short paragraphs are admirably suited to meditation. The *Imitation of Christ* is an apt title, for it is concerned with devotion to Christ and its emphasis is on him as 'The Christian's Pattern' (a seventeenth-century title for the work). But the little book does not invite or deserve the kind of criticism levelled at this type of piety by Lutherans, that it is set under the sign of the law, and suggests a mere outward imitation. Rather it is concerned with the life of Christ in the soul, in simple dialogue between the Lord and the believer, with plain but profound insight into the selfishness and frailty of the human soul. Somewhere here is the clue to its astonishing survival-value, and the reason why so many diverse Christians from William Law and John Wesley to Edith Cavell and Dietrich Bonhoeffer have turned to it for light and comfort.

The relation between the 'Modern Devotion' and northern humanism has been much debated in recent years, and it must be confessed that there is within it an ascetic and even an anti-intellectualist strain which did not tend to the improvement of learning. It seems to have led to the rigorist austerity of a Jean Standonck at Paris, and the obscurantism of the young 'barbarians' against whom the young Erasmus so vehemently reacted.

NICHOLAS OF CUSA (1401–64). In the thought of this great German churchman, theologian and seer, we see, even more clearly than with Gerson, how the rational scholasticism of earlier centuries came to be supplemented by other traditions, by the Augustinian and Platonic tradition in Pseudo-Dionysius, resting on the mystical learning of Eckhart and Raymond Lull, and able in consequence to turn to the new questions of the widening world of the Renaissance. Here Nicholas of Cusa, firmly rooted in his own age, stands between it and a new world struggling to be born. Like Gerson he was deeply committed to the struggle for reform: and for him too this was no academic matter but the fight through long years against the contradictions of both saints and sinners, in long, wearing and frustrating journeys, and at councils and synods, in the attempt to win back the Bohemians, the Greeks, to communion with the Western Church, and to confront Islam not simply with war and with polemic, but with reasonable understanding. No wonder that in our time, men have come to stress the modernity of his approach. And with all this there was that which came upon him daily, the care of the churches in Germany, and in his own diocese of Brixen, a struggle in an age of growing violence, in which he had to contend with the fierce antagonism of Duke Sigismund and that astonishing fire-breathing female dragon the Abbess Verena von Stuben. His literary, scientific, mathematical and astronomical studies, his philosophic and theological writings, and what we might call his concern for comparative religion need to be set in this context of practical achievement, and of conflicts for which he was perhaps unfitted by temperament.

Born at Cusa on the Moselle, he had thorough training in learning at Heidelberg and Padua, though he took his doctorate in law. At first a moderate Conciliarist, he came to see the Papacy as the only hope of lasting reform and became a valued servant first of Eugenius IV, then of Nicholas V and finally of his friend and fellow humanist, Pius II, in that brief moment when it seemed that the best humanist hopes might be realized and a reform achieved which might, as has been said 'have taken the wind out of the sails of Martin Luther'.

Though indebted to the Augustinian and Dionysian tradition, he developed his own views with astonishing independence. Against a rationalist tradition which would smooth and explain difficulties, Nicholas found a key to truth in recognizing the limitations of human knowledge of divine things, not the ignorance of brutes without understanding but a 'learned ignorance' (*docta Ignorantia*) in the presence of God: he underlines what Thomas and Eckhart and Dionysius had said about the *via negativa* and the *via eminentiae*, the partial analogies of all language and symbols. And he sustains and illustrates his points from his own great knowledge of mathematics and astronomy. God is the one who unites all opposites: there is in Him the true coincidence of all polarities of knowledge, just as God is the deep underlying cause of the unity of the universe and of the nature of man. These antinomies are not played down but accepted in their polarity, but without giving up in despair since God unites all apparent contradictions in his own Triune existence. This gives Nicholas his ecumenical and eirenical faith, for not only the stars in their courses, but God himself is on the side of unity and peace.

These views are startling against the background of the Hussite wars, of the deep antipathies between the Latin and Greek churches and the ominous nearness of Islam represented by Mahomet II the conqueror of Constantinople. Hence the marvel of his great eirenical writings, the *De Concordantia catholica* (1433). concerned with the harmony between body and soul of the Church, Empire and priesthood: his *De Pace fidei,* a Utopian vision of a concord of all faiths, signed in heaven, but summoning men on earth to seek what is true and Christian in all religions of the world, and his *Cribratio Alchemi* (Sifting of the Alchemist) which is not so much a refutation·of the errors of Islam as an invitation to dialogue. Against his humanist background he presents a forward-looking view of truth in relation to science, and the renaissance view of man which his own age could but partially appreciate, though some among the German humanists like Reuchlin and (startlingly) Thomas Müntzer appear to echo his eclectic Platonism. No wonder there are those who nowadays think of Nicholas of Cusa as a kind of fifteenth-century Teilhard de Chardin only now coming into his own.

MARSILIUS FICINO (1439–99) and *Florentine Platonism.* To turn from Nicholas of Cusa, in journeyings oft, to Marsilius Ficino, who never left his native Florence, is to turn to a contrasting personality, yet one who in the realms of the mind and imagination may have been the more daring voyager. A great deal of humanism was concerned with the revival of classical letters, with poetry, history and moralistic enquiry, but Florentine Platonism marks the convergence, as Trinkhaus has suggested, of philosophical and theological humanism in Italy.

Ficino himself, ordained in mature life, was a poet and man of medicine, a lover of music, and of friendship. There is about his circle and its relation to Lorenzo de Medici, something of that dilettantism never far from humanism, as perhaps Ficino's correspondence reveals. But it was his Greek learning which enabled him to become the translator and transmitter of ancient wisdom. Most important were his translations of Plato – the lovely bust of him at Florence shows him strumming a volume of Plato like a lyre. These were followed by important Neoplatonic writings and an edition of Dionysius. Of seminal influence was his publication of the writings of Hermes Trismegistus, whom his age took to be an ancient Egyptian sage whose teachings were older than Moses. Henceforth the Hermetic writings haunt Platonist writings until the time of Thomas Vaughan and the Cambridge Platonists. Ficino's most famous work was his defence of the immortality of the soul. It was the work of Ficino and his friend Pico della

Mirandola (1463–94) to express the Renaissance view of the indelible image of God in man, as in Mirandola's remarkable tract *Of the Dignity of Man*. To Ficino's mastery of Greek, the younger genius brought Hebrew and oriental study, and added to Platonic, Neoplatonic and Egyptian mysticism the speculations of the Jewish Cabbala. In a way perhaps only superficially similar to Nicholas of Cusa, Ficino and Mirandola sought clues to a primitive religion more ancient than Judaism and Christianity, a fundamental and reconciling point of unity behind all faiths, though they never denied the authenticity and uniqueness of the Christian revelation. There is an element in their thinking which edges off into the late medieval and renaissance underworld of magic, alchemy, astrology. Ficino believed in and practised white magic, as his use of the Orphic songs reveals. These diverse impulses had influence on northern humanism. Johannes Trithemius (1462–1516), though as a historian and book collector he is closer to the south German humanism of Celtis and Wimpfeling, shared a taste for daring speculation in the realm of white magic and in the mysteries of numerology. Reuchlin was a devoted Cabbalist whose interests passed to Osiander the Reformer of Nuremberg, while in England John Colet and in France Lefèvre of Étaples were immersed in the Pseudo-Dionysian writings. Erasmus, rather significantly, had no sympathy with this side of the Platonist revival, beyond some early dabbling in the mystical content of Egyptian hieroglyphs.

Fifteenth-century Scholasticism

While modern scholarship in the work of Ritter, Grabmann, Vignaux, Bohner and Oberman has modified the view of late scholasticism as a time of disintegration, there were causes, as we have noted, for the apparent eclectism whereby Nominalists and Realists were affected by cross-currents of Augustinian, Platonic thought or by mystical religion. There is evidence to support Lortz's view of an age dogmatically marked by 'Unklarheit' – an absence of definition, an ambivalence, as might be seen in Biel's eucharistic treatise with its absence of any real attempt to relate the uniqueness of the Cross to the repeated sacrifices of the Mass. But there is evidence to support the attacks by Erasmus and by Luther on sophistry and hair-splitting and the sectarian in-fighting to which Gerson had earlier referred. The great quarrel at Louvain (1465–75) concerning 'future contingents' not only set the University in uproar but penetrated to Rome on the one hand and even more devastatingly to Paris where Louis XI banned the Nominalists in 1473.

There are three scholastic theologians who have received perhaps more attention than they deserve (Bartholomew of Usingen and John Paltz may one day be seen as more interesting thinkers) by reason of Ullmann's famous study of them as *Reformers before the Reformation* [E. Tr. (1885)].

John of Wesel (c. 1400–81) attracts attention because he was a man of learning (D.D. Erfurt, 1456) and for a short time a Professor at Basle. He got into trouble, perhaps because he discussed in the pulpit matters which had he kept them to the schools might not have led to danger, as when he attacked Indulgences and the theology of the 'Filioque' clause (see p. 237).

In 1497 he fell among inquisitors and suffered the worst fate of all for a medieval heretic, a recantation followed by perpetual imprisonment until his death, which mercifully soon followed. *John Pupper of Goch* (d. 1475) was a secular priest who died as Rector of a Convent of Augustinian sisters at Sluis near Malines. He seems to have been a Nominalist theologian, with some Augustinian stresses. He gave high place to the authority of scripture and to the authority of the church only in so far as it expressed scriptural truth. He attacked monastic vows and the distinction between precepts and counsels. Augustinian perhaps is his teaching about man's acceptance by God as conditioned only by God's sovereign freedom, and perhaps his adherence to the doctrine of the ultimate fruition of God. Negatively he attacked the teaching of Thomas Aquinas about merit. He seems to have had no direct connection with the Brothers of the Common Life (R. R. Post).

Wessel Gansfort is the most impressive of the three. He was a layman and both in his own schooling and in his residence in their hostels came into close contact with the Brothers of the Common Life, while at the end of his life he returned to them and to the cultivation of the 'Modern Devotion'. He studied in Cologne, Heidelberg and Paris and spent some time in Italy. He was learned in medicine and in the sacred languages – if he anticipates anybody it is not Luther but Vadianus, the humanist doctor of St. Gall. He began as a realist but left the *via antiqua* for Nominalism, and then developed in the Gersonian way a growing sense of the importance of the life of contemplation. He showed himself severely critical of high papalist claims of indulgences, and of those who laid too great stress on the objectivity of sacramental teaching. He retired to Agnetenberg (1477–82) under the protection of the Bishop David of Utrecht. He influenced Jan Mombaer, and some of his writings (edited as the *Farrago* (1522) with a preface by Luther) had repercussions in the early days of the Reformation.

GABRIEL BIEL (c. 1420–95) is a more considerable figure than the three so-called 'reformers before the Reformation', a man of great learning if of limited genius, who combined his scholasticism with a career of pastoral care and preaching. Unlike Wesel, Pupper and Gansfort he was strongly Papalist and in the struggle between Pius II and Diether of Mainz he supported papal authority which he expounded in his *Defensorium Obedientiae Apostolicum* (1462). He was born in Speyer and went to Heidelberg, Erfurt and Cologne, ending as Professor at the new south German University of Tübingen. In 1468 he became Provost of the house of the Brothers of the Common Life at Butzbach and ended his days in another house of the order at Tübingen. In him the 'Modern Devotion' marked its deepest penetration into Germany and its most distinguished convert. His scholastic thinking is within the frame of late medieval spirituality (whether 'mystical' is a right word to use of him seems doubtful). His exposition of the Canon of the Mass was a famous text-book (Luther was trained on it) but most of it is gathered from other sources and it is of little originality. Similarly his 'Commentary on the Sentences' is rather a *Collectorium* of Ockhamist ideas. His preaching is important, for he took its theology very seriously and rated it more highly than attendance at Mass. There is a strong Mariological interest in his preaching. While, as a good Ockhamist' he stressed the liberty of God and the freedom of man and made full use of the dialectic of the 'Potestas absoluta' and 'Potestas ordinata' (see Index s.v.) he also made much of the doctrine of merit and the need for man to do what in him lies 'Facere quod in se est'. Oberman judges his thoughts to be semi-Pelagian and Luther vehemently attacked this element in Biel. But one must be careful about the word 'Pelagian' which easily becomes anachronistic in discussions about the later Middle Ages. In Peter of Auriol it seems to have stood for the view that a man can have rights over and against God (Vignaux); but often when a writer seems outrageously Pelagian he has a way of standing everything upon its head and ascribing all to grace. In Biel, too, much is made of the tension between fear and love, between the 'justitia' and the 'bonitas' and 'misericordia' of God which would some day be a stumbling-block to the young Luther. Among lesser figures in the half-century before Luther must be included Johannes Staupitz, in whom Augustinian elements are joined with a 'theologia crucis', linked with Tauler and the German mystical tradition.

ERASMUS (1469–1536), the greatest figure in the northern Renaissance, is an indispensable link between the overlapping themes of humanism and reformation, but in what sense he is important for the historian of doctrine is a complex problem, raised acutely in the recent fifth-centenary celebrations, which as distinct from earlier studies (Allen, Renaudet, Huizinga) probe the question of his theological status. The older views can still be accepted: he was an outspoken critic of the contemporary Church, as vehement in his way as Hutten or Rubeanus, and he did not fear to attack individual Popes (like Julius II, 'his most intimate enemy') for the obvious contrast between their life-style and that of the apostles. Yet he accepted the authority of the Church while stressing (with his friend Sir Thomas More) the importance of the 'communis sensus fidelium' – 'the consensus of the faithful'. But in matters where the church had not declared its mind Erasmus held it right to suspend judgment and even to follow in the path of the sceptics. He attacked, with Colet and More, that excessive legalism in late-medieval religion which Burnet called 'superannuated Judaism'. His combination of 'good' with 'sacred' letters was linked on the one hand with Italian humanism and on the other with the 'Modern Devotion'. He disliked Hebrew and concentrated on Greek and on New Testament studies, and to some extent filled his ethics with the best classical moralism. He was not only indebted to Platonism (this may have been exaggerated) but also to Stoicism and Epicureanism; and with Thomas More he shared a passion for Lucian. He is plainly in the Italian humanist tradition with its ideals of 'eruditio' and 'humanitas'. Béné has shown how deeply he was indebted to Augustine's *De Doctrina Christiana* and how he followed him in his discrimination of the extent to which Christians might 'spoil the Egyptians' of classical culture.

About his relation to the 'Modern Devotion' the last word has not yet been said. He hated the obscurantism of some of his fellow Augustinians who decried poetry and classical learning, or indeed any learning at all, and he had little sympathy with ascetic rigorism. Yet in his search for a simpler religion, his turning to the scriptures and above all to the 'philosophy of Christ' in the gospels and epistles, he is surely linked with the 'Modern Devotion'. There is some evidence that he never troubled to master scholastic teaching, and he certainly attacked the sophistries of the Scotists as heartily as Tyndale or Luther. But this 'philosophy of Christ', as he developed it from the time of his seminal tract the *Enchiridion* (1503) and in a series of edifying tracts, but above all in his New Testament manifestoes – his Prefaces to the New Testament (1516 and 1519) and his Letter to Volzius (1518), seeing it as a re-statement of the Christian religion as a divine life, is serious theology of first importance. Grounded on the humanist principles of Valla which sought the importance of a scriptural text in its strictly grammatical and philological context, he proceeded to seek a better Greek text of the New Testament and on its basis a new Latin version. To this he added a noble plea for the 'open Bible' and indicated a new method of biblical and theological study which was to be taken up by Melanchthon and by the reformed theologians Musculus, Bullinger and Calvin.

All this certainly gives Erasmus the status of a New Testament theologian. To this must be added the impact of the massive series of editions of the Fathers of West and East: if at the end he left the chores of editing to others, his was the over-all responsibility, and we must never underrate the importance of the availability for scholars of these new printed texts, let alone the explosive character of some of them such as the edition of Tertullian by Beatus Rhenanus and Erasmus's own publication of Origen. Beyond this it would be perilous to claim Erasmus as a considerable theologian. Those who have thought to find theological depth in him have in recent years concentrated on isolated texts, the *Enchiridion*, the New Testament prefaces, the Letter to Volzius. E. W. Kohls, who sees Erasmus as steeped in St. Thomas, and relying on that broad sweep of the plan of redemption as 'exitus-reditus' (all things 'going out from' God and 'returning to' God) which had been expounded from Erigena onwards – seems to read much into Erasmus and perhaps to misconceive what was really simply the acceptance by Erasmus of the common catholic tradition. Manfred Hofmann gives to Erasmus an epistemology of amazing depth, 'a philosophic system concentrated in Christology, of encyclopaedic breadth': but again one wonders if this is really Erasmus. Most persuasive of all G. Chantraine in his beautiful study of *Mystère et philosophie du Christ selon Érasme* (1971) shows that Erasmus certainly had a religion, and a spirituality of depth, but even he has to say that Erasmus 'does not love abstract arguments; he is an artist'. And the writer of the most detailed examination of the sacramental teaching of Erasmus (J. B. Payne) is constrained to make most damaging admissions, as that 'Erasmus is but little aware of the tension between God's love and his wrath, his mercy and his justice, he does not feel the need of Christ as an expiation and satisfaction for our sins'. When he goes on to say that Erasmus shared an 'Origenistic subordinationism about the Person of Christ' but that other facets of his teaching have 'an Antiochian ring', we may wonder how far the word 'theologian' can be applied, though it helps us to understand how in the next decade after Erasmus' death the city of Basle became a city of refuge for those who criticized accepted orthodoxy. It is not, therefore, simply the superficiality of much of his *De libero arbitrio* – hardly offset by the much more impressive second part of his *Hyperaspistes* – that raises doubts about his eminence as a theologian. He was a New Testament and patristic scholar of first-class importance (in the context of his time), and a pioneer in new educational and theological method: a Christian whose spirituality has depth, who can in no way be written off as an educationist whose thought centres in anthropology, but one who gives a central place to mystery and grace. Beyond this he would not seem to compare favourably with the greater schoolmen or the more eminent Reformers, or deserve to rank among those who have touched the great issues of Christian doctrine at the point of depth, from Augustine and St. Thomas to Calvin and Karl Barth.

A Note on Theology in the Christian East: the Fifteenth to Seventeenth Centuries

Kallistos Ware

A Note on Theology in the Christian East: the Fifteenth to Seventeenth Centuries

KALLISTOS WARE

Greek religious thought during the Turkish period – between the fall of Constantinople in 1453 and the outbreak of the Greek War of Independence in 1821 – is marked by two opposite tendencies: on the one hand an extreme conservatism, and on the other a movement towards westernization, either in a Roman Catholic or a Protestant direction. These two characteristics may seem at first sight contradictory, but both are easily intelligible in view of the situation which Orthodox Christendom occupied under the Turks.

(1) *Conservatism.* The Turkish period was not a happy era for the Greek Church. Oppressed as they were under Muslim masters, treated always as second-class citizens and kept in a position of social inferiority, Greek Christians naturally felt themselves on the defensive and developed a 'siege' mentality. Their great aim was survival – to keep things going in the hope of better days to come. They clung with marvellous tenacity to their Byzantine inheritance, but they had little possibility to develop that inheritance creatively. The vitality and originality which Greek theology displayed as late as the fourteenth century in the time of Palamas – and even in the mid-fifteenth century with such a writer as George Scholarios – disappeared almost entirely as the fifteenth century drew to a close. The 'ossification', which some historians unjustly attribute to the later Byzantine era, did indeed become a mark of Greek religious thought in the Turkish period. Theology became, in a way that it had not been in the eleventh or fourteenth century, a matter of repeating accepted formulae and defending entrenched positions. The prevailing outlook of unyielding traditionalism is well expressed by Patriarch Jeremias II of Constantinople in 1590: 'It is not the practice of our Church to innovate in any way whatsoever, whereas the Western Church innovates unceasingly . . . We do not dare to remove from the ancient books a single "jot or tittle", as the saying goes. So we were taught and such is our purpose – to obey and to be subject to those who went before us.' This conservatism had one great advantage: at least the Patristic tradition of the Christian east was never entirely forgotten, even though it was understood in an unduly narrow and inflexible manner.

(2) *Westernization.* 'Ossification', however, is but one side of the picture. Turkish rule had a second and somewhat different effect on Greek religious thinking. The prevailing poverty of the Greek world, the lack of libraries and of centres of scholarship, forced many Greeks to travel to the west for their university studies; and so they received their theological training from Catholic or Protestant masters. This background, Roman or Reformed, as

the case might be, was usually apparent in their writings: even when they strove to defend the Orthodox faith against western propaganda, they tended to use western types of argument and to apply western categories and terminology, foreign to that tradition of Patristic and Byzantine thought which was properly their own. In this way Greek theology underwent a kind of 'pseudomorphosis', being forced into alien moulds; and Greek theologians of the Turkish period can be divided into two main classes, the 'Latinizers' and the 'Protestantizers'. Many of them were deliberately eclectic, using whatever came most readily to hand – Roman arguments against the Reformers and Protestant arguments against Rome. In such a situation there was a real danger that the distinctive mentality of the Orthodox east might be lost or at any rate obscured. In this way, beneath an outward appearance of rigid traditionalism, Orthodoxy was steadily infiltrated by influences from the west.

The most important period for Greek theology of the post-Byzantine era was the hundred years between 1573 and 1672. During these ten decades Orthodoxy was brought face to face with the forces of the Reformation and Counter-Reformation, and was compelled to define its attitude towards the new religious situation that had arisen in the west. The confrontation occurred in three main stages:

(a) *Jeremias II and the Lutherans.* From the early days of the Reformation, the Lutherans looked to Orthodoxy for support in their conflict with Rome. 'The Orthodox Christians have the same faith as ourselves,' declared Luther in 1520, 'they baptize as we do, they live as we do.' The first serious attempt by the Lutherans at a theological 'dialogue' with the east was in 1573, when a group of scholars from Tübingen visited Constantinople; and after their return home these Tübingen theologians maintained an important correspondence with Patriarch Jeremias II during the years 1574–81. Among the topics discussed were the relations between grace and free will, between Scripture and Tradition, the nature of the sacraments – especially the eucharist and the priesthood – and the practice of praying for the dead and invoking the intercessions of the saints. The Lutherans evidently hoped to initiate some kind of reformation among the Greeks, but in this they were not successful. In his answers Jeremias adhered carefully to the traditional Orthodox teaching, without inclining either in a Protestant or a Roman direction.

(b) *Cyril Lukaris and the Calvinists.* The second important exchange between Orthodoxy and Protestantism occurred some fifty years later, when Cyril Lukaris was Patriarch of Constantinople (1621–38). Whereas Patriarch Jeremias had remained firmly loyal to the accepted Orthodox teaching, Cyril was more adventurous. Under Calvinist influence he composed – or at any rate appended his signature to – a *Confession of Faith*, published at Geneva in 1629. In this he adopted the standard Calvinist teaching upon predestination and election, and there is little to distinguish his doctrine of the Church and the sacraments from that of Protestantism. He states that the witness of Scripture is far higher than that of the Church (i.e., of the Ecumenical Councils); he rejects belief in the Church's infallibility, and stresses its invisible rather than its visible aspect; he teaches that there are two sacraments, not seven; he rejects transubstantiation, stating that Christ's presence in the eucharist is 'spiritual' only.

(c) *The Latinizing reaction.* Cyril Lukaris is the extreme example of a Greek 'Protestantizer'. Although he had some followers, his viewpoint was clearly unacceptable to the Orthodox world at large. His *Confession* was condemned by no less than six Orthodox councils between 1638 and 1691, the most important of these being the Councils of Jassy (1642) and of Jerusalem (1672). In direct reaction to Cyril, two other Orthodox hierarchs wrote *Confessions* of their own: Peter of Moghila, Metropolitan of Kiev (whose *Orthodox Confession* was ratified, after extensive modifications, at Jassy in 1642); and Patriarch Dositheus of Jerusalem (whose *Confession* was adopted at Jerusalem in 1672). Peter and Dositheus are the most notable of the Orthodox 'Latinizers': both, for example, employed the term 'transubstantiation',[1] and when discussing the state of the departed both approach close to the Latin notion of purgatory. But in their 'Latinism' they were far less radical than was Cyril Lukaris in his Calvinism. Cyril is a Protestant in the *substance* of his thought; Peter of Moghila and Dositheus are Latin in *method* and *terminology*, but Orthodox in their basic convictions.

The seventeenth century, while not a period in which Orthodox theology is to be seen at its best, possesses none the less a considerable importance for the history of doctrine in the Christian east. The Reformation controversies raised problems about the sacraments, and about the nature and authority of the Church, which neither the Ecumenical Councils nor the Church of the later Byzantine Empire had been required to face. It was important for Orthodoxy to clarify its teaching on these matters and to define its position in relation to the Protestant-Catholic debate. This was the task which the Councils of Jassy and Jerusalem, for all their shortcomings, managed to fulfil.

---

[1] The first Greek theologian to employ this term seems to have been George Scholarios in the fifteenth century. It reappears in the writings of Meletios Pigas and Gabriel Severus at the end of the sixteenth century and thereafter becomes frequent in Orthodox authors. But there were always some Orthodox theologians who deliberately avoided its use.

Martin Luther

Benjamin Drewery

Martin Luther

Introduction

BENJAMIN DREWERY

The history of Christian doctrine has been marked by a select succession of master-minds – S. Paul, Origen, Augustine, Aquinas – who have not only stamped their personal seal on the crises and advances of their day, but continue to fertilize and fructify the course of all subsequent theology. To this exalted company, beyond cavil, belongs Martin Luther. Protestantism in all its fissiparous manifestations has for nearly five centuries drawn on him as its earthly fountain-head, and the twentieth century has witnessed the overflowing of the Lutheran streams into the pasturage of Catholicism and even of Orthodoxy. Yet the exposition and evaluation of Luther's theology remains a matter of almost unparalleled complexity.

First, there is the sheer bulk of his writings; the great Weimar Edition, begun in 1883, approaches its completion in nearly sixty vast volumes. Then there is the unfamiliarity of his language and thought-forms, especially to the English-speaking. This is intensified by his complex historical setting; he was not so much *zwischen den Zeiten* as one who spans like no other the dying and the rising of two worlds. Nor does his temperament and character simplify the quest; tempestuous, prophetic, profoundly learned yet totally committed to the human drama, appealing and exasperating, argumentative, contradictory, ironical, with something of the mystic and much of the party manager, a man of the people and supremely a man of God – the last thing Luther intended was to make life easy for later systematic theologians. The very process of his development – the late medieval monk, the arch-rebel of the religious revolution, the matured father-figure of the Reformation – makes systematic analysis of his thought a hazardous and at times an almost despairing venture. To all this must be added the immense renascence of modern Luther-scholarship, beginning in Germany with Karl Holl and built up on the Continent and in Scandinavia into such a gigantic monument of learning that hardly a sentence can be written on Luther which some monograph or volume could not be found to have anticipated, modified or disproved.

'The phenomenon of the theology of Luther, to which one might give an altogether different name, is instructive enough for the dangers which threaten an "irregular dogmatics". Yet – it admitted of incorporation into the school-theology of Melanchthon and Calvin and their successors, and all that may have been lost in the process should not preclude acknowledgement that it was necessary.' Karl Barth is here (C.D. I/1, 32of.) setting out his own programme of 'regular dogmatics'; and his warning that such a discipline 'sleeps through' the existence of other forms of theology at its peril is illustrated by his own more numerous citations of Luther than of Calvin himself. Yet his claim is valid. If Luther admitted of no incorporation into a formulated theology – if he made no contribution even to a scientific dogmatics – this would undermine his status not only as a theologian but as prophet, preacher, scholar, 'religious genius' and everything else that has been claimed for him. In all these capacities he was consciously seeking or expounding *truth* – truth about God, man, salvation; and in the end the truth is one. The unity, the wholeness, the reality of the Christian faith are presuppositions that Luther never for one moment abandoned.

Luther's Theology in the Making

Luther was born in 1483 at Eisleben in Saxony. He grew up in Mansfeld where his father made money as a miner and became a local councillor. He was educated at the Cathedral School at Magdeburg, where he would (significantly) be taught by the famous 'brethren of the Common Life'; later at Eisenach, and from 1501 at Erfurt University, where he graduated in Arts. The law was then the obvious profession for a young man of his gifts, and his father was deeply angered when he entered the house of the Eremetical Order of St. Augustine at Erfurt (1505). Ordained priest in 1507, he was selected for advanced theological study at the new University of Wittenberg. In 1509 he was appointed lecturer in the Arts Faculty, and in spite of his own preference for theology he was apportioned the *Nicomachean Ethics* of Aristotle. In 1510 he was sent to Rome on business of his Order, and was shocked and disillusioned by the cynical professionalism and degrading luxury of the clergy and rulers. In 1512 he took his D.D., and succeeded Staupitz as Professor of Biblical Theology. Few things are more significant, either for him or for the whole history of Protestantism, than that Luther was a Professor of Biblical Theology from a date some years before his 'break-through' to the day of his death.

It was during his years as a monk that Luther underwent the experiences of mind and conscience that were to presage the Protestant revolution and the fine flowering of his theology. His novitiate had gone well, but Luther was not a man to do things by halves. The challenge of monasticism was nothing less than Christian perfection; and Luther had been brought up in a home where God was primarily the judge, and parental discipline laid on him that fear of God which was the beginning of wisdom. His conscience now became afflicted with sombre brooding at his own failures to satisfy the Divine imperative; his own description of that helpless remorse and futile struggling was *Anfechtung*, a word for which in Luther's case (as for that 'dark night of the soul' through which so many Christian saints have passed) a mere psychological evaluation reaches no further than the symptoms. At its heart lay Luther's ever-deepening apprehension of God the Righteous, and if there is one master-key to the whole of his theology it is his own thousandfold repeated *coram Deo* ('in God's presence', 'by God's standards'). 'Had not God come when the cool of the day arrived, Adam and Eve would never have noticed their sin. But when He came, they crept away –'

Theologically, Luther had been initiated at Erfurt into Nominalism, especially by the treatises of the Occamist Gabriel Biel (ob. 1495); and the Nominalist emphases on the sovereign freedom of God alongside the efficacy of the human will served to intensify rather than mitigate his own religious tribulations. The internal controversies of Nominalism found in Luther no whole-hearted partisan, but the tradition of Duns Scotus seems to have attracted him less than that of Occam, with his stress on God's simplicity of being and his use of the distinction between God's *potestas absoluta* (what God can and could do) and *potestas ordinata* (what God has in fact chosen to do), which opened the way to a tempering of God's arbitrary omnipotence by the liberty of divine mercy. But at Wittenberg this controversy became overlaid by the wider and deeper battle between scholasticism as a whole and the new humanism. The *Ad Fontes* ('Back to the Sources!') of the Renaissance, with its rediscovery of the fresh springs of classical antiquity, took its Christian shape, through men like Reuchlin and supremely Erasmus of Rotterdam, in a return to the Bible and the early Fathers, with a philosophical perspective marked by a revival of Platonism as against the Aristotelianism which, though or course in origin as 'classical' as its rival, had entered medieval Christendom centuries earlier through alien and suspect intermediaries. Philosophically, as Barth says (C.D. I/2.728), while the medieval scholastics – and the post-reformation Protestant scholastics – were unconcealed Aristotelians, Luther and Calvin were equally clearly Platonists, Luther more of the neo-Platonist, Calvin more the classical.

The works of Gabriel Biel included a commentary on the Sentences of Peter Lombard, which had been for centuries a kind of theological textbook; and for the Master of the Sentences, who significantly had antedated the invasion of Aristotelianism and its Christianized elaboration in Albert the Great and Thomas Aquinas, Luther had a life-long regard. But throughout the years at Erfurt and early Wittenberg the lines of development and controversy were opening the way to a greater name – Augustine, whom Luther began to explore with passionate enthusiasm, and who above all encouraged him to cut through the 'rancid rules of the logicians' to the ultimate authority of the Bible.

Luther's 'breakthrough', as it is called (although its date and nature remain the subject of learned controversy) can perhaps be described as the culmination and undermining of all his tribulations – spiritual and theological – by the identification and re-interpretation of the one dominant concept of the Righteousness of God. In perhaps every major historical 'conversion' – St. Paul, Luther, Wesley – it is possible to accuse the 'convert' of unfairness, conscious or unconscious, to the mentors, predecessors and traditions from which he claimed emancipation. The present century has duly witnessed from the Catholic scholar Denifle a massive attack launched on Luther at this very point, and still more learned rejoinders from Karl Holl and his school. What is hardly in doubt is that for Luther himself the spiritual pilgrimage through Nominalism and Medievalism in general to Augustine and Scripture had brought him to the ultimate *scandalon*, and that from his 'breakthrough', whatever its relation to the so-called *Türmererlebnis* (his 'experience in the tower' of the monastery at Wittenberg), there arose a Christian renascence which is still far from exhausted, and which falls into line with the road to Damascus and with Aldersgate

Street. The problem of the date of the breakthrough is not merely academic, but involves the interpretation of his own writings from 1513 to 1519 and its reconciliation with the evidence of his own autobiographical fragment of 1545.

From Staupitz Luther had garnered much that was now ripening for the harvest. Although Staupitz has been claimed as a herald of the Reformation, he remained himself a Catholic, and not in name only: he never broke through the theological presuppositions of merit and of spiritual discipline as an 'imitation' of Christ. Yet Luther testifies that it was through Staupitz that 'the light of the Gospel began first to shine out of the darkness of the heart'. Staupitz had fostered his concentration on Biblical study in depth; he had led him from Nominalism to the Augustinian emphasis on grace; he had met Luther's time-honoured dismay at the doctrines of predestination by an assurance which startlingly adumbrates the distinctive re-appraisal of the doctrine by Karl Barth: 'In the wounds of Jesus is predestination understood and found, and nowhere else.' He had above all ('as a messenger from heaven') brought Luther a liberating comprehension of the meaning of *penitence*. It was here that the conventional Latin translation of μετανοεῖν by *poenitentiam agere* had wrought such mischief, by bringing (originally no doubt unintentionally) overtones of human *works* of penitence, *acts* of 'satisfaction', which came to find ritual expression in the Sacrament of Penance and tended to obscure the motivating and empowering love of God. If 'penitence' means doing one's stint by way of reparation, then *coram Deo* it is self-defeating. If (as Staupitz showed Luther) it means a total change of mind, affections, heart, then here is truly a 'new creation' which begins and ends, like the creation of the universe, with the mercy, love, grace of God. Hence do the 'very commands of God grow sweet', and the way is open for the rediscovery of the Biblical revelation of God the Righteous.

This – the real 'breakthrough' – is best recounted in Luther's own words. 'I had been wondrously eager to understand Paul in the Epistle to the Romans, but hitherto I had been held up – by one word: "the righteousness of God is revealed in (the Gospel)" – as if it were not enough that miserable sinners, eternally ruined by original sin, should be crushed – through the law of the Ten Commandments, but that God through the Gospel must add sorrow to sorrow, and even through the Gospel bring his righteousness and wrath to bear on us. – At last, as I meditated day and night, – I turned my attention to the connection of the words – "The righteousness of God is revealed, as it is written: the righteous shall live by faith", and I began to understand that the righteousness of God is the righteousness in which a just man lives by the gift of God, in other words by faith, and that what Paul means is this: the righteousness of God, revealed in the Gospel, is *passive*, in other words that by which the merciful God justifies us through faith –. There and then the whole face of Scripture was changed; I ran through the Scriptures as memory served, and collected the same analogy in other words: *opus Dei* – that which God works in us; *virtus Dei* – that by which God makes us strong; *sapientia Dei* – that by which He makes us wise; and so the fortitude, salvation, glory of God.' Luther's specific problem must not be confused with the familiar and mistaken antithesis between the 'righteous God' of the Old Testament Law and the 'loving God' of the New

Testament Gospel. The *justitia Dei* which had baffled him was revealed equally by Law and Gospel, as was the liberating recovery of its true significance.

The breakthrough of the Reformation as an event of world-history is usually dated from the nailing of Luther's 95 Theses to the door of the Castle Church of Wittenberg on October 31st, 1517. Luther's theology is still, however, in the making. If we take the Theses along with the slightly earlier 97 against the Scholastics, the *Explanations* of the 95 and the *Theses* and *Proofs* for the Heidelberg Disputation of the next year, and set them in the context of the New Testament lectures (*Romans* 1515–16, *Galatians* 1516–17, *Hebrews* 1517–18) which Luther was delivering in these years of theological ferment, we shall see the directions into which Luther's personal breakthrough was leading him.

(1) The 95 Theses were primarily an attack on the current theory and practice of *Indulgences*. An Indulgence was strictly the commuting of the temporal punishment for sin by an act of satisfaction prescribed by the Church – that is, the substitution of one ecclesiastical penalty for another. In earlier times the penance, for example, of long-term fasting for man-slaughter could be replaced by enlistment for a Crusade. Almost inevitably the practice of financial commutation crept in, especially as growing financial embarrassments afflicted the Papacy. The Bull *Unigenitus* of Clement VI (1343) set out a theory of Indulgences based on the Papal claim to have acquired 'a great treasure (of redemption) for the Church militant' through Peter and his successors, which was constantly swollen by the merits of the Virgin, the elect, and the newly redeemed. Indulgences drawn on this treasury were extended by Pope Sixtus IV in his Bull *Salvator Noster* (1476) to the souls in purgatory; money payments by the living could shorten or terminate their time in this condition. Vital distinctions – between guilt and penalty, penitence and satisfaction, forgiveness and indulgence – had by Luther's time become blurred, and the whole *sacrum negotium* of financial commutation (even for such laudable aims as the building of St. Peter's) a crying scandal. Moralists and theologians were already protesting, and some German state authorities taking preventive action.

Luther's immediate concern in the Theses was not to deny but to circumscribe the authority of Pope and priest; remission or commutation, he insisted, was limited to penalties the Church itself had imposed. The guilt of sin and its forgiveness were reserved for the judgement of God, and the discretion left to His ministers was declaratory only. The outward sign – the submission of penance – while necessary, is nothing without inward penitence, and this penitence embraces the whole lives of believers. Moreover, the penitential canons apply only to the living; the real penalty of purgatory is the fear springing from consciousness of guilt in a dying man. The Papal power is not plenary – there is no 'power of the keys' – but intercessory; and true penitence properly understood (that is, *coram Deo*) is a privilege: 'true contrition seeks out and loves to pay the penalties of sin, whereas Indulgences relax the penalties and make men resent them.'

(2) Luther's reaction against scholasticism and Indulgences was serving

to distil from his own theological ferment a number of themes, antitheses, catchwords that his N.T. commentaries were simultaneously exploring and expanding into his matured theology of *1520* onwards. His deepening knowledge of Greek and Hebrew, his concentration on Augustine and St. Paul, are serving not merely to activate protest against current ecclesiastical abuses and theological infelicities, but to undermine the whole medieval structure of human merit and reward. As the Righteousness of God, newly interpreted, dominates more and more the theological landscape, any lingering validity of man's own 'works' gives way to a whole complex of associations centring on 'grace' and 'faith', the twin watchwords of the presence alike of the Risen Christ and the Holy Spirit in the life of the believer.

We find in antithesis 'God hidden'/'God revealed'; Christ's 'strange work'/ His 'proper work'; Law/Gospel; grace/nature; the bondage of the sinful will/ cheerful and un-selfregarding Christian obedience. God wills to save us, not by our own (*domesticam*) righteousness, but by a righteousness from without (*extrinsecam, alienam*), coming from heaven. Faith is not a human 'good work' but the obverse of grace, contrasting not with reason but with *sensus* ('wisdom of the flesh', self-confidence). Famous Lutheran phrases are now heard – *simul peccator et justus; semper peccator, semper penitens, semper justus;* 'the saints are inwardly always sinners and outwardly always justified'. We are given the dynamic progression from self-accusation through humility to faith. Above all there resounds the characteristic Lutheran 'alone' – *sola fide, sola misericordia, solo evangelio, sola gratia, per Christum solum.* In this context the Law ceases to be merely ceremonial or a passing phase in God's dispensation, and is seen as every demand made on the outward man which does not reach to the agreement of his will, just as 'concupiscence' is no longer the mere lusts of the flesh but the total inward-orientation of the self in its egoistic rebellion against God. Everything – including anthropology – is *coram Deo*, and we meet with the Lutheran use of *larva* ('mask', 'veil') for the face that is turned to the world, as contrasted with the inner self – the heart – which is seen by God. It is the Holy Spirit which converts faith from a mere *fides historica* or even a dogmatic structure into the very presence of Christ, and hence 'faith is indivisible'.

(3) But above all in these years there emerges the seminal Lutheran 'theology of the Cross'. The modern English reader, mindful of his own immediate theological ancestry, might presume an antithesis with 'theology of the Incarnation'. But Luther's antithesis is 'theology of Glory', by which he means the vain and presumptuous endeavour to penetrate directly to the 'naked majesty of God' either through the scholastic methods of inferential and speculative reason or through the *anagogé* – the 'ecstatic ascent' – of mysticism. The true knowledge of God is to be found only in the theology of the Cross, God's chosen way of self-revelation to the blinded vision, the stunted reason and the bruised conscience of man. 'The Cross alone is our theology'; 'the Cross proves everything'; 'the Cross of Christ meets us everywhere in the Scriptures'. Luther was never to outgrow these central affirmations, which were the real legacy of these formative years of

storm and stress, and which none of his opponents, with the possible exception of Cardinal Cajetan, came near to appreciating.

Scholastic speculation on the attributes of God, with its well-trodden pathways of the *analogia entis* and the *via negativa* (see Index s.vv.), was open from Luther's standpoint to fatal objections. From one aspect it led to a mere deification of sinful humanity. If man makes his own way to God, the God he attains is but himself writ large. From another, its *telos* ('goal') could only be a God who was a complex of abstract metaphysical concepts, progressively apprehensible by the increasingly rarefied subtleties of human intelligence. Such may well have been the ideal of Aristotle. Far different was the God of the Bible. If its 'ethical monotheism' is to be taken seriously, it implies of necessity, first, a God whose transcendence is apprehensible only through His own self-disclosure, and secondly, a God whose concern is not with the ethically neutral human intelligence in isolation, but with man in his totality, and hence the 'knowledge' so imparted broadens into that enlightenment of reason, conscience and will which can only be called 'salvation'. On both these grounds, the gap – or rather the abyss – between the infinite qualitative remoteness of God and the exceeding sinfulness of the sinner can only be bridged by a Mediator who in Himself embodies the glory of God accommodated to our suffering humanity, which indeed He shares – and shares to the lowest possible depths of its bitterness and desolation. Our sin and ignorance may bring us low enough in the scale of suffering and degradation; they are unlikely to bring us lower than the Cross – and Christ has been there. 'God is not to be found save in the Cross', and like Paul, Luther was determined to know nothing save Jesus Christ and Him crucified.

The mystical *anagogé* – the other form of the 'Theology of Glory' – raises the perplexing question of Luther's relation to Christian mysticism. In this matter he shows an ambivalence foreshadowing in some respects that of John Wesley, who could reverence the great Christian mystics while at the same time exercising an unsparing blue-pencil on mystical passages in his brother's finest hymns. Wesley's concern was the apparent by-passing by mystical 'quietism' of Church and sacraments; Luther's, more fundamentally, of Christ and His Cross. The overt villain of the piece was (pseudo)-Dionysius; but one can trace here a tradition going back at least to Origen. Origen's copiousness of thought and language does not make for systematic consistency; but in some moods at any rate he can suggest that the words of *I Cor.* 2.6f. were 'spoken to those who had no need of apprehending the Word of God in so far as He was made flesh, but in His capacity of Wisdom "hidden in a mystery" ' (Hom. Exod. XII.4). The incarnate and crucified Saviour is correlated with 'imperfect knowledge', whereas the Holy Spirit brings 'perfect wisdom' to the sanctified. The Cross is perhaps not so much by-passed as made obsolete; mere faith has been left behind, lost in Wisdom and no longer even relevant.

This was the real root of the mystical tradition which Luther was repudiating. Faith for him is never lost in Wisdom but in 'Sight', and not so much lost as transformed into adoration. The Cross of Christ is the eternal focus of a faith which is never outgrown even by the saints, whereas the mystical ascent is a denial of God's providential plan for mankind. 'God will not have thee thus ascend, but He comes to thee and has made a ladder, a way and a bridge to thee. His Son speaks – "This way, brother – keep thine eyes fixed on Me, through My humanity is the way to the Father." ' Or again: 'It is not sufficient for anyone, and it does him no good, to recognize God in His glory and majesty, unless he recognizes Him in the humility and shame of the Cross. Thus God destroys the wisdom of the wise —. So also, in *John* 14, where Philip spoke in the manner of the theology of glory: "Show us the Father." Christ forthwith set aside his flighty thought about seeing God elsewhere and led him to Himself. True theology and the recognition of God are in the crucified Christ.'

So much seems clear; yet the heritage of mysticism, which had contributed so largely to the revival of spirituality in late medieval Germany, was compounded of other elements as well as the *anagogé* of Origen and pseudo-Dionysius. There was, for example, as Professor Rupp has reminded us (*Luther for an Ecumenical Age* ed. Meyer, p. 70), 'an older Thuringian emphasis on the "wounds of Jesus" going back to the Gertrudes and Mechthilds of the 12th century', which brought to bear a mystical influence on some German theologians of our period, and especially on Staupitz. Through him Luther was introduced to Tauler, the fourteenth-century Dominican mystic, in whose sermons (which he annotated) he found adumbrated the theology of the Cross; and the anonymous *Theologia Germanica*, the first printed edition of which Luther supervised during the years of his 'break-through', seemed to him to distil the legitimate essence of Tauler himself. Luther's own theology of the Cross begins to glow with a mystical radiance which probably owes as much to this tradition as to its primary sources in Augustine and St. Paul. 'God's commands grow sweet indeed when we learn to read them not so much in books as in the Wounds of our Blessed Redeemer.' 'It is a great matter to be a Christian man, and to have a life hidden away, not in some place like a hermit, nor in his own heart, though that is an unsearchable depth, but in the invisible God himself, and to live thus in the world, but to feed on that which is never seen, except by way of the Word —'

The theology of the Cross takes up one strand of medieval mysticism while repudiating others. In the end, with Luther as with Wesley, there is something in Christian mysticism he cannot resist – provided that it is a mysticism of the Cross. He could have made his own the peerless words of Charles Wesley which speak for Christian mystics of all the ages –

> 'Ah! show me that happiest place,
> The place of Thy people's abode,
> Where saints in an ecstasy gaze
> And hang on a crucified God.

> 'Tis there I would always abide,
> And never a moment depart,
> Concealed in the cleft of Thy side,
> Eternally held in Thy heart.'

Luther's Matured Theology

1. SOLA FIDE equals SOLA GRATIA equals CHRISTUS

Luther the theologian is conventionally identified with 'Justification by faith', whether to his glory as the champion of Pauline-based Evangelicalism, or to his damnation for the 'heresy of solifidianism'. Four and a half centuries of controversy, often characterized by barren systematization or motivated by what C. H. Dodd taught us to call 'non-theological factors', have tended to degrade what was for Luther the most living and burning of realities into a petrified irrelevance. Leonard Hodgson (*For Faith and Freedom* I, 108ff.) suggests that the confusion is now so profitless that we should cease to speak of Justification by Faith at all. Yet experience – and analogy – suggest otherwise. The turning-point of the Second World War was the Battle of Alamein in 1942. Four years later (we are told) the sand had blown, slowly and inexorably, across the empty battlefield, and there was nothing left but the white crosses and the occasional bedouin camel picking its way through the sunken and rusted mines. (Moorehead, *Montgomery*, p. 141.) Yet after one short generation that same desert puts a fundamental question to the whole material and cultural future of the world – the power-problem of Arab oil. Even so have many of the great Christian 'revivals' of all ages sprung from the renewed and insistent self-assertion of 'Justification by Faith'. The watchwords of twentieth-century theology – 'liberalism', 'theocentricism', 'existentialism', 'eschatology', 'conservative evangelism', 'ecumenism', 'encounter', 'process', even 'secularity', may well have a legitimate source in contemporary 'challenge'; but their abiding relevance to the Christian Gospel can almost be measured by their fidelity to this Lutheran *articulus stantis aut cadentis ecclesiae* – the 'critical clause by which the Church stands or falls'. Nor should the theological dissection of this *articulus*, and the dialectical subtleties to which it necessarily led Luther and (still more) the later 'Protestant scholastics', obscure for one moment the overriding truth that for Luther the very heart of the Gospel is that free, willing, unconstrained, joyful obedience to God which comes from faith and never under the law. 'He who lives in faith and in the Spirit will serve God from the heart, in freedom and gladness, and walk in His ways – ways which he loves, because it is in love and from the depths of his heart that he walks in them.'

The decisive point is that here, par excellence, Luther is thinking *coram Deo*. *Sola fide* is not one item of a doctrinal series which may or may not admit of systematic explication: it is rather the setting of the whole enquiry in a divine context. Donald Tovey recounts that at the first performance of *Elijah* at Birmingham, Mendelssohn had to submit to the destruction of a vital musical motif because Victorian England would have thought it blasphemous to change the A.V. 'but according to my Word' so as musically to fit the rhythm of Luther's 'ich sage es denn', which 'looms ominously' throughout the following orchestral overture – and (he might have added) at vital moments throughout the whole oratorio. (*Essays and Lectures in Music*, p. 214.) *Ich sage es denn* —. The human arts and sciences have their own rationale and evaluation: did not Luther himself once estimate that Cicero would enjoy a situation in hell several degrees higher than the Cardinal of Mainz? But 'we must heed that the life of action and the life of speculation do not delude us: they are each very pleasing and quiet and on that account the more perilous until they be disturbed and tempered by the Cross'. 'It is an error to put faith and its work on a footing with the other virtues and works. For this faith must be held as being exalted above all these things and a sort of general and inaccessible influence above them: by the moving and agency of which it is that all the works which are done by man, move, act and flourish and please God.'

Coram Deo. The gods of other religions and philosophies may tolerate partners or rivals: the God of the Bible is One – exclusively; and the reflex of this divine 'One' is the Lutheran '*alone*' – by faith, grace, scripture, Christ *alone*. In his *Open Letter on Translating* (1530), Luther tells us that the papists are making a tremendous fuss because the word 'only' is not in St. Paul's key-text on justification (Rom. 3:28). He defends himself partly by comparative linguistics – German and Latin, still more by the sense itself, with a telling reference to Rom. 4:2: 'if Abraham was justified by works, he has something to boast about, but not before God'. He might have added the Dominical 'fear not, only have faith'. The apparently contradictory Lutheran *simul* – at once righteous and a sinner etc. – is in reality an explication of the *sola*: the continuing paradox of 'sinners' and 'justified' is the human predicament, but were it not *coram Deo* – the One, Supreme, Righteous God – the sharp edges of the predicament would resolve into a mere matter of degree – 'all cats are grey in the dark'.

In line with this, Justification by Faith is the reflex of creation – of *creatio ex nihilo*. 'God enjoys bringing light out of darkness and making things out of nothing. Thus He created all things and thus He justifies sinners.' 'We take all righteousness from men and ascribe it to the Creator who creates out of nothing.' 'Those who look for righteousness by their own works do nothing but try to become their own makers or creators.' The verdict of Ps. 100 – 'He has made us and not we ourselves' – is as true of the new life in Christ as of the first life from birth. Even if we *were* perfect, God would still save us by grace and mercy *alone* – even if (as Augustine suggested) the Holy Spirit added a kind of supernatural capacity to fulfil the law and earn merit thereby, justification would still be God's free gift through Christ – like creation, *ex nihilo*.

But what is 'justification'? The long debate down to our own day on the Pauline *dikaioun* has run parallel with the controversy on Luther. Is it 'make righteous' or 'declare righteous'? Linguistically, the case is inconclusive: if, in Greek, analogous words like *axioun* ('deem worthy') suggest the latter, yet the presumed underlying Hebrew *hitzdiq* can hardly be other than the former. Doctrinally, each alternative leads to confusion. To 'make righteous' is (ethically) a contradiction in terms. Yet to 'declare righteous' someone who is *ex hypothesi* a sinner seems a mere ethical or legal fiction. Not even God can declare that black is white. Perhaps the best word has been spoken by T. W. Manson (*Studies in Biblical Theology*, No. 38, ed. M. Black) who looks on *dikaioun* as God's declaration, not of an acquittal, but an *amnesty* – the act of a King rather than a Judge. The judicial metaphor is never far from Luther's mind, yet this view seems true to his central intent. It is the prerogative of a King to declare an amnesty without prejudice to his sovereignty. It is the prerogative of the All-Righteous God to restore, without prejudice to His own awful purity, a lost standing to a corrupt creature.

For this is where Luther began. 'How shall a guilty sinner stand before the Living God?' Luther's own *Anfechtung* is often dismissed as a psychological abnormality, or respectfully discounted as only one among many 'types' of human experience. 'Normal' people (it is claimed) who do not undergo such dark nights of the soul, are just as much children of God and equally entitled to their own rather less drastic 'grace'. Such a claim misses the point. Even in the every-day physical sphere life is a continuing tension of health and disease; 'normally' we may achieve an equilibrium, but our trivial ailments and serious illnesses warn us of the tension that is always there. Your 'general practitioner' can only cure you if research into disease-at-its-depth goes on without stint or fear, and the 'common' illnesses (like the cold) are often as intractable as the gravest. Mentally and morally the tension goes deeper, for here 'normality' is never more than apparent. Theologically it is all-embracing and reaches the heart of man, for here the very claim to 'normality' – the absence of any real conviction of sin – is the greatest sin of all. Those 'doctors of the soul' who can contribute most are precisely those who have seen God in His stainless purity and then looked with complete honesty at themselves.

For Luther the vision of God is the Cross of Christ, and in its light his sin stands disclosed. 'Original sin' or 'concupiscence' is far more than the traditional lusts of the flesh: it is the inward orientation of the whole personality – its self-seeking and rebellion (conscious or unconscious) against God. 'For Scripture describes man as *incurvatum in se* ('curved inwards'), so that not only bodily goods but spiritual goods also he turns to himself, and seeks himself in all things.' This egoism is always at work in the dark chambers of the soul. Hence, says Luther (using the current Latin version of Prov. 18:17) *justus in principio est accusator sui* ('The righteous man is first and foremost an accuser of himself'). This is no mere exaltation of ethical humility. It is *judicium coram Deo*: 'this crookedness and depravity is in the hidden depths of our nature, nay rather is nature itself, wounded and in ferment through the whole, so that not only is it impossible to remedy without grace, *but it is impossible fully to recognize it*'.

Justification, then, is the restoration of our lost 'standing' before God, made necessary by the 'Fall' – the sin of Adam, the 'original sin' of every-man, for which he is without excuse. Luther treats the Fall as implicitly 'from nature to sub-nature', as distinct from the scholastic 'super-nature to nature'. God's gifts to man – of creation, preservation and all the blessings of this life – were such that the creature should and could have spent his whole life glorifying God and enjoying Him for ever, and even so with no claim to merit *coram Deo*: for 'what hast thou that thou hast not been given?' The fatal twist, however – the 'incurvation' – turned all these gifts to poison, so subtly and profoundly that only in the even more searching light of God's renewed grace could the evil be recognized and diagnosed. How then can such a guilty sinner stand before the Living God?

Justification is by *faith*. Here Luther may best speak for himself, in the *Preface to the Epistle to the Romans* (1522):

'Faith is not that human notion and dream that some hold for faith. Because they see that no betterment of life and no good works follow it, and yet they can hear and say much about faith, they fall into error and say "Faith is not enough; one must do works in order to be righteous and be saved". This is why, when they hear the Gospel, they make for themselves, by their own powers, an idea in their hearts which say "I believe". This they hold for true faith. But it is a human imagination and idea that never reaches the heart, and so nothing comes of it and no betterment follows it.

'Faith, however, is a divine work in us. It changes us and makes us to be born anew of God; it kills the old Adam and makes altogether different men, in heart and spirit and mind and powers, and it brings with it the Holy Ghost. O, it is a living, busy, active, mighty thing, this faith; and so it is impossible for it not to do good works incessantly —.

'Faith is a living, daring confidence in God's grace, so sure and certain that a man would stake his life on it a thousand times. This confidence in God's grace and knowledge of it makes men glad and bold and happy in dealing with God and with all his creatures; and this is the work of the Holy Ghost in faith. Hence a man is ready and glad, without compulsion, to do good to everyone, to serve everyone, to suffer everything, in love and praise of God, who has shown him this grace; and thus it is impossible to separate works from faith, quite as impossible as to separate heat and light from fire —.

'Righteousness, then, is such a faith and is called "God's righteousness", or "the righteousness that avails before God", because God gives it and counts it as righteousness for the sake of Christ, our mediator, and makes a man give to every man what he owes him. — Such righteousness nature and free will and all our powers cannot bring into existence. No one can gives himself faith —; how then will he take away a single sin, even the very smallest? Therefore, all that is done, apart from faith, or in unbelief, is false; it is hypocrisy and sin, no matter how good a show it makes.'

From this passage, supplemented and illuminated in Luther a thousand times, central issues and difficulties in the whole doctrine become clarified.

(1) Faith is not a 'human notion or dream' or 'idea' or 'imagination'. Critics who have accused Luther of advocating salvation by 'sentiment',

'emotion', 'experience' – of a back-door re-admission of justification by works – ignore the explicit insistence that faith is a *divine work within us*. It is the way in which Christ gives himself to us, or alternatively 'the power which takes hold of' (*virtus apprehensiva*) Christ. 'Faith justifies because it takes hold of and possesses this treasure, the present Christ.' 'If God has made his righteousness mine, I am righteous with the same righteousness as his.'

The note of paradox, as with the Pauline 'I, yet not I', is inescapable. Faith and grace are, if one wishes, correlatives, or rather twin poles, of that mysterious tension we call 'personal relationship', whereby with every degree of 'influence' deepening to 'communion' and even 'mutual indwelling', the integrity of the individual person remains unimperilled. This is familiar enough in human relationships – above all that of love. But when God enters the scene, the paradox is complete. The communion is so close that faith, grace, and Christ – the 'mediator' – are one: yet there is no 'deification', after the fashion of the Greek Fathers. 'When the soul is united with the Word, it becomes like the Word, just as iron becomes red like the fire in which it is heated.' Yet the iron is still iron, and the fire is still fire. *Simul iustus ac peccator* – 'at once righteous and a sinner'. From the human side one can and must analyse 'faith' into assent, knowledge, trust, confidence. From God's side it is the free restoration of man's lost standing by 'grace' – by the personal indwelling of Christ in his heart.

(2) The righteousness that avails before God – man's restored 'standing' – is given by God and 'counted as' righteousness for the sake of Christ. Luther usually describes this process by the Pauline metaphor of 'imputation', and on this point controversy was to fasten. The very metaphor, from the world of commerce, has been thought unworthy of its theme. To this Professor Rupp has given a definitive answer. 'Those who complain of (St. Paul's) figures as abstract, and as unsuited to express personal relationships, might walk through the City of London, past the Royal Exchange, the Old Bailey and the Cathedral of St. Paul. They will find there . . . those same figures, the market, the law-court, the temple and be reminded that the language of transaction, of judgement and of sacrifice sums up a good deal of the life of man in its corporate existence' (*The English Protestant Tradition*, p. 159). If the metaphor of imputation fails to 'describe the indescribable', then so do its forensic and ecclesiastical companions. Its strength lies in its preservation of vital emphases: the righteousness of God is not impugned – He does not slacken His standards; the distinction of divine and human is maintained within an inexpressibly close and mysterious communion; the infinitely precious personal mystery of salvation is safeguarded from any hint of arithmetical 'accountancy', because the 'imputed righteousness' is a mere mask for the Living Christ; and any fear of what St. Paul calls 'boasting' on the ground of human merit is on principle excluded.

(3) But how does Luther's doctrine allow for real moral growth? What is the relationship between justification and sanctification? Is there indeed any intelligible place for ethics in his system?

Luther, as we saw, was almost lyrically emphatic at this point. 'O, it is a living, busy, active, mighty thing, this faith; and so it is impossible for it not to do good works incessantly.' He repeatedly dwells on the transformation of the life of the Christian through faith, of the conquest as well as the pardoning of sin through Christ, of our being justified 'more and more', of our growth in sanctification through the Holy Spirit, of our ever becoming 'more and more' new creatures in Christ. Indeed, while for Luther justification and sanctification may be distinguishable in theory, in reality they are inseparable. Clarly we must not be as hasty as some twentieth-century critics to convict him of antinomian immortality.

Yet it may be plausibly urged that the Thomistic-Scholastic tradition, to which Luther stood in conscious polemical contrast, offered a more generous and realistic assessment of man's ethical struggles and achievements. This tradition was not indeed uniform; in important respects it took a different form in Thomas from that of the later Scholastics, and in the Scholastics from the exaggerations and perversions of the still later Nominalists who were Luther's most immediate target. But the central position seems to have been somewhat as follows.

Aristotle had developed (especially in the *Nicomachean Ethics*) an influential doctrine of *Hexis* (*habitus*) – man's 'second nature', gradually perfected (on the analogy of technical or musical expertise) by *ethismos* or 'practice', and implying a persistent moral subject. In the guise given it by Christian Scholasticism, this *habitus* became a faculty added to nature and beyond its natural level – a gift of God's grace, developed no longer by self-acquisition but by supernatural 'infusion'. Hereby, however, man's true nature was not destroyed but perfected, as the persistent moral subject realized the potentialities of its divine creation – as it regained the forfeited 'likeness' and so perfected the abiding 'image' of God, and grew increasingly capable of a believing response to its Creator, a response with the merit of 'fittingness' if not of 'worthiness' – *de congruo* if never *de condigno*.[1] Good works remain the fruit of grace and never its cause or occasion; but 'infused grace' gradually dissolves the *simul peccator* and makes genuine moral growth a reality. There is no affront to the supremacy of Christ, to whom alone is given the 'grace of union' with God; but man's 'grace of habit', supernaturally infused and fostered, at least implies a substantive or ontological reference without which the original 'grace of justification' might well seem to have been given in vain.

Why could not Luther be satisfied with this? Not, to be sure, because of a presumed antithesis between an Aristotelian priority of 'works' and a Lutheran of 'persons' – between 'by doing right one becomes righteous' and 'by being righteous one does right'. Luther, it is true, often insists that 'the tree makes the fruit and not the fruit the tree'. But the Aristotelian *habitus* subtly and correctly transcends the antithesis: through a lifetime of growth and enrichment it is, like a tree, giving and receiving incessantly. Luther's objection is far more fundamental. The Aristotelian tradition betrays, at this point above all, the ultimately anthropocentric and legalistic bias against which his 'Copernican revolution' – *coram Deo* – was one unqualified protest.

[1] Cf. P. S. Watson in *Luther and Erasmus: Free Will and Salvation*, edd. Rupp and Watson (1969), p. 25.

If the authority of Aristotle is to be respected, then one might do well, like the Master of the Sentences, to identify the *habitus* with the Holy Spirit. But far better drop 'that rancid philosopher' (one thinks of Tertullian's 'miserable Aristotle'!) altogether, and with him the whole notion of 'infused grace'. This latter implies a 'pouring' of a divine element into some identifiable vessel within man – some *locus* in his personality, even for that matter the underlying metaphysical 'essence' – which thereby becomes at least relatively deified. Luther's anthropology, by contrast, is that of the *'whole man' coram Deo* – the person or being not as a complex of potentialities and moral activities but as a creature in relation to his Creator, a sinner in the presence of his Judge. There is no antithesis between 'personal relations' and 'ontological implications': the whole man as he really is only emerges *coram Deo*. His redemption is not achieved by the 'pouring in' of some new – even divine – ingredient known as 'grace'; for grace *is* Jesus Christ, and Christian ethics can only be gratitude. Such gratitude *coram Deo*, when the gift is the salvation of the 'whole man' – the guilty sinner, can only be unreserved and unqualified response of that selfsame 'whole man'. The distinctions of condign and congruous merit, of image and likeness, are in this context dangerously misleading: they presuppose divisions and grades of acceptability to God within the fulness of the personality: they suggest that man must be 'sanctified', in some part of him and by some means or other, as a precondition of salvation, and thus limit, distort, qualify, the sovereign freedom of grace – of that God who befriends publicans and sinners, and in whose presence a note (however muted) on the human trumpet (even the trumpet God gave him) betrays a shifting of the centre of gravity from God to man.

The scholastic view (in Philip Watson's brilliant analogy) represents God as 'a doctor who refuses to come into contact with his patients so long as they are ill, but is sufficiently well-disposed toward them to send them medicine through the post (sacramental grace!) with a promise that he will see them when they are recovered. According to Luther — we must think of God in Christ as a true physician, who without a thought for Himself enters the plague-stricken dwelling to tend the sick with His own hands and nurse them back to health.' (*Let God be God!* p. 68, n. 43.) But 'health' in this context – sanctification – is least of all a life of growing independence of the divine Doctor. Of 'ethical growth' there is plenty in Luther's teaching, but it is always a 'new beginning'. The Christian life is one long elaboration of gratitude. *Coram hominibus* we may well construct schemes of values, or criteria of ethical progress: *coram Deo* we never transcend the 'dynamic of justification', for the moment we look to ourselves and our own ethical attainments the old 'incurvation' of original sin destroys them. Indeed, Christian assurance – the bold, free, joyful living of the redeemed – is grounded wholly in the refusal to look for it within ourselves, but only in Christ, and there it is to be had in boundless measure. 'For faith is not — a *habitus*, quiet, snoring, sleeping in the soul: but it is always turned towards God with a straight and perpetually looking and watching eye: hence it comes to pass that it is the author and origin of all good works – and what else are the Psalms but certain definitions of faith, hope and love?' This progress in faith, hope, love is an increasing possession by the Righteousness of Christ, in the power of the Holy Spirit, through faith. It is a progress of the whole man, even though the *semper peccator* is never overcome – or rather is more clearly recognized for what it is by those who, 'justified more and more', are more keenly conscious of the awesomeness of the divine standards and the miracle of condescending grace. No 'theory of Christian ethics', we may be sure, will be Christian at all if it overlooks the truth expressed by the Victorian hymn-writer:

> 'And all, O Lord, crave perfect rest,
> And to be wholly free from sin:
> And they who fain would serve Thee best
> Are conscious most of wrong within.'

What, then, of *perfection*? Is it merely 'laid up in heaven' like a Platonic 'ideal', to be realized with decreasing inadequacy until we have 'taken flight thither whence we came'? There is, as we have said, something of Plato in Luther. 'Sanctification, once begun, daily increases; the Holy Spirit is continually at work in us – and daily forgiving us, until we reach that life where there is no more forgiveness, all persons there being pure and holy.' But this is only one element in Luther's eschatology. Central and dominant is the conviction that the eschatological ideal has been brought into the present, in the perfect and final righteousness of God in Jesus Christ, and apprehended here and now by man in faith, hope, and love. Yet faith is not sight, hope is not realization, love remains a tension between what Nygren was later to distinguish as *eros* and *agape*. The Christian life 'does not consist in being but in becoming, not in victory but in the fight —' The ideal, however, is not merely in the future, but in the past and the present, for the ideal is Christ, crucified and risen, whose perfect righteousness is available for us here-and-now.

Once this is remembered, ethical growth falls into place. 'We must constantly grow in sanctification and ever become more and more new creatures in Christ. The word is *Crescite* and *Abundete magis* ("grow" and "be more abundant") —' The mark towards which we must press is nothing less than perfect love – love which is disinterested (as the reverse of self-love), uncalculating (as looking neither for reward to oneself or to the worthiness of our neighbour), motivated by the desire to please God alone, and perfectly realized in the Cross of Christ as that divine compassion which seeks and saves that which was lost.

The later moral theology of Protestantism, best known to us in the Puritan casuistries of the next century, may have owed more to the systematizing genius of Calvinism than to Luther: but there was nothing unethical or impractical about the latter's endless emphasis on the fundamental primacy of the 'bruised conscience'. It may be an exaggeration to say, in the spirit of Karl Holl, that Luther's is above all a religion of conscience; but his letters of unwearying pastoral counsel for afflicted brethren bring into characteristic relief the distinctive paradox of the Gospel – ethics and grace, the God who condemns and forgives, the individual conscience in which God at once overwhelms us and gives us peace. 'If it is apparent that the Calvinist patterns provided something more stable and more practical than Luther's moral theology, it is also true that Luther's stress on the spontaneity of the Christian ethic, on the creative ferment of the new life and liberty of the Christian man, might have saved Protestantism from the intermittent petrification of its religious life into the recurrent moralisms of the last centuries' (Rupp, *Righteousness of God*, p. 252).

2. *GOD: MAN: THE LAW*

The threefold equivalence of faith: grace: Christ in Luther brings into focus a rich complex of theological insights. Some of the most important may be set out briefly as follows.

God hidden and revealed. Luther's *deus absconditus/revelatus* must be carefully distinguished from the scholastic *potentia Dei ordinata/absoluta* (see Index s.v.). The latter envisages a process of speculation, with the 'ordained' power as the factual premise and the 'absolute' as the metaphysical conclusion. Luther emphatically closes the door on such a dichotomy. 'His grace is sufficient for me'. God's purpose is to be known as revealed in Jesus Christ. Yet Luther's antithesis is not the simple one of God apart from His revelation in Christ/God thus revealed. The revelation in Christ is itself open only to faith, and might be and has been disputed and mistaken. The Incarnation is both a 'veil' and a 'mirror'; the divinity of Christ is 'hidden' in the humanity. There is in every self-disclosure of God a tension of hidden/revealed, of mystery/revelation. The supreme self-disclosure is the Cross, where the *paradox* is at its deepest. Glory is hidden in humiliation, power in weakness. 'If thou does possess Christ, so dost thou possess the hidden God in like manner to the revealed.'

Such at any rate is Luther's normal use of the antithesis, grounded as it is in his 'theology of the Cross', and suggesting a whole series of the most startling paradoxes. 'The outward appearance of grace is as it were pure anger –'; 'God's faithfulness and truth must always first become a great lie –'; 'God cannot be God unless he first becomes a devil, and we cannot go to heaven unless we first go to hell –'; 'the devil becomes and is no devil unless he has first been God.' That this is no mere Chestertonian dabbling in paradox for its own sake becomes starkly apparent when one looks, as Luther could, not only at the world's blindness to the truth of God in Christ ('for had they known, they would not have crucified the Lord of Glory'), but at the satanic potency of religion itself – even of Christianity – when the devil follows God's example and 'hides himself' in the theology and the praxis of the Church.

In the *Bondage of the Will* (1525) Luther uses the antithesis in a different way. He comes up against the traditional problem of why some are predestined to salvation and others not, and he gives the traditional answer: 'that hidden and awful will of God whereby He ordains by His own counsel which and what sort of persons He wills to be recipients and partakers of His preached and offered mercy. This will is not to be enquired into, but reverently adored —' This is simply Rom. 11.33, on which Augustine, for example, so often and so inevitably falls back in the same context. But Luther goes further. He distinguishes sharply between '(the will of) God as preached, revealed, offered and worshipped', and 'God as He is in His own nature and majesty'. Of the former Ezekiel may truly say that He 'desireth not the death of a sinner'; the latter we are to leave alone, for it is something that is no business of ours. 'God must therefore be left to Himself in His own majesty, for in this regard we have nothing to do with Him — God does many things that He does not disclose to us in His word — Thus He does not will the death of a sinner, according to His word; but He wills it according to that inscrutable will of His.'

Luther's language is not perhaps at its happiest in this passage, which *prima facie* might suggest two wills or even two Gods. But the contradiction between the two uses of God hidden/revealed is only apparent. The Incarnation reveals the hidden God; yet the God so revealed is still hidden. The revelation is still a veiling. Our apprehension of it is on three levels, which Luther later in the same treatise names 'the light of nature, the light of grace, the light of glory'. To the first – the wisdom of this world – there is no God, merely blind chance or fortune. To the second (falling, we remember, on the *simul justus ac peccator*), some problems which baffle the first, such as unmerited suffering or unearned prosperity, are problems no longer; yet a whole new range of higher problems emerges, such as the rationale of the divine theodicy. These will only be solved 'hereafter', when the light of glory will reveal those ultimate secrets of God, implicit indeed in the Cross, but not to be truly apprehended until the veil of sin and limitation is finally lifted from the redeemed in heaven.

Meanwhile, for our present knowledge and assurance, we turn to the Cross of Christ. The God so revealed may still be hidden; yet the hidden is there revealed. Both the hiding and the revelation are the will of the One God – adapted to our condition, and hence apprehensible 'by faith alone'. 'In whatever therefore God hides Himself and wills to be unknown to us, that is nothing to us: what is above us does not concern us.'

The knowledge of God and human reason. The knowledge of God is twofold – that which is 'general' (found in everyone) and that which is 'proper' (given alone through Christ). So Luther; our modern debates on 'natural' and 'revealed' theology are slanted on a different set of presuppositions, which recall the tradition explicit in St. Thomas and (with variations of balance and degree) dominant in scholasticism. This tradition envisages complementary areas or perspectives of theology, the 'natural' being attainable by the human reason (inferential or speculative) and the 'revealed' being reserved to faith. The relations between the two and their respective dimensions may then clearly be the subject of endless debate, but there can be no final contradiction. Revelation may well be above and beyond reason, but never beneath it; while that which reason could never of itself discover may nevertheless prove compatible with rational requirements. Faith is not folly, and grace is the perfection rather than the destruction of nature.

From this point of view, and recalling Luther's overwhelming emphasis on faith, we might be tempted to discuss what 'concessions' Luther makes to 'natural theology', in comparison (for example) with the much disputed 'concessions' of Calvin. The suggestion is ready to hand that whereas for Luther faith in Christ is everything, man's natural capacities have been so ruined by the Fall that his reason is incapable of any apprehension of God at all. Passages in Luther where (after his wont) he appears to assert the opposite with equal vehemence, are then either discounted as rhetorical flourishes or taken to prove that he was 'no systematic theologian'.

Yet if we steadily keep before us Luther's *coram Deo*, the whole perspective shifts, and the seemingly disparate utterances fall into line. Fundamentally, if the God we seek to know is the One God and Father of our Lord Jesus Christ, then all knowledge of Him – 'general' or 'proper' – must be of His own self-giving, prior to, undercutting, re-aligning, over-arching all our human seeking. Hence this 'general' knowledge – whatever its content – cannot be opposed to, or complementary to, or a 'concession' allowed by, this 'proper' knowledge. God is One and His knowledge is wholly of His grace. Such knowledge is never merely academic or curious, but salvation itself; and salvation is wholly of Christ and through faith. Any knowledge springing from any other source is knowledge of a false god – an idol of our making, whether a concrete figure of anthropomorphic worship or an abstract intellectual formulation.

Why, then, must the distinction between 'general' and 'proper' knowledge remain?

Luther's whole conception of God – God 'hidden' and 'revealed'; God wholly transcendent and yet coming to us in the Cross, which remains a paradox; the ultimate identity of faith, grace and Christ – implies that there can be no *unmediated* relationship between God and man. 'No man can see my face and love.' God's glory must be 'masked' or 'veiled'. The final, essential veil is Christ, above all Christ crucified; but the whole world is God's creation, and hence all His creatures, along with their rational and moral patterns and orders of life, are also His 'veils', and as He is the One God, the whole creation may be said to 'contain Christ'. Through such *larvae* or *involucra* God comes to meet man and so prepares him for the fulness of saving knowledge in Christ. Were it not so, there would be no 'point of contact', as we say, in man for the Gospel, nor could its claim be universal, on man-as-such.

This 'general' knowledge, mediated through the creation, embraces, for a start, the fact of God's *existence*, and the awareness that this world and all its life is His *creation* and the sphere of His *providence*; then the ineluctable consciousness that God has *moral demands* to make on us; then the conviction that some day in some unknown way we shall be called to account before Him as our *judge*. Evidence of such knowledge is the universal prevalence of religion and of the moral conscience as such.

Yet (and here is the sting of Luther's teaching) the moment man accepts such knowledge, he falls into the trap of interpreting and augmenting it by the light of his own reason, turned 'inwards' instead of upwards: and from this moment his knowledge becomes idolatry. Luther illustrates this by the familiar distinction between knowing a man by sight and knowing him (as we say) in person. The former gives, within its limitation, true knowledge; but immediately and inevitably we start to construct our own picture of the object by the use of our own imagination, instead of looking to him to fill out the visual picture by fostering with us a growing personal relationship. *Coram Deo* the distinction between the alternatives becomes absolute. Our reason has received the initial 'general' knowledge, but immediately and inevitably perverted it into an idolatrous structure of Fate, good works, anthropomorphism. The 'personal relationship' which alone can build the authentic 'proper' knowledge of God in Christ is initiated, sustained and perfected by grace alone.

Reason, the universal human function, is thus a double-edged sword. As an *instrument* – defining, deducing, inferring, distinguishing – it is God-given. But set it the wrong problems with the wrong presuppositions – material, for example, for theological construction that is derived from philosophy rather than grace, from man rather than God – then, as man's sharpest weapon, it will wreak havoc with his apprehension of the truth. 'Reason is the devil's whore', says Luther, using the well-known Old Testament imagery of idolatry in terms of whoredom – 'and can do nothing but shame and disgrace everything which God says and does.' It is the task of faith to 'strike it dead', to 'kill this beast, which heaven and earth and all creatures cannot destroy'. But this is when reason, in a more fundamental context than the Tennysonian antithesis of natural science and moral value, aspires to the rank of a divine' philosophy', hence to 'shoot beyond its mark' and become 'procuress to the lords of hell'. Herein lies the damnation of scholasticism with its 'theology of glory'.

This, however, as reason is God-given, is its *abuse*. There is a true use of reason, and on two levels, corresponding to the 'two Kingdoms' (which we shall discuss later). First, when reason, illustrated by the Spirit, becomes the handmaid of faith – 'reason regenerate'. It is then no longer an independent authority, as in the scholastic dichotomy, but (as B. A. Gerrish says in his study of *Grace and Reason* in Luther) 'Faith's cognitive and intellective aspects' (p. 26). Reason, thus 'illuminated by the Word' (in Luther's language) becomes an 'excellent instrument of godliness'. Luther is, in the last analysis, no irrationalist – even in the dimension of eschatology. Irrationalities which remain, even for the light of faith (for 'now we see through a glass, darkly') await for their resolving the final light of glory.

Nevertheless, as Prof. Gerrish has so well brought out, there is a second legitimate level of reason – of reason 'unregenerate' but still God-given: the level of the 'earthly Kingdom'. 'In temporal affairs and those which have to do with men, the rational man is self-sufficient. He needs no other light than the light of reason. Therefore, God does not teach us in the Scriptures how to build houses, make clothing, marry, wage war, navigate etc.' So Luther; but as Gerrish further insists, 'without the Humanists, as Luther well knew, there could have been no Reformation —. — the Biblical professor who won the admiration of Bucer, Melanchthon, and Oecolampadius; the scholar who produced the massive Wittenberg Bible – surely this man was no stranger to the *bonae literae* of the Humanists.' (p. 171) No man (one is tempted to add) has used his reason more persistently and remorselessly than Luther – either his 'natural' reason in the temporal realm or his 'regenerate' reason in the realm of faith. Perhaps the ultimate query lies against his conception of the relationship between the two 'reasons' – whether there is not at least an *analogy* of scope and function to correspond with what we shall term the 'interpenetration' of the two Kingdoms.

The Law. – The Word of God comes to man in the twofold guise of Law and Gospel, and the Law itself in a twofold form or 'use'. Yet the Word is one as God is One, hence there is a divine unity of Law and Gospel, as of the Law itself. 'There is one Law, effective in all ages and known to all men because it is written in everyone's heart. From the beginning to the end no one can excuse himself, for the Spirit never ceases to speak this Law in the hearts of all.' This unity may be diffracted by human blindness and sin, and the analysis of its 'uses' becomes necessary for the theologian (himself a sinner): but the analysis will be false if it blurs or ignores the original and ultimate oneness of Law and Gospel in the Word of God.

Hence when Luther treats of the 'first use of the Law' in the 'civil' or 'political' sphere, we must beware of an identification with the scholastic 'Natural Law' or the later emphasis of the Enlightenment on the 'Law of Nature' as a metaphysical category, grounded in universal human reason. It would be just as perilous as the identification of the Pauline law 'inscribed on the hearts' of the Gentiles with the natural law of the Stoics, after the fashion of Origen's 'common (innate) ideas'. Luther's 'first use' is the Word of God as it encounters the chaos and injustice in the universe and in human history; it is a function of God's creativity, a force – a *dynamis* – by which God contends for order and righteousness. In this sphere or 'use' the Word of God is necessarily 'veiled' or 'masked'; hence the level of goodness achieved in man's response is never more than 'relative' – *iustitia coram hominibus* ('as men see it'), even though Luther, in contrast with some later exponents of 'Pietism', never undervalues this limited target, least of all in his practical reactions to such historical crises as the Peasants' Rebellion. The 'first use' of the Law is the indispensable foundation of human relationships in society. It limits the power of sin; it compels an albeit outward and 'moral' conforming to its letter.

When Moses attempted to interpret the Law into the twin duties of man towards God and his neighbour, he was endeavouring to clarify what already existed but had been clouded and perverted by sin. What he achieved, however, as an adumbration of the 'second' – the 'theological' or 'spiritual' – use of the Law, by which righteousness is seen to be ultimately *iustitia coram Deo* – a demand for perfection and therefore impossible. As long as fallen man is 'under the Law' he cannot fulfil it; indeed, the Law serves to expose and even aggravate man's incapacity.

Here we are on familiar Pauline territory. Luther's distinction between the 'moral' and the 'spiritual' *observance* of the Law becomes sharply relevant: no mere outward confirming is relevant *in loco justificationis* – when our salvation is at stake. Luther uses a text from Isaiah 28[21]:

'For the Lord will rise up as on Mount Perazim,
He will be wrath as in the valley of Gibeon;
– to do his deed – strange is his deed! –
and to work his work – alien is his work'

(R.S.V.)

God's or Christ's 'strange work' is that by which His Word as Law condemns our sin within our own conscience and brings home our despairing helplessness to save ourselves. Within the mask of this 'strange work', however, is hidden the 'proper work' of God, to which it is the indispensable preliminary. 'The Lord humbles and terrifies us with the Law and the prospect of our own sins —. So that when we acknowledge and confess that there is no form nor comeliness in us, but we live in the hidden God (that is in naked confidence of his mercy) we have in ourselves the answer to sin, folly, death and hell — and this is what Is. 28 calls the "strange work" of God, that He may work His "proper work" – that is, that He may humble us in ourselves, making us despair, that He may exalt us in His mercy, causing us to hope.'

We 'live in the hidden God' – our salvation is 'veiled' in the Law of Moses: but the lifting of the veil, the disclosure of our salvation, is no simple matter. For the perfection which the Law demands is Love – pure, unsentimentalized, holy – that total self-giving to God and to others which cannot be produced to order, even the order of God's Law itself. Such love could only be realized by unfallen man in his innocency as a sheer gift of God; fallen man in a fallen world has erected a cosmic barrier which could only be pierced by a special divine intervention of cosmic significance. The barrier of evil was something dynamic, objective, aggressive – Sin personified, the Devil himself.

Luther's doctrine of the Devil is no mere superstition or psychological abnormality. At the same time Luther is no Manichaean; there is no 'ultimate dualism' in the universe. The Devil is evil in person – but his very deception and defeat by the Cross of Christ re-affirmed his unwilling submission to God by making him, in his own despite, the instrument of God's wrath, and hence also and necessarily of His salvation. 'For God's "proper work" is "life, peace, joy", and the other fruits of the Spirit. Yet, in this, God made marvellous His holy one, and is made wonderful in His saints, that He destroyed the Devil, not with the work of God, but even with the work of the Devil himself. — For thus God sets forward His own work and fulfils it by means of His strange work, and with wonderful wisdom forces the Devil by means of death to work nothing other than life —. For thus it was with the work of Christ, His death, which Christ through the immortality of His divinity swallowed up altogether and gloriously rose from the dead.'

In so far as he makes theological distinction between the two, Luther finds the 'strange work' of God revealed in the Cross, His 'proper work' in the Resurrection. The barrier of evil is divinely and cosmically shattered: the Law has been fulfilled, satisfied and *therefore* abolished by Christ. This brings us to the final feature of Luther's doctrine of the Law: *there is no* '*third use*'. This – the *usus didacticus* or whatever it may be – appears first in Melanchthon, and it may well be that by it the hardening and obscuring of 'Luther into Lutheranism' was substantially furthered. For Luther the Gospel is *not* a new Law, for the only 'norm' of the Christian is Christ – the righteous love of God incarnate. The work of Christ on our behalf must be carried through within us – the sharing of His sufferings and the conquest of sin, death and the Devil. This is achieved through the enabling of the Holy Spirit, and constitutes that 'royal freedom' of the Christian by which the law of Love is transformed into a spontaneous self-giving. The alleged 'third use' of the Law is thus in principle transcended into a free outpouring of the love of Christ through the faith-union of the believer with Him.

Yet – the Law, although abrogated, is yet in force, both in its civil and theological uses, because the Christian lives simultaneously in two spheres: 'in so far as he is flesh he is under the Law; in so far as he is spirit, he is under the Gospel' – where *caro* is human nature as it organizes itself against God, and *spiritus* is the life redeemed by Christ. *Simul iustus ac peccator.* Law and Gospel are not for two classes of people, but for all Christians all the time; and ethical progress follows from the fact that, in the end, Law and Gospel are functions of the one Word of God. The Gospel alone, for example, can reveal the true range and validity of the civil Law; secular righteousness can only be rescued from its inveterate temptation to self-justification *coram Deo* by faith; the freedom of the Spirit is that by which, among much else, we are qualified for sober and rational political, philosophical, ethical, social and personal well-doing. Luther, like St. Paul, will repudiate neither the Law (antinomianism) nor the Gospel (legalism). Such perfection as awaits us is (in the sense defined above) eschatological. '(The spirit of life) — has not yet freed us from death and sin, but it will free us at length, for we have yet to die, yet to labour against sins. But He freed us from the Law of sin and death, that is, from the *kingdom and tyranny* of sin and death, that sin indeed should be present, but with the tyranny taken away — and death is indeed present, but with the sting removed.'

The Word of God is one; but the complex pattern – the inner tensions – of Law and Gospel, of the 'strange' and 'proper' work of God, reflected in the multitudinous and often seemingly contradictory utterances of Luther on the theme, is a truer and more comprehensive presentation both of human nature in all its baffling inconsistencies and (still more) of the un-fathomable resources of the grace of God than any simplistic and 'systematic' scheme of sin and salvation.

Christian Liberty. The application of Luther's total view of God, man, the law to the hoary problem of free-will resulted in an intricate and bewildering controversy with Erasmus, reflected in the chaotic and contradictory expositions of subsequent interpreters and editors. It should, however, be clear enough by now that Luther's presuppositions, his *Weltanschauung*, his whole system of theology since his 'break-through' had placed him on a standpoint subtly but substantially alien to the Christian humanism of Erasmus, whose bitter contempt of monkish scholasticism went along with an instinctive and inherited scholasticism of his own. The contestants fired their salvoes with conviction and finality, and nearly always at the wrong target.

In 1520 Luther had published three seminal treatises which have been called the 'manifestoes of the German Reformation'. The third of these – *Concerning Christian Liberty* – begins with Luther's celebrated paradox. 'I first lay down these two propositions —: a Christian man is the most free lord of all, and subject to none; a Christian man is the most dutiful servant of all, and subject to everyone.' Human nature as it should be – 'before the Fall' – would have no will of its own but to obey God, yet with that *voluntary* and *spontaneous* obedience which is 'perfect freedom'. The Fall however had debased this willing servitude into a declaration of independence over against God – the triumph of the 'flesh' against the 'spirit', that jealous husbanding of mythical human prerogative which necessarily implies hostility and rebellion against its Lord. *Corruptio optimi pessima.* Fallen man is not a mere beast; his reason and will remain operative on a basis of some lingering awareness of God and His law. But they are *incurvata in se*, and hence they distort and falsify. God's gracious providence, the grace and the love which bring freedom, become from this perspective arbitrary and bureaucratic; and what should be in man a willing and whole-hearted spontaneity of response is replaced by circumspection and defiance. The kingdom of God is overshadowed by the kingdom of Satan.

Not that freedom is utterly destroyed: it remains in respect of 'things beneath man' – the ability to choose between alternatives in that sphere to which the 'first use of the Law' would apply. But in respect of 'things above him' – man's salvation – he is powerless. Luther would here align himself with Augustine in the insistence that if we make a wrong choice in this sphere we are no longer free but enslaved – and if we are left to ourselves we shall always so choose. Only the grace of God can give us the true freedom, which is 'not freedom to sin but freedom not to sin'. This is the glorious freedom of the redeemed, in which a man, redeemed by Christ, gladly 'empties himself' of the very liberty to seek salvation apart from good works, and 'takes upon him the form of a servant — and in every way acts towards his neighbour as he sees that God through Christ has acted towards him. All this he should do freely, and with regard to nothing but the good pleasure of God'.

It was not likely that such views would commend themselves to Erasmus, who in 1524 flung down the gauntlet in his *Diatribe on Free Choice*. Erasmus accepted without conscious question the scholastic view of the Fall. Before it, man's natural powers, reinforced by a supernatural gift of grace, enabled him to know and do the good and *merit* his salvation. Even after it man retains freedom of choice to apply himself to or to turn away from 'the things that lead to salvation'. If man does what in him lies, God will assist with grace; man can choose to cooperate or refuse – hence in the end *man* is responsible for his salvation or destruction. To deny this responsibility would be (in our modern idiom) to cut the ethical nerve and render meaningless the motivation to the 'good life'.

Luther's elaborate reply follows predictable lines; 'cooperation with God', for example, to Erasmus a condition of salvation, is for Luther a consequence. Salvation is to Erasmus a restoring of the 'supernatural' dimension which gives back humanity its acceptability before God and its rightful claim to eternal life; to Luther it is liberation from *subhuman* bondage and the free *gift* of the heavenly reward. The traditional enigmas in the out-workings of the problem of free-will are encountered with hardening divergences of perspective and answer. Erasmus meets the apparent evacuation by his doctrine of any significance in God's *predestination* by defining the latter as foreknowledge; and if, as Luther claims, even this must impose necessity, Erasmus will fall back on the scholastic distinction between 'necessity of the consequent' and 'necessity of consequence', the former being absolute and the latter (allowing contingency) conditional. Luther replaces this to him meaningless distinction by another – the 'necessity of coercion', the 'necessity of immutability'. Judas, on the first view, was not 'forced' to betray Christ, although God foreknew that he would: his action was no more than 'conditionally necessary' – on his not changing his mind. On the second view Judas likewise was not 'forced' – his action was 'voluntary', but being the man he was he could not have done otherwise – the 'necessity of immutability'. Why did not God act to *change* Judas? What of the choice of Jacob and the rejection of Esau? What of the 'hardening' of God's Word and the consequent increase of sin? Luther can here apply – as we saw, in a somewhat different perspective – his distinction of the hidden/revealed will of God, which is here to him (like the doctrine of predestination) a sign of the ultimate mystery into which theology cannot penetrate, but which nontheless offers a sure and certain pledge – pastorally and morally – that man's calling and election are the responsibility of the unfathomably gracious God, and not of his own free choice.

'Erasmus', says Professor Rupp in his verdict on the debate, 'does deeply and sincerely believe that Christianity is a religion of grace. The idea that men can be saved without divine assistance would have been wholly abhorrent to him. It may be that at the end of the day it will be conceded that as against Luther he grasps the importance of human responsibility and of an insistence on grace which yet does not take by storm the citadel of the soul. Yet at the end of the day, too, Luther could maintain the great Anselmian retort: 'Thou hast not considered the gravity of sin' – or what it means for man to have his existence *coram Deo*.'[1]

The 'Two Kingdoms'. No doctrine of Luther has been more persistently reprobated than the *zwei Regimente*, and nowhere has superficial and un-historical exegesis been more potent or baleful. He spans, here as always, they dying world of Western Medievalism and the birthpangs of the modern era; it is equally misleading to read him in terms of the earlier debates on the spiritual and temporal powers in Christendom, as to saddle him with the paternity of the notorious *cuius regio, eius religio* (which was not officially used until the Peace of Augsburg, nine years after his death, and represented a mere compromise sanctioned by Catholic princes as well as the Lutherans), or (worst of all) to declare, as did William Temple in 1941, that it is 'easy to see how Luther prepared the way for Hitler', and in the

[1] *Luther and Erasmus: Free Will and Salvation*, p. 12.

same sense to vilify Luther, with a pamphlet of the same period, as 'Hitler's spiritual ancestor'.

The problem of Church and State, in the Christian tradition, looked back to the dual Old Testament witness, on the one hand of the godly King, the Lord's anointed, who besides ruling over the people could on occasion build an altar and establish a priesthood, and on the other of the 'prophetic protest' – social and ethical as well as religious – in the name of God whose Word stands above people, priesthood and king alike. The Apocrypha, in altered historical settings, bears increasing witness to a 'tradition of rebellion'; the N.T. leaves, without resolving it, a tension between the Pauline 'powers-that-be are ordained of God' and the violent revulsion against the secular power in *Revelation*. In the first three Christian centuries the persecutions dominate the head-lines (in spite of the unsolved question of the legal underpinning of the right to persecute) to the relative neglect of the growing involvement of Christians in the structure and even the ethics of Graeco-Roman society. The conversion of Constantine raised as many problems as it solved, and the aspirations to 'theocracy' of an Ambrose were balanced by the outraged 'dualism' of a Martin of Tours, especially when the incursions of the former into the realm of Imperial sanctions and of the secular power into such scandalous exercises as the execution of Priscillian demonstrated at once the peril and the inevitability of a mutual interaction between State and Church. In the West the decline of Rome as a secular power and the consequent elevation of the Papacy (above all in such dominant representatives as Leo and Gregory the Great) to secular as well as spiritual supremacy, began to tilt the balance of the standard contemporary doctrine of the 'two swords' (the interdependent dualism of Church and State) towards the supremacy of the spiritual power. Throughout the Middle Ages this tradition on the whole preserved its dominance through all the set-backs and vicissitudes of Western European history. The Eastern tradition of 'Byzantine theocracy', especially after the final break between East and West in the eleventh century, ceased to be relevant. Luther grew up in a world in which the break-up of Medievalism threw the age-old problem once again into the melting-pot. The still menacing claims to absolutism of Rome, the dawning consciousness of nationalism (especially in Northern Europe), and the extremism of political and religious revolutionaries made his quest for a positive and consistent pathway peculiarly hazardous and perplexing.

The 'two kingdoms' is in any case a misnomer. The *zwei Regimente*, like the *basileiai* of the Gospels, refer to 'kingly rule' or 'reign' rather than 'kingdom' or 'realm' – to God's ways of saving men, rather than to the spheres of His authority. This recognition leads to the fundamental insistence of Luther that the whole question be set primarily and determinatively *coram Deo*. The two 'rules' are both God's; the whole creation is His *larva*. The so-called 'temporal' is as much under His providential control as the 'spiritual'. Hence at one stroke Luther stands apart from the earlier centuries, with their 'dualism' or 'interdependence', from contemporary Papal absolutism or Imperial theocracy, and from the modern dilemma. It is God's rule, and God is neither Pope nor Church, Emperor nor Diet, Priest, Parliament or people.

Within the sovereignty of God are two modes of rule, the 'spiritual' and the 'temporal'. The first is exercised through the preachers and the sacraments of the Church, and is designed to bring men to goodness of heart (Luther's 'passive' righteousness) and 'eternal peace'. The second is exercised through Princes, officers of State, fathers of families, and its aims are the forestalling of evil ('active' righteousness) and 'external peace'. The instrument of the first is the Word, of the latter the Sword. This is one form of the fundamental contrast of Gospel and Law, and Luther repudiates both the Catholic obtrusion of the latter into the first 'rule' and the left-wing extremists' of the former into the second.

Here we may pause to note Luther's characteristic emphases on *Obrigkeit* (authority), *Beruf* (vocation), *Stand* (station) and *Amt* (office). Those who accuse him of recklessly shattering the fabric of medieval Christendom in the interests of an individualist and antinomian 'fideism' know nothing either of Luther's predicament or of his doctrine. No concept more persistently exercises him than *Obrigkeit* – the authority, for example, of Scripture-as-a-whole or in its varying elements; of apostles, creeds, and councils; of tradition, of Princes, of rulers, of *justitia civilis*. His early monastic ideal of holy obedience never left his conscience free when it became clear that his own activities were leading the way to a break-down of Papal authority; his natural conservatism – so typical of the religious reformer who (like John Wesley) was also a scholar – revolted against the violent disturbances in state, town and university in the years following 1510. The current 'dynamism of unrest' could all too easily issue in the left-wing intellectualism of a Karlstadt, the mob-tyranny threatened by the Peasants, or an apathetic and cynical resentment of all authority. Yet it was not easy to maintain a clear and consistent doctrine of Christian obedience. His two prime Biblical texts – Rom. 13[1] ('Let every soul be subject to the higher powers —') and Acts 5[29] ('We must obey God rather than man') – may well be theoretically harmonious, but in practice always either the one or the other seemed paramount. This is well illustrated in his 1523 tract *On Temporal Authority* – 'When we have learned that there must be temporal government on earth, and now we should use it in a Christian and salutary way, we must then learn how long its arms reach, if it is not to stretch too widely and encroach upon God. For unbearable danger results if we give it too much scope; yet damage is also done if it is too narrowly constricted.'

This is the context in which we should see his use of the vocational terms. He distinguishes between *Christperson* (a man *coram Deo*) and *Weltperson* (a man *coram hominibus*). *Coram Deo* all men stand equal – and condemned; God offers forgiveness and salvation as the free gifts of His grace. *Coram hominibus* men are not equal, for here God 'calls' them to various 'stations' and 'offices', and here men do not receive the Gospel but work and serve at the behest of the Law. In this way God 'earths' His will in the ongoing and orderly life of His creation.

These 'stations' or 'offices' are the relationships in which we stand to our fellows, whether within the family, the state (law, politics, society), or the Church. The Church, indeed, somewhat disturbs the symmetry of Luther's thought at this point, for its Ministry (the *Priesterstand*) is hardly confined to the sphere of the Law. But the specific contribution of Luther to the doctrine of Vocation lies in the other spheres. 'For what is our work in field, garden, house, war, ruling, towards God but child's play, through which He gives His gifts to field and house and all the rest? They are the *larvae* of our Lord God through which He will remain hidden and yet do all.' Child's play to God – but to us a divine calling, a mask of the sovereign rule of God. To this should be added that Luther is fully aware of the *plurality* of every man's vocation, as also of its *mutability*. These features, while not prescribing a modern theory of 'situation-ethics', at least set a query against fixed standards of behaviour or codes of conduct.

Neither of God's 'rules' is subordinate to the other; neither can be thwarted by man – or the devil, who is to Luther the supernatural 'person-alized' essence of evil, and makes it a prime concern to interfere with man in his stations, and even to instigate the Catholic and antinomian corrosion of the two rules by intrusion of Law into the one and Gospel into the other. Yet the 'offices' are God's creation and do His will, whether or not the 'officers' intend it. If they set themselves against Him, He in His own good time will replace them. Meanwhile 'God governs the world through good rulers and through bad'; the 'office' is to be obeyed, even when there is injustice, and only those in authority have the right to rule and use the sword. Disobedience leads to chaos, which is worse than injustice, and rebellion is not certain to bring improvement – only chance, in which the innocent will suffer. Instead of rebelling, men should pray – and God will when He pleases raise up a Superman (*Wundermann*) to restore His sovereignty. This 'Superman' is indeed a rare bird. It is David, Hannibal, Augustus, Frederick the Wise, one or two of the right kind of lawyer (for example), who have been gifted by God with free, spontaneous insight into 'that noble jewel' of natural law, reason, and equity through which God has guarded the world from uproar and chaos. For the bulk of mankind the duty is to obey. Yet disobedience is not ruled out *in toto* – it can even be a Christian duty, but only when the ruler interferes in 'spiritual' affairs (where in naked truth 'we must obey God rather than man'), and with the reservation that an instrument is not force; the ruler alone has the right to the sword.

The two 'authorities' are distinct but related. The temporal for example can ensure peace, without which the spiritual is barred from its exercise. Nor is the Church wholly exempt from temporal interference; it may need reformation – but exceptionally, and with especial justification in each case; and the ruler's power of intervention is limited and defined by its derivation from his leading status in the Church itself. The spiritual authority 'inter-venes' by its unwearying admonitions that the temporal rule is itself of God and exercised for the service of man; by its encouraging and rebuking the ruler and magistrates through preaching of the Word; above all by making men Christians. But in the last resort it must not entrench on the Sword by bringing to bear the Gospel in that temporal sphere which is subject to the rule of the Law.

Such is, in outline, Luther's doctrine of the *Zwei Regimente*. It remains to note some of the points on which serious discussion has centred.

(1) It is suggested that the 'two rules' were relevant only for Christendom, and that the doctrine has ceased to be meaningful in the modern age, when Christians have to take seriously not only the rival world-religions but 'post-Christian secularism'. Yet Luther knew perfectly well that the world and Christendom were *not* co-terminous, even if in some of the most deplorable passages of his works he reacted with mere denunciation, above all of the Jews. He stands in a powerful tradition that would never cut the knot even of the modern problem by a simple devaluation of Christianity to 'one possible option', or an abandonment in principle of large areas of life to man's own devices.

(2) The notion of the Superman has been criticized on the ground that only in retrospect is he recognized as such; at the time he is a mere rebel. Yet God who raised the Superman might be expected to prepare for his recognition; and a Milton (as A. E. Taylor reminded us) is not likely to go through the world 'mute', in any case. Did not a large part of Northern Europe thrill to the coming of just such a superman in Luther himself?

(3) It is argued that Luther's analysis of the individual into *Christperson* and *Weltperson* sets up in him an impossible tension, as if he was a man of religion on Sundays and a man of the world the rest of the week. But the tension is there already, as any serious Christian living in the world already knows. Luther is far more 'realist' than doctrinaire thinkers such as Marx, for whom everything in a man's life is determined by one dimension (in Marx's case, his 'class'), whereas responsible living is in essence a radiation from the individual as a focal-point of vocations, interests, obligations of all kinds. Nor is the 'temporal' sphere for Luther itself exempt from God's rule, even if it be the rule of Law. It is indeed God's provision for all His children and all His creation – including the Grand Turk and his subjects! Home, daily life – the whole realm of the 'secular', are never exempt from God's rule, where the Word of God is itself the conscience of a city and a nation.

(4) Luther has been accused of insufficient provision for the *abuse* of its vocation by the temporal authority. He does not ignore this contingency, as we have seen. Yet it may well be maintained that his guide-lines are insufficient, and that on balance he is far too 'conformist'. We have tried to show that his personal history, set in the context of his place and time, made such a reaction inevitable. In principle it is identical with that of the eighteenth-century Tory High Churchman, Dr. Samuel Johnson: 'it is better in general that a nation should have a supreme legislative power, although it may at times be abused. – if the abuse be enormous, *Nature will rise up, and claiming her original rights, overturn a corrupt political system.*' (July 6th, 1763: Boswell's italics.) The difficulty is, of course, to lay down in advance a scientific diagnosis by which 'such times' may be recognized

the instant they occur, and the exact balance of advantage and disadvantage in rebellion be foreseen. Even S. Augustine, who also holds that the civil power is under the authority of God, can only add – in so far as it is founded on true righteousness and worship. Luther was never a systematizer, and while claiming (as we must) a profound inner coherence in his thought, we may perhaps admit that here more than anywhere he allows himself changes of stress and vocabulary under pressure of circumstance. He was not a pacifist, and in 1543 regretted that he was too old to enlist against the Turk. Yet none knew better that violence breeds worse violence, and that it is in the end the innocent – the children, the elderly – who suffer. In spite of this, the problems (from 1530 onwards) of the forceful repression of Anabaptists and armed resistance by inferior magistrates to the Emperor brought from him a positive response of growing passion, until we find him thinking of Pope and Emperor in apocalyptic terms, demonic and destructive rather than genuine 'authorities', spiritual or even temporal.

(5) The real weakness of Luther's position lies perhaps in the final difficulty. The lines of demarcation between the *zwei Regimente* are much too sharply drawn, as if each in principle excluded the other. If both are God's, this would in any case be surprising; and Luther's view in the end seems to clash both with the facts of living as we know them and with the witness of the Bible and sound theological reflection.

The service Luther has rendered in the establishment and delineation of the two rules of God is beyond question; but the *isolation* of each obscures their genuine interpenetration, and results in a more than marginal distortion. We saw one example of this in the vocation of the priest: *vocatio* can hardly be confined to the *Weltmensch* who acts solely according to the Law if the Ministry of the Church is in any sense a *vocatio*. On the other side, we should reject, along with so sound a Lutheran as Prof. Philip S. Watson, 'Luther's unqualified insistence that "one must not resist the government with *force*, but only with knowledge of the truth; if it is influenced by it, well: if not, you are innocent and suffer wrong for God's sake".' (*The State As a Servant of God*, p. 71, n. 1). These last words give the case away: it is not 'my innocence' that is at stake, but the redressing of an injustice to my neighbour. A 'Christian war', may well be, as Luther claims, a contradiction in terms, but hardly on the grounds he gives, that a man may not fight as a Christian but only as a 'temporal office-bearer'. If fighting is right (or wrong) for the one, it can hardly be different for the other. A Christian, says Luther, fights with prayer and the Word: an Emperor (at God's command) with the Sword. Yet Christians have been soldiers and Emperors Christians, each reinforcing the Sword with prayer and the Word. There may be real truth in the distinction, but it is far too clear-cut.

It is in the end impossible to deny that the Church – the whole body, not merely the 'Christian ruler' or the members as *Weltpersonen* – has a legitimate work in the political sphere; and it is equally clear that the righteousness – even the sanctions – of the Law may well be the temporal expression of that divine love which, as the supreme gift of grace, is the hallmark of the 'spiritual rule'. Luther, as we have shown, accepts the 'intervention' of each 'rule' on the other, but the intervention remains external and limited.

The doctrine of the Incarnation should have suggested an interpenetration that is, in principle at least, complete.

3. *CHURCH AND SACRAMENTS*

Tradition is as often the enemy of truth as its servant; and in the matter of the Church, a superficial understanding of Luther's 'priesthood of all believers' and his 'Church visible and invisible' has built on the *a-priori* assumptions that Luther's doctrine must in any case have been no more than a precipitate of his conflict with Rome, and that for one whose consistent watchword was 'justification by faith' the individual Christian must always be the primary theological unit and the Church a secondary afterthought.

One of Karl Holl's great services to Luther-studies was his demonstration that, in all essentials, Luther's doctrine of the Church may be recovered from his first course of lectures on the *Psalms*, dated as early as 1513–15, when he was still an ardent 'Catholic'. The later and more 'classical' sources, such as the first of the three Reformation manifestos of 1520 (*To the Christian Nobility of the German Nation*), the Schmalkaldic Articles of 1538, the tracts *Of Councils and Churches* (1539) and *Wider Hans Worst* (1541), witness the testing and tempering of his doctrine by the fires of controversy and the momentous march of events. In 1520 he made his personal break with Rome – 'farewell, unhappy, hopeless, blasphemous Rome. The Wrath of God has come upon thee as thou deservest. We have cared for Babylon and she is not healed. Let us then leave her that she may become a habitation of dragons, spectres and witches.' But it was during these years that Luther had been immersing himself in Bible study, in Church History – especially the Councils and the Decretals – and in theological controversy; and his maturing doctrine of the Church, so far from being a mere rationalization of his destruction of 'catholicity', constituted a protest in the name of the one, holy, catholic community against its corruption and degradation in current theory and practice.

(1) The Church is the *'special community'*, the *'proper work'*, *of the Holy Spirit* in the world. 'I believe that there is only one holy common Christian church on earth – This is nothing else than the community or gathering of the saints and of the godly, believing men on earth which the Holy Spirit gathers, preserves and rules.' So far from the Church being a human contrivance for the convenience of individual believers, it is as much a gift of God as faith itself; indeed, faith – like every primary Christian value – is what in modern jargon we should call a 'societary concept'. 'As Christ has become the common possession of us all, we should also become the common possessions of one another.' It is the Spirit of Christ that dwells in Christians, and through Him 'brothers become co-heirs, one body, and citizens of Christ'. 'The Church is the divine, the heavenly, the noblest brotherhood —, for here we have one baptism, one Christ, one sacrament, one food, one gospel, one faith, one spirit, one spiritual body, and each person is a member of the other.' The Church is a 'gracious blending of our sin and suffering with the righteousness of Christ and His saints'. 'When I suffer,

I suffer not alone, but Christ and all Christians suffer with me – and their strength becomes my own.' If ever there was (in the only true sense of the words) a 'High Churchman', it was Martin Luther.

(2) The Church of Christ is fundamentally the *communio sanctorum*. This venerable phrase has primary reference to the communion or fellowship of persons (*congregatio*); secondarily – but implicitly and of necessity – it also implies a sharing in holy things (*communicatio*), the 'things' including the whole range of God's precious gifts, material and spiritual. Luther disliked the word *Kirche*, and in his New Testament translated *ecclesia* by *Gemeinde*, 'assembly of people' rather than 'dedicated building'. 'If the words,' he says, 'had been used in the Creed, "I believe that there is a holy Christian people", it would have been easy to avoid all the misery that has come in with this blind, obscure word — for the common man thinks of the stone house which we call a Church. "Ecclesia" ought to mean the holy Christian people, not only of the time of the apostles — but right to the end of the world, so that there is always living on earth a Christian holy people in which Christ lives, works and reigns *per redemptionem* — and the Holy Spirit *per vivificationem et sanctificationem*.' These ideas were of course not new; they are firmly anchored in Bible, Creeds, Fathers. But their recovery, in the context of a stale and over-institutionalized late medievalism was revolutionary enough. 'Thank God,' said Luther in one of his most inspired simplicities, 'a child of seven knows what the Church is – the holy believers and the lambs who hear their shepherd's voice.'

The 'holy', the 'saints', are not, as with the rigorist schismatics of the early Church, an elevated group within or apart from the main body of Christians on earth, nor are they specifically and exclusively the souls of the righteous made perfect in heaven, but, as with Augustine, those 'called to' sanctity, whose holiness lies in their calling and is properly attributable to God alone – that is, the whole body of the Church, whether on earth or in heaven. Our own Christian service is primarily directed to the former. 'The living saints are your neighbours, the naked, the hungry, the thirsty, the poor.' The life of the departed is safe in God's keeping – 'let the dear saints rest where they are – and let God take care of them. We can neither know nor understand how they live in the world beyond.' So much for the medieval transfer of merits in the bank of heaven from one account to the other. Even the intercession for us by the saints in heaven, while not denied, is not stressed; such intercession too easily becomes 'meritorious' and encourages our veneration – which is idolatry.

(3) The Church, the new Israel, is, like the old, subject to the tension of '*Life after the flesh*'/'*life after the spirit*'. This formulation is preferred by Luther to the one he inherits from St. Augustine of 'visible'/'invisible', which is more patent of a Platonic interpretation, and which has led to modern accusations of a Lutheran devaluation of the apostolicity or sacramentalism of the Church, or even of the Incarnational principle itself. The distinction, indeed, between the twin antitheses tends to be somewhat finely-drawn; the *Epistle to the Hebrews*, with its 'earthly/heavenly', and St. Paul, with his 'temporal/eternal' appear almost to transcend it, and in Luther there is a deep (if rarely acknowledged) debt both in language and

thought to the pagan Plato, at this point perhaps above all. Yet on the main issue Luther is clear: 'When I call the Church a spiritual assembly, you have insultingly taken me to mean I would build a Church as Plato builds a state that never was.' The church was never for Luther a Tennysonian Camelot – 'never built at all, and therefore built for ever'. 'How massive', says Professor Rupp (*Righteousness of God*, p. 335) 'was his own concentration on the visible Church: the Bible, the Catechism, the hymns, the correspondence on ecclesiastical problems from every quarter of Christendom, the cure of souls, the care of the Churches.'

'Oh, it is a high, deep, hidden thing is the Church, which nobody may perceive or see, but can only grasp by faith in Baptism, Word and Sacrament.' With these famous words Luther points, in the matter of the Church, to a conflux of convictions, which (as we have seen) are integral to his theology as a whole. First: the Church is *sola fide perceptibilis*: its life is 'hid with Christ in God', while it remains 'despised and rejected of men'. It is the Church 'under the Cross' – its battle is never won, its suffering is a mark of its truth. Hence its members only become one in Christ and each other when they stand *coram Deo*; their bond of unity, like their Christian estate, stands rooted in the divine order. The Church, like the Incarnation itself, is a *larva* – a 'mask', at once a revelation and a veiling; and while the ultimate reality ('after the spirit') is 'not a bodily assembly but an assembling together of hearts in one faith', yet the outward form ('after the flesh') is a necessary instrument of providence of God for the salvation of the world. In its visible manifestation the Church is an accommodation to fallen humanity; its 'marks' or 'signs' are all God-given, though all are open to sinful misconstruction. Luther lists them as follows:

> preaching; Baptism; the Sacrament of the altar;
> the 'power of the keys'; the ordained Ministry;
> public worship; suffering.

These 'marks' can point us, if we 'attend and enquire', to the true community of the faithful, and there is one sure link between them: they are one and all bound up with the 'Word of God', which alone suffices to show the presence of the Church. 'For God's Word cannot be present without God's people, and God's people cannot be without God's Word.' 'The Church of God is present wherever the Word of God is spoken, whether it be in the middle of the Turk's land or the Pope's land or hell itself.' 'If I were the only one in the whole world who retained the Word, I alone should be the Church.' Luther can repeat in his own context the Cyprianic *extra ecclesiam nulla salus*, for outside the Church there is no Saviour, and the Saviour is only to be found where the Word is preached.

(4) *Priesthood and Ministry*. The 'priesthood of all believers' is a phrase with connotations in subsequent Protestantism – for example, of a degradation of the clerical office – which make it misleading as a label for the profound and Scriptural teaching of Luther. The first manifesto of 1520 appeals to the 'temporal power' to undertake the reforms where the 'spiritual power' has failed, and in support of this Luther elaborates from Rom. 12, I Cor. 12, I Peter 2:9 and Rev. 5:10 the twin doctrines (a) that

fundamentally (*coram Deo*) there is but one Christian estate (*Stand*), into which we enter by 'baptism, Gospel and faith', and in which we are all consecrated as priests by baptism; (b) within this 'royal priesthood' there may come to each Christian a different office (*Amt*). Priesthood is in essence the realization or activation of our corporate oneness in Christ – our responsibility *coram Deo* for one another. The way in which this is exercised depends on the special calling of God and the 'wish and command of the community'. 'That which is the common property of all, no man may arrogate to himself, unless he be called.' One consequence of this is that there is no 'indelible character' in the priestly *office*: a man deprived of it by the community is *in that sense* a 'priest' no longer. Another is that 'in cases of necessity every man can baptize and absolve, which would not be possible if we were not all priests (sc. by "estate")'. Yet another – of enormous importance for the later history of Lutheranism and inter-church relations – is that the true unity of the Christian Church lies in its one divine source – Word and Gospel – rather than a uniformity of liturgy or polity. There are Lutheran Churches with episcopal, presbyterian or congregational constitutions. God fulfils Himself in many ways: but it is equally true that the ultimate priesthood of all believers as Luther understood it not only admits but demands a properly called and consecrated 'ministry'.

(5) *Sacraments.* Among the 'marks' or 'signs' of the Church are included Baptism, the Eucharist and the 'power of the keys'. In the second of the 1520 manifestoes (*On the Babylonish Captivity of the Church*) Luther rejects the remaining traditional 'sacraments' as unwarranted by Scripture; even the three remaining are strictly 'sacramental signs', for ultimately there is but one Sacrament, the Word, by which God 'lays hold of and "puts on" the creatures' of water, bread and wine. Such sacramental 'signs' are the form in which we receive the Word, and through them comes a guarantee, a pledge, a seal of the promises of God. These signs are necessary, 'for when God reveals Himself in some sign, of whatsoever kind it may be, He is to be apprehended in it'; there is to be no 'theology of glory' which would by-pass alike the sign, the Word, and the gracious self-giving of God.

The *'power of the keys'* (Matt. 16:19, 18:18) is the declaratory authority of the ministry to pronounce absolution. This title is preferred by Luther to the traditional 'sacrament of penance'; the true 'absolver' – like the true 'baptizer' – is the living God, and the minister is yet another *larva Dei*. Further, absolution is hardly an independent sacrament of itself; it is rather a re-affirmation of baptism. 'Baptism will always hold good; and though some fall away and sin, they can always return to it in order to subdue again the old Adam. Repentance is nothing but a return and re-entry into Baptism'.

Baptism 'signifies two things: death and resurrection; that is, full and complete justification. When the minister dips the child into the water, this signifies death; when he draws him out again, this signifies life'. Hence baptism confers the whole of salvation – 'forgiveness of sins, deliverance from death and the devil, eternal life, both in body and soul'. Baptism conveys the entire grace of God, 'the entire Christ and the Holy Spirit with his gifts'.

We are baptized but once, yet the act is in the fullest sense eschatological: it sets its seal on our whole life, which is nothing else than a daily baptism, once begun and constantly lived in', nor do we 'perfectly fulfil the sign of baptism until the last day'. Baptism is indeed for Luther the 'outward and visible sign' of his whole doctrine of justification.

In various sermons and writings of the 1520s, and above all in his *Larger Catechism* of 1529, Luther defends infant baptism against the Anabaptists. He speaks (some may think surprisingly) of universal Christian tradition; God has at every period of the Christian era shown His approval of the practice by His undeniable bestowal of the Holy Spirit on those baptized as infants. Such a tradition could only be overruled if it were contradicted by the higher authority of Scripture, and Luther faces fairly the fact that infant baptism is neither commanded nor even specifically mentioned in the New Testament. His answer anticipates the familiar apologetic of modern paedobaptism. He cites the blessing of children and the 'forbid them not, for of such is the Kingdom' (Mk. 10 etc.); he appeals to the 'all nations' of Matt. 28:19, where no age-group is specified or excluded; he cites the 'household baptisms' of Acts ('children are certainly a substantial part of the household'). But his real defence lies in his whole theology of the Gospel, with its universal offer of salvation.

What, then, of faith? In Mk. 16:16, Luther admits, Christ puts faith before baptism; do infants in any intelligible sense possess such faith? To this still burning question Luther offers a variety of answers, without complete consistency. The faith in question is that of their sponsors or of the Church – or that which they will have themselves in the future; children who do not yet have 'reason' can have a 'closer faith' than adults because reason (our old friend the 'devil's whore') is as often as not the enemy of faith. Children *can* have faith, like John the Baptist who 'believed' while yet in his mother's womb. It is Christ Himself who arouses faith in children, as (unborn Himself) he did in John the Baptist, although the 'how' is to be left in the hands of God.

Yet in the end, however this problem is to be solved, the *validity* of baptism does not depend on any faith, infant or adult, but on the will and the Word of God. Faith does not constitute baptism but receives it. If it were otherwise, faith would itself become a human 'work', and hence idolatry.

The Lord's Supper. Luther's eucharistic thought develops in two main stages: until 1524 his main adversary is Rome, afterwards certain 'enthusiasts' and above all the Swiss movement centred on Zwingli.

Luther inherited from long tradition a conviction of the 'real presence' of Christ in the Sacrament. 'It is' (he says in a sermon of 1519) 'a divine sign, in which Christ's flesh and blood are truly present.' But in the second 1520 manifesto he repudiates 'transubstantiation', on the ground that this mirrors the 'captivity' of the sacrament to the Thomistic–Aristotelian philosophy of accident/substance. Both 'accidents' and 'substance' of the bread and wine remain constant, and the body and blood of Christ are given with them. Luther offers as an anology 'fire and iron, two different substances, which are so mingled in red-hot iron that every part of it is both fire and iron. Why may not the glorious body of Christ much more be in every part of the substance of the bread?' Luther is really replacing Aristotelian categories by those derived from Chalcedonian christology, to which he remained faithful: 'unconfusedly, unchangeably, indivisibly, inseparably'.

The controversy with Zwingli, which led to the Colloquy at Marburg in 1529, brought to a head various trends alien to Luther's central doctrine of the Real Presence: the Hussite bread and wine as bare symbols; the wide-spread interpretation of the Scriptural *est* ('this is my body') as *significat* ('represents'); Karlstadt's view that in the same passage 'this' (*hoc*) refers to the body of Christ and 'take', 'eat' to the bread; the version of Oecolam-padius, 'take and eat: this is a sign of my body'. Luther will have nothing of any qualification of the simple '*is* my body', quoting in support the 'I am' passage of the Fourth Gospel, none of which means 'represent' (not even 'the door', 'the true vine'). Zwingli's claim that the risen and glorified body of Christ is 'in heaven at God's right hand' and therefore cannot be localized at any sacrament on earth, is met by the Lutheran rejoinder that it cannot be localized in heaven either: 'God's right hand' is the place of His effective power and presence – wherever He wills to be; and when He comes to us in Christ it is likewise as He wills: at the sign of bread and wine. 'How this happens, or how He is in the bread, we do not know and are not to know. We should believe the Word of God, and not dictate ways and means to Him.' In the sacrament there is both a physical and a spiritual eating: 'as far as taste is concerned the mouth seems to be eating something other than Christ's body. But the heart grasps the words in faith and eats precisely the same body as the mouth eats physically. — How does it see this? — by looking at the word which is there, "Eat, this is my body". Yet there is only one body of Christ, which both heart and mouth eat, each in its own mode and manner.' This 'body of Christ' is a union of the two natures so organic that, as in Palestine the man Jesus was the bearer of the divine nature, so here in the sacrament there is the same 'hypostatic union 'of the body of Christ with us, spiritual and physical.

Luther rejects the medieval *ex opere operato* – the mere 'performance' of the sacrament does not secure its efficacy, otherwise, once again, a human 'work' would be at our disposal for the activation of God's grace; and in the same way it is not a 'sacrifice' offered to secure that grace, which is free and universal. Luther prefers the word 'testament' – a sure pledge, promise of God, to bestow 'from Christ's mouth forgiveness of sins, – God's grace, His Spirit, and all His gifts, protection, refuge, and strength against death, the devil, and all misfortunes'. To this should be added the cardinal grace of 'communion'. We are brought into 'communion' with Christ and all the saints' the sacrament is 'a sacrament of love, and as love and help have come to thee, even so must thou learn to show love and help in return to Christ and His needy followers'. Without faith these blessings are lost, yet faith (as in baptism) is not constitutive of the sacrament: even the 'un-worthy' receive the body and blood of Christ, though to their own damna-tion. The sacraments are constituted by the Word of God, Incarnate now as always in the fulness of Christ and the enabling power of the Holy Spirit.

We gave at the outset of this rapid journey through Luther's theology the constant *coram Deo* as its master-key. Its unifying principle, in which all his 'doctrines' subsist, we may now identify as the *Word of God* – *'ich sage es denn'*: for the God in question is uncomprisingly the *Christian* God, whose Word is the whole divine revelation, supremely incarnate in Christ, mediated through the living Gospel of prophets, apostles, church and sacraments. Faith and salvation: man and the law: Scripture and tradition: ministry, congregation, baptism, the altar: the 'secular' world of magistracies, home, family, work and play – they are one and all brought into a divine perspective as the searchlight of the Word blazes on and through them, or rather find their reality as its constitutive power continually creates them. 'Let the Word of God go free and conquer –' It may well be that the theology of the Word of God has won its greatest triumph not among the professed allies and friends of Luther in later days (and in Karl Barth above all), but in the Second Vatican Council itself, where it may be claimed as the underlying and unifying thread. Luther himself would have wished no more.

Ulrich Zwingli

Basil Hall

Ulrich Zwingli

BASIL HALL

The Reformation begun by Luther obtained in its early years wide-spread success moving into city after city and into one princely territory after another, yet it did not spread easily into south Germany and the upper Rhine region. The early success of Protestantism lay in its urban victories. If a city council decided for Protestantism it tended to associate particular social and political implications with it. The more wealthy and sophisticated cities of south Germany which had been affected by strong currents of humanist culture could be more politically self-conscious than the conservative north. This combination of humanist culture and political assertiveness in Basel and Strasbourg checked the advance of Lutheran theological orthodoxy, which was politically quietist, and they turned to theological views which could be adapted to the humanist social viewpoints of the city councillors. This tendency was encouraged by the powerful and independent Swiss Confederation, some of whose cantons turned to a Protestantism marked by a close identification of the civil community and the programme of religious reform. This development had been checked in the northern Lutheran regions by conservative political control through the princes who had taken over after the suppression of the Peasants' War, of Anabaptism and of the associated radical theological and social ideas of Thomas Müntzer and Andreas Karlstadt. The self-conscious communal sense of the Swiss Confederates was anti-princely and urban democratic, though this democratic principle had its power centre in the merchants and country land-owners who were unwilling to allow power to devolve to the artisans' guilds or to the peasants. Zürich was the important canton in the development of this socially and politically differentiated Protestantism which challenged and checked the spread of Lutheranism. Zürich was the city where Huldreich Zwingli undertook a Reformation on different lines from Luther – from a different starting point, with a different framework of theological ideas, personal life-style and character.[1] The powerful influence of Zwingli's Zürich on the progress of the Reformation was to be felt at Strasbourg and other cities of southern Germany as well as in Basel, and was to win over Berne, the most powerful Swiss canton. Its advance northwards was checked when a conservative Lutheran political and theological reaction occurred in the powerful city of Augsburg. Without capitulating to social and political determinist views in men's affairs it must be stated that the social and political aims of Zwingli and Zürich, and of those who

[1] G. R. Potter, *Zwingli*, Cambridge, 1976.

were influenced by them, were bound to challenge, because of their different purpose and proselytizing energy, the Lutheran movement. The breakdown of Protestant unity at Marburg in 1529 was rooted not only in certain theological differences but also in the social and political factors latent in Luther's conservative royalism and his imperial German disapproval of Swiss republicanism: it was also affected by what he thought of as the roughness of these mountain men, speaking a 'coarse' German, who though still officially part of the Empire yet in practice were opposed to it.

The Reformation in Strasbourg, Basel and Zürich was marked by the sense of the community – the urban community. It emphasized what was useful to the community in education and morals, as well as what provided it with its best support – apart from patriotism – the practice of piety. Zwingli, for example, as a parish priest began from the pastoral sense of what was good for the Confederation to which he belonged: his starting point was 'How could Christ best be honoured among the Swiss', whereas Luther, the friar, began from the need for a gracious God, a need powerfully felt by him in his conventual cell. Zwingli was different from Luther not only by being Swiss; but also by the nature of his training for the priesthood and his developing humanist commitment. Again the personal religious crisis through which both men went differed in origin and in their response to it. These influences and experiences led them to differing ways of undertaking reform in the Church, and of the kind of Church that should emerge from this reform. Zwingli was to become more radical than Luther in breaking free from the traditions and practices of the Roman Church. Luther was content to leave ceremonial and ecclesiastical customs and organization little touched if they were not shown to be gravely defective by the touchstone of justification by faith alone. Zwingli, on the other hand, insisted on a thorough transformation which left behind very little resemblance to the organization and practice of the Roman Catholic Church. This difference is usually expressed by saying that Zwingli abolished everything in Church life and practice which was not explicitly commanded in Scripture, but Luther retained from the Roman Catholic past what was not plainly forbidden in Scripture.

The question used to be much argued whether Zwingli was influenced by Luther or not: Lutheran scholars had no doubt of it. Seeberg wrote: 'There can be no doubt that Zwingli derived the idea of justification by faith, as well as his fundamental reforming views from Luther. . . . At the central point of his awareness of religious truth Zwingli is dependent on Luther.'[1] Loofs took a similar line: 'All those religious ideas basic to Zwingli's reformation activity he derived from Luther.'[2] But these are overstatements. Zwingli began by being stimulated to reforming views through the work of Erasmus. This led him to much greater concentration on the community in relation to a transformed Church, going beyond Erasmus in using biblical patterns from the Old as well as the New Testament in conceiving the Church's purpose and organization to be closely associated with Swiss cantonal structures. This more thorough-going Erasmianism united with

---

[1] R. Seeberg, *Textbook of the History of Doctrines* (tr. Hay), Grand Rapids, 1956, p. 307.

[2] F. Loofs, *Leitfaden zum Studium der Dogmengeschichte*, 4th ed., Halle, 1906, p. 795.

ideas taken from his earlier training in scholastic theology (particularly in his use of certain aspects of Thomism) gave a uniquely Zwinglian structure to his theology. It is true, however, that after 1519, and notably in the early twenties, he used the theological insights of Luther for his own purposes as can be seen from verbal similarities in his writings of this period with themes already expounded by Luther. It is this which lies behind the statement that Zwingli was unoriginal and reflected Luther's ideas, but it is not a basis for the charge of simple plagiarism since Zwingli used his own emphases and structures to form a distinct and positive pattern of theology of his own which was to be followed with modifications by his successors at Zürich, notably Bullinger, and through Bullinger was to influence English Protestantism and through this some theological developments later in English evangelical and nonconformist theology.

To understand the development of Zwingli's theology it would be useful to give an account of his early years before he openly committed himself to challenging the Church of Rome and its institutions. He studied for the priesthood at two universities, for two years at Vienna and for four years at Basel, before going to Glarus as parish priest in 1506. While he had some acquaintance with Nominalism, through Biel for example, Zwingli's major studies in Scholastic theology lay in the *via antiqua*, the Realism of Scotism and Thomism. The leading teacher at Basel in this field was Thomas Wyttenbach whom Zwingli studied under briefly, and from whom he learned first to question the value of Indulgences, and whose lectures on the *Sentences*, and particularly those on the *Epistle to the Romans* influenced him, in pointing him for example to the saving effect of the death of Christ. It was from the *via antiqua* that Zwingli obtained his philosophical framework and some of the themes suitably emended through which he set forth his reforming views. After 1514, however, Zwingli, who had already been strongly influenced by humanist methods at Basel, turned more and more to Erasmianism and began to scorn Scholastic theology in favour of reading the original texts of the Scriptures and of the Fathers of the early Church – though he never wholly rejected his early Realism, for his theory of knowledge and view of providence were grounded in the Aristotelian principles expounded by Scotist Realism. This should be remembered when the well-known conflict between Luther and Zwingli occurred at Marburg in 1529 concerning the Lord's Supper: they represented two opposed traditions in Scholastic philosophy. On the eucharistic elements what for Zwingli was a metaphysical impossibility, was for Luther the occasion for increase of faith.

Zwingli was not a man to call himself a committed disciple of any one theologian or writer. He was eclectic in his choices among the teachings of his predecessors, so that he cannot be described as a wholly committed Realist of the Basel school in 1514, but even in his most humanist phase he never lost sight of the philosophical and theological framework of his early training at Basel. Again, in the course of his early training he had been influenced to some extent by the *Devotio Moderna* which stimulated him to understand in theological terms his experience of the Christian life. But the most powerful influence on Zwingli after 1514 was undoubtedly Erasmus who had come to Basel that year and stirred up young Swiss scholars by his new approach to the nature of theological studies and his attractive programme of a moderate and meliorative process of Church reform. As early as 1513 Zwingli had begun to learn Greek: it was already plain to him what could be made of biblical study through the new humanist techniques of philological and historical methods to be seen in Jacques Lefèvre's *Psalterium Quintuplex*. Erasmus' New Testament, published in Greek and Latin in 1516 and annotated in a new and fresh style, further inspired Zwingli who made his own manuscript copy of the Pauline epistles in Greek and entered his own notes in the margins, one of which reads 'Christ alone'. Zwingli adopted wholeheartedly the Erasmian concern to return to the sources (that is the study of the Bible in the original languages without the traditional medieval method of exegesis), and the study of the Fathers – Zwingli was to owe something to Augustine and more to Origen, and for biblical exegesis he turned as Erasmus had done to Jerome and Ambrose. Also to Erasmus Zwingli owed his turning to a form of Christ-mysticism, that is, the focusing of religious ideas on what Christ taught in the Sermon on the Mount, and in His life of obedient piety shown in the Gospels; from these studies Zwingli came to emphasize the theme 'Christ alone' in theological study. Here, like Erasmus, he sees the starting point for a regeneration of Christendom. Christ alone is the teacher who has come from heaven, He alone can guide us, who is Himself eternal wisdom: He alone teaches salvation by being in Himself the Saviour, He alone fulfils what He promises. It is not surprising that Zwingli could write to Erasmus in 1516 in most exalted approval: 'O best of men, I am overwhelmed by the splendour of your erudition'.[1]

Two other aspects of Zwingli's thought – and for Zwingli to think was a preparation for action – were derived from his Erasmian view of the Christian social order. There was the need to correct abuses in society first through the renewal of inner piety and secondly, through changes in the practice of government involving both aims and methods. These themes, seen in the *Enchiridion* and *Institution of a Christian Prince* of Erasmus, had strongly attracted humanist-minded lawyers of the period, and these in turn were to influence laymen in positions of authority. This helped to make it possible for Oecolampadius at Basel, Bucer at Strasbourg and later Calvin at Geneva in varying degrees to find men to lead a reform movement deriving from these aims of renewing society through piety and new ways of social discipline. Zwingli looked about his native Switzerland and asked himself where the possibility of transformation lay, bearing in mind these proposed themes and methods. Before he became a Reformer the first subject he found was the Swiss custom of mercenary service in foreign wars which Zwingli denounced because of its corrupting influence on the Swiss, although he was not a pacifist like Erasmus since he was himself to die on the battlefield. His concern was for the men of the Swiss cantons who left a healthy life to be corrupted by the vices and greed of foreign service: rather he believed they should fight only to defend their country and, later, the Protestant Reformation. The second theme which he was to develop from his Erasmianism was to turn gradually from the traditional respect

[1] *Opus Epistolarum Des. Erasmi Roterdami*, ed. P. S. Allen, II, Oxford, 1910, p. 225.

for Christendom under papal government to the recognition that papal
curialism was secular minded and presumably incapable of itself of reforming the abuses of the Church which so grievously affected society. The years
1516 and again 1519 were significant in this development of Zwingli. In 1516,
at the age of thirty-two, he had been ten years a parish priest, popular,
outgoing, and becoming famous as a preacher. He had hitherto supported
the papacy believing that it should be defended against French interference
in Italy. He had received a pension for his services in obtaining Swiss
recruits for papal service and acting himself as an army chaplain in Italy.
But in that year he underwent disillusionment followed by religious dis-
quiet. Francis I and Leo X accepted the Concord of Bologna: this was a
complete reversal of papal policy which now supported the French against
the Emperor. For Zwingli the question arose whether the Pope could be
regarded as above political concerns, and was he not instead acting on the
same ruthless assumptions made by any secular prince? Should, therefore,
Swiss troops continue to support unscrupulous papal politics? When he
found his own parishioners willing to consider acting as mercenaries in the
French service Zwingli decided to leave for Einsiedeln to which he had been
invited as parish priest. For him henceforth the papal government of the
Church was now open to question and doubt.

In addition at this period a moral crisis arose in his life. As was not
uncommon at that period he had been guilty, though a priest, of sexual
relations with a woman in the parish. To a friend he wrote in excuse that
he had not, and would not, corrupt a virgin, nor approach another man's
wife nor seduce a nun. But his sense of guilt was possibly strong and may
have been increased by his close study of the Greek New Testament with
the warnings of Paul against 'the flesh'. In that year questionings about
abuses in the Church and his own loss of self-respect may have led him to
ask whether Erasmianism could prove sufficiently strong to change the
needs of society and the needs of sinful men. In 1516 he must have been
powerfully affected by his close study of the Greek New Testament, by his
sense of disillusionment with the papacy, and by his personal anxiety
through his moral lapse – an anxiety insufficiently satisfied by the moralism
of Erasmus's writings. Zwingli must have come to regard it as inadequate
to teach that virtue is a form of knowledge, and that by teaching it personal
lives, and society itself, could be transformed. This could lead him to a
further stage. Like Luther and, later, Calvin (and many another Catholic
who was to turn to Protestantism), Zwingli experienced a personal and acute
religious crisis: it was foreshadowed in 1516 but 1519 saw it brought to a head.

In 1519 he was called to the high office of 'people's priest' at Zürich, and
began to preach directly from the biblical text expounding section by section
the Gospel of St. Matthew. But that year the plague struck Zürich, and
Zwingli became a victim through his priestly duty of visiting the sick and
dying. His younger brother died, and he himself was at the point of death.
In his slow convalescence a further religious change can be seen in a poem
called the *Plague-Song*.[1] It has been plausibly argued that this poem has

---

[1] *Huldreich Zwinglis Sämtliche Werke*, ed. E. Egli, etc., 1905—, Berlin/Leipzig/Zürich,
I, pp. 67ff. Cf. A. Rich, *Die Anfänge der Theologie H. Zwinglis*, Zürich, 1949, pp. 104-119.

two main themes: it is a commentary on his earlier stage of religious experience before the plague struck him down, and it shows his being brought to a new view of his life before God by the nearness of death. There is a strong theocentric emphasis on the power and majesty of God and the mysterious workings of His providence. There is the need to rely wholly on God for salvation, for nothing that man can do merits salvation. He tells of the nothingness of the creature before divine transcendence. The movement of his mind here is existential and theocentric and is turning away from the Erasmian calm in seeking to follow Christ. Zwingli has changed, while never forgetting his debt to Erasmianism, from Christian humanism to what was becoming the Reformation nexus of providence, unmerited grace and justification by faith.

In his correspondence with friends Zwingli now began a positive attack on the papacy, which he accused of love of power and money, and of challenging by its authoritative claims the sovereignty of Christ alone. In 1520 he resigned his papal pension originally given for his zeal as a chaplain to Swiss troops supporting the papacy in 1514. So far Zwingli had reached independently of Luther hostility to the temporal power of the Papacy and its corrupting consequences and concern for the new doctrine of justification by faith – though he probably reached them in the reverse order from that of Luther. He had not yet achieved anything near the depth of theological insight which Luther had by then attained. This is probably seen in his being much less disturbed by the preachers of Indulgences in Switzerland than Luther had been by Tetzel in Germany. For Zwingli, as for many others of the Swiss humanists, Indulgences were an absurdity and an irrelevance, and therefore did not require a passionate commitment to opposing them. Even though Zwingli had begun to pass from his original attachment to Erasmianism he had not yet acquired the deeper theological insights, coherently arranged, which could transform him into a fully equipped protestant reformer. But he was becoming known in the south German cities as well as in the canton of Zürich, and he was going to make it the second focal point, after Saxony, of the German Reformation.

The influence of Luther on Zwingli must now be considered briefly, for in reading Luther's works Zwingli acquired a new theological energy which brought out the implications of his previous development from humanist criticism, anti-papal negation and the experience of sin and grace during his more recent years. From now on he will turn to revolutionary change in church order, in sacraments, and in ministry, using the force of Luther's insights, even though he denied that he owed a real debt to Luther. This attitude was due, however, to his wish to avoid, in these early stages of Protestantism, being caught up in the condemnation of Luther by Church and Empire after 1521, and also he seems to have felt unease from the first in being associated with Luther's eucharistic theology which was certainly different from that being developed by Zwingli in part from Erasmian principles. Since Zwingli's library contained over twenty works by Luther it could well be that Zwingli adopted from Luther characteristic themes such as the freedom of a Christian man in Christ. Certainly Luther's example, as well as his writings, helped Zwingli to deeper theological insights and turned him positively to full acceptance of what was going to be called in a few years Protestantism.

Two further influences may be mentioned before turning to an analysis of Zwingli's theology. In 1524 he received a letter from Cornelis Hoen (Honius) offering an interpretation of the presence of Christ in the eucharist which had been firmly rejected at Wittenberg but cautiously welcomed by Oecolampadius the reformer at Basel and sent on to Zürich. This letter made a deep impression on Zwingli and he caused it to be printed at Zürich in 1525.[1] Hoen argued that the Apostles had not written of the dogma of the real presence, and that the word 'is' in the account of the Lord's Supper ('This is my body') should be understood to mean 'signifies'. Erasmus had already been hinting in his correspondence that a literalistic interpretation of the words was misleading. Hoen was saying in effect that the eucharist commemorates what Christ had done in the past, and the participants now recollect by faith the atoning death of Christ in eating the bread. Zwingli was largely convinced by the extended argument of Hoen, of which the briefest statement has been given here. To it Zwingli added, among other things, the argument that the words of Christ, 'The flesh is nothing it is the spirit which vivifies', pointed to a spiritual eating.

The other, and negative, influence on Zwingli was the vigorous opposition made to his reform movement at Zürich by the Anabaptists, which compelled Zwingli to reconsider his teaching about baptism, and to give greater attention to the method of applying Scripture to theology, and the nature of the Church in relation to society than he had done before. This controversy clarified and deepened his theological work and made him look further into the implications of some of the statements he had made earlier.

To describe Zwingli's theology in detail poses the question: Where does one begin? It will be evident from what has gone before that Zwingli, as so many other protestant reformers, found the stimulus to his theological thinking in the intellectual and moral conditions of his environment and the contemporary state of the Church. This gave an existential note to his theology. All the protestant reformers were united in choosing as the two focal points of their challenge to what they believed to be the theological errors of the Church of Rome – errors which so distorted the Christian faith that leaving the Roman Church was imperative – the doctrine of grace (including the concepts of original sin, justification by faith, and, for many, predestination), and the appeal to Scripture as the only valid source of theological statements. Zwingli was less concerned than Luther to emphasize the doctrine of justification by faith, with its corollary the forgiveness of sins, because his religious experience had taken a different form from that of Luther. Some have seen in his thought the doctrine of providence and predestination as the fulcrum of his challenge to Roman Catholicism; others have seen his conception of the Bible as the source of theological truth, as the law book of rules laid down by God for a properly constituted Church and society, as the central theme. These emphases are strongly made by Zwingli but they should not let us lose sight of his

[1] Translation in H. A. Oberman, *Forerunners of the Reformation*, New York, 1966, pp. 268ff.

emphasis on Christ (in spite of his tendency to theocentrism associated with his doctrine of providence) and on the guidance of Christians by the Holy Spirit. However, Zwingli had barely ten years of vigorous reforming work in which he undertook a heavy load of activity, including many political and social conflicts as well as theological writing, and his books were hastily produced, though always well-written, often in response to a particular social or religious crisis. For this reason he left behind little that can be described as an ordered carefully balanced account of his theology seen as a whole. He left no equivalent to Melanchthon's *Loci Communes* or Calvin's *Institutio*.

This makes it difficult to organize the description of his theology without overemphasizing certain themes, or distorting their relationship to others. Take, for example, what comes first in order of time as a formal expression of his theology, his *Sixty-seven Theses* of January 1523, prepared for the Disputation with Catholic opponents at Zürich.[1] These theses could lead to the assumption that his thought was wholly controlled by Christocentrism. The first twenty-four theses are concerned with the work of Christ, the remainder attack papal abuses and urge the duty of the magistracy to reform these. The sum of the gospel is that Christ the Son of God has fulfilled for us the will of God our heavenly father, and through his guiltlessness delivered us from death and reconciled us to God. Christ is the salvation of all believers who form his body and it follows that all who live in Christ are members of Him and sons of God. This is the Church, the communion of saints, the bride of Christ, the catholic Church. Statements like these which show the influence of Erasmus and his New Testament studies, do not govern Zwingli's theology throughout his career. In two formal and carefully written treatises *On True and False Religion* (1525), and *On the Providence of God* (1530) Zwingli replaces his earlier christocentric emphases by the theocentric emphasis.[2] Here Zwingli writes of God showing man his loss, disobedience and depravity, and when man acknowledges his helplessness God then takes pity on him in merciful power. God is shown, in the later treatise, as known through the *analogia entis*, and providence is connected directly with predestination in a manner displaying the philosophical use of the doctrine of God's omnipotence through his eternal decree to act upon man in salvation and condemnation. It is difficult to see here where Zwingli's original christological purpose has gone. Too often it seems that for Zwingli the theme is: 'All is done by and from God, and nothing without Him.'

It would be preferable to begin the description of Zwingli's theology by setting forth his doctrine of Scripture for this is where he began his studies when, influenced by the call of Erasmus for Christian scholars to return to the sources of Christian truth (*ad fontes*), he wrestled with the interpretation of the Greek New Testament. Nevertheless, Zwingli did not forget his earlier

---

[1] *Zwinglis Sämtliche Werke*, I, pp. 485ff. Also B. J. Kidd, *Documents Illustrative of the Continental Reformation*, Oxford, 1911, pp. 412ff. Translation in A. C. Cochrane, *Reformed Confessions of the Sixteenth Century*, London, 1966, 36ff.

[2] *De Vera et Falsa Religione*, Zwinglis, *Sämtliche Werke*, III, 59off.: *De Providentia, Dei Anamnema. H. Zwinglis Werke*, M. Schuler and J. Schulthess, Zürich, 1828–42, IV, pp. 79ff.

training which had given him the scholastic juristic view of Scripture seen not only as the source of truth but also as the divine law which should govern the private and public life of men. At the Disputation in January 1523 with the Catholics at Zürich, Zwingli's theses emphasized the centrality of Scripture as the test of matters of belief without reference to the teaching and interpreting authority of the Church. All human traditions, authority of Councils, Fathers and papacy, are as nothing before the all competent self-authenticating authority of the Scriptures. At the Disputation his colleagues sat with open Bibles before them, in the original languages, to justify the challenges made by the theses. This is the first appearance in the Reformation period of the use of the scriptural principle (*sola scriptura*) as a fundamental article of faith. Luther and Melanchthon had made justification by faith the basic starting point. Scripture, affirmed Zwingli in his *On the Clarity and Certainty of the Word of God*, 1522, a sermon he preached to the nuns at Oetenbach, has no need to be confirmed by the authority of the Church; the Word of God speaks directly from the Scripture to the individual heart and mind.[1] The authority of Scripture is self-evident and the Holy Spirit moves the human heart to respond and recognize that irresistible authority. Zwingli emphasizes in this sermon the interior witness of the Holy Spirit which God will not refuse to those who seek it earnestly from him. He emphasized this again in Thesis 13 of January 1523, stating that to understand the Word of God men need to be enlightened by God. In sum, men must submit all their teachings about doctrine to the written text of Scripture.

But in his view of Scripture Zwingli differed from Luther in giving Scripture an almost juridical function, since he used Scripture to apply not only to God's saving work in Christ but also to the method of ruling in human society and the government of it. Again, unlike Luther he did not emphasize that in Scripture some parts had less or little authority in comparison with other parts. Zwingli tended to identify the authority of the Word of God in both Old and New Testaments as of equal importance and thus to blur the distinction between Law and Gospel which Luther made. Zwingli seemed to brush aside problems concerning the Scripture being obscure or self-contradictory. Either he failed to find time to see these problems, or he was so concerned to avoid any concession to the use of tradition or the authority of the church in interpreting Scripture that problems about understanding the Bible did not hold him from his course. (Melanchthon attempted to resolve this problem by recourse to the 'Testimony of the Fathers' and to Faculties of theology who were regarded as the means of arriving at a consensus of interpretation; Calvin, by the office of doctors of the church whose function it was to deal with these problems; but in the event this office tended to be shadowy in his writings.)

From Scripture we turn to Zwingli's doctrines of sin and grace which show the condition we are in through the fall of man, and how we are saved from that state. The whole race is dead in Adam through his sin, and this is the infirmity and defect of our ruined nature. Sin is a penchant to evil and to disobedience to God's will. We are so affected by original sin that

---

[1] *Zwinglis Sämtliche Werke*, I, pp. 338ff.

this defect which we inherit at birth, prevents us from living in innocence before God and obeying Him. But Zwingli is more mild than Luther or Calvin here. He states that we still have an indwelling desire for God so that even the pagans who lived before Christ felt something of the guidance of the Spirit though few realized it. When the natural man has glimpses of truth these are due to God's guiding. Nevertheless the defect of sin is sufficiently strong to prevent men from finding deliverance from it through their own strength. The Christian life consists in putting trust in God since we are assured by Christ of the divine mercy: by the example of Christ we die daily to sin and our condition is transformed by Christ. The basic affirmation here is Pauline and Christocentric – Christ on our behalf endured the punishment for sin on the Cross and fulfilled the works of righteousness. When we believe in Him and seek to follow Christ's example God regards us as righteous. Here faith is shown as trust and confidence in God's gracious purpose for us: this faith is worked in us by the Spirit of God and faith is born of the Word of God seen in Scripture showing us Christ's work. This distinguishes Zwingli from Luther who sees faith as directly related to Christ, whereas Zwingli sees the relationship as Christ-Scripture-faith. This concerns the means of knowing faith, but faith in itself is guided by the Spirit giving certitude and bringing peace of soul to the anxious sinner. This opens the question, Could there be a sacramental presence in view of this direct certitude through faith? In so far as an objective correlative to faith is desirable, for Luther it is to be found in the sacramental presence of Christ and for Zwingli it is to be found in Scripture. (Zwingli will use this concept of faith and its objective support when he comes to oppose Luther's doctrine of the real presence.) It is possible to express this differently by stating that Zwingli uses two aspects of faith, faith as giving immediate peace to the soul, and faith as conveyed to us through the Word of God, that is, Scripture. As did Luther, however, Zwingli insists that good works can only follow upon faith. We are shown the law of God in Scripture and it is our duty in faith to obey it and fulfil it; this is made possible by God working in us by His Spirit. Here, again, Zwingli differs from Luther: he gives the Law a positive emphasis in contrast to Luther's more negative attitude to the Law.

Zwingli was not content to see salvation as resting on faith alone: he sought also to link salvation more closely to God's sovereign election. God gives faith to those whom He choses, regardless of their merit, and this is God's secret decision into which it is no use for us to inquire. Good works are considered as the consequence of faith, therefore not meritorious, and they show that God's Spirit is working in us. They are the sign of our election and perseverance in faith: this is our regeneration. Here again comes an important distinction from Luther. With Luther faith is a starting point, and it needs external aids to increase it, that is, the mediation of the Word and the Sacraments. But for Zwingli faith, because of his radical immediate appropriation of its fruits in Christ, needs less mediation. We are instructed because of our election. Justification for Zwingli includes the process of regeneration indicated above: this is due, in part, to his being less aware of the appalling consequences of original sin than was Luther.

Zwingli set himself against the possibility of antinomianism which he believed lay in Luther's opposing Law to Gospel. He saw, however, as did Luther, how important it was to find deliverance from the Law in so far as it points only to sin and its dire consequences, but he also in addition gives it a more positive and abiding place as having a teaching role showing men a right way of life.

Providence is closely associated with election in Zwingli, for he had a powerful sense of the active omnipresent power of God which was no doubt based on his personal experience (see, for example, his *Plague-Song*), as well as being attractive to his philosophical interests. In his book on providence Zwingli, who claims to be a biblical and Christocentric theologian, shows a curiously logical, even scholastic interest in proofs for God's providential power. Since God in His very being is good, the good will finally win because of God's omnipresent and omnipotent power – evil has only an incidental existence here. This attitude approaches, if it does not become, metaphysical determinism in which contingency disappears. Nothing escapes God's foreknowledge concerning men and grace, so that Zwingli equates predestination with preordination; it is the way in which providence acts. Apparently without the thought disturbing him he affirms the division of mankind into the elect and the reprobate, and he makes divine uncontingent causality the ground of the rejection of the reprobate – this shows, in fact's God's justice. Election is represented as irresistible power. One ground of comfort is found in his assertion that the premature death of infants is a sign of election. The evil works of the reprobate are a sign of their reprobation, and the good works of the elect are a sign of their election. Zwingli, with his less insistence on the potency of sin and evil, has some degree of optimism about providence and predestination; he lacks the awe and fear shown, for example, in Calvin later. It may be that elements of contemporary Neo-Stoic thought, through the interest shown in the writings of Cicero and Seneca in Renaissance philosophy, influenced him here. He could even write that good pagans living before Christ could be among the elect by God's free choice. Predestination is the fulcrum by which Catholicism can be levered away: its insistence on the priority of good works can be overturned by it. This insistence on fixed election in predestination as the only ground on which a man can be sure of salvation is for Zwingli (as for other Reformers) the chief weapon against the Catholic doctrine of grace. However, for daily living, in moral practice and teaching, he tends to imply free-will by making the Gospel, so to speak, into a 'new Law': here is the moral law, now we must obey it. (Zwingli is rejecting Luther's opposition between Law and Gospel: he does so by making the New Testament take over and continue from the Old Testament, and by stressing the existence of 'the natural law'.) This again shows Zwingli's pragmatic attitude. He wishes to emphasize that our duty is not to talk about doctrine, including predestination, but to get on with good Christian living. However, as a theological weapon against both Catholics and Anabaptists Zwingli frequently used the doctrine of predestination to undermine any reliance on good works.

From the discussion of election it is easy to turn to Zwingli's doctrine of the Church since the Church is the sphere in which the Christian life is developed and the Church is grounded on election – the Church consists of the elect. By God's gift of faith the elect grasp the fact of their election and are assured of it, but their election can be understood only from within the Church. This corrects the assertion made by some writers who derive from his book on providence the assumption that he advocated metaphysical determinism without reference to the life of the Church. To assume this is to fail to grasp that Zwingli's main concern is pastoral, to being people into saving relationship with Christ. He is willing to make the charitable judgment that election is to be assumed in a person if there is no obvious evidence of a reprobate life – hence his acceptance of the salvation of good pagans and infant children. The Church is not only the company of the elect; it is also a covenanted society, the final stage of God's covenants with Israel. Here emerges a seed which was to take a very strong root later in the Reformed Churches in contrast with the Lutherans – the covenant and the covenanted people of God. The Church is, of course, seen in two ways; first the invisible company of all the elect in Christ who cannot be condemned, and secondly, the local communities, parishes and cantonal churches. But the latter are no mere construction of men, although they are in line with the particular political structures of a nation or city. They are part of God's will, and reflect His will in Christ towards mankind which works through such institutions. This Church must exercise discipline to exclude scandalous sinners and readmit the penitent, and have oversight of the work of the preachers. But the Church is not simply recognized by having discipline as the Anabaptists declared, nor the hierarchy as the Catholics insisted.

Zwingli's churchmanship was originally simplistic, as seen in his Theses of 1523, where he emphasizes the society of true believers who are held together by spiritual and non-institutional links. But he had to go further: it has been stated that Zwingli saw the Bible as containing regulative laws for Christians, and he takes this 'law of God' so far as to see it providing the guide for worship and organization in the visible or institutional church. This led him beyond Luther's view of the Church, by laying down rules he derived from Scripture for a particular organization of the Church. Luther tended to leave church organization to the territorial ruler guided by Melanchthon's principles, and saw no necessity for change from past patterns unless they interfered with the biblical doctrine of grace which he had expounded. Zwingli, however, believing that Scripture set down clear rules, made a clean sweep of things belonging to the past, and brought the greatest simplicity – no images, no organs, no vestments, no chalices and patens. Again, Zwingli seems to have been unaware of, or indifferent to, the need for finding a close link between the invisible and catholic church of the elect, and the visible congregations organized within a certain city or canton or nation.[1] Calvin later sought strongly to make close the link between invisible and visible partly through his sacramental emphasis. But Zwingli's visible churches seem to be more concerned with jurisdictional functions

---

[1] The final statement of Zwingli on the Church is in *Christianae Fidei . . . Expositio* (1531), *Zwinglis Werke*, IV, pp. 44ff.

than with the teaching and sacramental office of the Church. (For him a key passage in Scripture on the Church is S. Matthew, ch. 18, vv. 15–18.) Further his strong sense of being a good Confederate, a loyal Swiss, with commitment to the cantonal units of the Swiss Confederation, gave him a strong emotional sense of the need to relate the canton of Zürich with the life of the parishes: the parishes became very closely identified with the civil pattern and administration. Zwingli saw God's providence at work in the magistrates at Zürich abolishing Catholicism and setting up a biblically grounded reformed Church, and was willing therefore to encourage the identification of the Zürich Church with the Zürich state. The enforcement of the discipline of morals and church obedience with the sanction of excommunication was wholly in the hands of the magistracy: at first, Zwingli saw this as strength (it brought ready victory over the Anabaptists) but later realized that it involved too little independence for the Church as a spiritual society.

It was not that Zwingli believed the canton of Zürich was a wholly Christian society but that God had ordained that through this state, led by its Christian magistrates, an order was created through which the citizens could develop in the Christian life. He was convinced that there had to be a relationship between the magistrates governing the community on the one hand and the church on the other, doing so under the higher authority of the Word of God, so that the full preaching of that Word was made available to all and that every citizen was thus given the opportunity of obedience to it. The magistrate cannot create a true Christian community: only God through His Word can do this; but the magistrate is a God-appointed instrument to that end as long as he is obedient to God. For Zwingli the Roman Catholic Church, the Anabaptists and the Spiritualists were separatists and sectaries since they rejected the preaching, the sacraments and the discipline set forth by the Word of God and supported by the magistrates. Zwingli, in the event, gave away too much to the state which he saw as identified with the model of the Jewish state idealized in the Old Testament which for him represented both the civil order and the Church as having their sanction in God's law. He held to a straightforward, indeed oversimplified, theocracy. But it would be to misunderstand his purpose to say that he identified Church and state in the sense that the state had the primary place and that the outward forms of the Church in worship and discipline of themselves had saving power; since he believed that the Christian was not a Christian by being a citizen of Zürich – rather, he is a Christian by confessing his faith, by his obedience to the Word of God, by his dependence on God's promises in Christ, and ultimately by the mystery of his sovereign election by God.

Unfortunately, this view of the Church, in spite of Zwingli's qualification just stated implies a secondary place for the nature and status of the ministry and the sacraments they administer. If the Church's nature consists in confessing believers, elect and obedient to the rule of God in His Word, then traditional notions of priesthood, hierarchy, ministerial status and authority are all rejected or greatly reduced, and the sacraments tend to become aids to faith supporting a relationship already established otherwise between believers and God. The ministry of the Church consists of those called by God to be preachers of His Word, they have been taught by it, and are to expound it: this is recognized by the Church of Zürich through the magistrates who as representatives of the Church appoint ministers to the office of preachers in the community. Zwingli noted there were four kinds of ministry in Ephesians ch. 4 – apostle, prophet, evangelist, and pastor (bishop) or doctor. Since all these share the fundamental office of expounding the Word of God then there is really one ministry with a variety of expressions of it.[1] On behalf of the Church the ministers exercise discipline, which is intended to build up obedience to the Word of God and true brotherhood in Christ rather than to be merely penal. Because of the traditional severe consequences of excommunication the magistrates refused to leave this powerful weapon in the hands of the ministers and reserved the right to excommunicate to themselves. It has already been said that Zwingli came to regret this extensive claim by the state since it meant the association of the civil power and its punishments with the healing office of discipline, which was a dangerous linking of the civil law and Christian morality. This is worth noting in view of the possible criticism to which the Reformed churches were open later that they tended to moralistic legalism, for example, in seventeenth-century Presbyterianism. (Calvin was to labour hard to prevent the state from controlling excommunication at Geneva and won not much more than a compromise after a long struggle.) Since the ministers exercised discipline as well as preached as prophets of the Word, Zwingli emphasized this function by calling a minister not only a 'pastor' (*Hirt*) but also a 'watchman' (*Wachter*).[2] Later Zwingli came to emphasize more and more the conception of the minister as 'prophet' – here he saw the most significant rôle of ministry. Towards the end of his career as a reformer Zwingli added the notion of an 'elder' who was to be a layman, presumably elected by the individual congregation or parish, to help in the practice of discipline and oversight in the Church. Here is foreshadowed the distinctive office of the Reformed Churches, already suggested by Oecolampadius at Basel, to be developed by Calvin, and further enlarged in later Presbyterianism, though it does not seem to have been introduced in practice by Zwingli at Zürich.

On the Sacraments Zwingli markedly departed from Luther and created also difficulties for the development of the Reformed Churches since Calvin could not follow his views. It could be argued that in later history the Zwinglian and Calvinist views of the sacraments were never finally reconciled. For example, the influence of Bullinger and Laski in England and Knox in Scotland leaned more to Zürich than to Geneva on the sacraments. As was said above, Zwingli did not give a close link between the invisible and the visible church, and also with the sacraments he was so concerned not to confine, or to associate, God's grace closely with sensible signs that he separated the sign from the thing signified. His early training in Realist philosophy, and even more probably his interest in Platonism, may have influenced him to emphasize the difference between the 'ideal' in heaven

[1] *Zwinglis Sämtliche Werke*, IV, p. 390.
[2] *Zwinglis Sämtliche Werke*, III, pp. 5–68.

and the 'sensible' on earth. The suggestions of Erasmus and Hoen have been mentioned earlier as influencing Zwingli towards 'spiritualizing' the sacraments. He reduced the traditional number of sacraments to two, Baptism and the Lord's Supper, and he gave these a secondary place as supporting faith rather than making it possible and ensuring its growth. He used the history of the word *sacramentum* to demonstrate its pagan and secular origin, and wrote that he wished the word had not come into Christian usage. He avoided using it as relating to an action holy and grace-giving of itself, or even as a sign of grace being given to the believer. He regarded the two sacraments instituted by Christ as pledges reminding Christians to keep the faith: God is free and will not bind his gift of faith to the outward signs of water or bread and wine. Against Catholics and Lutherans he denied that these signs could convey 'holiness', or 'forgiveness' or 'grace'. Instead they are helps to the community (the congregation, *Gemeinde*), they are signs of, and for, faith within the community and not for the individual believer. Through Baptism we confess Christ's name in the congregation: through the Lord's Supper we show we are members together of the Church, which is Christ's body, and we remember His accomplished work of salvation and His victory on the cross. Since Luther insisted on the objective reality of grace given through the sacrament of Holy Communion, we can see that Zwingli was on a collision course – a course which split irrevocably the unity of the Protestant Reformation. Zwingli wrote: 'Let us affirm that these are signs, or ceremonies, by which the believer professes before the Church to be the disciple or soldier of Christ, and that they have as their aim to certify your faith to the Church, rather than to give you certainty for yourself.'[1] Here Zwingli has reversed the function of sacrament hitherto held in the Churches of the East and West, and continued by Luther. It relates more to what the believer does and affirms than to what he is given, and at the same time the believer is drawn from individual needs to solidarity with the community. (Here perhaps recurs the concern for the unity of good confederates.) This affirming and doing, this sense of solidarity, brings moral obligation with it since the sacrament is a pledge of loyalty and responsibility on the part of the believer. Nevertheless, though they are pledges of faith they are not subject to the arrangements of men: they were instituted by Christ to strengthen our faith in His saving work by recalling to us the fact and meaning of His Cross. In sum the sacraments for Zwingli do not have an instrumental value or force, as with the traditional views: their value lies in their psychological and teaching power.

On Baptism Zwingli had to face the vigorous attack of the Anabaptists, including Balthazar Hubmaier, an able writer, and one of the few professionally trained theologians among them, who adopted a position almost identical with that of the modern Baptists – Baptism witnesses to the experience of conversion and the baptized publicly declares his intention of living a new life.[2] Zwingli, like the Anabaptists, attached no importance to the water as indicating the purification of the soul, rather the washing by water is a sign of joining the community (*Gemeinde*) and carries with it the

---

[1] *Zwinglis Sämtliche Werke*, III, p. 761.
[2] Kidd (*The Anabaptists in Zürich*, 1525–32), pp. 451–7.

pledge to live the Christian life; and he regarded the action as having also a teaching significance. From Scripture Zwingli sees Baptism as continuing under the new covenant the intention of circumcision under the old, just as he also affirms that the Passover precedes and continues into the Lord's Supper. Zwingli gave no place to the old baptismal theme of washing away the stain of original sin since he saw this presumably as irrelevant to his stress on what circumcision had meant in Israel, and to his view of a sacrament as primarily a pledge. It was the taking together of the implication of circumcision in the Old Testament, and the lack of a declaration against infant baptism in the New Testament, which enabled Zwingli to oppose the Anabaptists on scriptural grounds. He went further and insisted that the New Testament taught infant baptism; his insistence was reinforced by his belief that it was essential for the sake of the Church as consisting of the whole community. Confining baptism to adults would introduce the sectarian principle which he vigorously rejected, since it divided and destroyed the community of Christian people. He brushed aside any suggestions that his view of Baptism did not cover all the statements relating to it in the New Testment. He was driven in this direction by the Anabaptists insisting on the New Testament evidence and isolating parts of it in their favour. In order to destroy the force of their argument he undermined their insistence on the primacy of Baptism following upon personal declaration of faith, by making it an external sign of obligation laid upon the parents to ensure the Christian education of their children now received into the Church community. To this he added, from the principle of Jewish circumcision, that children born to Christian parents are heirs of the covenant given in the Old Testament and renewed in the New Testament, and therefore baptism is not dependent on personal faith since it is a sign of the predestination of the elect. Here he shows once again his determination to separate the sign from the thing signified.[1]

While this affected less his view of Baptism, for other Protestants his determination to separate the sign from what it signifies sharply affected his view of the Lord's Supper and was to become the cause of acute division among Protestants not only in his own time but long afterwards. For Zwingli this sacrament can be no more than an aid to the strengthening of our faith: of itself it is not a means of grace. Like Baptism it is a public testimony to our faith in which we pledge obedience to God and give Him thanks for His goodness towards us. Zwingli was determined to find a means of destroying the basis of the Catholic and traditional conception of the Real Presence of Christ, as he had been determined to destroy the basis of the Anabaptists' argument on baptism. Luther's view of this sacrament as an objective correlative to faith, and as the grace-bearing presence of Christ in, with and under the elements of bread and wine, Zwingli saw as almost identical with the Catholic view, and therefore near to idolatry caused by the identification of the sign with the thing signified. It has been shown above that the cautiously expressed views of Erasmus, and the more positive view of Cornelis Hoen, in Zwingli's first beginnings as a Reformer, had led him to a spiritualizing and symbolizing conception of the sacrament

[1] *Zwinglis Sämtliche Werke*, IV, pp. 188–337; 577–642; V, 448–452; VI, 1–196.

congenial to his humanist training: he feared and disliked identifying spiritual reality with visible things – water, bread, wine, hierarchy etc. As with his treatment of Baptism Zwingli starts afresh with Scripture, accepting no traditional views on what the eucharistic passages mean. John ch. 6 is essential to the argument; all the expressions about feeding on Christ's flesh found therein are overthrown by verse 63 which shows that the intention is symbolical; John is not showing Christ as teaching a sacramental feeding upon Himself. What we feed on is faith in Christ, 'the flesh profits nothing', therefore the words of Christ 'my flesh is food indeed' mean His flesh was given up to death on the Cross and we feed on that saving truth by faith. Further, Zwingli wished to emphasize thanksgiving in a fellowship meal, recalling the pledge to identify with the Christian community and its solidarity in fellowship. If we are to seek the 'mystical body of Christ' then it is to be found symbolized by the community or *Gemeinde* and not enclosed within the elements of bread and wine. When the sacrament is ministered the words of institution (the words used by Christ at the last supper), 'This is my body' means no more than 'signify the body', and commemorate the death of Christ and its benefits to us. Christ's word 'is' means here 'signifies' as Hoen (Honius) had proposed – Zwingli noticed too that 'is' means 'signifies' in Luke 8, v. 11 and John 15, v. 1. We must carry our eyes away from what is visible, bread and wine, and set our minds and hearts on invisible God. Faith cannot depend on what can be seen, heard or touched. The Holy Spirit brings to us in the Lord's Supper the quickening of our faith in the saving power of Christ's death and His presence with the Church. Again, Zwingli insisted on the fact of Christ's Ascension to heaven to 'sit at the right hand of God'; since Christ dwells there He cannot be with bread and wine on earth. But what of I Corinthians 10, vv. 16–22? Zwingli answers this by saying that 'participation in the blood of Christ' means sharing in the blood of the covenant, and 'participation in the body of Christ' means sharing in the Church.[1]

The movement of Zwingli's thought on the sacraments and especially on the Lord's Supper began from a different basis than that of Luther and developed along lines which Luther was wholly unwilling to accept. Luther's intransigence towards Zwingli's eucharistic teaching began from Luther's acute suspicion of his former colleague Karlstadt, who had rejected Luther's assertion that the bread and the wine and the body and the blood of Christ are at the same time present – the 'Real Presence'. Since Karlstadt sympathized with sectarian extremists this meant he had become in Luther's eyes like them a 'fanatic' (*Schwärmer*) divisive and misleading to faithful Christians. Karlstadt, expelled from Saxony, visited Strasbourg, and Zwingli as well as Bucer came to know of his views. Luther suspected both Bucer and Zwingli thereafter as potential if not actual sympathizers with Karlstadt. Matters became worse when Oecolampadius of Basel published an account of the teachings of the early Church fathers on the Lord's Supper which were shown as more inclined to support Zwingli than Luther. Basel, Strasbourg and Zürich were all suspect now at Wittenberg. Several

[1] For the Eucharistic Controversy, cf. G. R. Potter, *Huldrych Zwingli* (Documents of Modern History), London, 1978, pp. 89–109.

writings were published from Saxony and Zürich, and in 1528 Luther published a treatise on the Lord's Supper in which he described those who did not hold to his interpretation as heretics. This division in Protestantism was not only disruptive among the churches but also politically dangerous, since a divided Protestantism might well fall before a Catholic counter-attack. The Landgrave of Hesse with Bucer of Strasbourg sought to resolve the differences by a conference at Marburg in 1529. A number of articles of doctrine were discussed and all agreed except one, that on the nature of Christ's presence in the Lord's Supper. Luther had developed from the teaching on the two natures of Christ declared at the Council of Chalcedon in 451, and the medieval scholastic notion of *communicatio idiomatum* ('communion of the properties', that is, the attributes of the one nature of Christ could be affirmed of the other), the view that the human nature of Christ participates in the powers of the divine nature including omnipresence, ubiquity, whereby His body could be present wherever the Lord's Supper is celebrated. A prolonged discussion on Christology ensued at Marburg – Zwingli insisting that the two natures of Christ are distinct and must not be confused, and that the body of Christ is localized in heaven. Superficially it might appear that Zwingli was taking the doctrine of the Incarnation more seriously than Luther, but in the writings of both on the controversy his position is far from being secure: in the end of the day Luther is emphasizing a living risen Christ present with us now similar to His presence on earth, and Zwingli is emphasizing a commemoration of Christ's death and insisting that His Ascension removes Him far from visible signs. To Luther Zwingli's Lord's Supper seemed to be one more human work, inefficacious, and without the fulfilled promise of Christ being intimately with His people. To Zwingli Luther still seemed to be obsessed with Catholic notions which were unscriptural.

Attempts were made to heal this division after Zwingli's death; Melanchthon and Bucer agreed to the Concord of Wittenberg in 1536 (but Melanchthon did not identify himself with Luther's own formulation and the Concord was not acceptable to later Lutherans). The successor of Zwingli at Zürich, Bullinger, refused to agree to the Concord since that might appear to be disloyalty to Zwingli's views. Bullinger eventually conceded some change, but not to Lutherans, when an agreement was made between Zürich and Geneva in 1549 on the Lord's Supper.[1]

---

[1] The *Consensus Tigurinus* (Kidd, pp. 652–6).

Philip Melanchthon and Martin Bucer

E. Gordon Rupp

Philip Melanchthon and
Martin Bucer

E. Gordon Rupp

At the heart of the modern developments in Reformation studies, which are still acquiring momentum, lie the new critical editions of the works of the Reformers. In the case of Luther, Zwingli and Calvin such editions have been the focus for a great complex of study, from dissertations and mono-graphs to secondary works of depth and intricacy. Now it is the turn of those important theologians who did not 'attain to the first three'. In the last decades, new editions of the works of Melanchthon, Bucer, Brenz, Osiander on the Lutheran side, Bullinger, Beza and Peter Martyr in the Reformed tradition have appeared, presenting a whole body of interesting material, such that the overall picture of reformation doctrine is likely to be profoundly modified, and a new alignment of theologians to result, in coming years. This is a time then, for tentative, provisional and interim judgments. These things are true in eminent degree about the assessment of

PHILIP MELANCHTHON (1497–1560)

Recent bibliographical works by Hammer, Fraenkel and Greschat have noted the acceleration in publications about the thought of Melanchthon and they have had to note that in some very important questions, the relation between his evangelical theology and his humanist anthropology, his agreements and differences with Luther, the relation of the young to the old Melanchthon, eminent scholars are still divided. What he wrote affected profoundly the religion of the German people, and his legacy to the Lutheran church, his influence on Protestant Orthodoxy and indeed on all subsequent Lutheran development was so fateful that he will always be a centre of controversy. This is not to deny consensus about the main events of his life, and a general admission of his greatness as an evangelical theologian. It seems reasonable, following Maurer, to recognize the deep impact upon his development of three men, his uncle Reuchlin, the great Erasmus, and Martin Luther. Through his birth and his relationship with Reuchlin, Melanchthon was placed within the context not only of the Northern renaissance, but of that South German humanism which owed much to Wimpfeling, and which joined him with other young men, like Oecolampadius and John Brenz, in the Universities of Heidelberg and Tübingen. His whole training was concentrated in the classics and the humanities, and it was as a Professor of Greek that, on his uncle's recom-mendation, he went to Wittenberg. That he was known as 'Master' Philip and did not advance beyond the degree of 'Baccalaureus Biblicus' marks him off from Martin Luther, who was very much a mediaeval Doctor of

Divinity and whose early lectures show striking expertise in that fifteenth-century theological tradition in which he grew and against which he rebelled.

Melanchthon was in his teens that tiresome figure, an academic prodigy, taking degrees, bursting into print in prose and poetry, and astonishing and delighting his elders, like Luther, with the maturity of the programme of academic reform which he adumbrated in his celebrated inaugural lecture in 1518. No doubt he inherited much from his uncle, such as an element of Platonism, though he did not share his uncle's relish for the Cabbala, or for the kind of eclectic mysticism which linked men like Reuchlin, Le Fèvre and Andrew Osiander (!) with the Florentine Platonists, and he had no sympathy with Florentine white magic, though he dabbled in astrology. But he shared his uncle's awareness of the importance of the sacred languages of Hebrew, Greek and a renovated Latin. But here his ideal was fulfilled in the work of Erasmus, from whom he learned the philological basis of scriptural study, and the beginnings of a new 'method' in theology. Like Erasmus he had a life-long interest in education and in edification, and was deeply influenced by classical, ethical and rhetorical traditions. Indeed so deep did these things persist in his thought and in his life-long and immense educational achievement that we perhaps get some idea in Melanchthon of what Erasmus might have done for the Reformation movement had he, like this young man, been early won to the evangelical doctrines.

And while it was Luther who turned him against scholastic theology and the perverse infiltration of Aristotle into revealed doctrine, he shared with Erasmus a revulsion against the muddled priorities of the schoolmen, their sectarian preoccupation with subtleties, and above all the new barbarism which he believed might lead to the destruction of all sound learning, and which Melanchthon continued to dread when signs of it appeared in the Reformation movement also. The Scriptures, properly interpreted, became for Melanchthon the supreme authority for Christian truth, but he did not in any way minimize the significance of the Fathers of the early centuries, and especially of St. Augustine. At the outset of his career Melanchthon thus found himself involved in a revolution in theological method: in the first place the return to Scripture, replacing post-Lombard theology with the writings of the Fathers. In this direct attention to the Bible itself he was at one with others in the fateful first decade of the reformation when Erasmus, Oecolampadius, Bucer, Zwingli began a great spate of directly Biblical commentaries. In the first place it was a Pauline renaissance, for Melanchthon and Bucer were pre-eminently Paul men (unlike Luther in whose thought there is a powerful Johannine element), but hardly less influential too, a return to the Old Testament and the writings of the Prophets.

But no more then than now was an entirely Biblical theology possible, and in the end the theological and philosophic scaffolding had to be re-erected. Melanchthon shared with Erasmus a concern for a new 'method' in theological exposition, the grouping of 'topics' and 'commonplaces' which were to become so important in coming decades. No doubt the idea owed something, as Erasmus explicitly said, to classical and humanist precedents, though the elements had never disappeared from the medieval theologies, from the 'Sentences' and 'Summae' of the twelfth and thirteenth centuries, to the 'quaestiones' of the latter Middle Ages, and the extended theological excurses – the 'Scholia' – of the Biblical commentaries.

But when Melanchthon came to Wittenberg he met in Martin Luther, not so much a colleague as a destiny (Bornkamm). To this young man Luther behaved with immense generosity and sensitivity and with an unflagging admiration for gifts which he regarded as superior to his own. Their training and temperament were very different, as were the qualities of their minds – but to an astonishing extent complementary, so that Lutheranism would have been unthinkable without either of them. And however relations between them might be strained – and one is bound to sympathize with Melanchthon at this point, in Luther's latter years especially – the bond held between them, adding unique poignancy to that last decade when Melanchthon had to soldier on, alone.

When all has been said about Melanchthon's humanism, about his ability to synthesize – about his 'Melanchthon – and' (as against 'Luther – or') eclecticism, he did fatefully and deeply understand what Luther meant by the gospel, and that what he received at this point, or rather what with Luther he re-discovered in the Bible, was not a set of notions or doctrines, but an initiation into the experience of salvation, of a forgiven and re-generated soul, set at peace and liberty by grace, and turned from disobedience to a new life, within the redeemed community, within a forgiven and edifying solidarity, through the action of the Word.

Scholars have by no means done with the investigation of Melanchthon's developing anthropology and psychology in his early lectures and the impact upon it of his immersion with Luther in the theological ferment attending the great church struggle in those fateful months between the Leipzig disputation and the Diet of Worms.

Obviously his concentration on the Epistle to the Romans and on the fifth chapter in particular was of critical importance and is reflected in the shape of the first edition of his *Loci Communes* in 1521 with their concentration on sin and law. Like the *Institutes* of Calvin it was to go through many revisions and editions and the final shape, in 1555, was to be a very different compendium. But here – succinct, lucid, seminal – was an intelligible presentation of the new affirmation of the gospel. Luther was ecstatic in his praise for it and it became rapidly of international influence. It was clear that at the moment when he was most needed, at the beginning of an era of polemic and confession, a man had appeared with a genius for definition, and a skill in theological formulation. This became still more evident at the fateful watershed of Augsburg (1530) when the *Confession* – Melanchthon's little masterpiece – became the frame for the new evangelical leadership and for the Lutheran churches. Though it became almost at once a confessional document, Melanchthon considered it his own theological property and he could add to it, or detract from it, while his own defence of it against the catholic counter-confession, his *Apology*, became his greatest piece of theological argumentation: no wonder that France and England tried again and again to win him to their territories.

There are manifest perils in definitions and formulae. The mystery of salvation is too profound and complex to be compassed in a hundred or even a thousand words. There were opposites and paradoxes of truth which Luther intuitively grasped and expounded unsystematically, occasionally, sometimes incoherently, though amazingly consistently, in a flood of tracts, sermons, commentaries. John Brenz wrote in some alarm in 1531 about the new definition of justification in forensic terms – 'gratis justificentur, propter Christum per fidem, cum credunt se in gratiam recipi, et peccata remitti propter Christum, qui sua morte pro nostris peccatis satisfecit. Hanc fidem imputat Deus pro justicia coram ipso' (CA art. 4) – '(they teach) – that men are justified freely on account of Christ through faith, when they believe that they are received into grace and their sins remitted on account of Christ, who made satisfaction by His death for our sins. This faith God imputes for righteousness in His sight'. He asked what had happened to the regenerating influence of the presence of Christ within the soul?. Here was in Melanchthon an emphasis on objectivities which held within it the root of the later conflict with Osiander.

But this was not only to misconceive Luther but also Melanchthon. He has been accused of stressing too much the element of knowledge within faith, of overemphasizing 'pure doctrine', of concentrating on the 'benefits of Christ' rather than on Christ himself; and perhaps rationalist and moralist were more evident than mystical elements in his thought. But when one reads his affirmations at length, in the later editions of his *Loci* and in the noble exposition of his *Confessio Saxonica* (1551), one cannot but observe how again and again religion breaks through, the thought of faith as centring in God's forgiving mercy, of the 'benefits of Christ' as being peace in one's conscience, a new liberty and the new life into which Christ brings the redeemed soul. Heinrich Bornkamm in one of the most luminous assessments of Melanchthon, stresses the importance for him of the concept of 'the heart'.

These evangelical doctrines and these emphases seem to be central to Melanchthon's view of the gospel, and they link him indissolubly with Luther. But he could not isolate these things. He had somehow to reconcile them with a view of human nature, and indeed of the very structure of the moral universe, and he valiantly attempted to construct a scaffolding of rational apologetic in which Stoic, Ciceronian and Aristotelian elements appear. His humanist concern for instruction and edification led him to innumerable writings of texts and studies, which branched out from biblical and linguistic texts to reflect his interest in the whole realm of learning, in dialectic and rhetoric, in law, and psychology, in medicine and astronomy, held together in a view of the wholeness of truth, and the centrality of theology, which earned him the label of being himself a 'one man university'.

His grasp of the dialectic between law and gospel did not mean for him (it did not for Luther, either) a disregard of the ancient and received notions of moral, natural and positive law. But Guido Kisch has impressively printed a number of orations and counsel's opinions of Melanchthon on legal matters, and in Luther's last years it was upon Melanchthon that the heavy task fell of keeping good relations between the legal and theological faculties in Wittenberg. Hand in hand with the creative task of preparing the tools of the new learning, came his vital office of restoring educational institutions of higher education, the immensely influential achievement which won him the enduring title of 'Praeceptor Germaniae'. From the first, too, he was involved in the restoration of ecclesiastical discipline – from the time of the Saxon Visitation (1527–8), and in the concern which he shared with Luther and his other colleagues for the raising of the standard of clerical education (his splendid set of questions *'for the Examination of Ordinands'* (1552) is an emblem of this concern).

Though he fully shared with Luther the view of the church as a communion of saints, a forgiven and edifying community, he came more and more and in the end in an un-Lutherlike way to stress the importance of the visible and institutional church. But this for him too was rooted in a profound awareness of the importance of the one holy catholic church of Christ, and so for the mending of the great and widening schisms between Christian men.

Hence his abhorrence of sectarianism, the recurring 'damnant Anabaptistas' ('our Churches condemn the Anabaptists –') of his Confession, his willingness to compass many lands (if not many seas) to come to agreement with the Emperor and if possible even with the Pope, the long and intricate negotiations which from 1530 onwards he willingly entered into in a great series of conversations and debates, which took their toll upon his spirit, and for which he was temperamentally quite unsuited, and which brought at the end, as to so many ecumenical conversationalists, a degree of disillusion.

With the death of Luther, and the appalling military and political disasters which befell the evangelical cause in 1547, a grim period began for Melanchthon, sharpened by intimate bereavements in his family. For the sake of unity, for the peace of church and Empire, Melanchthon was inclined to give wide limits to what were generally conceded to be 'adiaphora' ('things indifferent') and after the appearance of the Leipzig Interim, to bow in the house of Rimmon when many friends and colleagues went into exile. There came from some quarters a new attack on his integrity and a complaint that perhaps, throughout the years he had been led to fatal compromises with even Luther's inheritance, in his doctrines of faith in relation to works, in his definitions of sin, in his abandonment of the view of the complete passivity of the human will.

Somehow Luther had managed to hold together a number of doctrines in balance and tension and with a success which some of his students, colleagues and disciples could not compass. Soon Melanchthon found himself at the centre of half a dozen controversies, all of which at one point seemed aimed at himself. Most painful and bitter was that with Flaccius Illyricus and 'God's chancellery' at Jena, but also the accusation of crypto-Calvinism, and of compromise in the matter of the eucharist: and a whole series of angry debates with theologians in Prussia, with Osiander and then with Stancarus and Staphylus, ranging from the balance of subjective and objective elements in justification, to intricate problems of Christology and of the divine nature. Bornkamm says 'He had always understood what was decisive in Luther: but he did not understand it in its one-sidedness and exclusiveness and he sought to align it with the awareness of philosophic thought.' Justification by faith alone – with the necessary appeal for moral freedom: revelation and natural theology: Luther's thought of the church as a pure fellowship in faith, with the conception of a legal institution alongside other human corporations: the service of love for which Luther could call on Christian princes to serve their communities, with the humanist view that the prince has to care for all the welfare of his subjects – and we may add the view that the godly ruler has to watch over both Tables of the Law.

When one envisages those last stormy, lonely years, when internecine strife about 'pure doctrine' fatally divided Protestantism in a time of deadly peril, so that all the Catholics had to do, at angry conferences, was to sit back and watch the Protestants devour one another, one sees how the years had toughened Melanchthon, who knew better than in 1530 how and where to dig in his toes and refuse to compromise and who no longer dissolved in every emotional crisis into an Alice swimming in her pool of tears. The little paper found after his death is really most revealing. It shows his dedication to truth and wisdom: that burning intellectual curiosity which has some-times been put down to original sin, but which was really the massive 'Credo ut intelligam' – 'I believe that I may understand' – of the great Christian tradition, as it was to be the bastion for modern integrities.

> 'You will be redeemed from sin
> And set free from the cares and fury of *theologia*.'

And perhaps at the end a hint of that Christian Platonist tradition which had been his first infection

> 'You come to the light, you will look upon God
>   and His Son.
> You will understand the wonderful mysteries which
>   you could not understand in this life,
> Why we were made in this way and not in another,
> And in what the union of two natures in Christ
>   consist'

Not, it is said, one of the creative, original thinkers of mankind but one who belonged, as Dilthey said, to that great band of under-rated and under-estimated men who have had immeasurable influence for good, those great orderers of human thought who have put together and made comprehensible and articulate the thoughts of others, and enabled them to become a continuing inheritance for many generations.

MARTIN BUCER (1491–1552)

What is often distinctive and determinative about the theology of the Reformers, apart from context of life and gifts of temperament, is not the ingredients but the proportion of the ingredients. Most of the early Re-formers owed much to classical thought, more than they knew to medieval theology and spirituality; and for them isolated treatises like the *Epistle to the Romans* and Augustine's *Spirit and Letter* might be deeply influential. So there were many similarities in ingredients between Melanchthon and Bucer, but the overall result turned out to be strikingly different. Certainly Martin Bucer is one of those second-line Reformers whose reputation grows as his works are re-published and studied. The swarthy, stocky Alsatian with his large nose and his tendency to talk too much, yet with his warmth and sincerity was one of the 'characters' of the Reformation, and such over-statements as that he was the Pietist among the Reformers, and the Father of the Puritans, touch a real point.

He too owed much to the setting of South German and Alsatian humanism with its fine grammar schools like that at Sélestat, and its learning of which scholars like Wimpfeling and Beatus Rhenanus were real if minor glories. He was entered by his parents within the Dominican order at an age so young that he had little difficulty later on in securing canonical dispensation from his vows. He was bred in Thomist theology, but without taking theological degrees; and the extent to which Thomist ideas continued to influence his thought is still a matter of debate. But he soon became a whole-hearted Erasmian, whose works were the first priority among his possessions, and he eagerly turned, like Melanchthon, to the new method of Biblical, theological study using the linguistic tools, and to the new interest in the Fathers as against the schoolmen. He also shared with Melanchthon, though to a less degree, his addiction to the classics, and he fatefully read Plato's *Republic*. Then he met Martin Luther at the Heidelberg disputation (1518) and was completely won over, dining with his new hero, so that he became a devoted Martinian, prepared to suffer for his new loyalties. This initial debt to Luther was deep and lasting, and though he had, as Strohl says, almost a charisma for assimilating the ideas of others, he understood Luther's doctrine of justification and the need to cast oneself on the divine mercy. It may be true that, even more than Melanchthon, he stressed the element of intellectual assent in faith; and it is certainly true that his doctrine of predestination put justification by faith in another context. In 1523 he came to the city of Strasbourg, unemployed, alone, friendless: but within a few months he had become the soul of reform in the great community, which in the next years became not only a centre of Reformation, but a city of refuge for all kinds of radicals on the run, and so of an astonishing ferment of debate and discussion. He never dominated Strasbourg as Zwingli and Bullinger Zürich, or Calvin Geneva. The complexities of the Strasbourg situation itself: the fact that he joined a team which included the two Sturms, magistrate and educationist, and such formidable colleagues as Hedio, Zell and above all Wolfgang Capito, and the fact that the magistrates were always alert to the dangers of a new clericalism, meant that Bucer never dominated and in the end had to leave, at an age and in circumstances from which, unlike Calvin's initial departure from Geneva, there could be no triumphant return.

Of great importance for Bucer as for the young Melanchthon was the *Epistle to the Romans*; but whereas for the Wittenberg genius it was the fifth chapter which was crucial, it might seem that for Bucer chapters 8–12 were what counted most. For here there are doctrines of predestination, of the Spirit (Bucer has an interesting concern with the regeneration of all things, which through John Bradford entered the English tradition), and of Christian moral renovation. He had not an original mind, and there is still need for investigation as to why the doctrine of Predestination, which combined a view of salvation and an ecclesiology, should be so important. It was not at all the Martinian proportion of truth, and since we find it in the same area and at the same time in Martin Cellarius (*De operibus Dei*, 1527) and in the writings of Nicholas of Ulm, one has to ask questions about the persistence of Augustinian and even Wycliffite-Hussite notions, in these parts.

But it is important that Bucer's lectures and commentaries – on the Psalms, with its persistent dualism between the godly and ungodly – on Romans and Ephesians – are all concerned with predestination, not as a rationalist system but as expounded within a doctrine of God's saving mercy in Christ, warmed by a doctrine of the Holy Spirit, able to make important the unity both of the Old and New Testaments within one divine Plan of Salvation. Justification by Faith is set within what was to become the classic reformed presentation, with its roots in the great notions of the Epistle of Romans – of calling, of justification, of regeneration, sanctification and glorification. Like Melanchthon Bucer was an incurable moralist, concerned with all his powers about the church as an edified and edifying community and so immersed in liturgical and catechetical experiment. It has been noted that Bucer added to the existing three-dimensional pattern of the church – Word, Sacrament and the discipline of Christ, a notable and characteristic fourth dimension, love: the practical exercise of charity – a doctrine clearly set out in one of the loveliest of all reformation tracts – 'Das ym selbs niemant, sondern anderen leben soll, und wie der mensch dahyn kummen mög' (1523) ('that none must live for himself but for others: and how a man may achieve this'). Bucer had read his Plato in the light of the Bible and the doctrine of 'Commonwealth' – 'Gemeinnutz' – had for him, as for many others of that day, a talismanic importance.

He had to learn the hard way how to achieve reformation, through the agencies of guild and magistrate, in a city where there were always strong counter-agents at work, and this not only in Strasbourg, but with Conrad Sam in Ulm, and in the long abortive tug of war for the soul of Augsburg, where catholic bankers and humanists strove with Lutherans, Zwinglians and Anabaptists. It was in this setting and for this purpose that Bucer wrote one of his most striking writings, a dialogue setting out the duties and powers of the godly magistrate, which in some ways has been seen to anticipate Erastus. He kept to the medieval view of a 'Corpus Christianum' – but a doctrine already drastically modified (as Holl said of Luther) by the doctrine of Word and Sacrament. But he looked back gratefully to the example and legacy of the first days of the Christian Empire, to Constantine and Theodosius and Justinian, who accepted their responsibility for the whole welfare of their subjects, not just for material welfare and public order, but to protect their subjects against blasphemy and heresy. And though in regard to the Anabaptists he was more tolerant than most of his contemporaries – Capito was another exception (they had known the more godly Anabaptists) – his advice to Philip of Hesse on how to deal with the Jews, while based on quite different premises from the views of Luther, led him to similar cruel and depressing practical conclusions.

After the death of Francis Lambert of Avignon, Bucer became the leading theological adviser, with Melanchthon, of the Landgrave Philip of Hesse. Liturgical reform, instruction and education, were matters dear to Bucer, and one of his finest writings is his 'Grund und Ursach' ('Foundation and Origin') (1527) in which he offered an impressive rationale of the new liturgy, perhaps less notable theologically than an earlier document in which Osiander wrote his apologia for the changes in Nuremberg, but breathing the spirit of joy and spontaneity in worship, and undergirding the whole with his rich doctrine of the Holy Spirit. At a period when Word and Spirit were in some danger of being pressed against one another, Bucer combines the two doctrines in a way which as in other matters anticipates Calvin. His debates with the Anabaptists and his recognition that they had a case against a reformation which so far seemed to have led to little amendment of life, led him to a concern for Christian instruction, and for the discipline of the church, and indeed the recognition of the importance of the elements of 'Koinonia' which prompted him to a temporary attempt to foster smaller communities within the church, an anticipation of the later 'collegia pietatis'. The concern for discipline which had so exercised his friend Johannes Oecolampadius was something which continued to preoccupy him and resulted in the massive and important discussions in his treatise 'Von der waren seelsorge und dem rechten Hirtendienst' ('of true cure of souls and true pastoral service') (1538). The work is in the great tradition of pastoral cure, one of concern for the training of the ministry.

In it he gives proper place to the rights and duties of the godly magistrate and his use of the 'jus reformandi', but he is not less concerned with the duties of the congregations and of the ministry, in the exercise of a cure of souls, and a pastoral discipline which has different ends and uses other means than the sanctions of the temporal power. He outlines the four-fold ministry of pastors, teachers, elders and deacons which he conceived to be the New Testament pattern of ministry, and here too he anticipates John Calvin, as well as in the advocacy of the use of lay elders as 'Kirchenpfleger' ('Churchwardens'!): It is generally admitted that Bucer's views on these things must have influenced John Calvin during the important months (1538–41) when he was in Strasbourg as pastor of the French congregation, and we may admit also that Bucer must have learned much from his contacts with this prodigiously gifted younger man. In the matter of the eucharist Bucer should be seen as holding a genuinely mediating position between that of the Swiss and the Wittenberg theologians, though he won little thanks from either side from his attempts to bridge the gap between them. He believed with the Swiss that the presence of Christ in his human nature at God's right hand precluded a Real Presence, but he was prepared to use the realistic language of the Fathers to support the view that with the bread and wine the Body and Blood of Christ are truly exhibited to the faithful.

At Marburg in 1529 he came to see that he had misunderstood Luther to have believed in a localized presence, and from then on bent all his efforts to restore agreement, so that, while unable to convince the Swiss that he had not abandoned truth, he brought off with Melanchthon the important Wittenberg Concord of 1536, and friendlier personal relations with Luther whom he visited at the critical moment of his illness in 1537. With Melanchthon and Calvin he shared in the great series of dialogues and conversations with which the Emperor from 1539 onwards attempted to bring catholics and evangelicals to compromise, if not agreement, and at Hagenau, Worms and Regensburg Bucer took a manful part in intricate debates with the so-called 'mediating' Catholic theologians like Contarini, Pighius and Gropper. In a powerful joint exposition he and Melanchthon drew up an impressive document of liturgical and theological statement with a view to its implementation by Archbishop Hermann von Wied in Cologne – Melanchthon writing most of the theological articles, and Bucer, drawing on the experiments of the last two decades, the liturgical proposals. The document *Pia Deliberatio*, though practically abortive, had some real influence on the English Prayer Book.

In 1548 came the great crisis of conscience about the Imperial Interim, and though all the reformers agreed that there was a realm of things indifferent (*adiaphora*) where the magistrate might rule for the sake of peace and order, Bucer felt that this was no case of things indifferent, but that the whole matter of the Reformation was at stake. He went into exile, and it is characteristic of this old and sick man that, faced with invitations to take refuge in Prussia, Poland and England, he should choose the nastiest and most wearisome journey and turn to England, about which he had long had a conscience since the 1530s, in an evangelical concern for the spreading of the gospel. In Cambridge a few months, he delivered some lectures, became involved in a rumpus about Justification, and spent many weeks in bed. But he soon won hearts in a land not given to offering their affections to strangers – the Lady Jane Grey, Matthew Parker, the late-vocationed John Bradford and above all Grindal, another future Archbishop, were among his friends. When his health finally gave way he was given a great funeral in Cambridge at which those paid tribute to him who were not at all won to the evangelical cause. His advice had been sought and no doubt heeded by Goodrich and Cranmer when they came to revise the First Prayer Book, though most of his suggestions would have occurred, surely, to Cranmer himself, and the practical influence of his comments – the so-called 'Censura' – are not to be exaggerated. His real legacy to England was an extraordinary document, a vision of a godly commonwealth, into which he put his deepest concerns and the experience of a lifetime, his *De Regno Christi* ('On the Kingdom of Christ'). His own demise and the death of the young king made the document an academic blue-print, but it is to be recognized as an important theological document. Like the good Martinian he had been, he understood the folly of attempting reformation of great communities by public law and magisterial edict alone. The renovation of England must be preceded by an evangelical campaign conducted by able preachers in all parts of the country, and accompanied by what was also for Bucer a high priority, the regeneration of the Universities and places of learning, and above all of theological education, which must raise the appallingly low standards of clerical learning and integrity.

He went on to discuss public life, manners and morality, the needs of agriculture and industry, and the problem of the unemployed, and of the use of leisure. Much of this was not intended to be original, and he must have taken advice from Englishmen like Sir John Hales. The exception is the startling section – a very long one – in which he put forward views about Divorce too radical for his contemporaries, while some of his economic arguments would seem to repeat old fallacies. None the less it is a profound and noble vision, and in an amazing way foreshadowed the great movements of University and national renewal which in a few decades would emerge in Cambridge Puritanism. We have emphasized the importance of his last months in England, but he was after all a European figure, of impact on the whole western Reformation in many lands; and it is timely that modern scholarship is paying belated tribute to his depth and eminence, and the enduring qualities of that proportion of truth which he made his own, and which has yet fully to be investigated.

John Calvin

T. H. L. Parker

John Calvin

T. H. L. Parker

Jean Calvin (1509–64) is a theologian who gave evangelical theology a dogmatic form and at the same time related it to the main stream of the Catholic faith. His chief theological writings are the *Institutio Christianae religionis* and a large number of commentaries on the Bible. The former exists in four major recensions. The first edition (1536), in catechetical form, consisted of six chapters, on Law, Faith, Prayer, the Sacraments, the five so-called Sacraments, and Christian liberty. This became (1539) first a work of seventeen, and then (1543–50) of twenty-one chapters. The definitive edition (1559) was divided into four books containing eighty chapters. Without substantial change of doctrine between the various editions there is a difference of emphasis and of the doctrinal context. The increase in size is due to extended treatment of topics already dealt with briefly, to greatly enriched theological and historical references to previous writers and above all to the Scriptures, and to the inclusion of controversy against current movements of thought.

We will, for our exposition of Calvin's theology, expound briefly the 1559 *Institutio*.

Calvin's THEOLOGICAL METHOD is threefold. First, his general theological method consists in arranging and ordering the Biblical doctrines. 'Let this then be a settled principle, that there is no Word of God to which place should be given in the Church save that which is contained, first in the Law and the Prophets and secondly in the writings of the Apostles, and that the only right method of teaching in the Church is according to the prescription and rule of his Word' (IV.viii.8). But this demands a criterion both to judge of the inherent order of these doctrines and also to arrange them in such an inter-relationship as shall do justice to their inherent order. Calvin's criterion was Christological: 'how could they have comprehended the mysteries of God . . . unless by the teaching of him to whom alone the secrets of the Father are known? The only way, therefore, by which in ancient times holy men knew God, was by beholding him in the Son as in a mirror' (IV.viii.5). The Scriptures of both the Old and New Testaments refer in different modes to Jesus Christ. The second aspect of his method is that theology is the interpretation of God's relationship with man. The first sentence of the *Institutio*, constant from 1539 but present in a different form also in 1536, runs: 'Well-nigh the whole sum of our wisdom, so far as it may be considered true and substantial, consists in two parts, the knowledge of God and of ourselves' (I.i.1). The inter-relationship between the knowledge of God and the knowledge of oneself is throughout the *Institutio* taken as the necessary epistemological presupposition to theology.

Thirdly, whereas the first edition of the *Institutio* had a catechetical form, and was thus constructed around expositions of the Ten Commandments, the Creed, and the Lord's Prayer, the final edition used the Apostles' Creed itself as its framework. Book I on the knowledge of the Creator corresponds to 'I believe in God the Father Almighty, maker of heaven and earth'; Book II on the knowledge of the Redeemer in Jesus Christ corresponds to the Christological section of the Creed; Book III on *The way in which we obtain the grace of Christ* corresponds to 'I believe in the Holy Spirit'; and Book IV on *The external Means by which God invites us into the society of Christ*, corresponds to the concluding section.

Book I, on the KNOWLEDGE OF GOD THE CREATOR treats of five main topics: the nature of knowledge, the immediate object of the knowledge of God, the doctrine of God, the creation, and providence.

Man's wisdom consists almost entirely in the two knowledges which are inextricably and delicately interconnected. His self-knowledge, if genuine, will immediately lead him to knowledge of God in that he will attribute his endowments to his Creator and will also from the imperfections of his life learn that he stands towards God as child to Father. But on the other hand, self-knowledge is dependent on the knowledge of God. We are aware of our sinfulness only when we have 'seen' God's perfections. Calvin does not resolve this polarity; but for methodological reasons he begins with the knowledge of God.

By the KNOWLEDGE OF GOD Calvin intends more than a conception that God exists. It is rather an apprehension of God in relationship to ourselves, and thus a knowledge which issues in *pietas* (godliness, reverential love towards God), from which is born *religio* (religion, the service of God). *Pietas* and *religio* are the qualities of true humanity; without them man's life is perverted from its true end. God Himself imparts this awareness of Himself to men and so continually renews it that they can never be without it. Calvin combines this Stoic doctrine with the Pauline argument of inexcusability (Romans 1.20; 2.1, 15; 3.19). Awareness of the existence of God is given to men in order to make them inexcusable – that is, that they shall not be able to plead ignorance but shall be so 'shut up under sin' that only Christ shall be able to save them. The awareness itself does not lead to *pietas* and *religio*, for it is smothered or corrupted into idolatry (the invention of a god instead of obedience to revelation), into a practical atheism in which God is severed from the world, and into a pseudo-*pietas*, superstition or idolatry. It is, therefore, not knowledge of God but only a 'confused idea of God'. God has also established an external stimulus to awareness of himself in the beauty and physical machinery of the creation. All his works bear inscribed marks of his glory, so that the universe is a mirror in which the otherwise invisible God may be contemplated. Man in his physical, psychological and intellectual endowments is the choicest example of God's workmanship. This knowledge should arouse us to worship God and to hope for the future life. But man derives no immediate profit from the consideration of the universe. He beholds creation without thinking of the Creator, he interprets history as chance or fate instead of considering God's providence. The simple testimony of the creation is therefore insufficient. Nevertheless, this objective revelation in the creation has its purpose in making men inexcusable and therefore answerable for their godlessness.

In Chapters vi–ix Calvin comes to the 'other and better help', that is the teaching of the SCRIPTURES. That man may know his Creator, the Scripture, so to say, sorts out his confused notions into their true pattern, enlightening his mind to understand, his will to accept, the truth. In Scripture the universe is correctly interpreted as the creation, the work of God.

In Scripture God himself speaks, and that in such a way that as a whole and in its particulars it is a message from God. Hence it should be regarded as coming from heaven and should be granted an accordant authority. There is a divergence of opinion about Calvin's precise meaning. He often speaks in such a way as to make it appear that the human writers of Scripture are virtually unthinking stenographers, writing at the verbal dictation of the Holy Spirit. On the other hand, he is alive to differences of style and outlook between Biblical authors, and to minor discrepancies between one part of Scripture and another. What he above all wishes to emphasize is the divine authorship and therefore the divine authority of Scripture. But if this is so, the authority can rest on no extraneous proofs. Because God alone can bear sufficient witness to himself, Scripture is self-authenticating, *autopiston*; that is, by the inward illumination of his Holy Spirit God convinces us that Scripture comes from himself.

The doctrine of GOD THE CREATOR not only treats of God's *virtutes* (attributes or perfections) of goodness, mercy, righteousness, etc., in their reference to ourselves; it not only explains the concept of monotheism; but it also teaches that the Creator is the divine TRINITY. God distinguishes himself from all idols, and thus reveals himself as the one God, by declaring his tri-unity. Apart from this, the word 'God' is only a bare and empty *nomen*. Already then, in his doctrine of the Creator, Calvin makes it quite clear that he is not speaking of a 'natural' knowledge of God but of a revealed. It is often said that Calvin's Christology was 'Antiochene', in contrast to the 'Alexandrian' tendency in Luther; but this judgment has the weakness that: (1) it omits the 'Athanasian' influence of Hilary of Poitiers on Calvin; and (2) it forgets that all Antiochene Christology was not of one cast. If we generalize and say that Calvin was 'Antiochene' rather than 'Alexandrian', we must at once particularize and say that the Antiochene theology which chiefly influenced him was that of Chrysostom, with its strong resemblances to Athanasius and Cyril of Alexandria. It would, however, be misleading to attach Calvin too closely to any one of the early orthodox Christologies. A study of *Inst.* I.xiii will show his indebtedness to many different theologians – Tertullian, Hilary, Cyril, Chrysostom, Irenaeus and Gregory of Nazianzus among others. His chief endeavour is so to expound the doctrine as to think simultaneously unity and threefoldness, to think completeness of deity in each *hypostasis* simultaneously with the twofold relatedness of society of each. It would be better if we could keep to the simplicity of Scripture, that 'the Father, the Son and the Holy Spirit are one God; yet the Son is not the Father nor the Spirit the Son, but that they are distinguished by a certain "property" ' (I.xiii.5). Analogies of the Trinity are inappropriate, for God, being of his own nature, cannot be understood from the nature of that which is not God. Nevertheless, there is a certain revealed analogy of distinction in Scripture, in that the Father is 'the principle of activity, the fount and wellspring of all things' (I.xiii.18), the Son is 'wisdom, counsel, and the very charge (*dispensatio*) in activity' (ibid.) and the Holy Spirit is 'the power and efficacy of action' (ibid.). It should be noted that Calvin does not leave the doctrine of the Trinity behind him when he has completed *Inst.* I.xiii. It remains in all his thinking about God in other doctrines.

Chapters 14–15 treat of CREATION, or rather of God as Creator and other entities, angels, devils, men and universe as his *opera*. The source of this knowledge is not the *opera dei* themselves but Scripture. Enlightened by Scripture, we should delight in the creation and ponder its purpose. But the end of such knowledge is *pietas* and *religio*, that we should trust, call upon, praise, serve, and love God our Creator. Chapter xv on MAN as God's creature has to be understood against the Renaissance background. Here Calvin is dealing with the knowledge of man before the Fall. Man is composed of soul (sometimes in Scripture called 'spirit') and body. The soul is an 'immortal, but created, essence' (I.xv.2) and is not inseparable from the body. The *imago dei* was lost at the Fall, making the evidence of Genesis 1–2 insufficient foundation for the doctrine; hence, although he at once states that 'The image expresses Adam's integrity – his full possession of understanding, his affections subordinated to reason, all his senses in harmony, and his recognition that all these were gifts of God' (I.xv.3), yet his source for the statements is the New Testament witness to the restoration of the image in Christ. Thus in Col. 3.10 the image is knowledge, righteousness and holiness; in II Cor. 3.18 it is true *pietas*, righteousness, purity, intelligence. Calvin's definition therefore runs: 'The image of God is the perfect excellence of human nature which shone in Adam before his Fall, but afterwards was so corrupted and almost obliterated that from the ruin nothing remained but what is confused, mutilated and infected by taint' (I.xv.4). Calvin's concept of the soul is not free from unnecessary obscurity. He flirts with Plato's doctrine, shows that he is attracted by it as probable and true, but rejects it as obscure. He then condemns 'the philosophers' as confusing fallen with unfallen man. The soul consists of two faculties, understanding and will. Understanding is the leader and governor of the soul (τὸ ἡγεμονικόν), which distinguishes between objects and either approves or disapproves them. Included in understanding are the senses. The will depends upon and looks to the understanding in that it chooses and follows what the understanding calls good and rejects what it disapproves. In man as created, understanding and will were perfect in themselves and perfectly in accord. Moreover, he had freedom of will, so that by it he could have arrived at eternal life (the caveat must be entered that this is dependent on the Word of God). Thus 'Adam could have stood had he so willed, seeing that he fell solely by his own will' (I.xv.8). Why then did not God give him also the gift of constancy? The reason is hidden from us; our wisdom lies in submission to revealed truth.

PROVIDENCE (I.xvi–xviii) is not the driving of the mechanism of the world by some universal or generated motion but the upholding and cherishing of all created things by the Creator with a particular providence. Calvin's interest here is not philosophical but pastoral. We and all things are in the almighty hands of a loving Father. Events are neither fortuitous nor caused by 'fate' but are governed by God's secret purpose. God is omnipotent not potentially but in that He actually governs heaven and earth. Any attempt to remove God's activity from immediacy is rejected. Providence means that God 'holds the helm' (I.xvi.4), and relates not only to God's 'eyes' (*providere*) but also to his 'hands', that is, it is activity and not mere fore-knowledge. Creaturely contingency is not entirely denied, for what God has once determined flows on spontaneously. But necessity must be defined. Christian necessity lies in the power of God performing what he has decreed. Calvin approves the scholastic distinction between *necessitas secundum quid* and *necessitas absoluta* and between *necessitas consequentis* and *necessitas consequentiae*. What God has determined must so happen of necessity that nevertheless it was not necessary absolutely and of its own nature.

He goes on to show the relevance of providence to Christian living. Providence does not lead us to shift responsibility for our sin to God, does not drive to despair and suicide, does not make us neglect precautions, does not make prayer impossible. Precautions against danger, disease etc. are to be taken because God himself has given man relative foresight and also has given means (e.g. medicine) to preserve life. The consequence in life for believers is that they may trust God and pray to him, are grateful for blessings, patient in adversity, and incredibly free from anxiety (I.xvii.11). They will nevertheless reckon with secondary causes, they will thank others for help, will blame themselves for slackness or carelessness, will use common sense in worldly matters. The final chapter explains how God uses even the evil of evil men for his purposes without being defiled by their evil.

Book II, on the knowledge of God the Redeemer in Christ may be divided into four parts: Chapters i–v, man the sinner; Chapter vi, Christ the Saviour; Chapters vii–xi, the witness of the Old and New Testaments to Christ; Chapters xii–xvii, the doctrine of Christ.

MAN AS SINNER. The Fall concerned not one individual, but all mankind; for Adam passed on his sinfulness by propagation. But the solidarity of sin rests also in the determination of God. God gave gifts to Adam not only for himself but for all men. When Adam fell, God withdrew the gifts. It is not enough to say with some schoolmen that original sin is lack of original righteousness. It is *concupiscentia* of the whole man. Man by falling lost freedom of will. He chooses evil freely and not of compulsion; but he cannot of himself turn to God. Therefore his will is bound. The will is not destroyed by the Fall, or man would cease to be man, but it is turned totally to perversity. Reason also is not destroyed, but its soundness is impaired. In regard to 'inferior' things (political and social life, the arts, the sciences and technology) it has an ability; but for heavenly matters it is 'blinder than a mole' (II.ii.18). As for morality, man's reason can discern between good and evil because God has imprinted natural law in his heart. But the only purpose of this is to make man inexcusable. Man is therefore responsible for not willing the good but the bad. But more, he sins necessarily, not by external compulsion but by the movement of his own *libido*, by his depravity of nature (II.iii.5).

The conclusion comes in the title of Chapter vi: 'Redemption for lost man is to be sought in Christ'. The chapter shows that the emphasis rests on the word CHRIST. How Christ is Saviour, however, is not at once considered. First is declared his uniqueness as Mediator in the whole history of the world: 'God never showed himself favourable to the ancient people nor ever held out any hope of grace apart from the Mediator' (II.vi.2). Chapters vii–xi therefore treat of the witness of the Law and Gospel to Christ and of the relationship of the two covenants. The Old Testament no less than the New promised and assured the people of the hope of eternal life, not by their merits but by the mercy and calling of God and that through the one Mediator Christ. Hence both testaments have a common substance. The difference between them lies in the mode of dispensation. The New Testament reveals the truth of what had been shown as a shadow; the Old Testament is of the letter, the New Testament of the Spirit (and therefore the Old Testament condemns, and is transitory, the New Testament is the instrument of life and stands for ever); and the bondage of the Old Testament is contrasted to the freedom of the New Testament.

In considering the INCARNATION, the first question to be asked concerns its necessity. The necessity lay neither in Christ's being as the Son of God, nor in man's being either as creature or as sinner, but in God's determination not to destroy but to redeem. But, proceeding further, Calvin points to a necessity in the nature of the task and of its performer. The task was to make men into God's sons; only the Son of God could do this. Similarly, only life could swallow up death, only righteousness could overcome sin, only the Lord could conquer the devil. Hence, if Life, Righteousness, and Lordship are demanded, God alone is these. If the Son is demanded, then the Redeemer must be the Second Person of the Trinity.

Necessity lay also in the performing of the task. 'It was for man, who had perished through his disobedience, to offer obedience as a remedy, to satisfy God's judgment, and to pay in full the penalties of sin' (II.xii.3). When, therefore, the Son of God became man, he rendered complete obedience and paid in the flesh the penalty for sin. But here all depends on the two natures of Christ. As God, he could not experience death; therefore, if he was to die, it was necessary that he should become man. As man, he could not overcome death; therefore, to overcome death, it was necessary that he should be God.

Calvin's treatment of the two natures of Christ (Chapter xiv) is largely dependent on the *Quicunque vult*. He even follows the cautious analogy of the two 'substances' (i.e. essences) which compose man's soul and body. Neither is to be confused with the other. Each has its own properties. Sometimes, however, the properties of one may be referred to the other. So with Christ. Sometimes Scripture speaks of his humanity alone, sometimes of his divinity; sometimes it refers to one what is true of the other, by the figure of speech called *communicatio idiomatum*, the communication of properties. But Calvin's Christology throughout is ruled by soteriological considerations, by Christ's relation to his people. What Scripture says of the two natures together must be understood in the light of Christ as Mediator.

Chapter xv gives content to his office. It is threefold, corresponding to his anointing (Christ-hood) as Prophet, Priest, and King. Christ the Prophet or Teacher is not an educator but 'the herald and witness of the Father's grace' (II. xv.2). More, the office is both act and being: Christ not only teaches wisdom but *is* wisdom. In the kingship of Christ is emphasized its eternity and its spirituality. This is brought out more clearly in xv.5, that Christ is anointed, not with oil, but with the Spirit, to his threefold office. That he is anointed to priesthood means that he is anointed to his sacrificial priesthood, his sacrifice of himself, to make atonement for sins and reconcile God to us. But the whole Christ is the Head together with the Body. Therefore Christ's threefold office is the office of the whole Christ, Head and Body: 'he receives anointing, not only for himself that he might perform the office of teaching, but for his whole Body that the power of the Spirit might be present in the continued preaching of the Gospel' (II.xv.2). Believers share also in Christ's kingship; they live under the Cross, but they are protected by their King and look confidently to the possession of the Kingdom. Christ also receives them as his companions in the office of priest. 'For we, though polluted in ourselves, are priests in him and offer ourselves and our all to God, and freely enter the heavenly sanctuary, so that the sacrifices of prayer and praise which we offer are acceptable and of sweet odour to him' (II.xv.6).

The object of Christ's Mediatorial work is ATONEMENT, the reconciling of God to men, its substance the sacrifice of himself. The *How?* of atonement is the subject of Chapter xvi. Christ made atonement 'by the whole course of his obedience' (II.xvi.5). For Calvin the whole life of Christ on earth was saving; the Cross was the final intensification of all his previous obedience. He does not develop the theme in this chapter, however, but expounds the historical section of the Apostles' Creed. Each event has a heavenly counterpart or is an effectually enacted symbol. Christ's trial under Pontius Pilate means that he did not die in some chance or extra-legal way but was condemned to death by the mouth of a judge (II.xvi.5). The circumstances of his death therefore corresponded to its eternal meaning. That he was executed by crucifixion on the 'tree' signified that he suffered the curse of God upon sin (Deut. 21.22f.). The curse becomes accentuated in the next clause 'he descended into hell', which is to be interpreted literally, that Christ should not merely die physically but should experience in his soul 'the severity of God's vengeance' (II.xvi.10). But the suffering of hell was a 'fighting hand to hand with the power of the devil, with the horror of death, with the pangs of hell' in which 'our Prince won the victory' (II.xvi.11). In Christ's death, sin and death are abolished; in his resurrection, righteousness is restored and life established. In resurrection he began to reveal his glory, but his ascension truly inaugurated his reign. It was Christ's human body which ascended and reigned with the Father; his power and efficacy are shed abroad everywhere in heaven and earth. Christ is not in heaven as a private person, but as the Head of his people in their flesh. Hence they already possess heaven in Christ, with whom they are united. He is there also as the perpetual advocate and intercessor for his people. And thirdly, it is precisely because he ascended that he gives the power of his Spirit and therefore life and righteousness. His Second coming will be his visible presence in the same physical form that he had when last seen on earth at his ascension. He will come as Judge; but this is matter for comfort for his people, for their Judge will be their Redeemer.

In the last chapter of Book II Calvin returns to the *How?* of redemption and at the same time makes two vital points about the atonement. The obedience of Christ is both positive and negative; positive in that he kept the Law perfectly, neither transgressing the commandments nor failing to fulfil the righteousness demanded, negative in that he accepted the penalty for man's not keeping the Law. Moreover, it must be said that by God's grace Christ has merited eternal life and all blessings by his obedience. But he shares all his blessings with his people, not so much by gift as by union. Hence, what is his (eternal life and all blessings which he merited by his obedience) becomes ours. We must speak not only of the grace of *God* but also of the grace of *Christ*.

Book III carries on this point in its title: *The Way in which we receive the Grace of Christ, what benefits come to us from it, and what effects follow.* Strictly speaking, the book deals with only four, or perhaps five, subjects — the Holy Spirit and faith; the Christian life of penitence; justification and liberty; prayer; and predestination. The book's considerable length is due partly to anti-Romanist polemic on penance and justification, partly to the long sections on prayer and election.

Salvation is in Christ; it is therefore obtained through union with Christ. This union is twofold, on Christ's side and on ours. He makes himself one with us by taking our flesh in his incarnation and by dwelling within us through his SPIRIT. We on our side must be engrafted into Christ and 'grow into one body with him' (III.i.1). Union with Christ is effected by the Holy Spirit. Christ was anointed (*Christos*) by the Spirit to be prophet, king and priest. Union with Christ is therefore union with him in this anointing, so that Christ shares with his people his anointing with the Spirit. In all, the primacy remains with Christ. The Church, the believer, has no prophetic authority, no kingdom, no priesthood, apart from Christ's. The activity of the Spirit consists in uniting the elect with Christ, and this by creating in them FAITH, for faith is subjective union with Christ, their assuming of the union already established by God in the incarnation.

The schoolmen, says Calvin, failed to concentrate on Christ as the object of faith and referred faith too generally to 'God'. For 'the invisible Father is to be sought nowhere but in this image' [Christ] (III.ii.1). The object of faith is therefore Christ; but it is Christ 'clothed with his Gospel' (III.ii.6). Therefore the first step in Calvin's doctrine of faith is that Christ is its object, the second the permanent relationship between faith and God's Word. But Christ represents God's goodwill or grace towards men. Hence the definition that faith is 'a firm and sure knowledge of God's goodwill towards us, founded upon the truth of the freely given promise in Christ, both revealed to our minds and sealed in our hearts through the Holy Spirit' (III.ii.7). To call faith 'firm and sure', refers first to confidence in the object. There can never be assurance while we are doubtful as to whether we know God's will or whether he will be true to his Word. Secondly, it means that we accept God's promise for ourselves. There can never be assurance while we think of God's will as apart from ourselves. But the assurance lies in the virtue not of the faith but of its object. In explaining the foundation of faith, 'the freely given promise in Christ', Calvin connects assurance with union with Christ. Faith is not looking to a remote Christ; it is union with Christ: 'we must not separate Christ from ourselves or ourselves from Christ' (III.ii.24), 'Christ is not outside us but dwells within us. Not only does he cleave to us by an indivisible bond of fellowship, but with a wonderful communion he daily grows more and more into one body with us, until he becomes completely one with us' (III.ii.24). The Holy Spirit enlightens the mind and converts the will to understand and assent to the Gospel. He gives, so to say, a new mind which corresponds to the object. 'The Holy Spirit . . . begets in us another and a new mind.'[1] 'Illuminated by him, the soul receives, as it were, new eyes for the contemplation of the heavenly mysteries' (III.ii.34).

Since the connection of the arguments in this book is not clear at a first glance, we should note Calvin's careful explanations of his line of thought at the beginning of chapters. Chapters i–ii treat of faith as union with Christ; Chapters iiiff. of the scope and fruits of faith. To be one with Christ is to be one with him in his Cross and Resurrection, thus in forgiveness and reconciliation and in newness of life. We are immediately in the sphere of repentance and sanctification, a sphere of quite special importance for the Reformers in that they were engaged in correcting a long-established doctrine of grace and the penitential practice joined to it. Repentance is 'A real conversion of our life to God, proceeding from a sincere and serious fear of God, and consisting in the mortification of our flesh and the old man and the quickening of the spirit' (III.iii.5). Therefore repentance and regeneration are made identical and are related to the restoration of the image of God: 'I interpret repentance as regeneration, of which the aim is that the image of God . . . may be formed again in us' (III.iii.9). By calling the Christian life self-denial, Calvin intends a mortification of self-will and consecration of the will to God's service, and he sums it up in a series of telling variations on 'We are not our own; therefore . . .' and on 'But we are God's; therefore . . .' (III.vii.1).

JUSTIFICATION is inseparable from regeneration in that the justified is also regenerated, the regenerated also justified. But whereas regeneration is the work of God within the man, justification is the decision of God upon him. Man is on trial as a sinner before God. He is guilty and can plead nothing in excuse. The decision of the judge is that he is acquitted as innocent. The decision is righteous – it expresses the mind of the righteous judge and of the truth of the situation. The factor which makes the decision

[1] Comm. on Eph. 4.23 (ed. T. F. and D. Torrance, p. 190).

righteous is both that the law by which the sinner is tried has already been kept by the sinner's representative, Christ, and also that the representative has suffered the penalty of the broken law. Once again it is a question of the objective and subjective union with Christ. Justification is by faith and not by 'works'; that is, it is not earned by any virtue or virtuous act (not even by faith!) but is accepted as the truth declared in Christ.

The justified sinner has LIBERTY from the curse of the law (for Christ with whom we are united has suffered the curse), from the moral threatenings of the law (for to command to love is absurd; God 'calls us with fatherly kindness' (III.xix.5) to follow him), and from rigorism in the use of things indifferent. In this respect, however, the guide-line should be love for our brethren. Sufficient to be aware of freedom; we need not use it. And secondly, all that has been said of God's rich goodness and of man's poverty must be brought together in the consideration of PRAYER (this chapter, and that on the Lord's Supper, are the two longest in all the *Institutio*). That which God promises must be asked for – not in an attempt to coerce an unwilling God, but to make man aware of his needs and desires; and for what he gives, God is to be thanked and praised.

On PREDESTINATION Calvin followed deliberately in the steps of Augustine. Why, he echoes, does the preaching of the Gospel meet with acceptance by some, rejection by others? The answer lies in the hidden will of God, to attempt to penetrate which would be rashness. Here too, theology must keep to God's revealed will in Scripture. But theology must not be timid; it must follow to the limits to which Scripture leads. Calvin defines predestination as 'God's eternal decree, by which he determined within himself what he willed to become of each man. For all are not created in equal condition; rather, eternal life is fore-ordained for some, eternal damnation for others. Therefore, as any man has been created to one or the other of these ends, we speak of him as predestined to life or to death' (III.xxi.5). God's fore-knowledge is active and creative. He did not choose men whom he foresaw to be deserving of his grace; but those whom he foreknew as his own, in time believed because they were foreknown and chosen. God 'is not the spectator but the author of our salvation' (III.xxii.6). Although Calvin speaks of Christ as the author of election in common with the Father (III.xxii.7), it would seem that he means that 'God' elects in eternity and the incarnate Christ elects on earth. Hence, with Augustine he makes much of the Johannine passages where the Father is said to give to the Son those who already belong to the Father. Reprobation is not to be viewed as merely the negative side of election, the passing over of those not chosen (and it is in regarding predestination as both election and reprobation that Calvin seems to go beyond Augustine and Aquinas). It is rather a deliberate rejection for which the reason lies in the hidden will of God. Election is into Christ and therefore into faith in Christ. Pastorally Calvin's doctrine is rescued from moral scepticism and despair by his final insistence that we are assured of election by faith in Christ and not vice versa.

Book IV deals with the external means by which that which is objectively true in Christ becomes subjectively true in the believer. A very large part of the book is anti-Roman polemic, since Calvin is replacing the Roman with an evangelical Church order. The positive teaching is therefore relatively short.

The unity of the CHURCH is a unity within the one Christ. The foundation of the Church is the election of individuals into Christ and therefore into unity with him. Because they are one with him they are therefore one with each other. 'All the elect are so united in Christ that, as they are dependent on one Head, they also grow together into one Body . . . They are made truly one since they live together in one faith, hope, and love, and in the same Spirit of God. For they have been called not only into the same inheritance of eternal life but also to participate in one God and Christ' (IV.i.2). A vital corollary to this is that as Christ shares with his people all that is his, so each member shares his goods, spiritual or material, with the rest of the Body. Private possessions, while not forbidden, should be regarded as lent by God for the common good.

The Church is a mother to believers; 'There is no way to enter into life except this mother shall conceive us in her womb, give us birth, nurse us at her breast, and keep us under her care and protection until we put off mortal flesh and become like the angels' (IV.i.4). The way in which the Church gives and fosters life is by the self-giving of Jesus Christ, the bread of life, in the proclamation of the Gospel and the sacraments of Baptism and the Lord's Supper. The Church is therefore recognizable as Church by the two 'marks' of the preaching of the Gospel and the administration of the sacraments in the way that accords with their nature. Why these two marks? Because the Church consists of Christ and his people. Without Christ, the Head, there is no Church. But Christ is present with his people in the proclamation of the Gospel and in the sacraments of the Gospel. Take away these marks and the Body is deprived of its Head.

The MINISTRY of the Church corresponds to its nature and exists to effect Christ's saving work in the Church. It includes, besides the ministry of the Word and Sacraments (i.e. the doctors or teachers and the pastors – in the New Testament also called bishops and presbyters, or elders), also the ministry of discipline and of *diakonia*. The task of the doctors was to teach the Faith, whether by lecturing or by writing. The pastor, having oversight of a parish, preached, administered the sacraments, and joined in the ministering of discipline and the *diakonia*. *Diakonia*, the care of the needy, belonged to the order of deacons, and the discipline to the (lay) elders. DISCIPLINE is the evangelical substitute for the medieval penitential system. The power of the keys (Matt. 16.19), the power to loose and to bind (Matt. 18.15–18; John 20.23) is inherent in the promise attached to the preaching of the Gospel. To unlock the door of heaven, to loose from sin, is to proclaim Christ as the sole mediator between God and men and to assure men that, believing, their sins are forgiven and heaven is opened. To lock up heaven, to bind, is to warn unbelievers that, unless they repent and believe, heaven is shut against them. Beyond this, however, a special power of the keys is exercised in excommunication. The Church 'binds' the sinner when it excommunicates him and 'looses' him when it receives him again into communion.

A SACRAMENT is an external sign by which the Lord seals on our consciences his promises of good-will towards us, in order to sustain the weakness of our faith, and we in our turn testify our piety towards him, both in his sight and in the sight of angels and men (IV.xiv.1). God's Word, or promise, of which the sacraments are seals, is in itself completely sure and steadfast and needs no confirmation. But God has added sensible signs to confirm our weak faith in his sure promise. The sacraments are never to be separated from the Word – indeed, a sacrament consists of the Word and the outward sign. Sacraments express to the other senses what the Word says to the hearing. It may therefore be called a 'visible word', holding forth and offering to us Christ and the grace which he has merited for us. Just as the Word is powerless without the inward creative act of the Spirit, so also the whole efficacy of the sacraments lies in the creative power of the Holy Spirit.

BAPTISM 'is the initiatory sign by which we are admitted into the fellowship of the Church, so that, engrafted in Christ, we may be reckoned among the children of God' (IV.xv.1). It confirms our weak faith in God's sure promises in three respects. First, it is a sealed 'deed' of the promise of forgiveness in Christ. The washing by water signifies the removal of sin by the death of the Son of God. Secondly, the enactment of the rite signifies mortification and the new life, a uniting of the person with the death and resurrection of Christ (IV.xv.5). Thirdly, and more comprehensively, baptism is the sign of union with Christ himself, who is the 'true object of baptism'; but if with Christ, then into the fellowship of the Trinity. Infant baptism is to be retained as accordant with the will of Christ, who wishes to draw some of every age to himself.

The other sacrament, the [LORD'S] SUPPER or the EUCHARIST, is again a sacrament of union with Christ. Its signification of eating and drinking represents the image of Christ as the living bread. As God in baptism 'engrafts us into the fellowship of his Church and adopts us as his own' (IV.xvii.1), so, as a good Father he supplies the food 'to sustain and preserve us' (IV.xvii.1) in eternal life. The simple but lively activity of the eating and drinking confirms our weak faith in God's sure promise or covenant that he is our God, we his people through the atonement of Christ. But further: the Supper is the rite of life. The eternal Word of God was the fountain of life. When he became man he 'gave vigour' to his humanity, so that from his flesh 'a communion of life' might flow to us. The life-giving body and blood of Christ are brought to us by the Spirit, who 'truly unites things separated by space' (IV. xvii.10). Hence the Supper is not only a sign pointing away to the Jesus Christ of the first century or now in heaven but it is union with that Christ and therefore communion or participation in his body and blood.

On the basis of this teaching, Calvin rejects the doctrines of transubstantiation and consubstantiation. But he advances no theory of his own to interpret the *How?* of the presence of Christ: 'It is too high a mystery for my mind to comprehend or my words to express; and to speak more plainly, I rather feel than understand it . . . He declares that his flesh is my soul's meat, his blood my soul's drink; I give my soul to him to be fed with this food. In his holy Supper he bids me take, eat, and drink his body and blood under the symbols of bread and wine. I have no doubt that he will truly give and I receive' (IV.xvii.32). He rejects the sacrifice of the Mass because Christ was sacrificed once for all. This is not to be understood in the sense that his sacrifice is potential for every age. On the contrary, 'once for all' signifies 'eternally'; that is, his sacrifice is real and efficacious in every age, and if real, it does not need to be realized either by renewal or re-enactment.

The final chapter of the *Institutio*, on CIVIL GOVERNMENT, is little altered from the first edition. The State is a divine appointment for the well-being of God's creation. Although it is not to be confused with the kingdom of Christ, it has a duty 'to foster and maintain the external worship of God, and to defend sound doctrine and the condition of the church' (IV.xx.2). The magistracy (i.e. government) of a State is an office and ministry established by God. It is therefore responsible to God. On the relative merits of forms of government Calvin is undecided, but prefers a State 'where many bear rule, so that they may help, teach, and advise one another' (IV.xx.8), whether as an aristocracy pure and simple, or as a compound of aristocracy and democracy. Since the magistracy is ordained by God, the people should accept its authority as God-given and therefore to be obeyed as part of their obedience towards God. The private individual is bound to obey even the unjust and harsh laws of a tyrannical government. The one exception that Calvin makes is that God's law is the standard by which rulers may legislate and that therefore no law directly conflicting with divine law clearly stated in Scripture should be obeyed. No private citizen, again, may attempt to remove an unjust ruler. Nevertheless, in §31 Calvin not only delivers a plain warning to rulers that they are subject to the providential judgment of God, but he also lays it down as a principle that in any monarchy which also possesses a form of parliament (to use modern language) or any constitutional body bearing authority in the State (he instances the Three Estates in France), it is the duty of that body 'to curb the tyranny of kings', for they are 'by the ordinance of God the appointed guardians of the liberty of the people' (IV.xx.31).

The Council of Trent

Benjamin Drewery

The Council of Trent

BENJAMIN DREWERY

Tridentine studies have in recent years been almost revolutionized by the masterly studies of Hubert Jedin (*Geschichte des Konzils von Trient*, Band I – 1949; Band II – 1957; Eng. tr. *A History of the Council of Trent* by Dom Ernest Graf, Vol. I – 1957; Vol. II – 1961), the first volume setting out in intricate detail the enormously complex historical background and the tortuous processes of the Council, the second examining (in the light, among much else, of the twentieth-century revival of Luther and Reformation studies) the doctrinal and disciplinary discussions and formulations. Here is a simple outline of the history and an indication of the content of the most important doctrinal decrees.

The Council met in three prolonged but non-continuous periods between 1545 and 1563, embracing twenty-five 'sessions'. None of the five successive Popes attended it, and during the papacy of Paul IV (1555–9) it lapsed entirely; but the others endeavoured to control it through their legates, of whom Cardinal Morone (during the third period) was outstanding. Trent was chosen as being (nominally) in the Empire but in practice under Italian control; at the end of the first period the Council was transferred to Bologna, on the pretext of an epidemic at Trent, but after a four-year interval the second period was convened at Trent.

The two main concerns – fear of Protestantism and the internal desire of the Roman Church for reform – were complicated by other issues: the unwillingness of the Popes to commit themselves in advance to the findings of a Council without assurance of absolute control; the determination of the Spanish bishops and above all of the Emperor Charles V to entrust the Council with real powers and secure genuine reforms; the political desirability of conciliating the German Protestants with the Emperor; the standing hostility of the Emperor and the French King Francis I, and the consequent support from the latter for the procrastinations of the Popes. It was only after the Peace of Crépy, which included a secret agreement between King and Emperor to forward the matter, that the hand of the Pope was forced. By this time the frontiers of the Catholic/Protestant schism had probably hardened beyond the point at which mutual doctrinal understanding was possible.

The first period of the Council (1545–7: Sessions I–X) compromised on the priority of doctrine or discipline by determining that they should be treated concurrently; then –

Session III re-affirmed the Niceno-Constantinopolitan Creed (A.D. 381), including the *Filioque*;

Session IV dealt with Scripture and Tradition;

Session V with Original Sin;

Session VI with Justification;

Session VII with the Sacraments in general, and specifically with baptism and confirmation.

The second period (1551–2: Sessions XI–XVI) dealt –

Session XIII with the Eucharist;

Session XIV with Penance and Extreme Unction.

The third period (1562–3: Sessions XVII–XXV) dealt –

Session XXI with Eucharistic communion;

Session XXII with the sacrifice of the Mass;

Session XXIII with Orders;

Session XXIV with matrimony.

This gives three main themes of interest to the historian of doctrine – Scripture/Tradition; Justification; Sacraments – which we shall treat in order.

Scripture and Tradition

The decrees of the fourth session may be summarized as follows:

(1) 'The fountain of all saving truth and moral discipline is the Gospel';

(2) This truth and discipline is contained in the written books and in the unwritten traditions, which latter have come down to us at the dictation of the Holy Spirit by unbroken succession from the mouth of Christ himself or his apostles; hence we receive and venerate both scripture and tradition 'with equal piety and reverence';

(3) The canon of the O.T. which is listed, embraces the Apocrypha; in the N.T. *Hebrews* is given as the fourteenth Pauline epistle, and of course the traditional authorship of the Apocalypse reaffirmed;

(4) The authoritative version is the Vulgate;

(5) It is the prerogative of 'holy mother-church' to 'judge the true sense and interpretation of holy scripture'; no private judgment shall contradict the interpretations of the church or the 'unanimous consensus of the Fathers'.

For the last three points it may be said that the achievement of fixed and recognized standards in canon, version and interpretation, was of the highest importance, especially for the myriads of 'simple faithful', in the violent unsettlement of faith and morals that the Renaissance and Reformation had provoked. Even the inclusion of the Apocrypha was in one sense a gain, as a number of less edifying books, such as *Hermas*, were firmly excluded. Yet the cost was great; biblical scholarship in the Roman Church was to be fatally handicapped for more than three centuries in all the three spheres.

The first point is preceded by an emphatic declaration that the unvarying purpose of the Council is to preserve the purity of the Gospel: here, and still more in the first point itself, the Council is responding to the challenge of the Reformation by appropriating its claims for the Catholic Church. It is on the second point, reinforced by the fifth, that controversy has centred. Tradition is placed on a level with Scripture as a complementary source of truth in theology and ethics; the (Catholic) Church is at once the sole guardian of tradition and the sole judge of the interpretation of Scripture. It is clear from what we know of the discussions at the Council that the famous 'with equal piety and reverence' was in fact a compromise between those who demanded that priority should be given to Scripture and those (like the Jesuits) who demanded a declaration that the Church could not err in matters of faith, morals and practice. It is also clear that grave problems – the relation of Dominical and apostolic traditions, the respective functions of Popes and Councils in declaring the authoritative interpretations of 'holy mother-church' – are left untouched. The following comments, positive and negative, may be made in the light of subsequent discussions (not least of Vatican II) on the real issue as it was left by Trent.

On its behalf we may urge that the simple antithesis of Scripture and tradition and the exclusive attribution to the former of divine truth, characteristic of the more extreme Protestant sects, is false in theory and unworkable in practice. No Christian community can regulate its worship and the lives of its members exclusively by Scriptural precedent, and some non-Scriptural traditions come to be hallowed by them all. More fundamentally, there is a mutual invasion in Scripture and tradition themselves: the Bible is above all other writings a 'traditional book', as was evident long before the age of Form-criticism; and conversely Church tradition at point after point reflects the language and the practice of Scripture. But above all, the *right* of the Church to interpret Scripture, with some degree of 'privilege', is a principle recognized in other forms of human association and equally legitimate here. It is at bottom the necessity of interpretation 'from within'. John Sebastian Bach, for example, can never be understood in depth apart from the interpretations of musicians who have been bred and trained in the Western tradition of musical development and even (in his case) the tradition of Lutheran Christianity. Shakespeare remains a closed book unless the insights of European aesthetics are brought to bear on him. The ultimate significance of Scripture requires the experience, in depth, of the 'redeemed community' for its evaluation. Here the Council of Trent itself stands in valid succession to a tradition reaching back to Tertullian's *Praescriptio*.

Yet the Decree cannot ultimately stand, because it ignores the equally valid principle that *in some sense*, in spite of this, the *priority* of value and hence of 'reverence' remains with Scripture. Bach and Shakespeare are in the end supreme over their interpreters. There is a Scriptural *hapax* – a 'once-for-all' – pertaining to the mighty acts of God in creation and redemption of which subsequent tradition is, in a vital sense, but an unfolding, an elaboration. The precise definition of this priority has exercised the subtlest intelligence of modern scholarship, both privately and (for example) in Vatican II. But to ignore it by a simple equation with tradition is not only a denial of responsibility but an implicit authorization of any practice or *theologumenon* that subsequent Popes and Councils may promulgate.

Justification

The decree of the fifth session on *Original Sin* lays down the following:

(1) The sin of Adam lost him 'the holiness and righteousness in which he had been constituted', and so he incurred the wrath of God, death and captivity to the Devil;

(2) 'Bodily penalties' and 'sin which is the death of the soul' have been 'transfused' to the whole human race by Adam (through 'propagation', not 'imitation');

(3) 'This sin of Adam' is removed solely through the reconciling merit of Jesus Christ, applied through baptism (infant or adult) to humanity; the baptism of infants, guiltless of actual sin, is valid 'that what they contracted by generation may be washed away by regeneration'.

(4) By Christ the whole essence of original sin is removed, not merely 'alleviated' (*radi* lit. 'scratched') or no longer 'imputed'. Yet there remains after baptism 'concupiscence' or the *fomes peccati* (lit. the 'tinder' of sin i.e. the raw material, liability of sinning); this however in the regenerate is not properly 'sin' but 'of sin and inclining to sin'.

(5) The Blessed Virgin Mary is exempt from this *proviso*.

The decree of the sixth session on *Justification* may thus be summarized:

(1) Justification begins with the prevenient grace of God through Jesus Christ, that sinners 'through God's arousing and helping grace, may be disposed to convert themselves to their own justification by freely assenting to and cooperating with that grace'. God 'touches the heart through the illumination of the Holy Spirit'; man 'neither does absolutely nothing while receiving that inspiration, nor is yet able by his own free will, without the grace of God, to move himself to righteousness in His sight (*coram illo*)'. (caput V)

(2) The pre-baptismal preparation consists of belief, repentance, and resolve to begin a new life: thus are men 'disposed to righteousness' when they are 'aroused and helped by divine grace'. (c. VI)

(3) 'Justification is not only remission of sins but also sanctification and renewal of the inward man through the voluntary receiving of the grace and gifts whereby an unrighteous man becomes righteous'. 'The *final* cause of justification is the glory of God and Christ; the *efficient* is the merciful God; the *meritorious* is Jesus Christ by His passion; the *instrumental* is the sacrament of baptism; the *single formal cause* is the righteousness of God – not that by which He Himself is righteous, but that by which He makes us righteous'. 'Not only are we reputed but we truly are — righteous, each receiving our own righteousness within us, according to the measure which the Holy Spirit distributes to everyone as He wills, and according to each one's own disposition and cooperation.' 'In justification a man receives through Jesus Christ, to whom he is ingrafted, all these things together with remission of sins – faith, hope and love. For faith, unless hope and love be added, neither unites a man perfectly with Christ nor makes him a living member of His body. Hence it is most truly said that faith without works is dead and useless.' (c.VII) Justification 'freely' and 'by faith' is traditionally and correctly interpreted to mean that 'faith is the beginning of

salvation — and nothing that precedes justification – faith or works – merits that grace of justification.' (c. VIII)

(4) Justification neither follows from nor necessarily issues in 'confidence and certainty': 'no one can know with certainty of faith, which can be subject to no error, that he has obtained the grace of God.' (c. IX)

(5) 'Those justified — through observing the commandments of God and the church, faith cooperating with good works, increase in that righteousness received through the grace of Christ and are justified the more.' (c. X) Hence justification does not dispense from observance of God's commandments. (c. XI)

(6) Rash presumption that one is 'among the number of the predestined' is to be avoided: this can only be known 'by special revelation'. (c. XII) 'Perseverance' is a gift of God, not to be taken for granted. (c. XIII) Those who fall into sin after baptism can be justified again, but on condition no longer of mere repentance but of sacramental confession, satisfaction, absolution – i.e. of penance. (c. XIV)

(7) Eternal life is both a gift of grace and a reward of life-long merit. Jesus Christ 'continually infuses virtue into those justified, and this virtue always precedes, accompanies and follows their good works'. 'Thus neither is our own righteousness established as such because it comes from ourselves, nor is the righteousness of God ignored or repudiated; for what we call our righteousness, because we are justified by its inherence in us, is itself the righteousness of God, because it is infused into us by God through the merit of Christ.' 'Christ's goodness towards all men is such that he wishes His gifts to be their merits.'

The decree is followed by thirty-three 'canons' or anathemas, four against Pelagianism, the rest against Protestantism.

These decrees make clear how far the Council had moved from medieval Nominalism in the direction of the older Augustinian heritage; yet the whole way it could not go because of the Lutheran occupation of the Augustinian ground. Hence the impression of *compromise*, which Harnack (*Hist. Dogma* VII 56ff. E.Tr.) with perhaps over-refined subtlety, traced throughout these decrees and took to be the key to them.

There is, for example, no hint of the medieval Fall from super-nature to nature, instead of from nature to sub-nature. Original sin is not equated with concupiscence, nor the latter given restricting sexual overtones. But in rejecting, as a prime matter of principle, the Lutheran category of *imputation* and insisting that the whole essence of original sin is 'removed' (*tolli*), the Council compromises on the notorious fact of post-baptismal sin by an application of the *fomes peccati*, to which it is not in consistency entitled. The exception of the Virgin Mary from this application is another re-affirmation of Catholic tradition against the Reformation.

Again, the priority of the grace of God ('prevenient') in conversion and the exclusion of merit before justification, as also the endorsement of the Lutheran passive/active righteousness of God, work in one direction: in the other the category of 'transfusion', 'infusion' for the *modus operandi* of the divine grace, the narrowing in practice of 'faith' to 'belief', the confinement of justification itself to one element in the divine pattern of salvation instead of the presupposition of the whole, and above all the running dualism of grace and merit, which begins at the moment of justification and ends with eternal life with their practical identification. Luther would have claimed that a vital dimension of the Christian Gospel has here been lost. 'Whosoever will, let him take the water of life – freely' (Rev. 22:17) should be the last as well as the first word here, if the taint of semi-Pelagianism (of which it is hard to acquit the Council) is to be shunned.

The Aristotelian elaboration of the logical 'causes' of justification is perhaps harmless, and was in any case to be outdone by still more artificial exercises in Protestant scholasticism. The rejections of antinomianism and the Calvinist 'assurance' and 'perseverance' were to be expected, as was the doctrinally paradoxical insistence that sin after baptism can only be dealt with by the church, whereas the (presumably much less heinous) sin of the unconverted can only be dealt with by God. The old distinction of 'penance' from 'penitence' is of course reaffirmed.

The difficulty with any compromise is that in principle it lacks stability. In this central matter of justification the Council, while successfully fencing the Catholic Church against Protestantism and making doubly sure of this by its explicit concluding anathemas, yet admitted elements of Reformation insight sufficiently potent to make later development inevitable. The student should pass from the decrees on sin and justification to the work of Newman 300 years later and the subsequent decree of the second Vatican Council.

Sacraments

The multiple decrees on the sacraments may be dealt with, in a history of doctrine, more succinctly.

'Through the sacraments all true righteousness either begins or is increased or is restored' (VII Foreword). The seven were all instituted by Jesus Christ, although varying in 'worth' and they are all necessary for salvation. They confer grace *ex opere operato*, not by faith alone, and three of them (baptism, confirmation, orders) convey an indelible 'character' or stamp, and hence cannot be repeated. Administration by an authorized minister, 'with the intention of doing what the Church does', is mandatory, and even a minister 'in mortal sin' who observes all the essentials of the sacrament 'effects and conveys it'. (VII)

Baptism: the 4th Canon reaffirms the Augustinian 'validity of heretical baptism' provided it is given in the threefold name and with the same 'intention' as the Church; the efficacy of baptism is limited (Canons 9, 10) to sins committed before it, and the rôle of faith in baptism is consistently played down (VII).

Eucharist: The 'true, real and substantial' presence is affirmed – the 'whole and entire' Christ, both in His divinity and humanity (body and soul), and both body and soul complete in both wine and bread – through transubstantiation of the bread and wine. The Eucharist is an 'antidote (as it were) against daily' (= venial) 'sins and a safeguard against mortal sins'. The preeminence of the Eucharist among the Sacraments is argued somewhat obscurely – 'the other sacraments first have the power of sanctifying when one uses them, while in the Eucharist is the Author of sanctity Himself before it is used', the real point of this being the vindication of such practices as the worship of the Host and the festival of Corpus Christi (XIII).

The 'sacrifice of the Mass' is a 'representation' of the historical 'bloody sacrifice' on the Cross, with 'salutary efficacy' for the remission of daily sins and 'truly propitiatory' for the gravest. 'The victim is one and the same, the same now offering by the ministry of priests who then offered Himself on the cross, the manner of offering alone being different' (XXII).

Penance: the doctrinal basis for this Decree had already been laid in the decree on justification, and the elaboration of theory and practice in terms of inherited Scholasticism (cf. Harnack *op. cit.* 51ff.) (XIV). Nor is there any real departure from scholastic tradition in the discussion of the remaining sacraments, the concessions to Protestantism being of the faintest, for by the time of the third period of the Council all hope or intention of reconciliation with the Protestants was dead, and the dominant element in the discussions was by now the Jesuits.

There is, of course, much in these sacramental canons of permanent validity for Christian thought and practice. The present-day *rapprochement* between several major Christian traditions on sacramental theory (e.g. the *Agreed Statement* on *Eucharistic Doctrine* of an Anglican/Roman panel, Sept. 1971 – see *Theology*, Jan. 1972, pp. 4ff.), is based on a growing flexibility in the understanding of traditional concepts. A good example is offered by the Protestant R. H. Bainton (*Christendom*, Vol. II 1964, p. 195): 'The point is made by Catholic theologians that the scholastic distinction between accidents and substance is rendered untenable by modern physics, which looks upon matter as a form of energy. If (transubstantiation) means that one form of energy replaces another and that the food for the body may become food for the spirit, the "change" appears to be functional, an interpretation which most Protestants would find acceptable.'

The Council of Trent gave its Church at least a point of departure. The Aristotelian categories made a final defiance to a world that had already begun to leave them behind. The clear demarcation of the Catholic Church, and the bold reading back of the whole structure of doctrine, worship and ethics to the apostles or to Christ Himself, the circumvallation by an endless chain of anathemas against Protestantism and the sects, served to restore the Roman Catholic Church in the later sixteenth century by furnishing it with a measure of reform (even if not all that was desired), and a new discipline which was to be effective for more than three centuries. (For a detailed treatment of all this the student should consult e.g. A. G. Dickens *The Counter Reformation* (1968), and other works listed in the *Oxford Dictionary of the Christian Church* (2nd edition, 1974, edd. F. L. Cross and E. A. Livingstone), s.v. *Counter-reformation* p. 352.)

Sixteenth-Century Anglican Theology

H. F. Woodhouse

Sixteenth-Century Anglican Theology

H. F. WOODHOUSE

Before 1547, when King Henry VIII died, we really cannot say that there was any permanent doctrinal reform in England, save the repudiation of the papacy. He had controlled the Church and not made doctrinal changes. When these began, in our period we can speak of four strands, the first three being predominantly doctrinal. These we call the Catholic (not Roman), the Calvinist, the Lutheran, and (we may add concerning the relationship of Church and State) Erastian – though this latter belongs to a politico-sociological type. The result is that in Anglican theology through the period we get both Catholic and reformed elements and therefore varying emphases, often creating tension, yet always demanding comprehensive inclusiveness.

We find in the reign of Henry VIII that, partly for political reasons, the books called the Bishops' and the King's books had shown traces of Luther's teaching and that Thomas Cranmer himself (Archbishop of Canterbury 1532–56) was attracted to certain aspects of it. Nevertheless, tentative efforts, in the field of doctrine, seem to blow hot and cold, and the Six Articles at the end of Henry VIII's reign were definitely affirmations of what we would call medieval Roman teaching. They asserted transubstantiation, the needlessness of communion in both kinds, clerical celibacy, obligations to keep vows of charity, the necessity of private masses and auricular confession.

The prayer book of 1549 contains material showing definite moves in a reformed direction and this was greatly accelerated by the changes made in the prayer book of 1552. Cranmer was its chief compiler and creator, and it reflects much of his doctrinal outlook. Then followed the Marian reaction. Later, in the prayer book of 1559, we get an effort to combine the pre-reformation and reformation strands seen in the 1549 and 1552 books, e.g. the words of administration used in the communion office and retained in the 1662 book.

The next significant date is 1571, when we get the 39 Articles in their present form reflecting the official viewpoint of the Anglican church in the period. We shall often quote them and comment on them from different angles. There were also many controversial and often laborious tomes produced.

An important factor which must be remembered is that the Anglican church was fighting on more than one front. In the earlier part of the period the opponent was Rome. Later, although there was still a great deal of

414 *A History of Christian Doctrine*

literature produced against the Roman position, what we may call the 'Puritan controversy' also arose. Despite the sympathy of Edmund Grindal (Archbishop of Canterbury 1575–83) for elements of the Puritan position, John Whitgift (Archbishop of Canterbury 1583–1604) was their implacable opponent, and he enlisted Richard Hooker (c. 1554–1600) to help in defending the Anglican position. This was, however, more a matter of discipline than of doctrine.

There were questions about the ministry, especially the episcopate, and questions concerning ceremonies and free will; and on all three issues we may mention the name of Richard Bancroft, Whitgift's successor as Archbishop of Canterbury who had taken a leading part in flushing out the Puritans' printers. One result of all this was that shortly after 1603 we get the growth of an Arminian party stressing free will over against Calvinist predestination. Although our period ends at 1603, we must remember that the whole Anglican position remains somewhat flexible till after 1660; this applies to several areas of doctrine and to the whole ethos of the church in England during a century. Some would call it compromise and some would call it comprehension; Elizabeth herself, who was a dominant force in ecclesiastical affairs, did not want, as she herself said, to make 'windows into men's souls'.

It is against this background that we shall describe sixteenth-century Anglican theological thinking.

Broadly speaking, Anglican theology in the sixteenth century adopted the attitude of other reformed churches to Holy Scripture as that which contained 'all things necessary for salvation'.[1] This was a definite refutation of the prominent place that Roman Catholics gave to tradition at the time. Rogers, in his exposition of Article Six, said that Roman Catholics place their own 'doctrines, injunctions, precepts' on an equality with God's word, an attitude which he repudiated because it equated the authority of the church with that of the Gospel.[2] On the other hand Anglicans did not assume that every detail mentioned in scripture must be imitated 'even to the taking up of a rush or of a straw', as some of the Puritans insisted.

What Anglicans did assert was the supremacy and sufficiency of Holy Scripture. If we examine the Articles, such as those of 'good works', 'of works before justification', 'of works of supererogation', 'of Christ alone without sin' and 'of sin after baptism', we shall find that the standpoint is based on Holy Scripture and the teaching is made as agreeable to Holy Scripture as is possible. They describe words of supererogation which are over and above God's commandments by the words 'arrogancy' and 'impiety', and stress the scriptural phrase 'we are unprofitable servants'. It was on the teaching of Scripture that they based their repudiation of 'the Romish doctrines of purgatory, pardons, worshipping and adoration of images and relics, and invocation of saints'.[3] To speak in a tongue which was foreign to the majority of people was described as plainly repugnant,

[1] Article 6.
[2] T. Rogers, *The Catholic Doctrine of the Church of England* (Parker Society), pp. 78f.
[3] Article 22.

not only to the custom of the primitive church, but also to the word of God.

But deference should be paid to other authorities even though they were secondary. First, there were the Greek and Latin Fathers of the first six Christian centuries, for, as Jewel said, they were interpreters of the word of God and so 'we despise them not, we read them, we reverence them, and give thanks to God for them'.[1] Such leading Anglican divines as Cranmer, Hooper, Jewel and Whitgift used the Fathers widely in their writings, and were able to say that if heresies were practised in the Church of England they had been learned from the Fathers.

Tradition concerning both extra-credal doctrinal areas and also rites was respected, especially where it came down from antiquity; but some authors spoke very scathingly of 'man's tradition' comparing such to 'cockle and chaff'. Nor was the antiquity of the first constitution of the church proof of its truth or its soundness. Yet, as Hooker says, it was never safe to depart from the judgment of antiquity.[2] Article 34 spoke of the need to obey the traditions of the church where these were not repugnant to God's word.

Concerning the public ordering of church affairs, Hooker spoke of the necessity to give place and deference to intrinsic reasonableness, antiquity, church authority, suitability and necessity.[3] Thus these subsidiary authorities had their place but they were not essential, for no point of faith might be based upon them. This attitude, coupled with the supremacy given to scripture, was the sixteenth-century Anglican standard for matters of faith and order.

The first five Articles deal with faith in the Holy Trinity, Christ and the Holy Ghost. Concerning Christ, of the Homilies which were reprinted in 1562, we find that one was on the nativity, another was on the passion and another on the resurrection.[4] All these contain valuable teaching, though I would not say that it is specifically distinctive. But Article No. 31 has the title of 'The One Oblation of Christ offered upon the Cross' and makes plain that it was 'the perfect redemption, propitiation and satisfaction', and goes on to condemn the 'Sacrifices of masses' as 'blasphemous fables and dangerous deceits'. We should also note that little is said about the Virgin Mary and that there is condemnation of prayers to the Saints.

What was there distinctive about the doctrine of man held by these theologians? 'Both Anglicans and Puritans accepted the doctrine of original sin, but they estimated differently the seriousness of the effects of man's wounds. Anglicans found man to be deficient in spiritual capacity; his other powers were weakened, but not desperately wounded and in need of redemptive blood transfusions as the Puritans claimed. Man's reason was, for the Anglicans, unimpaired; it had a natural capacity to distinguish between good and evil in a moral order'.[5]

This quotation provides a fair summary and contrast with the Puritan

---

[1] *Works* (Parker Society), vol. 4, p. 1173f.

[2] *Laws of Ecclesiastical Polity* 5.7.1.

[3] *ib.* 5.6.9.

[4] For a fine discussion on the Incarnation, see Hooker, *op. cit.*, 5, chapters 51–56.

[5] Horton Davies, *Worship and Theology in England from Cranmer to Hooker*, 1534–1603, O.U.P., 1970, p. 54.

position, though both stand on the reformed side of the divide. Article 9 deals with 'original or Birth-sin' and says that 'man is very far gone from original righteousness and is of his own nature inclined to evil'. It goes on to state that this 'infection of nature' remains even in the regenerate. Thus man's free will is impaired and 'he cannot turn and prepare himself, by his own natural strength and good works, to faith and calling upon God'. Hence man needs to be justified. Good works before justification are of no value, nor can there be works of supererogation.

Thus we may say that the Anglican teaching in this period was a modified form of Augustinianism. There was great stress laid on man's sin and the effect of the fall.[1] Man was depraved in his nature rather than merely deprived of some additional benefit with which he had been created, but although he was very far gone from original righteousness he was not totally corrupt.[2]

On the other hand, equally great stress was laid on what God had done and man's need of grace; man could do nothing of himself, and so the reformed doctrine of justification by faith was centred upon Christ, and everything was done to prevent the possibility that by any stretch of imagination it could be regarded as man-centred or that man contributed anything to his own salvation. 'Catch thou hold of our Saviour' preached Hugh Latimer.[3] This stress on justification by faith in Jesus Christ through grace has to be viewed against the background of the times, although the final form of the Anglican article was printed after the Council of Trent ended. The decree of the latter gave an impression not merely of ambiguity but of evasion of this fundamental truth. Consequently, like their continental brethren, the Anglican reformers stated that 'we are accounted righteous before God, only for the merit of our Lord and Saviour Jesus Christ – we are justified by Faith only'.[4]

The homily on salvation stressed three things necessary for justification. These were: on God's part 'His great mercy and grace'; on Christ's part 'justice, that is, the satisfaction of God's justice'; and on our part 'true and lively faith in the merits of Jesus Christ'. But this faith is not ours but by 'God's working in us, and therefore it is the gift of God.'[5] The word 'alone' in the phrase 'justification by faith alone' was defended by a number of the Anglican reformers because it made clear that there was no human merit involved. Rogers, in his comment, puts the position neatly in three propositions stating that we are justified (1) 'only for the merit of our Lord and Saviour Jesus Christ', (2) 'only by faith', (3) 'not for our own works or deservings'.[6]

What has been said should make it very plain that the Anglican teaching on this subject does not refer to faith in isolation, because it stresses the merits of Christ and also the place of works as the inevitable consequence

---

[1] Cf. the confessions in the Prayer Book services.
[2] Hooker 1.1–8 and his Sermon on Justification *passim*.
[3] *Works* (Parker Society), vol. 1, pp. 329ff.
[4] Article 11.
[5] *Homilies* (ed. 1843), p. 22.
[6] *Op. cit.*, p. 108.

of a lively faith. Faith, therefore, was the cause, not the instrument of justification, and unless there were good works it was not a right faith but counterfeit. 'Works are an addition to the foundation'; they are 'pleasing and acceptable to God in Christ', springing 'necessarily of a true and lively faith'.[1]

Concerning predestination, Article 17 is both long and full, stating that predestination to life is the everlasting purpose of God and that God supplies grace and gifts to enable those so predestined to live the Christian life. It is a source of great comfort to those who enjoy it and it is the opposite to 'those who are curious and carnal persons, lacking the spirit of Christ'. The Article concludes by saying that we 'must receive God's promises in such wise, as they be generally set forth to us in Holy Scripture'. The conclusion would seem to be that while predestination to life is taught and affirmed there is no authorized teaching on double predestination. Rogers, in his commentary on this Article, states the following propositions:

(1) There is predestination of men unto everlasting life.
(2) Predestination has been from everlasting.
(3) They which are predestinate unto salvation cannot perish.
(4) Not all men, but certain, are predestinate to be saved.
(5) In Jesus Christ, of the mere will and purpose of God, some are elected, and not others, unto salvation.[2]

This last proposition is more difficult but it does not affirm predestination to condemnation. It can create difficulty for us but, on the whole, the Anglican reformers did not teach double predestination, though a number especially of the less prominent writers before 1570 seemed to lean towards it.

There were efforts in this direction, especially those connected with Whitgift and the Lambeth Articles. Whitgift became primate in 1583, and while he opposed the discipline of Calvin he contended for the doctrine of Calvin. In 1595 Whitgift and others put forward the Lambeth Articles consisting of nine propositions; among other matters, they spoke of the predestination of certain persons unto condemnation, and stated that the *number* of these was predetermined. Whitgift said these Articles were agreeable to the thirty-nine Articles, but we should note that they never received what we may call an official imprimatur.[3]

Next, let us turn to sanctification, using Hooker's sermon on justification, since we have already noted the emphasis laid on good works as the proof of a lively faith. Hooker stresses that we must work at sanctification, but we distinguish it from the righteousness of justification, and so there are two kinds of Christian righteousness 'the one without us, which we have by implication; the other in us, which consisteth of faith, hope, charity and other Christian virtues'. He makes it plain that both come from God.[4]

Concerning the other areas we are about to examine, we find that the Anglican reformers differed in some ways from the Roman Catholic church

---

[1] Hooker's Sermon on Justification, Section 29 and Article 12.
[2] *Op. cit.*, p. 143.
[3] For more detail see F. L. Cross, *Oxford Dictionary of the Christian Church* in loc.
[4] Section 2.

but in others agreed with it. On the other hand, in these same areas, we find differences between the Anglicans and the Puritans.

Before we discuss these varied emphases and tensions we should insert a note on the writers in the whole period. In the earliest period up to 1553 we had the tremendous wide-ranging learning of Cranmer, the acute brain of Ridley and many others whom we have not mentioned, e.g. Thomas Becon, who in calibre and scholarship did not fall much behind. The central period is characterized mostly by the massive learning of Jewel deployed against the Romanists, as were the efforts of those before him; towards the end of it we have Whitgift entering into his controversy with the Puritans. In the last section, in addition to men like Bancroft, Pilkington, Sandys, Saravia, Whitaker, we have the dominating figure of Hooker, yet we must remember that with the exception of doctrinal writing in the area of church, ministry and sacraments, we do not find a great deal of actual doctrine in Hooker. There is more than his title 'The Laws of Ecclesiastical Polity' would warrant, but this is because of his method of approach and his comprehensive thoroughness.

In the total period under review the whole nature and doctrine of the church was prominent, and the controversy on many topics was on the two fronts already mentioned.

Several Articles have a bearing on the church. 'The visible church of Christ is a congregation of faithful men, in the which the pure word of God is preached, and the sacraments be duly ministered according to Christ's ordinance.'[1] Rogers comments on this in the following propositions:

(1) There is a church of Christ, not only visible but also invisible.
(2) There is but one church.
(3) The visible church is a Catholic church.
(4) The marks and tokens of the visible church are the due and true administration of the words of the sacraments.[2]

Ridley, perhaps the most acute mind amongst the early reformers and a martyr under Mary, gives three meanings to the word church. First, it meant all who profess the name of Christ; secondly what Ridley calls the purer part of the church, i.e. those Christian in heart and truth; and thirdly, by an extension of this second meaning, the 'mingled' church as a whole.[3]

Several other writers stressed the relationship of the church to Christ, thus in one way anticipating modern writing on ecclesiology. Terms such as Head, Bridegroom, Prince, Protector, Spouse were used, and one reason for this was to provide an antidote to the claims of Rome. One inference drawn was that the church had no need for a visible head. Thus the relationship of the church to Christ was one of 'incorporation, dependence, obedience and representation; the church lives in Christ and by Christ'.[4] The usual notes of the church were given, that she was one, holy, catholic and apostolic; Christ was the centre, and also the source and maintainer of

---

[1] Article 19.
[2] *Op cit.*, p. 164.
[3] *Works*, p. 126f.
[4] H. F. Woodhouse, *The doctrine of the church in Anglican Theology 1547–1603*, S.P.C.K., 1954, p. 30f.

unity. This unity was both outward and inward, and had both outward and inward marks.

This enabled the Anglican writers to maintain that their church was not a novelty – an assertion made by their Roman opponents. Anglicans had done nothing contrary to the teaching of Christ and His apostles, but rather they had left a church whose errors were plain. Field, in his notable book on the church written just after 1603, stated that this applied to other reformed churches as well.[1] Indeed Anglicans and Puritans agreed that there were worse evils than schism; these were heresy and apostasy.[2]

Generally they held that the church was holy, not because of her actual holiness but because of her holy calling; some writers, however, stated that only those actually holy could be united to Christ as Head. Here we see the influence of a type of predestination, and how some writers spoke of the true church as being invisible.[3]

The church is also catholic, and the Church of England was part of this catholic Church, though this did not preclude the existence of local or particular churches which were always to be regarded as part of the Catholic Church.[4]

Apostolicity included right doctrine, for the church had her being 'out of the Gospel'.[5] So the apostolic faith had to be retained, heresy repudiated, schism overcome and the word read and preached. Thus stress was laid on doctrine.

Concerning the church, the adjectives visible and invisible were held in uneasy tension. While Article 19 has not the title with either adjective, the phrasing speaks of the visible church; but this does not deny that the church might also be invisible and, on the question of government, Whitgift definitely asserts the use of both adjectives. All the reformed theologians face a difficulty here, because if the question was asked 'Where was the church during the latter medieval centuries?' when there was in their opinion a great deal of corruption, the only answer they could give was that the true church was invisible and the members were known to God alone.

Probably it may be said that Jewel's words reflect a general opinion. 'Thus the general or outward church of God is visible, and may be seen; but the very true church of God's elect is invisible and cannot be seen as discerned by man, but is only known to God alone.'[6] The visible and invisible were neither identical nor mutually exclusive, and several other writers used the phrase invisible to mean the elect or sanctified individuals. For them membership depended on inward qualities rather than on outward marks – another difficulty which created various opinions amongst our writers. Generally preaching of the word and administration of the sacraments were given as 'marks'; also discipline or some such word was often

---

[1] Field, Vol. 1, p. 349; Jewel, Vol. 3, pp. 79 and 92.
[2] Hooker, 5.68.6.
[3] W. Whitaker, *Works* (Parker Society), pp. 66–67.
[4] Article 34; Hooker 3.1.14.
[5] Field, Vol. 3, p. 168.
[6] Jewel, *Works*, Vol. 4, p. 668.

added; but other marks were given which we might call subjective – charity, obedience and the like.[1]

Our next section deals with authority, that intractable heritage from the Reformation. 'The church has power to decree Rites or Ceremonies, and authority in Controversies of Faith' but yet the church has no authority 'to ordain anything that is contrary to God's Word written'.[2] The next Article deals with the authority of General Councils but states that they may err, and Article 34 deals with the traditions of the church, not only giving them a degree of authority in themselves but allowing 'every particular or national Church – authority to ordain, change and abolish ceremonies or rites –.'

Hooker speaks of the authority of the church to ordain what was new as well as to ratify what is old. 'That which the church by her ecclesiastical authority shall probably think or define to be true or good, must in congruity of reason overrule all other inferior judgment whatsoever'; therefore 'the bare consent of the whole Church' should stop those who 'dare presume to bark against it'.[3]

Authority was one of the main issues of contention with the Roman Catholic church especially concerning the question of the papacy and the extent of its authority. One of Rogers' propositions is that it had 'most shamefully erred' in life, ceremonies and matters of faith. He quotes a very vitriolic early Protestant writer, John Bale, once Bishop of Ossory in Ireland, that 'Roma' spelled backwards is 'Amor' and he condemns the life of the church of Rome for wrongful 'love out of kind'.[4] The gravamen of Anglican charges was that Rome did not truly preach the word or rightly administer the sacraments. Jewel maintained that Rome was in schism, in schism from the Greeks, from the primitive church and even from Christ Himself and the Apostles.[5] Far too much authority was claimed for the pope.[6] Despite these grave faults, Hooker held that Rome has not denied 'the foundation directly', and hence papal baptism was still valid and Roman Catholic priests had a calling, so that the present Roman church was still to some extent part of the visible church of God.[7]

When we consider questions concerning the ministry and particularly episcopacy, we find that these Anglican writers directed their controversy chiefly against the Puritans. Hooker devoted three chapters to the ministry, first about its nature; secondly, the powers given to men to execute the office; thirdly, the gift of the Holy Ghost in ordination and degrees of ministry.[8] We shall select a few sentences from these chapters as they reflect a general Anglican opinion. 'Without the work of the ministry religion by no means can possibly continue.'[9] 'The ministry of things

---

[1] For fuller details and evidence see Woodhouse, *op. cit.*, chs. 4 & 5 *passim*.
[2] Article 20.
[3] Book 5, ch. 8.
[4] Rogers, *op. cit.*, pp. 164 and 179.
[5] Vol. 3, pp. 91ff.
[6] Jewel, Vol. 1, pp. 338ff. and many others.
[7] Sermon 2, section 27; cf. section 17.
[8] 5, chs. 76–78.
[9] 5.76.1.

divine is a function which – God did Himself institute.' Those ordained are 'Christ's ambassadors and his labourers' and they bear His commission. 'The power of the ministry of God translated out of darkness into glory, it raiseth men from the earth and bringeth God Himself down from heaven, by blessing visible elements it maketh them invisible grace, it giveth daily the Holy Ghost.'[1]

Thus the ministry is indelible and it is also a distinct order.[2] Whether we preach, pray, baptize, communicate, condemn, give absolution or whatsoever, as disposers of God's mysteries, our words, judgments, acts and deeds are not ours but the Holy Ghost's.[3]

Later Hooker says that he uses the term presbyters rather than priests so as not to give offence, and later adds 'Seeing then that sacrifice is now no part of the church ministry how should the name of Priesthood be thereunto rightly applied?' He answers 'The Fathers of the Church of Christ' speak of the ministry using the word Priesthood 'in regard of that which the Gospel hath proportionable to ancient sacrifices, namely the Communion of the blessed Body and Blood of Christ, although it hath properly now no sacrifice'.[4] Thus the word Presbyter is more fitting than that of priest.

He summarizes this discussion thus: 'I may securely therefore conclude that there are at this day in the Church of England no other than the same degrees of ecclesiastical order, namely, Bishops, Presbyters, and Deacons which had their beginning from Christ and His blessed Apostles themselves'.[5] Concerning ministry we may briefly refer to two other points. One is that the unworthiness of the minister hinders not the effect of the sacrament.[6] The other is that the ministry has also the pastoral task of feeding the flock, teaching and the like.

We must however concentrate on the position concerning episcopacy, since the Puritans made a fierce attack upon it especially in the latter part of our period. The obvious answer that Anglican writers could have made, if it were possible to do so in honesty, would have been to assert the divine origin of episcopacy; but this was never done. Late in the period one or two writers tended towards this rebuttal. Bancroft, according to some, did assert the divine origin of episcopacy. He referred indeed to its apostolic origin, and it is possible a case could be made out that there were occasions when 'apostolic' was used with the same meaning as 'divine'. Another writer who was very definite in his claim was the foreigner Saravia, but it would seem that he was not episcopally ordained himself. Furthermore, investigation of some of the more notorious cases such as that of Whittingham and Travers show that the ground of their deprivation was not their lack of episcopal ordination.[7]

These writers asserted that they spoke of a constitutional type of

[1] 5.77.1.
[2] 5.77.2 & 3.
[3] 5.77.8.
[4] 5.78.2.
[5] 5.78.12.
[6] Article 26.
[7] For details see Woodhouse, *op. cit.*, pp. 84ff. and on Travers, pp. 100f.

episcopacy, exercising a fatherly and pastoral authority. It was not prelacy.[1] The duty of the bishop was to teach the word of God, to pray and to lead a good life. He had not superior power of order with regard to preaching and administering the sacraments, but a superior degree concerning matters of jurisdiction.

There are three other points upon which we should touch. The first concerns consecration. Article 36 affirmed the lawfulness of the consecration of bishops and ministers, but we note that this was something 'confirmed' by secular authority. However we must add that, in the case of Parker's consecration, which has been so hotly disputed, great care was taken concerning it. The second point is the question of relations with non-episcopal churches. These seem to have been most friendly and no aspersions were cast upon them in this period. The third point concerns succession. Over and over these writers stress the need for succession in doctrine, but in no case what one would call a pipeline succession.[2] In summary, then, with the possible exceptions of Bancroft, Bilson and Saravia, the arguments for episcopacy advanced by Anglican divines of this period were its place in safeguarding faith, in ordaining and confirming, and in maintaining unity. Concerning non-episcopal bodies, authors were willing to accept the plea that non-episcopal churches advanced, that they had been forced into abolishing the episcopal system.

Before we discuss the sacraments, two points deserve some attention concerning two authors. The first is Cranmer and the second is Hooker. Cranmer's doctrine of the sacraments, especially of the eucharist, is very hard to discover and scholars are still at variance over details. Two general remarks may help. The first is that during his life Cranmer changed his views, and also that he was much influenced by Ridley and the continental reformers.[3]

The difficulty concerning Hooker really stems from a single sentence. 'The real presence of Christ's most blessed body and blood is not therefore to be sought for in the sacraments, but in the worthy receiver of the sacraments.'[4] This sentence has been taken by some as the basis for an assertion that Hooker's view of the Eucharist was receptionist. But this seems to be clean contrary to the whole tenor of his chapter, in which he was trying to secure peace in an area of great dispute by getting men to concentrate on what they received rather than how they received the gift.[5]

Now let us turn rather to the teaching of the Articles, three of which specifically deal with the sacraments. The first point is that these Anglicans spoke of only two sacraments – baptism and the eucharist, which 'be not only badges or tokens of Christian men's profession' but rather 'sure witnesses and effectual signs of grace'. God uses them to quicken, strengthen and confirm faith. The five which are commonly called sacraments are rejected as not being sacraments of the Gospel, and certain Roman practices

[1] e.g., Field, Vol. 3, p. 214.

[2] For more detail concerning succession see my article in *Theology*, Oct. 1952, pp. 376ff. and on these three points my book, pp. 91ff., chs. 11, & 7 *passim* and references given there.

[3] P. Brooks, Thomas Cranmer's *Doctrine of the Eucharist*, Macmillan, 1965.

[4] 5.67.6.

[5] 5.67.12.

are also repudiated. The need for sacraments is stressed, for they have both 'generative force and virtue'.[1] They are 'visible signs of invisible grace' and 'powerful instruments of God to eternal life'.[2] They have a much wider and deeper function than that of merely teaching the mind, because 'Christ doth truly and presently give his own self in His sacraments; in baptism that we may put Him on; and in His supper, that we may eat Him by faith and spirit'.[3] They are also helps to exercise Christian charity, to develop godliness, to preserve us from sin, to remind us of the benefits of what Christ has done. So they are marks and 'means conditional' whereby God works within us. This does not mean that they contain 'in themselves' 'vital force or efficacy', for they are rather instruments of salvation; but yet God normally bestows the grace of sacraments by the sacraments. 'They really give what they promise and are what they signify'. Consequently Hooker, both in the quotation above and in his repudiation of the word 'bare' or 'naked' in connection with them, reflects general Anglican opinion.[4]

These general statements receive more particular treatment. In baptism we receive Jesus Christ; He is really the substance of baptism. Hooker also discusses scriptural teaching and the necessity of outward baptism. He devotes attention to certain things which Puritans have attacked e.g. baptism by women, the use of the cross in baptism, the questions asked of the godparents and the relation of baptism to confirmation.[5] Three propositions of Rogers on Article 27 concerning baptism may act as a summary – it is 'a sign of profession' to denote Christians; also a sign 'or seal' of new birth; and thirdly, that 'infants and young children – are to be baptized'.[6] The article states that the privileges consist of being grafted into the Church, the promises of the forgiveness of sin, and the adoption to be sons of God.

Hooker links baptism to the eucharist – 'the grace which we have by the holy eucharist doth not begin but continue life'.[7] This famous chapter covers a great deal of material and could be described as an aid to piety as well as an earnest plea for toleration and for concentration on things where Christians agree. It covers much controversial ground but always in an eirenical spirit.

Three short Articles assert that communion is to be given in both kinds, that the wicked do not eat the body of Christ and that the eucharist is in no sense a repetition of the sacrifices of Christ; here masses are strongly condemned.[8] Article 28 has the title 'Of The Lord's Supper'; it is not only a sign of the love of Christians but of our redemption, and is also a partaking of the body and blood of Christ. Transubstantiation is then condemned on the grounds that it cannot be proven by Holy Writ, is repugnant to scripture, overthrows the nature of the sacrament and has given rise to many superstitions. The next paragraph asserts that the 'body of Christ is

---

[1] Hooker 5.50.1.
[2] Hooker 5.50.3.
[3] Jewel, Vol. 3, p. 64; Vol. 2, p. 1106.
[4] Hooker 5.57.1-5 *passim.*
[5] Hooker 5.57-61 *passim.*
[6] *Op. cit.*, p. 274.
[7] 5.67.1.
[8] 30.29.31.

given, taken, and eaten, in the Supper only after a heavenly and spiritual manner'. The means whereby this is done is faith and the sacrament is not to be 'reserved, carried about, lifted up or worshipped'. These statements show that Anglicans gave an important place to the sacraments.

The matter of church government, polity or discipline (the words were almost synonymous) can be dealt with much more briefly. Hooker especially dealt with it in great detail, and his real objection was that Puritans asserted that their own method and approach was the only one, while he defended the scriptural legitimacy of the attitude of the Church of England. The government, according to Article 37, belonged chiefly to the King's majesty, but it was expressly stated that the Church of England does not give to princes the 'ministering either of God's Word or of the Sacraments' and the article also repudiates the jurisdiction of the Bishop of Rome. We mention this point because the identification of church and state was so close – 'the self same people, whole and entire, were both under one chief governor'. 'One God, one king, one faith, one profession, is fit for one monarchy and commonwealth.'[1] The Queen had supremacy in ecclesiastical causes, but not to execute ecclesiastical functions, to preach, minister the sacraments, or consecrate bishops.[2]

Both in matters of discipline and of doctrine these Anglican theologians were waging war on two fronts, and yet they did try to secure a *via media*. They were anxious to retain as much as possible of what they regarded as their scriptural and catholic heritage, but the criterion of their catholicity was scripture. On many matters, where Scripture was indefinite or silent, they sought a great deal of toleration.

When we come to the end of our period we do not find that a neat arrangement has been achieved. Puritans agreed with Anglicans in rejecting papal supremacy and in stressing justification by faith, but the latter also held a strong sacramental doctrine, adhered to the episcopal system and desired a 'church-type' Church. Furthermore, Anglicans had some affinities with the Church of Rome in the place they gave to the authority of the Church and in the retention of ceremonies, unless these were hindrances to faith or contrary to scripture.

While there was no 'finality', there was yet a 'tone and a direction' given to the Church of England by these, the first generation of its reformed theologians. Despite different types of pressures, they kept a specific object in view and this is found in a document ascribed to Parker, Elizabeth's first Archbishop of Canterbury, predicting that the result of the Reformation would be that God would have His honour truly and purely reserved to Him; that His word, and not men's fantasies, would provide the rule and way to everlasting salvation; that the sacraments should be ministered religiously and reverently; and finally that the primitive form of discipline might be restored.[3]

---

[1] Sandys, *Works* (Parker Society), p. 49.

[2] Whitgift, Vol 3, p. 592.

[3] J. Strype, *Life of Parker* (ed. 1821), Document No. 32.

The History of Doctrine in the Seventeenth Century

R. Buick Knox

The History of Doctrine in
the Seventeenth Century

R. Buick Knox

During the sixteenth century the Church of Rome and the Churches of the Reformation had defined their doctrinal position in Decrees, Articles and Confessions which had an air of finality and permanence. However, no theological position has ever been immune to criticism or to varying emphases and interpretations, and by the end of the century the processes of reassessment were already at work. The doctrinal schemes were felt by some to be insufficiently warranted by Scripture or by the experience of the Churches; they appeared to do less than justice to some aspect of the faith and experience of the Churches, and at several points they turned out to be unable to absorb fresh theological insights or increasing ranges of knowledge. Personal antipathies or attractions and the dominating magnetism of gifted and often extravagant leaders were also potent factors in directing the trend of agitations within the Churches and among the movements on the fringes of the Churches throughout the seventeenth century.

I

The Church of Rome had been slow to realize the seriousness of the challenge presented by the Reformation, but when at last it regrouped its forces it met the challenge with the Decrees of the Council of Trent, in which it crystallized trends which had been at work in the Church for generations, and also signified its rejection of the Protestant criticisms of its teaching on Scripture, Tradition, Justification, the Sacraments and the primacy of the Pope. The resurgent Church of Rome had also a powerful agent in the Society of Jesus. Several of its members had been influential figures at Trent, and another member, Cardinal Robert Bellarmine (1542–1621), was one of the ablest apologists and propagators of the Tridentine teaching. His most powerful controversial work[1] was composed in the sixteenth century but its scholarly and clear exposition of the Roman Catholic position was highly influential in the seventeenth century, as is proved by the flood of refutations produced by Protestant controversialists and especially by defenders of the Church of England. His effectiveness was enhanced by his moderation, especially in his careful limitation of the papal authority in temporal affairs. Moreover, he had a grasp of the issues raised by Galileo Galilei (1564–1642) and, while the Holy Office and the Inquisition forced Galileo to recant his views, Bellarmine was aware that here was new

[1] R. Bellarmine, *Disputationes de Controversiis* (1586–93).

knowledge which the Church would sooner or later have to digest. Nevertheless, on the issues then at the heart of controversy he was a formidable papal protagonist, and his thorough knowledge of the Scriptures and his use of them to defend the papal claims were a notable asset to the Church of Rome. One of his main theses was that prevenient grace was necessary to inaugurate repentance and faith, but this was followed by co-operating grace and by sufficient grace to transform the believer so that in the end he was justified not merely by imputed righteousness but also by his own inherent righteousness. Recent scholars have sought to show that Bellarmine and other apologists have comprised within their definition of justification what the Reformers meant by both justification and sanctification, and that the Reformers had no intention of minimizing the importance of the fruit of justification in good works; but the issue was one of the sharpest points of division in the seventeenth century.[1]

Within the Church of Rome itself there were rumblings against the dominance of the Jesuit outlook and these came to a head in the movement associated with the name of Jansen. The movement arose through a fresh interest in the writings of Augustine of Hippo whose influence had shaped much of the theology of the Middle Ages. However, his emphasis upon divine election and irresistible grace made him congenial to many Protestants. Any Roman Catholic scholars who adopted these strands into their teaching were liable to come under suspicion of being crypto-Protestants. In the sixteenth century, Michel Baius, a teacher at Louvain, had come under such suspicion and his teaching had been condemned.

Cornelius Jansen (1585–1638) was a native of Holland and studied at Louvain where he had a brilliant career. He sought admission to the Society of Jesus but was rejected, and this may have sharpened his later aversion to the Jesuits and their teaching. He also formed a lasting friendship with another student, a Frenchman, du Vergier, and they devoted themselves to a study of Augustine. In 1617 du Vergier became abbot of St. Cyran in central France and in the same year Jansen became president of the new Collège de Sainte-Pulchérie at Louvain and was also made professor of exegesis in the University. In 1630 he was promoted to the professorship of Sacred Scripture. He prepared commentaries on several books of the Bible in addition to compiling an extensive study of the teaching of Augustine. None of his works was published until after his death, which took place at Ypres (of which he had been made bishop in 1635). During his life he was a faithful son of the Church and it was only when his *Augustinus, seu doctrina S. Augustini de humanae naturae aegritudine, sanitate et medicina* (Augustinus; or the teaching of Augustine on the sickness, health and cure of human nature) was published in 1640 that a storm arose concerning his teaching. In this work he had dealt with Augustine's arguments against Pelagius and his treatment of the state of Adam before and after the Fall and of 'the grace of Christ the Saviour'. The will of fallen man, according to Jansen, was so enfeebled that by himself he was unable to choose the way of virtue and his only hope of salvation was when he was drawn and fortified by the irresistible grace of Christ.

[1] J. Brodrick, *Robert Bellarmine* (revised ed., 1961).

Ten doctors of the Sorbonne added their approval to this version of the teaching of Augustine, but the Holy Office condemned the work in 1641 and Urban VIII added his condemnation in 1643 in the Bull *In eminenti*. Technically, the condemnation was based on the ruling that no works on the subject of grace could be published without the consent of the Holy See, but underlying the decision was the fear that the work marked a revival of Baian teaching and that the authority of the Church was in danger of being undermined by the stress upon irresistible grace bestowed upon the elect. Moreover, it was feared that such teaching countenanced the Protestant position.

The alarm caused by Jansen's teaching was aggravated because it was being propagated by a school of disciples. Du Vergier, known to history by the name of his abbey at St. Cyran, had won the interest of the Abbess of Port-Royal, Angélique Arnauld, and, when St. Cyran died in 1643, her brother, Doctor Antoine Arnauld of the Sorbonne, continued to advance the Jansenist cause. Another Sorbonne official, Cornet, issued in 1649 five propositions distilled from the *Augustinus*. The first proposition stated that some of God's commands were impossible to keep, since even just men had not the grace sufficient to enable them to do so. The second was that man in his fallen state was incapable of resisting interior grace, which when given by God did not crush personal freedom but renewed the whole life, including its freedom. The third was that for any person to receive merit or demerit in the sight of God there must be freedom from external constraint but not from the pressure of interior necessity. The fourth was that Semi-Pelagianism, while it was correct in admitting the need for interior prevenient grace, was in error in holding that it could be resisted. The fifth branded as a further Semi-Pelagian error the teaching that Christ shed his blood for all men.

A papal commission examined these propositions for over two years and in 1653 Innocent X condemned them in the Bull *Cum occasione*, and the condemnation was backed by royal approval. The Jansenists retorted with the flimsy evasion that the five propositions were not verbatim citations from the *Augustinus* and therefore their condemnation was not a condemnation of Jansen or of those who followed his teaching. They held that while the Pope had authority to decide whether any teaching was orthodox or heretical, the decision as to what was or was not in a book was a decision on a matter of fact to which the papal infallibility did not extend and on which people were competent to make their own judgment; papal pronouncements on such matters need be received with no more than respectful silence and did not require interior assent. Many Jansenists were content to remain in the Church on the basis of these reservations, but the confrontation was continued by the precocious and penetrating genius, Blaise Pascal (1623–62), who in his *Lettres Provinciales* (Letters to a provincial) defended the propositions as a faithful digest of the teaching of both Augustine and Jansen and as theologically sound. He also widened the debate into an attack on the Jesuits and their own devious moral guidance. The Sorbonne dismissed Arnauld and sixty other doctors who shared his views, and in 1656 the French bishops by a majority decision supported the papal position. In the same year the new Pope, Alexander VII, reiterated the condemnation in the Bull *Ad Sanctam Beati Petri Sedem* and in 1664 followed this up by a constitution *Regiminis Apostolici*, by which all clergy were required to subscribe to the condemnation of the five propositions and of the teaching of Jansen. However, Louis XIV became apprehensive that such a repressive policy was likely to impair the liberties of the Gallican Church, and many bishops were also moved to assert that papal infallibility did not extend to matters of fact outside of revelation. The papal nuncio of Clement IX devised a conciliatory formula which by 1669 all the French bishops were able to sign.

The hostility of the Jansenists to the Jesuits had its roots not only in personal antipathies and in a distaste for the Jesuit zeal in furthering papal centralization and curbing local characteristics but also because the Jesuits had countenanced the teaching of Luis de Molina (1535–1600), a Spaniard, who in his *Concordia liberi arbitrii cum gratiae donis* (Concord of free will with the gifts of grace) (1588) taught that God bestowed his grace in the light of his foreknowledge of those who would freely co-operate with the gift of grace; Molina held that only in this way could human free will be safeguarded. This teaching was far removed from the doctrine of the irresistibility of grace and it aroused a fierce hostility in Jansenist circles and also in the far wider company of those in whose eyes it undermined the sovereignty of God. Its condemnation was only averted by the refusal of Paul V to bow to the clamour, and Molinism has remained a permissible view within the Church of Rome.

Between these opposed positions that man has freewill and that he has none, there is the third possible position that man has freewill but that his highest good is served by the annihilation of that freewill and by an abandonment to God so complete that there remains concern neither for heaven nor for personal salvation nor for virtue nor for mortification nor for love of Christ, but only for a resting in the presence of God in pure faith; added to this would be a submersion in God so entire that all thoughts and acts would be works of God himself. This doctrine, known as Quietism, had among its leading exponents in the Church of Rome another Spaniard, Miguel Molinos (c. 1640–97), who became a noted spiritual director in Rome and counted among his friends Cardinal Odescalchi who became Innocent XI. Molinos expounded his views in his *Spiritual Guide* (1675). It was this same Innocent XI who in 1687 issued the Bull *Coelestis Pastor*, in which he condemned sixty-eight points in Molinos's teaching. The peril of this doctrine was that under the conviction of being totally immersed in the will of God it was possible to place the divine *imprimatur* upon acts which would normally be regarded as sinful, and it is probably not without significance that Molinos was sentenced to life imprisonment on charges of immorality, though during his imprisonment he sustained the serenity of soul prescribed in his *Spiritual Guide*.

Among Molinos's sympathizers was Madame Guyon (1648–1717) who was also accused of heresy and suspected of immorality, but, though she was protected by Madame de Maintenon and defended by Archbishop Fénélon (1657–1715), her views were condemned at the Conference of Issy in 1695, and Fénélon who was Archbishop of Cambrai concurred in the sentence.[1] In 1697 he published his *L'Explication des maximes des saintes* (Expositions of the sayings of the saints) in which he gave evidence of a mystical spirituality which provided some ground for the suspicion that he had not fully abandoned his Quietism. Twenty-three propositions from his book were condemned by the Holy See in 1699 and he meekly accepted the condemnation. Though Quietism was condemned by the Church of Rome its influence continued to be felt in many areas and can be traced in the rise of Pietism in the Lutheran Church.

Among the defenders of the position of the Church of Rome was Bossuet (1627–1704) who became the bishop of Meaux and was one of the greatest preachers of the Church. His zeal and his power of argument were seen in his *Exposition de la doctrine catholique sur les matières de Controverse* (Exposition of the catholic doctrine on matters of Controversy) (1671) and in his *Histoire des variations des Églises Protestantes* (History of the divisions among Protestants) (1688). He was also zealous in securing the condemnation of Quietism in 1699 and had paved the way for it in his *Relation sur le Quiétisme* (Treatise on Quietism) (1698). On the other hand, this ebullient protagonist of the Church of Rome as the Church which through the centuries and amid the plethora of Protestant divisions had been the only custodian of the deposit of faith, was opposed to the ramifications of papal power and its encroachments upon the civil power, and he was responsible for the drafting of the four Gallican Articles of 1682; in these the French clergy asserted that the Pope had no authority in temporal and civil matters and could not dispense subjects from their allegiance; these Articles also declared that Popes were subject to General Councils of the Church, that the ancient liberties of the Gallican Church were inviolable, and that papal judgments were not irreformable.

These Articles were condemned by Alexander VIII in 1690, and it suited Louis XIV to add his condemnation in 1693 but they expressed an attitude of national independence which persisted in France in succeeding years.

II

At the end of the sixteenth century the common doctrinal standard of the Lutheran Churches was the Formula of Concord which had been drafted in 1577, and by 1580 had been accepted by most German states, though not without considerable pressure from the Elector of Saxony. This had become the definitive statement of doctrine and it dominated the Lutheran scene during the seventeenth century. No major theologian arose to disturb the concord, and there were many writers who produced vast treatises to expound and defend the teaching of the Formula. One of the most notable was Abraham Calovius (1612–86) who became a professor of theology at Wittenberg in 1652, and in 1655 began to produce his twelve-volume *Systema Locorum Theologicorum* (System of Theological Themes). His zeal for orthodoxy was said to have been shown by his morning and evening petition, 'Fill me, O Lord, with hatred of heretics'. In addition to the heavy

[1] P. Janet, *Fénélon* (1892).

pressure for conformity, the strain of the Thirty-years War and of the French attempts in the later part of the century to annex the Palatine was not conducive to fresh ventures in theological thought. Much of Germany was devastated, and the universities, in particular, were thrown into disarray.

Yet if there was little fresh theological thinking, it was not a century of religious stagnation. The times of terror awakened in many members of the Church a new awareness of the reality and presence of God; the God of the Creeds and the confessional standards became for them the living God. Johann Gerhard (1582–1637) was professor of theology at Jena and he produced one of the many contemporary expositions of Lutheran theology; his *Loci communes theologici* (Theological Commonplaces) which appeared from 1610 to 1622 became a standard work, but in 1606 he had already produced his *Meditationes Sacrae ad veram pietatem excitandam* (Sacred Meditations for the stirring up of true piety). This proved to be a very popular devotional work and the 'Pietas' in its title was a portent of the pietist movement which was to come. However, it was overshadowed by another work published in the same year. This was *True Christianity* by Johann Arndt (1555–1621), a Lutheran pastor, who was less concerned with the cogency of a theological system than with the work of Christ in the heart of man. This book was read and re-read in the years of adversity and became a source of deep spirituality and of social concern.

The spirituality was notable in the irenic attitude of George Calixtus (1586–1656) who became professor of theology at Helmstadt in 1614. He venerated the memory of Melanchthon and believed he was perpetuating his spirit in seeking to reconcile not only Lutherans and Calvinists but also the Roman Catholics on the basis of a common acceptance of the Scriptures, the Apostles' Creed and the deposit of faith to be found in the first five centuries by the application of the criterion of Vincent of Lérins. He went to a conference in Thorn in Poland in 1645 where his vision of reunion was the main theme but he was accused of a syncretistic blurring of doctrinal differences and he was strongly opposed by Calovius. The irenic project foundered but was revived later in the century by Gottfried Wilhelm Leibniz (1646–1716) in his *Systema Theologicum* (Theological System) (1686). He entered into correspondence with Bishop Bossuet but his efforts led to no tangible results. He was to gain more lasting fame in the next century by his writing on the philosophy of religion.

However, the main thrust of Arndt's influence was not towards ecclesiastical change but towards spiritual renewal as seen in the hymns of Paul Gerhardt (1607–76), in the sermons of Balthasar Schupp, and in the exotic and sometimes crude mystical writings of Jakob Boehme (1575–1624). This ferment issued in a lush growth of movements both inside and outside Germany, and all of them rather loosely related to the existing Churches. The most notable figure to emerge from the ferment was Philip Jakob Spener (1635–1705). He had a wide education in at least four universities, and in 1666 he became a Lutheran pastor at Frankfurt-on-Main, where he began to hold meetings for Bible study and for devotion. These meetings came to be called Collegia Pietatis, and they were the outstanding feature of the Pietist movement. Arising out of his experience and his belief in the need for a new birth and a new sharing of spiritual understanding he wrote his *Pia Desideria* (1675).[1] In this book he set forth a plea for devotional study of the Bible, for charity and an appeal to the heart in theological controversy, for higher standards of religious life among teachers and students in the theological departments of the universities, and for a new direction of preaching towards conversion and edification. In 1695 the University of Wittenberg claimed to have detected two hundred and sixty-four errors in Spener's teaching, but in 1694 a new university had been founded at Halle and its ethos was in line with Spener's programme. It gained great prestige, and its most famous figure was August Hermann Francke (1663–1727), the professor of Greek. He shaped the outlook of thousands of students, many of whom became Lutheran pastors, and he wrote many books to stimulate the Pietist movement and give it a theological framework. He also worked out his faith in a chain of charitable institutions, notably his orphanage at Halle, and also in encouraging the pioneer venture of Protestant foreign mission work.

In Francke the religious and social emphases of Arndt were combined. The social strand was also seen in the aspirations of Comenius and Andreae. John Amos Comenius (1592–1670) belonged to the Bohemian Brethren, but he became a scholar who travelled widely in search of knowledge or in flight from persecution. He had a vision of an educated humanity, and this vision sustained him amid the perversities of his time. He propounded educational methods which have won him an honoured place among pioneering pedagogues. Johann Valentine Andreae (1586–1654) embodied a vision of a pure society in his *Reipublicae Christianopolitanae Descriptio* (Outline of a Christian State) (1619); this plan covered many aspects of town planning, social services, cultural opportunity and religious accord, and it ranks as one of the most sober of the visionary schemes compiled across the ages.

Pietism deeply influenced Johannes Albrecht Bengel (1687–1752) whose biblical studies bore fruit in his *Gnomon* (1742) which was a rich mine of information on the text and interpretation of the New Testament. On the other hand, since Pietism was not primarily concerned with doctrinal precision, some of its followers tended to be critical of claims to doctrinal finality, and this paved the way for the growth of a rationalistic treatment of doctrinal statements; this trend can be seen in the writings of Thomasius (1655–1728), a colleague of Francke, and in those of Gottfried Arnold (1666–1714). Again, the Collegia Pietatis, which were intended to be centres of renewal within the Church, 'Ecclesiolae in Ecclesia', in some cases tended to become separate from the Church and to develop eccentric forms of sectarian teaching and practice and so to foster a spirit not always akin to piety.

III

The teaching set forth in the Churches of the Reformed tradition came under criticism in the Low Countries. James Arminius (1560–1609) was a

[1] *Pia Desideria, or Heartfelt Desire for a God-pleasing Reform of the true Evangelical Church*, translated and edited by T. G. Tappert (1964).

preacher at Amsterdam and in 1603 he became a professor at Leyden. He was asked to defend the Church's position on predestination but his studies led him to question the doctrine, and this led to a conflict in the university between himself and another theological professor, Gomarus. The conflict became complicated by political loyalties. Gomarus supported the monarchical rule of Prince Maurice of Orange, but Arminius supported the republican party led by Oldenbarnevelt. Arminius also wanted a national synod to be summoned to examine the position of the Church in relation to the Calvinist teaching as it was presented in the Belgic Confession and in the Heidelberg Catechism. He died in 1609 before he could secure any doctrinal revision, but forty-six ministers led by Uytenbogaert met at Gouda in 1610 and set forth the essence of the teaching of Arminius in five affirmations. First, 'God by an eternal and unchangeable purpose in Jesus Christ his Son before the foundation of the world hath determined out of the fallen sinful race of men, to save in Christ for Christ's sake and through Christ those who through the Holy Ghost shall believe on this his Son Jesus and shall persevere in this faith and obedience of faith through this grace, even to the end'; those who are incorrigible and unbelieving remain alienated from Christ and are left to endure the wrath of God. Second, as a consequence, when Jesus died he 'died for all men and for every man' and redemption was now available for all but was only enjoyed by those who believed according to the terms set forth in the Gospel. Third, no person is capable of choosing to believe; everyone is in a state of apostasy and sin and can neither 'think, will, nor do anything that is truly good' but needs 'to be born again of God in Christ through his Holy Spirit and renewed in understanding, inclination or will and all his powers'. Fourth, necessary as is the pressure of God's prevenient and assisting grace, people still have the power to resist the pressure of the Holy Spirit which is therefore not irresistible. Fifth, with the assisting grace of the Holy Spirit 'those who are incorporated into Christ by a true faith' have resources to 'strive against Satan, sin, the world and their own flesh' and against the assaults of temptation, but by negligence they may forsake the way of Christ and return to 'this present evil world' and so lose a good conscience and become devoid of grace.

These Articles are neither a declaration that God will save all people nor that all people have a freewill to choose to accept Christ. The mystery of election remains, but there is a universal intention to offer salvation to all, though those to whom it is offered may reject the offer or fall away from it if they do accept it. Nevertheless, the Remonstrance, as the Five Articles were called, aroused fierce controversy in both the University and Parliament. The successor of Gomarus was Episcopius, who became a leading exponent of the teaching of Arminius and was banished from his post. Arminius's own successor, Vorstius, tried to uphold his teaching but he too was silenced. In Parliament, Arminian teaching was alleged to contain thirty-six heretical tendencies, but a declaration was compiled from a catena of scriptural quotations and was safely piloted through Parliament. This did not satisfy the critics any more than the purely scriptural statements of the fourth-century Arians satisfied the followers of Athanasius.

The statement was piloted through Parliament by Hugo Grotius whose personal standing gave great weight to his views. He was a noted scholar and jurist and was eminent as a pioneer of international law, especially the law of the sea. He also made his mark as a theologian in 1617 when he published his work *On the Satisfaction of Christ*; he questioned the generally-accepted view that Christ had paid the penalty incurred by sinful men and had thus made a full satisfaction to appease the Father's wrath. Grotius said Christ died, not because God could not forgive unless atonement were made and his justice satisfied, but to expose the heinousness of sin; if no penalty had been exacted sinners might have thought that sin was trivial. Grotius' views were to be influential in later times, but when they were published they were abhorrent to the orthodox, especially to those who believed in the necessity for a precise atonement for the sins of the elect, and even the Arminians did not venture into this field of speculation. Orthodox alarm at the teaching of Arminius and his circle led to a full-scale confrontation at the Synod of Dordrecht (Dort) in 1618. This was an impressive assembly and included a group of divines sent by James I from England.

The Canons of Dort were a concentrated treatment of the five points of the Remonstrance.[1] The first section was devoted to the subject of predestination. It assumed, as had most of the prior Reformed statements, that God's choice of the elect had been made before the foundation of the world. However, there had been a divergence on the reason for the choice. Some said that God had foreseen and had resolved to permit mankind to fall from the state of innocence in which they were created, and then out of his mere good pleasure he had resolved to elect some to be delivered from the state of sin and misery into which they would fall; this was known as the infralapsarian view. Others took a starker view and held that election was a choice made without reference to man's fallen condition, and that the Fall and the way of salvation were subsequent stages in the process whereby God chose to bring the elect to salvation; this was the supralapsarian view. The Canons of Dort took the infralapsarian view; it was stated that no injustice would have been done if all had been allowed to perish, but God mercifully sent 'most joyful tidings to whom he will and at what time he pleases' and he 'graciously softens the hearts of the elect, however obstinate'; those not elected were left to the just reward of their obduracy. The Canons then stated that the death of Christ was 'abundantly sufficient to expiate the sins of the whole world' and the call to repent and believe had to be issued to all mankind but the quickening and saving efficacy of Christ's death only extended to the elect. All men had indeed glimmerings of natural light but this was quite insufficient to lead to a saving knowledge of God; God had to 'call effectually in time the elect from eternity' and he used the appointed means to make this effectual call and to bend the will 'to a true obedience in which true freedom resides'. God's elect persevered to the end and had an infallible pledge of eternal glory.

The next manifestation of turbulence in the doctrinal waters of the

[1] P. Schaff, *The Creeds of the Evangelical Protestant Churches*, III, Part Second; W. A. Curtis, *A History of Creeds and Confessions of Faith*, 238–250.

Reformed Churches took place in France at the Academy of Saumur where Gomarus, the opponent of Arminius, had taught before moving to Leyden. The appointment of John Cameron, a peripatetic Scottish scholar, to be a professor in the Academy in 1618 introduced a stimulating teacher to the scene,[1] and when in 1626 his pupil, Moses Amyraut (Amyraldus), was called to be a minister at Saumur and also appointed to be a teacher in the Academy the troubling of the waters began. In 1634 he published his *Brief Traité de la Predestination* (A Short Treatise on Predestination). The theological edginess of the time was revealed by the storm which was caused by so modest a restatement of the Reformed position. Amyraut believed his teaching to be both Scriptural and Calvinist, and he had indeed a great knowledge of Calvin's writings. He was supported at Saumur by Louis Cappel and Josué de la Place and also on the wider scene by Jean Daillé and David Blondel, the influential leaders of the Reformed Church in Paris. Amyraut was not a disciple of Arminius and he agreed with the decree of the Synod of Dort that God out of his own pleasure had elected some to salvation, but he held that this was the secret counsel of God and could not be plumbed by finite minds nor made the basis for the Church's doctrine. God had declared his public purpose in covenants in which he accommodated himself to human capacity. This purpose was an intention to save all mankind, an intention made a possibility by the universal sufficiency of Christ's redemptive act and by the ensuing external call which moved the elect to respond in faith. Amyraut also related this purpose to the doctrine of the Trinity and to the sweep of history; God the Father was primarily the source of the first Covenant between God and man in the state of innocence and of perfect obedience, and also in the period of the law when salvation was offered to fallen man upon condition of obedience to the law delivered to Moses; God the Son had established the Covenant of Grace whereby forgiveness and justification were offered to sinners without any inherent merit in themselves; salvation thus became potentially available to all who responded in faith, but this faith was itself a gift and was only possible when fallen men were persuaded by God the Holy Spirit, and this persuasion was exercised in accord with the mysterious and secret absolute will of God.[2]

Amyraut's teaching aroused hostility in many circles and the assault was led by two Leyden professors, Peter du Moulin and Frederich Spanheim. The main grounds of the attack were that Amyraut relegated to insignificance the great biblical teaching on predestination and presented a doctrine of God in utilitarian rather than in objective terms. He was assailed at the national Synod of Alençon in 1637, but in view of the widespread condemnation of his views the decision was surprisingly lenient; contestants were not to raise disputed issues in the pulpit nor to use new expressions likely to be misunderstood, and they were required to submit their books and their college curricula for approval by the provincial synods of the Church. However, in 1644 Amyraut reiterated his views in his *Defensio doctrinae J. Calvini de absoluto reprobationis decreto* (Defence of the teaching

---

[1] John Cameron, *De Triplici Dei cum homine foedere Theses* (1608: in *Opera*, 1642).

[2] Brian G. Armstrong, *Calvinism and the Amyraut Heresy* (1969), esp. chapters 2 & 4.

of J. Calvin concerning the absolute decree of reprobation) and this provided grounds for a further attack upon his teaching at the national synod
of Charenton in 1644 when two positions were reaffirmed: first, God's choice
and effectual calling were restricted to the elect only, since otherwise, if
God designed to save all, and all were not saved, as clearly all were not,
then the intolerable conclusion had to be drawn that God had failed in his
purpose; second, the original sin of Adam was not merely a corruption
handed on by hereditary transmission, but the guilt of the sin was actually
imputed to all so that all were counted sinners even before they themselves
had sinned. Yet Amyraut himself was not condemned but was confirmed
in his professorship and in the principalship of the Academy to which he
had been appointed in 1641 and in which he continued to his death in 1664.

In France the controversy spluttered on for several years, but in 1649 the
Duke of Thouars engineered an agreement that nothing more would be
written on the disputed topics. A rekindling of the controversy occurred
when Claude Pajon (1626–85), who had become professor of theology at
Saumur in 1666, developed Amyraut's teaching and suggested that God's
pressure upon the soul was exercised through the truth of the Gospel and
through the providential environment by which each person was surrounded. This pressure enlightened the intellect which then of its own
accord moved the will to respond to this working of the Spirit of God. This
was challenged by defenders of God's direct action in calling the elect, but
the menacing political clouds overshadowing the French Protestants at that
time prevented the outbreak of a full-scale controversy. Amyraut had
adopted a strong royalist position and was incensed by the execution of
Charles I of England, the brother-in-law of the late French king, Louis XIII.
This royalism estranged him from many of his fellow-Protestants who were
rightly apprehensive of the trends which led to the Revocation of the
Edict of Nantes in 1685.

In Geneva, Amyraut's teaching was adopted by Alexander Morus who
had succeeded Spanheim on his translation to Leyden, but Morus was forced
to renounce his position and leave Geneva. In 1675 Amyraut's teaching
was condemned in Switzerland by the *Formula Consensus* drawn up by
Heidegger of Zürich.

The use of the Covenant motif as the key to the presentation of doctrine
was brought to its climax by Johannes Cocceius (Koch) (1603–69), a
German who in 1650 became professor of theology at Leyden. He held that
the Bible was the history of God's purpose, each stage of which was marked
by a fresh Covenant. God moved to achieve his purpose in the first place by
a Covenant of works in which felicity was guaranteed so long as mankind
remained in the state of holy innocence. This Covenant was nullified by the
Fall of Adam which brought him and his posterity under the curse of God,
but God, whose purpose could not be defeated and who was rich in mercy,
then offered the Covenant of Grace; the first phase of this Covenant was a
Covenant with Abraham and his family, and this became more precise when
the written law was given to Moses and through him to the people of Israel.
It then reached its universal form in the coming of Jesus Christ whose
advent was also the fulfilment of a Covenant between himself and the

Father. The Covenant-offer at all stages was due to God's good pleasure, but in Christ it was extended to all people. Cocceius laid no emphasis upon predestination. He saw people, not as objects of divine selection but as persons created to receive the divine grace into their hearts, though also for Cocceius this reception was due to the persuasion of God who produced whatever good there was in man.[1] This federal theology, as it was called, aroused much hostility in orthodox circles, but there was in the churches a growing weariness of theological strife and so his teaching eventually secured a tolerated place in the Dutch universities and in the Reformed Church. Moreover, the scent of pietism was in the air and Cocceius's German origin made him and his disciples[2] sensitive to the changing climate.

Nevertheless, the dominant outlook among the Reformed Churches was still that of the accepted orthodoxy and this was expressed not only in the decrees of Dort and many subsequent synods but also in weighty theological treatises. One of the most notable writers was Francis Turretin (1623–87) who was a professor of theology at Geneva from 1648 until his death and who towards the end of his life prepared the extensive *Institutio Theologiae Elencticae* (System of Polemical Theology).[3] He had no hesitation about defending the orthodox system. Predestination, in his view, was one of the pillars of the Gospel; he repudiated any doctrine of universal grace which was propounded under pretext of exalting the glory of God. God's true glory was seen in his election according to his own good pleasure of those destined for salvation. It was, he claimed, the unanimous consensus of the Reformed Churches that God's election was purely gratuitous and apart from all knowledge or foreknowledge of works or of merits. Equally, reprobation to damnation was an inevitable concomitant of election; when God elected some he clearly disregarded others and thrust them aside. Nor had Turretin any place for a twofold will in God; it was 'contradictory to say that God intends the salvation of all and at the same time decrees to choose to love some and to hate and reject others'.[4] Moreover, if, as some said, Scripture taught that God willed the salvation of all, then, since many were not saved, God 'intended something which he knew with certainty he would never accomplish'. When it is said that 'God so loved the world', this applied only to the elect, 'a special privilege to the human race with respect to some parts so that the whole species will not be lost'.[5] Turretin claimed the support of Calvin, 'that distinguished man', for the view that Scripture did not teach that God willed all men to be saved; Calvin 'refers to classes of men, not to individuals'.[6] God was under no obligation to bless anyone, and 'no matter how great his mercy there is no reason why it should be universal in the sense of saving everybody'; 'God's love and mercy toward men do not suffer from this decree to leave the majority of mankind in their

---

[1] J. Cocceius, *Summa Doctrinae de Foedere et Testamento Dei* (1648).

[2] Franz Burmann, *Synopsis Theologiae et speciatim Oeconomiae Foederum Dei* (1671). Herman Witsius, *De Oeconomia Foederum Dei cum Hominibus* (1685).

[3] John W. Beardslee (ed.), *Reformed Dogmatics* (1965); this includes Locus IV of Turretin's *Institutio Theologicae Elencticae* (1680–83).

[4] Beardslee, *op. cit.*, 425.

[5] *ib.* 433.

[6] *ib.* 439.

sin'.[1] Turretin also rejected the view that God planned the coming of Christ before he nominated the elect; rather, God sent Christ to gain the salvation of those, and only those, whose election he had already planned:

'If Christ is concerned with individuals who have been given him by the Father, their election must of necessity be conceived as antecedent to the decree to send Christ.'[2]

At this point Turretin misrepresented the teaching of Amyraut; he said that Amyraut taught that because of Christ's satisfaction made to the Father, God called all people to salvation, but when none could respond because of their depravity 'he chose some people specifically by a special decree, leaving the lost in their voluntary unbelief and impenitence'.[3] This overlooks Amyraut's clear teaching about God's secret and absolute will.[4]

Turretin claimed to be in the tradition of Calvin and the Reformed Churches. Modern scholars have propounded the view that Calvin's basic theme was God's purpose in Christ and that he only dealt with election and predestination after he had set forth the universal reference of Christ's achievement, and therefore election was election in Christ and in the context of the universal offer. These scholars maintain that the subsequent dogmatic formulae of the Reformed Churches and the writings of their leading theologians have seriously distorted Calvin's teaching; by beginning with the doctrine of God and his eternal decrees of predestination and reprobation the Gospel was depersonalized and transformed from Good News to arid logic.[5] Yet it is in Book II of Calvin's *Institutes*, before he has reached the doctrine of Christ, that he says

It is God's election which so distinguishes among men. — It is through God's mercy that not all remains in wickedness. — Only those whom it pleases the Lord to touch with his healing hand will get well. The others whom he in his righteous judgment passes over waste away in their own rottenness until they are consumed.[6]

On the other hand, Turretin could reveal a warmth which belies to some extent his aridity; he said that God who had written the names of the elect in the book of life had also 'written the transcript of our election in the book of conscience and on tablets not of stone but of human hearts, not with ink but with the spirit of the living God by inscribing grace and law on our souls that he may assure us of his eternal love and of his everlasting care and protection'.[7]

On the fringe of the Reformed Churches and of the Lutheran Churches was the Socinian movement. Indeed, the only affinity between it and these Churches was a common rejection of the claims of the Church of Rome. Its distinctive teachings only help to show how small were the differences

[1] *ib.* 410.
[2] *ib.* 451–3.
[3] *ib.* 449.
[4] See supra, p. 436.
[5] e.g., see G. E. Duffield (ed.), *John Calvin.*
[6] *Institutes*, II, v, 3.
[7] Beardslee, *op. cit.*, 396.

within and between these Churches. Socinianism took its name and teaching from Lelio Francesco Sozzini (d. 1562) and his more famous nephew, Fausto Sozzini (d. 1604). Lelio was widely travelled and had made the acquaintance of Melanchthon and Calvin, and he was suspected of undermining the doctrine of the Trinity. Fausto carried on his uncle's speculations and denied the divinity of Christ. He found a responsive attention for his teaching in Poland, especially among the upper classes. A popular uprising in 1598 drove him from Cracow, but from the seed he had sown in Poland there arose groups of his followers, especially at Racow, and from them there emerged in 1605 the Racovian Catechism.[1] Claiming to base its teaching solely on the Scriptures, it held that man was a free agent, since without this freedom no action could have any moral quality; this being so, 'the notion of predestination is altogether false'. There followed an attack upon the doctrine of the atonement as a sacrifice to satisfy divine justice; God needed nothing in order to enable him to forgive and therefore Christ died, not to move God to forgive, but to influence men to seek forgiveness. Christ was not divine but was a man of marvellous life who at his resurrection was raised to divine power, and this made any doctrine of the Trinity irrelevant. These were the elements in the Catechism which caused alarm in the Churches. Yet even the Catechism did not jettison all the traditional doctrines. It stressed the need of enlightenment from above if men were not to perish eternally; they could not discover for themselves the way to avoid death. Moreover, Christ was referred to as mediator, propitiation, expiation, satisfaction, offering and sacrifice. Subsequent Socinian teaching has tended to eliminate these survivals of traditional doctrine.[2]

In Poland, Jesuit influence was instrumental in crushing the movement. The Catechism was burnt in England in 1614 by order of King James. Yet the leaven of the movement persisted in many countries, and in England it had a disciple in John Bidle whom Archbishop Ussher tried to win over to the Church.[3]

More than any other group the Socinians were the precursors of the outlook which made rationality the decisive test of what was acceptable in religion; what God revealed had to be rational, otherwise it was not acceptable.

IV

The doctrinal position of the Church of England had been set forth in the sixteenth century in the Thirty-nine Articles. There were many in the Church of England who wished for an even more pronounced Protestant platform so as to accentuate the repudiation of the Roman Catholic teaching and the kinship with the Churches of the Reformation on the Continent. The influence of the Reformed Churches was seen in the Lambeth Articles prepared by Archbishop Whitgift in 1585. At the turn of the century this

[1] Curtis, *op. cit.*, 357–370.
[2] A. C. McGiffert, *Protestant Thought before Kant* (new ed., 1962), pp. 107ff.
[3] R. B. Knox, *James Ussher, Archbishop of Armagh* (1967), p. 68; H. J. McLachlan, *Socinianism in Seventeenth-Century England* (1951).

Protestant stance was a strong feature of the Church and it was reinforced by a revulsion from what was believed to be a sure sign of a new papal aggression in the Gunpowder Plot. The Church of England at that time embraced the established Church of Ireland which had a constant struggle to survive amid a population predominantly loyal to the Church of Rome. To make its position clear, the Church of Ireland adopted in 1615 a new series of one hundred and four Articles which gave a sharper definition to the Protestantism of the Church. Not that there was anything novel in the Irish Articles. They were compiled by James Ussher, later to become the Archbishop of Armagh, and he used materials already to hand.[1] Thirty-six of the Thirty-nine Articles were embodied in whole or in part; the Lambeth Articles were adopted and condensed into five articles; the remainder were summaries of the Elizabethan Homilies. The Thirty-sixth English Article specifying the threefold ministry of bishops, priests and deacons was omitted; this might seem to signify that Ussher did not regard the threefold ministry as essential for the Church of Ireland, but the Twenty-third English Article was adopted and this stated that no one could minister unless 'he be lawfully called and sent to execute the same', and the lawful method of calling was by episcopal ordination. In a country where it was difficult to secure a sufficiency of ministers, it was presumably thought wise not to alienate those who had scruples about episcopacy but who were willing to conform so long as they were not required to give a positive assent to the episcopal form of government. Thus the Irish Articles did no more than accentuate the Protestant strand in Anglicanism and spell out the logical conclusion of the premiss in the Thirty-nine Articles which said that the elect were those chosen by God so as to 'deliver them from curse and damnation'.

There were, however, other emphases to be discerned in the Church of England. Archbishop Bancroft was less wedded to the Calvinist tradition which in his eyes signified not only a doctrinal outlook but also a leaning to a presbyterian form of ecclesiastical polity, and he was increasingly convinced of the strength of the claims of episcopacy.[2] Archbishop Abbot reversed the trend of Bancroft's policy in so far as it diverged from the Calvinist doctrinal position, but Abbot, like Bancroft, had little sympathy for a presbyterian polity, and, for practical if not for theological reasons, he was a strong advocate of conformity to the established system and he held it right to compel people to conform.[3] It was with his consent that James chose a deputation to attend the Synod of Dort. These English delegates approved the doctrinal articles of the Synod with their firm though not extreme Reformed attitude to the doctrine of predestination, and they concurred in the condemnation of Arminianism, but they did not concur in the articles on polity which were geared to a presbyterian system. This reluctance to adopt the full Dort position was not simply due to the fact

[1] R. B. Knox, *op. cit.*, pp. 16ff.

[2] S. B. Babbage, *Puritanism and Richard Bancroft* (1962); W. D. C. Thompson, 'A Reconstruction of Richard Bancroft's Paul's Cross Sermon', in *J.E.H.*, XX (1969), 253–66.

[3] P. A. Welsby, *George Abbot, The unwanted Archbishop* (1962).

that the Church of England had an episcopal form of government. It also arose from the awareness that there was in the Anglican outlook a persisting strand which stressed the autonomy of the Church of England and was averse to looking upon the Church of England as part of a pan-protestant block. It saw the Church of England as a national Church, closely linked to the sovereign, holding the central teachings of the undivided Church of the early centuries, and preserving a ministry whose pedigree could be traced across the ages and whose continuity was most clearly seen in the succession of bishops from apostolic times. This position was freshly expounded in the first half of the century by a company of learned men who have come to be known as the 'Caroline divines', among whom may be numbered Lancelot Andrewes, James Ussher, Joseph Hall, John Bramhall, John Prideaux, John Cosin, Robert Sanderson and Jeremy Taylor. All of these were sound defenders of the Protestant position of the Church of England; their sermons and writings included massive answers to the claims of the Church of Rome, and particularly to those claims as set forth by Bellarmine, and they also gave evidence of a heavy debt to the writings of the continental reformers, especially to those of Calvin, but it is worthy of note that they made extremely scant acknowledgment of this debt, while they copiously referred to the writings of the early Fathers, notably Cyprian, Augustine, Chrysostom and Gregory the Great, and made use of them to establish the catholicity and continuity of the Church of England.[1] They also laid a heavy emphasis upon the ethical consequences of faith and developed a distinctive school of casuistry which, while setting forth much of timeless value, was also directed to the justification of the existing ecclesiastical and monarchical structure of English society.[2] The outlook of these divines was translated into an effective policy within the Church of England during the ascendancy of William Laud who became Archbishop of Canterbury in 1633. Some of these divines were somewhat alarmed by the consequences of Laud's policy, but he himself never sought to escape the responsibility for that policy which he sought to enforce with the full weight of his legal and judicial powers. It has been common to regard Laud as an Arminian, but this was a title he never claimed for himself. He never renounced a doctrine of election and he used with approval the text, 'The Lord knoweth them that are his'. Moreover, the issues involved in Arminianism were not altogether novel in England; they had been discussed in Elizabethan days in controversies between conformists and puritans.[3] Doctrinal debates on Arminian issues were not central in Laud's career. He was driven by the desire to secure national conformity to the established system. If the puritan agitators were Calvinists, then it suited that Laud's party should be labelled as Arminian monarchists. This was indeed a curious development, since in the Low Countries it was the Arminians who were republicans over against the Calvinists who supported the Prince of Orange. Further, Laud's pressure

[1] P. E. More & F. L. Cross, *Anglicanism* (1935); H. R. McAdoo, *The Spirit of Anglicanism* (1965).

[2] J. Taylor, *Ductor Dubitantium*; R. Sanderson, *Nine Cases of Conscience*; T. Wood, *English Casuistical Divinity during the Seventeenth Century* (1952).

[3] T. M. Parker, 'Arminianism and Laudianism in Seventeenth-Century England', in *Studies in Church History*, I, pp. 20–34.

to push the Irish Articles into desuetude was not evidence of Arminian leanings but of a desire to make the Thirty-nine Articles the norm for the Churches of England and Ireland.[1]

Laud's intransigence contributed to the theological, political, economic, judicial and military issues which led to a growing rift among the ruling classes in England, and this percolated into society as a whole and led to the Civil War between the royalists and the parliamentarians. Parliament had economic strength but lacked the military power necessary to defeat the royalists, and so the 'Solemn League and Covenant' was made with Scotland in 1643. One of the conditions of military assistance from Scotland was that a plan would be made to secure a reform of the Church of England so that there might be in the two kingdoms a common form of church polity agreeable to the Word of God. To assist in preparing this plan, Scottish commissioners were invited to join the Assembly of Divines which met at Westminster from 1643 to 1647 with a desultory extension to 1648. The eight Scottish commissioners had an influence out of all proportion to their number, but even with all their pressure they were never able to secure approval for a system of church government in which final authority would be entrusted to Church courts of a presbyterian pattern. Even the English Presbyterians, who were the largest group in the Assembly, would not concede such a dominance, much to the annoyance of the Scots. The Assembly did produce a Confession of Faith and a Larger and a Shorter Catechism which set forth the doctrinal consensus of the various hues of the theological spectrum to be found in the Assembly. Under the labels of puritan and parliament were comprised not only the Presbyterians but also the Independents who ranged from those convinced of the New Testament prescription of congregational independence in ecclesiastical affairs to those of Erastian outlook. The Assembly was one of the most erudite gatherings of divines ever to meet in England and its doctrinal productions were couched in expansive and lucid prose. It has been said that the Confession was based on Ussher's Irish Articles, but these Articles were not an Ussherian novelty, and in any case the Confession was a far longer document and stands by its own right as a distinguished sample of vintage Protestantism.[2]

Beginning from the assertion that the works of creation and providence were sufficient to give an indubitable proof of the existence and power of God, the Confession moved on to assert that a saving knowledge of God was only to be found in the Scriptures which were 'given by inspiration of God to be the rule of faith and life'. Then followed sections on God and on the Holy Trinity and on the eternal decrees of God, who 'did freely and unchangeably ordain whatsoever comes to pass'.[3] Thereafter came a stark assertion of the doctrine of predestination in which the Arminian position was clearly rejected:

> 'Those of mankind that are predestinated unto life, God, before the foundation of the world was laid, according to his eternal and immut-

[1] R. B. Knox, *op. cit.*, 49–50.
[2] Schaff, *op. cit.*, III, Part Second, 598–703.
[3] Ch. I.

able purpose, and the secret counsel and good pleasure of his will, hath chosen in Christ unto everlasting glory, out of his mere free grace and love, without any foresight of faith or good works or perseverance in either of them, or any other thing in the creature, as conditions, or causes moving him thereunto, and all to the praises of his glorious grace.'[1]

This statement occurs before any mention has been made of the Fall of man, and, contrary to the view of Curtis that the teaching of the Confession is 'strictly infralapsarian', this statement has a supralapsarian ring.[2] The Confession then referred to 'the elect being Fallen in Adam', but this did not mean that the elect were chosen from those whose fall was foreseen but rather that the elect were not exempt from the fallen state of mankind. Scholars differ as to the meaning of the assertion that the choice was in Christ, but the prevailing view is that Christ was seen as the means by which God's good pleasure in choosing the elect would be effected. Those not elected have been ordained 'to dishonour and wrath for their sin, to the praise of his glorious justice'.[3] Admitting that the doctrine was a high mystery it was nevertheless said to 'afford matter of praise, reverence and admiration of God'.[4] The Confession then moved on to expound the person and work of Christ and asserted that 'to all those for whom Christ hath purchased redemption he doth certainly and effectually apply and communicate the same'.[5] These words imply that the atonement was made for the elect and for the elect only, and yet far from trying to name the elect or discouraging anyone from seeking to be among the elect, the Confession had a rapturous section on the 'evangelical grace' of repentance unto life; by it a sinner, who saw his sins as contrary to the holy nature and righteous law of God and who apprehended the mercy of God in Christ, was able to turn from sin unto God 'purposing and endeavouring to walk with him in all the ways of his commandments'.[6] Yet it was also said that the grace of faith was given only to the elect.[7]

The Confession also contained chapters on the Church and Sacraments. The Catholic Church was the Church of the elect known to God alone, but the visible Church comprised all those throughout the world that professed the true religion, together with their children, and was 'the kingdom of the Lord Jesus Christ, the house and family of God'; within this visible church there was the ministry and the sacraments. The two sacraments 'represent Christ and his benefits and confirm our interest in him'; their efficacy did not depend upon the intention or piety of 'him that doth administer them' but upon the work of the Spirit. Baptism was to be administered but once to any person, and was to be administered to believers and their children; but it was made clear that 'grace and salvation are not so inseparably

[1] Ch. III, v.
[2] W. A. Curtis, *op. cit.*, p. 271.
[3] Ch. III, vii.
[4] Ch. III, viii.
[5] Ch. VIII, viii.
[6] Ch. XV, i & ii.
[7] Ch. XIV, i.

annexed unto it that no person can be regenerated or saved without it'. The Lord's Supper was a remembrance of Christ's sacrifice and sealed its benefits to true believers and was a pledge of their communion with him and with one another. The doctrine of Transubstantiation was rejected, but it was admitted that the bread and wine were 'truly, yet sacramentally only' called by the name of the things they represent, to wit, the body and blood of Christ. The Confession claimed that the Church ought to be governed by synods or councils, though all such assemblies were capable of error.[1]

This Confession and the accompanying Catechisms were destined to have a great influence in the subsequent history of Presbyterian Churches, but they were overshadowed by the immediate aftermath of the Assembly. The increasing efficiency of the army under the tutelage of Oliver Cromwell soon obviated the need for Scottish help, and the victory of the army was followed up by the purging of Parliament to leave a Rump which concurred in the execution of the King. This left Cromwell in a dominating position, though he was never able to devise a stable form of government. In ecclesiastical affairs he made the keystone of his policy the provision of worthy ministers who satisfied the Triers set up to vet all applicants for appointment to parishes. This system enabled men of widely varying ecclesiastical leanings to secure appointments; several hundred presbyterian ministers and a much smaller number of Independents and Baptists were appointed and perhaps as many as six thousand Anglicans managed to remain in their parishes because of their personal integrity, their powerful friends in high places, the remoteness of their parishes or simply because there were not sufficient other ministers to take their place. A group of the Independent ministers met at the Savoy in London in 1658 and produced a statement of their ecclesiastical and doctrinal position. Doctrinally, they were at one with the Westminster Confession, and they adopted its first nineteen chapters. A chapter was added stressing the promise of Christ set forth in the Gospel; this promise was revealed only in the Word of God and was not available to those seeking it by the light of nature or to those who were destitute of that revelation. Chapters XXI to XXVI are verbal modifications of chapters XX to XXV in the Westminster Confession. The Savoy Declaration then proceeded to stress the autonomy of particular Societies or Churches, each of which had authority for carrying on all needful worship and discipline; each Church could choose its own pastors, teachers, elders and deacons to be over it and minister to it in the Lord.[2]

A confession akin in most respect to the Savoy Declaration was prepared by the Regular or Calvinistic Baptists in 1677, and this stressed the autonomy of each 'particular church gathered and completely organized according to the mind of Christ', and it introduced the special Baptist tenet that 'those who do actually profess repentance towards God, faith and obedicnce to our Lord Jesus, are the only proper subjects of this ordinance of baptism'.[3]

[1] Chh. XXV–XXXI.
[2] Schaff, *op. cit.*, III, Part Third, 707–729.
[3] Curtis, *op. cit.*, 301–2.

The era was also marked by an efflorescence of sectarian groups with a wide variety of beliefs and practices. This was part of the European spin-off of the Anabaptist phenomenon. These groups were noted for a profession of total dependence upon the Bible for their teaching, for a disregard of tradition, for a claim to immediate inspiration by God, and for the shaping hand of colourful leaders. One of the most remarkable of these groups was the Society of Friends led by George Fox, whose Journal is a spiritual classic. Since one of the Society's basic tenets was that each person is guided by the inner light of the Holy Spirit, it has been averse to defining firm doctrinal positions, but the Confession of Fifteen Theses compiled and defended by Robert Barclay has been widely allowed to be a statement of the Society's outlook.[1] God revealed himself immediately to the sons of men and this revelation is neither contrary to nor subordinate to 'the outward testimony of the Scriptures or right and sound reason' since all these proceed from God. Since the Scriptures 'are only the declaration of the fountain and not the fountain itself they are not to be esteemed the principal ground of all truth and knowledge nor yet the adequate primary rule of faith and manners', though they were to be esteemed as 'true and faithful testimony to the first foundation'. Every man was indeed fallen and 'subject unto the power, nature and seed of the Serpent' and had no natural light, but God had sent his Son to enlighten the hearts of all, and this light was as universal as the seed of sin. The love and the mercy of God were extended to all mankind. Christ died for all men and 'not only for all kinds of men, as some vainly talk, but for everyone of all kinds'. The common Calvinist view that Christ did not die for all was baseless, as was the Arminian teaching which denied any saving effect of Christ's work until there was knowledge thereof; Christ had enlightened everyone who came into the world whether they had knowledge of him or not. Nevertheless, there was great gain when 'Jesus was formed within us and working his works in us'; there was justification, sanctification and the leading to a perfect obedience. The leading of this light was also the ground of ordination and ministry and the guide to where, when and to whom every evangelist and pastor would minister; with this leading there was no need of any human commission, and without it no human commission had any weight. All true worship was the outcome of 'the inward and immediate moving of the Spirit'; fixed times and forms and even contrived extemporary effusions were 'all but superstitions, will-worship and abominable idolatry in the sight of God'. True baptism and communion were inward and spiritual workings of the Spirit, and the baptism of infants was a mere human tradition with no scriptural basis. In their early days members of the Society were severely hounded by the authorities of Church and State, and it is therefore no surprise to read that one of the Theses was that governments had no authority to force the conscience by 'killing, banishing, fining, imprisoning and other such things'.[2]

---

[1] Schaff, *op. cit.*, III, Part Third, 789–798.

[2] R. Barclay, *Catechism and Confession of Faith* (1673); *Apology for the True Christian Religion* (1678).

V

A further trend in the theological scene remains to be considered. This was not strictly a contribution to the formation or definition of doctrine, but was rather a consideration of the grounds for accepting any doctrine. The increased awareness of many world religions with age-long traditions and of the multiple divisions within Christianity raised questions about the assessing of the validity of the claim of any doctrine to be based on a divine revelation.

Lord Herbert of Cherbury (1583–1648) in his *De Veritate* (Concerning Truth) (1624) gave an impetus to an outlook which later came to be known as Deism. He found his standard of assessment in 'common notions' which were implanted in the human mind and were 'the only truly Catholic Church which does not err'. These 'common notions' included belief in a supreme God who worked out his purposes by both a universal and a special providence, and who was worthy of being worshipped by a life of virtue and piety; such a life was contrary to the wickedness which was common in the larger part of the human race, and there was therefore need of repentance. After this life there were rewards and punishments. All claims to possess a direct revelation from God or to have inherited a revelation given to persons in the past had to be authenticated either by 'the breath of the divine spirit immediately felt' or by a correct transmission through persons with convincing credentials. However, even this attenuated corpus of doctrine went far beyond what later thinkers would regard as tenable, and it was still much shaped by the Christian doctrinal tradition. A sign that Lord Herbert was still a child of his age can be seen in his confession that his reluctance to publish his *De Veritate* was overcome by hearing a loud but gentle noise from a clear sky.[1] He had not the temperament to gather around him a school of disciples, and he never became the focus of an influential party. Moreover, though the Deist movement which sprang from his teaching did not reach its full development until the next century, yet in 1626 Joseph Hall, later to be a bishop in the Church of England, denounced Deists as 'those monsters whose idol is nature, whose religion is secondary atheism, whose true region is the lowest hell'.[2]

More influential was William Chillingworth (1602–44) who because of scruples about subscribing to the Thirty-nine Articles delayed his ordination for some time. He was praised by Archbishop Tillotson for 'his worthy and successful attempts to make the Christian religion reasonable'[3] in his work, *The Religion of Protestants* (1638), but this did not mean that he had discarded respect for the doctrines of the Church. He laid down the 'express and certain warrant from God's Word' as the criterion of sound doctrine, and he attached great weight to the 'universal tradition' of scripture interpretation. When he declared that 'the Bible, I say, the Bible only, is the religion of Protestants' he was worlds away from any iconoclastic

---

[1] Ninian Smart (ed.), *Historical Selections in the Philosophy of Religion* (1962) Chapter VI.
[2] J. Hall, *Works* (ed. 1863), V, 249.
[3] J. Tillotson, *Sermons* (ed. 1743), XI, 4966.

rationalism. He held there were basic doctrines binding upon all Christians and he was satisfied that these were taught in the Church of England. His liberality has often been deduced from his famous statement:

> 'I will think no man the worse man nor the worse Christian, I will love no man the less, for differing in opinion from me.'

But it was on secondary matters that Chillingworth conceded there could be varying opinions. On fundamental matters God required belief, especially that the Scriptures were his Word, and there was a duty 'to endeavour to find the true sense of it and live according to it'.[1] Chillingworth was able to remain safely within the bounds of the Church of England. The use of reason did not make doctrine unnecessary but strengthened its claim to be accepted on its own persuasive merits.

Much more disturbing issues were raised by the teaching of Descartes and Hobbes.

René Descartes (1596–1650) in his *Discours de la Méthode* (Discourse on Method) (1637) examined the basis of knowledge. He began by a process of stripping away all assertions which he judged it possible to doubt, and came to the conclusion that the one thing it was impossible to doubt was his own existence: 'Cogito ergo sum' (I think, therefore I am). Then he proceeded to reconstruct a corpus of what he believed to be the necessary consequence of that basic certainty. He had ideas which had their origin in objects external to himself, and he held it reasonable to suppose that the ideas had a likeness corresponding to the external objects, though he admitted that ideas had often to be corrected in the light of fuller understanding. The sun at first seemed to be smaller than the earth but in fact it was not so. He also had ideas which were not the result of awareness of external objects. In sum, whatever ideas he had must result from an efficient cause, and the only efficient cause must be a total cause, 'an archetype in which all the reality that is found objectively or by representation in these ideas is contained formally and actually' and this archetype must be God. Indeed the ability to conceive of God implied his existence:

> 'I ought not to find it strange that God, in creating me, put this idea in my nature in much the same way as a craftsman imprints his mark on his work.'[2]

In a century which inherited so firm a tradition of scriptural and ecclesiastical authority such a method of thought based on a preliminary universal doubt was uncongenial and encountered much hostility from theologians.

Even more unwelcome were the speculations of Thomas Hobbes (1588–1679). He laid down in his *Leviathan* (1651) that the causal sequence observable in the world and the need for a system of rewards and punishments were sufficient to prove the existence of God. God created people and planned their salvation, but they could only be saved from their own ambition, assertiveness and cruelty by transferring their own individual

---

[1] W. Chillingworth, *The Religion of Protestants*, VI, lvi.
[2] Ninian Smart, *op. cit.*, Chapter VII.

rights to the custody of a sovereign power with sufficient strength to compel them to moderate their demands and so preserve their own and other peoples' lives. It was therefore the will of God that people should obey the sovereign power and not risk martyrdom for the sake of any private conviction. Scholars are divided on the significance of the place given to God by Hobbes in his writings. Warrender sees it as central to the coherence of Hobbes's system, but Plamenatz regards it as a superfluity which could be excised without serious loss to the argument, and which was only introduced to foster social stability in a turbulent period and even to secure his own safety in an age when there were penalties lying in wait for the avowed atheist.[1] However, even if the importance of the idea of God in the system is conceded, the contemporaries of Hobbes were repelled by his portrayal of God as the irresistible power whose fiat decided what was right and whose plans for preserving mankind involved unquestioning obedience to a sovereign however wicked his person and crooked in his policy. Bishop Bramhall expressed the outlook of many theologians when he said Hobbes's principles were 'not only destructive to all religion but to all societies, extinguishing the relation between prince and subject, master and servant, parent and child, husband and wife.[2]

Bramhall was a firm churchman with a strong interest in maintaining the established system of faith and order and it was not surprising that he was alarmed by novelties, but the teaching of Descartes and Hobbes eventually evoked an equally chilly reception from the 'Cambridge Platonists', who were credited with a notable hospitality and charity of mind towards contemporary trends of thought. Among the leaders of the group were Benjamin Whichcote (1609–83), Ralph Cudworth (1617–88), and Henry More (1614–87). Yet to read their writings is to meet men steeped in Scripture and in the Christian tradition.[3] Henry More, in particular, was soaked in the doctrinal tradition of the Church. 'The Bible', he said, 'is the truest ground of the certainty of faith that can be offered to our understanding to rest in.' The Bible, 'dictated by the Spirit of God, that is written by holy and inspired men, is sufficiently plain to the unprejudiced capacity in all points necessary to salvation'. The divine certainty of faith was 'corroborated by the spirit of life in the new birth and by illuminated reason'.[4] These Platonists, like Chillingworth, believed that the mysteries of faith were seen with additional radiance when examined under the light of reason. They held that both revelation and reason had their foundation in the Eternal God, and while they sought to commend and examine the faith in the light of reason, they were also men of spirituality, highly sensitive to the wonder of revelation. More's Christmas and Easter hymns are fine expressions of the creed of the Church.[5]

This Cambridge school helped to shape the outlook of those who came to be called Latitudinarians, but Bishop Stillingfleet and Archbishops Tillotson

[1] J. Plamenatz (ed.), *Leviathan* by T. Hobbes: H. Warrender, *The Political Philosophy of Hobbes* (1957).

[2] J. Bramhall, *Works*, IV, Discourse III, p. 507.

[3] G. R. Cragg (ed.), *The Cambridge Platonists* (1968).

[4] *ib.* pp. 146–7.

[5] *Songs of Praise*, 80; *Congregational Praise*, 152.

and Tenison were firmly anchored in the traditional teaching of the Church. They did not fall back upon the authority of ecclesiastical definitions of the faith but rather trusted to the inherent persuasiveness of the teaching of the Church upon unprejudiced hearers and readers, and they had no doubt that the doctrine of the Church of England had this self-authenticating power. Yet they never held that that teaching could have been devised without the special revelation in Christ whose claims were certified by his miracles, which were the necessary imprimatur for any new religion.

Tillotson found the doctrine of the Trinity perplexing, but he did not deny it or propose that it should be excised from the faith of the Church.[1] Stillingfleet came to the defence of the doctrine when he believed it was threatened by the teaching of John Locke (1632–1704).[2]

Locke was the harbinger of the empirical outlook which was to loom so large on the theological scene in the next centuries. He repudiated the teaching of Lord Herbert concerning common notions or innate ideas.[3] People, he held, began their life with minds free of any ideas at all, but through sensation and reflection they built up ideas and patterns of thought which ranged from simple irreducible ideas to complex constructions which were also capable of correction and refinement. Reason was the controlling agent in this process and it was able to 'discover the certainty or probability of such propositions or truths which the mind arrives at by deduction made from such ideas as it has got by the use of its natural faculties, viz. by sensation or reflection'. Such mental equipment was the basis of all further development. When a doctrine was taught purporting to convey the content of divine revelation in the past, it had to be in terms capable of being fitted into the existing mental patterns.

> 'No proposition can be· received for divine revelation or obtain the assent due to all such if it be contradictory to our clear intuitive knowledge.'

What God revealed was bound to be true, but it was reason which had to decide if it was revelation. Nothing contrary to the clear and self-evident dictates of reason had a right to be urged or assented to as a matter of faith. Such attempts had led in the past to the propagation of many absurdities. Locke's thought, however, was still sufficiently shaped by belief in God and by the Christian tradition to move him to concede that when God chose to reveal himself directly to any person this could break through the hedge of reason and implant new ideas; there were no bounds which could be set to God's action. Such a possibility of fresh revelation did not loom large in his thought. Nor did respect for doctrinal tradition or for ecclesiastical authority play a decisive role in his thinking. Hence, he was an advocate of toleration. He had moved beyond the thought of the Cambridge Platonists and beyond Stillingfleet and Tillotson, who held it to be sound wisdom to fall back upon tradition and authority whenever issues were cloudy and reason indecisive in its verdicts. The theologians through-

---

[1] J. Tillotson, *Works* (Folio Ed., 1707), 573–4.
[2] E. Stillingfleet, *The Bishop of Worcester's Answer*.
[3] Ninian Smart, *op. cit.*, chapter IX.

out the century were still men who lived within the inherited tradition and had the will to believe and wanted to be in a position to show that the tradition was credible. Some found their anchorage in tradition, others in ecclesiastical authority, and still others in the corroborative weight of reason. Locke had entered a new and uncharted avenue and was in a different pathway when he wrote

'Light, true light, in the mind is or can be nothing else but the evidence of the truth of any proposition, and if it be not a self-evident proposition all the light it has or can have is from the clearness and validity of those proofs upon which it is received.'[1]

[1] Ninian Smart, *op. cit.*, p. 140.

A Note on Theology in the Christian East: the Eighteenth to Twentieth Centuries

Kallistos Ware

A Note on Theology in the Christian East: the Eighteenth to Twentieth Centuries

KALLISTOS WARE

Two main developments occurred in the history of Christian doctrine in the east between 1700 and 1900: the 'Hesychast Renaissance' in Greece during the second half of the eighteenth century; and the rise of Russian theology in the middle of the nineteenth century.

(1) *The 'Hesychast Renaissance'*. In the last decades of the eighteenth century there was a striking renewal of interest in mystical theology. At the centre of this movement were two friends, St. Macarius Notaras, Metropolitan of Corinth (1731–1805), and St. Nicodemus of the Holy Mountain (1748–1809). At a time of profound discouragement in the Greek nation and of startling decadence in the Greek Church, they helped to preserve the tradition of St. Symeon the New Theologian and St. Gregory Palamas as a living reality. Their chief work was the *Philokalia*, a vast anthology of ascetic and mystical texts, published at Venice in 1782, which has proved one of the most influential books in modern Orthodox history. The 'Hesychast Renaissance' was a spiritual rather than a specifically doctrinal movement: its members were more interested in such things as the practice of the Jesus Prayer or frequent communion than, for example, the distinction between the essence and the energies of God. But in the Christian east of the eighteenth century, as in earlier times, it is impossible to distinguish sharply between spirituality and dogma:[1] Macarius and Nicodemus are, therefore, rightly entitled to a place in the history of Christian doctrine.

(2) *Russian theology*. Around 1850 the Russian Orthodox Church first began to produce theologians of originality and distinction. Hitherto Russia had been closely dependent on Greek religious thought. When the Byzantine missionaries began the conversion of Russia in the late tenth century, they brought with them a fully articulated system of Christian doctrine, which the Russians assimilated, but which they felt little need to supplement or reinterpret. Religious controversies in Russia usually involved ritual practice and canon law rather than doctrine.

In due course the Byzantine Hesychast movement of the fourteenth century extended its influence to Russia. St. Nilus of Sora (c. 1433–1508) was well acquainted with the works of St. Gregory of Sinai and St. Gregory Palamas. But Nilus is a faithful disciple rather than an original thinker, and his concern is with the practical teaching of the Hesychasts rather than their doctrinal foundations.

[1] See above, chapter on "Christian Theology in the East", p. 186.

During the late seventeenth and the eighteenth centuries Russian theology, like that in the Greek world, became subject to a heavy western influence. The same two tendencies emerge: on the one side, the 'Latinizers', led by Metropolitan Stephen Yavorsky (1658–1722), who owed his education to the Jesuits; on the other, the 'Protestantizers', led by Archbishop Theophan Prokopovich (1681–1736), a man of undisguised Lutheran sympathies. It is a curious and revealing fact that in Russian seminaries at this time the instruction was given neither in Slavonic nor in Greek, but in Latin.

Not until the period 1850–1900 did Russian theology come fully into its own. Two men in particular changed the whole spirit of Russian religious thought: the lay theologian Alexis Khomiakov (1804–60), and Philaret Drozdov, Metropolitan of Moscow (1782–1867). Khomiakov was opposed equally to the 'Latinizers' and to the 'Protestantizers'. In his view all western Christians, whether Roman or Reformed, share the same basic assumptions, whereas Orthodoxy stands apart from either. Orthodox must therefore stop using Protestant arguments against Rome and Roman arguments against Protestantism, and they must return to the genuine tradition of the Christian east, a tradition which is neither Roman nor Protestant, but distinct from both. Khomiakov devoted especial attention to the doctrine of the Church, its unity and authority. He saw the Church as a unique combination of freedom and unanimity, of diversity and unity: to express this notion, Russian theologians since Khomiakov's time have used the term *sobornost*, 'catholicity' or 'conciliarity'. Metropolitan Philaret, for his part, did much to revive a Patristic spirit in the Russian theological schools; and in his many sermons he made clearly manifest the deeply liturgical character of the Orthodox approach to the faith. In the words of a recent Russian scholar, Fr. Cyprian Kern, 'It was Philaret who laid the first stones of our scientific theology, and one returns constantly to the ideas which he formulated'.

The revolution of 1917 was a severe blow to the development of religious thought within Russia itself, but the traditions of Russian theology have been continued by a brilliant circle of writers in the emigration. Fr. Sergius Bulgakov (1871–1944), rector of the Russian theological institute in Paris, devised a highly original system centring upon the concept of *Sophia* or Divine Wisdom. His theories were fiercely criticized by two other Russians in Paris, Vladimir Lossky (1903–58), and Fr. George Florovsky (born 1893), who is now in the U.S.A. Reacting against the speculative and almost theosophical spirit of Bulgakov's 'Sophiology', Lossky and Florovsky insisted on the essentially Patristic character of all Christian theology; but they insisted also on treating the Fathers as living witnesses, not as dead texts or archaeological relics. Florovsky has summed up his theological programme in the phrase 'neo-Patristic synthesis'. Within the younger generation of contemporary Russian theologians, Fr. Alexander Schmemann (born 1921) has written on liturgical theology, while Fr. John Meyendorff (born 1926) has produced a standard work on St. Gregory Palamas, as well as a concise but comprehensive survey entitled *Byzantine Theology: Historical Trends and Doctrinal Themes* (London, 1975).

What is the chief contribution which Orthodox theology can make in contemporary ecumenical discussions? Many western Christians take the view that reunion with the east is, for the time being, no more than a very distant possibility: Catholics and Protestants, so they argue, should settle their own differences first, and only then can they begin to think seriously about *rapprochement* with the Orthodox. Such an outlook is perhaps short-sighted. For will western Christians ever succeed in overcoming their own disagreements, so long as they leave out of account the testimony of the Christian east? Precisely because Eastern Orthodoxy is seemingly so remote – because its background is different, because it has known no 'Middle Ages' in the western sense, no Reformation and Counter-Reformation – it can act as a catalyst in the western ecumenical debate. Theologians in the west, whether Roman or Reformed, are today seeking to escape from the closed circle of ideas in which the western world has moved since the twelfth century – a circle of ideas which Luther and Calvin, for all their protests against Rome, still shared with Peter Lombard and Thomas Aquinas. It is here that the east, with its continuing tradition of Patristic theology, can be of vital help. The east has never been restricted within the same closed circle as the medieval and post-medieval west. It has never ceased to think according to different and more ancient forms. Orthodox writers such as Lossky and Florovsky have indicated something of a contribution which eastern Christendom can make in this respect. The possibilities are immense, and as yet we have scarcely begun to take advantage of them.

Christian Theology in the Eighteenth to the Twentieth Centuries

John H. S. Kent

Christian Theology in the Eighteenth to the Twentieth Centuries

JOHN H. S. KENT

I

THE EIGHTEENTH CENTURY

The history of theology between 1760 and 1960 can without undue distortion be treated as a whole. It was a period in which the classical theologies of Catholicism and Protestantism (which this book has already described) had to fight for life against wave after wave of criticism from both inside and outside organized Christianity. To some extent this intellectual struggle followed its own inner logic: social and political change could not obliterate what Hume and Kant said, for example, so that even in the mid-twentieth century a hostile discussion of the case for Christian theism (in Anthony Flew's *God and Philosophy*, 1966, for instance) was still dominated by their arguments. Theology was also affected by sociological change, however, by the development of a mass, technological, urban society in which scientific progress seemed to confirm a rejection of the belief in the supernatural which had already taken place for the sophisticated in the eighteenth century.

This combination of social and intellectual change drove Christianity from the centre to somewhere near the margin of western society, a change symbolized in the way in which in the modern university Christian theology has become a minority subject, or a component part of 'the study of religion'. As for those who still retained their belief in the fixed dogmatic orthodoxy of the past, they saw themselves faced with the problem of how to restore the Church's past ascendancy in western society without compromising theological traditions which they had inherited. Another, more critical school of theologians became convinced that the intellectual and social changes were so far-reaching that they necessitated a theological transformation of Christianity. It was the widespread feeling that what was becoming a post-Christian society no longer accepted the claim of the Churches to possess an immutable, clearly defined body of revealed religious knowledge about both God and Man – the kind of theology which was summarized for the Reformed tradition, for instance in the *Compendium of Christian Theology* which Johannes Wollebius (1586–1629) published in 1626 – which gave a peculiar edge to the nineteenth-century controversies between orthodoxy and 'liberalism'. The stage had been set, however, in the previous century when the Church had failed as a whole to anticipate the impending collapse of the traditional social order and remained committed to the customary centres of power. Complacent Roman Catholic support for the crumbling French absolute monarchy, and an equally worldly Anglican involvement in the fortunes of the Hanoverian dynasty symbolized this failure and helped to fix the Enlightenment in an anti-Christian position. In Germany, Protestant religious institutions enjoyed a similar cultural prestige and also identified themselves with the *ancien régime*, a fact which is explicable if one accepts that, as Ernst Troeltsch maintained, the Protestant Reformation was not so much an expression of the beginnings of the 'modern spirit' as a movement strictly within the intellectual limits of medieval culture. Classical Protestantism flourished between 1517 and the end of the seventeenth century, but went into decline after 1700 and must be distinguished from the kind of Protestantism which then developed in association with the rationalist mood of the Enlightenment, as well as from the liberal Protestantism of the nineteenth century. In the eighteenth century the social function of theology – which is to provide a system of explanations and actions (or rituals) which will give meaning to life as a whole for the individual and also help to solidify a specific society – was being steadily eroded because the society itself was ceasing to hold the allegiance of some of the ablest men it produced. One cannot continue to pay social homage to religion in the sceptical style familiarized by Montaigne if one no longer believes in the value of the social system whose stability is to some extent reinforced by common religious practices and explanations. If one wants instead to destroy the social order, the religion which helps to bind it together becomes a part of the target. For a society which does not value itself, religion cannot exist on the strength of its alleged value to society. In the mid-twentieth century, when the situation has become more acute, some Christian theologians have reacted by demanding a theology of 'revolution', or a 'political' theology (as Harvey Cox, the author of *The Secular City* (1965), would call it), but most eighteenth-century theologians defended both the theological and the social past. As a result, they did not dominate the thought of the period: the British Deists, the French *philosophes* and the writers of the German Enlightenment like Reimarus and Lessing felt it necessary to attack both Christian institutions and Christian doctrine, and in doing so threw the theologians even more on to the defensive, so that the best-known English theological work of the period, Bishop Butler's *Analogy of Religion* (1736), was primarily composed as a reply to the Deists.

Various factors helped to change the intellectual climate of theological thought in the seventeenth and eighteenth centuries. Among them were geographical discovery, which meant contact with non-European cultures, the scientific discoveries of Isaac Newton, and the effect on the humanist tradition of the long series of 'wars of religion' and of the divisions of the western Church. Christian historiography has always exaggerated the decisiveness for the history of theology of the Reformation and Counter-Reformation, and has passed swiftly over the period between 1550 and 1700; but it was in these later years that the split in European culture became acute. This culture, which had never been completely unified in the medieval period on either a Classical or a Christian basis, began to fall radically apart during the sixteenth century, a process which the successive waves of Protestant and Roman Catholic religious renewal did little to check. The degree of religious doubt latent in Renaissance humanists like the Italian philosopher, Pomponazzi, is a matter of some dispute: one scholar has said that 'in the light of his passionate and consistent advocacy of a purely secular and this-worldly morality, as well as of his insistence in the *Apologia*, the *Defensorium* and the *De Nutritione*, that immortality is contrary to all the principles of natural reason, it remains a moot question how seriously he took his contention that immortality is nevertheless a "religious truth" ' (cf. *The Renaissance Philosophy of Man*. ed. E. Cassirer, 1959, p. 18). By the end of the sixteenth century, in any case, the sceptical tradition had established itself as an independent element in the cultural pattern, and it is significant that the most important source-book of the English Deists, Lord Edward Herbert's *De Veritate*, was published as early as 1624. Herbert (1583–1648) had little influence in his troubled life-time, but his assertion that God had, quite apart from Christianity, revealed to all men what was necessary for salvation, stood in sharp contrast to the bitter division between Laudian and Puritan which was one of the causes of what was not only a secular but also England's 'religious war'.

In general, the Churches were able to invoke the authority of the State to ban or censor direct attacks on Christianity itself, but the development of a religious alternative to Christianity – for this was what early eighteenth-century Deism set out to be – could only be delayed, not stopped. John Locke's *Reasonableness of Christianity as delivered in the Scriptures* (1695) was an attempt to reconcile the Christian claim to a direct divine revelation in the Bible with the kind of simple ethical theism which Lord Herbert had codified for his successors; it is also important as an example of the reduced sort of Christianity which was to appear again and again in the liberal tradition, a tradition which accepted the strength of the critical, rationalist attitude which had been developing since the Renaissance, but which clung with determination and even sometimes with passion to the value of the Christian religious tradition. In his essay on 'liberalism' in the *Apologia pro Sua Vita* (1865) John Henry Newman called it the 'Anti-Dogmatic Principle', and said that religious liberalism started from the mistake of subjecting to human judgment those revealed doctrines which in their very nature were beyond and independent of it, and of claiming to determine on intrinsic grounds the truth and value of propositions which rested for their reception simply on the external authority of the divine Word. It would certainly be fair to describe the kind of religious rationalism which Newman was attacking as at any rate 'non-dogmatic', for one of the enduring characteristics of the school was its comparative indifference to dogmatic orthodoxy, and especially to the doctrines of original sin (which John Locke, for instance, claimed to be unable to find in the Scriptures), the atonement (in most of its classical interpretations), eternal punishment (which Locke, once again, dispensed with), the sacraments, and the Church, a body which non-dogmatic liberals usually disliked, partly because religious institutions were often intolerant of doctrinal variation, and partly because institutionalized Christianity sometimes seemed more concerned with temporal than spiritual power. Ernst Cassirer (in *The Philosophy of the Enlightenment*, E.T., 1951) regarded as a fundamental principle of the Enlightenment the view that it was dogma and not doubt which was the true enemy of morality and religion; the non-dogmatic liberals carried this attitude over into the nineteenth century, strengthened by the anti-metaphysical influence of Kant.

The liberal tradition had other characteristics, however, to which Newman did not sufficiently refer, expecially that of Christocentricism – understood as an emphasis on the central rôle of the Jesus of the Gospels not only as a religious leader and teacher but also as the living source of an immediate freedom. Jesus was the justification of Liberal tolerance. One should be cautious, moreover, of accepting the assertion, still often made, that nineteenth-century Protestant Liberalism mainly developed as a response to the advances of natural science. The influence of nineteenth-century scientific method was confirmatory rather than primary; it sprang from and confirmed the value of the rationalist tradition, and produced the sort of results which rationalist theologians had anticipated, not in detail, but in general. This has been obscured in Britain by the immense controversy which surrounded the publication of Charles Darwin's *Origin of Species* in 1859. It was certainly true, as Paul Tillich said (in *Perspectives on 19th and 20th century Protestant Theology*. 1967) that after 1859 'Christian theology was like an army retreating in the face of another advancing army. With every new breakthrough of the advancing army Christian theology would attempt to protect the Christian tradition' [which here meant, of course, what we have called dogmatic orthodoxy] 'which still remained untouched. Then a new breakthrough would make the previous defence untenable, and so another retreat and setting up of a new defence would be necessary' (p. 158).

But it was dogmatic orthodoxy which retreated in the second half of the nineteenth century. Armed with its own, earlier rationalism, and with its immediate, undogmatic reliance upon the spirit of the living Jesus, Protestant Liberalism had not so much to retreat as to hold on to positions which theologians like Schleiermacher had established in the earlier part of the century. Even Albrecht Ritschl (1822–89), whose liberalism was certainly less than his Lutheranism, understood what was at stake, and wrote that 'in every religion what is sought, with the help of the super-human spiritual power reverenced by man, is a solution of the contradiction in which man finds himself as both a part of the world of nature and a spiritual personality claiming to dominate nature. For in the former rôle he is a part of nature, dependent upon her, subject to and confined by other things; but as spirit he is moved by the impulse to maintain his independence against them. In this juncture, religion springs up as a faith in super-human spiritual powers, by whose help the power which man possesses of himself is in some way supplemented and elevated into a unity of its own kind which is a match for the pressure of the natural world' (*Justification and Reconciliation*, iii, 1888, p. 199). Whatever else Ritschl meant by this – and he certainly did not exaggerate the extent to which the Christian could know that he was being supplemented and elevated by supernatural spiritual powers – he did not mean that a post-Kantian Christianity had to beat a retreat in the face of the advances of natural science.

From this point of view John Locke's *Reasonableness of Christianity* pointed towards the future. Locke tried to go behind the Biblical and dogmatic controversies which had divided seventeenth-century Christendom, and to read the Bible without the prejudices of either the Roman Catholic or classical Protestant theological systems, to take, as he claimed, 'the plain, direct meaning of words and phrases' (p.2). Read in this common-sense fashion the Scriptures seemed to add to, rather than contradict, Lord Herbert's 'natural religion' as to what was essential to salvation: men had to repent and acknowledge that Jesus was the Messiah; God would regard this faith as making up for the believer's failure to achieve moral perfection. Christ's significance in the history of religion was that his divine authority (which Locke in this essay established on the orthodox basis of his fulfilment of Old Testament prophecies and by his working of the miracles recorded in the New Testament) freed men from the polytheism and idolatry and perverted religious ritual of the past; Jesus assured men that the moral order was guaranteed by God and promised them that they might expect divine assistance in their attempts to behave well. It was Christ, so to speak, who first showed men what the true form of religion was, and it was his supernatural authority to do this which men were really acknowledging when they declared their faith in him as the Messiah. Like many later rationalist theologians, however, Locke was not prepared to commit himself to the proposition that faith in Jesus as the Messiah was necessary to salvation. In any case Locke rejected the classical context of the traditional doctrine of salvation in as much as he abandoned the ideas of original sin and eternal punishment.

Giving a guarded assent to the possibility that the Christian revelation offered a kind of divine supplement to or a confirmation of the religious insights obtained by human reason, Locke produced a reduced but recognizable Christianity. The principal Deist writers, however, wanted to replace Christianity, not to reform it; and the attack which John Toland (1670–1722) may be said to have started when at the age of twenty-six he published *Christianity not Mysterious* (1696) continued to spread throughout Europe for the remainder of the eighteenth century. It is inaccurate to speak of Deism as in decline by about 1730, or to suggest that Bishop Butler (by an appeal to reason) and John Wesley (by an appeal to religious experience) somehow obliterated the very memory of the Deist position. Toland exalted reason above revelation, which Locke had not done, and dismissed from Christianity all suggestions of mystery and miracle, as well as dogmas like that of the Trinity, which he said were unintelligible. Samuel Clarke (in *A Discourse concerning the Unchangeable Obligations of Natural Religion*, 1711) renewed the appeal to the knowledge of right religion which was held to be the possession of every man born into the world. Anthony Collins (1676–1729) criticized the traditional argument that Jesus proved his claim to be the Messiah by the fulfilment of Old Testament prophecies (see, for instance, his *Discourse of the Grounds and Reasons of the Christian Religion*, 1724). Matthew Tindal (in *Christianity as Old as the Creation*, 1730) objected to the Christian picture of God on moral grounds; Christianity had only perverted a natural religion which was old as the creation of man. A later powerful contribution to the Deist position was Conyers Middleton's *Free Inquiry into the Miraculous Powers which are supposed to have subsisted in the Christian Church* (1749).

The traditional picture of Deism has not been adequately revised since Leslie Stephen wrote his *History of English Thought in the Eighteenth Century* (1876). The Deist attack was not important as part of Christian theology itself, but as a vital part of the context within which Christian theology had to operate after 1700. Orthodox historians ignore the revolutionary nature of the Deist movement and emphasize instead the violence of its controversial methods – without seeing that these reflect the Deist sense of being a handful of Lilliputians in arms against a race of Gullivers. Orthodox church historians still stress the weaknesses of Deism, 'its lack of historical insight, its blindness to the power of evil, its tone of supercilious superiority, its consistent silence about Jesus Christ' (*Reason and Authority in the Eighteenth Century*, G. R. Cragg, 1964, p. 69). They miss the origin of the mood that inspired the Deists, their horror at what they felt to be the inadequacy of classical Protestantism with its emphasis on the supernatural, its morally questionable doctrines of the atonement, its lack of interest in the fate of those born outside the historical Christian community, its insistence on relating morality, of which the Deists approved, to beliefs which they regarded as a mass of superstition. The orthodox were shocked at the satirical vigour with which writers like Collins treated the Bible; they did not understand how the Bible itself shocked the Deists. They did not share the Deist feeling that classical Christian theology contradicted what Isaac Newton and other scientists were revealing about the true nature of God, who must have ensured that all men had an equal opportunity of knowing how he wanted them to live. It was a kind of rationalist and moral contempt which made Collins so biting in his attacks. The Tindal of 1730 apart, the Deists were young men in revolt: their stylistic ancestor was the Erasmus of such colloquies as *The Shipwreck*. (Erasmus' *Colloquies* were translated by Roger L'Estrange at the end of the seventeenth century, and again by N. Bailey in 1725). Once one sees that the Deists belong to the history of European religion rather than to the history of Christianity, one sees that it was no particular criticism of their religious sincerity to say that they were anti-Christian.

More relevant perhaps was the fact that the Deist campaign to discredit the alleged divine authority of the Christian Scriptures was not entirely unsuccessful. 'After the Deists it was far more difficult to treat Holy Writ as a simple, clear and unequivocal doctrinal authority. Its ambiguities and discrepancies had been probed into, some of its ethical crudities (especially in the Old Testment) had been exposed, and the twin pillars of the Evidences – prophecies and miracles – were already seen by a percipient few to be as much stumbling blocks as stepping stones to faith . . . Thus John Conybeare's *Scripture Difficulties Considered* (1732) allowed that the Bible contained many puzzling "darknesses", many apparent contradictions still unresolved by human scholarship. Francis Webber's *Jewish Dispensations Considered* (1737) ended on a note of near defeatism, remarking that "the difficulties which attend the Scriptures of the Old Testament are not insuperable". How many churchmen felt in moments of secret doubt what Conyers Middleton openly admitted, that it was no longer possible to maintain "that every single passage of Scripture . . . must needs be received as the very word and as the voice of God himself".' (J. Walsh, *Essays in Modern Church History* ed. Bennett and Walsh, 1966, p. 150; the quotation is from Middleton, *A Letter to Dr. Waterland*, 1731, pp. 44f.)

Locke and the Deists shared the conviction that religious knowledge consisted of (a) a number of propositions about God (which Locke, of course, was more willing to derive from the Scriptures than were the Deists) and (b) what may be called moral experience. The Deists accepted the summary of 'natural religion' arrived at by Lord Herbert, that God existed and ought to be worshipped; that the sincerest form of worship was virtuous behaviour – a view which Immanuel Kant reaffirmed powerfully at the close of the eighteenth century; that men ought to repent of their wrong-doing; and that God would allot rewards and punishments to men in a future life. The only religious 'experience' in their sense was moral experience, and Bishop Butler, for that matter, was taking a similar line when he criticized the religious revivalists. George Whitefield and John Wesley, for what he called 'pretending to extraordinary sayings and communications of the Holy Ghost': Butler was afraid that this new outburst of popular religion, which emphasized special providences and 'leadings' and 'promptings' of the Spirit, would lay the Church more open to the Deist contention that Christianity was full of irrational superstition.

This did not mean that the dogmatic orthodoxy which Butler was defending did not allow for the possibility of man's being capable not only of moral experience but also of a direct, sensible experience of God; but this capacity was carefully defined as God's freedom to invade the human personality and not as man's freedom to reach out and attain knowledge of the divine personality. The credibility, nature and value of alleged 'religious experiences' was often debated in the eighteenth century, one of the most interesting discussions being in the works of the American Calvinist theologian and philosopher of religion, Jonathan Edwards (1703–58), not least in his *Inquiry into the Modern Prevailing Notions concerning that Freedom of the Will which is supposed to be Necessary to Moral Agency* (1754). For Edwards, man was not free but preserved from self-destruction through sin only by the merciful will of God, who might at any time righteously withdraw his mercy allowing the sinner to fall, not into annihilation, but into fire. Edwards was a remarkable case, because whereas in an early book, *A Faithful Narrative of the Surprising Works of God* (1737), in which he gave an account of the religious revival which had followed his own evocative preaching in Northampton, Massachusetts, he tried to describe and analyse conversion as a variety of religious experience, he came in later years, as may be gathered from his treatise *On the Religious Affections* (1746), to doubt the validity of almost every kind of religious experience found in a typical religious revival, on the ground that it was almost impossible to distinguish significant from assumed symptoms. He seems to have been gradually driven to the conclusion that genuine and significant conversion was rare, an event to be associated with a particular kind of individual who was able to be radically changed by God. The mid-eighteenth-century religious revivals which characterized the Methodist movement involved John Wesley in similar discussions, but Wesley showed less analytical power than Edwards, and a greater willingness to accept his followers' religious experience without question.

This controversy about the possibility of human religious experience in a Christian sense (together with the controversy about the authority of the Bible), remained the fundamental question for the future of Christianity throughout our period. Schleiermacher, Soeren Kierkegaard, J. H. Newman, F. D. Maurice, von Hügel, and even paradoxically, Dietrich Bonhoeffer, all sought to protect Christianity against what they took to be the damaging assaults of the Enlightenment by establishing the rights, the validity of the kind of statement which John Baillie, for example, was still making in *Our Knowledge of God* in 1939: 'It is not as the result of an inference of any kind . . . that the knowledge of God's reality comes to us. It comes through our direct personal encounter with him in the Person of Jesus Christ his Son our Lord' (p. 143). This is the normal, orthodox assertion. For a modern version of the eighteenth-century criticisms of it one may compare *God and the Philosophers* (1966) by Anthony Flew. He was perhaps too easily satisfied with the argument that it is impossible to make direct and self-authenticating inferences from the character of subjective experience to conclusions about the supposedly corresponding objective facts. Theologians, on the other hand, have frequently been satisfied with very loose statements about our 'encounter with God'. Another acute criticism of the notion of a self-authenticating 'encounter' with God may be found in Ronald Hepburn's *Christianity and Paradox* (1958).

John Locke's formulation of the difficulties of such theological statements characterized one side of eighteenth-century opinion. It is to be found in chapter nineteen of the fourth book of *The Essay on the Human Understanding*, where Locke, having distinguished between faith and reason as grounds of assent, went on to speak of enthusiasm, or direct religious experience of God 'which, laying by reason, would set up revelation without it. Whereby in effect it takes away both reason and revelation and substitutes in the room of it the ungrounded fancies of a man's own brain, and subsumes them for a foundation of both opinion and conduct . . . Immediate revelation being a much easier way for men to establish their opinions and regulate their conduct than the tedious and not always successful labour of strict reasoning, it is no wonder that some have been very apt to pretend to revelation and to persuade themselves that they are under the peculiar guidance of Heaven in their actions and opinions . . . God, I own, cannot be denied to be able to enlighten the understanding by a ray darted into the mind immediately from the fountain of light; this they understand he has promised to do, and who then has so good a title to expect it as those who are his peculiar people, chosen by him and depending on him?' Such men, Locke said, 'see the light infused into their understanding and cannot be mistaken . . . they feel the hand of God moving them within, and the impulses of the Spirit, and cannot be mistaken in what they feel. But here, let me ask: this seeing, is it the perception of the truth of the proposition, or of this, that it is a revelation from God? . . . The question then here is, how do I know that God is the revealer of this to me; that this impression is made on my mind by the Holy Spirit? If I do not know this, how great soever the assurance is that I am possessed with, it is groundless, it is but enthusiasm . . . But how shall it be known that any proposition in our minds is a truth infused by God . . .? Here it is that enthusiasm fails of the evidence it pretends to. . . . The strength of our persuasions is no evidence at all of their rectitude. . . . If this internal light, or any proposition that under that title we take for inspired, be conformable to the principles of reason, or to the Word of God, which is attested revelation, reason warrants it and we may safely receive it for true, and be guided by it in our belief and actions: if it receive no testimony from either of these rules, we cannot take it for revelation, or for so much as true, till we have other mark that it is a revelation besides our believing it so. Thus we see the holy men of old, who had revelations from God, had something else besides that internal light of assurance in their own minds.' Moses, for instance, had the burning bush. 'It is not the strength of our private persuasion within ourselves that can warrant it to be a light or motion from God; nothing can do that but the written word of God without us, or that standard of reason which is common to us with all men.'

In the long run this line of argument culminated in the conclusion which Professor Flew, for example, formulated when he said that since the epistemological question (i.e. how do I know that God is addressing me directly?) is inescapable, 'and if, as everyone agrees, it cannot be met by reference to immediate observation or other common-place tests – then the whole argument from religious experience must collapse into an argument from whatever other credentials may be offered to authenticate the revelation supposedly mediated by such experience' (p. 139). Here the emotive word 'collapse' seems too strong: it is not impossible, for instance, to invoke the history of Christian sanctity (as von Hügel did) to support an assertion of the reality of God's existence.

For the other side of the argument in the eighteenth century one must turn to Bishop Butler (1692–1752), the ablest defender of orthodoxy and the author of *The Analogy of Religion, Natural and Revealed, to the Constitution and Course of Nature* (1736). In general, Butler opposed the Deists by emphasizing the limits of human reason: thus, just as men could not understand more than a small part of the working of nature, so they must admit that Christianity was a scheme quite beyond their comprehension as a whole, and one which they were not competent to criticize on the ground that it was not the kind of revelation, in form or content, that they would either have expected or preferred. On this ground, Butler advanced his general defence of the authority of the Bible:

'And thus we see, that the only question concerning the truth of Christianity is, whether it be a real revelation: not whether it be attended with every circumstance which we should have looked for; and concerning the authority of the Scripture, whether it be what it claims to be: not whether it be a book of such a sort and so promulgated as weak men are apt to fancy a book containing a divine revelation should. And therefore neither obscurity nor seeming inaccuracy of style, nor various readings nor early disputes about the authors of particular parts; nor any other things of the like kind, though they had been much more considerable in degree than they are, could overthrow the authority of the Scripture: unless the Prophets, Apostles, or our Lord, had promised that the book containing the Divine revelation should be secure from those things. Nor indeed can any objections overthrow such a kind of revelation as the Christian claims to be, since there are no objections to the morality of it, but such as can shew, that there is no proof of miracles wrought originally in attestation of it; no appearance of anything miraculous in its obtaining in the world; nor any of prophecy, that is, of events foretold, which human sagacity could not foresee. If it can be shewn, that the proof alleged for all these is absolutely none at all, then is revelation overturned. But were it allowed, that the proof of any one or all of them is lower than is allowed; yet, whilst any proof of them remains, revelation will stand upon much the same foot as it does at present as to all the purposes of life and practice.' (*Analogy*, Pt. 11, ch. 3, p. 185, ed. 1874.)

Here the question of 'moral' objections to Christianity referred to the question as to whether the Scripture contained things 'plainly contradictory to wisdom, justice or goodness; to what the light of nature teaches us of God' (*ib.* p. 193). In the *Analogy* (pt. 11, ch. 5) Butler considered and dismissed moral objections to the interpretation of Christ's death as offering a vicarious satisfaction for sin, objections which, as far as Protestantism was concerned, might be traced behind the Deist writers to late sixteenth-century Socinianism. He took as an example the view that the doctrine of Christ's being appointed to suffer for the sins of the world represented God as being indifferent whether he punished the innocent or the guilty. 'The world,' Butler replied, 'is a constitution or system whose parts have a mutual reference to each other: and there is a scheme of things gradually carrying on, called the course of nature, to the carrying on of which God has appointed us in various ways to contribute. And when, in the daily course of natural providence, it is appointed that innocent people should suffer for the faults of the guilty, this is liable to the very same objection we are now considering' (p. 223). In other words, this objection to the idea of vicarious satisfaction applied as much to the whole scheme of Theism and the whole notion of Religion as against Christianity, and could not therefore be safely used by the Deist writers as a criticism of the Christian system. Butler described Christ's death as both a 'satisfaction' and as 'a propitiatory sacrifice', but he left the terms undefined, adding that in any case 'we seem to be very much in the dark concerning the manner in which the ancients understood atonement to be made, i.e. pardon to be obtained by sacrifices' (*ib.* p. 221). He rejected the Deist view that human repentance sufficed by itself to save men from future punishment (*ib.* p. 212). That the world was in a state of ruin Butler held to be 'a supposition which seems the very ground of the Christian dispensation, and which, if not proveable by reason, yet is in no wise contrary to it (*ib.* p. 213). God, however, had mercifully provided that there should be an interposition to prevent the destruction of mankind, which men were themselves powerless to prevent, with or without repentance. God did this through the gift of his son, 'who interposed in such a manner as was necessary and effectual to prevent that execution of justice upon sinners which God had appointed should otherwise have been executed upon them' (*ib.* p. 214). At this point Butler was less obviously throwing light on the orthodox doctrine of the work of Christ than putting down a smoke-screen to obscure the cruder features of the position. His account differed sharply from the ideas of Locke and the Deists and was hardly likely to have impressed those in the rationalist tradition.

As for the miraculous, Butler argued that 'the extraordinary phenomena of nature' – he instanced electricity and magnetism – suggested that there could be no presumption against miracles which rendered them in any way incredible. Moreover, though a man might say that the historical evidence for miracles wrought in attestation of Christianity was not sufficient to convince him that they had happened, he could not deny that historical evidence existed. In the case of the argument from prophecy, Butler asserted that although his opponents might claim that the conformity between the prophecies and events was accidental, there were many instances in which the conformity itself could not be denied. It followed that both prophecy and miracle could still be invoked as evidence of the divine authority of the Christian revelation.

The argument from prophecy fell rapidly into the background as Biblical criticism developed in the nineteenth century. Nevertheless, Butler's position was still echoed as recently as 1938 in the official Report on *Doctrine in the Church of England,* a document which offered a fair summary of orthodoxy after the First World War, and which was produced by a committee whose chairman was William Temple. 'In the past,' it was said, 'as a part and consequence of the then current view of Scripture [as inerrant], emphasis was often laid on detailed prediction of facts, especially as concerns the life of Christ. We cannot now regard as a principal purpose or evidence of Inspiration the giving of detailed information about the future; but we recognise, as a consequence and evidence of Inspiration, such an insight into the Divine Mind and Will, and therefore such a general apprehension of the course of events to be expected in a world ruled by God, as in particular cases resulted in the prediction of events which subsequently came to pass. Nor do we rule out, as possibly a concomitant of Inspiration in certain cases, a direct prevision of detailed events, though it is not on such prevision that men should base their belief in the Inspiration of Scripture' (*op. cit.,* 2nd ed. 1950, p. 29). The Report implied a shift from the position that the fulfilment of prophecy made (inter alia) faith possible, to the position that faith might make possible belief in the fulfilment of prophecy. It could hardly be said, however, that on this subject the Report showed much awareness of the intellectual history of Christianity in the previous two hundred years.

The strength of Butler's position lay in his appeal to probability, to the steady building up of the possibility that Christianity might be true. In the nineteenth century he is the obvious master of John Henry Newman in a book like *The Grammar of Assent* (1870), which directly relates the idea of faith to the prior establishment of a high degree of probability, and of Mansel in *The Limits of Religious Knowledge Examined* (1858). The weakness of Butler's position, on the other hand, was that he still relied on being able to persuade his readers that there was at least a logical possibility that the Old Testament prophecies were fulfilled by Christ and that the miraculous events described in the New Testament actually took place. His method suffered from the drawback that 'the mere logical possibility of an event in no sense constitutes a *prima facie* case in its favour; it merely puts the statement in a form in which we can ask whether there is anything in its favour' (cf. the American theologian, Van A. Harvey, in *The Historian and the Believer*, 1967, p. 86: this is an objection often ignored by twentieth-century apologists whose attitude to the miracle narratives of the New Testament recalls that of the eighteenth-century bishop).

Butler's consideration of miracles had in any event lost its force by the middle of the eighteenth century. In 1748 the Scottish philosopher, David Hume, argued that 'a miracle can never be proved so as to be the foundation of a system of religion' (*An Enquiry concerning Human Understanding*, 1748, ed. Selby-Bigge, 1902, p. 127). Hume defined a miracle as 'a violation of the laws of nature' (p. 114), and made clear what he was referring to by the example that he chose: 'It is a miracle that a dead man should come to life; because that has never been observed in any age or country' (p. 115). Firm and unaltered experience had established such laws, and therefore the weight of the argument against a miracle – the Biblical reference needs no elaboration – was as absolute as argument from the uniformity of experience can possibly be. Hume said in effect that the narratives of miracles to be found in the Bible could not be defended in general terms – the only way in which Butler tried to defend them – but that each story must be defended in particular. In dealing with the evidence adduced for it the historian should not put aside his normal view of the natural order or his belief in the uniformity of experience. If these criteria were rigorously applied the evidence for a particular allegedly miraculous event would always be found to fall short of proof, so that one was left at most with the possibility that the event had taken place, but never with the certainty that it had actually happened, and this meant that the miracle story did not offer a foundation for a religious system. G. E. Lessing (1729–81) went further and said that even if it were possible to prove the truth of the stories of Christ's resurrection, the contingent event in itself offered no proper basis for eternal truth.

Butler's *Analogy* offers one example of eighteenth-century theological attempts to come to terms with the rationalist mood of the intellectual life of the period. At first sight John Wesley's Methodist movement looks like nothing more than a successful reassertion at the level of Christian behaviour of the orthodox theological Protestant system (Wesley's understanding of the doctrine of justification by faith, even his doubts about how to formulate it, existed within the traditional limits of the reformed schools): the response to his preachings belongs to the history of the Church rather than to the history of theology. Or if one broadens the concept of theological history so far as to include his preaching, it would be in order to note that there was still, in the England of the eighteenth century, a section of the population which, under the very guns of the Enlightenment, so to speak, clung to the theological forms of the previous century and thought of the Christian life in the terms of John Bunyan's *Grace Abounding*. The uniqueness of the Wesleyan response has been exaggerated, however: Lutheran Pietism, for instance, which, like Methodism, survived the eighteenth century, was a source, not a consequence, of the Methodist movement; French Protestantism also showed signs of a revivalist process in the first half of the eighteenth century; while the American revivalism which flourished between 1730 and 1760 (however divisive and destructive its final effects) had its own roots in the Colonial situation. No account of these national events which ignore what was happening elsewhere can be adequate, whether sociologically or theologically.

John Wesley's importance for the history of Christian doctrine lies elsewhere, in his doctrine of Christian Perfection, or Christian Holiness. The significance of his thought in this area becomes clear only if one places it within its European context. 'The period between 1648 and 1789', wrote E. Préclin (*Histoire de l'Eglise*, vol. xix, 1956, p. 519), 'broadly corresponds to the reigns of Louis XIV, Louis XV and Louis XVI. In that period developed the Cartesianism which in its turn provoked what has been called "the crisis of the European consciousness" and the anti-religious philosophical movement of the eighteenth century. At the same time, it is the period in which the political system of enlightened despotism installed itself and the bourgeois spirit formed. Secular attitudes became continually deeper and more powerful. It is not surprising that in this period conditions hardly favoured the foundation of new religious orders or new forms of the religious life.' In general, the dominant groups in eighteenth-century Europe rejected the traditional Christian model of the perfect life, the model of the man who had renounced marriage, money and freedom (including intellectual freedom), and for whom the highest form of sanctity remained in theory the absolute solitude of the hermit, an ideal which could be traced back to the Desert Fathers. This classical attitude had accepted the existence, on a lower spiritual plane, of the social Christian from whom less was demanded, who might marry, make money and act politically without incurring the wrath of God; but in the eighteenth century man in society began to deny the superiority of the ascetic, and even to deny his right to be an ascetic at all. Little serious contrast existed between the old ascetic model and the new secular one because little was tolerated: by the early eighteenth century the religious were widely despised and it is significant that in France, for example, the conventual life by no means cut off a woman altogether from participation in the society from which she had technically withdrawn. Professor J. McManners, in *French Ecclesiastical Society under the Ancien Régime* (1960), has powerfully illustrated the way in which the theology of poverty and withdrawal had ceased to function through the existing monastic institutions, which seemed both wealthy and interfering in a society no longer prepared to tolerate the contradiction between ideal and achievement for the sake of other, allegedly more spiritual benefits. One of the most convinced acts of the early French Revolution was the liberation – as its authors saw it – of monks and nuns from their vows; the secularization of conventual property in France was justified on the specific ground that the monasteries had no social contribution to make.

The Christian theology of holiness had always been torn between the needs and facts of a society at once hierarchical and wealth-producing on the one hand, and on the other the attractions of a theory of perfection which exalted the denial of one's self and the repudiation of anything which distracted one from the contemplation of God. Of course, sixteenth-century Protestantism had already abolished monasticism and the celibate priesthood, had glorified the ideal of marriage and had also found ways of permitting divorce which implied that an earthly marriage could cease to be. But this was a kind of half-way to humanism, for the distrust of human nature which dominated the Reformed view of man made it necessary to believe that even if the life of the present world were not inferior to monasticism (or the priesthood) in the eyes of God, this was only because all forms of human behaviour were equally displeasing to God because of the corrupting effect of original sin. The Reformed tradition accepted the natural man but did not glorify him. The Protestant world remained psychologically subject to the older model of perfection for generations, as John Wesley's attitude showed, and as appeared in the very limited revival of monasticism in the Church of England in the 1840s. Although theologically able to repudiate the institutionalized forms of the ascetic theological tradition, neither Luther nor Calvin could take a positive view of human existence. For them the model of the Christian life was the faithful steward of God's gifts and calling, one who no longer found it spiritually necessary to withdraw from everyday society because no greater conformity to the will of God could in the last resort be achieved outside than inside the normal human framework. This attitude flourished in a comparatively static society in which rapid and positive change was not expected.

John Wesley's originality for the historian of western religion and of Christian theology lies in his effort to devise a new model of the Christian life in an eighteenth-century culture which was rapidly divesting itself of the classical Christian assumptions about what constitutes human perfection – the model of the anti-economic men, as it might be called. The ideal Wesleyan was to achieve a perfection as complete as that possible for the Desert Father, but he was also to live and work in the ordinary world without allowing his relation to God to be corrupted by his immersion in civil society: he would attain the goal of Christian Holiness within the pale of the Wesleyan Methodist society but without withdrawing from the world. Wesley was trying to recover the ancient goal of the ascetic while accepting, instead of resisting, the extent to which western society had already expanded economically; he wanted to place limits on the enjoyment of the social possibilities offered by society, but he did not want to limit the possibility of holiness. Theologically, he was not only reviving the idea of spiritual perfection in Protestant circles, but also seeking to preserve the power of religion as a limiting force on the acquisitiveness of man.

Wesley's doctrine of Christian Perfection may be examined in terms of two documents, a sermon called 'Christian Perfection', published in 1741, and an essay called 'Thoughts on Christian Perfection', issued in 1760. Both may conveniently be found in *John Wesley*, an anthology edited by A. C. Outler (1964), though the editor's insistence on the importance of Byzantine sources (especially Gregory of Nyssa strained through the writings of Macarius the Egyptian) for the proper understanding of Wesley's teaching on Perfection should be treated with great caution. Both essays have to be read against the background of the traditional view, common to both the Calvinist and the High Anglican systems, that perfection was a gift sometimes bestowed on the righteous on their death-beds, but usually only bestowed after death had taken place. Wesley's defiance of this tradition gave offence both to Anglicanism and to Dissent. In the 1741 sermon he quoted those who said that perfection would not be given in this world, but only at death, and he answered: 'How are we to reconcile this with the express words of St. John, "Herein is our love made perfect, that we may have boldness in the day of judgement; because, as He is, so are we *in this world*". The apostle here, beyond all contradiction, speaks of himself and other living Christians, of whom (as though he had foreseen this very evasion and set himself to overturn it from the foundation) he flatly affirms that not only at or after death, but *in this world*, they are as their master' (Outler, p. 270). In the same early sermon he was already trying to meet the objections of those to whom it seemed absurd to speak of any one as 'perfect': he did not mean, he said, that the 'perfect' Christian became exempt from ignorance or error, infirmities or temptations: he meant that the 'perfect' did not commit deliberate, conscious infractions of the known laws of God. They might suffer from evil thoughts and evil tempers, but these were internal difficulties to be distinguished from sinful actions. In general, however, Wesley did not argue from personal experience (this counts for much more in the 1760 document) but appealed to Biblical quotations to support his claim that '*a Christian is so far perfect as not to commit sin*' (Outler, p. 267).

These points were elaborated in 'Thoughts on Christian Perfection', dated October, 1759, but published in 1760. The early 1760s saw the climax of perfectionist teaching in British Methodism; a second, theologically trivial, wave of Methodist perfectionism followed in the United States in the mid-nineteenth century. Here again Wesley distinguished between sins properly so called, voluntary transgressions of a known law, and sins improperly so called, involuntary transgressions of the divine law, known or unknown. Someone filled with the love of God might still fall into these involuntary transgressions (which 'you may call sins if you please'), but was nevertheless delivered through faith from what Wesley seriously regarded as sin.

A change so fundamental was to be attained 'in a zealous keeping of all the commandments; in watchfulness and painfulness; in denying ourselves and taking up our cross daily; as well as in earnest prayer and fasting and a close attendance on all the ordinances of God . . . it is true we receive it by simple faith; but God does not, will not, give that faith unless we seek it with all diligence in the way which he hath ordained' (Outler, p. 294). Because of the difficulties which he was experiencing in London with antinomian perfectionists who believed that their faith lifted them above all normal moral regulations, Wesley was anxious to emphasize in this pamphlet that Christian perfection included moral achievement. This pamphlet, however, has also to be read alongside the equally characteristic sermon on 'The Scriptural Way of Salvation', published in 1765, in which he said: 'Do *you* believe we are sanctified by faith? Be true, then, to your principle and look for this blessing just as you are, neither better nor worse; as a poor sinner that has still nothing to pay, nothing to plead but "Christ died". And if you look for it as you are, then expect if *now*' (Outler, p. 282). This emphasis on the possibility of a sudden and complete transformation of the personality explains the later use of the phrase 'instantaneous perfection'.

Wesley compared this transformation, this entire renewal in the image of God, with physical death, which might sometimes approach gradually but nevertheless took place at a particular moment. He described, as an event which he believed had happened to men he knew, a state in which they could say, 'I feel no sin, but all love. I pray, rejoice, give thanks without ceasing. And I have as clear an inward witness that I am fully renewed as that I am justified' (Outler, p. 290). No doubt it was possible to relapse from this condition, but the important thing for Wesley was that Christian Perfection should be attainable at all. In the 1740s he had not built the doctrine on the foundation of personal experience, but by 1760 he was prepared to say: 'For many years I have preached, "there is a love of God which casts out all sin". Convince me that this word has fallen to the ground, that in twenty years none has attained this love, that there is no living witness of it at this day, and I will preach it no more' (Outler, p. 298). His alleged authority, that is, was the New Testament illuminated by personal experience; he emphasized the fulfilment in human religious experience of the spiritual promises which he claimed to find in the New Testament. And this was probably why Wesley told the members of the Methodist societies that if they believed that they had died to sin they ought, on balance, to say so publicly – advice which ran alarmingly counter to the apparent common sense of the spiritual life and did not seem justified by its divisive results in Methodist history. Nevertheless, this advice – that the 'perfect' should testify to their perfection – played a prominent rôle in nineteenth-century American and British evangelical history; in a more extreme form it was taught that those who did not testify would lose the gift of perfection. Wesley came close to this himself in 'Thoughts on Christian Perfection' (cf. Outler, p. 289).

In the history of the Christian Church Wesley's perfectionism was a brief episode. He combined the ideas of moral and ritual goodness – fulfilling the divine ethical commandments and also sharing in the sacramental life of the ecclesia – with something quite different, an experience of personal deliverance from sin as such ('I feel no sin at all but love . . . have an inward witness that I am fully renewed'). Moral and liturgical obedience could be tested, but the state of grace which John Wesley described (without ever claiming it for himself), a state which was supposed to be obtained as a gift from God, given on account of faith and not works, could not be delineated with any exactness, or effectively tested from the outside, so that the pursuit of perfection was steadily discredited by some of those who actually said that they had achieved it. Wesley, on the other hand, was convinced that he had no right to disbelieve those who said that they had been fully renewed, and constantly urged his followers to seek and expect this same experience.

Wesley's theological confusion is evident; his distinction between voluntary and involuntary transgression was too crude to bear the weight he attached to it; the stress on 'the conscious and deliberate intention of the agent is the most formidable defect in Wesley's doctrine of the ideal', wrote Newton Flew in *The Idea of Perfection in Christian Theology* (1934). One cannot safely define perfection as the absence of conscious sin. A more important weakness, however, was Wesley's willingness to describe not only the goal of perfection, but the way in which it was attainable. A man became perfected in a specific event, a conscious experience of God's gift of holiness. Wesley did not mean to depreciate moral and ecclesiastical obedience – indeed, he insisted on the value of the second far more than did a theologian like Soeren Kierkegaard, who shared his passion for absolute obedience to God but who felt that ecclesiastical obedience (a reliance upon the Church's understanding of what obedience to God should involve for a layman) positively hindered absolute conformity to the divine. Wesley's tendency to describe 'perfection' as a personal 'knowledge' that one had been freed from all sin by a direct act of God, however, led others to see the pursuit of holiness as distinct from the moral and ecclesiastical context, so that some nineteenth-century professional revivalists, for example, would 'offer' 'sanctification' in the same way as they offered 'justification by faith'.

The root of the theological problem seems to lie in Wesley's lifelong admiration for Christian mystical writers, especially Roman Catholic authors of the late seventeenth century. He accepted their utter devotion to God and their claims to a special sense of God's presence in their lives, but he rejected the Catholic theological framework in terms of which they explained their spiritual life. Instead, he tried to reach the same goal of 'pure love' by means of the Protestant idea of salvation by faith. He wanted to democratize the mystical experience, to replace the Catholic idea of process, of grace extending and perfecting nature in a handful of great saints, with a picture of God's grace as dramatic action, transforming the static misery of any sinner at any moment if only he begged the gift of holiness in utterly trusting humility. Wesley said that the gift of entire holiness was open to every faithful member of the Wesleyan societies. His theology of perfection, despite the weaknesses created by the stiff framework of orthodox theology into which he had to force it, represented an effort to keep the concept of God-centred behaviour alive in a society which was already beginning to find new bases for action in the market economy, the bourgeois ethic and the modern state. His approach was sounder than that of the nineteenth-century Anglo-Catholic revival of monasticism which pitted the old order of ascetic values against the new values of the expanding West without seriously debating whether the conventual life offered the most appropriate form of expression for Christianity in an urban, industrialized society dominated by potential plenty, not potential scarcity. The process of rejecting a Christian understanding of human behaviour and a Christian definition of the highest form of human happiness – a rejection already there in the Deist writers for whom Wesley's idea of 'perfection' was a kind of insanity – reached its logical conclusion in Friedrich Nietzsche's *Antichrist* (1895) in which Christianity was condemned fiercely as a conspiracy 'against life itself', words which echoed powerfully through European culture in the following seventy years.

Eighteenth-century Catholicism also faced the problem of reconciling the traditional Christian model of the perfect life with the growth of the bourgeois spirit. On the one side the Dominicans, represented especially by Daniel Concina (1687–1756), whose *Theologia Christiana Dogmatico-Moralis* appeared in 1749, thought that there was too strong a move to conciliate the Christian life with the satisfactions of this world. They encouraged confessors to press upon the laity moral demands which had in the past been regarded as required only of those who aspired to the highest degree of perfection. Benedict XIV, Pope from 1740 to 1758 (and thus a contemporary of John Wesley in his most flourishing period), supported this reaction. Modern Catholic historians refer to Concina as 'half-Jansenist', by which they mean that his moral austerity had much in common with the mood of seventeenth-century Port-Royal.

This rigorism arose from a desperate anxiety to preserve the traditional grip of the ascetic ideal upon the lay imagination: one may interpret John Wesley's doctrine of holiness as a not dissimilar attempt to find a model of perfection which could be followed successfully in the world of the Enlightenment. More like Wesley, however, was Alphonso de Liguori (1696–1787), the greatest Catholic character of the eighteenth century, a man who won the prestige necessary for his accommodation of holiness to the social environment because he preserved in himself the ascetic image of the persecuted saint who abandoned the world. Liguori's *Theologia Moralis* (1752–55) slowly sapped the popularity of rigorism. It is impossible to summarize here the subtleties of the controversy which raged between 'probabilists', 'probabiliorists' and 'equiprobabilists': what was at stake was the degree of moral freedom which could be reconciled with Christian holiness in the laity. It is in Liguori and his order of Redemptorists (founded in 1732 as the Congregation du Saint Sauveur), and not in the medieval Franciscans, that the significant Catholic parallel with John Wesley is to be found. Liguori organized his order for the evangelization of the poor of the remoter Italian countryside; he preached many missions himself, taking as his favourite themes the fear of Hell and the safety of trust in the Virgin Mary. Theologically, of course, there was a clear distinction between the Catholic 'mission' tradition and Protestant Revivalism, which had roots in the seventeenth century, chiefly in the American colonies, and which aimed at the production in the individual of the outward and personal signs of justification by faith, as a precondition to admission into the full membership of the typical local Baptist, Congregationalist, or Presbyterian Church. Wesley and Liguori were not trying to do exactly the same thing, nor were their methods closely similar, but both reacted to the spiritual and intellectual isolation of the lower ranks of an excessively rigid, hierarchical society, and both wanted to awaken in people a greater awareness of the importance of translating theology into human existence, especially where the practice of holiness was concerned.

In its Protestant context, therefore, Wesley's doctrine of perfection represented an important attempt to revive the idea and pursuit of holiness (understood as a sinful condition, whatever the qualifications which Wesley sometimes applied), in a society which was now tempted to discard the idea of holiness altogether, and in which the Church, responding to the mood of the age, increasingly described the Christian life in limited moral terms. Wesley wanted to revive holiness as an absolute demand (as distinct from the instinctive relativism of the true moralist who knows – as Alphonso de Liguori knew, for example – how difficult moral choices really are), and yet at the same time leave a man free to fulfil his social rôle. To solve the contradictions which he created Wesley invoked grace on God's side and faith on man's side. His socio-economic dictum, 'get all you can, save all you can, give all you can', made peace with the new acquisitive market society which had broken with the scholastic economic theory. The scholastics had established the ethical basis of the just wage and the just price and had condemned unearned income in the form of interest. 'Get all you can' echoed the ethos of a society in which the self-centred pursuit of material gain was destroying the social character of property. This was not a revolution historically avoidable at that juncture, but a new theology of the Christian's life in the world was needed to cope with the results of the social changes involved. Give all you can, however, was not a solution to the problems created by capitalism; it only reflected the pre-industrial belief that individual charity was the appropriate Christian reaction to social problems. Wesley died before the full effects of the industrial revolution had shown themselves, but it was unfortunate that his search for a theology of intra-mundane holiness (the word 'asceticism' here only confused the issue, because it pointed back to the Desert and not forward to the factory) did not lead to a clearer understanding of the shape which society was taking and so to an earlier Christian self-consciousness about the full consequences of the expanding production of wealth.

The issue is important, because a theology of holiness can only really be assessed in practice. In the early nineteenth century Evangelical Tory parsons were among the pioneers of the Factory Movement, the agitation to reduce working hours and improve working conditions in cotton mills in northern England. The Evangelical attitude was summed up by George Stringer Bull (1799–1864), who said that people must have time 'to reflect, to improve their minds, to instruct their families and worship their God' (quoted in *The Factory Movement* (1962), by J. T. Ward, p. 423). The Evangelicals believed that the factories were forming a generation which could have no knowledge of the Gospel and must therefore inevitably be damned; the Evangelicals were freer to act in terms of this analysis because they were not socially identified with the men who were driving industrialization forward. The Wesleyan Methodists, however, remained for the most part hostile to the movement for factory reform: this was partly because their social connections put them on the side of the mill-owners, but partly because Wesley's concentration on the subjective evidence for personal holiness, his confusion of absolute obedience to God with states of emotional experience, blunted the practical edge of his teaching. By the end of the nineteenth century the position of the two groups had reversed: the Wesleyans supported the Social Gospel, which contained a very mild programme for moral, rather than social, reform; that is, they concentrated on symptoms of social disorder rather than on offering a new structure for society; the Evangelical Anglicans now saw any sort of social Christianity as a dangerous substitute for the all important issue of conversion, and so kept aloof.

The significance of industrialization for the history of theology is obviously hard to decide. There is often a tendency to assume that eighteenth-century European, and especially British, society had a moral and religious unity within which moral and metaphysical questions could be raised in terms understood by the society as a whole, even if there were no final agreement about the answers suggested. The Industrial Revolution, including as it did among its consequences not only urbanization but also the formation of class divisions, is supposed to have destroyed this unity and to have accelerated the secularization of society. In the twentieth century 'there remains no framework within which the religious questions can be systematically asked. For different classes the loss of a religious framework proceeds in different ways at different rates and in different periods, but for all there are left at last only fragments of a vocabulary in which to ask or answer these questions' (*Secularisation and Moral Change*, 1967, A. MacIntyre, p. 30).

Such an analysis does not seem to correspond to the real history of theology in the eighteenth century. Eighteenth-century society was already sharply divided into worlds which had no basic understanding of one another. Part of the social explanation of the rise of Methodism, for example, was that substantial groups of people who felt themselves excluded from the mainstream of English life and culture reacted by emphasizing their withdrawn status and by setting up a new society of their own, of which Wesleyanism, as an institution and theology, was the religious expression. The withdrawal of the Wesleyan societies from the Church of England was neither an historical accident nor the result (as John Henry Newman thought) of the absence of a concerted, conciliatory episcopal policy, but followed from the social origins of Methodism itself; the Wesleyan doctrine of Christian Perfection fitted in here again, as it happened, as a theological way of creating a separate Methodist identity. Eighteenth-century Methodism was not as potentially anti-social as seventeenth-century Quakerism had been in the person of George Fox; but Methodism should not be seen exclusively through the eyes of John Wesley, the quasi-Anglican loyal to the Establishment, for some of his ablest eighteenth-century lay preachers expressed through their Wesleyanism a rejection of the status quo.

In the same way, it is clear from the intellectual history of the Enlightenment that throughout the eighteenth century Europe was intellectually divided. Paul Hazard has emphasized the active desire of the Deist writers to be rid of Christianity: 'What the historian of ideas must first put down to their account is the immense effort which they made to transform into a non-Christian Europe the Christian Europe which confronted them'

(*European Thought in the Eighteenth Century*, 1963, p. 110). The myth of cultural unity, on the other hand, was defended by the American scholar, Carl Becker, who saw the philosophes as seeking to demolish the Heavenly City of Augustine only in order to rebuild it with more up-to-date materials. Becker's view, however, that the Enlightenment was a secularization of Christian attitudes, has not found favour with other scholars. R. R. Palmer, in *Catholics and Unbelievers in Eighteenth Century France* (1961), and L. G. Crocker, in *Nature and Culture: Ethical Thought in the French Enlightenment* (1963), agreed that although the anti-Christian writers were firmly embedded in a Christian environment, they were nevertheless advocating a new faith, one which involved a new stress on the possibilities of science, on the growth of the State, as well as a denial of the doctrine of original sin and all its alleged consequences. Crocker said that the controversy between philosophe and Catholic was concerned with moral rather than religious issues. In any traditional form the moral standpoint of Christianity contradicted that of the Enlightenment, and this meant not only that European culture in the eighteenth century no longer had a common basis, but also that in future European culture would not be limited to the kind of intellectual and emotional support which Christianity could provide. In its traditional shape, in fact, Christianity would become one marginal source of criticism of a culture which was accepting new presuppositions.

These changes took place in an intellectual context, from which social and industrial consequences followed, rather than *vice versa*. Between 1700 and 1750, when the French state was still able to prevent the publication of anti-Christian literature, deist and atheist manuscripts circulated clandestinely. There is an excellent account of these writings in J. S. Spink's *French Free Thought from Gassendi to Voltaire* (1960); through them the influence of the British Deists gradually permeated first France, and then Germany. The inevitable explosion came in the 1750s. In 1751 the abbé Martin des Prades, who was known to be a collaborator of Diderot's in the *Encyclopaedia*, published *La Jérusalem Céleste*, an essay in which he cast doubt on the apologetic value of the healing narratives in the New Testament. Pope Benedict XIV condemned des Prades' essay, and the Parlement of Paris suppressed the first volume of the *Encyclopaedia* in 1752; this made clear that official Catholicism, obsessed with its internal struggle with Jansenism and apparently careless of the sceptical influence of the Cartesian philosophy which the Jesuits had introduced into the seminaries, had no intention of trying to adapt to the rapidly changing intellectual climate of Europe. The Jesuits also bitterly attacked Helvétius' *De L'Esprit* in 1758: Helvétius, then a Deist, wanted to establish a science of ethics on the basis of John Locke's sensationalist psychology; his was a utilitarian system to which the pleasure-pain principle was fundamental. The persecution which he encountered shocked Helvétius into moving from Deism to atheism, and in *De L'Homme*, published after his death in 1772, he argued on mechanistic lines that all men began life with the same potential and that education could therefore be used to create an egalitarian, instead of the existing hierarchical, society. He proposed the redistribution of landed property as a further means towards the formation of a more democratic state. Down to about 1750 men of various shades of belief thought that it might still be possible to stand in a positive relation to the Roman Church, but by 1760 even this idea of cultural unity had also disappeared.

The weakening in the social prestige and cultural centrality of orthodox Christianity, which was the most important theological event of the period, and which went on parallel to the slow disintegration of the Ancien Régime, depended far less upon the effects of the Industrial Revolution than upon the Church's theological failure successfully to counter-attack the intellectual and political revolution which was also developing throughout the eighteenth century. What might be called the Church's social theology weighed heavily here, for rationalists like Diderot, Helvétius and Voltaire were all the more bitterly anti-Christian because of the justificatory rôle of the Church in the existing social order, and because of its willingness to use legal and political means to prevent the free circulation of ideas. Diderot's shift from deism to atheism between 1746 and 1749 coincided with his growing discontent with the state of French society as he struggled to publish the first volume of the *Encyclopaedia* against the opposition of the state and ecclesiastical censors. His imprisonment in the fortress of Vincennes (a state prison which also housed Jansenists in the eighteenth century) left him a convinced opponent of any religious institutions and of the non-democratic organization of the State. Even Voltaire, at one time an admirer of enlightened despotism, showed sympathy towards Genevan democracy in his later life. The intellectual atmosphere which these men formed made it increasingly difficult for either Catholic or Protestant orthodoxy to survive. The criticism of classical dogma from outside the Churches showed signs of succeeding where older internal forms of questioning, such as Socinianism in the late sixteenth and early seventeenth centuries, had failed.

External criticism did not shift power from the hands of those who opposed change, though it contributed to the suppression of the Jesuits in France in 1763. The internal demand for reform was theologically linked with Jansenism, which steadily became more of an attitude than a party after the Papal condemnation of the movement in the Bull *Unigenitus* (1713). The chief Jansenist leader of the early eighteenth century, Pasquier Quesnel (1634–1719) advocated an extreme form of the ideas of Edmond Richer, whose *On ecclesiastical and political power* had been published as far back as 1611. Richer said that although the Church was a spiritual monarchy with Christ as its King, the government of the Church on earth should be in the hands of bishops and priests united in one order and taking the advice of local synods, instead of in the hands of monarchical bishops with the Pope acting as both the source and sum of their diocesan authority. Quesnel now extended the rôle of the laity, saying that only the whole Church had the power to declare a member excommunicate, for example, a position which orthodox Catholic commentators treated as meaning that the laity might claim the right not to be excommunicated without their own consent – a liberty which official circles considered would be fatal to all ecclesiastical authority. Yet another eighteenth-century French advocate of a fusion of the Jansenist and Richérist traditions was

Nicholas Travers (1674–1750), who frequently suffered official persecution, and who, in his *Legitimate Powers of the First and Second Orders of Clergy* (1744), said in effect that parish priests ought to be free from episcopal interference. These ideas grew in popularity as the gap widened between the aristocratic and often very wealthy French episcopate and the more and more poverty-stricken parish clergy. The highest point of these attacks on the system came at the gatherings of the curés which preceded the meeting of the States General in Paris in 1789. Many of the curés wanted a national, presbyterian Church, almost all of them wanted a thorough democratization of the system.

These hopes of change were not fulfilled in the French Revolution; a powerful reaction followed revolutionary attempts first to reform the Catholic Church and then to set up a new, deistic religious system in its place. In the meantime it was German, rather than French or British, theologians who tried to cope with the changing ethos of western culture. The ablest of these were Immanuel Kant (1724–1804) and J. A. Semler (1725–91). Kant summarized, in *Religion within the Limits of Reason Alone* (1793), a form of Christianity which might survive the criticism of contemporary rationalism; Semler, on the other hand, wanted to reform the presentation of Christianity from within the Christian community, applying to the Lutheran tradition in which he had been raised both historical and rationalist criticism. The difference that matters here is perhaps Semler's greater historical sense.

Kant began from the assumption that God existed as the moral ruler of the universe. This God did not require either the possession of conscious religious experience (in the sense of pietism, for example), or the deliberate performance of liturgical actions (orthodoxy) as a condition of obtaining his favour. Indeed, Kant laid it down as a principle which needed no proof, that 'whatever, over and above good life-conduct, man fancies that he can do to become well-pleasing to God, is mere religious illusion and pseudo-service of God'; steadfast diligence in morally good life-conduct was all that God wanted from his subjects. It was characteristic of Kant's position that he argued that the Lord's Prayer expressed the spirit of prayer so well as to make its own verbal repetition a contradiction; prayer was an attitude, not an incantation. If men really needed supernatural assistance in order to serve God, then God would provide it; the man who was striving for complete obedience to the moral law could trust God to assist him even if he personally remained quite unconscious of the divine presence.

Kant did not deny that man's nature was radically evil, in as much as he was a being capable of subordinating the moral law, of which he could not plead ignorance, to his own self-loving inclinations. Nor could the solitary individual overcome this radical evil in himself, and therefore it would be natural for him to join others in the formation of an ethical commonwealth, which Kant said might be called 'a people of God' because its purpose was to impress the laws of virtue upon the whole human race. The power of human evil, however, prevented the actualization of this community of virtue, and so Kant, ironically perhaps, called it 'the invisible Church'. The visible religious institutions of mankind were historical examples of man's desire to bring the ideal down to earth. They had anthropological, not supernatural, significance.

Kant linked this austere system to Christianity by arguing that true Christianity (which was not, of course, the Christianity available in the eighteenth century) came closest to the ideal. Christianity was the religion of Jesus and had no vital connection with Judaism (here Semler agreed). Jesus showed his understanding of natural religion when he said that religious practices such as forms of confession and weekly worship were religiously irrelevant, but that moral faith, which alone made a man holy as his Father in heaven was holy, was the only saving faith. Jesus' death was an act of perfect obedience to God, but the narratives of his resurrection and ascension had no value for rational religion; indeed, the concept of resurrection to be found in the New Testament writings was incompatible with any valid hypothesis of the spirituality of rational world-beings. When Jesus said that he would be with his followers to the end of the world he was thinking of the survival of the memory of his own teaching, example and merit. At every step in the interpretation of the New Testament the miraculous and the metaphysical must be subordinated to the moral. Jesus did not found the true religion because this had always existed, devoid of dogma (by which Kant meant especially doctrines such as the doctrine of the Atonement), engraved on the hearts of men. Jesus was instead the founder of the first true Church.

Even so, in the concluding section of the book Kant reduced the value of this best of all possible Churches almost to nothing. He disbelieved in the content of what was usually alleged to be religious experience and insisted that men could know nothing at all about supernatural aid. This made him regard the setting up of religious institutions as hazardous because religious rites, rituals and ceremonies constantly tempted men to believe that they were the witnesses of miraculous events within themselves. Kant, that is, did not believe that men should attach any importance to self-conscious religious experience. It was difficult for a man to be religious by himself, but once he associated with others in a visible 'Church' he was still more liable to fall into fanaticism and superstition. The Church's justification was that it stood as a sign of man's radically evil nature, but even this self-understanding men did not owe to the Church as a bearer of divine revelation; men could understand themselves well enough if they used their reason. The Church did not possess supernatural 'means of grace' in the sense that John Wesley, for example, would have interpreted the term.

The continuity between the attitudes of Kant and Locke is obvious. In the *Essay on the Human Understanding* Locke had already suggested that religious experience, which he called 'enthusiasm', held no significance for the truth of Christianity. Kant denied even more explicitly that there was an identifiably authentic, or validly self-authenticating religious knowledge of God available to men. He had no contact with such movements as eighteenth-century Wesleyanism, for instance, but it is not likely that he would have been impressed by the individual Methodist's claim that he had consciously received a divine gift of holiness. For Locke (in *The Reasonable-*

ness of Christianity), the religious significance of Jesus lay in his divine authority, so that when men accepted his claim to be the Messiah they also accepted his claim to show them the true form of religion, which Locke described in ethical terms much as Kant did. Kant, however, reduced Jesus to the founder of the 'true Church', since true religion needed no special divine revelation. The chief Deist positions seemed to both of them to be immemorial and immutable. They did not think of man's nature as a problem for which some kind of a metaphysical explanation was necessary; they therefore dismissed the classical Christian dogmatic system of divine special creation, fall (the doctrine of original sin), and redemption through the crucifixion of Christ, as well as the elaborate descriptions of the person of Christ (the Chalcedonian statement, for example) which this system required; they shared a rejection of the traditional concept of eternal punishment.

Kant did not bulk largely in the consciousness of most nineteenth-century professional theologians. They could do nothing with a man who sincerely thought that one would not go to church if one valued one's relation to God. In Germany, the influence of the Enlightenment on religion diminished during the national uprising against Napoleon; the Biblical critics, who traced their origin to Richard Simon and Semler, not to Kant, found themselves opposed by a revival of Evangelical conservative Biblicism generalled by E. W. Hengstenberg (1802–69). By the 1830s Hegelianism, especially as manipulated by D. F. Strauss (1808–74) seemed a more dangerous philosophical approach to theology; then in England Charles Darwin transformed the theological question of man into a historical question, and began to undermine Victorian self-confidence about the absoluteness of moral values. Ritschl (1822–89) is sometimes thought of in Kantian terms, and it is true that he rejected metaphysical speculation as a source of knowledge about God, but there was little that was Kantian in his return to religious experience, and to the Gospels naively accepted as the authentic record of the mind of Jesus, as data for a new, pragmatic exploration of the religious nature of man. Indeed, there was positive intellectual failure in Ritschl's assumption that only western religious experience was of any significance for his task, and that even in the west one should ignore mystical, pietist and Roman Catholic sources.

Kant's influence, sometimes undoubtedly at second-hand, can perhaps be detected in characteristic asides like Benjamin Jowett's dismissal of the Church as 'a figment of theologians'; or in Matthew Arnold's by now too often quoted assertion that men could not do without Christianity (like Ritschl, of course, he was thinking of Europeans), but that they could not do with Christianity as it was. Kant seemed to subordinate something he called 'religion' to something else which he called 'morality', whereas one hope of the nineteenth century – really in reaction against the Enlighten- ment – was to find a way of understanding religious experience which would justify not only the inherited western moral code (which had its roots in Classical Greece as much as in Christianized Judaism), but also speculative theology. Unfortunately, after Schleiermacher the task seemed to be too much for those who attempted it. There is no danger, in any case, of producing a Whig interpretation of theological history at this point; nineteenth-century liberals were writing on the retreat, disputing every inch of the ground but not contesting the verdict of history.

The Victorian liberal – Matthew Arnold for example – did not believe that the preservation of a religious interpretation of experience and the use of reason to examine the foundations of Christianity were mutually exclusive, but if he had to choose between the free use of reason and the survival of traditional religious positions he felt obliged to put reason before religion, as Arnold himself did when he argued that western religious culture had simply abandoned the concept of miracle in any common-sense meaning of the term. This acceptance of the autonomy of reason (rather than its omnicompetence) really entered the theological field in the second half of the eighteenth century; Christian Wolff (1679–1754), of Halle, for example, did not go so far; it was Semler's work that was fundamental to the change.

Kant and Reimarus had both seen the problem of Christianity from the outside; Semler was much more of a Lutheran, but a Lutheran in whom the historical, as well as the existential approach was deeply rooted. He was not prepared to abandon the idea of some kind of special biblical revelation altogether, but he restricted its use and importance drastically by a destructive (but to many of his contemporaries, liberating) historical analysis of the orthodox Lutheran theories about (a) the Canon of Holy Scripture, and (b) the Verbal Inspiration of the biblical text.

Semler historicized the Canon which, he said, was only accepted as such in the fifth century A.D. (Cf. his *Abhandlung von freier Untersuchung des Kanons*, 1771–75). This historicization was perhaps even more significant in its way than the late twentieth-century Roman Catholic historicization of the Tridentine documents. Semler argued that the Early Church spread through preaching, while collections of documents differed in different areas. A Christian could therefore be in the same position as Stephen, who had not read a line of what was to be the New Testament but who knew enough of the Christian faith to become a martyr. Only from the beginning of the fifth century A.D. did one find any striving for a single, agreed Canon. The institution had followed the Gospel, imposing a legal definition of membership, a creed and a standard documentary authority: in other words, the formation of the Canon was a practical and ecclesiastical act, which had no absolute authority. (Once again one encounters the disagreement between those for whom the ecclesia is in essence a supra-natural body, and those for whom the ecclesia remains in essence a human institution). Semler said that if the formation of an agreed Canon was not essential to the initial spread of Christianity the existing Canon could not be made into a law for Christian faith and thought. He went further, because he held that for Christians only the New Testament message had a normative character, since Christ was the only ground of Christian faith: his dismissal of the Old Testament to an inferior status was again a portent for the future.

This demotion of the Canon meant, in effect, that one could not assume that every phrase in each book of the New Testament must have some profound religious significance because it occurred within a supranaturally inspired text. On the idea of Verbal Inspiration Semley was only a little less sweeping. He traced the notion back to the legend of the seventy translators of the Septuagint, who were all led by the Holy Spirit to use exactly the same words; while this fable was believed, it was natural that something like it should be extended to the New Testament. There was no evidence of a verbal inspiration theory in the New Testament itself, however; John and Paul, for example, appealed to quite other sources of authority for their statements, their acquaintance with Jesus or with the tradition which came from him. Semler thought that the development of the verbal inspiration theory could be attributed to an institutional need to guarantee the contents of the Bible, an attitude which caused his critics to accuse him of scepticism, and to see themselves as defenders of the whole Bible. According to orthodox Lutheran theory, the Scriptures might have been written down by men, but they were not men's words, but God's Word; it had even been claimed that the Holy Spirit dictated every word through passive human instruments.

At this point Semler parted company with the purely rationalist approach to biblical problems. He made a distinction between religion and theology. By 'religion' he meant an inner experience, a practical knowledge of the truth of God which was 'revealed' – he did not want to drop the word altogether – in the Bible. This 'revelation', however, was not to be lightly identified with the external words of the Bible. He substituted for the orthodox thesis that Holy Scripture *is* the Word of God, the view that the Holy Scripture *contains* the Word of God; and held that in working out the content of this revelation one should stick firmly to the historical method, trying to understand the text as the original author understood it, and not coaxing a mystical sense out of every text in the Pietist manner.

For Semler theology had become the scientific study of religious documents, a definition which he opposed to the orthodox Lutheran understanding of theology as a 'science of faith', and against the claim that the orthodox theological system, itself extracted as articles from the allegedly verbally inspired text of Scripture, ought to be binding on the faith of the individual. Semler, that is, like many later Lutheran theologians from Schleiermacher to Rudolf Bultmann, did not reject the essence of the Lutheran position, its concentration on the idea of personal justification through faith in Christ. He was prepared to affirm this in terms of his own inner religious experience, but he thought, as Bultmann was to think in a different intellectual context, that Lutheran orthodoxy had no intellectual right to make this inner reality a ground for requiring verbal adhesion to detailed confessional statements, to which, indeed, the historical method should also be applied. It was not surprising that he should have attacked Lessing's publication of Reimarus in his *Answer to the Fragments of an Unknown* (1779), though German scholars have sometimes seen this as a betrayal of Semler's own liberal principles. This was how Lessing took the book, for it cost Semler Lessing's friendship, but Lessing had in any case reached the view that the Bible was superfluous to the survival of Christianity, and found narratives like those of the Resurrection little more than an embarrassment in which there was no religious value. Semler, on the other hand, believed that the New Testament should remain a constitutive part of the Christian religion, a norm against which to test the empirical and existential approach; he had no sympathy with the Deist impulse (so strong in Reimarus) to clear the ground of Christianity in order to reveal the obscured simplicities of natural religion. One advantage of his so-called 'accommodation-theory', which proposed that Jesus was not completely committed to the Jewish thought-forms which dominated his sayings, was that it should enable the liberal theologian to separate a New Testament message from an Old Testament context, a context which Reimarus and many others had exploited against Christianity. (It may be added here that Karl Barth's influential account of Semler – in his *Protestant Thought in the Nineteenth Century* (1952, E.T. 1972) – which included him among the advocates of 'natural religion', was seriously misleading.)

In Semler many of the principal themes of nineteenth-century critical theology stand out already: the historical approach; the concomitant rejection of Verbal Inspiration theories; anti-dogmatism; the tendency to prefer existentially defined 'religion' to creeds, confessional statements and propositional theology in general. In 1800, however, such ideas had made little headway in the Christian community as a whole.

THE NINETEENTH CENTURY

The most important aspect of the history of nineteenth-century theology was the struggle for domination between two closely related theological outlooks or systems, orthodoxy, and what must still, for want of a better word, be called liberalism. On the whole, the initiative lay with the liberals in Protestantism and with the orthodox in Roman Catholicism.

In Protestantism the liberals sought to obtain general acceptance of the eighteenth-century historical-critical method of analysing the Bible. They tried to relax the binding-force on priests and laity of the historic creeds, denominational confessions, and other statements of doctrine like the Anglican Thirty-Nine Articles; they wanted to diminish the power and freedom of religious institutions to exclude laymen or ministers from the visible church on doctrinal grounds. Many liberals criticized orthodoxy as such, especially the traditional forms of such doctrines as the Trinity (see Schleiermacher's criticisms in *Christian Faith*, sections 170–172); the Person of Christ (see Matthew Arnold, *Literature and Dogma*, chapters 8 and 9); and the doctrine of the Atonement (see B. Jowett, 'On Atonement and Satisfaction', in his commentary on the Epistle to the Romans). The liberals promoted a non-dogmatic, and sometimes even anti-dogmatic approach to religious belief. They accepted willingly the advances of nineteenth-century science, which the orthodox were sometimes anxious to reject, but the direct effect of scientific thinking on liberal theology has been exaggerated by writers who have ignored liberalism's deep roots in eighteenth-century philosophy and historical method. Liberal theologians were not for the most part liberal because of the repercussions of a conflict between science and religion, or *Genesis* and geology; they were liberals because they already accepted the principle of free inquiry, which separated them from those theologians who advocated the absolute claims made for the religious authority of the Bible, Tradition, the Creeds, the Church or the Papacy.

Liberals did not accept, that is, the idea of a system of christian doctrine as a *revelatio revelata*, a definite message from God to man distinctly conveyed by his chosen instruments (the language is Newman's) to be acknowledged on the grounds of its being divine, not as true on intrinsic grounds, or as probably or partially true, but as absolutely certain knowledge guaranteed by the interposition of a power greater than human teaching or human argument. It was the finality of this conclusion, and the willingness of ecclesiastical authority, Protestant as well as Roman Catholic, to enforce it, which dismayed the liberal mind.

Schleiermacher, for example, did not dispute the use of the word 'revelation' to stand for a divine casual activity, but he did not think that revelation operated on man as a cognitive being, because that would make revelation essentially *doctrine*; instead, revelation was to be thought of as the appearance of a thinking being who worked upon the self-consciousness of those into whose circle he entered by his total impression upon them: doctrine was implied, but what was revealed and revealing was not doctrine in itself (*Christian Faith*, section 10). He then widened the idea, suggesting how difficult it was to draw any clear dividing line between what was revealed and what came to light through inspiration in a natural way. Moreover, if a religious body wanted to establish the validity of its own claim to revelation as against the claims of others, it could not do so by asserting that its own divine communication was pure and entire truth, while that of others contained falsehood. For if God revealed himself in this total way the finite human mind would be unable to grasp or use what was given to it. On the other hand, Schleiermacher added, an awareness of God which developed in a barbarous, degraded society might still be a revelation, even though it was grasped imperfectly in the mind in which it arose.

Here, cautiously, for he did not mean his words to be given too wide an application, Schleiermacher was arguing that if one started from the position that any kind of communicating relationship was possible between man and God, one was logically obliged to admit the possibility that 'revelation' took place outside as well as inside Christianity, whose claims to a unique and absolutely certain knowledge were correspondingly limited. Throughout the century the view that Christianity was one of a family of religions was to grow steadily in popularity; it was powerfully advocated by Ernst Troeltsch at the beginning of the twentieth century; the more exclusive view reappeared in the 1930s, but the liberal attitude returned strongly in the 1970s.

One has also to recognize the impact on the formation of the liberal tradition not so much of biblical criticism in the more technical sense – the historical effect of this has always been exaggerated – but of a freer kind of speculation about the historical career of Jesus, and about the reasons for the historical expansion of Christianity after the death of Jesus. The miraculous growth of Christianity, to take the second first, had been a fundamental part of traditional apologetics; as late as 1870 one finds Newman still defending the idea against Gibbon's purely historical interpretation:

It was the thought of Christ, not a corporate body or a doctrine, which inspired that zeal which the historian so poorly comprehended . . . Now all this will be called cloudy, mystical, unintelligible; that is, in other words, miraculous. I think it is so. How, without the Hand of God, could a new idea, one and the same, enter at once into myriads of men, women and children of all ranks, especially the lower, and have power to wean them from their indulgences and sins, and nerve them against the most cruel tortures, and to last in vigour as a sustaining influence for seven or eight generations, till it founded an extended polity, broke the obstinacy of the strongest and wisest government which the world has ever seen, and forced its way from its first caves and catacombs to the fulness of imperial power?[1]

By the 1870s, however, this was already rather old-fashioned; the relative position of Christianity in world-history was better understood, and it was becoming clear that it was no more of a problem to give a purely historical account of the rise of Christianity than it was to do the same for Buddhism or Islam, religions whose supernatural origin was steadily denied by the vast majority of western theologians. And the failure of christian missions, at the height of European and American world-influence in the nineteenth century to do more than establish marginal churches in China, India and the Middle East – there was no question of replacing the local relgious culture on any significant scale – reinforced the impression of late Victorian liberalism that the world's 'great religions' were culturally bounded. In Africa, Islam proved as lively as Christianity. And this slow change in the psychological situation of Christianity reflected the changes in its historical situation. For in Western Society in the nineteenth century the cultural initiative largely passed to the secular minority. Quantitatively, religious groups remained strong, but their rôle was never the same after the American and French revolutions. A modern historian, E. J. Hobsbawm, even claimed that 'in the ideologies of the American and French revolutions, for the first time in European history, Christianity is irrelevant . . . The ideology of the new working-class movements was secularist from the start.'[2]

This was not the whole of the truth. The American revolution was followed by a revival of Protestant evangelicalism which continued for most of the nineteenth century; the language of this tradition was not as irrelevant to the American Civil War as Hobsbawm implied. In France, it was also an exaggeration to say that major political and social changes were secularized: the revolution left France divided, but Roman Catholicism proved strong enough not only to provide vital support to Louis Napoleon, but also to endow the Vichy régime of the early 1940s with a social philosophy. In general, however, his judgment stands, for neither the American nor the French nor the later Marxist revolutions were based in christian thinking, and a sense of the growing exclusion of Christianity from western politics and much of western culture, steadily weakened, as far as liberal theologians were concerned, any belief that a special providence had watched over the rôle of the ecclesia within an otherwise 'fallen' society, either in the first five centuries of the western Christian era or in the nineteenth century itself. And of course a similar feeling of incipient cultural superfluousness helped to stimulate the romantic conservatism of theologians like Joseph de Maistre (1753–1821), the young Lamennais (1782–1854), S. T. Coleridge (1772–1834), and F. D. Maurice (1805–72).

As has already been suggested, liberal theology was also deeply affected by the so-called 'quest for the historical Jesus'. The most prominent

[1] J. H. Newman, *An Essay in Aid of a Grammar of Assent* (1870), pp. 458–59.
[2] E. J. Hobsbawm, *The Age of Revolution* (1962), p. 220.

contributors to the nineteenth-century succession of 'lives of Jesus' were D. F. Strauss (1808–74), M. Arnold (1822–88), J. E. Renan (1823–92), F. Nietzsche (1844–1900), Johannes Weiss (1863–1914), and A. Schweitzer (1875–1965). The series of radically different images of Jesus which they produced had really become logically inevitable once Reimarus (see above) had shown that a coherent secular view of Jesus, in complete contradiction to the portrait enshrined in the orthodox theological systems, was possible in terms of the New Testament evidence. These new images of Jesus served many purposes, including the orthodox 'lives' which contained a composite biography designed to confirm belief in the traditional picture of Jesus as the God-Man. All those mentioned here, however, were intended to help men to free themselves either from Christianity altogether (as in Renan and Nietzsche, for instance), or from Christian dogmatic systems which were interpreted by the writers as crippling or corrupting western man – Strauss, Arnold and Schweitzer all shared this theme. At the same time, the sheer variety and subtlety of the 'lives' sapped the foundations of the liberal assumption that New Testament scholarship, once freed from the restrictions of ecclesiastical censorship (which continued throughout the nineteenth century in the Roman Church), would arrive at 'agreed results', and so at an agreed historical and theological understanding of the life of Jesus. Orthodox theologians naturally welcomed the gradual diminution of the prestige of New Testament scholarship; they thought that the discovery that scholarship could not give final answers to the questions which it raised would facilitate the reintroduction of a dogmatic reading of the New Testament, and a reassertion of the Chalcedonian definition of the Person of Christ. Liberal theologians, however, felt that what was happening was the disappearance of the New Testament as 'scripture' (the kind of document on which a religion bases its claim to absolute authority) and its replacement by the New Testament as a literary document, not dissimilar to the Homeric or Shakespearian writings. The distinction between the two groups may be put in this way: that when the orthodox considered the possibility that the New Testament was a book like any other, they rejected it, whereas the liberals were not sure that the possibility could be rejected. Behind this distinction lay another. The central argument of nineteenth-century conservatism, accepted by all, Catholic and Protestant, may be summed up in Newman's statement:

> Natural religion is based upon the sense of sin; it recognises the disease, but it cannot find, it does but look out for the remedy. That remedy, both for guilt and moral impotence, is found in the central doctrine of Revelation, the Mediation of Christ.[1]

In these terms Newman had spoken of the image of Jesus as the 'image of Him who fulfils the one great need of human nature, the Healer of its wounds, the Physician of the soul'.[2] Taking the nineteenth century as a whole, the movement of liberal theology was away from that description of human nature, and consequently from that picture of the function of Jesus.

[1] J. H. Newman, *The Grammar of Assent* (1870), p. 480.
[2] *ib.* p. 458.

Like Reimarus, Strauss, in his *Life of Jesus* (1835–6) tried to give a non-supernatural explanation of the origins of the Christian religion; but whereas Reimarus had cut Jesus down to a failed Jewish politician, Strauss interpreted him as a Jew who came to believe that he was the Messiah. Historically speaking, Jesus had probably been a Jewish religious teacher who had denounced sinners, foretold the Woes that would come at the End, and invoked the blessedness which would be the reward of the righteous. Popular Jewish feeling, soaked in a messianic literature, constantly pressed on him the rôle of behaving as though the supernatural intervention which he was prophesying had actually already begun. When Jesus died a community developed which, drawing heavily on the Old Testament, created a complete mythology, including the stories of Jesus's birth, childhood, miracles, transfiguration, predictions of the Passion, resurrection and ascension.

For Strauss, therefore, both Jesus and his successors were totally absorbed in a local primitive Jewish methology; it was legitimate, from Strauss' point of view, to say that if Jesus and the New Testament were to have any surviving significance, it would have to be in nineteenth-century terms, and in the closing sections of the book he used his own variety of Hegelianism to illustrate this. This was not a failure of interpretation, as is often said, but rather the assertion (which Strauss himself found it hard to hold on to in the 1830s but which came out strongly in his later work) that the New Testament mythology could only be given meaning if it was torn clean out of its historical matrix. If Jesus believed himself to have been the Messiah, he was essentially Jewish, and to take him seriously one would have to be a Jew; as for the ideas of incarnation and resurrection, for example, these could be restated in nineteenth-century terms, and this was the only way in which they could be given meaning:

> Humanity is the union of the two natures – God become man, the infinite manifesting itself in the finite, and the finite spirit remembering its infinitude; it is the child of the visible Mother and the invisible Father, Nature and Spirit . . . it is the sinless existence, for the course of its development is a blameless one, pollution cleaves to the individual only, and does not touch the race or its history. It is Humanity that dies, rises, and ascends to Heaven, for from the negation of its phenomenal life there ever proceeds a higher spiritual life; from the suppression of its mortality as a personal, national and terrestrial spirit arises its union with the infinite spirit of the heavens. By faith in this Christ, especially in his death and resurrection, man is justified before God: that is, by the kindling within him of the idea of Humanity, the individual man participates in the divinely human life of the species.[1]

After Strauss, the unity of the New Testament, and agreement between the historical Jesus and the primitive Christian community could never again be taken for granted; and in general liberal theologians were those who

[1] D. F. Strauss, *The Life of Jesus Critically Examined* (ET 1846), vol. 3, p. 438. There is a modern edition, P. C. Hodgson (1972).

reacted strongly to this uncertainty. There was, in any case, a considerable difference between saying that the New Testament contained historical evidence that Jesus consciously claimed to be the Messiah, or to be the divine Son of God, and saying that the primitive Christian community believed him to have been divine, etc.

On the conservative side, in the course of the nineteenth century, this was balanced by the view, already strongly held by Coleridge, for example, that the problems of the New Testament could be solved by turning from scholarship to religious experience. This was an appeal to experience to confirm tradition, whether Catholic or Protestant, rather than an appeal to theological tradition to interpret experience. One finds it in Coleridge's posthumously published *Confessions of an Inquiring Spirit* (ed. H. N. Coleridge 1840), where it was a step *behind* Kant not an advance from him, inasmuch as it was obvious that the experience was likely to confirm the documents when they were tested within the religious culture which they had formed. Moreover, in mid-nineteenth-century Europe there were fewer people really prepared to transpose their discontents into the language-game of the New Testament: anxiety and authority were shifting else-where. In 1843, for example, Karl Marx said, in his essay on *The Jewish Question*:

> We do not turn secular questions into theological questions. We turn theological questions into secular questions. History has been resolved into superstition long enough. We are now resolving superstition into history; the question of the relationship of political emancipation to religion becomes for us the question of the relation of political emancipation to *human* emancipation.[1]

This was a more seminal passage than anything in Coleridge, for Marx meant that the search for individual salvation, with which Coleridge was personally obsessed, was irrelevant at least until the social liberation of humanity was accomplished.

Although Marx, rather than Coleridge, wrote the agenda for the following century, the theological appeal to experience did not vanish. Thus the Roman Catholic theologian, Friedrich von Hügel (1852–1925), said not long before his death, and after a very close acquaintance with the personalities and ideas of the Catholic Modernist movement:

> But above all, and without any emphasis upon future possibilities, the essential, the most indispensable of the dimensions of religions is, not breadth, but depth, and above all, the insight into sanctity and the power to produce saints. Rome continues – of this I am very sure – to possess this supernatural depth – possess it in far greater degree than Protestantism, and still more than quite unattached moderns.[2]

This position – the verdict on Rome apart – might be shared by two distinct groups. The conservative proper could argue that if a particular

[1] K. Marx, *Early Writings*, trans. G. Benton; Penguin, in association with New Left Review, p. 217.

[2] L. F. Barmann, *Baron Friedrich von Hügel and the Modernist Crisis in England* (1972), p. 251; from a letter to Norman Kemp Smith, the philosopher, 31 Dec. 1921.

theological system produced sanctity there could not be much wrong with the attendant interpretation of the New Testament. A very moderate liberal like von Hügel, however, argued that if the orthodox theological systems produced saints, then their indefensible attitude to nineteenth-century biblical scholarship (and he had no real doubt that it was indefensible) might be endured. Of course, the use of the word 'sanctity' begged many questions, and it could be said that von Hügel had been educated into approval of a certain kind of person nurtured in a particular variety of the ascetic tradition; it was Simone Weil (1909–43), rather than von Hügel himself in his studies of Roman Catholic mysticism, who succeeded in making asceticism central to a twentieth-century religious outlook; but she had genius. The moves from religious experience to tradition and thence to the Bible raised another question, whether the spiritual patterns character-istic of the various theological systems could stand alone without the New Testament, which they were being used to interpret. This was the position which Renan and Matthew Arnold exploited in a liberal direction, the first without much respect for the Roman Catholicism which he had abandoned in 1845, the latter with more feeling for Anglicanism as he understood it.

It is sometimes said that the theological influence of Renan's *Life of Jesus* (1863) was negligible, that the book was only a stage in the discovery that there was insufficient material for a biography of Jesus which excluded the supernatural. This is an exaggeration, because it misses the sense in which Renan (and also Nietzsche) was concerned with theology as well as with biography. Renan used the biographical method to dramatize the difference, as he saw it, between the Jesus of the Gospels and the elaborate ecclesiastical and sacramental systems which claimed his authority. Jesus – Renan said – showed us for the first time the nature of pure worship, unbounded by either time or place, 'la religion absolue', in which the inhabitants of other planets could also believe. Here was the ultimate spiritualization of religion, with neither rites, priests, nor temples, a cult without a cultus, based on the Sermon on the Mount, in flat opposition to the actual historical develop-ment of all the major Christian churches, the Church of Rome included.

When Renan turned to the christological question, he said that it was permissible to call Jesus 'God', but not in the sense that he had totally absorbed the divine, or was somehow identical to it, but in the sense that Jesus was the individual who had enabled his species to make its biggest step towards the divine. With calculated vagueness, Renan implied that the universe had a spiritual core, and that Jesus had once and for all purified men's apprehension of how to find a personal relationship with this hidden source of being, 'l'âme cachée de l'univers'. No trinitarian doctrine was necessary, because the relationship between Jesus and the hidden source of all being was not different in kind from that which any man might now have with the ideal. Jesus had enabled men to take their biggest step towards the divine, but once the step had been demonstrated any one could imitate it who chose to do so. Much has been made of Renan's 'ambiguity', but he was not inevitably insincere when he said at the close of the famous preface to the thirteenth edition of the *Life of Jesus* (1867), that 'the least of the simple, provided that he worships from the heart, is more enlightened about the reality of things than the materialist who believes that he can explain everything in terms of chance and the finite'.[1]

It was said that Renan replaced legend with a novel: he certainly regarded the Gospels as legends, to be approached in the same way as European scholars approached islamic or buddhist documents. He said (in 1867) that if one limited one's account of the life of Jesus to what was historically certain, the result would be a few lines only:

> He existed. He came from Nazareth in Galilee. He preached attractively and left in the memories of his disciples aphorisms which embedded themselves deeply. His two chief disciples were Cephas and John, the son of Zebedee. He excited the hatred of orthodox Jews, who managed to have him put to death by Pontius Pilate, then procurator of Judaea. He was crucified outside the gate of the city. Soon afterwards some believed that he was resurrected.[2]

Everything else was a matter of opinion, and the Gospels frequently furnished arguments for opposing theses. One could only suppose (this was the plot of Renan's novel) that somehow the ethical genius of the Sermon on the Mount was forced by the pressure of popular messianic expectation into a morally-ambiguous position, especially on the issue of miracles, from which death was the only escape. Death, however, liberated his pure conception of religion from the limitations of Palestinian Judaism.

Neither Reimarus nor Strauss had described a Jesus who was capable of founding a world-religion; in both cases the largely anonymous community had been the decisive factor. Renan's Jesus sounded like a religious genius, all the more so for coming into conflict with both Jewish orthodoxy and popular religious feeling; and Renan made him more plausible by the very act of historicizing him, by treating him, that is, not as the unique divine vehicle of revelation, but as a man who, over a quite brief period, saw deeply into the nature of the universe. And so Lessing's question about the gospel-stories, which had seemed so menacing – how could one base one's eternal happiness upon historical knowledge? – was at once answered and put aside. What mattered in the gospels was not, for example, the resurrection-narratives at which Lessing had jibbed, but the ethical understanding which could be tested in action. There was still a religious attitude here, Renan implied, and a valuable one, but it was simply not the religious system which the Christian churches claimed to have found in the gospels. Renan's way of interpreting the Jesus-figure appealed to the middle-classes in France, and to the working-classes in England.

The kind of distinction which was being made can be measured if one looks at Soren Kierkegaard's attempt, about twenty years earlier, and with Lessing's question specifically in mind, to decide what would be the minimum possible content of the Christian tradition. Kierkegaard's underlying anxiety was to make a case for the orthodox idea of salvation, an idea which seemed to Lessing to ask too much of one's reason:

[1] E. Renan, *Vie de Jésus* (Gallimard, Paris, 1974), p. 59.

[2] *ib.* pp. 44–45.

If the contemporary generation had left nothing behind them but these words: 'We have believed that in such and such a year the God appeared among us in the humble figure of a servant, that he lived and taught in our community, and finally died', it would be more than enough. The contemporary generation would have done all that was necessary; for this little advertisement, this *nota bene* on a page of universal history, would be sufficient to afford an occasion for a successor, and the most voluminous account can in all eternity do nothing more.[1]

Lessing had baulked at the traditional summary of Christianity because it required unconditional assent to allegedly historical events which could never in themselves achieve more than a high degree of probability, certainly not the absoluteness required before one could make them the basis of religious commitment. Renan's summary of the historically certain element in the life of Jesus, by its sheer brevity, delicately enforced Lessing's point, but left the possibility of an ethical theism based on the teaching of Jesus. Kierkegaard was prepared to grant that one could not base eternal happiness on historical knowledge (Lessing was right on his own terms), but argued that to stop there was to miss the point. The 'true' minimum historical account of Jesus was one which pointed back to the moment of God's self-revelation in the form of a servant as the first believers experienced it; this account was adequate to afford another man the occasion to encounter God's revelation – 'there is no disciple at second-hand, the first and the last are essentially on the same plane'.[2] At this point the statement that 'God appeared' was obviously a description of the belief of those who encountered Jesus in the flesh, the 'God in the humble figure of a servant'; as such, this belief was historical, and open to the historical method, there were even historical analogies. In Kierkegaard's mind, however, revelation did not consist in information which could be learned and passed on, nor was it simply given, to be taken or rejected, in the Bible: revelation was the self-authenticating act of God who revealed to a man his sinfulness and God's willingness to save him. Even if he had only the clues given in the short summary of the life of Jesus quoted above, a man could hope for the divine encounter, though its actually taking place would depend on God. What Kierkegaard had done was to surround human religious experience with the interpreting medium of a particular pietist tradition; the God who appeared in the humble figure of a servant had the rules laid down for him. Kierkegaard's attempt to show that Christian faith was independent of historical knowledge was to reappear in the twentieth-century theology of, for example, Barth, Bultmann and Tillich.

Kierkegaard, then, whose influence was to be felt after 1900, returned to the classical Protestant polarization of the repentant individual face to face with the God and Father of the Lord Jesus Christ, who in wrath yet remembered mercy. But mid-nineteenth-century Europe was not the world

[1] S. Kierkegaard, *Philosophical Fragments*, ed. D. Swenson, N. Thulstrup, H. V. Hong (Princeton University Press, New Jersey, 1967), pp. 130–31.
[2] *ib.* p. 131.

of the Reformation; the liberal, critical mood of the period may be summed up in John Stuart Mill's view, in *On Liberty* (1859) that 'the beliefs which we have most warrant for, have no safeguard to rest upon, but a standing invitation to the whole world to prove them unfounded'. In this atmosphere sensitive writers on religion like Matthew Arnold felt that they had to abandon an apologetic based on the appeal to prophecy, miracle, and the necessity of a divine mediator whose death was an atoning sacrifice, and to work out instead a version of Christianity more closely associated with the teaching and personality of the Jesus of the Gospels. As he put it in *Literature and Dogma* (1873):

> The great prophecies of Isaiah and Jeremiah are, critics can easily see, not strictly *predictions* at all; and predictions which are meant as such, like those in the Book of Daniel, are an embarrassment to the Bible rather than a main element of it. The 'Zeit-Geist', and the mere spread of what is called *enlightenment*, superficial and barren as this often is, will inevitably before long make this conviction of criticism a popular opinion held far and wide. And then, what will be their case, who have been so long and sedulously taught to rely on supernatural predictions as a mainstay?[1]

As for miracles, 'our point is that the objections to miracles do, and more and more will, without insistence, without attack, without controversy, make their own force felt; and that the sanction of Christianity, if Christianity is not to be lost along with its miracles, must be found elsewhere'.[2]

Religion, therefore, had to be recast, and the first step towards that was an understanding that the language of the gospels was fluid, passing and literary, not rigid, fixed and scientific. The Bible, Arnold said, was not a talisman to be taken and used literally, nor was any existing Church, whatever its pretensions, a talisman for giving the absolute interpretation of the Bible. Neither the historian, nor the New Testament scholar, nor the traditional theologian, could save Christianity as it was. The cultured layman who (as Arnold put it) had acquainted himself with the best that had been known and said in the world, would have in the future to work out his own interpretation of the Jesus of the gospels. If he followed Arnold's personal interpretation he might, by means of the method (self-analysis, repentance, self-renunciation) and the temper (sweet-reasonableness) of Jesus find the joy and peace which came from the pursuit of righteousness. For beyond Jesus existed an 'eternal power, not ourselves, which makes for righteousness'. It is not clear how far Arnold thought that one could observe the activity of this power in oneself. Certainly, he regarded his description of God as verifiable; he substituted it for the orthodox assumption, which he rejected on the ground that it was unverifiable that there was 'a Great Personal First Cause, the moral and

---

[1] M. Arnold, *Literature and Dogma* (1873), p. 152.
[2] *ib.* p. 189.

intelligent Governor of the universe,[1] from whom the Bible derived its authority; and he called the doctrine of the Trinity 'the fairy-tale of the three supernatural men'.[2] What he was trying to affirm was an ethical idealism which could still find in the Jesus of the gospels a principal source of personal moral power; to the extent that his position depended on Kant, he did not seem to see the force of the criticisms which could be made of the authority of the moral consciousness.

Arnold tried to compel Christianity to face the possibility of a purely human Jesus; he failed, and Anglican liberalism retreated into late Hegelian schemes for a Christ who would still be both human and divine; the same Hegelian pattern may be found in J. F. Bethune-Baker (1861–1951) and J. A. T. Robinson in the 1970s. Arnold failed, partly because he lacked Renan's ability to fashion a new Jesus-myth out of the old Jesus-myth; and partly because, once he had reduced Jesus to a Teacher of Righteousness, ethical imprecision set in. He has to be compared with Leo Tolstoy (1828–1910), for whom the teaching of Jesus (in whose divinity he also did not believe) was not just a matter of repentance, self-negation and (of all things) sweet reasonableness (as though Jesus had been a rather refined Oxford don), but meant non-resistance to evil, loving one's enemies, breaking up the traditional property-basis of western society, and so on. Arnold wanted to recast religion for the sake of stabilizing a threatened society; Tolstoy threatened society, and traditional western religion as well. One must not press this too much. Few Englishmen in the 1860s and 1870s grasped the quantity of human suffering which underlay national prosperity; in the Russia of the 1880s and 1890s Tolstoy was by no means the only intellectual who shuddered at the ignorance, poverty and oppression of the peasantry. Theologically, what mattered was that two such men should have agreed in turning to the ethical teaching of the Jesus of the gospels (however variously they understood it), and not to orthodox theologians who wove a supernatural concept of Christ into salvation-systems, Catholic and Protestant. 'If we now speak to a modern educated man', Tolstoy wrote in 1886, 'about the fall of the angel and of Adam, or about redemption, he will not attempt to argue or to prove the falsity of it, but will ask with perplexity: What angel? Why Adam? What redemption?'[3]

Orthodox theology had lost its grip on the culture, which in its turn was getting a grip on the gospels. The reassessment of Jesus was carried to a brilliant limit in Nietzsche's *The AntiChrist* (written in 1888, published in 1895), the most remarkable of the nineteenth-century studies of Jesus. Nietzsche dismissed New Testament criticism as irrelevant, because of the absence of adequate parallel non-Christian material from the primitive period. One could not arrive at what Jesus said, what he did, or how he really died, one could only try to reconstruct the psychological type of the redeemer.

Nietzsche interpreted Jesus as carrying to the furthest extreme a revolt against reality which he thought had become characteristic of the later

---

[1] *ib.* p. 12 (from the Preface of 1873).
[2] *ib.* p. 361.
[3] L. Tolstoy, *What Then Must We Do?* (1886, ET 1925), p. 236.

Jewish religious system. By flight from reality Nietzsche meant that Judaism, already before Christianity, had used the categories of sin, guilt and punishment to falsify the ideas of God and morality. God became a God who made demands, in place of a God who assisted men; and morality, instead of being an expression of the conditions under which a nation lived and grew, became abstract, the antithesis of life – morality as a fundamental degradation of the imagination, an 'evil eye' for everything. The offending and repenting Jew, as well as the wayward Jewish people, constantly needed the priest and the sacrificial system in order to approach God at all. Even Jewish history was rewritten, so that the great epoch of the Jewish monarchy became a period of decay, and the Exile an endless punishment for the sins of the great epoch. (Nietzsche would have noted with interest that the Second Vatican Council was still struggling with the question of the alleged responsibility of the Jewish people for the death of Jesus.)

Jesus, Nietzsche argued, rebelled against the Judaism of his period, and Nietzsche would have approved of this if he had believed that the rebellion was directed towards a recovery of the natural values of existence, of the instinct for life. Jesus, however, seemed to Nietzsche to want to retreat even further from reality in the direction of a purely inner world. In his interior kingdom Jesus stood outside

> all religion, all conception of divine worship, all history, all natural science, all experience of the world, all acquirements, all politics, all psychology, all art – his 'knowledge' is precisely the pure folly of the fact that anything of this kind exists. He has not so much as heard of culture, he does not need to fight against it – he does not deny it . . . The same applies to the state, to society and the entire civic order, to work, to war – he never had any reason to deny the 'world', he had no notion of the ecclesiastical concept 'world' . . . Denial is precisely what is totally impossible for him.[1]

In order to show Jesus in complete revolt against the Judaism he experienced, Nietzsche had to assert that the ideas of sin, guilt, reward and punishment were absent from the gospel which Jesus himself preached. For Jesus every kind of distancing relationship between man and God (like sin) was abolished – this was the essence of the 'glad tidings'. Blessedness was not promised as something to come, or as tied to conditions, but was the present reality. Jesus spoke only of the inmost thing: 'life' or 'truth' or 'light' was his expression for the inmost thing – everything else, the whole of nature, and language itself 'possess for him merely the value of a sign, a metaphor'.[2] A new mode of behaviour, not a new system of belief, distinguished the Christian. Jesus no longer required formulas or rites for communicating with God, not even prayer. He had settled his accounts with the Jewish penance-and-reconciliation doctrine; he knew that it was through the practice of one's life that one felt 'divine', 'blessed', 'a child of God', not through penance and praying for forgiveness:

---

[1] F. Nietzsche, *The AntiChrist*, tr. R. J. Hollingdale, 1968, p. 145.
[2] *ib.* p. 144.

The profound instinct for how one would have to live in order to feel oneself in 'Heaven', to feel oneself 'eternal', while in every other condition one by no means feels oneself 'in Heaven': this alone is the psychological reality of redemption.[1]

Once Jesus died, Nietzsche said, his position was abandoned: 'the "Evangel" died on the Cross'.[2] Nothing could have been less like Jesus than the ecclesiastical crudity of describing God as a 'person', or of talking about a Kingdom of God which came 'upon earth'. Jesus had done away with the idea of 'guilt', had denied that there was a chasm between God and man, and had acted out of this unity of man and God as the heart of his 'glad tidings'; but the early Christians, inspired by Paul, unable to forgive or to understand Jesus's death, interpreted it as the sacrifice of an innocent man for the sins of the guilty. This was to construct the Church out of the antithesis of the gospel of Jesus. There had been no Christians at all in Jesus's sense, Nietzsche said; but instead a religion which feared and hated reality had taken his place, absorbed in an individualistic and superfluous doctrine of redemption. For Nietzsche, modern Christianity was the continuation of Judaism by other means. He denounced the orthodox Christian psychology of man, and said that in future men would have to find the courage to live without religious presuppositions, accepting their humanity, and neither asking their god to forgive them for it, nor hoping that their god would change it for them. Both the dogmatic, the ethical, and the simply historical images of Jesus had become irrelevant to the future of mankind.

The question of relevance was at the heart of the last significant nineteenth-century studies of the life of Jesus, those of J. Weiss, whose *Preaching of Jesus on the Kingdom of God* appeared in 1892, and of A. Schweitzer, whose essay, *The Secret of the Messiahship and the Passion*, A sketch of the Life of Jesus, came out in 1901. Both claimed that a 'true' life of Jesus must be based on a thorough-going eschatology, and allow for Jesus's apparent belief that the end of the age was imminent. When he summed up his views (with great éclat) in *The Quest of the Historical Jesus* (1906, E.T. 1910), Schweitzer argued that what he called the 'quest for the historical Jesus' had been an attempt to manufacture a 'modernised', 'relevant' Jesus, who would fit naturally into the feelings and aspirations of 'modern man' (whom Schweitzer himself did not like), whereas the 'true' historical Jesus had been a world-negating spirit, committed to the eschatology of his culture, and as alien to the nineteenth century as that century was alien to him. So far he resembled Nietzsche (whom he did not mention), but at this point he abandoned Nietzsche's line of advance and retreated into a liberal Protestant stance, for he said that although the historically knowable Jesus was irrelevant to the nineteenth century, there was also a Jesus spiritually arisen within men, to whom they could turn for religious leadership. Schweitzer's vague, ambiguous conclusion harked back to the positive side of Renan, but gave little purchase for further development.

[1] *ib.* p. 146.
[2] *ib.* p. 151.

If Renan's Jesus, ironically, was an eternal success, to whose simple spiritual religion all good men could return at any time, the typical Jesus-figure of the nineteenth century was a historical failure, whose teaching and example had been falsified by the ecclesiastical and theological systems which claimed him as a founder – a view which both reflected and influenced liberal ecclesiology. Renan and Nietzsche knew that no 'final' historical truth about Jesus could possibly be arrived at within the limits of the existing evidence; what they were challenging was the authority of orthodox theology, Catholic and Protestant, on the ground that neither could prove reliable links between the life and teaching of Jesus and their theological edifices. In the short term, this challenge hardly affected the history of theology, because there was an academic tendency to keep theories about the historical Jesus separate from 'dogmatic theology'. But the attempt to work from the Jesus of the Gospels towards a theology, instead of from a ready-made 'dogmatics' towards an image of Jesus, survived, and might be seen, for example, in later twentieth-century writers like Van Buren in the United States and D. Z. Phillips in Wales, who felt that the movement in modern philosophy associated with Wittgenstein had almost eroded the possibility of doing theology in the traditional manner, and who therefore saw Jesus as the focus of a group of stories which might become part of the imaginative sustenance of man's spiritual life, but could not legitimately serve as the basis of a metaphysical system (see also *An Empiricist's View of the Nature of Religious Belief*, 1955, by R. B. Braithwaite, who underlined the links between his position and that of Matthew Arnold).

The conclusion of the nineteenth-century liberal movement, then, was a growing tendency to appeal from the authority of Scripture, Dogma or Church to an experience of the Spirit of Jesus risen, as Schweitzer said, among men. It became increasingly difficult for ecclesiastical authority to require allegiance to the language of the past, to the words of the Bible, the Creeds, the verbal statements of popes, bishops and Councils. Older views of authority had expected assent to the original description of scriptural events – the Ascension of Jesus, for example – quite as much as to the 'event' understood as symbol; now, not only the historical aspect of the 'event' was questioned, but also the value of 'spiritual', 'poetic' or 'mythic' interpretations of it. A Catholic Modernist like George Tyrrell, or a French Protestant like Auguste Sabatier (1839–1901), whose *Religions of Authority and the Religion of the Spirit* came out posthumously in 1903, held that the most that the official Church could do was ask for obedience to the Spirit of Jesus. This Spirit, however, was to be encountered primarily in the present, so that institutional authority as well as the creative theologian had to respond first to what was actually given in the present, instead of simply appealing to the record of a revelation given once and for all in the remote and perhaps inaccessible past. By the end of the century, in fact, the would-be transformers of the Christian tradition were no longer content with the idea that what was needed was to change the definition of the Gospel in order to bring it into line with 'modern thought'; they had ceased to believe in absolute theological definition or dogma; they were coming to believe that Christianity might have to learn how to survive without any ascertainable divine revelation at all.

This line of thought has to be traced back to Schleiermacher, who was one of a small group of Protestant theologians – the American, Horace Bushnell (1802–76), Kierkegaard and F. D. Maurice, for example – who were neither strictly liberal nor strictly orthodox (the word 'conservative' would often be more appropriate) and who, when they appealed to religious experience, did so on the assumption that experience would confirm what they still regarded as divine revelation, not provide a substitute.

Schleiermacher described Christian theology as the intellectual refinement of the Christian's redemption in Jesus Christ, a refinement related to the New Testament, but not unduly limited by its historically localized language. He took for granted that eighteenth-century criticism had weakened the authority of the New Testament, and that one should no longer use the Bible in the naive, non-historical fashion of seventeenth-century Lutheran dogmatists. (This recognition, however, had still not become finally established in the late twentieth century, and Karl Barth devoted his professional life to the assurance – rather than the proof – that Schleiermacher was wrong.) And he solved the problems raised by the Old Testament by arguing that 'we should entirely discard the Old Testament proofs for specifically Christian doctrines, preferring to put aside what chiefly rests on such support'. (Christian Faith, sect. 132.) The real meaning of the fact would be clearer, he said, if the Old Testament followed the New as an appendix, because the standard relative position of the two made it look as though one must first work one's way through the whole of the Old Testament if one was to approach the New by the right avenue. No more than his contemporaries was Schleiermacher able to cope theologically with the continuing existence of Judaism, but pressure to modify the orthodox Christian use of the Old Testament increased during the century.

In the opening sections of *The Christian Faith* Schleiermacher, over against Kant, argued for the trustworthiness of the subjective experience of absolute dependence which seemed to him the deepest element in human self-consciousness. It is generally agreed nowadays that 'a sense of being utterly dependent' is a better translation of *schlechtin abhängig*, the key phrase in the German, than the older version, 'a *feeling* of absolute dependence', because these words lead to Schleiermacher's being understood to refer to a shallow level of emotion quite distinct from the profound self-analysis to which he was directing attention. Nor was Schleiermacher adopting a pantheist position: he was saying that human self-consciousness included, and might even be summed up in, a sense of personal dependence on that which was outside and apart from the self, an experience which pointed overwhelmingly towards God. He made clear that he was not offering a proof of God's being (see *Christian Faith*, sec. 33). He defined the sense of utter dependence not as though it were an abstract proposition, but as an existential awareness that the whole of one's spontaneous activity came from a source outside oneself (see *Christian Faith*, sec. 4); this is best understood as Schleiermacher's paraphrase of the statement that in God we live and move and have our being. The consciousness of being absolutely dependent, he said, was the same thing as being in relation with God; on the other hand:

> any possibility of God being in any way *given* is entirely excluded, because anything that is outwardly given must be given as an object exposed to our counter-influence, however slight this may be. The transference of the idea of God to any perceptible object, unless one is all the time conscious that it is a piece of purely arbitrary symbolism, is always a corruption.[1]

Schleiermacher held that this primary relation with God was a universal element in human experience, and he explained the positive atheism of the eighteenth century by saying that while one source was no more than a sickness of the soul, a second and more important cause was 'a reasoned opposition to the current more or less inadequate representations of the religious consciousness. The atheism of the eighteenth century was for the most part a struggle against petrified, anthropomorphic representations of doctrine, a struggle provoked by the tyranny of the Church,' (*The Christian Faith*, sect. 33).

Christianity itself, however, could not have been worked out from this ultimate existential awareness of being in relation with God. 'There is only one source from which all Christian doctrine is derived, namely, the self-proclamation of Christ' (*The Christian Faith*, sect. 19). Christianity was distinguished from all other religions by the fact that in it everything was related to the redemption accomplished by Jesus of Nazareth (*Christian Faith*, sect. 11). In ordinary men the encounter between the divine and the human which was the underlying form of the human self-consciousness led only to unsatisfactory adumbrations of the relation between God and man. Jesus, however, had not just the normal human limited awareness of being in some kind of imperfect relation to God: in him the consciousness of God was so pure and entire that one might properly speak of God existing in him, something which could not be said of any other historical being. Of Jesus, Schleiermacher said, 'we posit the God-consciousness in his self-consciousness as continually and exclusively determining every moment, and consequently also the perfect indwelling of the Supreme Being as his peculiar being and inmost self' (*Christian Faith*, sect. 94). Christianity, therefore, did not develop from human self-understanding, or from purely human subjective aspiration after a possible god, but from God's prior act of existence in Jesus Christ, to which Christ himself bore witness in his proclamation of his relation to God.

Karl Barth, therefore, must be said to have been mistaken when he said, in his influential *Protestant Theology in the Nineteenth Century* (1952, E.T. 1972) that 'man, human self-awareness, determined namely as pious self-awareness, was undoubtedly the central subject of Schleiermacher's theological thought. In the very places where the theology of the Reformation

---

[1] F. Schleiermacher, *The Christian Faith*, ed. H. R. Mackintosh, p. 18, from 2nd German ed. 1830; 1st ed. 1821–22; I use this as the basis of Schleiermacher's mature view. See also R. B. Brandt, *The Philosophy of Schleiermacher* (Westport, Conn., U.S.A., 1941, repr. 1971).

had said "the Gospel" or "the Word of God" or "Christ" Schleiermacher, three hundred years after the Reformation, now says religion or piety . . . Schleiermacher reversed the order of this thought. What interests him is the question of man's action in regard to God.'[1] The idea of God acting creatively upon and within man through Christ was essential to Schleiermacher's system. Writing in 1917, Rudolf Bultmann, in many ways one of Schleiermacher's heirs, said that the Christian faith was a relationship of God to man 'which is achieved neither by rational considerations nor by natural necessities but by experiences which are given to man outside reason and nature, which overpower him, to which he surrenders himself freely, which he describes as revelation, grace; in which he knows that he is not independently creative, as in other areas of culture, but quite simply dependent'.[2] This theocentric emphasis was constantly present in Schleiermacher's dogmatics, and was characteristic of his christology, which was a courageous attempt to replace the static logical impossibilities of the chalcedonian Christ of the two natures with something more dynamic and more intelligible.

In Schleiermacher's account the existence of God in the Redeemer was posited as the fundamental power within him. Everything in him that was human simply constituted the organism for this fundamental and divine power, and was related to it in the same way as in ordinary people all other human powers were related to the controlling intelligence. Since the Redeemer's human activity depended entirely upon God's presence with him, it was reasonable, Schleiermacher argued, to say that in his case (and in his alone) God became man. His human life sprang out of the divine. (See *Christian Faith*, sect. 96, pp. 397–8).

Many German Protestant theologians followed Schleiermacher in his rejection of the Chalcedon settlement (see *Christian Faith*, sect. 95–97, pp. 389–413), including Ritschl and Troeltsch. His skill in moving between liberal necessities and conservative absolutes was also clear in his treatment of the doctrine of the Virgin Birth. To begin with, he said that the Redeemer could not have come into being through natural procreation, because he must not belong to the corporate life of human sinfulness. Moreover, 'the reproductive power of the species cannot be adequate to produce an individual through whom something is to be introduced for the first time into the species which was never in it before' (*Christian Faith*, sect. 97). To achieve the desired end one had to postulate, in addition to the reproductive power of the species, a creative activity combined with the human activity. 'In this sense anyone who assumes in the Redeemer a natural sinlessness' – and Schleiermacher argued that sinlessness was natural, not unnatural, to man – 'and a new creation through the union of the divine with the human, postulates a supernatural conception as well'. Nevertheless, the assumption of a virgin birth in the traditional sense was superfluous, because 'the being of God in life cannot be explained by its origin from a virgin without sexual intercourse'. Consequently, everything turned upon 'the higher influence which as a divine creative activity could alter

---

[1] K. Barth, *Protestant Theology in the Nineteenth Century* (ET 1972), pp. 458–59.

[2] W. Schmithals, *Introduction to Bultmann's Theology* (ET 1968), p. 8.

both the paternal and the maternal influence in such a way that all ground for sinfulness was removed, and this although procreation was perfectly natural . . . The general idea of a supernatural conception remains . . . essential and necessary if the specific pre-eminence of the Redeemer is to remain undiminished. But the more precise definition of this supernatural conception as one in which there was no male activity has no connection of any kind with the essential elements in the peculiar dignity of the Redeemer; and hence, in and by itself, is no constituent part of Christian doctrine.'

Schleiermacher allowed that one might accept the traditional doctrine on the ground of the narratives contained in the New Testament, but anyone who could not accept these stories as literally and historically true was still free to hold a doctrine of the supernatural conception constructed along the lines which Schleiermacher suggested. In the same way, belief in the traditional doctrines of Jesus's resurrection, descent into Hell, ascension and return in judgment was not an independent element in the original faith in Christ, of such a kind that one could not accept him as the redeemer or recognize the being of God in him if one did not know that he had risen from the dead and ascended into heaven and so forth: all that was required from a Protestant, Schleiermacher said, was that he believe in these stories as far as he thought they were adequately attested in the New Testament – a conclusion which meant that these propositions belonged to the area of biblical studies – where they would remain indefin-itely – and not to the doctrine of the Person of Christ at all (*Christian Faith*, sect. 99).

Schleiermacher, that is, was discounting the impact of biblical criticism before many Catholics or Protestants had begun to feel its full power. He sought to persuade his contemporaries that they did not have to defend the literal and historical sense of every New Testament story, as though the truth or untruth of Christianity as a religion of redemption through Jesus Christ depended upon the credibility, for instance, of the resurrection stories as traditionally understood – a position as hazardous, though often adopted in the mid-twentieth century, as that which committed the cause of Victorian Christianity to the historical reliability of the Genesis creation-stories. On the one hand, the basic element in 'religion' (the sense of utter dependence) was a universal and necessary part of human experience; it could exist without either the knowledge of, or assent to, doctrines as such, because it was an immediate existential relation to God. On the other hand, given that every human being had an innate capacity for being religious, 'Christianity' in particular was the result of the play of Jesus's perfect religious consciousness on the developing religious consciousness of those human beings who were brought within the field of influence of the Christian tradition. From Schleiermacher's point of view, his systematic theology was an empirical description of the experience of those who had been redeemed by the activity of Christ and made members of a spiritual community whose creative energy came from Christ. He could therefore demonstrate inadequacies in both the New Testament and traditional theological systems by comparing them with the empirical evidence of experience. For him, the New Testament was simply the original but not inherently final attempt to describe the nature of Christian redemption, while documents like the Creeds and the Confessions of the Reformation tradition (which he discussed at length in *The Christian Faith*)[1] were equally imperfect attempts to reduce piety to language, a process which frequently confused philosophical and religious method.

The value of Schleiermacher's enterprise depended, of course, on the question of the relationship between religion and philosophy. At times in *The Christian Faith* he seemed only to claim that theology was a description of the content and convictions of the religious consciousness, and did not raise the question of their truth. At other times, he seemed to assert that a religious person had a direct experience of the divine object, and that this made religion independent of philosophy. In the second instance, he has been criticized for not clearly facing the issue of the truth or falsity of the claim: to do so would have taken him back into philosophical territory.[2]

If one says that Schleiermacher was neither strictly liberal nor strictly orthodox, but perhaps 'conservative', it is because a candid reading of *The Christian Faith* leaves the impression that Schleiermacher was trying to restate in acceptable ethical and psychological terms as much as possible of the traditional doctrinal pattern, in which a more than human Christ redeemed the human race from sin and bound it together in a new company of perfect love: this was the barest possible summary of the Christian 'myth', without which a recognizable Christian tradition would have ceased to exist; that it was not easy to demonstrate the truth of the myth did not mean that it was no more than false. Thus he could write: 'Just as the redemptive activity of Christ brings about for all believers a corporate activity corresponding to the being of God in Christ, so the reconciling element, that is, the blessedness of the being of God in him, brings about for all believers, as for each separately, a corporate feeling of blessedness.' In this spiritual process their former personality, the 'old man' of traditional theology, died, to be replaced by a new kind of self-identity, which owed its whole existence to the creative activity of Christ. A 'new man' took the place of the old, a 'new man' who, nevertheless, somehow retained continuity with his individual past. There was no question of the redeemed losing their identity in a vague, corporate holiness; instead, they attained a new kind of individuality, perfectly related to one another in Christ (*Christian Faith*, sect. 101, p. 436).

Such an exposition was based entirely, Schleiermacher said, on the inner experience of the believer; it could make no claim to be proof of the absolute truth of what was stated; but unless something like this was the case there would be no special possession of divine grace in Christianity at all. This distinction between a moral consciousness (the chief ground of the liberal position) and a state of consciousness which was held to contain an immediate experience of God, linked Schleiermacher with conservatives like Coleridge, Maurice and Kierkegaard. His position was much closer to orthodoxy than the rather vague appeal to the Spirit of Jesus as a divine

---

[1] See e.g. Section 109, pp. 496–505, where Schleiermacher comments on the doctrine of justification.

[2] See R. B. Brandt, *op. cit.*, pp. 294–98.

agent of change, an Arnoldian moral leader with a programme as well as a method, which was to characterize late-nineteenth-century liberalism. Both, in turn, were menaced by the tightening, in Germany in particular, of the anti-supernatural screw, first by Ludwig Feuerbach (1804–72), the materialist philosopher, who said in *The Essence of Christianity* (1841, E.T. by George Eliot, 1854) that men made themselves unhappy by projecting as an idea of 'God' a dream of human perfection which they could never realize, and that so-called 'religious experiences', while real enough, were nevertheless no more than subjective: Feuerbach, however, like some twentieth-century Christian liberals, assumed that 'religious' behaviour was part of the essence of human nature, and would continue even when deprived of its supernatural object. Second, by Karl Marx (1818–83), in his *Critique of Hegel's Philosophy of Right* (1844) and the *Theses on Feuerbach* (1845), who said that the religious sentiment was not a matter of individual psychology, as Feuerbach thought, but a social product. Certainly, man made religion and not religion man, but he did so only because the conditions of a particular society in historical time alienated him from his potential self. Religion might be the sigh of the oppressed but it was also the opium of the people. To ask men to give up their religious comforts and illusions was to ask them to give up the social conditions which made the illusions necessary. Revolutionize the society and religions would disappear, because it would no longer be socially generated.

Although few orthodox theologians can have read Marx they were aware that the connection between the 'natural' and the 'supernatural' had somehow to be maintained, and it is significant that this was a period of intense christological ingenuity. G. Thomasius (1802–75) and W. R. Gess (1819–71), among others, proposed a kenotic ('self-divesting') christology, in which they implied that the Eternal Son suppressed as much of his divinity during his earthly life as was necessary to make the idea of the incarnation credible theologically in the nineteenth century. In Gess's version the suppression was actually total, so that throughout his Palestinian existence the Eternal Son was simply a man. This was a desperate, unorthodox orthodoxy, aware that a case had to be made for the divinity of Christ but driven to make it by emphasizing his humanity. Moreover, romantic moves to revive the great theological systems of the past in order to establish the roots of modern orthodoxy in heroic soil, such as one sees in Anglo-Catholicism and Anglican Evangelicalism, or in the German Reformed 'Mercersburg Theology' in the United States (1844–53), failed in so far as they were unable to restate the supernatural argument convincingly. In British terms the change of mood could be seen clearly in the bitterness with which H. P. Liddon (1829–90), a rigid Anglo-Catholic of Keble's school, who had produced in *The Divinity of Our Lord and Saviour Jesus Christ* (1867) a consciously naive, biblicist and patristic, orthodox christology, received as a betrayal the belated kenotic speculations of Charles Gore (1853–1932) in the collection of Anglo-Catholic essays, *Lux Mundi* (1889). It was obviously not an accident that Gore belonged to the generation of Anglo-Catholics who preached Christian Socialism and founded monastic orders, just as Ritschl, though anti-socialist politically, vaguely identified the Kingdom of God with a regenerated world-common-wealth and, in abandoning Chalcedon, substituted a moral appraisal of a traditionally visualized New Testament Jesus who was held to have the value of God for the mind of faith. A slow shift of interest was taking place from what had in the past been believed or felt about a supernatural Christ, to what could be allegedly recognized as evidence that God (or Christ) was at work in the world.

This shift of interest stranded – as far as fashion went – the great conservatives of the period, Kierkegaard and Newman; even Maurice owed his nineteenth-century influence to his social teaching (see p. 548). For Maurice, who combined a Platonic epistemology with biblical ideas of God as the personal will of love acting in and through Christ, was convinced that man could participate in the eternal world when the true knowledge of reality was given him by Christ.[1] This was why he reacted so violently against the Oxford philosopher of religion, H. L. Mansel (1820–71) when he said in *The Limits of Religious Thought Examined* (1859) that man's knowledge was conditioned by time and space and that therefore he could not conceive God as he truly is; neither a sense of dependence nor a sense of moral obligation contained a direct intuition of God, but that men were entirely dependent for real knowledge of God on an objective, divine self-revelation, by which Mansel meant the Bible. 'Religion, to be a relation between God and Man at all, must rest on a belief in the Infinite, and also on a belief in the Finite: if we deny the first, there is no God; and if we deny the second, there is no Man. But the co-existence of the Infinite and the Finite in any manner whatever is inconceivable by reason; and the only ground that can be taken for accepting one representation of it rather than another, is that one is revealed and the other is not revealed.'[2] Strictly speaking, Mansel regarded the Bible, Old as well as New Testament, as set apart from any kind of criticism, to be accepted or rejected as revelation; but since he held that speculative theology was only a product of man's limited reason, he thought of the Bible as containing what he called 'representative revelation', revelation, that is, by means of symbols drawn from human experience, anthropomorphic, and therefore inevitably less than a full revelation of the nature of God. Mansel's book was a sign of what was to come philosophically; indeed, it probably helps to explain why Matthew Arnold was so willing to criticize the freedom with which many Victorian theologians talked of their 'knowledge' of God.

For Maurice, however, as for Coleridge, it was axiomatic that all men possessed a faculty by which they could attain direct communion with God, provided they reached out toward him and let him impart it. In Kantian terms, Maurice simply asserted that God gave men the direct knowledge of himself which the Pure Reason could not obtain according to Kant, because it was limited to regulative or constitutive ideas which had only an empirical use and could not be extended to objects which transcended experience, like God. Maurice's efforts to defend his position rarely got

---

[1] T. B. Christensen, *The Divine Order, a Study in F. D. Maurice's Theology* (Leiden 1973), pp. 65–73.

[2] H. L. Mansel, *The Limits of Religious Thought Examined* (1859), p. 125.

further than a vague mysticism: 'There is a light within you, close to you . . . Turn from these idols that are surrounding you – from the confused, dark world of thoughts within you. It will reveal itself to you . . . I mean a reality; I mean that which has to do with your innermost being; I mean something which does not proceed from you or belong to you; but which is there searching you and judging you . . . I mean that this light comes from a Person . . . from the Word, the Son of God . . . Turn and confess his presence. You have always had it with you.'[1]

At this point, at which the familiar Victorian attempt to personalize conscience – it was the core, for example, of Newman's *Grammar of Assent* (1870) – was transformed into the assertion that the Person of Christ was always actively present in each individual, one is reminded of Schleiermacher's idea of salvation, and there were other similarities, in Maurice's implicit universalism and vigorous rejection of penal substutionary theories of the atonement. Both men had a profound belief in the existence of a Divine Order (as opposed to disorder) which had to be revealed (not restored). In the long run, however, it was Maurice's *social* exposition of his principles which found disciples (see p. 533); it was only in the twentieth century that A. M. Ramsey, for instance,[2] praised Maurice for holding the 'classic' conception of the Cross as the divine victory over the powers of evil. The Danish authority on Maurice, T. B. Christensen (in 1973) criticized this assertion on the ground that the 'classic' theory presupposed exactly the kind of *disorder* in the universe which Maurice found theologically incredible.[3] Maurice's brilliant combination of the Bible and Plato, Christensen concluded, had not exercised any great influence on the emergence and shaping of modern English theology. This was partly because Maurice did not cope adequately with the problem of the authority of the Bible, and partly because later theologians (von Hügel being the obvious exception) did not find Platonism a solution to their difficulties with contemporary philosophy. Much the same comment might be made on Coleridge, whose influence in this field has been exaggerated, especially by literary critics.

Although Soeren Kierkegaard was a greater writer and theologian than Maurice, he was equally isolated in the nineteenth century. He started with the handicap of writing in Danish, but even if he had been translated more quickly he would probably still have been disregarded, for he not only denied that the God of Danish Lutheranism had any significant relation to the God of Luther, but he also rejected the Hegelian alternative of a God identifiable with, and discoverable in, the historical process. Moreover, he remained faithful to the eighteenth-century pietist tradition at the very time – 1800 to 1848 – when Pietism in general, and German Pietism of the Hengstenberg era in particular, was abandoning its old indifference to social and political concerns and becoming the staunch ally of those who were resisting political change, a development which reached a fateful climax in 1848 when most Protestant leaders opposed the liberal political revolutions.

[1] F. D. Maurice, *Theological Essays* (1853), pp. 117–18.
[2] See A. M. Ramsey, *F. D. Maurice and the Conflicts of Modern Theology* (1951).
[3] Christensen, esp. pp. 197–220.

Kierkegaard was nearer the heart of the Pietist tradition when he claimed that the demands of God, properly understood, could only destroy society in any normal form. It was not possible, he said, to love God in the Christian sense and to be happy in this world. With a very different emphasis from Maurice's, he said that the Christian God was in opposition to the fallen creation; indeed, Kierkegaard's late enthusiasm for celibacy was a way of expressing this position: Christianity was not only salvation from the human race, but it also aimed at stopping the human process.

For Kierkegaard was so far outside the contemporary approach to truth through history – to be found in Hegel, Marx, Spencer, and even Maurice when, as in *The Kingdom of Christ* (1838), he upheld both the nation and the British Established Church as divine institutions serving divine purposes – that he denied that Christianity had any history at all after the historical paradox of its origin, that the eternal came into existence *once* in time (see *Authority and Revelation*, E.T. Princeton 1955). Christendom, by which he meant the unity of state, religion and society which had been so familiar to Europe as to be accepted without question as of divine origin, might have had a history, but this was irrelevant, except in so far as it tempted men to rely on 'the faith of their fathers' for salvation, instead of facing the New Testament for themselves and Christ as their contemporary. For Kierkegaard, Christianity-as-Truth had been revealed once and for all, and historical time was dangerous, because the human apprehension of divine truth actually appeared to lessen as time went on: nineteenth-century Danish Lutheranism was further from the New Testament truth than Luther himself had been.

As for Hegel, his assertion that divine truth was not given once and for all, but unfolded itself gradually through the history of the race and the universe, inevitably involved a claim to judge the Christ-event itself, when it was by the Christ-event that men themselves were to be tested. In effect, by saying that absolute truth appeared only at the end of the historical process, Hegel relativized truth at any particular point of time, and Marx dramatized this when, in *The Communist Manifesto* (1848), he relativized the leading ideas of any epoch as being only the ideas of its ruling class. Both subsumed the individual in the general history of race and class, denying that he could experience any kind of eternal truth for himself.

Kierkegaard reversed this. The Christian category was the single person – the individual denied reality if he hid himself in history, or merged himself in a race or a class or a church. This was the meaning of the assertion that subjectivity was truth, that Christianity was not another system of knowledge to be studied, but a paradox, an absurdity, to be believed. The absurd was that eternal truth had come into being in time, that God had come into being, had been born, had grown up, and so forth, precisely like any other individual human being (see *Concluding Unscientific Postscript*, E.T. Princeton 1941, p. 188). Only by becoming a Christian could one 'know' Christianity. Becoming a Christian meant the setting-up in a leap of faith of an existential relationship between the self and the God-Man. This relation to Christ, though passionately inward, did not mean for Kierkegaard the discovery of an immanent 'ground of being' in the self, an idea with a long history which Paul Tillich revived in the twentieth century. That kind of immanent religious consciousness would have seemed to Kierkegaard only a step towards a truly Christian faith, which he always described as a relation to that which was outside the anguished, suffering, consciously sinful self. An absolute, passionately inward devotion to the Absolute relativized the finite, but it did not relativize the Absolute. And the end of the relationship was a new creation of the self, a gift of God, and radically discontinuous with the old.

It is not hard to see why Kierkegaard had little influence on Victorian theology. He could understand the liberal tradition, but he did not sympathize with it, because its kind of Kantian base excluded the existentialism which he developed. Nor was he attracted by an orthodox liturgical revival like Anglo-Catholicism. And while other conservatives, Maurice and Newman for example, wanted to restore the Church, Protestant or Catholic, to its pre-revolutionary rôle as the source and arbiter of morals, education, and training in social obedience, Kierkegaard attacked Christendom because he believed that religious institutions were bound to connive at social man's desire to replace truly primitive Christianity (which meant the renunciation of the earthly), with a religion which legitimized the disappearance of renunciation. More powerful secular movements, such as nationalism and various forms of socialism, appealed to men as mass in motion; Kierkegaard could only appeal to individual people's inward restlessness. Even in the twentieth century, when he became famous as one of the precursors of existentialism, he was more the subject of academic theses than of theological attention. Simone Weil was his nearest modern equivalent, but not his disciple. In both, much more than in any other theological writers of their period, isolated readers found a passionate inward grasp of the being of God and the immorality of man.

Roman Catholic theology in the nineteenth century suffered the same inner conflicts which have just been described in the case of Protestantism, but the process was complicated by the rapid revival of the papacy as the centre of Catholic authority after 1815. Nineteenth-century popes sharply opposed theological liberalism; even Newman's conservatism had a cool reception in Rome; Pius IX (1846–78) actually tried to strengthen the position of orthodoxy by making it more explicit. A few theologians might have ecclesiastical influence, but the reigning pope had power, and this was used, both at the first Vatican Council, and in the Modernist crisis after 1900, against any attempt to modify the orthodox concept of revelation; conservatism was distrusted, because its primary appeal to religious experience was seen as unwise and unnecessary.

The official condemnation of the resolutions of the liberal synod of Pistoia (1786) has usually been interpreted as the closure of the account marked Jansenism and Febronianism; in fact, however, the anti-clerical atmosphere of nineteenth-century north-Italian nationalism may be traced back partly to the failure of the Enlightenment campaign for ecclesiastical reform. As a whole, the Roman Church emerged from the Napoleonic wars weakened in France, Spain and Italy: hence, for example, the French

Catholic demand for the restoration of church property seized during the Revolution, and for a conscious repudiation of the ideology of the Revolution itself; but neither the property nor the national repentance was really forthcoming. Theologically, Rome itself continued to assert the traditional doctrine of the divinely-given authority of the teaching Church. The seminaries, which had been one of the targets of the synod of Pistoia, remained isolated in a seventeenth-century intellectual universe long after 1815. Chateaubriand's (1768–1848) romantic invocation of the rôle of Roman Catholicism in the European past, *Le Génie du Christianisme* (1802), had no theological force, but the appeal to authority, the authority of the past, was typical of the Catholic mind at this period. Lamennais' *Essai sur L'Indifférence en matière de religion* (vol 1, 1817; vol 2, 1820), similarly urged men to put aside the claims of their own individual reason, and to trust instead to the general reason, or *sensus communis,* to what humanity, guided by God, had always understood and believed, a religion which the Catholicism of Jesus had finally and fully revealed. In the long run Lamennais substituted the authority of the race for the authority of the pope, and abandoned Roman Catholicism for the Deism and revolutionary politics which were already logically implicit in the *Essai.*[1] Those who had doubted his orthodoxy from the start could argue that they had been justified; those who suspected J. H. Newman's *Essay on the Development of Christian Doctrine* (1845) of unsoundness were less evidently proved correct.

In Roman Catholic teaching as it was defined at the commencement of the nineteenth century revelation was defined as the content of the Old and New Testaments understood in the medium of tradition and expounded in the Church, through the Creeds, the Patristic writers, the Councils (including Trent) and specific papal pronouncements. Nothing could be added to the basic material, nor could there by any question of any new divinely revealed material. For the scholastic theologian dogmatic change took place through the logical elucidation of this original data. Since Newman was not convinced that theological change or development could be defended in this way, he needed a theory which would answer the Protestant assertion that Roman Catholicism had made illegitimate additions (the Marian theology, for example) to the original deposit of necessary faith. Once proposed, the theory had also to accommodate the papal proclamation of the dogma of the immaculate conception of the Virgin Mary (*Ineffabilis Deus,* 1854), and the first Vatican Council's definition of the infallibility of the papacy (*Pastor Aeternus,* 1870).

Newman broke with the view that theological development was a matter of logic. He took as his model the development of an *idea,* and described the process as the germination, growth and perfection of some living truth in the minds of men over a sufficient period of time. Put in this way, the development of the *idea* of Christianity might seem dangerously subjective, but Newman thought of this essentially divine idea as regulative, living its own life, gradually excluding false developments and extending itself in the

---

[1] For Lamennais, see the section on *Social Theology.* For the more strictly philosophical aspects of nineteenth-century French Catholic thought, see *Liberalism and Tradition,* B. Reardon (1975).

human consciousness. Once again one has the post-Kantian attempt to unite subjective experience with an objective self-giving of the Absolute; Newman tried to weaken the risk of subjectivity by saying that the developmental process took place in the mind of the whole Church, laity included. And there was, in any case, the organ of infallibility which, divinely guided, protected men troubled by the ambiguities of theological discussion, or tempted by the arrogant wilfulness of an unilluminated human reason. As a general defence of the possibility of some kind of doctrinal development the theory was persuasive, especially when Newman spoke of the Church as the most sacred and august of poets;[1] but it offered little help to those who were quite prepared to believe that the dogma of the Assumption of the Virgin had developed historically, being probably unknown before the fourth century, but who interpreted its germination, growth, and perfection as a constant development away from the original idea of Christianity.[2] In such a case, Newman's theory was too elastic to mollify Protestant suspicion, and his emphasis on the need to consult the laity in the process of infallible definition did not seem a significant safeguard. It was hardly surprising that conversations in the 1970s between Anglican and Roman Catholic theologians made no process on subjects like infallibility. Within the Roman Church, however, Newman's view of development became a powerful engine in the hands of those who, without approaching what in Protestant terms would have been a liberal position, wanted to make Roman Catholicism more open to change, and who welcomed the fresh impetus given by the second Vatican Council. Even so, by the 1970s theories of development in general were losing their charm. Coherent versions of human history as guided towards a goal, whether Catholic, Marxist or Protestant, seemed to lack plausibility. The world seemed more as it had seemed to Soeren Kierkegaard, for whom Christ was simply a contemporary, neither developed from the past, nor developing into the future; or to Simone Weil, for whom the apparent momentum of history was a force to resist. Through the eighteenth and nineteenth centuries, justification by development had been a popular move in both conservative and liberal circles; now the idea looked more obviously imposed on the past than derived from it.

Officially, however, the Roman Catholic Church reaffirmed orthodox intransigence under Pius IX, who had suffered from political liberalism in the Roman revolution of 1848–49. In the *Syllabus Errorum* of December, 1864, Pius condemned eighty propositions which he considered typical of the errors of mid-century Italy and Europe in general. The *Syllabus* attracted attention above all because of its famous eightieth condemnation, when Pius denied that he either could or should reconcile himself to, or agree with, progress, liberalism, and civilization as they were then fashionably defined. In Italian terms the *Syllabus* meant that the Pope would not agreed to Piedmontese demands for a secular education system and the

---

[1] J. H. Newman, *Essays Critical and Historical*, vol. 2 (1901), p. 442. Originally written in 1846.

[2] The Assumption was defined *ex cathedra* by Pius XII in 1950 in *Munificentissimus Deus*.

abolition of monasticism, that he would not make peace with the coolly triumphant, anticlerical Cavour. Some interpreters have said that no wider application existed in Pius' mind, but the decision of the first Vatican Council to proclaim the infallibility of the Pope when speaking *ex cathedra* on matters of faith or morals, put the earlier statement in its proper perspective.

The unification of Italy as a typical modern state underlined the failure of the social and political restoration of 1815; the eighteenth-century campaign for freedom from the Church was still continuing, and with growing success. The new, middle-class states were setting up civil, largely secular education systems and introducing legislation to sanction civil marriage and divorce. The modern state was freeing itself from organized religion, something which Jansenism had not foreseen, and which the ecclesiastics who had believed that they had 'defeated' Jansenism had not foreseen either. In the circumstances, Pius IX's assertion that the Catholic Church and the Papacy were the essential element in western (and by implication, all human) society, was inevitable. In 1864–70 the Pope seemed to be saying that orthodoxy was directly and permanently opposed to human progress in the widest meaning of the words; but the opposition looked natural to Pius because he could not voluntarily accept the reduction of Christianity to one among several religious options, and one to which society no longer admitted any official, absolute obligation. (In fact, of course, many Protestants, in England for example, also resisted every manifestation of the separation of Church and State.) Pius IX was himself personally committed to a papal form of definition of the infallibility of the Church, but he was in any case bound to insist on some kind of declaration of theological *certainty* – not to have done so would have seemed to him a surrender of the Roman Church's theological claim to be the channel and servant of a unique, divine revelation. From the orthodox point of view, infallibility was always involved in the struggle with religious liberalism, and this was just as true in Protestantism as in Catholicism. To agree that religious *certainty* was unavailable, either in terms of religious experience or as dogmatic definition, was to shift the locus of religion from the divine to the human, and to banish doctrines like that of the Trinity to the wilderness of speculation.

Pius IX, that is, was not a 'reactionary' as a theologian; rather, he made it clear that orthodoxy was at risk and had to be defended. He refused any premature surrender of the principle that all human life, individual and corporate, was lived within a hierarchical, divinely ordered structure, within which salvation was thought of as 'coming down from heaven' in the Person of Christ, who took flesh and lived among men, but whose capacity to redeem the human race depended on his being divine. For Christ to be a cosmic saviour he must also be a cosmic figure; humanity alone was not equal to the task of restoring or revealing a world-order on a supernatural scale. It was of the essence of the traditional theology that one be intensely suspicious of any proposal for change which had no better authority than the critical use of the human mind. As far as Pius IX and Pius X (1835–1914, Pope from 1903) were concerned, revelation had been given once and for all in the mission of Christ, and had been given clearly in language which stood for ever immune from historicizing forces. Some kind of development of doctrine was tolerable if it meant no more than building extensions to the system; Catholic Modernism, however, had to be resisted, because it implied that one might pull part of the building down.

It was all the more unfortunate that the precipitating factor in the controversy was the attempt by the liberal Protestant ecclesiastical historian, Adolf Harnack (1851–1930), to tackle the problem of theological change in his very successful book, *What is Christianity?* (1900). Harnack tried to make way for change in a characteristic manner which could be traced back to John Locke and the eighteenth-century reductionists. He dismissed the doctrinal elaboration of Christianity in favour of a minimal, allegedly primitive Christian gospel: 'God the Father, Providence, the position of men as God's children, the infinite value of the human soul, (in these) the whole Gospel is expressed'. He extended the sixteenth-century rejection of medieval theology to cover Protestant classicism as well. Perhaps it was the best that he could do, but one is reminded of Newman's epigram, that many a man would live and die upon a dogma, but no man would be a martyr for a conclusion. And Harnack's conclusion was that neither the gospel as systematic theology, nor the Church as a visible institution, nor the Christological dogma as traditionally received, were really part of Jesus's message: it was a case, Harnack said, not of distortion but of total perversion; Catholicism was superfluous and Protestantism only half-reformed. Harnack's was a brilliant presentation of the liberal view of Christianity as the product of the creative insights of the essentially human moral consciousness of Jesus. Indirectly, of course, Harnack was challenging all theories of development, including Newman's, on the ground that development ought not to have taken place.

This was a traditional Protestant argument, which played an important part in the Reformation, but it left Harnack wide open to the reply of Alfred Loisy (1857–1940, a Catholic biblical scholar, in *The Gospel and the Church* (*L'Évangile et L'Église*, 1902). Loisy said that of course, if one started from an abstract, unreal conception of revelation and dogma, one ended by condemning all the results of Christian reflection on Christianity. Clearly, if the unchangeable essence of the Gospel was simply faith in God the Father, then all the later development of Christianity, in doctrine, ecclesiastical order and liturgy, became a vast aberration. However, quite apart from the fact that the Gospel could not be reduced to such a simple faith, it was absurd to suppose that the proclamation of the Gospel could either remain unchanged, or be regarded as unchangeable: Christian doctrinal development was bound to take place, and was therefore legitimate in principle. Taken as a whole, development had served the Gospel, which would not have survived as a rarefied essence but which, perpetually translated into living doctrine, had gone on living through these doctrines, a result which legitimized development as a matter of fact.

The strength of Loisy's position in relation to Harnack, though not in relation to Catholic orthodoxy, was that he was prepared to distinguish between the overall effects of change, which he was ready to defend, and particular instances of development which he might regard as regrettable or mistaken. But while this flexibility made his conception of development more sophisticated than Newman's, it brought him into conflict with Rome. A small group of Catholic intellectuals, including Loisy, the philosopher Maurice Blondel (1861–1949), Lucien Laberthonnière (1860–1932), George Tyrrell (1861–1909) and Friedrich von Hügel (1852–1925) all shared a common disapproval of the intransigeance with which Catholic orthodoxy faced the modern world. Their agreement did not go much further, and it is an exaggeration to speak of a 'Modernist movement'; neither Blondel nor von Hügel, for example, was as committed to the need for theological change as were Loisy and Tyrrell, though both were impressed by the achievements of nineteenth-century Protestant biblical scholarship.

By 1902, in fact, Loisy had already reached the furthest point of the developmental argument. The earlier dogmas, he said, were rooted in the preaching and ministry of Christ and in the experience of the Church; they found their development in the history of Christianity and in theological reflection, and it could not have been otherwise. And what was no less natural was that creeds and dogmatic definitions should be *en rapport* with the general state of human knowledge at the time and the social context in which they were drawn up. It followed, however, that any considerable change in the state of knowledge would make necessary a fresh interpretation of the original formulae, and such a change had been taking place steadily since the beginning of the eighteenth century. One had now to distinguish between the material sense of the formulae – the sense in which they had been *en rapport* with the current ideas of the Ancient World into which Jesus was born – and their fundamental religious meaning, which could still be reconciled with modern views of existence and the nature of things.[1] 'Only truth is immutable', Loisy wrote, 'but not the image of truth in our minds. Faith holds to this unchanging truth by means of formulae which are inevitably inadequate, capable of improvement, and consequently alterable . . . The Church does not require faith in its formulae as though they were the adequate expression of absolute truth, but presents them as the least imperfect expression of the truth which is morally possible.'[2]

It was not surprising that Loisy was felt to have gone too far, and that the anti-Modernist Decree, *Lamentabili* (1907), specifically condemned Loisy's historical relativism, rejecting, for example, the proposition that some articles of the Apostles' Creed (Loisy had instanced the descent of Christ into Hell) did not have the same meaning for twentieth-century Christians as they had had for Christians in the primitive period. Pius X wanted to lay down, not only that the original dogmatic language must be retained, but that the original intention of the words (about which the authors of the encyclical apparently had no problem) must also be accepted. In *Christianity at the Cross-Roads* (1909), actually published after his death, Tyrrell, who had learned from Loisy to see the gospels in eschatological terms, attacked such theological immobilism with specific reference to Jesus himself. What, Tyrrell asked, were the categories and concepts of Jesus to

[1] Alfred Loisy, *L'Evangile et L'Eglise* (1902), pp. 161–65.
[2] *ib.* pp. 166, 174.

men now? Were they to frame their minds to that of a first-century Jewish carpenter for whom (the echo of Nietzsche was obvious) more than half the world and nearly the whole of its history did not exist; who cared nothing for art or science or history or politics or nine-tenths of the interests of humanity, but solely for the Kingdom of God and its righteousness? It was the spirit of Jesus that mattered, not the religious ideas and apocalyptic imagery which were that spirit's inadequate embodiment.[1]

In such an utterance Tyrrell rejected the conservative Catholic concept of development (that theological ideas could grow, but had always to remain consistent with their past). The view of change which he was advocating (that when theology grew it cast off its past as part of the process) cut the ground from under the liberal Protestant idea of development as well. In a choice which ranged over Strauss, Renan, Nietzsche, Arnold, Weiss, Liddon and Loisy, the 'spirit of Jesus' became indefinable. Tyrrell died in conflict with the official Church, Loisy withdrew after excommunication in 1908; it was not surprising that von Hügel gave up a struggle for which he had no intellectual enthusiasm – he was not committed to a 'modernist' theological view, but only to a campaign for freer research and discussion, and this Pius X would not tolerate.

In Catholic terms, this left obedience to the Church as the channel and interpreter of revelation as the only resource, and Pius XII was to reiterate this position as late as 1950 in his encyclical, *Humani Generis*. Modernism was not really vindicated until the second Vatican Council (1962–65). The controversial *Declaration on Religious Freedom* contained the conclusion: 'It is therefore in accord with the nature of faith that in matters religious every manner of coercion on the part of men should be excluded.'[2] This statement reversed the traditional teaching of the Roman Church on religious liberty, and indirectly repudiated the *Syllabus of Errors*. It could not be squared very convincingly with Newman's view of development, because the jettisoning of the past involved a discontinuity which amounted to contradiction. This willingness to go beyond the possibilities of theological development by slow, consistent aggregation, and to accept that contradiction might be the result of sudden but nevertheless valid, radical religious change, was the core of Modernism as Loisy and Tyrrell understood it. And when the Declaration began by saying that a sense of the dignity of the human person had been impressing itself more and more deeply on the consciousness of contemporary man, it was pointing, as Loisy had pointed, to the importance of the human cultural background of theological statements. Historically, the Declaration reflected the emergence of the United States as a Catholic power.

Any attempt to assess the significance of the second Vatican Council would still be premature, but theologically, the significant element seemed to be the recognition of co-existence as intellectual and ecclesiastical possibility. Broadly, the Council affirmed: the co-existence of the Roman

---

[1] G. Tyrrell, *Christianity at the Cross-Roads* (3 ed., 1910), p. 270.

[2] W. M. Abbott, ed., *The Documents of Vatican II* (New York, 1966), p. 690. One of the principal authors of the Declaration was an American Jesuit, John Courtney Murray (1904–67).

Church with other Churches and with secular political philosophies like Marxism; the co-existence of the idea of revelation as the unique self-disclosure of God in Christianity with science (as in biology, where conflict between the magisterium and Catholic biologists has been reduced to a minimum);[1] and co-existence of the traditional dogmatic system, especially where the doctrine of Christ is concerned, with great practical freedom for Catholic biblical scholars.

---

[1] See Wolfhart Pannenberg, *Theology and the Philosophy of Science* (1976), for the most exhaustive recent attempt to examine the 'scientific' status of revelation. For Catholic teaching on evolution, see K. Rahner, *Hominisation* (1965).

III

THE DOCTRINE OF THE CHURCH IN
THE WHOLE PERIOD

Two topics require special consideration in this discussion of modern theology. One is the doctrine of the Church, the other is what may be called social theology, the analysis of the relations between Church and society. In the case of the doctrine of the Church, the nineteenth and twentieth centuries have seen an astonishing variety of ideas, ranging from defences of the highest views of Papal supremacy to the conclusion that one may dispense with the Church altogether. The ecumenical movement has also affected the theological description of the Church. As for social theology, the nineteenth century witnessed a gradual but drastic revolution in theological opinion, the abandonment of the ancient western view that society already expressed the divine will and ought not to be radically changed, and the adoption of the view that society was necessarily in permanent flux and that theology must come to terms with a perpetually altering social structure. We shall examine the history of the doctrine of the Church first.

One may distinguish between the immediate social situation which underlies and explains the formation of a particular doctrine of the Church and the way in which this doctrine is then established within the intellectual tradition and discussed by later theologians in an essentially abstract manner which divorces the theological definitions from their origins. Thus any discussion of the fate of the doctrine of the Church in the eighteenth century must come to terms with the Methodist movement because the Methodists represented the obvious eighteenth-century challenge to accepted ways of thinking about ecclesiastical institutions. John Wesley's basic principle was that dogma took precedence over institutions. The purpose of ecclesiastical institutions was primarily to guard purity of dogma, to organize evangelism and to foster the converts. Existing eighteenth-century Anglican institutions, including the episcopate, were theoretically adequate to do this and might therefore be accepted and obeyed as long as they were faithful to their responsibilities, but if the existing institutions neither ensured purity of doctrine nor evangelized in terms of it, but tolerated a clergy which Wesley, in his sharper mood, could dismiss as ignorant of doctrine and idle in evangelism, then one had both the duty and the right to form new institutions.

Wesley did not regard this as involving schism; he neither unchurched the Church of England nor intended to set up a new national Church. To argue as to whether Wesley himself did or did not intend his followers to separate from the Church of England is to miss the point. He meant them to use Wesleyan institutions to guard and spread the Wesleyan interpretation of the Anglican tradition as contained in the Homilies and the Articles – and he believed the Wesleyan interpretation of these to be the 'pure' one, whose preservation was all important as against either the true High Church or Evangelical Anglican interpretations – until the Establishment reformed itself along similar lines, when the Methodist institutions might dissolve themselves. Wesley did not suppose that he was laying the foundations of permanent institutions which contained the absolute truth in themselves, as had earlier non-episcopal Protestants from the Society of Friends to the Presbyterians; but he thought of himself as creating temporary institutions, pragmatically designed and intended to shelter doctrines which were absolutely true. It is obvious, however, that John Wesley did not consider that episcopacy was one of these eternal truths or he could not have acted as he did. Nor can his behaviour be squared with the theology of obedience to ecclesiastical authority which John Henry Newman taught in his Roman Catholic days. Wesley was practising rather than advocating a theology of pragmatic disobedience. It is interesting to compare Wesley's position with the argument which Newman advanced in the *Apologia*, the *locus classicus* of ecclesiastical obedience:

> There is a time for everything, and many a man desires a reformation of an abuse, or the fuller development of a doctrine, or the adoption of a particular policy, but forgets to ask himself whether the right time for it has come; and, knowing that there is no one who will be doing anything towards its accomplishment in his own lifetime unless he does it himself, he will not listen to the voice of authority, and he spoils a good work in his own century, in order that another man, as yet unborn, may not have the opportunity of bringing it happily to perfection in the next. He may seem to the world to be nothing else than a bold champion for the truth and a martyr to free opinion, when he is just one of those persons whom the competent authority ought to silence; and, though the case may not fall within that subject-matter in which that authority is infallible, or the formal conditions of the exercise of the gift may be wanting, it is clearly the duty of authority to act vigorously in the case.[1]

Methodism, however, was not limited by such subtle considerations. And one reason for this may also have been that Wesley's actions and their theological justification could serve as a rationalization of a social schism which had developed in English society in the seventeenth century. This social division had been reflected in the formation of the Puritan movement in the Church of England and in the formation of the Baptist, Independent and Presbyterian local churches, but these had declined as a result of defeat in the Civil War and its aftermath. The spread of the Wesleyan societies was in many ways a reassertion in the religious sphere of the continuing social divisions of the country (which were not the same as the class-structure which grew up in the nineteenth century). John Wesley's attitude to religious institutions fitted pragmatically into this situation.

[1] J. H. Newman, *Apologia Pro Sua Vita* (M. J. Svaglic ed. 1967), p. 232.

For social and economic reasons Methodism proved unable to maintain a single set of institutions either in Britain or in the United States in the nineteenth century. A period of progressive fragmentation which lasted until the setting up of the Salvation Army in the 1870s (the teaching about holiness which distinguished the Army in its early days had American Methodist roots) deprived the Methodists of any great influence on the ecclesiology of the mainstream Churches, all of which remained committed officially to more absolute theories of the Church's nature. The pragmatic tradition survived in Methodism, however, as for example in this modern American Methodist statement on the doctrine of the Church:

> There remains a deep, almost instinctive awareness among us that our foremost and final justification for being the Church that we are is still precisely the same as the justification for our having first been an evangelical order within the ecclesia Anglicana – namely, Christianity in dead earnest, distinguished chiefly in our evangelical concern for the Christian mission, witness, nurture – 'holiness of heart and life'. I cannot myself point to any contemporary formulation or formula that I would acknowledge as the Methodist doctrine of the Church . . . The drift of these comments is that Methodism has never lost the *essence* of a *functional* doctrine of the Church but that, by the same token, it has never developed – on its own and for itself – the full panoply of bell, book and candle that goes with being a 'proper' Church properly self-understood. This makes us une église manquée, theoretically and actually.[1]

Outler uses the word 'evangelism' in a wide sense, so that it included Wesley's idea of doctrinal fidelity. In the twentieth century, of course, the suggestion that the Gospel is readily and absolutely definable is much more questionable than it was in the eighteenth century and does not provide an easy way of determining the Church-status of a particular religious body. It may seem, nevertheless, one of the tragedies of the historical development of the ecumenical movement that this pragmatic, or functional, attitude to the visible Church dropped so far into the background in the course of the nineteenth century. The renewed emphasis on the ecclesiological centrality of episcopacy which stemmed from Tractarianism retarded the advance of ecumenism without securing corresponding pragmatic advantages. John Wesley's view of the Church ruled out the idea that episcopacy was of the *esse* of the Church.

In the eighteenth century as a whole the doctrine of the Church did not attract much attention in Church of England and Roman Catholic circles. The inherited ecclesiastical structures were taken for granted except when at the political level the interests of Church and State clashed, as they did, for example, in the Austria of Joseph II. As long as ecclesiastical leaders could take it for granted that Christendom still existed, as long as they could assume that people generally accepted the partnership of Church and State as the divinely ordained pattern for the government of mankind, they did not greatly worry if men often ignored the ideal in practice. It was

[1] D. Kirkpatrick, ed., *The Doctrine of the Church* (1964), p. 25.

characteristic of nineteenth-century ecclesiology that theoretical defences of this allegedly organic relationship continued to appear in England, where the establishment of the Church of England was challenged, modified, but never finally abolished. S. T. Coleridge and F. D. Maurice both wrote from this point of view. Church establishment, in various forms, had been the standard form, and it was one of the significant changes of the period that all over Europe, in Roman Catholic as well as in Protestant countries, the State moved to bring the union to an end, setting up secular institutions for education, for instance, and for marriage, and permitting an increasing degree of religious competition, which in the past had been regarded as injurious to the State's own interests. In the United States of America establishment did not long survive the Revolution. It was one of the profound insights of the Danish theologian, Soren Kierkegaard, that he recognized not only that Christendom had collapsed but also that one could not make a successful programme out of a desire to restore the religious *ancien régime*. Many who admitted the futility of dreaming of a political restoration still hoped for a religious one.

The situation differed radically from what had happened in England in the seventeenth century when two powerful groups had fought for supremacy *within* the Church of England, both taking the idea of Christendom for part of the divine revelation. In the nineteenth century European states shifted rapidly towards a position of greater independence – it does not make much difference whether one calls this secularization or not. Broadly speaking, only a minority of right-wing, normally conservative political groups struggled very hard against this process. It was this political withdrawal from the old compact which compelled theologians to re-examine the doctrine of the Church, and the pre-occupation has continued. To speak, as has sometimes been done, of a theological rediscovery of the doctrine of the Church in the 1930s is misleading: the doctrine was central to Victorian theological perplexities, because after the French Revolution no one knew what the rôle of the Church was in a modern state.

Indeed, the modern ecumenical movement partly originated in the anxiety of church leaders to replace the vanished social order in which the Churches had played an accepted part with a united ecclesiastical institution capable of holding its own as an independent structure with the increasingly independent and secular state. The question which John Henry Newman, then still Anglican, asked in the first of the famous Oxford *Tracts for the Times* (1834) was therefore already in dead earnest:

> Should the Government and the country so far forget their God as to cast off the Church, to deprive it of its temporal honours and substance, on what will you rest the claim of respect and attention which you make upon your flocks? Hitherto you have been upheld by your birth, your education, your wealth, your connexions – should these secular advantages cease, on what must Christ's ministers depend?

Precisely the same problem confronted the Roman Catholic Church in France after the Revolution of 1830 had replaced the restored but unimproved Bourbons with a July monarchy which carefully avoided any open identification of itself with the Catholic Church, the traditional spiritual expression of the ancient French monarchy. There the suddenly inspired Lamennais took the opposite, liberal solution which Newman never seriously considered. In Italy, the question raised itself in the still sharper form of the Papal knowledge that Italian nationalism must sooner or later challenge the Church's temporal power in central Italy, where the Papal states, to complicate matters, were not conspicuously well-governed, and that the city of Rome itself had little enthusiasm for the Pope as a ruler. The alternative to the old alliance did not seem as simple then as necessity has made it seem since. 'We know,' Newman wrote, 'how miserable is the state of religious bodies not supported by the State. Look at the Dissenters on all sides of you and you will see that their ministers, depending simply upon the people, become the *creatures* of the people. Are you content that this should be your case? Alas, can a greater evil befall Christians than for their teachers to be guided by them, instead of guiding? Is it not our very office to *oppose* the world? Can we then allow ourselves to *court* it? To preach smooth things and prophesy deceits? To make the way of life easy for the rich and indolent and to bribe the humbler classes by excitements and strong intoxicating doctrine? Surely it must not be so – and the question recurs – on what are we to rest our authority when the State deserts us?'[1]

The issue was not one, in other words, of establishment or disestablishment. As such, the latter would bring no authority. The British state, while not actually disentangling itself entirely from the Anglican Church in England, was becoming more independent in spirit. If an act of disestablishment were passed through parliament it would be an act of recognition, not an act of revolution. A social order was falling apart, and Newman argued the case for a doctrine of the Church which would guarantee spiritual power both to the institution and to its ministers. 'Christ has not left his Church without claim of his own upon the attention of men. Surely not. Hard master he cannot be, to bid us oppose the world, yet give us no credentials for so doing.' Newman rejected in advance some of the solutions popular with his contemporaries. 'There are some who rest their divine mission upon their own unsupported assertion; others, who rest it upon their popularity; others, on their success; others, who rest it upon their temporal distinction. This last case has, perhaps, been too much our own; I fear we have neglected the real ground on which our authority is built, our apostolical descent.' His explanation of 'apostolical descent' showed why the idea attracted him. 'We have been,' he said, 'born not of blood, nor of the will of the flesh, nor of the will of man, but of God. The Lord Jesus Christ gave his Spirit to his Apostles; they in turn laid their hands on those who should succeed them; and these again on others; and so the sacred gift had been handed down to our present Bishops who have appointed us to be their assistants, and in some sense representatives.'[2]

Such an assertion – for it was in fact simply an assertion – placed the origin and authority of the Church (at any rate of the Anglican part of it, which was all that Newman was concerned with at that particular moment)

[1] *Tracts for the Times*, I (J. H. Newman), 1834.
[2] *ib.*

beyond the power of secular institutions which no longer cared to claim a divine origin and authority for themselves. In the past politicians had assumed that the Church was a necessary and useful element in human society, even if they had not embraced the high doctrine of the Counter-Reformation, exemplified in the treatises of Robert Bellarmine (1542–1621), and sometimes repeated in Roman Catholic circles even in the mid-twentieth century, that a civil state which acknowledged the laws of the Roman Catholic Church was a useful element or function within the mystical body of Christ which formed the primary notion and stuff of society. The disintegration of this theoretical unity, however regarded, of which Newman was certainly aware (as was Kierkegaard), meant that to survive the hostility or indifference of the nineteenth-century state, itself a child of the Enlightenment in many ways, the Church must claim a spiritual origin and an authority derived directly from Christ himself.

Here episcopal ordination came in as a convenient way of giving concreteness to the assertion of spiritual independence – 'if we trace back the power of ordination from hand to hand of course we shall come to the Apostles at last – we know we do, as a plain historical fact'.[1] This assertion, however, which Newman made with a fine disregard of the historical problems involved, was about the basis of the Church, not about the natural succession of bishops. In the Eleventh Tract Newman, anxious to conciliate, laboured to show that the Bible pointed to God's having set up a permanent, visible Church which Christians (as a general rule) were bound to join, so that to believe in Christ was not a mere opinion or secret conviction, but a social and even political principle; but the biblical evidence, like the episcopal succession, was essentially corroborative as far as Newman was concerned. His final withdrawal from the Anglican communion showed that for him the Anglican episcopal succession had not proved able to maintain a close enough continuity with that Primitive Christianity which had become his fundamental standard. It was the inner logic of the historical situation in the nineteenth century which compelled him to seek such an absolute authority for the Church, as was clear from his description of the world order in the *Apologia*:

> What a scene, what a prospect, does the whole of Europe present at this day. And not only Europe, but every government and every civilisation throughout the world, which is under the influence of the European mind. Especially, for it most concerns us, how sorrowful, in the view of religion, even taken in its most elementary, most attenuated form, is the spectacle presented to us by the educated intellect of Europe, France and Germany. Lovers of their country and their race, religious men, external to the Catholic Church, have attempted various expedients to arrest fierce wilful human nature in its onward course and to bring it into subjection. The necessity of some form of religion for the interests of humanity, has been generally acknowledged; but where was the concrete representation of things invisible which would have the force and the toughness necessary to be the breakwater

[1] *ib.*

against the deluge? Three centuries ago the establishment of religion
. . . was generally adopted as the best expedient for the purpose in
those countries which separated from the Catholic Church; and for a
long time it was successful; but now the crevices of those establishments
are admitting the enemy.[1]

It is significant that in the United States of America, which had abandoned the principle of church establishment, which kept up a kind of
conscientious objection to the *ancien régime,* and where the influence of
organized Christianity had come to rely in the early nineteenth century on
the work of the revivalist tradition, Anglicanism produced, at about the
same time as Anglo-Catholicism appeared in England, but without any
obvious English prompting, a movement very similar to Tractarianism and
committed to much the same view of the nature of the Church. Those who,
because of their inheritance of the habit of close association with the state,
saw more clearly the change that was taking place, were the most determined to find a supernatural sanction for the Church's visible being, a
sanction which, however dependent on the Bible for its intellectual backing,
might also serve as an answer to German historical-critical reassessments
of the Scriptures. The authority of the Church, established outside the realm
permitted to human reason, might support or replace the weakened
authority of the Book. It was significant that Kierkegaard, who was
accustomed to a state Church in Lutheran Denmark, came to speak of
religious authority as to be found only in a divine invasion of the present
age, when God chose to reveal himself, however darkly, through a particular
individual. Kierkegaard, that is, also tried to locate authority beyond the
power and influence of nineteenth-century secularizing society, whether it
was represented by the political state or the philosophical critic.

Following such a line of thought, it was not unnatural that Newman
should, in his Roman Catholic phase, defend the concept of the Church's
infallibility, as he did in the *Apologia,* where he related the idea to the
despairing picture of human culture which has already been quoted:

> Supposing it, then, to be the Will of the Creator to interfere in human
> affairs, and to make provision for retaining in the world a knowledge
> of Himself, so definite and distinct as to be proof against the energy of
> human scepticism, in such a case – I am far from saying that there was
> no other way – but there is nothing to surprise the mind if He should
> think fit to introduce a power into the world invested with the pre-
> rogative of infallibility in religious matters. Such a provision would be
> a direct, immediate, active and prompt means of withstanding the
> difficulty . . . And thus I am brought to speak of the Church's infalli-
> bility as a provision adapted by the mercy of the Creator to preserve
> religion in the world, and to restrain that freedom of thought, which
> of course in itself is one of the greatest of our natural gifts, and to
> rescue it from its own suicidal excesses . . . a power, possessed of
> infallibility in religious teaching, is happily adapted to be a working
> instrument, in the course of human affairs, for smiting hard and

[1] J. H. Newman, *Apologia,* p. 219.

throwing back the immense energy of the aggressive, capricious, untrustworthy intellect . . .[1]

And since an infallibility which never pronounced judgement would be little better than no infallibility at all, this argument – for men like Pius IX shared Newman's dread of the immense energy of the untrustworthy intellect – led on either to a declaration of Papal infallibility, as happened at the first Vatican Council (1870) or to some kind of committee infallibility (usually on the basis of the episcopate), an idea which has sometimes been mentioned in twentieth-century ecumenical and Roman Catholic discussion. It must be realized, however, that Newman himself did not think of papal infallibility as simply the individual activity of a particular Pope who weighed up the evidence on a point concerning faith or morals and gave an *ex cathedra* decision. He thought of infallibility as a process, which might take place over a long period and involve a conflict between ecclesiastical authority and reason, so that when authority finally felt called on to pronounce a decision, the decision had already been reached within the proper scope of reason. The wilfulness, scepticism and destructiveness of reason dominated the society which surrounded the Church; domiciled within the Church, however, human reason regained its purpose and moved towards truth. And in religious issues part of the truth, for reason, consisted in recognizing the limits of mere rationalism. Reason was not infallible, but infallibility did not destroy the freedom of the intellect.

Newman apart, however, the importance of the Anglo-Catholic movement in the development of modern ecumenicalism has been under-estimated because of the intransigent rejection of the ministries of non-episcopal Churches which was one of its first products. Speaking of ordination in the apostolic succession in *Tract One* Newman said that 'we must necessarily conclude none to be *really* ordained who have not been *thus* ordained', and the point once made remained a thorn in the side of the Protestant ecumenical movement. One has to view this in perspective. When Anglo-Catholicism gave an official description of its position in 1947 in the report entitled *Catholicity*, the authors said that 'the Anglican knows that wherever he worships throughout the Anglican Communion he will find the Holy Scriptures read and the public worship conducted in the vulgar tongue; he will find the historic Creeds recited alike in the rite of Holy Baptism and in the offices; he will find the Sacrament of Confirmation administered by the Bishop; and he will know that the celebrant at the Eucharist is a priest whom a Bishop, standing in the Apostolic Succession, has ordained. These things may be differently valued by churchmen, and even by theologians, but it is upon the constancy of these things in one single pattern that the unity of the Anglican communion rests, with the frank conviction that some parts of the pattern which are not held to be of the *esse* by some Anglicans are held to be of the *esse*, with conviction, by others.'[2]

In fact, the Anglo-Catholic emphasis on the origin and essence of the

[1] *ib.* pp. 219–20.
[2] *Catholicity*, A Report presented to the Archbishop of Canterbury (1947), pp. 55–6.

Church as a supernatural body which should be visibly and episcopally one was to penetrate Protestantism – and Anglo-Catholicism was 'protestant', however much some Anglo-Catholics disliked the label – more and more in the later nineteenth century. This influence was increased by the way in which the Oxford movement assisted in the professionalization of the clergy. As one Anglican observer, C. A. Whittuck, said (in 1893), clergy of the Tractarian pattern sought 'to eliminate from their lives any tendency to unclericalise themselves in their intercourse with other men'.[1] The ministerial training seminary, whose introduction throughout Protestantism was a marked feature of nineteenth-century religious history, was conceived as an instrument for the spiritual and professional rather than intellectual formation of the ministry. There was resistance from the older school, 'happy', as Whittuck said, 'in their intercourse with the mixed life of this world',[2] but a revolution slowly took place which implied a new theology of the ministry. The mid-twentieth-century appetite for what was called a 'secular theology', or even, in Harvey Cox's phrase, a 'political theology', implied a reaction against this ascetic view of the priesthood and against the concept of the Church linked with it. Perhaps one may see here the terminus of a mood which had begun as far back as the 1830s.

If eighteenth-century theologians had been able to assume the traditional idea of the Church, whether Roman or Protestant, and had defended the general truth of Christianity rather than the specific doctrine of the Church, nineteenth-century theologians felt obliged to defend the existence and nature of the Church because of the collapse of Christendom, the expansion of the modern state, and increasing criticism of the Church as an institution (and a property-holding institution at that) in human society. It is interesting here to compare Newman's solution of the problem with that of Lamennais, the French Catholic theologian who withdrew into a romantic humanism in the 1830s – he was the arch-example of the impatient, disobedient reformer whom Newman so distrusted. Newman's doctrine of the Church in the 1830s was very much a theoretical one; he did not, as an Anglican, campaign for disestablishment, or do anything to weaken in England the surviving outward signs of the old agreement between state and Church, nor did he seek to organize the Anglican Church to oppose the state: his normal target was the ecclesiastical authorities. Lamennais, on the other hand, perhaps more acutely conscious of the socio-political changes which were taking place in Europe, actually wanted the Roman Church to accentuate the breach with the French monarchy which had opened in 1830, to abandon the principle that the state ought to support the Church with all the means at its power. He wanted to loosen as quickly as possible the ties between French Catholicism and the monarchical world with which the French episcopal hierarchy continued to identify itself long after the Revolution of 1789. Newman wanted a spiritual declaration of independence from the state, coupled with some effort to prevent the state's further secularization – he was still committed psychologically to the idea of Christendom. Lamennais accepted as inevitable the progressive

[1] C. A. Whittuck, *The Church of England and Recent Religious Thought* (1893), p. 24.
[2] *ib.* p. 26.

dechristianization of the state; he wanted to make the Church politically as well as spiritually free so that it need not oppose but might even enter into a democratic system, the form of the new society which he believed was forming. Newman's doctrine of the Church was ascetic; the supernatural society existed on earth in time as the embodiment of grace both offered in the sacraments and received in the saints. Lamennais, like Kierkegaard in Denmark at the same period (1830–50) lacked Newman's willingness to discern such a Church in the existing pattern of institutions and thought that there must be an ecclesiastical revolution as a complement to the socio-political revolution which was still developing.

By the 1850s, in other words, lines had been laid down which led to the twentieth-century controversy about the nature of the Church and the ecumenical movement. From John Wesley, who believed in Protestant orthodoxy without hesitation but who was eighteenth-century enough to remain unimpressed by traditional institutions, there derived an ecclesiastical pragmatism in which doctrinal fidelity took precedence over ecclesiastical form. From the Tractarians stemmed both the idea of corporate visible unity, as distinct from the common nineteenth-century view that Church unity meant the voluntary association for common purposes of individual Christians without any question of organic union – and the stickiness about episcopal ordination which marred modern gropings after unity. From Catholic liberals like Lamennais there followed a view, not unlike John Wesley's, that religious institutions were a means, not an end in themselves: 'I am a follower of Christ, not of the Church', Lamennais said, rejecting all theological schemes which fused the two; but Lamennais also insisted that the vital factor was neither episcopacy nor doctrine but the European cultural revolution, an attitude which was to lead to the Catholic Modernist movement (1900), and the efforts of the French worker-priests to transform French Catholicism after the Second World War. In the 1960s the second Vatican Council reflected a movement away from Newman's emphasis on Christendom and institutional tradition, without any substantial movement in Lamennais' direction.

This summary does not exhaust the creativity of nineteenth-century theology. There was also the strongly individualistic attitude of Soeren Kierkegaard, who thought that the Church (epitomized for him in the state Church of Denmark) was a limiting factor on the chances of Christianity's survival. Whereas Newman in thinking about Christendom looked back to the old order as a lost but loved ideal, and Lamennais wanted to reconstitute it on a democratic basis so that the religion of the state was a religion which emanated from the people instead of being imposed upon them from above, Kierkegaard used the term 'Christendom' as one of abuse. The famous *Attack upon Christendom* (1854–55) was a formal repudiation of the religious results of the *ancien régime*. 'Every effort to bring about a Christian state and a Christian nation is *eo ipse* unchristian, anti-christian', he said, 'for every such effort is only possible in virtue of a reduction of the definition of a Christian, and is therefore against Christianity, and tending to establish the false claim that we are all Christians, and that it is therefore very easy to be Christian. In the New Testament Christianity is the performance of "duties towards God", and now it has long been decided that there are really no duties towards God – yet we are Christians, and in fact this is precisely what constitutes Christendom.'[1]

Kierkegaard felt that Protestantism as institutionalized Christianity had sacrificed the Gospel to the exigencies of human nature:

> If Protestantism is to be anything but a necessary corrective at a given moment, is it not really man's revolt against Christianity? If Christianity is to be proclaimed as it essentially is in the Gospels, proclaimed as, and actually being, imitation or following, sheer suffering, groaning and lamentation, heightened by a background of judgement in which every word must be accounted for, then it is a terrible series of suffering, *angst*, and trembling. Indeed, yes. But where do we read in the Gospels that God wishes this earthly existence to be otherwise? What human nature constantly aims at, on the other hand, is peace, *nil beatum nisi quietum*, peace to carry on with finite things, to enjoy life here. Is not Protestantism then man's revolt against Christianity? We will and must have peace – peace for Christianity. So we turn the whole of Christianity around, and out of the terrible pessimism which Christianity is in the New Testament we obtain an insipid optimism . . .[2]

This passage showed the influence of the *zeitgeist*, for Kierkegaard's description of Protestantism as a system for taking the sting out of Christianity was remarkably similar to John Keble's quite independent Anglo-Catholic criticism of the doctrine of justification by faith as practised in the Anglican Evangelicalism of his day as meaning self-justification – as though, Keble said, a man failed entirely to see the seriousness of sin but simply paused and apologized to God, and passed on convinced that he would be saved in the end by his faith alone. All this concerns the doctrine of the Church because Kierkegaard regarded the Church as the set of institutions through which the Gospel had been made impotent; Keble, on the other hand, turned, like Newman, *to* the Church as the only possible objective defence against what seemed to him the corrupt subjectivity of popular Protestantism. The Danish theologian's essential pietism came out in his horror of objectivity, his certainty that religion exists only in the personal relation between God and the believer: 'Nothing is more dangerous than that something which should be practised is transformed into learned knowledge'. At times the Church seemed to exist for him simply as an intrusive temptation to be satisfied with an objective, philosophical religion, which he symbolized as reliance on the fact of infant baptism. He was aware that Luther had attained salvation after 'a score of years filled with fear and trembling and temptation', but he found in nineteenth-century Lutheranism only the transformation of Luther's experience into a bourgeois non-event, so that membership of the state Lutheran Church meant security and complacency instead of fear and trembling.

> Christianity is so arranged that it is related to the individual. And it is
> in this that the immense ideality and effort of being a Christian

---

[1] S. Kierkegaard, *The Last Years* (ed. R. G. Smith, 1965), p. 334.

[2] *ib*. pp. 49–50.

consists, in being related to God as an individual, not protected by any abstraction, which, if you like, softens the blow . . . But what everything human aims at is to be quit of God. This is the common aim. The method is then twofold . . . The first way is to rebel against God, or to deny that there is a God. I do not speak of this. The second way is the more refined. It is under the pretext of zeal for God and the things of God to place an abstraction between God and oneself. Such an abstraction is the 'Church'. Men have struck on the idea of turning it into a person, and by first speaking of it spiritually as a person, about its birth and the course of its life and so on, in the end grow accustomed to identifying the Church with the Christians – and there are no Christians in any sense but this . . .[1]

Once again one notes the power of the *zeitgeist* and the English parallel, for Benjamin Jowett of Balliol, the leading Anglican liberal theologian, confided to his notebooks in the mid-nineteenth century the dismissal of the Church as 'a figment of theologians'. Of course Kierkegaard wrote as the pietist for whom only absolutely certain (and yet always absolutely uncertain) salvation would do; as the pietist whom the Church in history always horrified by its social and political behaviour; as the pietist for whom the Church, if it must be there at all, must be as a common subjectivity united in a common apprehension of the mercy of God in Christ. But he was also more serious than orthodox commentators have sometimes suggested in his analysis of the Church as the vehicle of human, not supernatural religion. He did not really accept the 'Church' as a supernatural guide, or regard it as the natural source of religious authority in the present world. If one compares him with a late nineteenth-century liberal Protestant theologian like Harnack, for example, Kierkegaard's individualism seems deeply religious and Harnack's much more political:

as Protestants we ought to know that we belong, not to an 'invisible' Church, but to a spiritual community which disposes of the forces pertaining to spiritual communities; a spiritual community resting on earth, but reaching to the Eternal . . . This community embraces Protestants inside and outside Germany, Lutherans, Calvinists, and adherents of other denominations. In all of them, as far as they are earnest Christians, there lives a common element, and this element is of infinitely greater importance and value than all their differences . . . And when we are reproached with our divisions and told that Protestantism has as many doctrines as heads, we reply, 'So it has, but we do not wish it otherwise; on the contrary, we want still more freedom, still greater individuality in utterance and doctrine . . . we are well aware that in the interests of order and instruction outward and visible communities must arise . . . but we do not hang our hearts upon them, for they may exist today and tomorrow give place . . . to new organizations; let anyone who has such a Church have it as though he had it not . . .[2]

[1] *ib.* p. 297.
[2] A. Harnack, *What is Christianity?* (ET E. B. Saunders, 1900), pp. 274–77.

Harnack's anti-dogmatic liberalism led him on to an individualistic praise of freedom which was attractive to many in the late nineteenth century, but was anathema to Kierkegaard, whose subjectivism was a subjectivism of religious experience, of encounter with God as the Absolute who made absolute demands for obedience upon his creatures; Harnack's was more of a revolt against absolutes, on the ground that the individual Christian must choose for himself what he would or would not believe, because there were no trustworthy sources of absolute authority in the finite world. Harnack's liberal idea of the Church conceded that institutions were necessary for practical purposes but sought to deny them power over the life of the individual; his position depended upon the assumption that the Gospel was 'so simple, so divine, and therefore so truly human, as to be most certain of being understood when it is left entirely free'.[1] Kierkegaard started from the opposite assumption that men did not want to be Christians in the vital sense, and that to leave them free would therefore accomplish nothing at all. To rely on the Church, however, as a method of defeating the human determination to pervert the Gospel, was to rely on the means of perversion which men had most frequently used. Harnack thought that Christianity could be saved by men who had set themselves free from ecclesiasticism; Kierkegaard would have unhesitatingly identified Bismarckian Protestantism as the same well-fed avoidance of the religious problem which he had marked down in Denmark fifty years before. He would probably also have called in evidence the *Kulturkampf*, the synthetic conflict which Bismarck generated between the new German Empire and the Catholic Church in Germany (1870–78).

This comparison may be supplemented by a brief discussion of two other theological writers whose work casts light on Kierkegaard's position. The first was Anton de Lagarde (1827–91), who was German despite the name which he took in 1854. A weather-beaten signpost to wrong roads that were followed later, the German historian, Golo Mann, called him. Lagarde's outlook was permanently affected by the abortive German revolutions of 1848. He incarnated all too perfectly the nationalist revulsion against any radical changes in the structure of society. He wanted to purge Christianity of all traces of Judaism, in order to replace it with a truly German religion in which the soul of the nation would find expression. Thus he was one of the fore-runners of the willingly anti-semitic German-Christian Church which briefly served Hitler's purposes in the 1930s. For Lagarde, suffering from the same social climate as Kierkegaard, the conclusion was not individualism but a frightened totalitarianism which merged the Church into the nation-state, and invented a new, more hysterical kind of revivalism, for which Jewishness became the presence of the Devil, and salvation a superficial loss of identity in the oneness of the group, not in the least like the profound destruction of the self relentlessly pursued by a serious student of renunciation like Simone Weil.

'The nation is an organism', Lagarde said, 'and must have a soul. This soul must have a unity. It is surely a misfortune if Germany remains divided in two or more parts. Germany does not want a Catholicism minus

[1] *ib.* p. 275.

the Pope, nor a Protestantism minus a greater or smaller number of dogmas, but a new life which would put the old life to death.' He used Judaism as the symbol of everything that he hated, the materialism of the post-1870 Empire, for example. 'The Jews, as their prophets have often said, are a stiff-necked people . . . But the Gospel seeks salvation not in the will, but in the breaking of the will, in the Cross, which the Jew rejects as foolishness. Only when each nation crucifies the will of the Jew will the Jew be redeemed from himself, and in that way, and only in that way shall we be saved from the Jew.' Lagarde's reputation in middle-class German Protestantism was too great for one simply to dismiss this as unrepresentative or insane.

It may seem unkind to compare Lagarde's destructive religious nationalism with F. D. Maurice's eagerness to reinforce the idea of the 'nation' with the mystical offices of the 'Church'. Maurice was, of course, untouched by anti-semitism and the worst that his enthusiasm for the 'national Church' may be said to have legitimized was a handful of imperialist episcopal speeches at the time of the South African War (1899–1902). Maurice, nevertheless, was reacting to the same cultural pressures as were affecting Lagarde, and this British blend of Church and state fell on the same side of the line as the German's headier theology. Like Lagarde, Maurice was deeply affected by the social division of industrialized society; he feared the onset of a radically pluralistic culture. He expressed his reaction in theological terms by saying that the Church was the servant of the divine order which God willed for men, and must therefore seek to reconcile the hostile classes to one another; to foster the emergence of social harmony was essentially the task of the National Church. Maurice had a Burkean sense of social and political continuity, and this has often won him the sympathy of later conservative-minded theologians. For him the union between Church and state in England was hallowed by time and providence, an object of veneration Even as late as 1870 he still believed that the clergy of the Church of England possessed the secret of 'nation-forming', a process of spiritual education which was denied to both the state and Nonconformity. He could not tolerate any suggestion of ecclesiastical discontinuity, though he did not share Newman's enthusiasm for episcopal succession as the specific symbol of the unity of the past; his defence of church establishment was as absolute as Kierkegaard's criticism of it.

Kierkegaard's individualism about the Church has therefore to be understood against the background of these other attitudes, this Victorian romanticism about the historical Church on the one hand, and Lagarde's much more vicious and political version of the organic doctrine on the other. There was never any question in the Victorian period of the doctrine of the Church either being neglected or of shrinking to a mere religious individualism: Kierkegaard's existentialist approach, which had little impact before 1900, contrasted strongly with the corporate theologies of the Church which dominated both Catholicism and Protestantism. It was in the twentieth century, and as often as not in the books of biblical critics, that the most extreme rejection of the idea of the Church was to be found. Summarizing the position in *Jesus and His Church* (1938) R. N. Flew said that the statement that Jesus founded no Church' had become almost a dogma of critical orthodoxy: E. F. Scott had declared that Jesus 'had not consciously formed a society', though the historical Church was 'the inevitable outcome of his work'; Troeltsch assumed that the first outstanding characteristic of the ethics of Jesus was an unlimited, unqualified individualism, and then asserted that during the lifetime of Jesus there was no sign of an organized community.[1] Such writers did not want to abolish the Church but regarded it as formed historically by the voluntary association of baptized or converted people; they thought that the institutionalization of the sacraments was a human, not a divine decision. In the light of the gradually changing religious crisis which has been described in these pages this was not surprising; there had been moments in modern Christian history when the survival of the possibility of belief had seemed much more important than the status of membership of the Church.

After 1918, however, the context of the doctrine changed as the ecumenical movement grew. Many causes (see, for example, B. Wilson, *Religion in a Secular Society*, 1966) combined to foster its growth. Historically, however, the breach between the traditional Churches and the modern state, and the further separation between the older religious culture and a newer, much less religious one, had thrown the Church as a whole back on itself, while on the mission-fields away from Europe and North America this feeling of isolation was reinforced by the increasing resistance of non-Christian religious cultures. There was no longer any question, as had been assumed in the over-confident early nineteenth-century missiology, of the rapid disintegration of the outworn Buddhist, Hindu or Islamic interpretations of existence. Unity began to seem a socially and politically desirable religious goal in the west. Theologians returned to the discussion of the nature of the Church and of the Church's unity, trying to do two separate things:

(a) to find new, or more convincingly stated, grounds for asserting the supernatural nature of the Church over against the aggressive surrounding societies (a repetition of the psychological pressures which had produced Tractarianism in the 1830s purely in terms of the collapse of the *ancien régime*);

(b) to find new or more convincing grounds for affirming the priority of visible ecclesiastical unity as such, as against, for example, the Harnackian position (see above) that institutional plurality, or variety, was of the essence of true Christianity.

The ecumenical movement produced no major writing, but an orthodoxy emerged that based itself on a fresh appeal to the evidence about the Church to be found in the Bible, here often treated as though the historical-critical method somehow did not apply. The primary point was that the Church should not be thought of as secondary to the Gospel. 'Any such conception of the relation between Gospel and Church is not true to the Bible, where Israel is constituted the People of God by faith. Throughout the New Testament justification by faith has corporate no less than individual reference. By faith in Christ a man becomes a member of the body. In the New Testament, moreover, this is wholly consistent with the

[1] R. N. Flew, *Jesus and His Church* (1938), pp. 24–5.

recognition of the individual and his personal encounter and communion with God in Christ . . . The privileges of the Gospel involve the believer in duties (worship, service) many of which can only be performed corporately.'

It was therefore possible to argue that 'God in Christ by the Spirit takes the initiative in bringing into being a people which is his Church; in entrusting it, though not as its own property, with means of grace . . . Such a community must have an order, not merely in the sense of disciplinary rules, such as any voluntary society needs, but as structure, so as to be itself and perform its proper functions. The essential structure of the Church is divinely determined, since it is Christ's Church, not ours. For this, as for Christian faith in general, we look to the Bible to discover "the given", i.e. what God has appointed.'

And so the very explicit conclusion might be reached that 'what is given in Order includes worship, word, sacraments, ministry, pastoral care, discipline of members, and participation of members in regulating the common life. These are gifts of the one Spirit and should operate harmoniously. It is true that the New Testament provides no fixed and self-evident pattern in which all these cohere, but some of the given elements help to shape other elements in Order. For example, the sacrament of Holy Communion involves the saying of certain words and the performing of certain actions, and requires rules as to who shall say and perform them and who shall be admitted to it.'

These passages on organic unity come from the 1963 *Report* of the Conversations between the Church of England and the Methodist Church (pp. 20–21) and they typify the ecclesiology of a generation. God brought those whom he saved into a single community (which men had wrongly divided), which had an essential (not arbitrary or widely variable) structure which was not only divinely determined but scripturally revealed, so that ministry, pastoral care and discipline of members were gifts of the one Spirit, for example. And this Report went on to say that although it might not be possible to prove from first principles that Church Order required a separated, specialized ministry, 'the real reason for having it is that the ministry is "given" in the New Testament, i.e. it both exists and is described as given by God' (p. 22). The ecclesiology of the period constantly assumed the need for a single, world-wide set of visible, ecclesiastical institutions, hierarchically organized on the basis of the 'historic episcopate', though it was significant of a deeper level of disagreement that the British Methodist representatives who accepted these premises in practice added that of course the Methodist Conference did not claim that either episcopacy or any form of organization even in the Apostolic Church should be determinative for the Church for all time.

This ecclesiology became more important after the Second Vatican Council (1964) under the inspiration of Pope John XXIII had made moves which suggested that the monarchical interpretation of the Papal office, which had been especially dominant since the Council of 1870, might now be modified. The documents of the Council called the Pope 'the pastor of the whole Church', rather than, more traditionally, 'the head of the Church'; the papal primacy was described as arising from the idea and existence of the Church, rather than the Church being described as deriving its being from the primacy. The position of the Roman Catholic episcopate in relation to the Pope was strengthened when the Council laid down that bishops received their full authority from their consecration and not from their appointment by the Pope; this was an old issue which the Council of 1870 had left unsettled but which as recent a Pope as Pius XII had tried to determine in favour of papal authority in his encyclical *Mystici Corporis Christi* (1943). Not only was it now held that the primacy was a ministry of service rather than a dominion or source of power, but some effort was made to set up institutions to embody the idea that the Pope and his bishops shared a collegial responsibility for the government of the whole Church. The pressure of Roman history was obvious in all this; the Council must have seemed at times thronged by silent, shadowy witnesses; every word that was spoken had multiple references in the past. Nothing that happened was decisively liberal and Paul VI did not maintain the Johannine momentum of the Council, but the ecumenical possibility remained that an episcopally united majority of Protestantism might in the not too distant future come to terms with a Catholicism less papal, less curial and less clerical.[1]

Theologically, the post-1918 approach assumed that the idea of the Church as a supernatural as well as a historical body could be found in the New Testament and that the structure of the Church – institutions essential to its existence – was also divinely revealed in the Scriptures. Moreover, the Church thus revealed could be recognized in history; what was divinely given could be historically identified. Driven from the cultural centre of modern western civilization the Church must unite in order to re-evangelize what was in danger of becoming a lost planet.

Thus one side of nineteenth-century ecclesiology – that which emphasized the unity, sanctity and necessity of the visible, hierarchical Church to which every Christian must belong – had largely triumphed. The triumph had come late, however. There was less theological satisfaction with their general doctrine than the new ecumenical school admitted. At the moment when ecclesiological unanimity seemed to have dawned theology swung off into a more critical position. At the first Assembly of the World Council of Churches (1948), for example, Karl Barth, without invoking the historical-critical attitude to the Bible, questioned the view that the Church possessed a divinely given structure continuously visible in history especially in terms of creeds, ministry and sacraments; for Barth, the Church was to be thought of as occurring in history as a discontinuous series of faith-events. A similar line was taken by Rudolf Bultmann, for whom it was only in a paradoxical sense that the Church was identical with ecclesiastical institutions which might be observed as sociological phenomena in secular history; the true Church was an eschatological phenomenon which might possess a congregational visibility but was nevertheless a part of the age to come,

[1] See *Authority in the Church*, a statement agreed by the Anglican-Roman Catholic International Commission (1977), especially p. 18, where the Commission seemed to envisage that in any future union the see of Rome should hold a modified universal primacy.

secularly *in*visible, but to be grasped by the eye of faith. Bultmann always expounded his understanding of the Church in the context of the saving event, so that the Church's transcendent life in Christ might not be concealed by its visible institutions, such as the ministry.

At first sight what was happening was a recrudescence of the old antithesis between institutionalized religion and what the late nineteenth-century French anti-dogmatic liberal theologian, André Sabatier, called the 'religion of the Spirit'. This was certainly Emil Brunner's thesis in *The Misunderstanding of the Church* (1953), a kind of exaggerated version of Harnack's *Essence of Christianity* (1900), in which Brunner (himself a contemporary of Barth and Bultmann) said that the Church of the New Testament period was a spirit-filled community which vanished as soon as it institutionalized itself; the true Church could not be given institutional form, and so what was institutionalized was not the true Church. Brunner did not want to abolish the existing Church, however. For him, as for Karl Barth, the model of the ideal Church was really a small local organism living in as close a relation as possible to the age to come. In the Protestant past, this model had been used by very diverse groups, the Puritan Independents, for example, and by F. D. Maurice and the early Christian Socialists.

There was a Roman Catholic parallel to this movement of ideas, in such books as *Do We Need the Church?* (1969) by Richard McBrien, and Hans Küng's *The Church* (1967). Küng, like the Protestant ecumenical theologians, appealed to the New Testament as his authority for the doctrine of the Church. His conclusion, however, was less conventional. Describing what he took to be the meaning of the Pauline evidence, he said that (a) there appeared to be no monarchical episcopate in the Pauline communities at all; (b) there was no uncontrovertible evidence that the office of presbyter existed in these communities; (c) that the Pauline letters contained no clear evidence of ordination.

Paul, Küng said, would not have regarded his church-order as provisional. It was all the more important, therefore, that in the type-case of Corinth 'the burden of proof lies with those who wish to assert that there existed in the Corinthian community in Paul's time an office of leadership, whether elders or the later kind of monarchical episcopate', (p. 403). In Küng's opinion the elder-episcopate developed separately on a Palestinian basis. Neither system could claim to be original. (There was not, in other words, according to the Catholic exegete, the divinely-given structure, accessible in both the New Testament and in later history, to which the Anglican-Methodist documents of the 1960s, for instance, had appealed). And so Küng used language very similar to Emil Brunner's: 'a frightening gulf separates the Church of today from the constitution of the original Church' (p. 413).

Küng said that traditional ecclesiology had turned to history and tradition in general to defend its arbitrary conclusions, ignoring or minimizing the extent to which the earliest New Testament data failed to confirm what was asserted. He wanted to avoid what he called the Protestant tactic of taking sides, specifically of taking an anti-institutional side. In the light of the Pauline evidence as he interpreted it, however, he under-lined the difficulty of justifying 'any special commission to the ministry by men, given that each man has received his charism, his vocation, directly from God. Is the inner impulse not sufficient?' (p. 422).

As Küng said, one could solve the problem by arguing that as a matter of fact the bureaucratization of charisms was the natural course of the historical development of any religion, but this solution left the Christian ministry only one more example of 'ministry' in general. One could also appeal to the need for order (and this reminds one of the Anglican-Methodist *Report* of 1963 which specifically claimed that order was not contrary to the gospel; its function was to express the gospel and to contribute to its fulfilment in life). Küng was not impressed by this argument, because the alleged chaos of the cults did not strike him as necessarily worse than the sterility which could be imposed by the systematization of ministry. Pastors had done as much harm as prophets, he said (which was not the usual opinion of the ecumenical theologians), and the statement was really a significant concession to historical evidence in a subject (ecclesiology) which had never taken kindly to inconvenient data. The pastoral quest for power, Küng said, dissolved the original unity of West and East. In balancing arguments like this he was keeping faith with his original premise that neither the Pauline nor the Palestinian church-type represented the form of the true Church which had subsequently been corrupted. Küng might not want to contradict the statement that 'the essential structure of the Church is divinely determined', if only because the alternative was so far-reaching in its effects, but he showed no confidence that such a structure could be deduced from the contents of the New Testament.

Küng's own solution of the problem – to describe the Pauline communi-ties as having an interim, eschatological structure – was unsatisfactory, all the more so because he wished to reform the Roman Church in the direction of the Pauline rather than the Palestinian position. Nor could he find a secure New Testament basis for the papal primacy, which he redefined as a primacy of service which could be attained 'through the voluntary renunciation of the power which has in practice become associated with the Petrine ministry, through a long and problematical historical development, and has partly helped it and also seriously injured it' (p. 472).

In Küng's work, radical in its Catholic context, one sees another example of the working-out of the historical-critical method in the field of ecclesio-logy. His use of the biblical material was not as definitive as he supposed, however. Like most Protestant ecumenical scholars, he could not rid him-self of the belief that there must exist somewhere an authoritative way of using the New Testament data, that one must be able to arrive at an un-ambiguous conclusion which would serve as an absolute basis for decision today. In reality, the vital point about the New Testament data about the Church was their ambiguity, their Pauline-Palestinian content (as Küng himself put it). The history of the Church, as well as the history of the doctrine of the Church, has oscillated between these models of the perfect community; but history does not justify the assumption that a single, essential and definable structure was nevertheless divinely and clearly revealed in the Scriptures. Unity was a relative term, more and less useful in different historical contexts.

The question of historical context was becoming as important as the question of what the New Testament said, and some of the darker sayings in *Letters and Papers from Prison* (E.T. 1953), by Dietrich Bonhoeffer (1909–45), seemed to imply that the church-types of the past, whether Pauline or Palestinian, had lost their relevance because they were based on cultural assumptions which no longer held good. If the European way of life had become secularized, one could only speak of God by using the secular as a mode of the transcendent, and this applied as much to the forms of the Church as to the language of theology. If a time was coming when men could no longer be religious at all, then Christianity itself would have to become 'religionless' as well. Bonhoeffer's theology was orthodox enough; what had changed for him was the world outside the Church. His cruel experience had driven him beyond Matthew Arnold's conclusion: now men *could* do without Christianity, human nature had changed, there was no religious *a priori*, and therefore one did not really know how to alter the form of the Church. Thirty years later the disappearance of religion no longer seemed as inevitable, because even alienation could be historicized, and so ceased to threaten a permanent condition; but it was still not clear how the form of the Church should be changed.

Bonhoeffer's prison writings pointed towards a new development of the doctrine of the Church to which he did not survive to contribute. The ecumenical theologians had concentrated on the problem of unity and therefore on problems of church-structure. Karl Barth and Rudolf Bultmann had restated the characteristic Protestant criticism that personal faith must take precedence over structure, that faith was more often in danger from organization than organization from personal faith. Hans Küng had given theological expression to the new demand for ecclesiastical reform which swept through the Roman Catholic Church at the time of the second Vatican Council, and which produced, for example, a long agitation for the abandonment of sacerdotal celibacy. All these theologians, however, took for granted the survival of the ecclesia in unbroken visible continuity with the traditions of the past; they perpetuated the Mauricean belief that nothing was worse than a breach of continuity, that Burke (to put it in English terms) was your only political theologian of the Church. Some of Bonhoeffer's successors suspected, however, that the cultural revolution (of which Kierkegaard had already foreseen the probable result) was reaching a climax in which a fundamental social discontinuity was beginning to take shape. This meant that the gravest weakness of the twentieth-century western Church was its deep sociological involvement as a set of historical institutions in precisely the cultural order that was passing away. A passion for continuity might now be no more than a death-wish. It was true that the Church as an institution had survived the collapse of the Roman world and had even to some extent determined the form of the medieval culture which had followed it, but the history of Europe between 1500 and 1914 did not prove that the Church had adapted itself significantly to change. Now in the twentieth century a new situation was crystallizing in which a hierarchical ecclesia which laid claim to absolute powers of discipline and dogmatic definition no longer seemed particularly appropriate. The concept of a 'divinely-given structure', which had had a long run since its revival in the 1830s, was beginning to fall into the background theologically. This did not entail the substitution of a third church-type for both the Pauline and Palestinian forms; nor did it mean that the idea of ecclesiastical institutions was called permanently in doubt; rather, there was a growing feeling that new forms of the ecclesia must be allowed to manifest themselves as society transformed itself; that, instead of trying to deduce the structure of the Church from some form of the doctrine of the Church, one must allow the doctrine of the Church to reflect the life of the actual Christian community as it finds itself moving from one new historical situation to another.

There remains one deep area of disagreement between orthodox and liberal theologians. Liberals cannot really accept the view that the Church as a visible institution has a special competence to proclaim and safeguard the gospel, and therefore must have effective means to do so. Orthodox theologians, on the other hand, while granting that such institutions have not always acted correctly, believe in the indefectibility of the Church, which Christ will never desert and which the Holy Spirit will lead into all truth. When the Anglican-Roman Catholic International Commission reported on 'Authority in the Church' in 1976 it could still maintain that when the Church met in ecumenical council its decisions on fundamental matters of faith excluded what was erroneous because, being faithful to Scripture and consistent with Tradition, they were protected from error by the Holy Spirit.[1] The strict liberal view might be that liberation from error was not so easily obtained, and that truth had to be possessed in faith, not in such relative certainty.

---

[1] *ib.* pp. 16–17. The Report was dated Venice, 1976, and published 1977.

IV

SOCIAL THEOLOGY IN THE WHOLE PERIOD

Social theology began to change rapidly in the nineteenth century. This was because the ongoing industrial revolution, and the social revolution which was bound up with it – both of which must be taken for granted here – changed the data with which the theologian had to work and compelled him, in some cases at any rate, to re-examine his assumptions about the social teaching of the Bible. Over a short period of time western society moved from conditions of comparative poverty, insecurity and dependence upon nature to comparative wealth, security and freedom of choice; the hierarchy of the *ancien régime* became the class structure of Victorian society; secular political assumptions and goals altered.

These social changes, and the intellectual activity they generated, affected theologians all the more profoundly because by the mid-eighteenth century they had come very much to terms with the *ancien régime*. Roman Catholic theology, for example, had committed itself so deeply to the idea that monarchy was the proper form of Christian government that it was not until the late nineteenth century that Leo XIII, realizing that the restoration of the French monarchy in any form had now become extremely unlikely, officially granted the possibility of a divine republic; in *Diuturnum Illud* (1881) he said that popular democracy could be reconciled with the traditional doctrine as to the right origin of political power, because the electors only chose the holders of authority and were not the source of the authority itself.

Protestantism, though not as devoted as Roman Catholicism to the monarchical principle, had certainly reconciled itself to the established order by about 1750. In its earlier, more extreme period, Protestant sectarianism had encouraged a politics of withdrawal from society. The remnant of the saints no longer hoped to change the world as a political reality but moved out into the wilderness to offer God perfect service, as in the case of the Puritans who sailed to America in the seventeenth century; there could be a similar kind of withdrawal in Roman Catholicism, as when the late-seventeenth-century Jansenists opted out of politics in despair at the apparent invincibility of French absolutism. In the Protestant world the fires of apocalyptic imagery had burnt low and the new energy of eighteenth-century evangelicalism ran into pietist movements like British Methodism whose leader, John Wesley, summed up his attitude to political authority in words which were not so very different from those which a contemporary Roman Catholic might have used:

'The supposition, then, that the people are the origin of power is every way indefensible. It is absolutely overturned by the very principle on which it is supposed to stand; namely, that a right of choosing governors belongs to every partaker of human nature. If this be so, then it belongs to every individual of the human species; consequently, not to freeholders only, but to all men; not to men only, but to women also; nor only to adult men and women, to those who have lived one and twenty years, but to those who have lived eighteen or twenty; as well as those who have lived threescore. But none ever did maintain this, nor probably ever will. Therefore this boasted principle falls to the ground, and the whole superstructure with it. So common sense brings us back to the grand truth, "There is no power but of God".'[1] The conclusion of the argument comes, of course, from St. Paul's Epistle to the Romans. The common sense which Wesley was defending was the common sense of revelation as he interpreted it, leading, in his own case, to passionate support for George III against the American revolutionaries.

The opposite, more radical tradition did not die out altogether. One can trace a line from the seventeenth-century republican propagandist, James Harrington (1611–77), through Moses Lowman, a presbyterian whose *Dissertation on the Civil Government of the Hebrews* was published in 1740, to the young and temporarily radical S. T. Coleridge, who stated in his 'Lectures on Revealed Religion', delivered in Bristol in 1795 but not published in his lifetime, that 'Jesus Christ forbids to his disciples all property and teaches us that accumulation was incompatible with their salvation'. Coleridge did not actually advocate equality of possessions, but rather the having all things in common, adding, however, that 'this part of Christian doctrine, which indeed is almost the whole of it, soon was corrupted'. The same lectures contained a sharp rejection of commerce and urban life:

'The smoakes that rise from our crowded Townes hide from us the face of Heaven. In the country, the Love and Power of the great Invisible are everywhere perspicuous, and by degrees we become partakers of that which we are accustomed to contemplate. The beautiful and the Good are miniatures on the Heart of the contemplater as the surrounding landscape on a convex mirror. But in Cities God is everywhere removed from our sight and Man obtruded upon us – not Man, the work of God, but the debased offspring of Luxury and Want.'[2]

It is interesting that the young Coleridge reasserted the world-renouncing themes of primitive Christianity just when the pace of industrial change was quickening. That Christianity, properly defined, could not come to terms with the economic expansion of the west was frequently to be maintained in the course of the nineteenth century, sometimes in unexpected quarters, as in the writings of Nietzsche or Franz Overbeck (1837–1905). Coleridge, of course, abandoned his youthful radicalism, and did not develop the deeper questions about the nature of Christianity which this ascetic, world-renouncing interpretation of its early history implied; in his later years as an apologist for the Church of England he was to emphasize the

[1] J. Wesley, 'Thoughts Concerning the Origin of Power', in *Works*, vol. 11 (1865), p. 50.
[2] S. T. Coleridge, *Works*, ed. L. Patton and P. Mann, vol. 1 (1971), p. 226.

oneness of a society from which it was inconceivable that Christians should want to withdraw at all.

The handful of Christian radicals apart, most eighteenth-century theologians accepted the permanence of a static, divinely ordained society on a hierarchical pattern, in which Church and State were closely united – a community in which, historically speaking, change had generally occurred too slowly in the past to become an issue in itself. Eighteenth-century German Lutheranism offers an example of the way in which the critical, liberal rationalism of the Enlightenment had only a limited effect on Christian social thought. In the German Lutheran Churches the change to a more rationalist outlook took place in the 1760s. Until then preaching had remained for the most part either orthodox – concerned with the faithful as part of the Lutheran Confession, which had to be clearly distinguished from the Calvinist Reformed as well as the Roman Church; or pietist – concerned more with the subjective side of the religious life, and with man as needing to be saved and needing to bear witness to salvation. Then the change came. The Lutheran preachers of the Enlightenment wanted to end what for them had become a tiresome battle over obscure and trivial theological distinctions; they also rejected the orthodox description of this life as a vale of tears. The preaching of morality (instead of doctrine) began as an escape from the past, not only into a more tolerant atmosphere but also into a life which actually seemed more religious, because more committed to sincere behaviour than to formal belief.

This new Lutheranism did not look forward to any new order of society. Even the most rationalist of the later eighteenth-century Lutheran preachers advised domestic servants, for example, that their duty and happiness lay in making their masters free and happy. 'Masters will always be masters and servants will always be servants', wrote C. F. Sintenis (1750–1820). For the most part the Lutheran preachers supported the existing regime of German princely states, though Sintenis sometimes spoke of the possibility of the prince's advisers having been elected by the people. The ideal prince would himself be 'enlightened'; he would identify with the bourgeoisie instead of with the aristocracy; he would promote men on account of merit instead of birth; he would keep out of war and seek to improve his country's economic position. The most that these theologians wanted politically was a gentle modification of the *ancien régime* in favour of the bourgeoisie and at the expense of the landed class; they neither foresaw nor wanted revolution. They had transformed the sixteenth-century idea of 'vocation' or 'calling', fundamental to Martin Luther's own view of society, into a doctrine of social obedience, which was used to persuade the lower orders to content themselves with their limited existence.

At the end of the eighteenth century, therefore, Christian opinion still largely supported the traditional idea of a hierarchical society ordained by God and incapable of major useful change; some theologians, however, like the Lutherans referred to above, reflected the demands of the bourgeoisie for greater intellectual freedom and economic power. (Among the theological offshoots of this campaign for intellectual liberty was the secularist movement, which in England was rooted in the writings of Tom Paine, from whom the tradition passed to Carlile (1790–1843), the more compromising Holyoake (1817–1906) who was willing to work with groups like the Christian Socialists, and Charles Bradlaugh (1833–91), who presided over the last aggressive phase between 1860 and 1900.) The most radical political thinkers of the early nineteenth century, Saint-Simon (1760–1825), Robert Owen (1771–1858) and Charles Fourier (1772–1837), rejected orthodox Christianity together with the existing social system, though Saint-Simon, like Rousseau, invented his own religious system because he did not believe that human society could function successfully without one.

What the utopian schemes of this group of socialist thinkers underlines was that the collapse of Christendom was leaving western society without any generally accepted sanction or source of common authority in economic affairs. As Emile Durkheim wrote in his study of the Saint-Simonians: 'What is needed if social order is to reign is that the mass of men be content with their lot. But what is needed for them to be content is not that they have more or less, but that they be convinced that they have no right to more.' (Which was the social outcome of hierarchical societies in general.) 'And for this it is absolutely essential that there be an authority whose superiority they acknowledge and which tells them what is right. For an individual committed only to the pressure of his needs will never admit that he has reached the extreme limit of his rightful portion. If he is not conscious of a force above him which he respects, which stops him and tells him with authority that the compensation due to him is fulfilled, then inevitably he will expect as due to him all that his needs demand . . . For it to be otherwise, a moral power is required whose superiority he recognizes and which cries out "You must go no further". This was precisely the rôle played in the older society by the (religious) powers whose progressive dethronement Saint-Simon notes. Religion instructed the humble to be content with their situation at the same time as it taught them that the social order is providential, that it is God himself who has determined everyone's share; and giving them glimpses beyond this earth of another world where everything will be balanced, it stopped them from feeling aggrieved.'[1]

This decline of the religious sanction on human economic expectation coincided with the rapid growth of industry and technology. One consequence, especially in the more developed industrial countries, was the gradual replacement of the older hierarchical structure by a new kind of class structure to which Christian theology was bound to take time to adjust itself. It was natural for some theologians to interpret this new pattern of classes as only the former hierarchy in a modern dress, to fix the stamp of the divine approval on Capital and Labour, for example, and to assume that correct Christian political solutions would always be found by creating harmony between the two. A God of Love must be served through social co-operation, not through social conflict, it was assumed, and the idea of co-operation was seen as excluding the possibility of basic changes in the given social structure. One can exaggerate the extent to

[1] E. Durkheim, *Socialism* (New York, 1967), pp. 242–43.

which the underprivileged had ever willingly borne the deprivations which the European social system had inflicted upon them; in any case, after 1815 the class structure itself became a vehicle of working-class demands for change. Theologians who argued that Capital must always be Capital and Labour must always be Labour were not well-placed to satisfy these demands theologically.

Variations on this theme dominated much of the social theology of the nineteenth century. After 1815, as after most periods of intense, prolonged warfare, there was a widespread desire in the wealthier classes for a return to a golden age of international peace, social stability and religious certainty. Theologians, both Roman Catholic (de Maistre, for example), and Protestant (Coleridge), reaffirmed the very unity of society and Christianity which the eighteenth-century philosophes had ridiculed and the revolutionaries had done their best to abolish. By 1848, however, it was clear that such a unity would have to be restored, not preserved, and it was the importance of the Christian Socialism advocated by J. M. Ludlow in 1848 that he asserted that one could no longer defend the existing social and economic system as ordained by God. In 1849, after the terrible fighting between the French workers and the middle classes in Paris, Ludlow said:

> In the name of a God of love let us not lose the warning. Capital and Labour cannot thus be suffered to remain at issue with one another. They must be harmonized, they must be associated. It is not a machinery that will do this, without God's grace shed abroad in our hearts; but can it be done without a change in machinery? Is it Christian, is it human, to leave labour – that is, the nerves, the muscles and lifeblood of our fellow-creatures – to the scientific operation of the 'laws of supply and demand'? to deem oneself justified in paying the 'current rate of wages' when that current rate of wages is not sufficient to support life? Look to the four days slaughter in Paris; see whether they are not the logical result of the competitive, the selfish system.[1]

Ludlow published this in *Politics for the People*, the weekly paper which the Anglican Christian Socialists (Ludlow, Charles Kingsley, F. D. Maurice) issued in 1848–49. They were entitled to call themselves 'Christian Socialists' because to some extent they believed that the social problems of the time could not be solved by a change of attitudes alone, by that mysterious warming of the heart on which many religious writers relied to bring about social transformation – as though Charles Dickens's *Christmas Carol* offered a serious image of the way in which men were moved to reform their behaviour and their society. A reversal of the trend towards unlimited individualism must, they thought, be embodied in visible economic institutions, the industrial co-operative, for instance, and trade unions inspired by a radical Christian understanding of the proper forms of social advancement for their members. Maurice, it is true, easily fell back on the language of feeling, exhorting both Capital and Labour to look 'not for differences but agreement, seeking to reconcile divisions and not to make them'; then everybody

[1] *Politics for the People*, p. 197.

would understand and feel 'what a blessing and privilege it is to be a member of the Great English Partnership'.[1] All the Christian Socialists agreed that a merely secular socialism could not reunite society into a harmonious co-operative enterprise. Charles Kingsley said that 'men will never be joined in true brotherhood by mere plans to give them a self-interest in common, as the Socialists have tried to do. No, to feel for each other they must first feel with each other. To have their sympathies in common, they must have, not an object of gain, but an object of admiration in common; to know that they are brothers, they must feel that they have One Father.'[2]

Kingsley, Ludlow and Maurice were reacting against the secularization of politics which had set in since the late eighteenth century and which produced its most famous document, *The Communist Manifesto*, in 1848, the same year which witnessed the appearance of the short-lived *Politics for the People*. The Christian Socialists wanted to capture the revolutionary socialist tradition for Christianity, and Ludlow dreamed briefly of introducing a new economic system of industrial organization through the formation of producer as well as distributor co-operatives: once these associations had expanded on a national scale (for he did not think in terms of revolution) they would be able to decide on wages and prices nationally and for the public good. Ludlow believed in what he called 'Collective Mastership' in a self-governing community. 'So long as each labours for all as all labour for him', he wrote, 'and endeavours always to do his best, because he knows that he will receive the best that can be given him, Communism, pure Communism, will, I feel sure, exhibit the very type of a flourishing society.'[3] This new society was the highest earthly embodiment of the Christian Church. For Ludlow, in the first flush of the Christian Socialist movement at any rate, the gospel of Christ was wholly incompatible with a political economy which proclaimed self-interest to be the pivot of social action, or with a system of trade based wholly on the incentive of private profit. A theologically true society could be created only by faith in Christ working through a true Church, but, Ludlow admitted in 1850:

> I feel more and more that it is utterly impossible to make Christian Socialism what it ought to be, a true Church-movement among the people, unless we can Americanise the Church by giving her true self-government in convocation . . . it seems quite clear to me that, with what I have called an Americanised Church we could fairly conquer the working-classes of this country, that is to say, the very heart of English society, for Christ, and that if we do not, nobody else will, and that we never shall, without sweeping church-reform.[4]

Such ideas only alarmed Maurice, who rejected democracy on his own biblical grounds and who dismissed all schemes for human organization

---

[1] *ib*. p. 274.
[2] *ib*. p. 185.
[3] *The Christian Socialist*, vol. I, p. 234.
[4] T. Christensen, *Origin and History of Christian Socialism* (1962), p. 161.

beyond the parish level as 'the organisation of evil powers for the sake of producing good effects'. Maurice, who resembled Coleridge, the political conservative, much more than Ludlow ever did, was fundamentally a symbolist, not a technologist. The Divine Order, which rested on fellowship and co-operation, already existed; God himself constantly renewed men's willingness to live in brotherhood. The value of the idea of association to Maurice was simply as a way of proclaiming this already given divine order, but he explicitly denied in the first of the *Tracts on Christian Socialism* that he wanted to create 'a great combination for the reorganising all the trades of the cities and the agriculture of the country'. As he saw it, there could not be a more divine order than what was already given, because any new social system would be exposed to the same strains from the selfishness, ignorance and competitiveness of man. His view of society was largely psychological: he did not separate an industrial system, which might be more or less 'christian', from the individual people, capitalists as well as workers, who made up the industrial structure which he knew. Maurice's habit of seeking to limit Christian action to the proclamation of truth on a parochial scale suggests that he was more of an evangelical pietist than he consciously admitted. Ludlow's failure to convert his leader to the need for nationally organised action symbolized his wider failure to democratize the Church of England or to persuade the majority of its members to accept as their personal social ideal the model of society which he advocated. One must not exaggerate the significance of his failure. There was never any chance of success. Maurice finally abandoned the Christian Socialist movement in 1854 for the more congenial field of the London Working Men's College. It remains true that after 1860 religious bodies had little influence on the development of the Labour Movement in England – as elsewhere, the revolutionary tradition absorbed Marx, not Christian Socialism.

Ludlow's case was not altogether dissimilar from that of Lamennais (1782–1854), the ablest of the nineteenth-century French liberal Catholics. Once he had been forced to give up, by 1834, the hope that the Papacy could be persuaded to preside over the democratization of the Roman Catholic Church, Lamennais ceased to believe that ecclesiastical institutions could be used to transform society as a whole. Interpreting the struggle of the people for political power as a mystical projection of the will of God, he substituted faith in a revolutionary people for faith in a revolutionary Church. This was a step which Ludlow was not able to take; he could not identify himself totally with the working-classes unless the working-classes first identified themselves with the Church of England, a position made all the more desperate by the fact that, like Lamennais, he had a low opinion of the Anglican Church as he found it. Lamennais was less politically inhibited. No one, he said, was born into the world with a right to command others; therefore, there should be no intermediary between God and the people. 'I am a disciple of Christ, not of the Church', he said, a remark which rejected the value of a hierarchical society. Both Ludlow and Marx (but not Coleridge or Maurice) wanted to change the economic structure of society, Ludlow in order to enable men to express the communal core of the Gospel through their social institutions, Marx – religiously speaking – in order to make men realize that they did not depend on God at all, and that they did not need to project him. Lamennais' interests remained more strictly political – he believed that the people would express the will of God if they were given the opportunity through a democratic system based on universal suffrage. If one compares F. D. Maurice, Ludlow and Lamennais in terms of their attitude to the decisive social fact of the nineteenth century, the change from a static to a dynamic economic system in the west, one finds that Maurice, apart from a brief period when he was influenced by Ludlow, attached little importance to the forms of society or to the likelihood of being able to change them, but constantly asked men to look through the superficial structure of society to the divine order which always underlay it; that Ludlow, while temperamentally opposed to this platonic conservatism, and convinced that the Gospel required a new socio-economic form – 'there must be a Socialist politics and a Socialist medicine, Socialist literature and Socialist art, Socialist science and Socialist law, as well as Socialist trade and industry' – believed that such social changes must be inspired by a religious rather than a political movement, but despaired once he realized that Maurice was not the man to lead one; while Lamennais, politically much the most sophisticated of the three, the clearest in his conviction that the religious forces of Europe could not indefinitely deny, though they might indefinitely lament, the passing of the *ancien régime*, was also the least able to translate his political understanding into specifically Christian language; he provided a political, but not a religious substitute for Roman Catholicism.

Lamennais' withdrawal from Roman Catholicism into a religious position not unlike that of David Strauss may have helped to stimulate the blanket condemnation of Communism, Liberalism and Socialism which figured in Pius IX's *Syllabus of Errors* (1864). The *Syllabus* made clear that traditional Catholic ideas about the relation between the family and the state, and between the state and the Church were not open to revision nor even, essentially, to discussion. Pius IX refused to make any concessions to the emerging secular and omnicompetent modern state which regarded the Church as one more voluntary society to which it owed no other kind of obligation than those which it recognized to all other voluntary societies. This attitude did not die out in later nineteenth-century Catholicism; it affected the way in which, in *Graves de Communi* (1901), Leo XIII distinguished between Social Democracy and Christian Democracy.

Social Democracy, he said, aimed at putting all government in the hands of the people, reducing all ranks to the same level, abolishing all distinctions of class, and introducing community of goods. The right of ownership was to be abrogated, and whatever property a man possessed, or whatever means of livelihood he had, was to be common to all. The acquirement and enjoyment of corporal, external goods constituted the whole of man's happiness. As against this, Christian Democracy, by the fact that it was Christian, was necessarily built on the principles of the divine faith, and provided for the betterment of the masses, with the ulterior object of availing itself of the occasion to fashion their minds for things everlasting. For Christian Democracy, justice was sacred; the right of acquiring and possessing property could not be impugned; and the various distinctions and degrees which were indispensable to every well-ordered commonwealth must be safeguarded. Finally, Christian Democracy must try to preserve in every human society the form and character which God ceaselessly impressed upon it. Christian Democracy and Social Democracy had nothing in common. They differed as much as the sect of socialism differed from the profession of Christianity.

Christian Democracy, the encyclical continued, did not necessarily mean popular government, but simply a benevolent and Christian movement on behalf of the people. This statement has to be understood in the light of the earlier encyclical, *Rerum Novarum*, 'The condition of Labour' (1891). *Rerum Novarum*, still the foundation of modern Roman Catholic social theology, started from the assertion that 'some remedy must be found, and quickly found, for the misery and wretchedness which press so heavily on the large majority of the very poor'. The encyclical then dismissed the humanist remedy, socialism, as emphatically unjust, because socialist proposals would rob the lawful possessor, bring the state into a sphere which was not its own and cause complete confusion in the community.

In both papal pronouncements, property was seen as basic to the argument. *Rerum Novarum* said that when a man worked for money he did so in order to obtain property which he then wanted to keep in his private possession. Every man had by nature the right to property of his own: this was an appeal to natural law, which the socialists had no authority to disobey. The primary community in which this property-holding individual lived was the family, which was ideally and historically anterior to the state – a proposition which flatly contradicted the view of its own powers which the state had been developing steadily since the sixteenth century, and also ran counter to the Marxist thesis that neither family nor state had an extra-historical essence, but that both words could have very different meanings and mutual relations at different historical times. *Rerum Novarum* denounced the idea that class was naturally hostile to class; the contrary was the truth, for 'Capital cannot do without Labour, nor Labour without Capital', a statement that might have many different political meanings, and which could also be found in common use in various Protestant circles.

Rerum Novarum had no fresh insight into the causes of poverty. The encyclical relied on the view that the distribution of money depended upon the interplay of 'fortune' and 'misfortune'. That the poor might object to their poverty being interpreted as simply the result of uncontrollable chance did embarrass the authors, who said that as for those who did not possess the gifts of fortune, they were taught by the Church that in God's sight poverty was no disgrace and that there was nothing to be ashamed of in seeking one's bread by labour. There was also, however, a somewhat conflicting tendency to argue that infidelity and poverty were linked, for it was claimed that Christian morality, when it was adequately practised, conduced of itself to temporal prosperity, for it merited the blessing of God who was the source of all blessing. The Encyclical criticized those who wanted to replace charity with a system of state-organized relief: 'no human methods will ever supply the place of the devotion and self-sacrifice of Christian charity'.

The Encyclical concluded with practical proposals. Strikes, which were said to be normally harmful for all involved, were to be prevented as far as possible by removing the causes of conflict between employer and employee. Hours of labour should be regulated; children excluded from factories; women were not suited to certain trades, 'for a woman is by nature fitted for home-work'. Wages should be sufficient to support the wage-earner in reasonable and frugal comfort. If all this were done a new race of property-owning workers would arise, for if a workman's wages were sufficient to keep his family in reasonable comfort he would not find it hard, if he were a sensible man, to put by a little property. Such men had a natural right to form trade unions, and the state must protect natural rights. A Christian worker ought not to join a union run on principles incompatible with Christianity, and the Encyclical urged them to join the associations of Catholic employers and employees which it was one of Leo XIII's aims to promote.

It can be argued, and indeed in the long run it had to be argued, that *Rerum Novarum* was not meant to lay down rules from which a detailed Catholic policy could be worked out. Once again, as in the *Syllabus*, the Vatican was defining the relationship between the Church and the world. Capitalism was acceptable, as long as it conceded the workers' natural rights, which embraced a reasonable wage, good working conditions and unionization; socialism was not acceptable, if socialism meant the abolition of private property. Religion must take precedence over everything else as the only permanent foundation for a right relationship between capital and labour.

There was a wide gap between J. M. Ludlow's position, that the application of the Gospel to society required a new socio-economic structure, and the attempt of documents like *Rerum Novarum* to assimilate the modern industrial world and the mass urban society which it was producing to the hierarchical forms of organizations with which the churches had been familiar in the past. Many later nineteenth-century British and American Protestants, unwilling to ignore the poverty and misery of town life for the majority of people, nevertheless sided implicitly with the Encyclical in rejecting any demand for radical social change on theological grounds. Instead, they advocated the so-called Social Gospel: gambling, drinking and prostitution were denounced as the alleged causes of the troubles of the working-classes; enthusiastic, but not very successful, attempts were made to limit such behaviour. Protestant pietists seemed reluctant to look beyond symptoms and a moral judgement passed on individuals. They wanted the existing social order, but they wanted it administered in a tidier, more moralistic style. This was also the revivalist period *par excellence*, the age of Moody and Sankey, when many religious writers really thought that the working-man had only to will a change in his own behaviour, and largely ignored the extent to which individual conduct was enmeshed in an economic and social structure.

The social theology of two later nineteenth-century German writers,

Albrecht Ritschl (1822–89) and Wilhelm Herrmann (1846–1922) offered sophisticated examples of the negative way in which Protestant theology met the problems of a dynamic industrial society. For Ritschl, though he was a devoted admirer of Bismarck and the unified German Empire which he created, the state had no positive Christian function. The object of the state as such was order, the formation of an ethical community; this did not include the Christianization of the community, and one could not speak properly of either a Christian state, or of a Christian political party within a state. As the richest form of natural organization the state prepared men for the emergence of the Kingdom of God. This Kingdom, as Ritschl understood it, was a kind of international ethical-religious spiritual community which would express a world-wide consciousness of human solidarity. It was true that when this universal spiritual community had been established it would be clear that the theological understanding of history coincided with the history of European culture; non-European cultures had nothing to contribute beyond their capacity to enter into the western religious inheritance; but Ritschl was not aware of being a German nationalist, he regarded the idea of the Kingdom of God as the one safeguard against nationalism and other kinds of particularism. Perhaps his most striking statement of this idea was to be found in *Justification and Reconciliation*:

> Moral fellowship, viewed in these two characteristics of possessing the widest possible extension and being animated by the most comprehensive motive, can only be conceived as the Kingdom of God. This idea Christ expresses in such a way that He transcends the view of the national State, and takes up an attitude essentially opposed to it.[1]

Here was the basis of a radical Christian reply to the passionate nationalism of the nineteenth and twentieth centuries, but Ritschl was not as critical of Bismarckian Germany as his conception of the Kingdom of God might lead one to expect. Positively, he said that in post-1870 Germany Protestantism must transform the nation by forming a cultural community which would both strengthen the state and also lead onward to the Kingdom of God. At the same time, however, he attacked Social Democracy, Liberalism and Roman Catholic Ultramontanism (a comparison with the targets of the *Syllabus of Errors* is interesting) as destructive of the harmony of the new State. In 1887, not long before his death, he gave a famous public lecture in which he tried to show that these three groups did not oppose Bismarck as a matter of coincidence but were inspired by a common belief in natural law which they drew from medieval sources but which might also be traced back to pre-Christian times, a fact which Ritschl found especially damning. In effect, he made his own version of Protestant political conservatism the only possible Christian political stance, and showed little awareness of the importance of the 'social question' at all.

One reason why Ritschl related the modern state and the Kingdom of

---

[1] A. Ritschl, *Justification and Reconciliation*, ed. H. R. Mackintosh (New York, 1966), p. 252.

God so loosely together was that he combined a confidence in the divine direction of human history with an optimistic faith in the possibilities of nation-state behaviour – all this must somehow help to usher in the moral integration of humanity in the Kingdom of God. As for the individual, he said that 'moral action in our calling is the form in which our life-work as a totality is produced as our contribution to the Kingdom of God'.[1] But he had little to add to the eighteenth-century Lutheran downgrading of the Reformation idea of vocation. 'A man's vocation', he said, 'as a citizen denotes that particular department of work in human society in the regular pursuit of which the individual realises at once his own self-end and the ultimate end of society. Every civil vocation is an ethical vocation, and not a means of egoism, in so far as it is pursued under the view that in society as a whole and in the individual the moral law ought to be fulfilled, and the highest conceivable goal for the race obtained. The varieties of ethical vocation, according to their natural origin, divide themselves in manifold fashion into vocations which have their origin in the family, those which are concerned with the production, manipulation and distribution of the means of the physical life, those connected with the state and with religion, vocations in the sphere of science and art.'[2]

Ritschl's interpretation of vocation expressed only a vague sacralization of the traditional order of things. It was all very well to make this the basis of a moral integration of humanity into the divine kingdom, but men were only likely to accept such a lofty spiritualization of human relationships if they already accepted the social structure on which it rested, and in effect, whether Ritschl recognized it or not, both the secular authority of the European social order, which Marx had challenged, and its Christian status, which writers like Ludlow had questioned, had declined in his lifetime. For Ritschl himself, the decisive political events had been first, the failure of the 1848 revolution in Prussia, after which he gave up his initial liberalism; and second, the triumph of Bismarck's drive to unite Germany politically. He overvalued these events and the kind of unity which they represented. As a result, he interpreted the evident alienation of the German working-classes from the German Churches in the industrial areas after 1850 as a breach of this new, and for him God-given, harmony. His remedy was theological, not political, because as far as he could see there was nothing political in the situation which he needed to repudiate. What had alienated the working-class, he argued, was the Lutheran habit of preaching about the consciousness of one's sinfulness to such a degree that men felt that their work had no value in the eyes of God. Protestantism must break out of this disastrous subjectivity, must accept and consecrate the labours of mankind; if the Churches integrated the worker into their own spiritual community he would soon find his place in the moralized community of the state. In practice, however, it was the hard-working, prosperous middle-class German Protestants who welcomed this change of style and were pleased to see God's attention drawn to their contribution to the new German Empire. Despite the potential critical power of his idea

[1] *ib.* p. 668.
[2] *ib.* p. 445.

of the Kingdom of God, then, Ritschl ended by asserting that the working-classes must adjust themselves spiritually as well as politically to the existing frame of society; he was as socially conservative as the popular apologists of the Social Gospel.

If Ritschl's theology expressed something of the widespread feeling in the western middle-classes that industrial expansion was not only good in itself but also a guarantee of the planet's future peace and prosperity, Wilhelm Herrmann, who had originally been a pupil of Ritschl's but in his later years broke with his master's ideas, gave expression to some of the doubts which were simultaneously arising in the same areas of society about what was happening. To some observers in the late nineteenth century it seemed not only that traditional values were being destroyed in the teeming cities of the west, where materialism apparently dominated, but also that the only effective new systems of value were those of socialism or marxism, which such observers identified with the denial of the existence of God, the abolition of private property and the rejection of the aesthetic standards of the past. In so far as he understood the situation in this way, Ritschl assumed that in a conflict between the spiritual and the material the spiritual would be bound to conquer, and he therefore opposed the view that Christianity necessarily implied or required any kind of withdrawal from the everyday, material world; the coming Kingdom of God would not turn out to be the justification of monasticism as the highest form of the Christian life.

In his later work, however, Herrmann stopped using the Kingdom of God as a theological category, and began to interpret the ethical commands of Christianity as world-renouncing. Herrmann attached great importance to ethical experience as such, because he regarded this as the ground on which modern religious belief could be rebuilt; he did not foresee, any more than similar liberal Protestant theologians like Tennant or Rashdall saw, that the authority of the so-called moral experience would soon be questioned as sharply as the authority of religious experience had been already. Herrmann, therefore, did not regard the 'social question' as important in itself – he was not a political theologian at all – but only as one more by-product of the inescapable inner struggle between the ethical-religious life of the individual man and the this-worldly demands of concrete living. The importance of Herrmann's position for social theology was that he changed what had come to be called *Kulturprotestantismus*, the Ritschlian desire to unite the spiritual and cultural, completely; his overriding interest in personal, and therefore individual, religious and moral experience destroyed the system as a theology of society at a time when some such social theology was, after all, desperately needed. Herrmann held that Christian ethics should be concerned with the inner spiritual growth of the individual, who should be led to see his primary ethical experience of life as an unsatisfactory conflict between world-renunciation and world-absorption, a conflict which could only be resolved beyond the sphere of the ethical in the sphere of the religious; the highest ethical achievement was open to man only as a divine gift. From this lofty height Herrmann explained the opposition of many Social Democrats to Christianity as the result of the personal life; the proper business of the state was simply to protect and strengthen the family, which formed the creative environment of both the ethical and religious spheres.

Herrmann's view could be assessed in various ways. At one level he was a religious existentialist who thought that men might best be persuaded to return to religion if they first followed the path of ethical self-analysis to what he took to be its inevitable end in shame and self-accusation. At the level of social theology his attitude suggested that even at the beginning of the twentieth century some Protestant theologians were still tempted to think that the new industrial society offered no significantly altered situation for theology. An acute contemporary, Ernst Troeltsch (see p. 574), said that Herrmann's theology still resembled much too closely the ethical system of orthodox Lutheranism with its doctrine of the two realms and its tendency to leave the responsibility for the context of human action to the orders of creation. Herrmann's best-known book, *The Communion of the Christian with God* (1886, 6th ed. 1908), was subtitled 'described on the basis of Luther's statements', but he did not provide a satisfactory answer to the question as to whether Luther's theology was relevant to the modern world. This was not a question which came naturally to most Lutheran theologians, but it came naturally enough to those who were not.

When one of the leaders of the next generation of German theologians, Karl Barth, in *Protestant Theology in the Nineteenth Century* (1947), accused Ritschl of subordinating the ideas of sin, justification, Christ and God to the needs of man, so that for him Christianity seemed to exist simply in order that the bourgeoisie should have the spiritual power and cultural ease to enjoy the age of Bismarck with a good conscience, he was implying that Ritschl was defending theologically the kind of Protestant self-satisfaction which Kierkegaard had satirized in his *Attack on Christendom* (1855). There was some truth in this, but Barth was not entirely fair to either Ritschl or Herrmann, whom he regarded as typical figures of the Liberal Protestantism which he himself was criticizing. For Ritschl certainly distinguished between reconciliation as a religious activity fixed in God, and ethical activity taking place in the sphere of personal relations; he did not suppose that the busy middle-class was justified in God's sight by its mere industriousness, or that the kingdom of God amounted to nothing more than a perpetually expanding German Empire. And Herrmann, though more of a social individualist than Ritschl, and therefore more justifiably criticized in this respect by Barth, drew back from any identification of the purpose of man with the purpose of God, saying that if men enjoyed the world they must do so as simultaneously standing apart from it, having it as though they had it not. And in the 1920s Barth's own political theology, with its strong impulse to leave the historical context to the unchecked destructiveness of the political pseudo-creativity of man, resembled that of Herrmann much more than he seems to have appreciated.

Nevertheless, the belief that modern western society rested on ideological premises unacceptable to Christianity, and that there ought to be an alternative which was religiously preferable, grew steadily between the 1890s and the end of the First World War, reaching its peak at the end of the

1920s. There were those in the English Anglo-Catholic tradition, for instance, who were so dismayed by the spectacle of mass industrialized society that they looked for a solution in a return to the past, to a medieval Christian model of society, an approach which had little positive result because it was so divorced from reality. A. J. Penty, for example, in an essay called 'The Obstacle of Industrialism', anticipated a time when once again agriculture and craftsmanship (in a very limited sense) would be exalted as the foundation of national prosperity, and when a Just and Fixed Price would be maintained by a system of Guilds covering the country (*The Return of Christendom*, by a Group of Churchmen, 1922).

Others, like the American Baptist, Walter Rauschenbusch (1861–1918), whose work was another comment on the popular but muddled belief that the weakness of Liberal Protestantism lay in its excessive individualism, sought to develop the Ritschlian system from its original form. One of the key chapters of Rauschenbusch's best-known book, *Christianity and the Social Crisis* (1907), was headed 'The Social Aims of Jesus', and concluded:

> Jesus has been called the first socialist. He was more; he was the first real man, the inaugurator of a new humanity. But as such he bore within him the germs of a new social and political order . . . Theologians have felt no hesitation in founding a system of speculative thought on the teachings of Jesus, and yet Jesus was never an inhabitant of the realm of speculative thought. He has been made the founder and organiser of a great ecclesiastical machine, which derives authority for its offices and institutions from him, and yet 'hardly any problem of exegesis is more difficult than to discover in the gospels an administrative or organizing or ecclesiastical Christ'. There is at least as much justification in invoking his name today as the champion of a great movement for a more righteous social life. He was neither a theologian, nor an ecclesiastic, nor a socialist. But if we were forced to classify him either with the great theologians . . . or with the mighty popes and princes of the Church . . . or with the men who are giving their heart and life to the propaganda of a new social system – where should we place him?[1]

Rauschenbusch's emphasis fell on the need to abolish the competitive and individualistic socio-economic order. Primitive society, he said, was 'communistic'. So were the most valuable institutions in the modern world, the family, school and Church. Even the state was essentially 'communistic', and was now becoming more so. Rauschenbusch insisted that Christianity had more in common with cooperative systems than with competitive disunity; it ought to help society to evolve from the existing phase of economic individualism to a higher kind of community. And since idealists alone were unable to change the world, Christianity should ally itself with the working-classes; once they controlled the means of production, industry could be reorganized on the basis of cooperation; this was the first vital step to the Christianization of the social order.

There was, of course, no serious question of the early twentieth-century

[1] See *The Social Gospel in America*, ed. R. T. Handy (1966).

American Churches supporting the under-organized American proletariat in a campaign to storm the heights of American capitalism. Teetotalism was closer to the Protestant heart, and the women's suffrage movement benefited from the belief that women, if given the vote, would use it against the liquor interest. Yet Rauschenbusch put his finger on the problem which was to dominate political theology for the next seventy years. Should organized Christianity simply be content to try to moralize the economic status quo; should it work for a radical reform of society in the not so distant future; or, going beyond Rauschenbusch's immediate horizon, should it support potentially violent revolutionary groups which were committed to seizing power? Behind this lay another, older distinction between those theologians who interpreted history pessimistically, believing that human society would steadily deteriorate until the abrupt return of Christ brought secular history to an end; and those who believed that both Church and Society would steadily grow better and better until an age of perfect peace and prosperity painlessly ushered in the Second Coming. With the aid of the historical-critical method Rauschenbusch unhesitatingly recruited Jesus for the second point of view.

> Jesus, like all the prophets and like all his spiritually minded country-men, lived in the hope of a great transformation of the national, social and religious life about him. He shared the substance of that hope with his people, but by his profounder insight and his loftier faith he elevated and transformed the common hope. He rejected all violent means and thereby transferred the inevitable conflict from the field of battle to the antagonism of mind against mind . . . He postponed the divine catastrophe of judgement to the dim distance and put the emphasis on the growth of the new life that was now going on . . . The tone of sadness in his later ministry was not due simply to the approach of his own death but to the consciousness that his purpose for his nation had failed . . . He began then to draw his disciples more closely about him and to create the nucleus of a new nation within the old . . . He also rose then to the conviction that he would return and accomplish in the future what he had hoped to accomplish in this earthly life.[1]

This Jesus was saddened by events, rejected by the society to which he came, yet still determined to create a new life for mankind – the catastrophe of judgement was postponed into the distant future. This picture reflected Rauschenbusch's own situation. He had published a programme called 'Practical Socialism' in 1901, precisely on the ground that the revolution for which the doctrinaire socialists were waiting would take a long time to come, and that it was immoral to put off reform in the present for the sake of changes which might or might not happen in the future. He suggested, among other schemes, the municipalization of electricity, gas and water; the extension of local education; library and museum services; and an inheritance tax. This might have been regarded as 'Fabianism' in the England of the same period, and one should distinguish between 'social gospel' as the name for a kind of moral crusade about behaviour (drinking,

[1] W. Rauschenbusch, *Christianity and the Social Crisis* (1907), pp. 65–6.

gambling, etc.), and 'social gospel' as the name for programmes which were more concerned with altering the social environment and less with personal behaviour.[1]

In Germany, events moved faster than in America, as was to be expected in a country where even before 1914 the Social Democratic Party had become a powerful organ of opposition to the Prussian idea of a united Germany. Harnack attached importance to the problem of what was to be done to re-integrate the social-democratic world into the general community and in this he was more realistic than Herrmann; the move away from the more moralistic version of the Social Gospel (which had its German equivalent, the 'evangelisch-sozial') came at the opening of the twentieth century. The first new leader was C. F. Blumhardt (1842–1919), who in late middle-age emerged as the centre of what was called a movement of 'Religious Socialism'. He was the mildest of the group; he used biblical language to paint a picture of God coming near to the poor and wretched in the Kingdom; he taught that Jesus had planted a seed in the human race which had grown among the Jews and atheists as well as among the Christians; the socialist utopia was therefore itself an offshoot of the Kingdom of God. Blumhardt sat as a social-democratic member of the Württemberg Diet from 1900 to 1906, whereas the British Free Church ministers who sat in Parliament in the Edwardian period did so as members of the Liberal Party. Even before the outbreak of war in 1914 the Religious Socialists were moving on to more dramatic statement, however; one of Blumhardt's associates, the Swiss theologian, Hermann Kütter, said in 1912, that the Social Democrats were revolutionary because God was revolutionary; they were men of revolution because God was the great revolutionary; the Religious Socialists must advance with them because so must the Kingdom of God.

Fundamental to Religious Socialism was the idea which Paul Tillich developed after 1918, that the Christian faith was a response to the Christ-event which, once freed from the narrowing effects of confessionalism which helped to bind men to their own social and economic self-interest, required and also made possible a comprehensive understanding of the will of God for society. This meant that the traditional opposition between the Church and the world was replaced by the idea of confrontation between God and his whole creation, the Church being regarded in its institutional form as one of the varieties of human rebellion against God. This was originally a point of agreement between Tillich and Karl Barth, who began his career close to the Religious Socialists, and with a similar impulse to criticise the visible Church. The political controversy about the proper economic form of society had added detail and sophistication to the traditional attack on the Church for becoming too involved in 'the world', a tradition which reached Barth, for example, through Kierkegaard.

Barth, however, refused to support the Christian Labour movement which the Religious Socialists wanted to start among the proletariat; he said

[1] See P. d'A. Jones, *The Christian Socialist Revival 1877–1914* (Princeton, 1968), for an account of how the later Christian Socialists failed, by and large, to set out a distinctively *christian* socialism.

that his earlier attacks on the Church had been 'churchly', not 'anti-church', that they had been made from a stance consciously *inside* the Church and with no intention of seeking to supersede what existed. Barth was perhaps less moved by the political upheavals which followed the German loss of the war in 1918 than was Tillich. For Tillich the post-war years in Germany seemed to present a chance to realize the evangelical principle in the specific social-democratic case now that the whole nation had fallen into what he interpreted as a revolutionary situation. Theologians have tended to agree with Barth in dismissing Tillich and the Religious Socialists as misguided, and certainly theologians cannot hope to manipulate the Church into doing politically what the majority of its members do not actually want to do. Nevertheless, the historical conclusion of the 1920s was the victory of Adolf Hitler, and this suggests that Tillich's campaign to persuade the German Churches to accept a socialist Weimar – which many German Catholics and Protestants were loath to do, whether for religious, nationalist, or anti-marxist reasons – was politically justifiable. The survival of Weimar was hardly the worst that could have happened. Barth, despite his theoretical approval of the Social Democratic Party, an approval which he maintained after 1933 on the ground that the Party stood for the working-class and for the German anti-militarist tradition, took little or no part in Social Democratic affairs during the Weimar Republic's short lease of Germany. On the other hand, when Tillich said in 1919 that the Religious Socialists stood on the ground of the Socialist Revolution, as distinct from the 'evangelisch-sozial' position, he was bound to antagonize many in the German Churches.

It is enlightening to look at the different approaches of Ludlow, Kütter, Tillich, and the later Czech. Protestant leader, Josef Hromadka (1889–1969), to the problem of a Christian politics. What affected Ludlow most deeply, for example, was not the sufferings of the working-classes but the way in which a section of the commercial classes bought cheap, sold dear and claimed that wages ought to be settled in the same non-moral atmosphere: he lived at a time when social reformers still hoped to modify the attitudes of the possessing groups, and before pseudo-Darwinian images of 'struggle' and 'survival' had increased the total effect of Malthus on the early Victorian imagination. Kütter, when he published *Sie Müssen* in 1904, no longer believed that it was possible to educate the forces which he collectively labelled 'Mammon'; he felt that the oppressive behaviour of capitalist society justified revolution to the extent that Christians could not oppose it in the name of order or decency or the will of God; he wrote as though revolution was historically inevitable, as though the proletariat would certainly be victorious, and as though what mattered therefore was the attitude which the Churches adopted to the new order which was coming. God was on the side of the revolution, because this revolution would be for the sake of His people, the poor and the helpless. Going much further than either Ludlow or his successors in England, Kütter said: 'The class war exists. It was there from the first moment that the oppressed lay at the foot of the oppressor' (*Sie Müssen*, p. 111). Mammon was to blame for the class struggle; strikes were justifiable because the employing class made concessions only under duress. The whole argument is interesting, because it was to recur, *mutatis mutandis*, after the Second World War with relation to the Third World, and especially to South America, where minority Catholic theologians defended Christian involvement in a struggle for economic, social and cultural liberation in very similar terms. (See G. Gutiérrez, *A Theology of Liberation* (1973); H. Assmann, *Practical Theology of Liberation* (1973); and J. M. Bonino, *Revolutionary Theology Comes of Age* (1975).) Throughout the twentieth century, in fact, the problem of the Christian attitude to violence as a political method was never far from the mind of the sophisticated theologian.

For all his fire, however, Kütter in 1904 did not really expect that revolution would happen soon. In 1919, on the other hand, Tillich believed for a moment that revolution had taken place. He therefore repeated Kütter's argument that the Churches should side with the revolution, but the slow collapse of Weimar, like the weakness of the far from revolutionary British socialist governments in 1923 and 1929, showed that the Russian Revolution had not after all heralded the total disintegration of western capitalism. And as the Nazi movement tightened its hold on Germany the Christian groups were forced into so negative a position that Dietrich Bonhoeffer seriously considered the place of the assassination of Hitler in a Christian programme.

For Hromadka the historical circumstances were different again. Tillich had soon to face the fact that the Germany of the 1920s was not going to become a socialist state. Hromadka, however, quickly realized that the Communist takeover in Czechoslovakia in 1948 would last his lifetime, which it did. By the end of the 1950s, he said, the structure of the socialist state had been consolidated; not even those most opposed to socialism still believed that it would be possible, by force or by secret infiltration, to liquidate the new political order. But for that very reason Czech Protestants faced a complex question of what to do in order that the individual might become a convinced and responsible partner in the building of the new society, and so that he might bring to it everything from the Protestant past and from that of the rest of the world which had helped to raise the level and dignity of human life. There must therefore be a Christian-Marxist dialogue which would cover not only questions of philosophical theology, but also the Marxist and Christian attitudes to the deep social divisions of human society. The class struggle, Hromadka said, was not just a slogan, but pointed to the gap between riches and poverty, whether in individuals or nations.[1] There were signs of such a dialogue beginning in France in the 1960s, between writers as distinguished as the Roman Catholic theologian, Karl Rahner, and Roger Garaudy, at one time a prominent member of the French Communist Party, but who was expelled in 1970.[2] In his *Theological Investigations* (volume XII, 1974) Karl Rahner insisted that political theology was still in its infancy, that the task of criticizing society which belonged to the official Church had still not achieved any theological definition. There was no absolute political

---

[1] J. L. Hromadka, *Thoughts of a Czech Pastor* (1970), p. 90.
[2] See R. Garaudy, *The Turning-Point of Socialism* (1969) and *The Whole Truth* (1971).

theology. A social encyclical like *Mater et Magistra* (1961) was not doctrine or binding prescription, but something that was recommended to the historically created freedom of man. He accepted much of the criticism of the visible Church. Where the Church was not directly threatened by the institutions of the society and the state, he said, and where the leaders of Christian thought did not feel themselves directly injured by institutionalized injustice, the task of the Church as a social critic was largely neglected. The case of South America was not far from Rahner's mind, and he recalled that Pius XI, in *Firmissiman Constantiam* (1937) had said that when a social order threatened the ultimate basis of human living and rights, revolutionary force might not only be permitted but even prescribed to Christians. Rahner said that *Spes et Gaudium*, a social document from the second Vatican Council, accepted that there might be complete political disagreement between groups of conscientious Christians, and implied that although in such situations individual groups could not claim the authority of the official Church, they could appeal to the authority of the Gospel.[1] There was no question here of a reconciliation of the Catholic and Marxist understandings of Man and God; Rahner was suggesting, however, that in the political area at least (and this included issues like education policy and toleration) the claims of revelation could be defended and discussed without the intransigeance of the *Syllabus of Errors*: doctrinal and political pluralism were not impossible from his point of view. For Rahner the Church was one social group within a pluralistic society; even natural law did not yield absolutely unreserved and concrete imperatives such as would deprive man and society of the power to commit themselves to historical decisions, in other words, to change things. The recognition that cultures have histories has profoundly affected Catholic social theology, so that the rôle assigned to property in *Rerum Novarum*, for example, might now be thought of as a historical case, rather than necessarily as a normative proposition.[2]

As for Britain, the Christian Socialist tradition did not collapse overnight after the First World War. It was still possible in 1923 for an official Anglican committee on 'Christianity and Industrial Problems', for example, to report that the fundamental evil of modern industrialism was that it encouraged competition for private gain instead of co-operation for public service. This perversion of motive, the Report said, fostered an organization of industry which treated the workers as hands rather than persons. This encouraged conditions of poverty which did not arise from the personal defects of individuals or from natural scarcity, but which existed side by side with excessive riches. There was an attitude of mutual antagonism and suspicion between the different parties engaged in industry. And it stated categorically that the concept of industry as a selfish competitive struggle was unchristian. Industry ought to be regarded primarily as a social service, based on the effort of every individual to discharge his duty to his neighbour and the community.[3] The Committee recommended the

---

[1] K. Rahner, *Theological Investigations*, vol. 12 (1974), p. 246.

[2] K. Rahner, *Theological Investigations*, vol. 14 (1976), 'The Unreadiness of the Church's members to Accept Poverty', pp. 270–79, is a good example.

[3] E. Talbot, ed., *Christianity and Industrial Problems* (1918), pp. 50–74.

principle of a living wage, unemployment insurance, and the setting up of an industrial parliament to represent the statesmanship of all parties in industry, an idea which recurred steadily down to 1939, especially in circles influenced by corporatist theories.

This condemnation of the spirit of capitalism was reminiscent of Maurice's denunciation of the assertion that competition was a law of the universe, but the Report said little about the structure of industry. This was because the Committee was chiefly moved (as the Christian Socialists had been in 1848) by a sense of the alienation of the working-classes from organized religion. The 1916 Report on *Church and State* had said that the hostility of the working-class originated partly in the belief that the Church was the moral policeman that the propertied classes used to protect their own interests, and partly in the belief that the moral teaching of the Church was against progress, and social change.[1] Apart from asking for more working-class priests (but not suggesting how they could be found if the case was as stated) the later *Report* advocated improved education, including a *compulsory* scheme for half-time school attendance by factory-workers between the age when full-time schooling stopped and that of eighteen; it was high-handed as well as high-minded.[2]

Between 1918 and 1939 the Anglican and Roman Churches in Britain suffered from a conflict between the recognition that organized Christianity had really very little influence on what happened in industry (as was clear in the General Strike of 1926), and a conviction that they ought as Churches to play a reconciling rôle in society. This was the social theology of the majority of the clergy (not social radicalism), who always thought of themselves as exercising a ministry of reconciliation in a static but disharmonious world. They could not believe that the real world of the inter-war years was in flux, and that the majority of the laity thought that the official Churches should not play an independent political rôle on the basis of an allegedly Christian programme.

William Temple (1881–1944), who was Archbishop of Canterbury for the last two years of his life, was therefore perhaps unduly optimistic when, between 1941 and 1944 he tried to form what he called 'a body of influence guided by Christian principles' to plead in the post-war period for aims such as proper housing and adequate nutritional standards for the whole nation. Temple believed that the Church had the right to lay down the principles which should govern the ordering of human society, because the Church possessed a divine revelation which illuminated every phase of human conduct. It was the ease with which such generalizations could be translated into 'principles' which was growing old-fashioned, and the post-war period in fact offered evidence for the mutability of 'Christian principles' when, in 1958, for example, the Lambeth Conference finally abandoned the position that artificial contraception could be permitted only in cases of exceptional social or medical need; instead, a case was now made for 'positive parenthood', which meant the 'planned family'. It was even

[1] *Report of the Archbishops' Committee on Church and State* (1916), p. 253.
[2] See E. R. Norman, *Church and Society in England 1770–1970* (1976), for a discussion of the influence of class-background on Anglican social thinking.

stated in 'The Family in Contemporary Society' that 'those who carelessly and improvidently bring children into the world trusting in an unknown future or a generous society to care for them, need to make a vigorous examination of their lack of concern for their children and for the society of which they are a part'.[1] Although the Lambeth Committee produced an exposition of *Genesis* which justified the change of view, this was a kind of ingenuity which only underlined the historically relative nature of the shift in policy. And this throws light on the demand for 'theologians of revolution': it is the post-revolutionary period which matters most, and at that point the dogmatist, whether religious or secular, has become obsolete.[2]

In general, then, the second half of the twentieth century has not seen the formulation of an agreed social theology. This is hardly surprising when one remembers that industrial societies have themselves been sharply divided by rival theories of the ideal state. Theologians who believe that Christian institutions should seek to foster social reconciliation in terms of the existing system instead of supporting social conflict in terms of some possible future system naturally do not want to choose between (for example) capitalism and socialism, and their position relates easily to those passages in the New Testament which reflect the early Christian acceptance of the hierarchical society of the Roman Empire in which the new religious movement came to life. The christians of the first five centuries did not consciously set out to turn the Mediterranean world upside down in a socio-political sense. They inhabited a culture in which critical groups often contracted out; fourth and fifth century monks and hermits, for example, expressed by withdrawal a widespread intellectual distaste for what they regarded as a decadent urban way of life. In the twentieth century the loss of social power by religious institutions, their inability to prevent, for instance, secular legal systems from developing an attitude to marriage which ignores ecclesiastical tradition, has increased the attractiveness of this kind of theology, which should not be confused with the kind of political conservatism which uses classical Christian pessimism about human nature as a justification for the rejection of socialism. Opposition to political activity may spring (as it did in Karl Barth's case in the 1920s) from a profound insight into the possible rôle of the Christian community as the symbol of the coming Kingdom of God; Christians, Barth thought, should not commit themselves either to the political left or the political right, as though one or other of these secular political attitudes embodied the divine society in its programme. God worked out his purposes through his own people, whose loyalty to him must transcend other loyalties of whatever kind.

Barth's point of view must be distinguished not only from the neo-Hegelian long-haul optimism of the older versions of the 'social gospel', as well as from the more desperate social eschatology of the 'revolutionary' Christians of the 1970s, but also from the so-called 'Christian realism' of the American theologian, Reinhold Niebuhr (1892–1971), who rejected the

[1] The Lambeth Conference, 1958, Report 5, 'The Family in Contemporary Society', Part 2, p. 146.
[2] See Hugo Assmann, *Practical Theology of Liberation* (1975), pp. 143–44.

political idealism of Rauschenbusch and his successors, which seemed to him only political innocence, not least in the context of totalitarianism. It might even be said of Niebuhr that his latent criterion of Christian political thinking was its degree of political success; it was certainly part of his criticism of the Christian social radicals that they often seemed to make almost a cult of political failure. His social theology was contained in *Moral Man and Immoral Society* (1932), *An Interpretation of Christian Ethics* (1935) and *Christian Realism and Political Problems* (1954). Niebuhr combined a sense of sin which tempted him to political cynicism, and therefore to an overeasy acceptance of power politics and concepts like the Cold War, with a religious perfectionism which prompted a desire for social change and led him to reintroduce those ideas of moral and social 'progress' against which he had reacted in his earlier books. Niebuhr was able to see through the naiveté of much of the idealistic ecclesiastical political talk and action which abounded in the 1930s; but his cult of 'realism' did not prove as reliable a guide after 1950, when the United States was drifting towards total engagement in Vietnam as well as into urban and racial chaos. Both Barth and Niebuhr approached politics from the orthodox side of the nineteenth-century theological tradition; both saw the danger of assuming that speculations about the continuity and coherence of history – whether idealist or materialist – formed part of the Christian understanding of man and his existence; both were well aware of the temptation, institutional as well as individual, to read politics into religion and come to absolute conclusions. Both, however, accepted the view that major theologians must make political pronouncements. Perhaps neither fully appreciated the position which Rahner was to hold in the 1960s, that even the deepest theological insight would not yield absolute political imperatives such as would deprive men and society of the power to commit themselves to decisions in history: politics was not a simple material to be moulded with a few unchanging principles.

Nevertheless, theologians of society had certainly not retreated to the static theology of the *ancien régime*. Positions had in fact been modified in the second half of the twentieth century. Social change was still theologically accepted; what had slackened was belief in the immediate future. The revolutionary myth, secular as well as theological, had lost some of its potency for the first time since 1789. Theologians tended to invoke the eschatological language and imagery of the Bible, the promise of a final divine intervention, in order to assert that at least the conclusion of history would make moral and religious sense. Many western marxist intellectuals were just as unhappy about the present age, seeming to have lost faith in the revolutionary potential of the working-classes. Secular society itself had lost some of its enchantment, and although monasticism had collapsed as a serious alternative way of life, it seemed as though a new theology of withdrawal was in the air, a spiritual withdrawal of consent from the contemporary organization of man. Such views neither repeated nor endorsed any previous theology, and lacked authoritative formulation; but the tide of secularization, which had run so strongly throughout the period which has been discussed here, seemed checked or turned. It is true that there was still disagreement in the 1970s as to whether the Christian Churches either could or should support violent or non-violent political action against the existing regimes in parts of the world like South Africa or South America; but this was only a symptom of a more subtle theological disengagement from some of the assumptions which had come to dominate modern industrial, urban, nationalist and aggressive society.

V

THE TWENTIETH CENTURY

Granted that at the beginning of the twentieth century traditional doctrines seemed more than usually in question, there were still those theologians who were prepared to defend the orthodox position. In England, for instance, Darwell Stone (1859–1941) advanced an unmodified High Anglican theology in his *Outlines of Christian Dogma* (1900); while P. T. Forsyth (1848–1921) made a brave reaffirmation of the Reformed position in such books as *The Person and Place of Jesus Christ* (1909), though his *The Christian Ethic of War* (1916), a passionate attack on conscientious objection as the evil fruit of a generation of theological liberalism, showed that traditionalism was just as subject to the pressures of circumstances as liberalism was said to have been.

If such writers were not very influential, one reason was that the problems which theologians were being called upon to solve were changing. Late nineteenth-century Protestant theological systems still centred on the individual. One can illustrate this in the case of popular religion, where the American Ira D. Sankey's once famous *Sacred Songs and Solos* (1873 onwards) exploited for revivalism such themes as the anxious, loving father who waited patiently for the return of his repentant 'wandering boy', whom he would then forgive and restore to all the joys of 'home'; and in the case of more formal theology, in the example of Ritschl, for whom the individual's moral experience formed the core of the anti-ontological theology which, as Paul Tillich said, provided a theological foundation for the growth of the strong, active, morally disciplined bourgeois individual of the period.[1] Both attitudes implied a definite relaxation of the intensity with which Soeren Kierkegaard had passionately restated Christianity in terms of an individual who alone could achieve the impossibly absolute relation to the Absolute. In *The Social Teaching of the Christian Churches* (1912, E.T. 1931), Ernst Troeltsch described Christian history largely as a permanent tension between 'the idealistic anarchy and love-communism, which with radical indifference or antipathy toward the other orders of the world embodies the love-idea in small circles', and a socially conservative tradition which preferred some kind of adaptation to the existing social order;[2] but he went on to argue that in the twentieth century both the world-accommodating Church and the world-denying Sect had become intolerable to the educated mind, for whom the religious institution remained possible only in the form

[1] P. Tillich, *Perspectives on Protestant Theology* (1967), pp. 215–19.
[2] E. Troeltsch, *Social Teaching of the Christian Churches* (1931), p. 75.

of the liberal protestant voluntary association.[1] Nietzsche's piercing cry that God was dead made no impact on the theologians who replied to him: J. N. Figgis (1866–1919), for example, in *The Will to Freedom* (1917). Kierkegaard might have understood Nietzsche, but his influence was still to come.

The First World War made a tremendous impact on a generation which had inherited a theology of evil, guilt, repentance and forgiveness conceived on a domestic scale for individual people. The war in France sickened and exhausted men beyond what they could either endure or interpret through their traditional Roman Catholic or Protestant world-views. It was the experience of many men that the normal springs of religious confidence, religious belief and religious feeling perished under such violent pressure. The question of God's existence, of the possibility and credibility of religious experience, seemed much more important than questions of personal guilt, repentance and divine forgiveness. The Stalinist terror, the Nazi persecution of the Jews, the dropping of atomic bombs on Japan, the bitter conflicts in Algeria and the destruction in Vietnam after 1945, all prolonged the reaction, and seemed to exceed the human capacity to find face-saving explanations for God's apparent tolerance of evil. The old theological appeal to human free will as a moral explanation of such events had worn thin after 1914, when a British officer could write, after the Somme battle, which was the real turning-point of feeling in that war:

> It did not seem possible that a gentleman could abandon, so fully as Providence appeared to have done, his servants to the cruelties of the world, on the specious ground that human agency must have a free hand. Except ye believe (not serve) Me, ye shall in no wise enter my Kingdom – a harsh threat, I thought, that no gentleman would utter to any servitor who, not in this world of his own accord, nevertheless carried out his duties to the best of his ability, maybe giving his life for them.[2]

In its fascist and marxist forms, totalitarianism also helped to make men feel that what was happening showed that the universe had no sort of underlying purposive structure: existence had no meaning beyond what men arbitrarily imposed themselves.[3] In an essay, 'Can a truly contemporary person not be an atheist?', Dr. J. A. T. Robinson included, as part of a threefold argument, the assertion that God was morally intolerable. He linked together writers like Feuerbach, Proudhon, Nietzsche, Dostoievsky, Camus and Sartre and said that this variety of atheism drew its strength from the seriousness with which it took the problem of evil: Camus' novel, *The Plague* (1947), a study of innocent suffering, spoke for a whole generation.[4]

If the theologians failed to cope with the task of explaining the ways of God to man, part of the trouble lay in their inability to absorb the scientific

[1] *ib.* p. 381.
[2] J. Terraine, ed., *General Jack's Diary 1914–18* (1964), p. 158.
[3] See the writings of Hannah Arendt, especially *Between Past and Future* (1961).
[4] J. A. T. Robinson, *The New Reformation?* (1965), p. 112.

understanding of biological evolution into the pattern of classical Christian orthodoxy. In a popular account of nineteenth-century church history, for example, A. R. Vidler said that by about 1890 'theologians, at least in the universities, were no longer making reluctant concessions to advances in the natural sciences but were claiming them almost as a godsend', and he quoted the totally undarwinian view of Aubrey Moore (1849–90), a theologian in the anglo-catholic tradition, that 'apart from the scientific evidence in favour of evolution, as a theory it is infinitely more Christian than the theory of special creation'.[1] This apparent acceptance of evolutionary theory often amounted to no more than the adoption of a pre-Darwinian, Enlightenment belief that history, now defined so as to include the biological pre-history of man and the other forms of life, revealed a process of development in which Spirit progressively dominated matter, and it was precisely this easy commerce with teleology which crumpled in the twentieth century. An Anglican anthropologist of the Edwardian period, W. H. L. Duckworth, for instance, said that 'the past history of man fails to reveal to scientists the evidence of a sudden degradation like that implied in the expression "fall". On the contrary, the general tendency has been upwards, though the path has been by no means straight, deviations have been numerous and mistakes frequent.'[2] Here at least the optimism was qualified, but the Scottish theologian, Henry Drummond (1851–97), imagined that in the evolutionary process the altruistic struggle for the life of others (as he called it) emerged from the primitive struggle for existence and became the over-rising impulse:

> In that new social order which the gathering might of the altruistic spirit is creating now around us, in that reign of love which must one day, if the course of evolution hold on its way, be realised, the baser elements will find that solvent prepared for them from the beginning in anticipation of a higher rule on earth . . . Evolution is nothing but the Involution of Love, the revelation of Infinite Spirit, the Eternal Life returning to itself.[3]

Drummond's rhetoric has become unreadable with time, but it is interesting to compare his optimism with a much later discussion of the doctrine of the fall of man:

> Now it is in this sense that man is fallen. Man has innate a genius (they call it the image of God), a genius for absolute generosity which is the essence of goodness. But as yet man cannot fully actualise this genius. He cannot give himself as he knows he has it in himself to give himself. *This is not his fault.* He was born that way. But, none the less, it makes him fall short of his full stature. He is fallen from what in God's Providence he one day will be.[4]

Here 'providence' is the dominating Spirit, man the malleable creature. Drummond's real heir, however, was Teilhard de Chardin (1881–1955) the

[1] A. R. Vidler, *The Church in an Age of Revolution* (1961), p. 121.
[2] H. B. Swete, ed., *Cambridge Theological Essays* (1905), p. 173.
[3] H. Drummond, *The Ascent of Man* (1894), pp. 45–6.
[4] H. A. Williams, *The True Wilderness* (1965).

Jesuit priest and scientist, who injected a similarly optimistic note into his highly speculative application of the idea of a evolutionary process to the universe as a whole. Teilhard, however, was not representative of the Roman Catholic position: until the first decade of the twentieth century the theory of evolution was almost unanimously rejected by theologians: a decree of the Biblical Commission of 1909 still said that a special creation of the first man was to be held as the literal historical sense of the second chapter of the book of Genesis.[1]

The most positive attempt made in the early twentieth century to combine biology and the Christian tradition was contained in *The Origin and Propagation of Sin* by F. R. Tennant (1866–1957). Tennant rejected the traditional Christian pessimism about man, as it had been developed from the Bible, especially from the combination of Genesis with the Pauline epistles. He assumed that the story about Adam and Eve and the serpent was a theologically irrelevant fragment of folklore, the exact intention of which it was impossible to decide. Instead, he appealed from the Scriptures understood in the light of tradition to the evidence of the evolutionary process as he was aware of it. This process seemed to him to have produced man as originally an impulse-governed, lawless organism, fulfilling the nature necessarily his and therefore the life which God willed for him, a man who could not therefore accurately be called 'rebellious'. (The idea of man as 'rebellious' was to be strongly revived in the 1920s by Karl Barth and Emil Brunner: later still, Barth was to call Adam 'the man who sinned at once', who was no sooner man at all than he was also proud man, in rebellion against God.)[2]

In this original man the moral consciousness awakened only slowly – there was no question of some catastrophic change for the worse in his relationship with God, nor was there, at a later stage in man's development, a 'radical bias towards evil' because of the Fall. Tennant was not unreasonably irritated when critics accused him of explaining sin and its sinfulness away, when in fact he made the process of moral growth, which in itself inevitably involved a constantly more acute sense of the nature of evil, the fundamental theme in the story of humanity. 'The sinfulness of sin', he wrote, 'is really more stoutly maintained by a theory which makes all sin actual and a matter of personal accountability, however less guilty its earlier stages may be than its later, than by a theory which finds the source of sinfulness in a supposed hereditary state for which no person is accountable'.[3]

Tennant absolutized the moral sense (in the Victorian fashion) by attributing its awakening directly to God. The Infinite was immanent in each human being and the phenomena of man's sensitive life were due to his agency. Tennant, however, stopped short of the panentheism which the idea of evolution in its broadest sense had made popular on the Continent; instead, he asserted the reality of man's finite freedom. In his *Philosophical Theology* he defended an ethical theism 'which takes the realisation of

[1] See K. Rahner, *Hominisation* (1965), p. 29.
[2] K. Barth, *Church Dogmatics*, vol. 4, *The Doctrine of Reconciliation*, Part 1, pp. 358–514.
[3] F. R. Tennant, *The Origin and Propagation of Sin* (2 ed. 1908), Preface, p. xx.

personality and moral values to be the raison d'être of the world',[1] and this ethical theism was also the basic presupposition of his Christian theology. God revealed the ideal, prepared the heart, supplied the inspiration, but the activity which in human response warred against 'the flesh' – by which Tennant understood the natural and essential, and in themselves not immoral, instincts and impulses of man's animal ancestors – was man's own. Certainly, man was divided, his animal basis conflicting with his acquired human conscience, but the traditional theological question as to how such discord could arise in human life when everything pointed to its proper condition as one of unity and harmony rested (in Tennant's view) on an incorrect presupposition, on the preconception that man had been created at a single stroke both intelligent and elementarily moral, without the background of any prior development. Tennant was quite ready to tolerate the picture of man which he believed followed from the data supplied by modern western science: he regarded 'human nature' as a variable, flowing quality, indefinable in any classical, once-for-all sense. It was as true to say that God was still making man as to say that God had made him, and the origin and meaning of sin had similarly to be sought in the process of becoming.

Nor did Tennant accept the theory which was expressed in several contemporary reviews of *The Origin and Propagation of Sin*, that the 'myth' of the creation of man in the book of Genesis still contained the material for a proper doctrine of human nature. What, Tennant asked very reasonably, was the test of the validity of a doctrine derived from it? Was it the alleged divine inspiration of the story? There would seem to be no other possible guarantee that the narrative of the 'Fall' supplied what might be called a set of theological facts. But, Tennant objected, 'we must define inspiration in this connexion in the light of an inquiry into whether that which the narrative asserts is positive fact, rather than assume its assertions to be true because they occur in the pages of a book which we regard as inspired'.[2] He also rejected the attempt made by such writers as Aubrey Moore to salvage the prestige of Genesis by arguing that the evidence of history showed that one was bound to assume a permanent bias toward evil in human nature. In the preface to the 1908 edition he wrote:

> I am aware that because, from the first dawning of his knowledge of what he ought to do, every human being has failed always to avoid doing what he has known he ought not to do, some philosophers as well as theologians have attributed a 'bias' to the human will, or spoken of 'radical evil'. But I have given full reason, I trust, for holding that what is 'radical' cannot, *ipso facto*, be evil, and have shown that post-Kantian psychology, or at least the recent sciences of child-psychology and race psychology, render the assumption of any warp in our nature unnecessary and improbable, if not impossible. The hypothesis of a bias is purely gratuitous, and would never have presented itself, but for the dominion over men's minds of the doctrine of Original Right-

[1] F. R. Tennant, *Philosophical Theology* (1928), vol. 2, p. 258.
[2] Tennant, *The Origin and Propagation of Sin* (2 ed. 1908), Preface, pp. xxviii–xxix.

eousness . . . it is at least as legitimate to go out of our way in search for a bias towards good, to explain cases where the moral sanction is obeyed, as for a bias towards evil to explain cases where it is disobeyed.[1]

In effect, Tennant refused to be impressed by the view which Karl Barth was to revive, that sin was a mysterious intrusion into the divine plan. He tried to draw a line between the traditional theological position that the relationship between God and man was one of human rebellion, and the view of some nineteenth-century German protestant theologians that sin was an inevitable, or even necessary, part of human development.[2] According to his carefully restricted formula, 'the existence of moral evil would seem to be the most easily justified to reverent speculation if it be looked upon as the contingent product of a moral world, and not as having an absolute purpose in the universe or in the self-manifestation of God'.[3] If sin were the contingent product of a moral world, it was not an inexplicable mystery, nor was it evidence of a 'massive disorder' in the universe, or of a 'pathology' extending through the whole of existence.

Both these phrases occurred in a modern example of the continuing traditional view of the relationship between God and man:

> Perhaps no one would deny that when we look at actual human existing, we preceive a massive disorder in existence, a pathology which seems to extend through all existence, whether we consider the individual or the community, and stultifies it. Because of this prevalent disorder, the potentialities of existence are not actualised as they might be, but are lost or stunted or distorted.[4]

The appeal from revelation to history did not dispose of Tennant's argument against asserting the self-evidence of a 'bias towards evil'. In its High Anglican context it was an appeal designed essentially to protect the argument that because of the universality and solidarity of human disorder, there was within the human situation no remedy to hand that was adequate, that only God, acting through Jesus, could redeem man from his tragic destiny. Here, traditional theological propositions took precedence over any biologically-based interpretation of man's history, and history itself was interpreted in monotone, as pathological.

After 1930, in fact, few writers pursued Tennant's effort to bring the two disciplines together, Essays in the more empirical tradition appeared in *Biology and Personality* (1965), a symposium edited by I. T. Ramsey, who was both philosopher of religion and bishop of Durham, but the contributors were chiefly concerned with problems like that of the status of human personality in the light of brain operations. Only occasionally, as in J. A. T. Robinson's study in christology, *The Human Face of God* (1973), did the

---

[1] Tennant, *The Origin and Propagation of Sin* (2 ed. 1908), Preface, pp. xxviii–xxix.

[2] For example, K. G. Bretschneider, *Dogmatics* (1838); Alexander Schweizer, *Christian Doctrine* (1877); H. Lüdemann, *Christian Dogmatics* (1926). Hegelian philosophy is more important than science in these writers.

[3] Tennant, *The Origin and Propagation of Sin* (2 ed. 1908), p. 137.

[4] J. Macquarrie, *Principles of Modern Theology* (1966), p. 59.

tension between mythology and biology come clearly out into the open. At an early stage of his argument Robinson said that in terms of modern biological knowledge the doctrine of the Virgin Birth had become meaningless: one could only properly speak of a 'man' if one meant someone born into the human evolutionary continuum, for being a man was given historically, within a temporal series of births; one could not just be 'as a man', but had to be a particular person, and this requirement was simply not met either by the classical idea of *anhypostasia*, according to which Christ was a divine person who assumed human nature without assuming human personality, or by the later modification of that position, *enhypostasia*, according to which the essence of humanity exists within the divinity of the Son, so that the human hypostasis or ego of Jesus had always existed within the Trinity. The 'divinity' of Jesus – which Robinson was prepared to affirm – did not depend on his being the incorporation of a heavenly figure from his birth. It depended on the quite different assumption that the Jesus-figure was being created by God from the beginning of the universe. There was no question of adoptianism: from his birth Jesus was the expression of the purpose of God. He was a man, Robinson said, who in all that he said and did as man was the personal representative of God. 'He stands in God's place, he *is* God to us and for us.'[1] But this capacity to represent God so fully that people naturally said of him that God was in him emerged in the process of evolution, within a series of temporal births. No discontinuity was involved, at either the natural or supernatural level. God raised Jesus up through the normal process of heredity and environment and made him his decisive word to men.

Up to this point Robinson had really been showing how readily specific scientific findings, like the data of biological evolution, can be integrated with a religious system: neither biology nor the doctrine of the divinity of Christ had suffered much so far. In the later part of the book, however, driven perhaps by his conviction that in an increasingly secularized western society men were not going to credit much longer a deity situated somehow outside his creation but intermittently intervening in it, Robinson tried, with the help of ideas drawn from Teilhard de Chardin, Dorothee Sölle[2] and (in the background) Hegel, to provide a workable myth of a god *inside* the creation. He turned to the myth of a human race which has to incarnate the World-Spirit. God is not yet immanent in our history because the race has not yet brought him fully into self-consciousness, and so he has to be represented. Jesus, Robinson said, was the sign of a new mutation in the world of Spirit, he was evidence of the reality of a coming new spiritual humanity in which all men would have a part, just as they had done in the order which linked them to the evolutionary past. Here, however, biology had become little more than the source of a handy metaphor ('mutation') which could be used to justify looking for discontinuity in the human future and so to bring back eschatology, the old Jewish hope that God would intervene in the present world-order and change the rules, with a slightly scientific air. And – partly because the conclusion was mediated by Hegel

---

[1] J. A. T. Robinson, *The Human Face of God* (1973), pp. 113–14.
[2] Dorothee Sölle, *Christ the Representative* (1967).

and Teilhard – one was not far from the vulgar progressivism which had flourished at the end of the nineteenth century.[1]

This free use of untestable myth was characteristic of one side of twentieth-century theology. This was true, for example, of Paul Tillich (1886–1974), whose *Systematic Theology* (2 vols 1951–57) was a restatement of Lutheranism in existentialist terms. In the 1920s (see p. 558) Tillich had hoped for a rapprochement between the German Protestant churches and the Social Democrats; driven out of Germany by the triumph of ecclesiastical conservatism and Nazi politics he went to the United States, where his theology became less revolutionary and his vocabulary much more Heideggerian.[2] The problems of 'Man' and society were shifted to a mythological level and attributed to man's tragic destiny, as fallen into a finite existence and incapable of 'authentic being'. 'Man as he exists is not what he essentially is', Tillich wrote, 'he is estranged from the ground of his being, from other beings, and from himself'.[3] Man might, according to Tillich, experience a finite freedom, but this freedom did not enable him to break out of his estrangement, but only to feel himself responsible for every act in which his estrangement was actualized. Sin and guilt were thus translated into the new idiom, and redemption followed, in the form of the 'new being' (Christ), a power from beyond man which healed his existential estrangement. In this pattern the underlying assumption, which had its antecedents in classical Christian theology, was that men and women as we encounter them are unable to be, and yet at the same time are responsible for not being, what their creator intended them to be. This was the assumption which Tennant wanted to drop, and which he argued was not somehow 'revealed' either in the book of Genesis, or in Paul's use of the Adam-story. Tillich, on the other hand, said that theology must represent the Fall, not as a story which happened once upon a time, but as a symbol of the universal human situation. Similarly, J. A. T. Robinson described the creation and fall stories as ways of giving theological expression to processes and experiences which were going on all the time. Robinson also applied this to the Parousia, which did not – he said – refer to a historical event in the future, but was part of a myth designed to clarify what was meant by seeing all things new in the Kingdom of God. 'It asserts that the reality depicted by the Fall, the truth of all things "in Adam", is not the only or final truth about the cosmic scene.'[4]

No doubt this approach, which is to be found in many other writers, is a means of saving traditional language from complete disuse – not many people talk about the Parousia, nowadays. But Tillich and Robinson seem

---

[1] Marxism and modern theology share an unwillingness to believe that human history is not moving towards an *end*. As Walter Benjamin wrote, thinking of the first half of the century, 'Social Democratic theory, and even more its practice, have been formed by a conception of progress which did not adhere to reality but made dogmatic claims' (*Illuminations*, 1970, p. 262).

[2] M. Heidegger (1889–1976) published *Being and Time* in 1927: 'what Heidegger did was to give philosophical seriousness, professorial respectability, to the love affair with un-reason and death that dominated so many Germans in this hard time' – P. Gay, *Weimar Culture* (Penguin 1974),p. 85.

[3] P. Tillich, *Systematic Theology*, vol. 2, p. 51.

[4] J. A. T. Robinson, *The Human Face of God*, p. 117.

automatically to attribute truth to the myths which they select, as though, once they have decided to treat them as mythical instead of historical, their truth has been established. It is the truth-value of stories like the Fall-story which is in question, however. Of course the Parousia is a myth designed to interpret existence, but this gives no status to the attempt at interpretation. Nor can the Fall suddenly be taken for granted as a serious description of the position of mankind in the eyes of God *because* it no longer has to be, or can be, defended as historical event. In fact, if one drops the appeal to history in the case of the Fall, for example, one is left with a myth proper, similar to all other myths from China to Peru; as such, the myth becomes testable by experience in the present: a historical Fall was indisputable, a mythological Fall can be no more than an assertion, whose truth-value depends on its being able to give imaginative coherence to deeply-lodged human needs for meaning in existence. The myth no longer guarantees its own truth, one has to give grounds for supposing that in some sense the myth may point in the direction of reality. 'The conclusion one is driven to', wrote Van Harvey, the American theologian, 'is that the content of faith can as well be mediated through a historically false story *of a certain kind* as through a true one, through a myth as through history. Everything depends on the form and structure of the symbolism and the myth. But having said this, one must also say that the conditions of belief vary from age to age. What may have been intelligible to and valid for Augustine and Francis may not be so for those of us who live after the advent of biblical criticism.'[1] Myths, one might add, survive only as long as they can bear the destructive testing in time of human experience.

If one asks why Tillich (or Rudolf Bultmann, for example) should have turned to existentialism for assistance with theology, the answer is not to be found in the theology itself so much as in the reasons why existentialism gained ground among European intellectuals after 1920, and these reasons belong to the general history of western culture.[2] If one thinks of existentialism in this period as often the substitution of action for argument, of decision for cartesian doubt, Tillich's use of the approach was analogous to Karl Barth's more conventional fideism, and one senses a deeper continuity with Newman's growing horror, a century before, at the anti-dogmatism of the – as they seemed to him – rationalist liberals. But the attempt to lift the discussion onto another level, beyond the reach of rationalism if not necessarily of 'reason', was not always successful, because for many people by the beginning of the twentieth century the central theological problem had become: how much longer could the Christian religion maintain its claim to possess uniquely revealed, absolute religious truth? or should one now interpret Christianity as a stage in the spiritual development of one of humanity's larger cultural centres? Early nineteenth-century Hegelian theologians had objected to the implication of the classical doctrine of the Person of Christ, that the ideal man/god could be manifested in a single

---

[1] Van A. Harvey, *The Historian and the Believer* (1967), pp. 280–81.
[2] For trenchant criticism, see T. W. Adorno, *The Jargon of Authenticity* (Frankfurt, 1964, E.T. 1973).

historical existence; they dismissed such a view of the life of Jesus as an intolerable foreshortening of the historical process. Now, what had been put forward as philosophical speculation – the relativity of all historical religions and their tendency to converge upon an ultimate unity as yet unattained – was alleged as the inevitable consequence of an enlarged understanding of human history, religious as well as biological.

The best example of this trend was Tennant's German contemporary, Ernst Troeltsch (1865–1923), though Troeltsch was not a theologian in Tillich's or Barth's sense, but a historian of religion and a powerful philosopher of history: he was also influenced by his friend, Max Weber, the sociologist.[1] As a historian, Troeltsch rejected the classical theology which isolated Christianity from the rest of history on the basis of miracle – the incarnation and the resurrection, for example. He could see no ground for admitting a specifically Christian miraculous causality at these points, when Christian writers denied a similar miraculous causality to other world-religions which claimed miraculous events as part of their main tradition; and when Protestants, indeed, normally denied the reality of all Roman Catholic alleged miracles, and that on what were historicist grounds. Nor did he feel any inner religious need to grant as a faith-act (in the style which Karl Barth made familiar again in the 1920s) the extra-historical historicity of the incarnation and resurrection, events whose probability he had already criticized on the historical level. Christianity, as far as Troeltsch was concerned, was not to be limited to what could be defined in terms of these particular stories. Attacked by General Superintendent Kaftan of Kiel, Troeltsch said in the 1911 edition of *The Absoluteness of Christianity* that he did not mind the designation 'Christian Neoplatonist' bestowed on him by Kaftan and added: 'I comfort myself with the thought that God is not the General Superintendent of the universe and therefore continue unperturbably to regard myself as a Christian'.[2]

For Troeltsch, therefore, the uniqueness and absoluteness of Christianity could not be shown by an appeal to a supernatural divine revelation and incarnation. What could be shown was its historical individuality as the religious expression of a particular historical, western culture; but as Troeltsch also came to accept the individuality and self-sufficiency of the other great world-religions, this made it difficult for him to take the idealistic-evolutionary view, as he called it, that Christianity was absolute as the realization of the essence or idea of Religion itself. He did not believe that Hinduism, for example, had to seek its fulfilment in Christianity.

In his last lectures Troeltsch said that his study of the history of European civilization and of Christianity had led him to emphasize the historical individuality of both, and to attach much less significance to the idea of the supreme validity of either. Christianity's primary claim to any validity (not to *supreme* validity) was that only through Christianity had Europe become what it was, and that only in terms of it could Europe preserve the religious forces that were essential to its further development. He wrote:

[1] See especially E. Troeltsch, *The Absoluteness of Christianity* (1901, E.T. 1972). Also *Protestantism and Progress* (1912) and *Christian Thought* (1923).

[2] Troeltsch, *The Absoluteness of Christianity*, pp. 171–72.

We cannot live without a religion, yet the only religion that we can endure is Christianity, for Christianity has grown up with us and has become a part of our very being. Christianity could not be the religion of such a highly developed racial group if it did not possess a mighty spiritual power and truth; in short, if it were not, in some degree, a manifestation of the Divine Life itself. The evidence we have for this remains essentially the same, whatever may be our theory concerning absolute validity – it is the evidence of a profound inner experience. This experience is undoubtedly the criterion of its validity, but, be it noted, only of its validity for us. It is God's countenance as revealed to us . . . it is final and unconditional for us because we have nothing else . . . But this does not preclude the possibility that other racial groups, living under entirely different cultural conditions, may experience their contact with the Divine Life in quite a different way, and may also possess a religion which has grown up with them, and from which they cannot sever themselves as long as they remain what they are . . .[1]

Troeltsch applied his position logically to the case of Christian missions. Although missionary enterprise, he said, had always been in part simply a concomitant of the political, military and commercial enterprise of a state or nation, in part it was also an outcome of the religious enthusiast's passion for conversion. This latter aspect was directly connected with the claim of Christianity to possess absolute religious validity. Troeltsch distinguished between the (as he thought) crude religious systems of small tribes which were being morally and spiritually disintegrated by contact with western civilization, and which might be said to need the assistance of one of the so-called higher religions, and these great philosophical world-religions themselves. These non-Christian great religions had to be recognized as expressions of the general religious consciousness corresponding to certain definite types of culture, and it was their duty to increase in depth and purity by means of their own interior impulses, a task in which Christianity might assist them. But there should be no further question of thinking in terms of the conversion of the East, for example, to Christianity: a certain interpenetration of the great religious systems was all that was seriously conceivable.

Troeltsch died before the full secularizing effect of western culture on other societies had become apparent, and long before marxism had become the state-philosophy of China; his historical relativism was itself conditioned by the time at which he was writing; although he sometimes spoke as though Christianity might be replaced by another religious form, he usually assumed that the existing world-religions would survive through any foreseeable future; he also exaggerated the extent to which Christianity and western culture were bound together. Nevertheless, it was a pity that ideas of this kind did not develop more quickly out of the experience of missionary work in the nineteenth century: Christian missions in China, for instance, showed little appreciation of Chinese religion and culture in the nineteenth

---

[1] Troeltsch, *Christian Thought*, pp. 25–26.

century. When the Edinburgh Missionary Conference commission on the Christian message in relation to non-Christian religions reported in 1910 it admitted the 'wholly unnecessary alienation and misunderstanding which have thereby been created', but still spoke cheerfully, a few pages later, of 'the spectacle of the advance of the Christian Church along many lines of action to the conquest of the five great religions of the modern world'.[1]

The conclusion which Troeltsch reached, that the western Christian churches should give up the struggle to overthrow the non-Christian world-religions, represented the confluence of humanist ideas of toleration, philosophical and scientific ideas about development, the growth of a less dogmatic theological attitude (and the rapid general disappearance of belief in the moral standing of Hell), together with the all-pervasive effects of historical relativism. When one adds that Troeltsch expected the European religious tradition to move towards increasing individualism, one sees how unadapted to the immediate future were those religious factors which must have seemed, about 1914, most attuned to change. Racial and religious co-operation or interpenetration, toleration and individualism were not to be the obvious characteristics of the mid-twentieth century. Indeed, this synthesis of the legacy of the Enlightenment with Christian doctrine disintegrated overnight: after 1914 there came 'neo-orthodoxy'; a partial revival in some Protestant circles of the traditional authority of the Bible as the Word of God, an authority which the historical-critical method had seemed to have shattered for ever; of the classical Christian pessimism about human nature; and of the claim of Christianity to possess absolute religious truth, a claim which, as we have just seen, was virtually abandoned by theologians like Troeltsch who, nevertheless, did not want to abandon Christianity. The extent of the change becomes evident if one compares Troeltsch's views of the rôle of Christian missions with those of the Dutch theologian, Hendrik Kraemer (1890–1968), the most distinguished missionary theologian of the century.

Kraemer began, in terms which Troeltsch might have accepted, by rejecting the early nineteenth-century Protestant missionary assumption 'that this universe of living non-christian religions was adequately conceived by taking it to be a vast, degrading and decaying section of the spiritual life of mankind, steeped in darkness and error . . . The annals of modern missions testify to the natural vitality and tenacious strength as well as the inertia of these religions. They are the product of man's great efforts in the field of religion.'[2] Drawing on Karl Barth, not on Troeltsch, Kraemer extended this judgement to institutional Christianity itself, in as much as empirical, historical Christianity had also, he thought, to be understood as at least in part a specimen of human effort in the religious field. This human effort (and its *human* origin is the significant factor for Kraemer) produced various religious types – the naturalistic, the mystical, the moralistic and so forth – and these types of man's religious self-expression could be found in Christianity as well as in other religions.

[1] *World Missionary Conference 1910*, report of Commission iv, *The Missionary Message in relation to Non-Christian Religions*, p. 269, and p. 273.
[2] H. Kraemer, *The Christian Message in the Non-Christian World* (1938), pp. 284–85.

Man's religious consciousness, however, could not match the self-revelation of God in Christ: in historical Christianity what derived from man always led 'to the misapprehension of the prophetic religions of biblical realism'.[1]

In fact, although Kraemer sometimes referred to a general revelation, he deprived it of content. Even the Old Testament contained nothing more than a forward-looking glimpse of the revelation in Christ: Judaism itself was not a revealed religion. (There is a terrifying obtuseness in this readiness, in the 1920s and 1930s, to say that Judaism existed positively only to the extent that it served the interests of Christianity.) Christ was the one way of salvation, in him God became flesh, judged man, and made clear his purposes for man and the world. Kraemer spoke as though this revelation was an objective fact, independent of historical context or theological interpretation; he disclaimed any burden of proof – the burden lay on men themselves, who must surrender in faith to what stood before them objectively in Jesus. As for other religions, Kraemer judged them in terms of the norm given by God in Jesus Christ, and concluded that they were only the products of the human religious consciousness, in flight from God or in rebellion against him.

All this amounted to a familiar traditional theology, though now a provincial one. Faced with Troeltsch's acceptance of the historicity of all knowledge, Kraemer appealed to 'revelation', but could not show in what way its specific source, the Bible, was to be exempted from historicity and from the problems of language. At the meeting of the International Missionary Council in India in 1938 he exhorted the missionaries to witness to Christianity as the *truth*. He said that reluctance to convert or proselytise, the preference for social service or for a sharing of religious experience with people of other faiths as the only valid Christian missionary method, sprang from a fundamental confusion: conversion was the missionary duty.

> 'In the field of religion there was only one alternative. Either the paramount thing in a religion was that it contained objective truth, or its truth-quality was of secondary or even minor importance, and left one permanently trapped in relativism.'[2]

Whatever qualifications Kraemer might make, he was still defending the thesis of a radical discontinuity between Christianity and the other world-religions. Twenty years later the ecumenical leader, Visser't Hooft, described his book as a decisive factor in the turning away from a relativistic missionary ideology to a christocentric theology of missions. At a greater distance of time one may attribute Kraemer's success to missionary nostalgia for the theological certainties of a vanished era. Within a year of Tambaram the world war had begun, which was to bring about a marxist victory in China, and speed up the advance of the 'third world' to political independence of the West, and this foreshadowed the end of Christian missions in the sense in which Kraemer was still thinking about them in 1938. It was not surprising that by the 1960s more was heard of 'dialogue' than of 'discontinuity' in missionary circles. Nevertheless, the neo-orthodox

[1] *ib.* p. 285.
[2] *ib.* p. 296.

theological revival of which Kraemer formed a part characterized the years between about 1920 and 1950. After the Second World War the sheer complexity of the intellectual, moral and political problems facing Christianity compelled the re-appearance of a more liberal theology, which had for the moment despaired of 'revelation' and returned to 'reason' as the source of religious truth. The principal difference between the 'radical theology' of the 1960s and the 'liberalism' of the 1900s was that the old optimistic philosophical idealism had less influence in the later period.

Kraemer's defence of the duty of Christianity to replace the other world-religions in their own cultures, to do to them what it had failed in the long run to do to Judaism, reflected the recovery of the more conservative point of view from the 1890s. Throughout the nineteenth century, as has been seen, two theological moods had conflicted: one, broadly optimistic, which involved an acceptance that the structure of western society was changing and would continue to change, and another, which might be called Christian pessimist, which was often found associated with deep hostility to the industrial, urban, technological and mass-democratic aspects of the modern world. In the background lay the shock of the Russian revolution of 1917, which seemed to embody all that the pessimists feared without producing what the optimists wanted. Post-war chaos, the brief prosperity of the 1920s, the 1929 depression, set the background of a decade in which what had seemed harmless ideologies, the quirks of irrelevant, eccentric men, transformed themselves into political forces of terrifying efficiency: in the 1930s economic misery, Fascism, Nazism and Stalinism dominated men's minds. To the extent that Russian marxism was officially anti-Christian, and to the extent that the institutional churches had become permeated by the collective hysteria of nationalism, which had its own anti-modernising strain of violence, theological pessimism was strengthened. Theologians reacted much as they had done to a similar psychological condition in the early nineteenth century and reasserted the supernatural origin and theological centrality of the ecclesia. One had to believe in the survival of the Church in order to believe in Christianity, and the survival of the visible Church seemed to require supernatural support: if the Church *was* the Gospel, the Church was secure, and with the Church secured, there might yet be time to save the Gospel.

This was part of the context of the ecumenical movement, the theological drive for the unification of the Churches which is usually dated from the World Missionary Conference which was held in Edinburgh in 1910. Part of its causation was social: the mounting hostility of western society to organized Christianity, the formation of competitive anti-Christian movements – Fascism, Marxism, Third World nationalism, the weakness of the individual Churches as generators of the idea of God in human society – all these factors pushed institutional Christianity towards organic unity of some kind.[1] The theological discovery that the New Testament might be said to favour this goal was hardly new; what was new was the willingness of various Protestant bodies to devise, or try to devise solutions to the

[1] For the sociological view that the unity movement was a response to the weakness of the individual churches concerned, see B. R. Wilson, *Religion in a Secular Society* (1966).

problems which the achievement of unity presented. In the past, when the Churches had thought of themselves as religious 'states', unity had been conceived either as the object of a kind of ecclesiastical imperialism, or perhaps as the outcome of a process of voluntary surrender by some Churches to others. In the 1930s and 1940s, however, the Protestant Churches seemed as though they might be about to break out of the fixed lines of the post-Reformation denominational system and to transcend this 'foreign policy' conception of the search for unity. Social change seemed to be making more fruitful negotiations possible, and theologians appeared to be able to rationalize the altered situation: the consequent theology, the work of committees rather than individuals, may be examined in the Reports of the long series of international conferences: Stockholm (1925), Lausanne (1927), Edinburgh and Oxford (1937), and Amsterdam (1948). Characteristic was the emphasis on the 'sins of our divisions'; on the certainty that Jesus's prayer that his followers might be one must be answered in terms of visible institutional and sacramental unity; and on episcopacy, with whatever necessary ambiguities of definition, as the basic structural form of the priesthood of the 'coming great Church', as it was sometimes called.

Theologically-speaking, however, the Protestant ecumenical movement had lost its momentum by the 1950s. Then in 1958 John XXIII was elected Pope and at the second Vatican Council in 1962 a new, essentially Roman Catholic ecumenical phase began, whose theological boundaries had not become completely clear by the 1970s. It looked, however, as though ecumenicity had slipped back into the 'diplomatic' forms of encounter, in which concepts like the papal primacy, Mariology, and the possession of valid ministerial orders were discussed with very traditional seriousness. Neither two centuries of Biblical criticism, nor our steadily accumulating knowledge of the history of institutional Christianity – whether in 'western' contexts or in 'overseas mission-fields', nor the growth of a highly sophisticated philosophical attitude to the use of words and myths in theology, had affected the confidence with which many ecumenical theologians handled such ideas. One example must be sufficient:

> The real presence of Christ's body and blood can, however, only be understood within the context of the redemptive activity whereby he gives himself, and in himself reconciliation, peace and life to his own. On the one hand, the eucharistic gift springs out of the paschal mystery of Christ's death and resurrection, in which God's saving purpose has already been definitively realised. On the other hand, its purpose is to transmit the life of the crucified and risen Christ to his body, the Church, so that its members may be more united with Christ and with one another.[1]

One could expound such sentences on the ground that they involved a specifically Christian mythological use of language, and that a Christian had as much right to arrange experience in *his* way as a marxist had to

[1] *An Agreed Statement on Eucharistic Doctrine* (1971 republished, unaltered 1973), iii.6. This was a Roman Catholic-Anglican statement.

arrange experience in *his* way; but such an argument, which took a plurality of doctrinal positions for granted, was alien to the convictions of those who made doctrinal statements like these. In the ecumenical world, on its post-Vatican II basis, the united ecclesia, the coming great Church, was its own, essentially supernatural authority, and could sanction the traditional dogmatic system which liberalism had abandoned in despair. It looked clear in the 1970s that organic unity would be achieved by moving closer to the Roman Catholic system.

Again, only one example can be given: in this case the movement towards a consensus on the doctrine of the eucharist. This emerged in a remarkable series of documents: *A Lutheran-Roman Catholic Statement: the Eucharist as Sacrifice* (St. Louis, Missouri, 1967); *The Eucharist in Ecumenical Thought*, a World Council of Churches paper finally agreed at Louvain in 1971; the Anglican-Roman Catholic *Agreed Statement on Eucharistic Doctrine* (1971); and a statement worked out by French Reformed and French Roman Catholic theologians, usually referred to as the *Les Dombes* statement (1972).

These documents proposed a common understanding of the idea of the presence of Christ in the eucharist. To quote the *Agreed Statement*:

> Communion with Christ in the Eucharist presupposes his true presence effectually signified by the bread and wine which, in this mystery, become his body and blood . . . the elements are not mere signs; Christ's body and blood become really present and are really given. But they are really present and given in order that, receiving them, believers may be united in communion with Christ the Lord.[1]

A footnote on the word 'transubstantiation' made the approach clear:

> The word is commonly used in the Roman Catholic Church to indicate that God acting in the eucharist effects a change in the inner reality of the elements. The term should be seen as affirming the *fact* of Christ's presence and of the mysterious and radical change which takes place. In contemporary Roman Catholic theology it is not understood as explaining *how* the change takes place.[2]

There was nothing very new theologically in this quiet dropping of the Aristotelian pilot, or in the way in which the word 'fact' was introduced into the passage: the roots of the consensus ran back to *The Fulness of Sacrifice* (1930) by F. C. N. Hicks, and to *The Christian Sacrifice* (1932) by E. Masure. These documents might be said to show that liberal theology, in the best meaning of the words, had never finally established itself ecclesiastically, however prominent individual liberal theologians might have been. It was not clear whether the *Agreed Statement*, for example, was intended to rule out Receptionism (or Virtualism) altogether as alternative positions, but it was clear enough that only one doctrinal interpretation of the rite was mentioned. The authors of the statement said that they intended to reach a consensus on the level of faith, so that all might be able

---

[1] *Modern Eucharistic Agreement* (1973), pp. 28–29.
[2] *ib.*

to say, within the limits of the document itself, 'this is the christian faith of the eucharist'. This implied that if one did not agree with the view expressed there, that in the eucharistic rite the bread and wine *become* (the word was used frequently) the body and blood of Christ, one was rejecting part, at least, of the Christian faith of the eucharist. To some this might seem obviously true; to others, however, it might well seem a rejection of the idea of a plurality of doctrinal interpretation, an idea which is fundamental to any 'liberal' sharing in the eucharistic rite, and also to the liberal theological position as such.

In Protestant circles the dominant figure in conservative academic theology was that of Karl Barth (1886–1968). Barth reacted against the whole cultural situation in which Liberal Protestantism existed only as a minor theme; he wanted Christianity to cut itself free, not just from the anthropocentricism and historical relativism which he felt had corrupted German religious thought from Schleiermacher to Troeltsch, but from every positive trend in western culture. This is the point at which to recall his most striking contribution to twentieth-century theology, his *Commentary* on the Epistle to the Romans, first published in 1918, much altered in the second edition of 1921. This edition was not subsequently changed, but short prefaces revealed the author's reaction to criticism; the sixth edition was translated into English by Sir Edwyn Hoskins in 1933, by which time the sharpness of the original was already blunted by events. The later *Church Dogmatics*, begun in 1932 and left unfinished at his death, was broadly anticipated in the Romans Commentary, but the desire to make the dogmatic system totally christocentric over-indulged Barth's taste for speculative theology, and explained why Dietrich Bonhoeffer thought that Barth had lost sight of the importance of the Word as God's intention to communicate with men. If Troeltsch saw the absoluteness of the Christian revelation dissolving in the haze of historical relativism, Barth's primary vision was of a revelation so absolute that it reduced everything human to a common level of helpless inadequacy or wilful rebellion. Given the total adequacy of God, however, Barth in his later years defended the idea of universal salvation.

This attitude was the strength and weakness of Barth's position. In a sense he simply turned Feuerbach, whose analysis of the origin of religious he thought especially penetrating, against himself. He agreed that all historical religion, much of what passed for Christianity included, was a product of the human spirit alone, but whereas Feuerbach had said that western man projected as his idea of God a noble idealization of man, Barth argued that human ideas of God, precisely because they *were* human, were distortions which led away from God himself. This was the root of the trouble in his debates in the 1920s with von Harnack, who saw no virtue in rejecting natural theology as a genuine source of knowledge about God. But for Barth only God himself could reveal himself, and he had done so only once, in Jesus Christ, the Word of the Father who became flesh for our salvation, and returned to the Father, to be present for ever in the Church through the Holy Spirit. This revelation, moreover, was recorded once and for all in the Bible. Logically, man, unable to look into himself for truth, could not expect to be able to read the truth about God for himself in the Bible; he had to depend on the working of the Holy Spirit to reveal Christ to him as the Word within the Scriptures. Scripture had to 'become' the Word of God, and Barth used this as a way of distinguishing between himself and the 'fundamentalist' theologians who, he thought, treated the Bible as a thing instead of an event, relying too much on the words and not enough on the Word. Barth, that is, tested everything by what he regarded as the Reformation understanding of the idea of justification by grace; at the same time he reaffirmed one important difference between Protestantism and Roman Catholicism, which, as recently as the First Vatican Council, had restated the medieval belief that reason was more than a sinfully distorted instrument.

Barth's brilliant writing could not always conceal the weakness of his theological method, which left him with only one argument, the appeal to the Bible as the one divine revelation. Human creativity had always to be pinned down as necessarily a source of error in theology; Kierkegaard, for example, at first seized on as a nineteenth-century fore-runner, was finally dismissed as an anthropocentric theologian. The absoluteness of the method helps to explain the opaqueness of his treatment of Schleiermacher in *Protestant Thought in the Nineteenth Century* (1952, E.T. 1972, chapter 13): to make any concessions to what Schleiermacher was actually trying to do would have meant admitting that his predecessor, schooled in such writers as Lessing and Semler, had foreseen·the troubles which would come to a Protestant theology which staked everything on an appeal to the Jewish-Christian writings as the unique self-revelation of God. It was a logical corollary of his commitment to this view of revelation that Barth should be obliged to give up the traditional doctrine of analogy (*analogia entis*), which implied that some kind of being was common to God and man, so that man did not depend entirely on divine revelation for his knowledge of God but could argue, for example, from what he knew of ordinary human love to the idea of love as it might be found in God, and to substitute the analogy of grace (*analogia gratiae*), according to which it was only because God had first revealed to us the nature of divine love (or fatherhood, or personality) that man was able to understand human love or fatherhood. (One is reminded of the way in which most Victorian missionaries took it for granted that what they believed to be the 'christian' idea of marriage must become the accepted form of marriage in every culture which they encountered.) The idea was dramatic rather than intelligible. (For a brilliant discussion of the subject, see *Analogy*, by H. Palmer, 1973.) Barth, in his study of Anselm, *Fides Quaerens Intellectum* (1930), insisted that man made no existential contribution to his own enlightenment at that point; there was no 'leap of faith' in his later revelational theology. Once a divinely and miraculously given 'faith' had taken over, human reason could understand what it was given to understand by and about God.

Barth's rejection of the critical or liberal style in theology was total: such thinkers had chosen the wrong place to start, and this invalidated what they said. This helps to explain the unfairness of the judgment which put Schleiermacher among the 'particular fathers' of the theological errors whose final phase was the 'German-Christian' movement which welcomed Nazism in the early 1930s. 'The doctrinal attitude of the German-Christians', Barth wrote in 1933, 'is nothing but a particular result of the entire neo-protestant development since 1700'.[1] In its historical context one follows the generalization, but it was the behaviour of the whole of German Protestant-ism since 1789, not just one part of it, that was on trial between 1918 and 1945. Perhaps in that confused situation Barth's gift was that of the preacher rather than the theologian – he excelled in the kind of language which reawakened men's belief in the relevance of a transcendent, omni-potent and righteous God who chose to reveal himself in Christ and justified men by grace alone. This may be illustrated by a passage on the resurrection of Christ:

> The resurrection is not a historical event which may be placed side by side with other events. Rather it is the 'non-historical' happening by which all other events are bounded, and to which events before and on and after Easter Day point . . . Were there a direct and causal con-nexion between the historical 'facts' of the resurrection – the empty tomb, for example, or the appearances detailed in 1 Cor 15 – and the resurrection itself; were it in any sense a 'fact' in history, then no profession of faith or refinement of devotion could prevent it being in the see-saw of 'Yes' and 'No', life and death, God and man, which is characteristic of all that happens on the historical plane . . . The con-ception of the resurrection, however, wholly forbids this method of procedure: why seek ye the living among the dead? The conception of the resurrection emerges with the conception of death and with the conception of the end of all historical things as such.[2]

This was the younger, paradoxical and perhaps more convincing Barth who was prepared to assert that just because the resurrection-stories of the New Testament offered problems to the historian, *belief* in the resurrection offered no problems at all: one had simply to grasp that the 'resurrection' was a 'non-historical' event with which 'appearances' and the 'empty tomb' had no essential link, that this was a spiritual disclosure and apprehension of God in Jesus.

Years later, however, in *Church Dogmatics*, Barth, perhaps now less willing to balance Christ against the Scriptures in a manner worthy of Luther, so altered his language as to convince many of his critics that he was now affirming the historicity of the resurrection after all. 'It is sheer superstition', he said, 'to suppose that only things which are open to 'historical' verification can have happened in time. There may have been events which happened far more really in time than the kind of things which Bultmann's scientific historian can prove. There are good grounds for supposing that the history of the resurrection of Jesus is a pre-eminent instance of such an event.'[3] Looked at more closely, however, his later

[1] K. Barth, *The German Church Conflict*, ed. T. H. L. Parker (1965), p. 16; the judgement on Schleiermacher is on p. 27.

[2] K. Barth, *The Epistle to the Romans*, tr. E. C. Hoskyns, 1933, pp. 203–205.

[3] K. Barth, *Church Dogmatics* (ET 1960), III/2, p. 446.

statements still seem to depend on the very unsatisfactory category of 'non-historical history'. The difference between the earlier and later versions seems to be that whereas in the commentary on *Romans* Barth used a very vague description of the resurrection (while vigorously asserting its status as non-historical history), in *Church Dogmatics*, on the other hand, the description of the resurrection became much more traditional, with the *bodily* nature of the 'appearances' and the story of the empty tomb now firmly in the foreground. He did not answer the questions which the historical critic raises about these narratives, however, but asserted that they described an event beyond the reach of historical research or description. This amounts to saying that the appearances of Jesus had a 'non-physical physicality', and that the state of the tomb was that of a 'non-empty emptiness'. Paradox breaks down when it is pushed so far. As Van Harvey commented, on the one hand Barth appealed to the seeing and hearing of the risen Jesus by the disciples as though it were a matter of the employment of common-sense categories like sight and hearing; on the other hand, he immunized the stories against assessment by saying that they were not literal or historical.[1]

Barth believed – and here he was at the very root of the problem of the modern theologian – that the Bible was the sum total of the sources in terms of which Christianity could be defined. Human religious experience, and human reflection on that experience, became irrelevant if one wanted to decide what God had revealed in Jesus Christ. Traditional literalism had lost its authority, however, and so Barth constantly invented categories which would express his Coleridgian conviction that the unique Word of God was in the Bible. A good example of this was his treatment, in *Church Dogmatics*, of the biblical doctrine of creation. The statement that God created the heaven and earth and man could not, he said, be advanced on any sort of human ground. The impregnable basis of this fact was that it was in the Bible, in the twofold creation narrative in *Genesis*, and in later recollection and comment on them in the Bible itself. These narratives should not be accepted as self-authenticating in some human fashion, however, but had to be understood through Christ. Thus Barth established his *credo ut intelligam*: I believe in Jesus Christ in order to understand that God created the heaven and the earth, and if I did not understand the former I could not understand the latter.

Nevertheless, the status of the creation stories had still to be established: how, if they were 'historical', could they have been recorded? Barth introduced a distinction between what he called 'saga' and 'myth', defining saga as an intuitive and poetic picture of a pre-historical reality of history which had been enacted once and for all in time and space. The creation stories were pure saga, and therefore worked on the divine level, whereas myth worked only on the level of human experience and explanation. Only the Holy Spirit, of course, could guide the faithful reader into knowing which parts of the Bible were saga and which were myth. The content of saga was, inevitably, 'non-historical history', which was now called the soul of history in the ordinary sense. The authors of the biblical sagas were

[1] Van A. Harvey, *The Historian and the Believer* (1967), p. 159.

summoned, claimed and committed to exploit the possibilities of historical divination and poetry, and to make himself explicit Barth said that the authors had been encountered by God. Yet his use of the phrase 'intuitive and poetic' suggested that he was aware of the weakness of his own argument in his own terms – that he was attributing divine creative power to the human imagination, and he fell back rather lamely on the assertion that in the last resort one had to receive and accept the witness of the Bible through the power of the Holy Spirit. This was what Dietrich Bonhoeffer meant when he spoke, in *Letters and Papers from Prison* (E.T. 1967, p. 152), of Barth's 'positivism of revelation', his take-it-or-leave-it-position. Barth, moreover, had left himself without any objective means of distinguishing between Christian miracles and non-Christian miracles, or Christian sacred writings and non-Christian sacred writings, though in both the non-Christian cases he was obliged to deny any question of a divine revelation, in act or word.[1]

Finally, the strength and weakness of Barth's theology become obvious if one examines his exposition of the doctrine of the work of Christ in *Church Dogmatics*, 11/1, *The Doctrine of God* (E.T. 1957). Barth intended this version of the doctrine to be pauline. Expounding *Phillipians* 2.6 he wrote that Christ 'shared in the status, constitution and situation of man in which man resists God and cannot stand before him but must die. How could God resist himself? How could God sin? The Son of God knew no sin. But he could enter into man's mode of being, being in the flesh, in which there is absolutely no justification before God (Romans 3.20) but only sin. God could – and not only could but did – allow his Son to be in the flesh, and therefore make him to be sin for our sakes, to become the object which must be the object of his own anger' (pp. 397–98). In a powerful attempt to explain how God could stage this internal interplay of mercy and righteousness Barth said that our criticism of God's justice was fundamentally a failure to recognize our own sinfulness. He continued:

> In a complete resignation not of the essence but the form of his godhead (Christ), took upon himself our own human form . . . he stepped into the heart of the inevitable conflict between the faithfulness of God and the unfaithfulness of man . . . He was not only the God who is offended by man. He was also the man whom God threatens with death, who falls a victim to death in face of God's judgement[2].

The strength lay in the coolness with which Barth stated the unknowable. The weakness came out in the final contrast: 'he was not only the God who is *offended* by man, he was also the man whom *God* threatens with death.' In his perpetual anxiety to safeguard the primacy of God Barth made him the major partner in the second clause as well as in the first. Whereas, if the balance which is inherent in the (admittedly obscure) concept of incarnation were to be preserved, one would have expected something like: 'he was also

---

[1] K. Barth, *Church Dogmatics* (ET 1959), 111/2: the argument is taken from pp. 1–93; the definition of saga is on p. 81.
[2] K. Barth, *Church Dogmatics* (ET 1957), 11/1, p. 397.

the man who makes his case against God's wrath'. Of course, Barth could not say this. He had even written, earlier in the same passage, that 'he (Christ) and not Israel is the one who really suffers in all that the Jews of today have to endure',[1] a comment which summed up the whole of Jürgen Moltmann's later discussion of Auschwitz in *The Crucified God* (E.T. 1974), but which pushed the idea of substitution beyond any serious intellectual or moral reality. Barth eschewed the liberal tradition, from Schleiermacher through Jowett to Tennant, too completely; he did not remember that – as Tennant, for example, would certainly have insisted – no theological method is trustworthy which obliterates men and women so entirely. A generation even before Schleiermacher, J. G. von Herder, a humanist-Christian in the German Enlightenment, had warned that there must be no *Favoritvolk*: 'the negro is as much entitled to think the white man degenerate as the white man to think the former a black beast'.[2] He rejected colonialism, whether military or missionary. A historical relativist, he valued the individual creativity of seemingly incommensurable cultures, and he did not suppose that God would prove less discriminating. *Mutatis mutandis*, Troeltsch was to say much the same thing, but in general the lesson had been lost as Europe moved through industrial expansion to the racialism, militarism and social inhumanity of the late nineteenth century. Barth believed that he had a mission to protest against a Christian humanism – which he often identified as 'neo-protestantism' – which was secularizing the Christian religion. He misunderstood his period: it was not from excessive humanism, whether Christian or otherwise, that the first half of the twentieth century suffered.

Those who thought – as Barth did, and as others still do – that Liberal Protestantism was the natural religious expression of every anthropocentric tendency in western culture, and who, somewhat perversely, also blamed Liberal Protestantism for the failure of Roman Catholic as well as Protestant orthodoxy to prevent the rise of the great totalitarian political movements, and for whom, in the second half of the century, 'Communism' remained the principal enemy, were horrified by the quiet academic recovery of liberal theology in the 1960s, when the influence of Bultmann, Tillich, and a rediscovered and partially misinterpreted Dietrich Bonhoeffer (1906–45) began to counter-balance that of Barth and the neo-orthodox, ecumenical movement. Yet this was hardly a revival of the philosophically naive, socially optimistic, science-orientated liberalism of the Edwardian period at its worst, as in *Liberal Christianity* (E.T. 1903) by the French theologian Jean Réville (1854–1907), or, with Hegelian overtones, *The New Theology* (1907), the product of a brief flirtation with radicalism by R. J. Campbell (1867–1956). The liberalism of the 1960s was much more a liberalism of desperation. Earlier liberals had usually assumed that some kind of 'modernisation' was the key to a general renewal of Christian belief, but their successors increasingly thought of critical theologies as the safeguard of a minority, not the watchword of a majority. This explains the popularity of Bonhoeffer's posthumously published *Letters and Papers from Prison*

---

[1] *ib.* p. 395.
[2] See I. Berlin, *Vico and Herder* (1976), p. 198.

(E.T. 1955). For although he saw the problem too much as one of communication (the theory that the problem was how to translate the known and unchangiᵤg gospel into 'modern' terms), at least Bonhoeffer started from the assumption (which the later liberals shared) that western culture was moving towards what would be a completely non-Christian phase; and when he asked himself the relevant question, how was one to speak of Christianity in a society which had no shared Christian or other religious assumptions, he did not suppose that either Barth's biblicism, or existentialism in the manner of Bultmann and Tillich, would provide an answer. Troeltsch had thought that western culture and western Christianity were indissolubly bound together, but Bonhoeffer thought that the links were dissolving, and he grasped something of the predicament of a religion without a culture, unable (unlike the Church in the European Dark Ages) to impose itself on the new environment. Barth, in as far as he had understood what was happening, had chosen to believe that this stateless and cultureless condition was the natural form of Christianity – this was the root of his political and ecclesiological views, and this was the point at which he and Bonhoeffer stood in profound agreement, over against all those who now disinterred various kinds of panentheism, progressivism, Hegelianism, 'christian-marxism' and so forth, in order to be able to declare that despite appearances, western culture would not and could not enter a non-religious phase.[1] Bonhoeffer dismissed Tillich, for example, as setting out to interpret the evolution of the world, *against its will*, in a religious sense. Nevertheless, Bonhoeffer disagreed with Barth's acceptance of a kind of extra-territorial status for the ecclesia: instead, he thought that the followers of Jesus had to struggle back into the secular culture, but that they could do this only by reinterpreting their biblical concepts from inside it. Because of his tragic death, his ideas remained obscure at this point, but he seems to have thought that the alternative to (a) theological development, which was proving as untenable as other ideas of historical continuity, and to (b) a pure eschatological theology which tried to behave as though religious ideas were changeless and had no cultural existence at all, was a theology of historical adaptation, in which one pole would be the 'lordship' of Jesus over all cultures conceivable, and the other the actual historical environment, which obeyed neither a secular marxist necessity nor the hidden hand of divine providence. Two problems followed. First, how to fill out, in theory or in experience, the idea of the Lordship of Christ; and second, that at a time when change was self-conscious and continual, the concept of a particular and definable historical environment seemed to recede indefinitely.

This illustrated the way in which liberal theology always seemed to come back to the same difficulties. His anti-dogmatic programme, part moral in origin, part philosophical, threw the liberal theologian back on the New Testament and on the personality and teaching (rather than Person and

---

[1] Theologians like the American Charles Hartshorne (b. 1897), and the British L. S. Thornton (1884–1960), who made use of the work of scientific philosophers like A. N. Whitehead (1861–1947); Tillich and Teilhard de Chardin, and their popularizers, are other instances.

Work) of Jesus. At the same time, however, his historical method, which was based on questions of probability in terms of evidence, and not on an *a priori* rejection of miracle as the neo-orthodox often misleadingly asserted, made the New Testament version of the teaching of Jesus less authoritative and the historical personality less acceptable. From the early nineteenth century onwards, therefore, the liberal theologian turned for assistance to religious experience, hoping, as Schleiermacher already clearly hoped, that the religious experience of the individual in the ecclesia would confirm that both Christian dogma, and the Christian tradition about the Person of Jesus, were inherently part of the conceptual and psychological structure of the ordinary human being.

It was in this way that Bultmann's demythologizing approach to the New Testament could be regarded as radical. One went *behind* the biblical myths, announcing not only what they had meant in the past, but also their alleged meaning in the present experience of a Lutheran-type Christian. Bultmann, like Tillich, crossed from the biblical myths to contemporary, more especially western experience through existential philosophy (especially that of Heidegger). Bultmann tried to bring justification by faith and existentialism together by describing salvation as a present, self-authenticating experience of deliverance from existence as an intolerable burden of suffering, guilt and the fear of death – what Heidegger called 'inauthentic existence'. Religious revelation was not a divine communication of knowledge, propositions to be believed, but an event (the life, death and resurrection of Jesus) taking place here and now, which abolished death and put the man who accepted faith into a new situation – authentic existence in Heidegger's language, Tillich's 'new being'. Exactly how Bultmann and Tillich related this secular existential experience of the mystery of being to the Christian symbolic system was never altogether clear, but Bultmann, for example, said that divine revelation did not present men with an objective world-view; indeed, world views were useless, because they led a man away from the self-understanding that he needed. Nor was revelation a matter of asserting that certain historical events happened in the past, or that one should believe certain extraordinary dogmatic statements. Rather the man of faith grasped the self-understanding which was divinely offered him in his existential present so that he understood himself, not only as one who came from a sinful past and stood under God's judgment, but also as one who was freed from this past by the divine grace which encountered him in the world.[1]

At this stage Bultmann moved back to a conservative, partially Lutheran position. Human experience, he claimed, at any rate as contained in twentieth-century existential philosophy of some kinds, offered a self-understanding which might be seen as a secular version of Pauline and Johannine anthropology. (Since Bultmann denied that revelation consisted of a world-view, he could not, of course, claim that this anthropology had absolute value.) This philosophical discovery, however, gave no positive standing either to humanism or to other religious systems, for, Bultmann

---

[1] R. Bultmann, *Existence and Faith* (ET 1964), p. 101. From 'The Concept of Revelation in the New Testament' (1929).

said, it was only the prior act of God in the Christ-event which made men capable of faith, love and authentic human existence. How this happened Bultmann could not say, except that the Christ-event negated human self-assertion and human values, a view rather like that on which Albert Schweitzer fell back at the end of the *Quest of the Historical Jesus*. Out of this negation, presumably, one passed into faith.

The success of Bultmann's argument obviously depended on confining the discussion of the religious consciousness and its secular analogue to western Christian and philosophical sources, but there was no reason why writers from other traditions should accept this limitation. Moreover, if one appeals to the existential result – to the Christ-event as the one possible source of authentic human being – one is appealing to the evidence of the human self-consciousness in historical time. Twentieth-century Christian theologians still make this claim about the transforming effect of the Christ-event on human nature with extraordinary confidence. Non-Christian cultures, however, which by now have considerable experience of the western world, would not necessarily agree with the flattering view which the west – in Bultmann, for example – took of Christianity as deliverance to faith, love and authentic human existence; they might prefer the kind of human being moulded in other religious traditions; they might equally argue that these same non-Christian traditions produced 'authentic human existence' quite as often as did the western religious tradition itself. Few modern Christian theologians, however liberal they may deem themselves to be, take seriously enough the attitude expressed in Herder's aphorism, that the negro is as much entitled to think the white man degenerate as the white man to think the former a black beast. And like all theologians Bultmann tended to exaggerate the finality of his interpretation of the New Testament gospels; it was arguable, for instance, that Jesus, as far as the traditions about him are reliable, spoke more of divine forgiveness than he did about a divine transformation of human nature; Luther himself was perhaps a safer guide than Bultmann at this point.

For the liberal theologians, then, the appeal to the Spirit of Jesus led to the problems of history; the appeal to 'myth', or 'the poetic use of language' ended in comparative literature; the appeal to the religious consciousness ended in the problem of the relationship between Christianity and other faiths. In the last case, the logical conclusion may be found in a book like *God and the Universe of Faiths* (1973) by John Hick, for whom Christianity was one of a group of world faiths, each of which provided the principal path of salvation for a large section of the human race. He argued that the view that Jesus proclaimed himself to be God incarnate, and to be the one point of saving contact between God and man, lacked adequate historical foundation. The fact – which he accepted – that Christians experienced salvation through Christ did not mean that salvation could not be experienced in any other way. 'The alternative possibility is that the ultimate divine reality – in our Christian terms, God – has always been pressing in upon the human spirit, but always in ways which leave men free to open or close themselves to the divine presence.'[1] He used the phrase, 'the universe

[1] J. Hick, *God and the Universe of Faiths* (1973), p. 145.

of faiths', to express the hypothesis that at their experiential roots all the great religious systems came into contact with the same ultimate reality. He also spoke of 'the Copernican revolution in theology', by which he meant that there was taking place a shift from the dogma that Christianity was at the centre of the theological universe to the realization that God must be thought of as the centre, while all the religions of mankind, including the western Christian religion, serve and revolve around him. This was language not unlike Troeltsch's, but strengthened by the fact that it was spoken in a post-colonial and not an imperialistic period as far as the west was concerned: a post-colonial west needs a post-colonial theology.

How, then, did the state of theology appear in the 1970s? Orthodoxy and critical liberalism had, not for the first time, reached a potential point of parting. Karl Rahner, as a senior Roman Catholic theologian, and the kind of German Protestant thinking associated with such men as Gerhard Ebeling, Jurgen Moltmann and Wolfhart Pannenberg, represented continuing orthodoxies which still took for granted the essential truth of such dogmas as: the divinity as well as the humanity of Christ; the need for a supernatural, self-sacrificing mediator to restore an allegedly broken fellowship between created and creator; the supernatural origin of the Church; the necessity of at least two sacraments, in one of which it may be said that the elements *become* the body and blood of Jesus Christ. Propositions of this kind are regarded in practice as knowledge, in the sense that they can be *taught* (in schools, for example), not just discussed. Movements in art, philosophy and science, not to speak of social change, have not substantially modified these positions since 1800, though they have modified the way in which individual orthodox theologians present them. The mainstream churches have neither modified the historic creeds since 1800, nor changed their liturgical significance. At the wider level of practising religious communities orthodoxy spills over into movements like pentecostalism, which have more psychological and social interest than theological value. The debate about secularization, which has gone on intensely in sociological circles since 1945, was really about the extent to which this general orthodoxy had ceased (or continued) to provide the mental framework through which ordinary men and women in the west interpreted the broader meanings of their life-experience. (The best modern discussion of the subject was in *The Secularisation of the European Mind in the Nineteenth Century*, 1975, by Owen Chadwick.)

Critical liberalism certainly failed, between 1800 and the 1970s, to replace the varieties of orthodoxy as far as the mainstream churches were concerned. This was perhaps because statements of the critical position, *The Remaking of Christian Doctrine* (1974) by Maurice Wiles, for example, inevitably seemed parasitic on the kind of orthodox propositions which have just been mentioned. Liberal theologians were committed, as long as they wanted to remain theologians in the Christian tradition, to the belief that western religious thought and behaviour must stem from the Bible and the Church in history, whatever other sources were drawn on in addition. They were like politicians who perpetually proposed legislative changes which somehow never reached the statute-book. On questions of ethics, especially sexual ethics, theological liberals had powerful social support which helped them, as in the case of the Anglican Church's volte-face on contraception, to obtain important results. But pure theology had only an ecclesiastical environment, it had no other social roots by the 1970s. Those outside the Churches were no longer interested in the liberal theologian's desire to qualify rather than replace what the Churches officially said in the realm of pure theology. They made little of the difference between saying that Christ was divine, and saying that it was supremely through Jesus that God's purposes and the experience of grace had been made effective in the world. Liberalism was available to the individual, but it was not available to the institution. And so a certain split had taken place. Certain kinds of religious behaviour belonged to and took place within the environment of the Churches; certain styles of religious thinking had for the moment ceased to belong to the environment of the Churches. J. S. Bezzant diagnosed this situation accurately some years ago:

> I think it is entirely reasonable for any man who studies the spirit of the facing of life as Christ faced it, and his recorded teaching, to decide that by him he will stand through life, death or eternity rather than join in a possible triumph of evil over him. Whether or not any Church will regard such a man as a Christian is nowadays wholly secondary and manifestly relatively unimportant.[1]

---

[1] J. S. Bezzant, in *Objections to Christian Belief* (1963), pp. 109–110.

Index of Names

Index of Subjects